GLEIM® CMA REVIEW

2017 EDITION

PART 1
FINANCIAL REPORTING, PLANNING, PERFORMANCE, AND CONTROL

 Official Marketing Partner

by

Irvin N. Gleim, Ph.D., CPA, CIA, CMA, CFM

and

Dale L. Flesher, Ph.D., CPA, CIA, CMA, CFM

Gleim Publications, Inc.
P.O. Box 12848
University Station
Gainesville, Florida 32604
(888) 87-GLEIM or (888) 874-5346
(352) 375-0772
Fax: (352) 375-6940
Internet: www.gleim.com
Email: admin@gleim.com

For updates to this edition of ***CMA Review: Part 1***
Go To: www.gleim.com/CMAupdate
Or: Email update@gleim.com with **CMA 1 2017-1** in the subject line. You will receive our current update as a reply.
Updates are available until the next edition is published.

ISSN: 2474-0322

ISBN: 978-1-61854-066-9

This edition is copyright © 2016 by Gleim Publications, Inc. Portions of this manuscript are taken from previous editions copyright © 1981-2015 by Gleim Publications, Inc.

First Printing: October 2016

ALL RIGHTS RESERVED. No part of this material may be reproduced in any form whatsoever without express written permission from Gleim Publications, Inc. Reward is offered for information exposing violators. Contact copyright@gleim.com.

ACKNOWLEDGMENTS

The authors are indebted to the Institute of Certified Management Accountants (ICMA) for permission to use problem materials from past CMA examinations and other ICMA exam information. Questions and unofficial answers from the Certified Management Accountant Examinations, copyright © 1982 through 2016 by the Institute of Certified Management Accountants, are reprinted and/or adapted with permission.

The authors are also indebted to The Institute of Internal Auditors, Inc., for permission to use Certified Internal Auditor Examination Questions and Suggested Solutions, copyright © 1985 through 1996 by The Institute of Internal Auditors, Inc.

The authors also appreciate and thank the American Institute of Certified Public Accountants, Inc. Material from Uniform Certified Public Accountant Examination questions and unofficial answers, copyright © 1981-2016 by the American Institute of Certified Public Accountants, Inc., is reprinted and/or adapted with permission.

Environmental Statement -- This book is printed on recyclable, environmentally friendly groundwood paper, sourced from certified sustainable forests and produced either TCF (totally chlorine-free) or ECF (elementally chlorine-free).

The publications and online services of Gleim Publications and Gleim Internet are designed to provide accurate and authoritative information with regard to the subject matter covered. They are sold with the understanding that Gleim Publications and Gleim Internet, and their respective licensors, are not engaged in rendering legal, accounting, tax, or other professional advice or services. If legal advice or other expert assistance is required, the services of a competent professional person should be sought.

You assume all responsibilities and obligations with respect to the selection of the particular publication or online services to achieve your intended results. You assume all responsibilities and obligations with respect to any decisions or advice made or given as a result of the use or application of your selected publication or online services or any content retrieved therefrom, including those to any third party, for the content, accuracy, and review of such results.

ABOUT THE AUTHORS

Irvin N. Gleim is Professor Emeritus in the Fisher School of Accounting at the University of Florida and is a member of the American Accounting Association, Academy of Legal Studies in Business, American Institute of Certified Public Accountants, Association of Government Accountants, Florida Institute of Certified Public Accountants, The Institute of Internal Auditors, and the Institute of Management Accountants. He has had articles published in the *Journal of Accountancy*, *The Accounting Review*, and *The American Business Law Journal* and is author/coauthor of numerous accounting books, aviation books, and CPE courses.

Dale L. Flesher is a professor, associate dean, and holder of the Roland and Sheryl Burns Chair in the School of Accountancy at the University of Mississippi and has written over 300 articles for business and professional journals, including *Management Accounting*, *Journal of Accountancy*, and *The Accounting Review*, as well as numerous books. He is a member of the IMA, AICPA, The IIA, American Accounting Association, and American Taxation Association. He is a past editor of *The Accounting Historians' Journal* and is a trustee and past president of the Academy of Accounting Historians. He is a former vice president of finance for the American Accounting Association. In 2011, he received the AICPA's highest award for educators, The Distinguished Performance in Accounting Education Award, which is a lifetime achievement award. Previously, in 1990, he received The Institute of Internal Auditors Radde Award as the Outstanding Auditing Educator worldwide.

REVIEWERS AND CONTRIBUTORS

Garrett Gleim, B.S., CPA (not in public practice), is a graduate of the Wharton School at the University of Pennsylvania. Mr. Gleim coordinated the production staff, reviewed the manuscript, and provided production assistance throughout the project.

Grady M. Irwin, J.D., is a graduate of the University of Florida College of Law, and he has taught in the University of Florida College of Business. Mr. Irwin provided editorial assistance throughout the project.

Michael Kustanovich, M.A., CPA, is a graduate of Ben-Gurion University of the Negev in Israel. He is a Lecturer of Accountancy in the Department of Accountancy at the University of Illinois at Urbana-Champaign. He has worked in the audit departments of KPMG and PWC and as a financial accounting lecturer in the Department of Economics of Ben-Gurion University of the Negev. Mr. Kustanovich provided substantial editorial assistance throughout the project.

A PERSONAL THANKS

This manual would not have been possible without the extraordinary effort and dedication of Calvin Adams, Julie Cutlip, Blaine Hatton, Kelsey Olson, Bree Rodriguez, Teresa Soard, Justin Stephenson, Joanne Strong, and Elmer Tucker, who typed the entire manuscript and all revisions and drafted and laid out the diagrams, illustrations, and cover for this book.

The authors also appreciate the production and editorial assistance of Jacob Bennett, Melody Dalton, Jim Harvin, Jessica Hatker, Kristen Hennen, Katie Larson, Diana León, Jake Pettifor, Shane Rapp, and Drew Sheppard.

The authors also appreciate the critical reading assistance of Felix Chen, Paul Davis, Solomon Gonite, Jared Halper, Andrew Johnson, Jacey Johnson, Jessica Joseph, Josh Lehr, Melissa Leonard, Ross Li, Monica Metz, Sharon Sabbagh, Daniel Sinclair, Diana Weng, Josie Zhao, and Lily Zhao.

Finally, we appreciate the encouragement, support, and tolerance of our families throughout this project.

Returns of books purchased from bookstores and other resellers should be made to the respective bookstore or reseller. For more information regarding the Gleim Return Policy, please contact our offices at (800) 874-5346 or visit www.gleim.com/returnpolicy.

TABLE OF CONTENTS

	Page
Detailed Table of Contents	vi
Preface for CMA Part 1 Candidates	viii
Preparing for and Taking the CMA Exam	1
Study Unit 1. External Financial Statements and Revenue Recognition	9
Study Unit 2. Measurement, Valuation, and Disclosure: Investments and Short-Term Items	45
Study Unit 3. Measurement, Valuation, and Disclosure: Long-Term Items	81
Study Unit 4. Cost Management Concepts	117
Study Unit 5. Cost Accumulation Systems	141
Study Unit 6. Cost Allocation Techniques	179
Study Unit 7. Operational Efficiency and Business Process Performance	215
Study Unit 8. Analysis and Forecasting Techniques	247
Study Unit 9. Budgeting -- Concepts, Methodologies, and Preparation	285
Study Unit 10. Cost and Variance Measures	337
Study Unit 11. Responsibility Accounting and Performance Measures	375
Study Unit 12. Internal Controls -- Corporate Governance	399
Study Unit 13. Internal Controls -- Controls and Security Measures	437
Appendix A: PV/FV Tables	463
Appendix B: Sample Financial Statements	467
Appendix C: Glossary of Accounting Terms U.S. to British vs. British to U.S.	471
Appendix D: ICMA Content Specification Outlines and Cross-References	473
Appendix E: ICMA Suggested Reading List	477
Index	479

DETAILED TABLE OF CONTENTS

Page

Study Unit 1. External Financial Statements and Revenue Recognition
- 1.1. Concepts of Financial Accounting 9
- 1.2. Statement of Financial Position (Balance Sheet) 12
- 1.3. Income Statement and Statement of Comprehensive Income 15
- 1.4. Statement of Changes in Equity and Equity Transactions 18
- 1.5. Statement of Cash Flows 22
- 1.6. Revenue Recognition -- Revenue Recognition after Delivery 27
- 1.7. Revenue Recognition -- Long-Term Construction Contracts 30
- 1.8. Essay Questions 42

Study Unit 2. Measurement, Valuation, and Disclosure: Investments and Short-Term Items
- 2.1. Accounts Receivable 45
- 2.2. Inventory -- Fundamentals 49
- 2.3. Inventory -- Cost Flow Methods 54
- 2.4. Inventory Measurement in the Financial Statements -- Lower of Cost or Market 58
- 2.5. Classification of Investments 59
- 2.6. Equity Method 63
- 2.7. Business Combinations and Consolidated Financial Statements 63
- 2.8. Different Types of Expenses and Liabilities 66
- 2.9. Essay Questions 79

Study Unit 3. Measurement, Valuation, and Disclosure: Long-Term Items
- 3.1. Property, Plant, and Equipment 81
- 3.2. Impairment and Disposal of Long-Lived Assets 85
- 3.3. Intangible Assets 87
- 3.4. Leases 90
- 3.5. Income Taxes 94
- 3.6. Accounting for Bonds and Noncurrent Notes Payable 100
- 3.7. Essay Questions 115

Study Unit 4. Cost Management Concepts
- 4.1. Cost Management Terminology 117
- 4.2. Cost Behavior and Relevant Range 120
- 4.3. Cost Classification 123
- 4.4. Costing Techniques 126
- 4.5. Essay Questions 137

Study Unit 5. Cost Accumulation Systems
- 5.1. Job-Order Costing 141
- 5.2. Activity-Based Costing 144
- 5.3. Process Costing 152
- 5.4. Life-Cycle Costing 160
- 5.5. Essay Questions 175

Study Unit 6. Cost Allocation Techniques
- 6.1. Absorption and Variable Costing -- Theory 179
- 6.2. Absorption and Variable Costing -- Calculations 185
- 6.3. Joint Product and By-Product Costing 185
- 6.4. Overhead Allocation and Normal Costing -- Theory 189
- 6.5. Overhead Allocation and Normal Costing -- Calculations 195
- 6.6. Allocating Service Department Costs -- Theory 195
- 6.7. Allocating Service Department Costs -- Calculations 199
- 6.8. Essay Questions 211

Study Unit 7. Operational Efficiency and Business Process Performance
- 7.1. Just-in-Time Inventory and Lean Operation 215
- 7.2. Enterprise Resource Planning and Outsourcing 218
- 7.3. Theory of Constraints and Throughput Costing 221
- 7.4. Capacity Management 225
- 7.5. Value-Chain Analysis 227
- 7.6. Other Process Improvement Tools 230
- 7.7. Essay Questions 245

Detailed Table of Contents

	Page

Study Unit 8. Analysis and Forecasting Techniques
    8.1.   Correlation and Regression 247
    8.2.   Learning Curve Analysis 251
    8.3.   Expected Value 253
    8.4.   Sensitivity Analysis 256
    8.5.   Strategic Management 258
    8.6.   The Balanced Scorecard 265
    8.7.   Strategic Planning 270
    8.8.   Essay Question 283

Study Unit 9. Budgeting -- Concepts, Methodologies, and Preparation
    9.1.   Roles of Budgets and the Budgeting Process 285
    9.2.   Budgeting and Standard Costs 292
    9.3.   The Master Budget 293
    9.4.   Budget Methodologies 296
    9.5.   Operating Budget Calculations -- Production and Direct Materials 300
    9.6.   Operating Budget Calculations -- Others 301
    9.7.   Projecting Cash Collections 306
    9.8.   The Cash Budget 306
    9.9.   Sales Forecasts and Pro Forma Financial Statements 308
    9.10. Essay Questions 332

Study Unit 10. Cost and Variance Measures
    10.1. Variance Analysis Overview 337
    10.2. Static and Flexible Budget Variances 341
    10.3. Direct Materials Variances 344
    10.4. Direct Labor Variances 346
    10.5. Mix and Yield Variances 348
    10.6. Overhead Variances 349
    10.7. Comprehensive Example 353
    10.8. Sales Variances 356
    10.9. Essay Questions 373

Study Unit 11. Responsibility Accounting and Performance Measures
    11.1. Responsibility Centers 375
    11.2. Performance Measures -- Cost, Revenue, and Profit Centers 377
    11.3. Performance Measures -- Investment Centers 379
    11.4. Comparing Performance Measures for Investment Centers 381
    11.5. Allocating Common Costs 382
    11.6. Transfer Pricing 384
    11.7. Essay Questions 397

Study Unit 12. Internal Controls -- Corporate Governance
    12.1. Corporate Governance and Legal Aspects of Internal Control 399
    12.2. Risk and Internal Control 408
    12.3. Internal Auditing 419
    12.4. Essay Questions 435

Study Unit 13. Internal Controls -- Controls and Security Measures
    13.1. Control Procedures 437
    13.2. Systems Controls and Information Security 443
    13.3. Security Measures and Business Continuity Planning 449
    13.4. Essay Questions 461

PREFACE FOR CMA PART 1 CANDIDATES

The purpose of this book is to help **you** prepare **yourself** to pass Part 1 of the two-part CMA examination. The overriding consideration is to provide an inexpensive, effective, and easy-to-use study program. This manual

1. Explains how to optimize your grade by focusing on Part 1 of the CMA exam.
2. Defines the subject matter tested on Part 1 of the CMA exam.
3. Outlines all of the subject matter tested on Part 1 in 13 easy-to-use-and-complete study units.
4. Presents multiple-choice and essay questions from past CMA examinations to prepare you for questions in future CMA exams. The multiple-choice answer explanations are presented to the immediate right of each question for your convenience. Use a piece of paper to cover our explanations as you study the questions.
5. Suggests exam-taking and question-answering techniques to help you maximize your exam score.

The outline format, the spacing, and the question-and-answer formats in this book are designed to facilitate readability, learning, understanding, and success on the CMA exam. Our most successful candidates use the Gleim Premium Review System*, which includes CMA Gleim Instruct, the largest test bank of multiple-choice and essay questions, expertly authored books, and the Gleim Access Until You Pass guarantee; or a group study CMA review program. (Check our website for live courses we recommend.) This review book and all Gleim CMA Review materials are compatible with other CMA review materials and courses that are based on the ICMA's Content Specification Outlines.

To maximize the efficiency and effectiveness of your CMA review program, augment your studying with the *CMA Exam Guide* (available at www.gleim.com/PassCMA). This booklet has been carefully written and organized to provide important information to assist you in passing the CMA examination.

Thank you for your interest in our materials. We deeply appreciate the thousands of letters and suggestions we have received from CIA, CMA, CPA, and EA candidates; accounting students; and faculty during the past 5 decades.

If you use Gleim materials, we want YOUR feedback immediately after the exam and as soon as you have received your grades. The CMA exam is NONDISCLOSED, and you must maintain the confidentiality and agree not to divulge the nature or content of any CMA question or answer under any circumstances. We ask only for information about our materials, i.e., the topics that need to be added, expanded, etc.

Please go to www.gleim.com/feedbackCMA1 to share your suggestions on how we can improve this edition.

Good Luck on the Exam,

Irvin N. Gleim
Dale L. Flesher
October 2016

*Visit www.gleim.com or call (800) 874-5346 to order.

PREPARING FOR AND TAKING THE CMA EXAM

Read the Gleim CMA Exam Guide	1
Overview of the CMA Examination	1
Subject Matter for Part 1	2
Learning Outcome Statements	2
Which Pronouncements Are Tested?	2
How Ethics Are Tested	2
Nondisclosed Exam	3
The ICMA's Requirements for CMA Designations	3
Maintaining Your CMA Designation	3
Eligibility Period	3
How to Use the Gleim Review System	4
Gleim Knowledge Transfer Outlines	5
Time-Budgeting and Question-Answering Techniques for the Exam	6
Learning from Your Mistakes	7
How to Be in Control While Taking the Exam	8
If You Have Questions about Gleim Materials	8
Feedback	8

READ THE GLEIM *CMA EXAM GUIDE*

Obtain a free copy of the Gleim **CMA Exam Guide** by visiting www.gleim.com/PassCMA. Then, note where to revisit later in your studying process to obtain a deeper understanding of the CMA exam.

The Gleim **CMA Exam Guide** has seven study units:

Study Unit 1: The CMA Examination: An Overview and Preparation Introduction
Study Unit 2: ICMA Content Specification Outlines
Study Unit 3: Content Preparation, Test Administration, and Performance Grading
Study Unit 4: Multiple-Choice Questions
Study Unit 5: Essay Questions
Study Unit 6: Preparing to Pass the CMA Exam
Study Unit 7: How to Take the CMA Exam

OVERVIEW OF THE CMA EXAMINATION

The total exam is 8 hours of testing. It is divided into two parts, as follows:

Part 1 – Financial Reporting, Planning, Performance, and Control
Part 2 – Financial Decision Making

Each part consists of 100 multiple-choice questions and 2 essay scenarios, and testing lasts 4 hours (3 hours for the multiple-choice questions plus 1 hour for the essays). The exams are only offered during the following three testing windows: January/February, May/June, and September/October.

The CMA exam is computerized to facilitate easier testing. Prometric, the testing company that the IMA contracts to proctor the exams, has hundreds of testing centers worldwide. The suite of Gleim products, including the Gleim CMA Review Course, CMA Mega Test Bank, and CMA Exam Rehearsal provide exact exam emulations of the Prometric computer screens and procedures so you are prepared to PASS on exam day.

SUBJECT MATTER FOR PART 1

Below, we have provided the ICMA's abbreviated Content Specification Outline (CSO) for Part 1. The percentage coverage of each topic is indicated to its right. We adjust the content of our materials to any changes in the CSO.

Candidates for the CMA designation are expected to have a minimum level of business knowledge that transcends both examination parts. This minimum level includes knowledge of basic financial statements, time value of money concepts, and elementary statistics. Specific discussion of the ICMA's Levels of Performance (A, B, and C) is provided in Appendix D, which is a reprint of the ICMA's discussion of "Types and Levels of Exam Questions."

Part 1: Financial Reporting, Planning, Performance, and Control

External Financial Reporting Decisions	15%
Planning, Budgeting, and Forecasting	30%
Performance Management	20%
Cost Management	20%
Internal Controls	15%

Appendix D contains the CSOs in their entirety as well as cross-references to the subunits in our text where topics are covered. We have studied the CSOs while developing our materials and can assure you they are aligned with the most current CSOs. Accordingly, you do not need to spend time with Appendix D. Rather, it should give you confidence that Gleim CMA Review is the best review source available to help you pass the CMA exam.

LEARNING OUTCOME STATEMENTS

In addition to the CSOs, the ICMA provides Learning Outcome Statements (LOSs). The LOSs are more specific and describe in greater detail what the candidate needs to know about each section of the CSOs. Gleim materials cover these LOSs thoroughly. Also, for your convenience, we provide a complete reproduction of the LOSs in the CMA Review Course.

WHICH PRONOUNCEMENTS ARE TESTED?

New pronouncements are eligible to be tested on the CMA exam in the testing window beginning 1 year after a pronouncement's effective date.

In conjunction with an IFRS released in 2016, the FASB in the U.S. has issued a new lease accounting standard. The new standard will not be testable on the CMA exam until 1 year after its effective date, which is December 15, 2018. Thus, the new standard is not covered in this edition of Gleim CMA Review. Rest assured that Gleim updates our materials as appropriate when any new standard is testable and will only cover what candidates need for the current CMA exam.

HOW ETHICS ARE TESTED

Ethical issues and considerations are tested from the perspectives of both the individual and the organization in Part 2. Candidates will be expected to evaluate the issues involved and make recommendations for the resolution of the situation in both the multiple-choice section and the essay section of Part 2 of the exam.

NONDISCLOSED EXAM

As part of the ICMA's nondisclosure policy and to prove each candidate's willingness to adhere to this policy, a confidentiality agreement must be accepted by each candidate before each part is taken. This statement is reproduced here to remind all CMA candidates about the ICMA's strict policy of nondisclosure, which Gleim consistently supports and upholds.

I hereby attest that I will not divulge the content of this examination, nor will I remove any examination materials, notes or other unauthorized materials from the examination room. I understand that failure to comply with this attestation may result in invalidation of my grades and disqualification from future examinations. For those already certified by the Institute of Certified Management Accountants, failure to comply with the statement will be considered a violation of the IMA's Statement of Ethical Professional Practice and could result in revocation of the certification.

THE ICMA'S REQUIREMENTS FOR CMA DESIGNATIONS

The CMA designation is granted only by the ICMA. Candidates must complete the following steps to become a CMA:

1. Become a member of the IMA, enter the certification program, and register for the part(s) you are going to take. The Gleim *CMA Exam Guide* contains concise instructions on the membership and certification application and registration processes as well as a useful worksheet to help you keep track of your process and organize what you need for exam day.
2. Pass both parts of the exam within 3 years.
3. Satisfy the education requirement.
4. Satisfy the experience requirement.
5. Comply with the IMA's *Statement of Ethical Professional Practice*.

MAINTAINING YOUR CMA DESIGNATION

When you have completed all requirements, you will be issued a numbered CMA certificate. This certificate is the property of the ICMA and must be returned upon request. To maintain your certificate, membership in the IMA is required. The annual CMA maintenance fee for regular members is $30. You are also required to comply with the IMA's *Statement of Ethical Professional Practice* and all applicable state laws. The final requirement is continuing professional education (CPE).

Beginning the calendar year after successful completion of the CMA exams, 30 hours of CPE must be completed, which is about 4 days per year. Qualifying topics include management accounting, corporate taxation, statistics, computer science, systems analysis, management skills, marketing, business law, and insurance. All CMAs are required to complete 2 hours of CPE on the subject of ethics as part of their 30-hour annual requirement.

ELIGIBILITY PERIOD

Candidates must register for an exam part within the first 12 months after being admitted to the Certification Program. In addition, all candidates are required to pass both parts of the exam within 3 years of being admitted to the CMA program. If a candidate is not able to pass both parts within this time period, the Certification Entrance Fee will have to be repaid and the passed part will have to be retaken.

HOW TO USE THE GLEIM REVIEW SYSTEM

To ensure that you are using your time effectively, we have formulated a three-step process to apply to each study unit that includes all components together.

Step 1: Diagnostic

a. Multiple-Choice Quiz #1 (30 minutes, plus 10 minutes for review) – In the CMA Review Course, complete Multiple-Choice Quiz #1 in 30 minutes. This is a diagnostic quiz, so it is expected that your scores will be lower.

  1) Immediately following the quiz, review the questions you marked and/or answered incorrectly. This step is essential to identifying your weak areas. Refer to "Learning from Your Mistakes" on page 7 for tips.

Step 2: Comprehension

a. Audiovisual Presentation (30 minutes) – This CMA Review Course presentation provides an overview of the study unit. Use the Gleim CMA Audio Lectures instead when you are on the go!

b. Gleim Instruct - CMA Video Series (30-90 minutes) – These videos are for candidates who prefer live instruction to the slide-show style of the audiovisual presentations. Gleim Instruct videos include lectures featuring professors from accredited universities, multiple-choice questions, and detailed examples.

c. Focus Questions (45 minutes) – Complete the Focus Questions in the CMA Review Course and receive immediate feedback.

d. Knowledge Transfer Outline (60-90 minutes) – Study the Knowledge Transfer Outline, particularly the troublesome areas identified from your Multiple-Choice Quiz #1 in Step 1. The Knowledge Transfer Outlines can be studied either online or in the books.

e. Multiple-Choice Quiz #2 (30 minutes, plus 10 minutes for review) – Complete Multiple-Choice Quiz #2 in the CMA Review Course.

  1) Immediately following the quiz, review the questions you marked and/or answered incorrectly. This step is an essential learning activity. Refer to "Learning from Your Mistakes" on page 7 for tips.

Step 3: Application

a. CMA Test Prep (60 minutes, plus 20 minutes for review) – Complete two 20-question quizzes in CMA Test Prep, a component of the Mega Test Bank, using the Practice Exam feature. Spend 30 minutes taking each quiz and then spend about 10 minutes reviewing each quiz as needed.

b. Essay Scenario (30 minutes, plus 10 minutes for review) – Complete the essay scenario in the CMA Review Course. Budget 30 minutes to complete the scenario and spend about 10 minutes reviewing.

Additional Assistance

1. Gleim Instruct Supplemental Videos (watch as needed) – These videos discuss multiple-choice questions and essay scenarios that test the topics candidates find the most difficult.

2. Gleim Essay Bank – For additional practice answering essays, complete scenarios from the Essay Bank, a component of the Mega Test Bank, as needed.

3. Core Concepts – These consolidated documents provide overviews of the key points of each study unit that serve as a foundation for learning.

Final Review

1. **CMA Exam Rehearsal (4 hours/240 minutes)** – Take the Exam Rehearsal at the beginning of your final review stage. It contains 100 multiple-choice questions and 2 essay scenarios, just like the CMA exams. This will help you identify where you should focus during the remainder of your final review.

2. **CMA Mega Test Bank (10-20 hours)** – Use the Mega Test Bank to focus on your weak areas identified by your Exam Rehearsal. This software gives you access to the largest test bank of multiple-choice and essay questions so you can work on the topics and question-answering techniques you struggle with the most. Also, be sure to do a cumulative review to refresh yourself with topics you learned at the beginning of your studies. View your performance chart to make sure you are scoring 75% or higher.

The times mentioned above and on the previous page are recommendations based on prior candidate feedback and how long you have to answer questions on the actual exam. Each candidate's time spent in any area will vary depending on proficiency and familiarity with the subject matter.

GLEIM KNOWLEDGE TRANSFER OUTLINES

This edition of the CMA Part 1 Review book has the following features to make studying easier:

1. **Examples:** Longer, illustrative examples, both hypothetical and those drawn from actual events, are set off in shaded, bordered boxes.

EXAMPLE

In Year 1, Creditor made a $100,000 sale. The cost of the item sold was $70,000, and Year 1 collections equaled $50,000. In Year 2, collections equaled $25,000. The net receivable (receivable – deferred profit) was $0 at the end of Year 2. The following entries are based on the cost-recovery method:

Year 1:	Receivable	$100,000	
	Inventory		$70,000
	Deferred gross profit		30,000
	Cash	$50,000	
	Receivable		$50,000
Year 2:	Cash	$25,000	
	Deferred gross profit	5,000	
	Receivable		$25,000
	Realized gross profit		5,000

---

2. **Gleim Success Tips:** These tips supplement the core exam material by suggesting how certain topics might be presented on the exam or how you should prepare for an issue.

Management accountants are expected to know the theory and how to complete detailed calculations for the topics covered in this study unit. To provide a more focused approach to studying, Gleim has broken up the theoretical questions and computational questions of the different cost allocation techniques into separate subunits. CMA candidates should expect a mix of both theory and computational questions on the CMA exam.

3. **International Standards Differences:** When international standards differ significantly from U.S. GAAP, we note the differences. Currently, this feature applies to the Financial Reporting section of Part 1 only.

IFRS Difference

The completed-contract method is not used. When the outcome of a long-term construction contract cannot be reliably estimated, revenue recognition is limited to recoverable costs incurred. Contract costs must be recognized as an expense in the period in which they are incurred.

TIME-BUDGETING AND QUESTION-ANSWERING TECHNIQUES FOR THE EXAM

Expect 100 multiple-choice questions and 2 essay questions on each part with a 240-minute total time allocation (180 minutes max for multiple-choice questions and at least 60 minutes for the essays). Study Units 4 and 5 in the Gleim *CMA Exam Guide* contain additional discussion of how to maximize your score on multiple-choice questions and essays.

1. **Budget your time.**
    a. We make this point with emphasis. Just as you would fill up your gas tank prior to reaching empty, so too should you finish your exam before time expires.
    b. You have 180 minutes to answer the 100 multiple-choice questions, i.e., 1.8 minutes per question. We suggest you allocate 1.5 minutes per question. This would result in completing 100 questions in 150 minutes to give you 30 minutes to review questions that you have marked.
    c. Before beginning the multiple-choice questions, prepare a Gleim Time Management Sheet as recommended in Study Unit 7 of the Gleim *CMA Exam Guide*.

2. **Answer the questions in consecutive order.**
    a. Do **not** agonize over any one item. Stay within your time budget.
    b. Mark any questions you are unsure of and return to them later as time allows.
    c. Never leave a multiple-choice question unanswered. Make your best educated guess in the time allowed. Remember that your score is based on the number of correct responses. You will not be penalized for guessing incorrectly.

3. **For each multiple-choice question,**
    a. **Try to ignore the answer choices.** Do not allow the answer choices to affect your reading of the question.
        1) If four answer choices are presented, three of them are incorrect. These choices are called **distractors** for good reason. Often, distractors are written to appear correct at first glance until further analysis.
        2) In computational items, the distractors are carefully calculated such that they are the result of making common mistakes. Be careful, and double-check your computations if time permits.
    b. **Read the question** carefully to determine the precise requirement.
        1) Focusing on what is required enables you to ignore extraneous information, to focus on the relevant facts, and to proceed directly to determining the correct answer.
            a) Be especially careful to note when the requirement is an **exception**; e.g., "A statement of financial position provides a basis for all of the following **except**"
    c. **Determine the correct answer** before looking at the answer choices.
    d. **Read the answer choices carefully.**
        1) Even if the first answer appears to be the correct choice, do **not** skip the remaining answer choices. Questions often ask for the "best" of the choices provided. Thus, each choice requires your consideration.
        2) Treat each answer choice as a true/false question as you analyze it.

e. **Click on the best answer.**
   1) You have a 25% chance of answering the question correctly by blindly guessing.
   2) For many multiple-choice questions, two answer choices can be eliminated with minimal effort, thereby increasing an educated guess to a 50-50 proposition.
f. As you answer a question, you can mark it by pressing the "Mark" button or unmark a marked question by pressing the "Marked" button. After you have moved through all 100 questions, you will be presented with a review screen that shows which questions you did not answer and which you marked. You then have the option of revisiting all of the unanswered and/or marked questions.
   1) Make sure you go back to all unanswered questions and at least make your best educated guess.
   2) Go back to the marked questions and finalize your answer choices.
   3) When you are back at the review screen again, verify that all questions have been answered.
g. **If you don't know the answer:**
   1) Again, guess; but make it an educated guess and select the best possible answer. First, rule out answers that you think are incorrect. Second, speculate on what the ICMA is looking for and/or the rationale behind the question. Third, select the best answer or guess between equally appealing answers. Your first guess is usually the most intuitive. If you cannot make an educated guess, read the stem and each answer and pick the most intuitive answer. It's just a guess!
   2) Make sure you accomplish this step within your predetermined time budget.

LEARNING FROM YOUR MISTAKES

Learning from questions you answer incorrectly is very important. Each question you answer incorrectly is an **opportunity** to avoid missing actual test questions on your CMA exam. Thus, you should carefully study the answer explanations provided until you understand why the original answer you chose is wrong, as well as why the correct answer indicated is correct. This study technique is the difference between passing and failing for many CMA candidates.

Also, you **must** determine why you answered questions incorrectly to learn how to avoid the same errors in the future. Reasons for missing questions include

1. Misreading the requirement (stem)
2. Not understanding what is required
3. Making a math error
4. Applying the wrong rule or concept
5. Being distracted by one or more of the answers
6. Incorrectly eliminating answers from consideration
7. Not having any knowledge of the topic tested
8. Employing bad intuition when guessing

It is also important to verify that you answered correctly for the right reasons. Otherwise, if the material is tested on the CMA exam in a different manner, you may not answer it correctly.

HOW TO BE IN CONTROL WHILE TAKING THE EXAM

You have to be in control to be successful during exam preparation and execution. Control can also contribute greatly to your personal and other professional goals. Control is a process whereby you

1. Develop expectations, standards, budgets, and plans
2. Undertake activity, production, study, and learning
3. Measure the activity, production, output, and knowledge
4. Compare actual activity with expected and budgeted activity
5. Modify the activity, behavior, or study to better achieve the desired outcome
6. Revise expectations and standards in light of actual experience
7. Continue the process or restart the process in the future

Exercising control will ultimately develop the confidence you need to outperform other CMA candidates and PASS the CMA exam! Obtain our Gleim *CMA Exam Guide* from www.gleim.com/PassCMA for a more detailed discussion of control and other exam tactics.

IF YOU HAVE QUESTIONS ABOUT GLEIM MATERIALS

Gleim has an efficient and effective way for candidates who have purchased the Premium CMA Review System to submit an inquiry and receive a response regarding Gleim materials directly through their course. This system also allows you to view your Q&A session in your Gleim Personal Classroom.

Questions regarding the **information in this introduction and/or the Gleim *CMA Exam Guide* (study suggestions, study plans, exam specifics)** should be emailed to personalcounselor@gleim.com.

Questions concerning **orders, prices, shipments, or payments** should be sent via email to customerservice@gleim.com and will be promptly handled by our competent and courteous customer service staff.

For **technical support**, you may use our automated technical support service at www.gleim.com/support, email us at support@gleim.com, or call us at (800) 874-5346.

FEEDBACK

Please fill out our online feedback form (www.gleim.com/feedbackCMA1) immediately after you take the CMA exam so we can adapt our material based on where candidates say we need to increase or decrease coverage. Our approach has been approved by the ICMA.

Learn even more about successful candidates' study habits and preparation methods in our free *CMA Exam Guide*. You can view this booklet online at www.gleim.com/PassCMA.

STUDY UNIT ONE
EXTERNAL FINANCIAL STATEMENTS AND REVENUE RECOGNITION

(24 pages of outline)

1.1	Concepts of Financial Accounting	9
1.2	Statement of Financial Position (Balance Sheet)	12
1.3	Income Statement and Statement of Comprehensive Income	15
1.4	Statement of Changes in Equity and Equity Transactions	18
1.5	Statement of Cash Flows	22
1.6	Revenue Recognition -- Revenue Recognition after Delivery	27
1.7	Revenue Recognition -- Long-Term Construction Contracts	30
1.8	Essay Questions	42

This study unit is the **first of three** on **external financial reporting decisions**. The relative weight assigned to this major topic in Part 1 of the exam is **15%**. The three study units are

Study Unit 1: External Financial Statements and Revenue Recognition
Study Unit 2: Measurement, Valuation, and Disclosure: Investments and Short-Term Items
Study Unit 3: Measurement, Valuation, and Disclosure: Long-Term Items

If you are interested in reviewing more introductory or background material, go to www.gleim.com/CMAIntroVideos for a list of suggested third-party overviews of this topic. The following Gleim outline material is more than sufficient to help you pass the CMA exam; any additional introductory or background material is for your own personal enrichment.

1.1 CONCEPTS OF FINANCIAL ACCOUNTING

1. **The Objective of General-Purpose Financial Reporting**
    a. The objective of general-purpose financial reporting is to report financial information that is **useful in making decisions** about providing resources to the reporting entity.
    b. The information reported relates to the entity's economic resources and claims to them (financial position) and to changes in those resources and claims.
        1) Information about economic resources and claims helps to evaluate liquidity, solvency, financing needs, and the probability of obtaining financing.
    c. Users need to differentiate between changes in economic resources and claims arising from (1) the entity's performance (income statement) and (2) other events and transactions, such as issuing debt and equity (balance sheet). Information about financial performance is useful for
        1) Understanding the return on economic resources, its variability, and its components;
        2) Evaluating management; and
        3) Predicting future returns.
    d. For general-purpose financial statements to be useful to external parties, they **must be prepared in conformity with accounting principles that are generally accepted in the United States (GAAP)**.

    NOTE: The CMA exam also tests some knowledge of International Financial Reporting Standards (IFRS). When international standards diverge significantly from U.S. GAAP, the differences are highlighted. If there is no specification between GAAP and IFRS, use GAAP.

e. Financial accounting differs from management accounting.

1) Management accounting assists management decision making, planning, and control. Management accounting information is therefore primarily directed to specific internal users, and it ordinarily need not follow GAAP.

2. **Users of Financial Statements**

   a. Users may directly or indirectly have an economic interest in a specific business. Users with direct interests usually invest in or manage the business, and users with indirect interests advise, influence, or represent users with direct interests.

      1) Users with direct interests include

         a) Investors or potential investors
         b) Suppliers and creditors
         c) Employees
         d) Management

      2) Users having indirect interests include

         a) Financial advisors and analysts
         b) Stock markets or exchanges
         c) Regulatory authorities

   b. **External users** use financial statements to determine whether doing business with the firm will be beneficial.

      1) Investors need information to decide whether to increase, decrease, or obtain an investment in a firm.
      2) Creditors need information to determine whether to extend credit and under what terms.
      3) Financial advisors and analysts need financial statements to help investors evaluate particular investments.
      4) Stock exchanges need financial statements to evaluate whether to accept a firm's stock for listing or whether to suspend the stock's trading.
      5) Regulatory agencies may need financial statements to evaluate the firm's conformity with regulations and to determine price levels in regulated industries.

   c. **Internal users** use financial statements to make decisions affecting the operations of the business. These users include management, employees, and the board of directors.

      1) Management needs financial statements to assess financial strengths and deficiencies, to evaluate performance results and past decisions, and to plan for future financial goals and steps toward accomplishing them.
      2) Employees want financial information to negotiate wages and fringe benefits based on the increased productivity and value they provide to a profitable firm.

3. **Features of Financial Statements**

   a. Financial statements are the primary means of communicating financial information to external parties. Additional information is provided by financial statement notes, supplementary information (such as management's discussion and analysis), and other disclosures. Information typically disclosed in notes is essential to understanding the financial statements.

      1) The notes are considered part of the basic financial statements. They amplify or explain information recognized in the statements and are an integral part of statements prepared in accordance with GAAP.

         a) The first footnote accompanying any set of complete financial statements is generally one describing significant accounting policies, such as the use of estimates and rules for revenue recognition.
         b) Financial statement notes should not be used to correct improper presentation.

b. A full set of financial statements includes the following statements:
   1) Statement of financial position (also called a balance sheet)
   2) Income statement
   3) Statement of comprehensive income
   4) Statement of changes in equity
   5) Statement of cash flows
c. To be useful, information presented in the financial statements must be relevant and faithfully represented. To enhance the usefulness, the information should be comparable with similar information for (1) other entities and (2) the same entity for another period or date. Thus, **comparability** allows users to understand similarities and differences.
d. Financial statements are prepared under the **going-concern assumption**, which means that the entity is assumed to continue operating indefinitely. As a result, liquidation values are not important. It is assumed that the entity is not going to be liquidated in the near future.

4. **Financial Statement Relationships**

   a. Financial statements complement each other. They describe different aspects of the same transactions, and more than one statement is necessary to provide information for a specific economic decision.
   b. The components (elements) of one statement relate to those of other statements. Among the relationships are those listed below:
      1) Net income or loss from the statement of income is reported and accumulated in the retained earnings account, a component of the equity section of the statement of financial position.
      2) The components of cash and equivalents from the statement of financial position are reconciled with the corresponding items in the statement of cash flows.
      3) Items of equity from the statement of financial position are reconciled with the beginning balances on the statement of changes in equity.
      4) Ending inventories are reported in current assets on the statement of financial position and are reflected in the calculation of cost of goods sold on the statement of income.
      5) Amortization and depreciation reported in the statement of income also are reflected in asset and liability balances in the statement of financial position.

      NOTE: See Appendix B for a complete set of financial statements. The complementary relationships among these statements are lettered.

5. **Accrual Basis of Accounting**

   a. Financial statements are prepared under the accrual basis of accounting. Accrual accounting records the financial effects of transactions and other events and circumstances when they occur rather than when their associated cash is paid or received.
      1) Revenues are recognized in the period in which they were earned even if the cash will be received in a future period.
      2) Expenses are recognized in the period in which they were incurred even if the cash will be paid in a future period.

      NOTE: Under the cash basis, revenues are recognized when cash is received and expenses are recognized when cash is paid. Under GAAP, financial statements cannot be prepared under the cash basis of accounting.

Stop and review! You have completed the outline for this subunit. Study multiple-choice questions 1 through 3 beginning on page 32.

1.2 STATEMENT OF FINANCIAL POSITION (BALANCE SHEET)

1. **Overview**
   a. The statement of financial position, also called the balance sheet, reports the amounts of assets, liabilities, equity, and their relationships at a moment in time, such as at the end of the fiscal year. It helps users to assess liquidity, financial flexibility, and risk.
   b. The basic accounting equation presents a perfect balance between the entity's resources and its capital structure. The entity's resources consist of the assets the entity deploys in its attempts to earn a return. The capital structure consists of the amounts contributed by outsiders (liabilities) and insiders (equity).

   $$Assets = Liabilities + Equity$$

2. **Elements of Balance Sheet**
   a. **Assets** are resources controlled by the entity as a result of past events. They represent probable future economic benefits to the entity. Examples include inventory; accounts receivable; investments; and property, plant, and equipment.
   b. **Liabilities** are present obligations of the entity arising from past events. Their settlement is expected to result in an outflow of economic benefits from the entity. Examples include loans payable, bonds issued by the entity, and accounts payable.
   c. **Equity** is the residual interest in the assets of the entity after subtracting all its liabilities. Examples include a company's common stock, preferred stock, and retained earnings. Equity is affected not only by operations but also by transactions with owners, such as dividends and contributions.
      1) **Investments by owners** are increases in equity of a business entity. They result from transfers of something of value to increase ownership interests. Assets are the most commonly transferred item, but services also can be exchanged for equity interests.
      2) **Distributions to owners** are decreases in equity. They result from transferring assets to owners. A distribution to owners decreases the ownership interest in the company.
   d. Assets and liabilities are separated in the statement of financial position into **current** and **noncurrent** categories.
      1) Assets are generally reported in order of liquidity.
   e. Some variation of the following classifications is used by most entities:

Assets	Liabilities
Current assets:	Current liabilities:
Cash	Accounts payable
Certain investments	Current notes payable
Accounts and notes receivable	Current maturities of noncurrent liabilities
Inventories	Noncurrent liabilities:
Prepaid expenses	Noncurrent notes payable
Noncurrent assets:	Bonds payable
Certain investments and funds	**Equity**
Property, plant, and equipment (PPE)	Investments by owners
Intangible assets	Retained earnings
Other noncurrent assets	Accumulated other comprehensive income
	Noncontrolling interest in a consolidated entity

   NOTE: A comprehensive example of statements of financial position can be found in Appendix B.

3. **Current and Noncurrent Assets**
    a. An asset is classified as **current** on the statement of financial position if it is expected to be realized in cash or sold or consumed within the entity's operating cycle or 1 year, whichever is longer.
    b. The following are the major categories of current assets: (1) cash and cash equivalents; (2) certain individual trading, available-for-sale, and held-to-maturity securities; (3) receivables; (4) inventories; and (5) prepaid expenses, etc.
    c. **Noncurrent assets** are those not qualifying as current.
    d. The following are the major categories of noncurrent assets:
        1) **Investments and funds** include nonoperating items intended to be held beyond the longer of 1 year or the operating cycle. The following assets are typically included:
            a) Investments in securities made to control or influence another entity and other noncurrent securities.
            b) Certain available-for-sale and held-to-maturity securities may be noncurrent.
            c) Funds restricted as to withdrawal or use for other than current operations, for example, to (1) retire long-term debt, (2) satisfy pension obligations, or (3) pay for the acquisition or construction of noncurrent assets.
        2) **Property, plant, and equipment (PPE)** are tangible operating items recorded at cost and reported net of any accumulated depreciation. They include
            a) Land and natural resources subject to depletion, e.g., oil and gas
            b) Buildings, equipment, furniture, fixtures, leasehold improvements, land improvements, assets held under capital leases, noncurrent assets under construction, and other depreciable assets
        3) **Intangible assets** are nonfinancial assets without physical substance. Examples are patents and goodwill.

4. **Current and Noncurrent Liabilities**
    a. **Current liabilities** are expected to be settled or liquidated in the ordinary course of business during the longer of the next year or the operating cycle.
        1) Generally speaking, current liabilities are expected to be settled or liquidated within 1 year from the balance sheet date.
    b. The following are the major categories of current liabilities:
        1) **Trade payables** for items entering into the operating cycle, e.g., for materials and supplies used in producing goods or services for sale.
        2) **Other payables** arising from operations, such as accrued wages, salaries, rentals, royalties, and taxes.
        3) **Unearned revenues** arising from collections in advance of delivering goods or performing services, e.g., ticket sales revenue.
        4) **Other obligations** expected to be liquidated in the ordinary course of business during the longer of the next year or the operating cycle. These include
            a) Short-term notes given to acquire capital assets
            b) Payments required under sinking-fund provisions
            c) Payments on the current portion of serial bonds or other noncurrent debt
            d) Long-term obligations that are or will become callable by the creditor because of the debtor's violation of a provision of the debt agreement at the balance sheet date

c. Current liabilities **do not include** short-term debt if an entity
   1) Intends to refinance them on a noncurrent basis and
   2) Demonstrates an ability to do so.
      a) The ability to refinance may be demonstrated by entering into a **refinancing agreement** before the balance sheet is issued.
d. **Noncurrent liabilities** are those not qualifying as current. The noncurrent portions of the following items are reported in this section of the balance sheet:
   1) Noncurrent notes and bonds
   2) Liabilities under capital leases
   3) Most postretirement benefit obligations
   4) Deferred tax liabilities arising from interperiod tax allocation
   5) Obligations under product or service warranty agreements
   6) Deferred revenue

5. **Equity**
   a. Any recognized transaction that does not have equal and offsetting effects on total assets and total liabilities changes equity. The following are the major items of equity:
      1) **Capital contributions by owners** (par value of common and preferred stock issued and additional paid-in capital).
         a) Additional paid-in (contributed) capital is the amount received in excess of par value at the time stock was sold.
      2) **Retained earnings** are the accumulated net income not yet distributed to owners.
      3) **Treasury stock** is the firm's own stock that has been repurchased.
         a) Treasury stock is reported either at cost (as a deduction from total equity) or at par (as a direct reduction of the relevant contributed capital account).
         b) Treasury stock is reported as a reduction of the total equity.
      4) **Accumulated other comprehensive income** items not included in net income.

6. **Balance Sheet Elements Are Permanent Accounts**
   a. Assets, liabilities, and equity are recorded in **permanent (real) accounts**. Their balances at the end of one accounting period (the balance sheet date) are carried forward as the beginning balances of the next accounting period.

7. **Major Balance Sheet Note Disclosures**
   a. Footnote disclosures and schedules specifically related to the balance sheet include
      1) Investment securities
      2) Maturity patterns of bond issues
      3) Significant uncertainties, such as pending litigation
      4) Details of capital stock issues

8. **Limitations of the Balance Sheet**
   a. The balance sheet shows a company's financial position at a single point in time; accounts may vary significantly a few days before or after the publication of the balance sheet.
   b. Many balance sheet items, such as fixed assets, are valued at historical costs, which may not equal their fair value.
   c. The preparation of the balance sheet requires estimates and management judgment.

Stop and review! You have completed the outline for this subunit. Study multiple-choice questions 4 through 8 beginning on page 33.

1.3 INCOME STATEMENT AND STATEMENT OF COMPREHENSIVE INCOME

1. **Income Statement Elements**

    a. The income statement reports the results of an entity's operations over a period of time, such as a year.

    The Income Equation

    ```
    Income (Loss) = Revenues + Gains - Expenses - Losses
    ```

    b. The following are the elements of income statement:

    1) **Revenues** are inflows or other enhancements of assets or settlements of liabilities (or both) from delivering or producing goods, providing services, or other activities that qualify as ongoing major or central operations.
    2) **Gains** are increases in equity (or net assets) other than from revenues or investments by owners.
    3) **Expenses** are outflows or other usage of assets or incurrences of liabilities (or both) from delivering or producing goods, providing services, or other activities that qualify as ongoing major or central operations.
    4) **Losses** are decreases in equity (or net assets) other than from expenses or distributions to owners.

    c. All transactions affecting the net change in equity during the period are included in income except

    1) Transactions with owners
    2) Prior-period adjustments (such as error correction or a change in accounting principle)
    3) Items reported initially in other comprehensive income
    4) Transfers to and from appropriated retained earnings

    d. Revenues, expenses, gains, and losses are recorded in **temporary (nominal) accounts** because they record the transactions, events, and other circumstances during a period of time. These accounts are closed (reduced to zero) at the end of each accounting period, and their balances are transferred to real accounts.

    1) For example, income or loss for the period (a nominal account) is **closed to retained earnings (a real account)** at the end of the reporting period.

2. **Typical Items of Cost and Expense**

    a. The **expense recognition principles** are associating cause and effect, systematic and rational allocation, and immediate recognition.

    1) **Matching** is essentially synonymous with **associating cause and effect**. Such a direct relationship is found when the cost of goods sold is recognized in the same period as the revenue from the sale of the goods.

    b. Cost of Goods Sold

    1) For a retailer, cost of goods sold is calculated based on changes in inventory:

Beginning inventory	$10,000
Plus: net purchases	14,000
Plus: freight-in	1,000
Goods available for sale	$25,000
Minus: ending inventory	(5,000)
Cost of goods sold	$20,000

2) For a manufacturer, cost of goods sold is calculated as follows:

Beginning raw materials inventory	$3,000	
Purchases during the period	3,000	
Ending raw materials inventory	(1,000)	
Direct materials used in production		$5,000
Direct labor costs		5,000
Manufacturing overhead costs (fixed + variable)		4,000
Total manufacturing costs		$14,000
Beginning work-in-process inventory		5,000
Ending work-in-process inventory		(4,000)
Cost of goods manufactured		$15,000
Beginning finished goods inventory		6,000
Ending finished goods inventory		(11,000)
Cost of goods sold		$10,000

c. Other Expenses

1) General and administrative expenses are incurred for the benefit of the enterprise as a whole and are not related wholly to a specific function, e.g., selling or manufacturing.

   a) They include accounting, legal, and other fees for professional services; officers' salaries; insurance; wages of office staff; miscellaneous supplies; and office occupancy costs.

2) Selling expenses are those incurred in selling or marketing.

   a) Examples include sales representatives' salaries, commissions, and traveling expense; advertising; sales department salaries and expenses, including rent; and credit and collection costs.

   b) Shipping costs are also often classified as selling costs.

d. Interest expense is recognized based on the passage of time. In the case of bonds, notes, and capital leases, the effective interest method is used.

3. **Income Statement Formats**

   a. The single-step income statement provides one grouping for revenue items and one for expense items. The single step is the one subtraction necessary to arrive at net income.

   b. The multiple-step income statement matches operating revenues and expenses in a section separate from nonoperating items. The most common way to present the income statement is the condensed format of the multiple-step income statement, which includes only the section totals.

   1) The following is an example of a condensed multiple-step income statement.

EXAMPLE

Income Statement

Net sales	$ 200,000
Cost of goods sold	(150,000)
Gross profit	$ 50,000
Selling expenses	(6,000)
Administrative expenses	(5,000)
Income from operations	$ 39,000
Other revenues and gains	3,500
Other expenses and losses	(2,500)
Income before taxes	$ 40,000
Income taxes	(16,000)
Net income	$ 24,000

A more detailed example format can be found in Appendix B.

4. **Reporting Irregular Items**

    a. When an entity reports a **discontinued operation**, it must be presented in a separate section after income from continuing operations.

        1) Because these items are reported after the presentation of income taxes, they must be shown net of tax.
        2) The term "continuing operations" is used only when a discontinued operation is reported.

    b. **Discontinued operations**, if reported, may have two components:

        1) Income or loss from operations of the component that has been disposed of or is classified as held for sale from the first day of the reporting period until the date of disposal (or the end of the reporting period if it is classified as held for sale)
        2) Gain or loss on the disposal of this component

5. **Major Note Disclosures**

    a. Note disclosures and schedules specifically related to the income statement include the following:

        1) Earnings per share
        2) Depreciation schedules
        3) Components of income tax expense
        4) Components of pension expense

6. **Limitations of the Income Statement**

    a. The income statement does not always show all items of income and expense. Some of the items are reported on a statement of other comprehensive income and not included in the calculation of net income.
    b. The financial statements report accrual-basis results for the period. The company may recognize revenue and report net income before any cash was actually received. For example, the data from the income statement itself is not sufficient enough for assessing liquidity. This statement must be viewed in conjunction with other financial statements such as the balance sheet and statement of cash flows.
    c. The preparation of the income statement requires estimates and management judgment.

7. **Statement of Comprehensive Income**

    a. **Comprehensive income** includes all changes in equity (net assets) of a business during a period except those from investments by and distributions to owners. It consists of (1) **net income or loss** (the bottom line of the income statement) and (2) **other comprehensive income (OCI)**.

        1) Certain income items are excluded from the calculation of net income and instead are included in comprehensive income. The following are the major items included in other comprehensive income:

            a) The effective portion of a gain or loss on a hedging instrument in a cash flow hedge
            b) Unrealized holding gains and losses due to changes in the fair value of available-for-sale securities
            c) Translation gains and losses for financial statements of foreign operations
            d) Certain amounts associated with accounting for defined benefit postretirement plans

b. All items of comprehensive income are recognized for the period in either

 1) **One continuous financial statement** that has two sections, net income and OCI, or
 2) **Two separate but consecutive statements**.

 a) The first statement (the income statement) presents the components of net income and total net income.
 b) The second statement (the statement of OCI) is presented immediately after the first. It presents a total of OCI with its components and a total of comprehensive income.

c. The following is an example of a separate statement of comprehensive income:

EXAMPLE

Net income		$70,000
Other comprehensive income (net of tax):		
Loss on defined benefit postretirement plans	$(15,000)	
Gains on foreign currency translation	6,000	
Gains on remeasuring available-for-sale securities	4,000	
Effective portion of losses on cash flow hedges	(3,000)	
Other comprehensive income (loss)		(8,000)
Total comprehensive income		$62,000

Stop and review! You have completed the outline for this subunit. Study multiple-choice questions 9 through 14 beginning on page 35.

1.4 STATEMENT OF CHANGES IN EQUITY AND EQUITY TRANSACTIONS

1. **Statement of Changes in Equity**

 a. A statement of changes in equity presents a reconciliation for the accounting period of the beginning balance for each component of equity to the ending balance.
 b. Each change is disclosed separately in the statement. The following are the common changes in the equity component balances during the accounting period:

 1) Net income (loss) for the period, which increases (decreases) the retained earnings balance.
 2) Distributions to owners (dividends paid), which decreases the retained earnings balance.
 3) Issuance of common stock, which increases the common stock balance. If the amount paid for the stock is above the par value of stock, the balance of additional paid-in capital is increased for the difference.
 4) Total change in other comprehensive income during the period.
 5) Repurchase of common stock (treasury stock) decreases the total shareholders' equity.

> **EXAMPLE**
>
> CI Company
> Statement of Changes in Equity (in millions)
> For the Year Ended December 31, Year 1
>
> | | Total Equity | Retained Earnings | Accumulated Other Comprehensive Income | Common Stock | Additional Paid-in Capital | Treasury Stock |
> |---|---|---|---|---|---|---|
> | **Beginning balance** | $500 | $350 | $100 | $40 | $ 30 | $(20) |
> | Net income for the period | 110 | 110 | | | | |
> | OCI for the period | 25 | | 25 | | | |
> | Common stock issued | 90 | | | 10 | 80 | |
> | Dividends declared | (60) | (60) | | | | |
> | Repurchase of common stock | (15) | | | | | (15) |
> | **Ending balance** | $650 | $400 | $125 | $50 | $110 | $(35) |
>
> A comprehensive example of a statement of changes in equity can be found in Appendix B.

2. **Statement of Retained Earnings**

    a. A statement of retained earnings reconciles the beginning and ending balances of the account. This statement is reported as part of the statement of changes in equity in a separate column.

        1) The following is a common example of retained earnings reconciliation:

            Retained earnings beginning balance
            + Net income (loss) for the period
            − Dividends distributed during the period
            + Positive (negative) prior-period adjustments
            Retained earnings ending balance

        2) Prior-period adjustments include the cumulative effect on the income statement of **changes in accounting principle** (e.g., change in inventory valuation method) and **corrections of prior-period financial statement errors**. These items require **retrospective application** (i.e., adjustment of the carrying amounts of assets, liabilities, and retained earnings at the beginning of the first period reported for the cumulative effect of the new principle or the error on the prior periods).

            a) Thus, correction of prior-period errors and the cumulative effect of changes in accounting principle **must not** be included in the calculation of current-period net income.

            b) However, **change in accounting estimate** (e.g., change in the percentage of credit sales for estimation of bad debt expense) requires **prospective application** (i.e., the effect of a change in accounting estimate is accounted for only in the period of change and any future periods affected).

    b. **Retained earnings** are sometimes appropriated (restricted) to a special account to disclose that earnings retained in the business (not paid out in dividends) are being used for special purposes. An appropriation must be clearly displayed within equity.

        1) Purposes include (a) compliance with a bond indenture (bond contract), (b) retention of assets for internally financed expansion, (c) anticipation of losses, or (d) adherence to legal restrictions.

        2) The appropriation **does not set aside assets**. It limits the availability of dividends. A formal entry (debit retained earnings, credit retained earnings appropriated) or disclosure in a note may be made.

        3) Transfers to and from an appropriation do not affect net income.

3. **Common and Preferred Stock**
    a. The most widely used classes of stock are common and preferred. The following basic terminology is related to stock.
        1) Stock authorized is the maximum amount of stock that a corporation is legally allowed to issue.
        2) Stock issued is the amount of stock authorized that has actually been issued by the corporation.
        3) Stock outstanding is the amount of stock issued that has been purchased and is held by shareholders.
    b. The **common shareholders** are the owners of the firm. They have voting rights, and they select the firm's board of directors and vote on resolutions. Common shareholders are not entitled to dividends unless so declared by the board of directors. A firm may choose not to declare any.
        1) Common shareholders are entitled to receive **liquidating distributions** only after all other claims have been satisfied, including those of preferred shareholders.
        2) Common shareholders ordinarily have **preemptive rights**. Preemptive rights give current common shareholders the right to purchase any additional stock issuances in proportion to their ownership percentages. This way the preemptive rights safeguard a common shareholder's proportionate interest in the firm.
    c. **Preferred stock** has features of debt and equity. It is classified as an equity instrument and presented in the equity section of the firm's balance sheet. Preferred stock has a fixed charge, but payment of dividends is not an obligation. The payment of dividends is at the firm's discretion. Preferred shareholders tend not to have voting rights.
        1) Preferred shareholders have the right to receive
            a) Dividends at a specified fixed rate before common shareholders may receive any and
            b) Distributions before common shareholders, but after creditors, in the event of firm bankruptcy (liquidation).
        2) The following are common features of preferred stock:
            a) **Cumulative preferred stock** accumulates unpaid dividends (called dividends in arrears). Dividends in arrears must be paid before any common dividends can be paid.
            b) Holders of **convertible preferred stock** have the right to convert the stock into shares of another class (usually common stock) at a predetermined ratio.

4. Equity Transactions – Issuance of Stock

a. Cash is increased (debited), the appropriate stock account is increased (credited) for the total par value of stock issued, and additional paid-in capital (paid-in capital in excess of par) is increased (credited) for the difference.

EXAMPLE

A company issued 50,000 shares of its $1 par-value common stock. The market price of the stock was $17 per share on the day of issue.

Cash (50,000 shares × $17 market price)	$850,000
Common stock (50,000 shares × $1 par value)	$ 50,000
Additional paid-in capital -- common (difference)	800,000

The balances of cash, common stock, and additional paid-in capital were increased by $850,000, $50,000, and $800,000, respectively.

---

b. Direct costs of issuing stock (underwriting, legal, accounting, tax, registration, etc.) must not be recognized as an expense. Instead, they reduce the net proceeds received and additional paid-in capital.

5. Equity Transactions – Cash Dividend

a. On the **date of declaration**, the board of directors formally approves a dividend. A declaration of a dividend **decreases** (debits) the **retained earnings** account.
b. All holders of the stock on the **date of record** are legally entitled to receive the dividend.
c. The date of payment is the date on which the dividend is paid.

EXAMPLE

On September 12, a company's board of directors declared a $3 per-share dividend to be paid on October 15 to all holders of common stock. On the date of declaration, 40,000 shares of common stock were outstanding.

September 12 -- Declaration date			October 15 -- Payment date	
Retained earnings (40,000 × $3)	$120,000		Dividends payable	$120,000
Dividends payable		$120,000	Cash	$120,000

---

6. Equity Transactions – Property Dividend

a. When an entity declares a dividend consisting of tangible property,

1) First, the property is **remeasured to fair value** as of the date of declaration, and any gain or loss on the remeasurement is recognized in the statement of income
2) Second, the carrying amount of retained earnings is decreased for the fair value of the property to be distributed
3) Third, the property is distributed as a dividend

EXAMPLE

On August 1, a company's board of directors declared a property dividend (land) to be distributed on December 1 to holders of common stock. On August 1, the carrying amount of the land to be distributed is $50,000 and its fair value is $80,000. The journal entries to record the declaration and distribution of the property dividend are as follows:

August 1 -- Declaration date

Land ($80,000 – $50,000)	$30,000		Retained earnings	$80,000
Gain on land remeasurement		$30,000	Property dividend payable	$80,000

December 1 -- Payment date

Property dividend payable	$80,000
Land	$80,000

7. **Equity Transactions – Stock Dividend and Stock Split**
    a. A stock dividend involves no distribution of cash or other property. Stock dividends are accounted for as a reclassification of different equity accounts, not as liabilities.
        1) The recipient does not recognize income. It has the same proportionate interest in the entity and the same total carrying amount as before the stock dividend.
    b. The accounting for stock dividends depends on the percentage of new shares to be issued.
        1) An issuance of shares **less than 20% to 25%** of the previously outstanding common shares should be recognized as a **stock dividend**.
        2) An issuance of **more than 20% to 25%** of the previously outstanding common shares should be recognized as a **stock split in the form of a dividend**.
    c. In accounting for a **stock dividend**, the **fair value** of the additional shares issued is reclassified from retained earnings to common stock (at par value) and the difference to additional paid-in capital.

EXAMPLE

On May 1, a company's board of directors declared and paid a 10% stock dividend on the 45,000 shares of common stock outstanding ($1 par value). The stock was trading for $15 per share at the declaration date.

May 1 -- Declaration and payment date

Retained earnings [(45,000 shares × 10%) × $15 market price]	$67,500	
Common stock [(45,000 shares × 10%) × $1 par value]		$ 4,500
Additional paid-in capital (difference)		63,000

---

    d. For a stock dividend that is accounted for as a **stock split in the form of a dividend**, the **par value** of the additional shares issued is reclassified from retained earnings to common stock.

EXAMPLE

In the preceding example, assume that a 40% stock split in the form of a dividend was declared.

May 1 -- Declaration and payment date

Retained earnings [(45,000 shares × 40%) × $1 par value]	$18,000	
Common stock		$18,000

---

    e. **Stock splits** are issuances of shares that do not affect any aggregate par value of shares issued and outstanding or total equity. Stock split reduces the par value of each stock and increases the number of shares outstanding.
        1) No entry is made, and no transfer from retained earnings occurs.

Stop and review! You have completed the outline for this subunit. Study multiple-choice questions 15 through 19 beginning on page 36.

1.5 STATEMENT OF CASH FLOWS

1. **Overview**
    a. The **primary purpose** of the statement of cash flows is to provide relevant information about the cash receipts and cash payments of an entity during the period. To achieve this purpose, the statement should provide information about cash inflows and outflows from the operating, investing, and financing activities of an entity. This is the accepted order of presentation.
        1) The statement of cash flows should help users assess the entity's ability to generate positive future net cash flows (liquidity), its ability to meet obligations (solvency), and its financial flexibility.

b. The statement of cash flows explains the change in cash and cash equivalents during the period. It reconciles the period's beginning balance of cash and cash equivalents with the ending balance.

EXAMPLE

The following is an example of the summarized format of the statement of cash flows (only the headings). The amounts of cash and cash equivalents at the beginning and end of the year are taken from the balance sheet.

Entity A's Statement of Cash Flows for the Year Ended December 31, Year 1

Net cash provided by (used in) operating activities	$20,000
Net cash provided by (used in) investing activities	(5,000)
Net cash provided by (used in) financing activities	9,000
Net increase (decrease) in cash and cash equivalents during the year	$24,000
Cash and cash equivalents at beginning of year (January 1, Year 1)	6,000
Cash and cash equivalents at end of year (December 31, Year 1)	$30,000

A more detailed example format can be found in Appendix B.

---

2. **Operating Activities**

   a. Operating activities are all transactions and other events that are not financing or investing activities. Cash flows from operating activities are primarily derived from the principal revenue-producing activities of the entity. They generally result from transactions and other events that enter into the determination of net income.

   b. The following are examples of **cash inflows** from operating activities:

      1) Cash receipts from the sale of goods and services (including collections of accounts receivable)
      2) Cash receipts from royalties, fees, commissions, and other revenue
      3) Cash received in the form of **interest** or **dividends**

   c. The following are examples of **cash outflows** from operating activities:

      1) Cash payments to suppliers for goods and services
      2) Cash payments to employees
      3) Cash payments to government for taxes, duties, fines, and other fees or penalties
      4) Payments of **interest on debt**

   d. The two acceptable methods of presentation of cash flows from operating activities are the direct and the indirect methods.

      1) The only difference between these two methods is their presentation of **net cash flows from operating activities**. The total cash flows from operating, investing, and financing activities are the same regardless of which method is used.
      2) The CMA exam requires candidates to know how to prepare the statement of cash flows using the indirect method.

3. **Investing Activities**

   a. Cash flows from investing activities represent the extent to which expenditures have been made for resources intended to generate future income and cash flows.

   b. The following are examples of **cash outflows (and inflows)** from investing activities:

      1) Cash payments to acquire (cash receipts from sale of) property, plant and equipment; intangible assets; and other long-lived assets
      2) Cash payments to acquire (cash receipts from sale and maturity of) equity and debt instruments of other entities for investing purposes
      3) Cash advances and loans made to other parties (cash receipts from repayment of advances and loans made to other parties)

4. **Financing Activities**

   a. Cash flows from financing activities generally involve the cash effects of transactions and other events that relate to the issuance, settlement, or reacquisition of the entity's debt and equity instruments.

   b. The following are examples of **cash inflows** from financing activities:

      1) Cash proceeds from issuing shares and other equity instruments (obtaining resources from owners).
      2) Cash proceeds from issuing loans, notes, bonds, and other short-term or long-term borrowings.

   c. The following are examples of **cash outflows** from financing activities:

      1) Cash repayments of amounts borrowed
      2) Payments of cash dividends
      3) Cash payments to acquire or redeem the entity's own shares
      4) Cash payments by a lessee for a reduction of the outstanding liability relating to a capital lease

5. **Noncash Investing and Financing Activities**

   a. Information about all **investing and financing activities** that affect recognized assets or liabilities **but not cash flows** must be disclosed in the notes, outside the body of the statement of cash flows.

   b. The following are examples of noncash investing and financing activities:

      1) Conversion of debt to equity
      2) Acquisition of assets either by assuming directly related liabilities or by means of a capital lease
      3) Exchange of a noncash asset or liability for another

6. **Indirect Method of Presenting Operating Cash Flows**

   a. Under the indirect method (also called the reconciliation method), the net cash flow from operating activities is determined by adjusting the net income of a business for the effect of the following:

      1) **Noncash revenue and expenses** that were **included in net income**, such as depreciation and amortization expenses, impairment losses, undistributed earnings of equity-method investments, and amortization of discount and premium on bonds
      2) Items **included in net income** whose cash effects relate to **investing or financing cash flows**, such as gains or losses on sales of property and equipment (related to investing activities) and gain or losses on extinguishment of debt (related to financing activities)
      3) All **deferrals** of past operating cash flows, such as changes during the period in inventory and deferred income
      4) All **accruals** of expected future operating cash flows, such as changes during the period in accounts receivable and accounts payable

      NOTE: The net income for the period as it reported in the income statement was calculated using the accrual method of accounting. Therefore, adjustments must be made to reach the amount of cash flow from operating activities.

   b. The reconciliation of net income to net cash flow from operating activities must disclose all major classes of reconciling items. At a minimum, this disclosure reports changes in (1) accounts receivable and accounts payable related to operating activities and (2) inventories.

EXAMPLE

During Year 2, Bishop Corp. had the following transactions:

- Inventory (cost $9,000) was sold for $14,000, with $13,000 on credit and $1,000 in cash.
- Cash collected on credit sales to customers was $12,000.
- Inventory was purchased for $6,500.
- Bishop paid $8,500 to suppliers.

The following is Bishop's income statement for the year ended on December 31, Year 2:

Sales	$14,000
Cost of goods sold	(9,000)
Net income	**$ 5,000**

The following are Bishop's balance sheets on December 31, Year 1, and December 31, Year 2:

	December 31			December 31	
Current assets	Year 1	Year 2	Current liabilities	Year 1	Year 2
Cash	$10,000	$14,500	Acc. payable	$ 5,000	$ 3,000
Net acc. receivable	6,000	7,000	Equity		
Inventory	14,000	11,500	Common stock	21,000	21,000
			Retained earnings	4,000	9,000
Total assets	$30,000	$33,000	Total liability and equity	$30,000	$33,000

Under the indirect method, the net cash flow from operating activities is determined by adjusting net income for the period.

Bishop's Statement of Cash Flows for the Year Ended on December 31, Year 2
(Using the indirect method)

Cash flows from operating activities:

Net income			$ 5,000
Increase in accounts receivable ($7,000 – $6,000)		$(1,000)	(1)
Decrease in inventory ($11,500 – $14,000)		2,500	(2)
Decrease in accounts payable ($3,000 – $5,000)		(2,000)	(3)
Total adjustments			(500)
Net cash provided by operating activities			**$ 4,500**
Cash at beginning of year			10,000
Cash at end of year			**$14,500**

Explanation:

(1) The amount of accounts receivable increased during year by $1,000, implying that cash collections were less than credit sales. The net income for the period is an accrual accounting amount. Thus, the increase in accounts receivable during the period must be subtracted from net income to determine the cash flow from operating activities.

(2) Inventory decreased by $2,500, implying that purchases were less than the amount of cost of goods sold. Thus, it must be added to net income to determine the cash flow from operating activities.

(3) Accounts payable decreased by $2,000, implying that cash paid to suppliers was greater than purchases. Thus, it must be subtracted from net income.

The following rules will help reconcile the net income to net cash flow from operating activities under the indirect method:

Increase in current operating liabilities	Added to net income
Decrease in current operating assets	Added to net income
Increase in current operating assets	Subtracted from net income
Decrease in current operating liabilities	Subtracted from net income

EXAMPLE

During Year 2, Knight Corp. had the following transactions:

- On December 31, Year 2, a machine was sold for $47,000 in cash. The machine was acquired by Knight on January 1, Year 1, for $50,000. Its useful life is 10 years with no salvage value, and it is depreciated using the straight-line method.
- On December 31, Year 2, the $31,500 due on a loan (principal + accumulated interest) was repaid. The term of the loan was 1 year from December 31, Year 1. The annual interest rate was 5%.
- During Year 2, Knight received $14,000 in cash for services provided to customers.

The following is Knight's income statement for the year ended on December 31, Year 2:

Revenue	$14,000
Depreciation expense ($50,000 ÷ 10)	(5,000)
Interest expense ($30,000 × 5%)	(1,500)
Gain on machine disposal [$47,000 − ($50,000 − $10,000)]	7,000
Net income	**$14,500**

The following are Knight's balance sheets on December 31, Year 1, and December 31, Year 2:

	December 31				December 31	
Current assets	Year 1	Year 2	Current liabilities		Year 1	Year 2
Cash	$10,000	$39,500	Loan		$30,000	$ 0
Fixed assets			Equity			
Machine at cost	50,000	0	Common stock		21,000	21,000
Accumulated depreciation	(5,000)	0	Retained earnings		4,000	18,500
Net fixed assets	$45,000	$ 0				
Total assets	$55,000	$39,500	Total liability and equity		$55,000	$39,500

Under the indirect method, the net cash flow from operating activities is determined by adjusting net income for the period.

Knight's Statement of Cash Flows for the Year Ended on December 31, Year 2
(Using the indirect method)

Cash flows from operating activities:			
Net income			$ 14,500
Depreciation expense		$ 5,000	(1)
Gain on sale of machine		(7,000)	(2)
Total adjustments			(2,000)
Net cash provided by operating activities			**$ 12,500**
Cash flows from investing activities:			
Proceeds from sale of machine		$47,000	
Net cash provided by investing activities			47,000
Cash flows from financing activities:			
Repayment of loan		(30,000)	
Net cash used in financing activities			(30,000)
Net increase in cash			$ 29,500
Cash at beginning of year			10,000
Cash at end of year			**$ 39,500**

Explanation

(1) **Depreciation expense** is a noncash expense included in net income. Thus, it must be added to net income to determine the net cash flow from operating activities.

(2) **Gain on sale of machine** is an item included in net income. Its cash effect is related to investing activities. Thus, it must be subtracted from net income to determine the net cash flow from operating activities.

The following rules will help reconcile net income to net cash flow from operating activities under the indirect method:

Noncash losses and expenses included in net income	Added to net income
Losses and expenses whose cash effects are related to investing or financing cash flows	Added to net income
Noncash gains and revenues included in net income	Subtracted from net income
Gains and revenues whose cash effects are related to investing or financing cash flows	Subtracted from net income

7. **Direct Method of Presenting Operating Cash Flows**

    a. Under the direct method, the entity presents major classes of actual gross operating cash receipts and payments and their sum (net cash flow from operating activities). At a minimum, the following must be presented:

    1) Cash collected from customers
    2) Interest and dividends received
    3) Other operating cash receipts, if any
    4) Cash paid to employees and other suppliers of goods and services
    5) Interest paid
    6) Income taxes paid
    7) Other operating cash payments, if any

    b. If the direct method is used, the reconciliation of net income to net cash flow from operating activities (the operating section of the indirect method format) must be provided in a separate schedule.

        1) Most entities apply the indirect method because the reconciliation must be prepared regardless of the method chosen.

Stop and review! You have completed the outline for this subunit. Study multiple-choice questions 20 through 25 beginning on page 38.

1.6 REVENUE RECOGNITION -- REVENUE RECOGNITION AFTER DELIVERY

1. **Revenue Recognition Principle**

    a. According to the revenue recognition principle, revenues and gains should be recognized when **(1) realized or realizable and (2) earned**.

    1) Revenues and gains are realized when goods or services have been exchanged for cash or claims to cash. Revenues and gains are realizable when goods or services have been exchanged for assets that are readily convertible into cash or claims to cash.

    2) Revenues are earned when the earning process has been substantially completed, and the entity is entitled to the resulting benefits or revenues.

        a) Thus, revenue on sales can be recognized in the statement of income even if the cash from sales is not received yet.

IFRS Difference

For a **sale of goods**, revenue is recognized when **five conditions** are met. (1) The entity has transferred the significant risks and rewards of ownership, (2) the entity has neither continuing managerial involvement to an extent associated with ownership nor effective control over the goods, (3) the revenue (measured at the fair value of the consideration received or receivable) can be reliably measured, (4) it is probable that the economic benefits will flow to the entity, and (5) transaction costs can be reliably measured.

For the **rendering of a service**, if the outcome can be reliably estimated, revenue (measured as described above) is recognized based on the stage of completion (the percentage-of-completion method). The outcome can be reliably estimated when (1) revenue can be reliably measured, (2) it is probable that the economic benefits will flow to the entity, (3) the stage of completion can be reliably measured, and (4) the costs incurred and the costs to complete can be reliably measured.

2. **The Installment Method**

   a. The installment method is only acceptable when receivables are collectible over an extended period and no reasonable basis exists for estimating the degree of collectibility.

   b. The installment method recognizes a **partial profit** on a sale as each installment is collected.

   1) This approach differs from the ordinary procedure, that is, recognition of revenue when a transaction is complete. Thus, when collection problems (bad debts) can be reasonably estimated, the full profit is usually recognized in the period of sale.

   c. The amount recognized each period under the installment method is the **realized gross profit**. This amount equals the cash collected on installment sales for the period times the gross profit percentage on installment sales for the period.

$$\text{Gross profit percentage} = \frac{\text{Gross profit on installment sales}}{\text{Installment sales}}$$

EXAMPLE

A TV costing $600 is the only item sold on the installment basis in Year 1. The TV was sold for a price of $1,000 on November 1, Year 1. Thus, the gross profit percentage is 40% [($1,000 sales – $600 cost of goods sold) ÷ $1,000 sales]. A down payment of $100 was received, and the remainder is due in nine monthly payments of $100 each. Because all payments are due within 1 year, no interest is charged. The entry for the sale is

Cash	$100	
Installment receivable, Year 1	900	
Cost of installment sales	600	
Inventory		$ 600
Installment sales		1,000

d. At the end of the period, a portion of deferred gross profit is realized.

EXAMPLE

In December, when the first installment is received, the entry is

Cash	$100	
Installment receivable, Year 1		$100

At December 31, installment sales and cost of installment sales are closed, and deferred gross profit is recognized. Moreover, deferred gross profit must be adjusted to report the portion that has been earned. Given that $200 of the total price has been received, $80 of the gross profit ($200 cash collected × 40% gross profit percentage) has been earned. The entry is

Installment sales	$1,000	
Cost of installment sales		$600
Deferred gross profit		400
Deferred gross profit (Year 1)	$80	
Realized gross profit		$80

Net income should include only the $80 realized gross profit for the period. The balance sheet should report a receivable of $800 minus the deferred gross profit of $320. Thus, the net receivable is $480.

Balance sheet:
Installment receivable (net of deferred gross profit of $320)	$480

e. The gross profit percentage for the period of the sale continues to be applied to the realization of deferred gross profit from sales of that period.

EXAMPLE

In Year 2, the remaining $800 is received, and the $320 balance of deferred gross profit is recognized. If only $400 were received in Year 2 (if payments were extended), the December, Year 2, statements would report a $400 installment receivable and $160 of deferred gross profit.

3. **Cost-Recovery Method**

   a. The cost-recovery method may be used only in the same circumstances as the installment method. However, no profit is recognized until collections exceed the cost of the item sold. Subsequent receipts are treated entirely as revenues.

EXAMPLE

In Year 1, Creditor made a $100,000 sale. The cost of the item sold was $70,000, and Year 1 collections equaled $50,000. In Year 2, collections equaled $25,000. The net receivable (receivable − deferred profit) was $0 at the end of Year 2. The following entries are based on the cost-recovery method:

Year 1:	Receivable	$100,000	
	Inventory		$70,000
	Deferred gross profit		30,000
	Cash	$50,000	
	Receivable		$50,000
Year 2:	Cash	$25,000	
	Deferred gross profit	5,000	
	Receivable		$25,000
	Realized gross profit		5,000

4. **Deposit Method**

   a. This method is used when cash is received, but the criteria for a sale have not been met. Thus, the seller continues to account for the property in the same way as an owner. No revenue or profit is recognized because it has not been earned, e.g., by transferring the property. The entry is

   Cash $XXX
      Deposit liability $XXX

Stop and review! You have completed the outline for this subunit. Study multiple-choice questions 26 and 27 on page 39.

1.7 REVENUE RECOGNITION -- LONG-TERM CONSTRUCTION CONTRACTS

1. **The Completed-Contract Method**

   a. The completed-contract method is used to account for a long-term project when the percentage-of-completion method is inappropriate.

      1) It **defers all contract costs** in the inventory account **construction in progress** until the project is completed. It records progress billings in the contra-inventory account **progress billings**.
      2) Revenue and gross profit are recognized only upon completion of the contract.

2. **The Percentage-of-Completion Method**

   a. Percentage-of-completion is the preferable method. It records (1) all contract costs in construction in progress and (2) all amounts billed in progress billings. However, the percentage-of-completion method differs from the completed-contract method because it recognizes revenue on long-term contracts when the

      1) Extent of progress toward completion, contract revenue, and contract costs are reasonably estimable;
      2) Enforceable rights regarding goods or services to be provided, the consideration to be exchanged, and the terms of settlement are clearly specified; and
      3) Obligations of the parties are expected to be fulfilled.

   b. The **amount of gross profit recognized** in a period is calculated as follows:

      1) Calculate the estimated total gross profit on the project.

EXAMPLE

A contractor is constructing an office complex for a real estate developer. The agreed-upon contract price was $75,000,000. As of the close of Year 4 of the project, the contractor had incurred $44,000,000 of costs. By its best estimates as of that date, costs remaining to finish the project were $19,000,000. Gross profit of $6,255,000 had been recognized as of Year 4.

Contract price	$75,000,000
Minus: costs incurred to date	(44,000,000)
Minus: estimated costs to complete	(19,000,000)
Estimated total gross profit	$12,000,000

---

   2) Calculate the percentage of the project completed as of the reporting date, determined by the ratio of costs incurred thus far to estimated total costs.

EXAMPLE

Total estimated costs for the project as of the end of Year 4 are calculated as follows:

Costs incurred to date	$44,000,000
Estimated costs to complete	19,000,000
Total estimated costs	$63,000,000

The project is therefore 69.8% complete ($44,000,000 ÷ $63,000,000).

3) Subtract the gross profit recognized so far.

EXAMPLE

The contractor will recognize $2,121,000 in gross profit for Year 4, calculated as follows:

Estimated total gross profit	$12,000,000
Times: percentage complete	× 69.8%
Gross profit earned to date	$ 8,376,000
Minus: gross profit recognized in prior periods (given)	(6,255,000)
Gross profit for current period	$ 2,121,000

---

c. As soon as an **estimated loss** on any project becomes apparent, it is recognized in full, under both the completed-contract and percentage-of-completion methods.

3. **Comparative Journal Entries**

EXAMPLE

A contractor agrees to build a bridge that will take 3 years to complete. The contract price is $2,000,000 and expected total costs are $1,200,000.

	Year 1	Year 2	Year 3
Costs incurred during each year	$300,000	$600,000	$550,000
Costs expected in future	900,000	600,000	0

By the end of Year 1, 25% ($300,000 ÷ $1,200,000) of expected costs has been incurred. Using percentage-of-completion, the contractor will recognize 25% of the revenue or gross profit that will be earned on the project. The total gross profit is expected to be $800,000 ($2,000,000 − $1,200,000), so $200,000 ($800,000 × 25%) of gross profit should be recognized in Year 1.

	Percentage-of-Completion		Completed-Contract	
Year 1: Construction in progress	$300,000		$300,000	
Cash or accounts payable		$300,000		$300,000
Construction in progress	$200,000		--	
Construction gross profit		$200,000		--

At the end of Year 2, total costs incurred are $900,000 ($300,000 + $600,000). Given that $600,000 is expected to be incurred in the future, the total expected cost is $1,500,000 ($900,000 + $600,000), and the estimate of gross profit is $500,000 ($2,000,000 contract price − $1,500,000 costs). If the project is 60% complete ($900,000 ÷ $1,500,000), $300,000 of cumulative gross profit should be recognized for Years 1 and 2 ($500,000 × 60%) under percentage-of-completion. Because $200,000 was recognized in Year 1, $100,000 should be recognized in Year 2.

	Percentage-of-Completion		Completed-Contract	
Year 2: Construction in progress	$600,000		$600,000	
Cash or accounts payable		$600,000		$600,000
Construction in progress	$100,000		--	
Construction gross profit		$100,000		--

At the end of the third year, total costs are $1,450,000. Thus, the total gross profit is known to be $550,000. Because a total of $300,000 was recognized in Years 1 and 2, $250,000 should be recognized in Year 3, using percentage-of-completion. *

	Percentage-of-Completion		Completed-Contract	
Year 3: Construction in progress	$550,000		$550,000	
Cash or accounts payable		$550,000		$550,000
Cash	$2,000,000		$2,000,000	
Construction in progress		$1,750,000		$1,450,000
Construction gross profit		250,000		550,000

* This is the first recognition of gross profit under the completed-contract method.

4. Progress Billings

a. Ordinarily, progress billings are made and payments are received during the term of the contract. The entries are

The customer is billed:
Accounts receivable $XXX
   Progress billings $XXX

The customer pays:
Cash $XXX
   Accounts receivable $XXX

1) Neither billing nor the receipt of cash affects gross profit. Moreover, billing, receipt of payment, and incurrence of cost have the same effects under both accounting methods.

b. The difference between **construction in progress** (costs and recognized gross profit) and progress billings to date is reported as a **current asset** if construction in progress exceeds total billings and as a **current liability** if billings exceed construction in progress.

Closing entry:
Progress billings $XXX
   Construction in progress $XXX

IFRS Difference

The completed-contract method is not used. When the outcome of a long-term construction contract cannot be reliably estimated, revenue recognition is limited to recoverable costs incurred. Contract costs must be recognized as an expense in the period in which they are incurred.

Stop and review! You have completed the outline for this subunit. Study multiple-choice questions 28 and 29 on page 40.

QUESTIONS

1.1 Concepts of Financial Accounting

1. A primary objective of external financial reporting is

A. Direct measurement of the value of a business enterprise.
B. Provision of information that is useful to present and potential investors, creditors, and others in making rational financial decisions regarding the enterprise.
C. Establishment of rules for accruing liabilities.
D. Direct measurement of the enterprise's stock price.

Answer (B) is correct.
   REQUIRED: The primary objective of external financial reporting.
   DISCUSSION: According to the FASB's Conceptual Framework, the objectives of external financial reporting are to provide information that (1) is useful to present and potential investors, creditors, and others in making rational financial decisions regarding the enterprise; (2) helps those parties in assessing the amounts, timing, and uncertainty of prospective cash receipts from dividends or interest and the proceeds from sale, redemption, or maturity of securities or loans; and (3) concerns the economic resources of an enterprise, the claims thereto, and the effects of transactions, events, and circumstances that change its resources and claims thereto.
   Answer (A) is incorrect. Financial reporting is not designed to measure directly the value of a business. Answer (C) is incorrect. While rules for accruing liabilities are a practical concern, the establishment of such rules is not a primary objective of external reporting. Answer (D) is incorrect. The objectives of financial accounting are unrelated to the measurement of stock prices; stock prices are a product of stock market forces.

SU 1: External Financial Statements and Revenue Recognition 33

2. Which of the following is **true** regarding the comparison of managerial and financial accounting?

A. Managerial accounting is generally more precise.

B. Managerial accounting has a past focus, and financial accounting has a future focus.

C. The emphasis on managerial accounting is relevance, and the emphasis on financial accounting is timeliness.

D. Managerial accounting need not follow generally accepted accounting principles (GAAP), while financial accounting must follow them.

Answer (D) is correct.
REQUIRED: The true comparison of managerial and financial accounting.
DISCUSSION: Managerial accounting assists management decision making, planning, and control. Financial accounting addresses accounting for an entity's assets, liabilities, revenues, expenses, and other elements of financial statements. Financial statements are the primary method of communicating to external parties information about the entity's results of operations, financial position, and cash flows. For general-purpose financial statements to be useful to external parties, they must be prepared in conformity with accounting principles that are generally accepted in the United States. However, managerial accounting information is primarily directed to specific internal users. Hence, it ordinarily need not follow such guidance.
Answer (A) is incorrect. Managerial accounting may be no more precise than financial accounting. For example, it relies on allocations of certain product costs (e.g., overhead) that are based on assumptions rather than on cause-and-effect relationships. Answer (B) is incorrect. Only managerial accounting is forward-looking. Financial accounting essentially records what has already occurred. Answer (C) is incorrect. Choices of financial accounting information to be reported must balance relevance (including timeliness) and reliability. External parties will not find financial accounting information useful if it is timely but unreliable.

3. Notes to financial statements are beneficial in meeting the disclosure requirements of financial reporting. The notes should **not** be used to

A. Describe significant accounting policies.

B. Describe depreciation methods employed by the company.

C. Describe principles and methods peculiar to the industry in which the company operates, when these principles and methods are predominantly followed in that industry.

D. Correct an improper presentation in the financial statements.

Answer (D) is correct.
REQUIRED: The improper use of notes in financial statements.
DISCUSSION: Financial statement notes should not be used to correct improper presentations. The financial statements should be presented correctly on their own. Notes should be used to explain the methods used to prepare the financial statements and the amounts shown. The first footnote typically describes significant accounting policies.

1.2 Statement of Financial Position (Balance Sheet)

4. A statement of financial position is intended to help investors and creditors

A. Assess the amount, timing, and uncertainty of prospective net cash inflows of a firm.

B. Evaluate economic resources and obligations of a firm.

C. Evaluate economic performance of a firm.

D. Evaluate changes in the ownership equity of a firm.

Answer (B) is correct.
REQUIRED: The purpose of a statement of financial position.
DISCUSSION: The statement of financial position, or balance sheet, provides information about an entity's resource structure (assets) and financing structure (liabilities and equity) at a moment in time. According to the FASB's Conceptual Framework, the statement of financial position does not purport to show the value of a business, but it enables investors, creditors, and other users to make their own estimates of value. It helps users to assess liquidity, financial flexibility, profitability, and risk.
Answer (A) is incorrect. Providing information to help assess the amount, timing, and uncertainty of cash flows is an objective of the statement of cash flows. Answer (C) is incorrect. The primary focus of financial reporting is information about an enterprise's performance provided by measures of earnings and its components. Hence, an income statement is more directly useful to investors and creditors for evaluating economic performance. Answer (D) is incorrect. Disclosures of changes in shareholders' equity, in either the basic statements, the notes thereto, or a separate statement, help users to evaluate changes in the ownership equity of a firm.

5. When classifying assets as current and noncurrent for reporting purposes,

A. The amounts at which current assets are carried and reported must reflect realizable cash values.
B. Prepayments for items such as insurance or rent are included in an "other assets" group rather than as current assets as they will ultimately be expensed.
C. The time period by which current assets are distinguished from noncurrent assets is determined by the seasonal nature of the business.
D. Assets are classified as current if they are reasonably expected to be realized in cash or consumed during the normal operating cycle.

Answer (D) is correct.
REQUIRED: The true statement about the classification of current assets.
DISCUSSION: For financial reporting purposes, current assets consist of cash and other assets or resources expected to be realized in cash, sold, or consumed during the longer of 1 year or the normal operating cycle of the business.
Answer (A) is incorrect. Current assets are measured using different attributes, for example, lower of cost or market for inventory and net realizable value for accounts receivable. Answer (B) is incorrect. Prepayments may qualify as current assets. They often will be consumed during the operating cycle. Answer (C) is incorrect. The classification criterion is based on the normal operating cycle regardless of the seasonality of the business.

6. A corporation uses a calendar year for financial and tax reporting purposes and has $100 million of mortgage bonds due on January 15, Year 2. By January 10, Year 2, the corporation intends to refinance this debt with new long-term mortgage bonds and has entered into a financing agreement that clearly demonstrates its ability to consummate the refinancing. This debt is to be

A. Classified as a current liability on the statement of financial position at December 31, Year 1.
B. Classified as a long-term liability on the statement of financial position at December 31, Year 1.
C. Retired as of December 31, Year 1.
D. Considered off-balance-sheet debt.

Answer (B) is correct.
REQUIRED: The balance sheet treatment of maturing long-term debt that is to be refinanced on a long-term basis.
DISCUSSION: Short-term obligations expected to be refinanced should be reported as current liabilities unless the firm both plans to refinance and has the ability to refinance the debt on a long-term basis. The ability to refinance on a long-term basis is evidenced by a post-balance-sheet date issuance of long-term debt or a financing arrangement that will clearly permit long-term refinancing.
Answer (A) is incorrect. The company intends to refinance the debt on a long-term basis. Answer (C) is incorrect. The debt has not been retired. Answer (D) is incorrect. The debt is on the balance sheet.

7. The purchase of treasury stock is recorded on the statement of financial position as a(n)

A. Increase in assets.
B. Decrease in liabilities.
C. Increase in shareholders' equity.
D. Decrease in shareholders' equity.

Answer (D) is correct.
REQUIRED: The accounting for the purchase of treasury stock.
DISCUSSION: The purchase of treasury stock is recorded on the statement of financial position as a decrease in shareholders' equity.
Answer (A) is incorrect. Treasury stock cannot be reported as an asset. Answer (B) is incorrect. Treasury stock cannot be reported as an asset nor is it associated with liabilities. Answer (C) is incorrect. The purchase of treasury stock is recorded on the statement of financial position as a decrease in shareholders' equity.

8. A statement of financial position provides a basis for all of the following **except**

A. Computing rates of return.
B. Evaluating capital structure.
C. Assessing liquidity and financial flexibility.
D. Determining profitability and assessing past performance.

Answer (D) is correct.
REQUIRED: The item for which a statement of financial position is not useful.
DISCUSSION: The statement of financial position, also known as the balance sheet, reports an entity's financial position at a moment in time. It is therefore not useful for assessing past performance for a period of time. A balance sheet can be used to help users assess liquidity, financial flexibility, and risk.
Answer (A) is incorrect. The statement of financial position reports the amount of invested capital necessary for computing rates of return. Answer (B) is incorrect. The statement of financial position reports the details of an entity's capital structure, i.e., the levels of debt and equity. Answer (C) is incorrect. The statement of financial position reports current and noncurrent assets and liabilities. Thus, it is useful for assessing liquidity and financial flexibility.

1.3 Income Statement and Statement of Comprehensive Income

9. In a multiple-step income statement for a retail company, all of the following are included in the operating section **except**

A. Sales.
B. Cost of goods sold.
C. Dividend revenue.
D. Administrative and selling expenses.

Answer (C) is correct.
REQUIRED: The item excluded from the operating section of a multiple-step income statement of a retailer.
DISCUSSION: The operating section of a retailer's income statement includes all revenues and costs necessary for the operation of the retail establishment, e.g., sales, cost of goods sold, administrative expenses, and selling expenses. Dividend revenue, however, is classified under other revenues. In a statement of cash flows, cash dividends received are considered an operating cash flow.
Answer (A) is incorrect. Sales is part of the normal operations of a retailer. Answer (B) is incorrect. Cost of goods sold is part of the normal operations of a retailer. Answer (D) is incorrect. Administrative and selling expenses are part of the normal operations of a retailer.

10. The profit and loss statement of an entity includes the following information for the current fiscal year:

Sales	$160,000
Gross profit	48,000
Year-end finished goods inventory	58,300
Opening finished goods inventory	60,190

The cost of goods manufactured by the entity for the current fiscal year is

A. $46,110
B. $49,890
C. $110,110
D. $113,890

Answer (C) is correct.
REQUIRED: The cost of goods manufactured.
DISCUSSION: The entity's cost of goods manufactured can be calculated as follows:

Sales	$160,000
Less: gross profit	(48,000)
Cost of goods sold	$112,000
Add: ending finished goods	58,300
Goods available for sale	$170,300
Less: beginning finished goods	(60,190)
Cost of goods manufactured	$110,110

Answer (A) is incorrect. Improperly beginning with gross profit instead of sales results in $46,110. Answer (B) is incorrect. Improperly beginning with gross profit instead of sales, then improperly subtracting ending finished goods and adding beginning finished goods results in $49,890. Answer (D) is incorrect. Improperly subtracting ending finished goods and adding beginning finished goods results in $113,890.

11. Which one of the following would be shown on a multiple-step income statement but **not** on a single-step income statement?

A. Loss from discontinued operations.
B. Gross profit.
C. Extraordinary gain.
D. Net income from continuing operations.

Answer (B) is correct.
REQUIRED: The item on a multiple-step income statement not shown on a single-step income statement.
DISCUSSION: A single-step income statement combines all revenues and gains, combines all expenses and losses, and subtracts the latter from the former in a "single step" to arrive at net income. Gross profit, being the difference between sales revenue and cost of goods sold, does not appear on a single-step income statement.
Answer (A) is incorrect. Loss from discontinued operations is shown on both a multiple-step and a single-step income statement. Answer (C) is incorrect. Extraordinary gain is no longer used. Answer (D) is incorrect. Net income from continuing operations is shown on both a multiple-step and a single-step income statement.

12. The financial statement that provides a summary of the firm's operations for a period of time is the

A. Income statement.
B. Statement of financial position.
C. Statement of shareholders' equity.
D. Statement of retained earnings.

Answer (A) is correct.
REQUIRED: The financial statement that provides a summary of the firm's operations for a period of time.
DISCUSSION: The results of operations for a period of time are reported in the income statement (statement of earnings) on the accrual basis using an approach oriented to historical transactions.
Answer (B) is incorrect. The statement of financial position reports a firm's resources and claims to those resources at a moment in time. Answer (C) is incorrect. The statement of shareholders' equity presents a reconciliation in columnar format of the beginning and ending balances in the various equity accounts. Answer (D) is incorrect. The statement of retained earnings presents the changes in an entity's retained earnings during a period of time.

13. Comprehensive income is **best** defined as

    A. Net income excluding extraordinary gains and losses.
    B. The change in net assets for the period including contributions by owners and distributions to owners.
    C. Total revenues minus total expenses.
    D. The change in net assets for the period excluding owner transactions.

Answer (D) is correct.
REQUIRED: The definition of comprehensive income.
DISCUSSION: Comprehensive income includes all changes in equity of a business entity except those changes resulting from investments by owners and distributions to owners. Comprehensive income includes two major categories: net income and other comprehensive income (OCI). Net income includes the results of operations classified as income from continuing operations and discontinued operations. Components of comprehensive income not included in the determination of net income are included in OCI, for example, unrealized gains and losses on available-for-sale securities (except those that are hedged items in a fair value hedge).
Answer (A) is incorrect. Extraordinary gains and losses are no longer used. Answer (B) is incorrect. The change in net assets for the period including contributions by owners and distributions to owners is the change in equity. Answer (C) is incorrect. Total revenues minus total expenses is operating income.

14. Given the following data for a company, what is the cost of goods sold?

Beginning inventory of finished goods	$100,000
Cost of goods manufactured	700,000
Ending inventory of finished goods	200,000
Beginning work-in-process inventory	300,000
Ending work-in-process inventory	50,000

    A. $500,000
    B. $600,000
    C. $800,000
    D. $950,000

Answer (B) is correct.
REQUIRED: The cost of goods sold.
DISCUSSION: The company's cost of goods sold can be calculated as follows:

Beginning inventory of finished goods	$ 100,000
Add: cost of goods manufactured	700,000
Less: ending inventory of finished goods	(200,000)
Cost of goods sold	$ 600,000

Answer (A) is incorrect. The amount of $500,000 results from failing to include beginning finished goods inventory. Answer (C) is incorrect. The amount of $800,000 results from failing to subtract ending finished goods inventory. Answer (D) is incorrect. The amount of $950,000 results from improperly including work-in-process inventories.

1.4 Statement of Changes in Equity and Equity Transactions

15. Unless the shares are specifically restricted, a holder of common stock with a preemptive right may share proportionately in all of the following **except**

    A. The vote for directors.
    B. Corporate assets upon liquidation.
    C. Cumulative dividends.
    D. New issues of stock of the same class.

Answer (C) is correct.
REQUIRED: The item that is not a right of common shareholders.
DISCUSSION: Common stock does not have the right to accumulate unpaid dividends. This right is often attached to preferred stock.
Answer (A) is incorrect. Common shareholders have the right to vote (although different classes of shares may have different privileges). Answer (B) is incorrect. Common shareholders have the right to share proportionately in corporate assets upon liquidation (but only after other claims have been satisfied). Answer (D) is incorrect. Common shareholders have the right to share proportionately in any new issues of stock of the same class (the preemptive right).

16. On December 1, a corporation's board of directors declared a property dividend, payable in stock held in a company. The dividend was payable on January 5. The investment in the company had an original cost of $100,000 when acquired 2 years ago. The market value of this investment was $150,000 on December 1, $175,000 on December 31, and $160,000 on January 5. The amount to be shown on the corporation's statement of financial position at December 31 as property dividends payable would be

    A. $100,000
    B. $150,000
    C. $160,000
    D. $175,000

Answer (B) is correct.
REQUIRED: The amount of property dividends payable on the corporation's statement of financial position.
DISCUSSION: When a property dividend is declared, the property is remeasured at its fair value as of the declaration date. This amount is then reclassified from retained earnings to property dividends payable.

SU 1: External Financial Statements and Revenue Recognition   37

17. The statement of shareholders' equity shows a

A. Reconciliation of the beginning and ending balances in shareholders' equity accounts.
B. Listing of all shareholders' equity accounts and their corresponding dollar amounts.
C. Computation of the number of shares outstanding used for earnings per share calculations.
D. Reconciliation of net income to net operating cash flow.

Answer (A) is correct.
REQUIRED: The content of the statement of shareholders' equity.
DISCUSSION: The statement of shareholders' equity (changes in equity) presents a reconciliation in columnar format of the beginning and ending balances in the various shareholders' equity accounts. A statement of changes in equity may include, for example, columns for (1) totals, (2) comprehensive income, (3) retained earnings, (4) accumulated OCI (but the components of OCI are presented in another statement), (5) common stock, and (6) additional paid-in capital.
Answer (B) is incorrect. A listing of all shareholders' equity accounts would provide little useful information. Answer (C) is incorrect. The computation of the number of shares outstanding used for EPS calculations is disclosed in the income statement. Answer (D) is incorrect. The reconciliation of net income to net operating cash flow is presented in the statement of cash flows.

18. Which one of the following statements regarding dividends is **correct**?

A. A stock dividend of 15% of the outstanding common shares results in a debit to retained earnings at the par value of the stock distributed.
B. At the declaration date of a 30% stock dividend, the carrying value of retained earnings will be reduced by the fair market value of the stock distributed.
C. The declaration of a cash dividend will have no effect on book value per share.
D. The declaration and payment of a 10% stock dividend will result in a reduction of retained earnings at the fair market value of the stock.

Answer (D) is correct.
REQUIRED: The correct statement regarding dividends.
DISCUSSION: When a small stock dividend is declared (less than 20% to 25% of the previously outstanding common shares), retained earnings is debited for the fair value of the stock.
Answer (A) is incorrect. When a small stock dividend is declared (less than 20% to 25% of the previously outstanding common shares), retained earnings is debited for the fair value of the stock. Answer (B) is incorrect. When a large stock dividend is declared (more than 20% to 25% of the previously outstanding common shares), retained earnings is debited for the par value of the stock. Answer (C) is incorrect. When a cash dividend is declared, a portion of retained earnings is reclassified as a current liability.

19. An appropriation of retained earnings by the board of directors of a corporation for bonded indebtedness will result in

A. The establishment of a sinking fund to retire bonds when they mature.
B. A decrease in cash on the balance sheet with an equal increase in the investment and funds section of the balance sheet.
C. A decrease in the total amount of retained earnings presented on the balance sheet.
D. The disclosure that management does not intend to distribute assets, in the form of dividends, equal to the amount of the appropriation.

Answer (D) is correct.
REQUIRED: The effect of an appropriation of retained earnings.
DISCUSSION: The appropriation of retained earnings is a transfer from one retained earnings account to another. The only practical effect is to decrease the amount of retained earnings available for dividends. An appropriation of retained earnings is purely for disclosure purposes.
Answer (A) is incorrect. The establishment of a sinking fund is entirely independent of appropriating retained earnings. Answer (B) is incorrect. Cash is unaffected. Answer (C) is incorrect. The total retained earnings will not change; however, the total will appear as the sum of two retained earnings accounts instead of one.

1.5 Statement of Cash Flows

20. When preparing the statement of cash flows, companies are required to report separately as operating cash flows all of the following **except**

    A. Interest received on investments in bonds.
    B. Interest paid on the company's bonds.
    C. Cash collected from customers.
    D. Cash dividends paid on the company's stock.

Answer (D) is correct.
REQUIRED: The item not reported separately as an operating cash flow on a statement of cash flows.
DISCUSSION: In general, the cash flows from transactions and other events that enter into the determination of income are to be classified as operating. Cash receipts from sales of goods and services, from interest on loans, and from dividends on equity securities are from operating activities. Cash payments to suppliers for inventory; to employees for wages; to other suppliers and employees for other goods and services; to governments for taxes, duties, fines, and fees; and to lenders for interest are also from operating activities. However, distributions to owners (cash dividends on a company's own stock) are cash flows from financing, not operating, activities.

21. All of the following should be classified under the operating section in a statement of cash flows **except** a

    A. Decrease in inventory.
    B. Depreciation expense.
    C. Decrease in prepaid insurance.
    D. Purchase of land and building in exchange for a long-term note.

Answer (D) is correct.
REQUIRED: The item not classified as an operating item in a statement of cash flows.
DISCUSSION: Operating activities include all transactions and other events not classified as investing and financing activities. Operating activities include producing and delivering goods and providing services. Cash flows from such activities are usually included in the determination of net income. However, the purchase of land and a building in exchange for a long-term note is an investing activity. Because this transaction does not affect cash, it is reported in related disclosures of noncash investing and financing activities.

22. A company entered into the following transactions during the year:

- Purchased stock for $200,000
- Purchased electronic equipment for use on the manufacturing floor for $300,000
- Paid dividends to shareholders of the company in the amount of $800,000

The amount to be reported in the investing activities section of the company's statement of cash flows would be

    A. $200,000
    B. $500,000
    C. $800,000
    D. $1,300,000

Answer (B) is correct.
REQUIRED: The amount to be reported in the investing activities section of the statement of cash flows.
DISCUSSION: The statement of cash flows classifies an enterprise's cash flows into three categories. Investing activities typically include the purchase and sale of securities of other entities and the purchase and sale of property, plant, and equipment. Thus, the amount to be reported in the investing activities section of the company's statement of cash flows is $500,000 ($200,000 + $300,000).
Answer (A) is incorrect. The amount of $200,000 results from failing to include the purchase of manufacturing equipment. Answer (C) is incorrect. The amount of $800,000 is the cash flows from financing activities. Answer (D) is incorrect. The amount of $1,300,000 results from improperly including the dividend payment.

23. All of the following should be classified as investing activities in the statement of cash flows **except**

    A. Cash outflows to purchase manufacturing equipment.
    B. Cash inflows from the sale of bonds of other entities.
    C. Cash outflows to lenders for interest.
    D. Cash inflows from the sale of a manufacturing plant.

Answer (C) is correct.
REQUIRED: The cash flow not from an investing activity.
DISCUSSION: Investing activities include the lending of money and the collecting of those loans; the acquisition, sale, or other disposal of debt or equity instruments; and the acquisition, sale, or other disposition of assets (excluding inventory) that are held for or used in the production of goods or services. Investing activities do not include acquiring and disposing of certain loans or other debt or equity instruments that are acquired specifically for resale. Cash outflows to lenders for interest are cash from an operating, not an investing, activity.
Answer (A) is incorrect. The purchase of equipment is an investing activity. Answer (B) is incorrect. The sale of bonds issued by another entity is an investing activity. Answer (D) is incorrect. The sale of a plant is an investing activity.

24. To calculate cash flows using the indirect method, which one of the following items must be added back to net income?

A. Revenue.
B. Marketing expense.
C. Depreciation expense.
D. Interest income.

Answer (C) is correct.
REQUIRED: The components of the indirect method of stating operating cash flows.
DISCUSSION: The indirect method begins with accrual-basis net income or the change in net assets and removes items that did not affect operating cash flow. Depreciation is a non-cash item and thus does not affect the cash flows. This amount must be added back to net income because it decreased net income even though it had no cash effect.
Answer (A) is incorrect. Revenues are not added back to net income when using the indirect method of cash flows. Revenues affect cash flows. Answer (B) is incorrect. Marketing expenses are not added back to net income when using the indirect method of cash flows. Marketing expenses affect cash flows. Answer (D) is incorrect. Interest income is not added back to net income when using the indirect method of cash flows. Interest income affects cash flows.

25. A company acquired land by assuming a mortgage for the full acquisition cost. This transaction should be disclosed on it's statement of cash flows as a(n)

A. Financing activity.
B. Investing activity.
C. Operating activity.
D. Noncash financing and investing activity.

Answer (D) is correct.
REQUIRED: The classification of an acquisition of land by assuming a mortgage.
DISCUSSION: The exchange of debt for a long-lived asset does not involve a cash flow. It is therefore classified as a noncash financing and investing activity.
Answer (A) is incorrect. To be classified as a financing activity, the transaction must have involved a cash flow. Answer (B) is incorrect. To be classified as an investing activity, the transaction must have involved a cash flow. Answer (C) is incorrect. To be classified as an operating activity, the transaction must have involved a cash flow.

1.6 Revenue Recognition -- Revenue Recognition after Delivery

26. Revenues of an entity are usually measured by the exchange values of the assets or liabilities involved. Recognition of revenue does **not** occur until

A. The revenue is realizable.
B. The revenue is realized and earned.
C. Products or services are exchanged for cash or claims to cash.
D. The entity has substantially accomplished what it agreed to do.

Answer (B) is correct.
REQUIRED: The appropriate timing of the recognition of revenue.
DISCUSSION: According to the FASB's conceptual framework, revenues should be recognized when they are realized or realizable and earned. Revenues are realized when products, merchandise, or other assets are exchanged for cash or claims to cash. Revenues are realizable when related assets received or held are readily convertible to known amounts of cash or claims to cash. Revenues are earned when the entity has substantially accomplished what it must do to be entitled to the benefits represented by the revenues.
Answer (A) is incorrect. Revenue also must be earned. Answer (C) is incorrect. Exchange for cash or claim to cash does not suffice for revenue recognition. Answer (D) is incorrect. Revenue also must be realizable.

27. An individual who recently founded a company that produces baseball bats and balls wants to determine their policy for revenue recognition. According to the revenue recognition principle, the **most** appropriate time to recognize revenue would be when

A. The sale occurs.
B. Cash is received.
C. Production is completed.
D. Quarterly financial statements are prepared.

Answer (A) is correct.
REQUIRED: The most appropriate time to recognize revenue.
DISCUSSION: Revenues are normally recognized when they are realized or realizable and earned. Revenues are realized (or realizable) when goods or services have been exchanged for cash or claims to cash (assets readily convertible to cash). Revenues are earned when the earning process is substantially complete, and the entity is entitled to the resulting benefits or revenues. The revenue recognition criteria are ordinarily met at the point of sale (time of delivery of goods or services).
Answer (B) is incorrect. Under the accrual basis of accounting, revenue is not necessarily recognized when cash is received. Answer (C) is incorrect. The criteria for revenue recognition ordinarily have not been met until the product is sold. Answer (D) is incorrect. Under the accrual basis of accounting, revenues are normally recognized when they are realized or realizable and earned, regardless of when the financial statements are prepared.

1.7 Revenue Recognition -- Long-Term Construction Contracts

28. A company uses the percentage-of-completion method to account for long-term construction contracts. The following information relates to a contract that was awarded at a price of $700,000. The estimated costs were $500,000, and the contract duration was 3 years.

	Year 1	Year 2	Year 3
Cumulative cost to date	$300,000	$390,000	$530,000
Costs to complete at year end	250,000	130,000	--
Progress billings	325,000	220,000	155,000
Collections on account	300,000	200,000	200,000

Assuming that $65,000 was recognized as gross profit in Year 1, the amount of gross profit the company recognized in Year 2 was

- A. $35,000
- B. $70,000
- C. $135,000
- D. $170,000

Answer (B) is correct.
REQUIRED: The amount of gross profit.
DISCUSSION: Determining the annual recognized gross profit requires calculation of the estimated total gross profit.

	Year 1	Year 2
Contract price	$700,000	$700,000
Minus: estimated total costs		
Costs to date	$300,000	$390,000
Estimated costs to complete	250,000	130,000
Estimated total costs	$550,000	$520,000
Estimated total gross profit	$150,000	$180,000

The completion percentage for Year 2 is the ratio of costs incurred to date to estimated total costs ($390,000 ÷ $520,000 = 75%). The cumulative gross profit recognized at the end of Year 2 is therefore $135,000 ($180,000 × 75%). Because $65,000 was recognized in Year 1, the amount recognized in Year 2 is $70,000 ($135,000 – $65,000).
Answer (A) is incorrect. The amount of $35,000 is the gross profit recognized in Year 3. Answer (C) is incorrect. The amount of $135,000 is the cumulative gross profit recognized at the end of Year 2. Answer (D) is incorrect. The amount of $170,000 is the total gross profit recognized over the term of the contract.

29. A company appropriately uses the completed-contract method to account for a long-term construction contract. Revenue is recognized when progress billings are

	Recorded	Collected
A.	No	Yes
B.	Yes	Yes
C.	Yes	No
D.	No	No

Answer (D) is correct.
REQUIRED: The effect of progress billings on the recognition of revenue.
DISCUSSION: GAAP require that revenue be recognized when it is realized or realizable and earned. Under the completed-contract method, revenue recognition is appropriate only at the completion of the contract. Neither the recording nor the collection of progress billings affects this recognition.

Access the **CMA Review System** from your Gleim Personal Classroom to continue your studies with exam-emulating multiple-choice questions!

1.8 ESSAY QUESTIONS

Scenario for Essay Questions 1, 2

Ambyt, Inc., a manufacturer of high-value integrated control devices, became a publicly owned company through an initial public offering less than 2 years ago. The company had been a privately held firm for over 15 years and has retained its senior management team. The CEO recommended to the CFO that they hire an assistant to prepare the additional reports required of a public company rather than continuing to rely on the outside accounting firm that has been preparing them since the IPO. Wayne Grant, who has experience preparing SEC filings, was hired 6 months ago to fill this role and reports to the CFO. On July 3, Grant prepared the quarterly reports for the period ending June 30, with information from the Sales and Accounting Departments. Ambyt treats sales and administrative expenses as period expenses; these expenses average about 14% of sales. Parts of the statements are shown below.

Income Statement for Period Ending June 30

Sales	$14,321,000
Less: returns and allowances	128,000
Net sales	$14,193,000
Cost of goods sold	9,651,000
Gross profit	$ 4,542,000
Selling & administrative expenses	2,024,000
Income from operations	$ 2,518,000

Partial Balance Sheet as of June 30

Current assets		
Cash	$ 269,419	
Accounts receivable	2,278,444	
Notes receivable	558,000	
Inventories	896,000	
Short-term investments	532,000	
Prepaid expenses	24,222	
Supplies	58,798	
Total current assets		$4,616,883
Current liabilities		
Accounts payable	$1,639,000	
Notes payable	580,000	
Accrued wages	421,000	
Taxes payable	187,000	
Other liabilities	66,000	
Total current liabilities		$2,893,000

On July 4, Grant learned from the shipping supervisor that a large order of control devices scheduled to be shipped on June 28 would not be ready until July 6 due to an unauthorized work stoppage by the production machinists. Later in the same day, Grant learned that the manager for the Sales Department had included the sale in the June 30 report because the work stoppage was not authorized by the machinist union and therefore was beyond their control. The revenue reported for this sale was $1,250,000, with an associated cost of goods of $715,000.

SU 1: External Financial Statements and Revenue Recognition 43

With this information, Grant determined that he should change the reports he prepared for the period. He discussed this situation with the CFO. The CFO refused to consider the change, explaining that consistent earnings growth is a primary driver of share price, and with Ambyt shares trading at a P/E of 22, the share price would likely fall even though there was no real problem with production. The CFO stated that although production delays were not common, they had occasionally occurred throughout his years with Ambyt and that it was not a "big deal."

Questions

1. Should the large shipment originally scheduled for June 28 be included in Ambyt's June 30 Income Statement? Explain your answer.

2. Assuming Grant revises the reports to exclude the sale from the period,
    a. Calculate the revised income from operations for the period ending June 30
    b. Describe the changes that would be made to Ambyt's June 30 balance sheet
    c. Explain how the revisions will impact Ambyt's cash flow statement

Essay Questions 1, 2 — Unofficial Answers

1. Revenue for a manufacturing company is usually properly recognized when the product is delivered. The product was not delivered during the period, and the revenue cannot be recognized during the period. The reason for the delay in delivery has no bearing on the timing of the revenue recognition.

2. a. The entry for sales will be decreased by the $1,250,000 sale amount. The entry for cost of goods sold will decrease by $715,000, resulting in a net adjustment of $(535,000) to the income from operations entry. The income from operations will be $1,983,000 ($2,518,000 − $535,000). The selling expenses and administration expenses are period expenses and are not affected by the timing of the sale.
   b. Accounts receivable will decrease by the amount of the sale to $1,028,444. Inventories will rise by only the cost of goods sold amount of $715,000, not the full sales amount.
   c. The income statement change will be accompanied by changes to the inventory and accounts receivable entries on the balance sheet. The cash flow statement entries for changes in inventory and changes in accounts receivable will be altered (as will the net income entry if using the indirect method to construct the statement). Entries to income taxes payable will also be altered.

Access the **CMA Review System** from your Gleim Personal Classroom to continue your studies with exam-emulating essay questions!

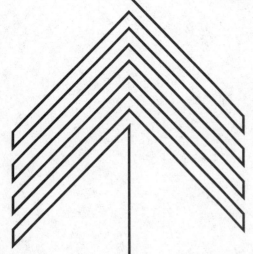

GLEIM Updates

We make it easy to keep your CMA materials current.

gleim.com/CMAUpdate

Updates are available until the next edition is released.

STUDY UNIT TWO
MEASUREMENT, VALUATION, AND DISCLOSURE: INVESTMENTS AND SHORT-TERM ITEMS

(24 pages of outline)

2.1	Accounts Receivable	45
2.2	Inventory -- Fundamentals	49
2.3	Inventory -- Cost Flow Methods	54
2.4	Inventory Measurement in the Financial Statements -- Lower of Cost or Market	58
2.5	Classification of Investments	59
2.6	Equity Method	63
2.7	Business Combinations and Consolidated Financial Statements	63
2.8	Different Types of Expenses and Liabilities	66
2.9	Essay Questions	79

This study unit is the **second of three** on **external financial reporting decisions**. The relative weight assigned to this major topic in Part 1 of the exam is **15%**. The three study units are

Study Unit 1: External Financial Statements and Revenue Recognition
Study Unit 2: Measurement, Valuation, and Disclosure: Investments and Short-Term Items
Study Unit 3: Measurement, Valuation, and Disclosure: Long-Term Items

If you are interested in reviewing more introductory or background material, go to www.gleim.com/CMAIntroVideos for a list of suggested third-party overviews of this topic. The following Gleim outline material is more than sufficient to help you pass the CMA exam; any additional introductory or background material is for your own personal enrichment.

2.1 ACCOUNTS RECEIVABLE

1. **Overview**

    a. Accounts receivable, often called trade receivables, are the amounts owed to an entity by its customers.

    b. The recording of a receivable, which often coincides with revenue recognition, is consistent with the accrual method of accounting.

    c. Receivables should be separated into **current and noncurrent** portions. Most of the entity's accounts receivable are classified as current assets because they are expected to be collected within 1 year or the entity's normal operating cycle.

    1) **Current** accounts receivable are reported in the balance sheet at **net realizable value (NRV)**, i.e., net of allowance for uncollectible accounts, allowance for sales returns, and billing adjustments.

    $$\text{Gross accounts receivable} - \text{Allowance for uncollectible accounts} = \text{NRV of accounts receivable}$$

    2) **Noncurrent** receivables are measured at net present value of future cash flows expected to be collected.

    d. The direct write-off method expenses bad debts when they are determined to be uncollectible. It is **not acceptable under GAAP** because it does not match revenue and expense when the receivable and the write-off are recorded in different periods. But this method is used for tax purposes.

2. **Allowance for Customers' Right of Sales Return**

    a. A provision must be made for the return of merchandise because of product defects, customer dissatisfaction, etc.

b. To be consistent with the matching principle (recognition of revenue and related expense in the same accounting period), the revenue from the sale of goods and the expense for the estimated sales returns must be recognized on the same date.

  1) Accordingly, an **allowance** for sales returns should be established.

EXAMPLE

A company has $500,000 of sales in July, its first month of operations. Management estimates that total returns will be 1% of sales.

Recognition of revenue from sale		Recognition of allowance for sales returns	
Cash/accounts receivable $500,000		Sales returns (contra revenue)	$5,000
Sales	$500,000	Allowance for sales returns (contra asset)	$5,000

---

3. **Allowance for Uncollectible Accounts and Bad Debt Expense**

   a. Because collection in full of all accounts receivable is unlikely, the allowance for uncollectible accounts must be recognized. This method attempts to match bad debt expense with the related revenue.

   b. The principal measurement issue for accounts receivable is the estimation of net realizable value for balance sheet reporting and the related **uncollectible accounts expense** (bad debt expense) for the income statement.

   c. The bad debt expense recognized for the period increases the allowance for uncollectible accounts. The allowance for uncollectible accounts is a contra account to accounts receivable. Thus, the recognition of bad debt expense decreases the balance of accounts receivable.

   d. The two most common methods of measuring bad debt expense and the allowance for uncollectible accounts are the **percentage-of-sales method** (an **income statement approach**) and the **percentage-of-receivables method** (a **balance sheet approach**). Both approaches have the goal of measuring accounts receivable at net realizable value.

      1) Note, the direct write-off method (i.e., expense bad debts only when they are determined to be uncollectible) is **not acceptable under GAAP**. This method does not match revenues and expenses. Occasionally, a small company will use the direct write-off method under the assumption that the difference between it and the allowance method is immaterial. In other words, the material principle is used as an excuse to violate the matching principle.

4. **Income Statement Approach (Percentage of Sales)**

   a. The **income statement approach** calculates bad debt expense as a percentage of credit sales reported on the income statement.

EXAMPLE

A company's year-end unadjusted trial balance reports the following amounts:

Gross accounts receivable	$100,000 Dr
Allowance for uncollectible accounts (year-beginning balance)	1,000 Cr
Sales on credit	250,000 Cr

According to past experience, 1% of the company's credit sales have been uncollectible. The company uses the income statement approach to calculate bad debt expense. The bad debt expense recognized for the year is $2,500 ($250,000 × 1%). The company records the following adjusting journal entry:

Bad debt expense	$2,500	
Allowance for uncollectible accounts		$2,500

The total adjusted balances of allowance for uncollectible accounts and bad debt expense are $3,500 ($1,000 + $2,500) and $2,500, respectively. The company reports **net accounts receivable** of **$96,500** ($100,000 – $3,500) in its balance sheet and **bad debt expense** of **$2,500** in its statement of income.

Balance sheet presentation:

Accounts receivable, net of allowance for uncollectible accounts of $3,500	**$96,500**

5. Balance Sheet Approach (Percentage of Receivables)

a. The **balance sheet approach** estimates the balance that should be recorded in the allowance based on the collectibility of ending gross accounts receivable. Bad debt expense is the amount necessary to adjust the allowance.

EXAMPLE

Using the data from the previous example, assume that the company uses the balance sheet approach and that based on the company's experience, 6% of accounts receivable are determined to be uncollectible.

Thus, the ending balance of the allowance for uncollectible accounts is $6,000 ($100,000 × 6%). Because the allowance currently has a balance of $1,000, the following journal entry is required:

    Bad debt expense ($6,000 – $1,000) $5,000
        Allowance for uncollectible accounts $5,000

Balance sheet presentation:
Accounts receivable, net of allowance for uncollectible accounts of $6,000   **$94,000**

---

b. An entity rarely has a single rate of uncollectibility for all accounts. Thus, an entity using the balance sheet approach generally prepares an **aging schedule** for accounts receivable.

EXAMPLE

Using the data from the previous example, assume that the company uses the following aging schedule to determine the ending balance of the allowance for uncollectible accounts:

Aging Interval	Balance	Estimated Uncollectible	Ending Allowance
Less than 30 days	$ 70,000	2%	$1,400
30-60 days	18,000	5%	900
61-90 days	10,000	13%	1,300
Over 90 days	2,000	20%	400
Total	**$100,000**		**$4,000**

Thus, the ending balance of the allowance for uncollectible accounts is $4,000. Because the allowance currently has a balance of $1,000, the following journal entry is required:

    Bad debt expense ($4,000 – $1,000) $3,000
        Allowance for uncollectible accounts $3,000

Balance sheet presentation:
Accounts receivable, net of allowance for uncollectible accounts of $4,000   **$96,000**

---

6. Write-Off of Accounts Receivable

a. Some customers are unwilling or unable to satisfy their debts. A write-off of a specific debt is recorded as follows:

    Allowance for uncollectible accounts $XXX
        Accounts receivable $XXX

1) Thus, the write-off of a particular bad debt has no effect on expenses.
2) Write-offs do not affect the carrying amount of net accounts receivable because the reductions of gross accounts receivable and the allowance are the same. Thus, they also have no effect on working capital.

b. Occasionally, a customer pays on an account previously written off.

    Cash $XXX
        Allowance for uncollectible accounts $XXX

1) Bad debt expense is not affected when an account receivable is written off or when an account previously written off becomes collectible.

The following equation illustrates the reconciliation of the beginning and ending balances of gross accounts receivable (accounts receivable before adjustment for allowance for uncollectible accounts):

Beginning accounts receivable
Plus: Credit sales during the period
Less: Cash collected on credit sales during the period
Less: Accounts receivable written-off during the period
Ending accounts receivable

The following equation illustrates the reconciliation of the beginning and ending balances of the allowance for uncollectible accounts:

Beginning allowance for uncollectible accounts
Plus: Bad debt expense recognized for the period
Less: Accounts receivable written off
Plus: Collection of accounts receivable previously written off
Ending allowance for uncollectible accounts

Under the income statement approach, bad debt expense is a percentage of sales on credit, and the ending balance of the allowance is calculated using the equation above.

Under the balance sheet approach, the ending balance of the allowance is a percentage of the ending balance of accounts receivable, and bad debt expense is calculated using the equation above.

7. **Factoring of Accounts Receivable**

   a. **Factoring** is a transfer of receivables to a third party (a factor) who assumes the responsibility of collection.

   b. Factoring discounts receivables on a **nonrecourse**, notification basis. Thus, payments by the debtors on the transferred assets are made to the factor. If the transferor (seller) surrenders control, **the transaction is a sale**.

      1) If a sale is **without recourse**, the transferee (credit agency) assumes the risks and receives the rewards of collection. This sale is final, and the seller has no further liabilities to the transferee. Accordingly, the receivables are no longer reported on the seller's books.

      2) If a sale is **with recourse**, the transferor (seller) may be required to make payments to the transferee or to buy back receivables in specified circumstances. In this circumstance the transfer might not qualify as a sale. The parties account for the transaction as a secured borrowing with a pledge of noncash collateral. Accordingly, the receivables are still on the seller's books and it must recognize a liability for the amount of cash received.

EXAMPLE

A factor charges a 2% fee plus an interest rate of 18% on all cash advanced to a transferor of accounts receivable. Monthly sales are $100,000, and the factor advances 90% of the receivables submitted after deducting the 2% fee and the interest. Credit terms are net 60 days. What is the cost to the transferor of this arrangement?

Amount of receivables submitted	$100,000	
Minus: 10% reserve	(10,000)	
Minus: 2% factor's fee	(2,000)	
Amount accruing to the transferor	$ 88,000	
Minus: 18% interest for 60 days	(2,640)	[$88,000 × 18% × (60 ÷ 360)]
Amount to be received immediately	$ 85,360	

-- Continued on the next page --

SU 2: Measurement, Valuation, and Disclosure: Investments and Short-Term Items

> **EXAMPLE -- Continued**
>
> The transferor also will receive the $10,000 reserve at the end of the 60-day period if it has not been absorbed by sales returns and allowances. Thus, the total cost to the transferor to factor the receivables for the month is $4,640 ($2,000 factor fee + interest of $2,640). Assuming that the factor has approved the customers' credit in advance (the sale is without recourse), the transferor will not absorb any bad debts.
>
> The journal entry to record the transaction is
>
> | | | |
> |---|---:|---:|
> | Cash | $85,360 | |
> | Due from factor | 10,000 | |
> | Loss on sale of receivables | 2,000 | |
> | Prepaid interest | 2,640 | |
> | Accounts receivable | | $100,000 |

    c.   The main reasons for factoring transactions are as follows:

        1)   A factor usually receives a high financing fee plus a fee for collection. Furthermore, the factor often operates more efficiently than its clients because of the specialized nature of its services.

        2)   An entity (seller) that uses a factor tries to speed up its collections. Also, it can eliminate its credit department and accounts receivable staff. In addition, bad debts are eliminated from the financial statements. These reductions in costs can offset the fee charged by the factor.

    d.   Credit card sales are a common form of factoring. The retailer benefits by prompt receipt of cash and avoidance of bad debts and other costs. In return, the credit card company charges a fee.

Stop and review! You have completed the outline for this subunit. Study multiple-choice questions 1 through 5 beginning on page 69.

2.2 INVENTORY -- FUNDAMENTALS

1.   **Overview**

    a.   Inventory is the total of tangible personal property

        1)   Held for sale in the ordinary course of business,

        2)   In the form of work-in-process to be completed and sold in the ordinary course of business, or

        3)   To be used up currently in producing goods or services for sale.

            a)   Inventory does not include long-term assets subject to depreciation.

    b.   Inventories are generally classified as current assets in the financial statements. They are expected to be realized in cash or sold or consumed during the normal operating cycle of the business.

        1)   Long-term assets either subject to depreciation or retired from regular use and held for sale are not classified as inventories.

    c.   The inventories of a **retailer** (trading entity) consist of goods purchased to be resold without substantial modification.

    d.   The inventories of a **manufacturer** consist of (1) goods to be consumed in production (materials), (2) goods in the process of production (work-in-process), and (3) finished goods.

    e.   The **gross profit** for the period is measured and presented in the income statement as the difference between the amount of sales and the amount of cost of goods sold.

        1)   The calculation of cost of goods sold for a retailer and a manufacturer is discussed in Study Unit 1, Subunit 3.

2. **Cost Basis of Inventory -- Initial Measurement**
   a. The **cost of inventory** includes all costs incurred in bringing the inventories to their existing location and ready-to-use condition.
   b. The **cost of purchased inventories** includes
      1) The price paid or consideration given to acquire the inventory (net of trade discounts, rebates, and other similar items);
      2) Import duties and other unrecoverable taxes; and
      3) Handling, insurance, freight-in, and other costs directly attributable to (a) acquiring finished goods and materials and (b) bringing them to their present location and condition (salable or usable condition).
   c. The **cost of manufactured inventories** (work-in-process and finished goods) includes the costs of direct materials used and conversion costs. Conversion costs consist of
      1) Direct labor costs and
      2) Manufacturing overhead costs.

3. **Inventory Accounting Systems**
   a. A **perpetual inventory system** updates inventory accounts after each purchase or sale. This system is generally more suitable for entities that sell relatively expensive and heterogeneous items and requires continuous monitoring of inventory and cost of goods sold accounts. Automobile dealers are an example. Under this system,
      1) Purchases and other items related to inventory costing are charged directly to inventory.
      2) Inventory and cost of goods sold are adjusted as sales occur.
   b. An **advantage** of the perpetual inventory system is that the amount of inventory on hand and the cost of goods sold can be determined at any time. A **disadvantage** of the perpetual inventory system is that the bookkeeping is more complex and expensive.
      1) A perpetual system is more often used when individual inventory items are of high value because a perpetual system provides better internal control.
   c. In the **periodic inventory system**, inventory and cost of goods sold are updated at specific intervals, such as quarterly or annually, based on the results of a **physical count**. Bookkeeping is simpler under this system. Thus, entities with relatively inexpensive and homogeneous items, such as grain dealers, that have no need to continuously monitor their inventory and cost of goods sold generally use this system. Under the periodic system,
      1) Goods bought from suppliers and other items related to inventory costs are tracked during the period in a separate temporary account **(purchases)**.
      2) The beginning inventory balance remains unchanged until the end of the period when the purchases account is closed.
      3) Changes in inventory and cost of goods sold are recorded **only at the end of the period**, based on the physical count.

> **EXAMPLE**
>
> Entity A's January 1, Year 1, inventory consists of 1,000 units with a cost of $5 per unit. The following are Entity A's Year 2 transactions:
>
> April 1: sold 600 inventory units for $4,800 in cash.
>
> May 1: purchased 250 inventory units for $5 in cash per unit.
>
> The year-end result of the physical count was 650 inventory units. The following are Entity A's journal entries under the perpetual and periodic systems:
>
> | Perpetual System | | | Periodic System | | |
> |---|---|---|---|---|---|
> | **Inventory sale April 1:** | | | | | |
> | Cash | $4,800 | | Cash | $4,800 | |
> | Sales | | $4,800 | Sales | | $4,800 |
> | Cost of goods sold (600 × $5) | $3,000 | | | | |
> | Inventory | | $3,000 | | | |
> | **Inventory purchase May 1:** | | | | | |
> | Inventory (250 × $5) | $1,250 | | Purchases | $1,250 | |
> | Cash | | $1,250 | Cash | | $1,250 |
> | **After the physical count on December 31:** | | | | | |
> | No journal entry is needed because the physical count equals the amount of inventory on the books (1,000 – 600 + 250 = 650). | | | Inventory (year-end) (650 × $5) | $3,250 | |
> | | | | Cost of goods sold (difference) | 3,000 | |
> | | | | Inventory (beginning) | | $5,000 |
> | | | | Purchases | | 1,250 |
>
> | | |
> |---|---|
> | Beginning inventory (1,000 × $5) | $5,000 |
> | Purchases of inventory during the period | 1,250 |
> | Ending inventory | (3,250) |
> | **Cost of goods sold** | **$3,000** |
>
> The perpetual and periodic systems have the same result. However, under the periodic system, the amounts of inventory and cost of goods sold are updated only at the end of the period after the physical count.

4. **Inventory Period-End Physical Count**

    a. An annual period-end **inventory physical count** is necessary under both the perpetual and periodic inventory accounting systems. The amount of inventory reported in the annual financial statements should be based on a physical count.

        1) Under the **perpetual system**, a physical count helps to detect (a) misstatements in the records and (b) thefts of inventory. The differences between the physical count and the inventory in the books (inventory shortages and overages) are recognized in cost of goods sold account or as a separate line item in the current period income statement.

        2) Under the **periodic system**, the amounts of inventory and cost of goods sold can be determined based only on the results of a physical count. Thus, the amount of cost of goods sold for the period includes both (a) inventory cost of goods sold and (b) inventory shortages and overages.

b. For a physical count to be accurate, the entity must count all items considered to be inventory and eliminate all items that are not. Items to be counted as inventory include the following:

1) **Goods in transit** – Items in transit are inventories that on the physical count date (a) are not on the entity's premises and are on the way to the desired location and (b) whose legal title is held by the entity; i.e., the entity bears the risk of loss on inventory in transit. The following are the most common shipping terms:

    a) **FOB shipping point** (sometimes called FOB Factory) – Legal title and risk of loss pass to the buyer when the seller delivers the goods to the carrier. The **buyer** must include the goods in inventory during shipping.

    b) **FOB destination** – Legal title and risk of loss pass to the buyer when the seller delivers the goods to a specified destination. The **seller** must include the goods in inventory during shipping.

2) **Goods out on consignment** – A consignment sale is an arrangement between the owner of goods (consignor) and the sales agent (consignee). Consigned goods are not sold but rather transferred to an agent for possible sale. The consignor records sales only when the goods are sold to third parties by the consignee.

    a) Goods out on consignment are included in the **consignor's** inventory at cost. Costs of transporting the goods to the consignee are inventoriable costs, not selling expenses.

    b) The **consignee** never records the consigned goods as an asset.

EXAMPLE

Entity A's December 31, Year 1, warehouse inventory physical count results in the amount of inventory of $50,000. The following is additional information regarding Entity A's year-end inventory:

- During the year, Entity A consigned goods with a total cost of $60,000 to Entity B (the consignee). The annual statement that was sent from Entity B to Entity A states that 60% of the consignment goods were sold for $42,000.
- Merchandise costing $40,000 shipped FOB shipping point from a vendor on December 29, Year 1, and was received by Entity A on January 4, Year 2.
- Merchandise costing $70,000 shipped FOB destination from a vendor on December 30, Year 1, and was received by Entity A on January 5, Year 2.
- The goods billed to the customer FOB destination on December 27, Year 1, had a cost of $25,000. The goods were shipped by Entity A on December 28, Year 1, and were received by the customer on January 3, Year 2.

In the December 31, Year 1, balance sheet, Entity A reports an inventory amount of $139,000. This amount consists of

Warehouse physical inventory count	$ 50,000
Goods held on consignment ($60,000 × 40%)	24,000
Merchandise shipped FOB shipping point (title and risk of loss passed to Entity A on December 29, Year 1, at the time of shipment)	40,000
Goods shipped FOB destination to customer (title and the risk of loss will pass to the customer only on January 3, Year 2)	25,000
December 31, Year 1, inventory balance	**$139,000**

---

5. **Inventory Estimation**

    a. An estimate of inventory may be needed when an exact count is not feasible, e.g., for interim reporting purposes or when inventory records have been destroyed. The gross profit method may be used for inventory estimation, even when the inventory may have been stolen or destroyed by fire.

    1) **Gross profit margin** (gross profit percentage) equals gross profit divided by sales.

    $$Gross\ profit\ margin\ (\%) = Gross\ profit \div Sales$$

> **EXAMPLE**
>
> A retailer needs to estimate ending inventory for quarterly reporting purposes. The firm's best estimate of the gross percentage is its historical rate of 25%. The following additional information is available:
>
> | | | |
> |---|---|---:|
> | | Net sales | $1,000,000 |
> | | Purchases | 300,000 |
> | | Beginning inventory | 800,000 |
>
> | | | |
> |---|---:|---:|
> | Beginning inventory | | $ 800,000 |
> | Purchases | | 300,000 |
> | Goods available for sale | | $1,100,000 |
> | Sales | $1,000,000 | |
> | Gross profit (Sales × Gross profit margin) | (250,000) | |
> | Cost of goods sold [Sales × (1 – Gross profit margin)] | | (750,000) |
> | Ending inventory | | $ 350,000 |

6. **Inventory Errors**

    a. These errors may have a material effect on current assets, working capital (current assets minus current liabilities), cost of goods sold, net income, and equity. A common error is inappropriate timing of the recognition of transactions.

        1) If a purchase on account is not recorded and the goods are not included in ending inventory, cost of goods sold (BI plus purchases minus EI) and net income are unaffected. But current assets and current liabilities are understated.

        2) If purchases and beginning inventory are properly recorded but items are excluded from ending inventory, cost of goods sold is overstated. Net income, inventory, retained earnings, working capital, and the current ratio are understated.

    b. Errors arising from recording transactions in the wrong period may reverse in the subsequent period.

        1) If ending inventory is overstated, the overstatement of net income will be offset by the understatement in the following year that results from the overstatement of beginning inventory.

    c. An **overstatement error in year-end inventory** of the current year affects the financial statements of 2 different years.

        1) The **first year's** effects may be depicted as follows:

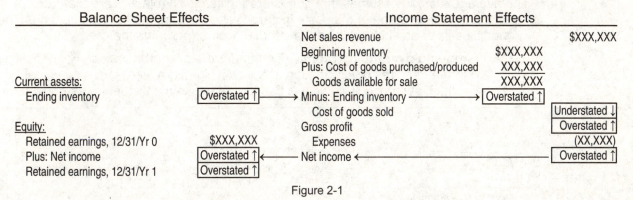

Figure 2-1

2) At the end of the **second year**, retained earnings is correctly stated as follows:

Balance Sheet Effects		Income Statement Effects	
		Net sales revenue	$XXX,XXX
		Beginning inventory [Overstated ↑]	
		Plus: Cost of goods purchased/produced	XXX,XXX
Current assets:		Goods available for sale [Overstated ↑]	
Ending inventory	$XXX,XXX ⟶	Minus: Ending inventory ⟶	$(XXX,XXX)
		Cost of goods sold	[Overstated ↑]
Equity:		Gross profit	[Understated ↓]
Retained earnings, 12/31/Yr 1	[Overstated ↑]	Expenses	(XX,XXX)
Plus: Net income	[Understated ↓] ⟵	Net income ⟵	[Understated ↓]
Retained earnings, 12/31/Yr 2	$XXX,XXX		

Figure 2-2

Stop and review! You have completed the outline for this subunit. Study multiple-choice questions 6 through 9 beginning on page 70.

2.3 INVENTORY -- COST FLOW METHODS

1. **Specific Identification Method**

    a. **Specific identification** requires determining which specific items are sold and therefore reflects the actual physical flow of goods. This system is appropriate for (1) items that are not ordinarily interchangeable and (2) items that are segregated for a specific project. It can be used for blocks of investment securities or special inventory items, such as automobiles or heavy equipment. Any item that has a serial number on it would be a candidate for the specific identification method.

        1) Specific identification is the most accurate method because it identifies each item of inventory.

        2) However, it requires detailed records and may not be feasible or cost effective.

    b. When the inventory items purchased or produced are identical and interchangeable, specific identification is not appropriate. In such circumstances, several assumptions about the flow of cost, such as **average, FIFO,** or **LIFO**, may be appropriate for the measurement of periodic income. The method selected should be the one that, under the circumstances, most clearly reflects periodic income.

2. **Average Method**

    a. The average method assumes that goods are indistinguishable and are therefore measured at an average of the costs incurred. The average may be calculated on the periodic basis or as each additional purchase occurs (perpetual basis).

        1) The **moving-average method** is used under the **perpetual** inventory accounting system. It requires determination of a new weighted-average inventory cost after each purchase. This cost is used for every sale until the next purchase.

EXAMPLE

The following data relate to Entity A's Year 1 activities:

Date	Transaction	Number of units	Purchase price per unit ($)	Sale price per unit ($)
January 1	Beginning balance	100	20	
March 1	Purchase	20	32	
April 1	Sale	70		40
June 1	Purchase	30	14	
October 1	Sale	40		24

--Continued on the next page --

EXAMPLE -- continued

Under the **moving-average method**, the year-end inventory and Year 1 cost of goods sold are calculated as follows:

Date	Activity	Units	Price	Cost of inventory purchased/sold	Inventory total balance	On-hand units	Cost per unit
January 1	Beg. bal.	100	$20		$2,000 (100 × 20)	100	**$20**
March 1	Purchase	20	$32	$640 = 20 × $32	$2,640 (2,000 + 640)	120	**$22** ($2,640 ÷ 120)
April 1	Sale	70	**$22**	($1,540) = 70 × $22	$1,100 (2,640 – 1,540)	50	**$22** ($1,100 ÷ 50)
June 1	Purchase	30	$14	$420 = 30 × $14	$1,520 (1,100 + 420)	80	**$19** ($1,520 ÷ 80)
October 1	Sale	40	**$19**	($760) = 40 × $19	**$760** (1,520 – 760)	40	**$19** ($760 ÷ 40)

The cost of **inventory** on December 31, Year 1, is **$760**. The Year 1 **cost of goods sold** is **$2,300**.

Beginning inventory	$2,000
Purchases ($640 + $420)	1,060
Ending inventory	(760)
Cost of goods sold ($1,540 + $760)	**$2,300**

2) The **weighted-average method** is used under the **periodic** inventory accounting system. The average cost is determined only at the end of the period. The weighted-average cost per unit is used to determine the ending inventory and the cost of goods sold for the period. It is calculated as follows:

$$\frac{\text{Cost of beginning inventory (\$)} + \text{Cost of purchases during the period (\$)}}{\text{Units in beginning inventory} + \text{Number of units purchased during the period}}$$

EXAMPLE

Under the **weighted-average method**, Entity A's ending inventory and Year 1 cost of goods sold are determined as follows:

First, the weighted-average cost per unit is calculated.

$$\frac{\text{Cost of beginning inventory} + \text{Cost of purchases during the period}}{\text{Units in beginning inventory} + \text{Number of units purchased}} = \frac{\$2,000 + \$1,060}{100 + 20 + 30} = \$20.40$$

Second, the ending inventory and Year 1 cost of goods sold are calculated using the weighted-average cost per unit (WACPU).

Beginning inventory	$2,000	
Purchases	1,060	
Ending inventory	**(816)**	(40 × $20.40) = (WACPU × Units in ending inventory)
Cost of goods sold	**$2,244**	(110 × $20.40) = (WACPU × Units sold during the period)

3. **First-in, First-out (FIFO)**

   a. This method assumes that the first goods purchased are the first sold. Thus, ending inventory consists of the latest purchases.
   b. Cost of goods sold includes the earliest goods purchased.
   c. Under the FIFO method, year-end inventory and cost of goods sold for the period are **the same** regardless of whether the perpetual or the periodic inventory accounting system is used.

> ### EXAMPLE
>
> The number of units in Entity A's ending inventory is 40. Under the FIFO method, the cost of these units is the cost of the **latest purchases ($740)**.
>
> | Date of purchase | Units | Price per unit | Total cost |
> |---|---|---|---|
> | June 1, Year 1 | 30 | $14 | $420 |
> | March 1, Year 1 | 10 | $32 | $320 |
> | **Ending inventory** | **40** | | **$740** |
>
> The Year 1 cost of goods sold is **$2,320**.
>
> | | |
> |---|---|
> | Beginning inventory | $2,000 |
> | Purchases ($640 + $420) | 1,060 |
> | Ending inventory | (740) |
> | Cost of goods sold | **$2,320** |
>
> NOTE: The results are the same under the periodic and perpetual systems.

4. **Last-in, First-out (LIFO)**

   a. The LIFO (last-in, first-out) method assumes the newest items of inventory are sold first. Thus, the items remaining in inventory are the oldest. Under the LIFO method, the perpetual and the periodic inventory accounting systems may result in different values for year-end inventory and cost of goods sold.

      1) Under the **periodic** inventory accounting system, the calculation of inventory and cost of goods sold are made at the end of the period.

> ### EXAMPLE
>
> The number of units in Entity A's ending inventory is 40. Under the LIFO method, the cost of those units is the cost of the **earliest purchases** (beginning inventory) of **$800** (40 units × $20). The Year 1 cost of goods sold is **$2,260**.
>
> | | |
> |---|---|
> | Beginning inventory | $2,000 |
> | Purchases ($640 + $420) | 1,060 |
> | Ending inventory | (800) |
> | Cost of goods sold | **$2,260** |

      2) Under the **perpetual** inventory accounting system, cost of goods sold is calculated every time a sale occurs and consists of the most recent (latest) purchases.

> ### EXAMPLE
>
> | Date | Activity | Units | Cost per unit | Cost of inventory purchased/sold | Inventory total balance | Number of units |
> |---|---|---|---|---|---|---|
> | January 1 | Beg. bal. | 100 | $20 | | 100 × $20 = $2,000 | 100 |
> | March 1 | Purchase | 20 | $32 | 20 × $32 = $640 | January 1, layer 100 × $20 = $2,000
March 1, layer 20 × $32 = 640
$2,640 | 120 |
> | April 1 | Sale | 70 | | 20 × $32 = $ 640
50 × $20 = 1,000
$(1,640) | January 1, layer 50 × $20 = $1,000 | 50 |
> | June 1 | Purchase | 30 | $14 | 30 × $14 = $420 | January 1, layer 50 × $20 = $1,000
June 1, layer 30 × $14 = 420
$1,420 | 80 |
> | October 1 | Sale | 40 | | 30 × $14 = $ 420
10 × $20 = 200
$(620) | January 1, layer 40 × $20 = **$800** | 40 |
>
> -- Continued on the next page --

> **EXAMPLE -- continued**
>
> Entity A's cost of ending **inventory** is **$800**, and the Year 1 **cost of goods sold** is **$2,260** ($1,640 + $620).
>
> NOTE: The results of the LIFO method under the perpetual and periodic systems are the same in this example but may differ in other situations.

> **IFRS Difference**
>
> LIFO is not permitted.

5. **Cost Flow Methods -- Comparison**

    a. The cost flow model selected should be the one that most clearly reflects periodic income.

> **EXAMPLE**
>
> Follows are Entity A's varying results under each of the five cost flow methods:
>
> | | Ending Inventory | Cost of Goods Sold |
> |---|---|---|
> | Moving average | $760 | $2,300 |
> | Weighted average | 816 | 2,244 |
> | FIFO | 740 | 2,320 |
> | LIFO periodic | 800 | 2,260 |
> | LIFO perpetual | 800 | 2,260 |

   b. An advantage of FIFO is that ending inventory approximates current replacement cost.

      1) A disadvantage is that current revenues are matched with older costs.

   c. Under LIFO, management can affect net income with an end-of-period purchase that immediately alters cost of goods sold.

      1) A last-minute FIFO purchase included in the ending inventory has no such effect.

   d. Under LIFO, if fewer units are purchased than sold,

      1) The beginning inventory is partially or fully liquidated and
      2) Old costs are matched against current revenues in the year's income statement.

   e. In a time of **rising prices** (inflation), use of the LIFO method results in the lowest year-end inventory, the highest cost of goods sold, and the lowest gross profit. LIFO assumes that the oldest (and therefore the lowest-priced) goods purchased are in year-end inventory, and that cost of goods sold consists of the latest (and therefore the highest-priced) goods purchased.

      1) The results for the FIFO method are the opposite of those for the LIFO method.

During a period of inflation	Ending Inventory	Cost of Goods Sold	Gross Profit (Net Income)
LIFO	Lowest	Highest	Lowest
FIFO	Highest	Lowest	Highest

Stop and review! You have completed the outline for this subunit. Study multiple-choice questions 10 through 13 beginning on page 72.

2.4 INVENTORY MEASUREMENT IN THE FINANCIAL STATEMENTS -- LOWER OF COST OR MARKET

1. **Statement of Rule**
    a. In the annual financial statements, inventory is measured at the **lower of cost or market (LCM)**. Inventory must be written down to market if its utility is less than its cost at the end of the annual reporting period.
        1) The difference (write-down) should be recognized as a loss in a separate line item of cost of goods sold in the current-period income statement.
        2) Reversals of write-downs of inventory are **prohibited** in subsequent periods.
2. **Market**
    a. **Market** is the current cost to replace inventory, subject to certain limitations. Market should not (1) exceed a ceiling equal to **net realizable value (NRV)** or (2) be less than a floor equal to NRV reduced by an allowance for an approximately **normal profit margin**.
    b. Net realizable value is the estimated selling price in the ordinary course of business minus reasonably predictable costs of completion and disposal.
        1) Thus, current replacement cost must not be greater than NRV or less than NRV minus a normal profit.

EXAMPLE of How to Calculate Inventories, Market, and the Year-End Measurement

The following information is related to a company's year-end inventories:

Cost per inventory unit	Item A	Item B	Item C
Estimated selling price	$80	$70	$44
Minus: Cost of completion	(20)	--	(3)
Minus: Cost of disposal	(6)	(5)	(2)
NRV **(ceiling)**	$54	$65	$39
Minus: Normal profit margin	(3)	(7)	(4)
NRV – NPM **(floor)**	51	$58	$35
Current replacement cost **(CRC)**	$53	$55	$40
(a) Market	$53 Ceiling > CRC > Floor	$58 Floor > CRC	$39 CRC > Ceiling
(b) Historical cost per unit	$50	$60	$45
Lower of cost (b) or market (a)	$50 Cost < Market	$58 Market < Cost	$39 Market < Cost

---

3. **Applying LCM**
    a. Depending on the nature of the inventory, the LCM rule may be applied either directly to each item or to the total of the inventory. The method should be the one that most clearly reflects periodic income.
        1) Once inventory is written down, the reduced amount is the **new cost basis**.
        2) Most entities use LCM by item. This method is required for tax purposes.

> **EXAMPLE**
>
> Allotrope Co. has the following information about its inventory at the end of the fiscal year:
>
> | | |
> |---|---|
> | Historical cost | $100,000 |
> | Current replacement cost | 82,000 |
> | Net realizable value (NRV) | 90,000 |
> | Normal profit margin | 5,000 |
>
> Inventory is measured at the lower of cost or market (current replacement cost subject to certain limitations). Market cannot be higher than NRV ($90,000) or lower than NRV reduced by a normal profit margin ($90,000 – $5,000 = $85,000). Thus, market is $85,000. (The current replacement cost of $82,000 is below the floor.) Because market is lower than cost, the inventory is reported in the balance sheet at market of $85,000. The write-down of inventory of $15,000 ($100,000 – $85,000) is recognized as a loss in the income statement. The journal entry is as follows:
>
> | | | |
> |---|---|---|
> | Loss from inventory write-down | $15,000 | |
> | Inventory | | $15,000 |

IFRS Difference

Inventories are measured at the lower of cost or net realizable value (NRV). NRV is the estimated selling price less the estimated costs of completion and disposal. NRV is assessed each period. Accordingly, a write-down may be reversed but not above original cost. The write-down and reversal are recognized in profit or loss.

Using the data from the example above, NRV ($90,000) is lower than cost ($100,000). Thus, the inventory is reported in the statement of financial position at its NRV ($90,000). The write-down of inventory of $10,000 ($100,000 – $90,000) is recognized in profit or loss. The journal entry is as follows:

Loss from inventory write-down	$10,000	
Inventory		$10,000

Stop and review! You have completed the outline for this subunit. Study multiple-choice questions 14 through 16 beginning on page 73.

2.5 CLASSIFICATION OF INVESTMENTS

1. **Investments in Debt and Equity Securities**

   a. A **debt security** represents a **creditor** relationship with the issuer.

      1) The accounting for debt securities depends on the **investor's intent** with respect to holding the securities. The diagram below depicts the possible classification of debt securities:

Investor's Intent	Classification
To hold primarily for sale in the near term	Trading securities
To hold until maturity date	Held-to-maturity securities
No specific intent (i.e., not to sell in the near term and not to hold until maturity date)	Available-for-sale securities

      2) In addition to the classifications described above, the entity may choose the fair value option (FVO) as its accounting method for most recognized investments in debt securities. Investments accounted for under the FVO are accounted for in essentially the same manner as trading securities.

b. An **equity security**, such as a share of common stock, is an **ownership** interest in an entity or a right to acquire or dispose of such an interest.

1) The accounting method used by the investor for its investment in equity securities depends on its **presumed influence** based on the **ownership interest** held. This diagram depicts the three possibilities:

% Ownership	Presumed Influence	Accounting Method
100% – 50%	Control	Consolidation
50% – 20%	Significant	Equity Method or FVO
20% – 0%	Little or none	Fair Value Measurement

2) When the investor has **little or no influence** over the investee (holds less than 20% of voting interests), the investment in equity securities may be classified as either (a) trading or (b) available-for-sale. A third possibility is to elect the FVO.

3) When the investor has **significant influence** over the investee (holds between 20% and 50% of voting interests), the investment in equity securities can be accounted for using either (a) the fair value option (FVO) or (b) the equity method (discussed in Subunit 2.6).

4) Consolidation is required when the investor owns more than 50% of the outstanding voting interests (discussed in Subunit 2.7).

2. **Held-to-Maturity Securities -- Amortized Cost**

   a. An investment in a **debt security** is classified as held-to-maturity when the holder has both the **positive intent** and the **ability** to hold the security until its maturity date.

   b. Held-to-maturity securities are reported at **amortized cost**.

   c. **Presentation -- balance sheet.** Held-to-maturity securities are presented net of any unamortized premium or discount.

   1) Amortization of any discount or premium is reported by a debit (credit) to held-to-maturity securities and a credit (debit) to interest income.

   2) No re measurement to fair value at the end of the reporting period is required.

   d. **Presentation -- income statement.** Realized gains and losses and interest income (including amortization of premium or discount) are included in earnings.

3. **Trading Securities -- Fair Value Through Earnings**

   a. Trading securities (debt or equity securities) are bought and held primarily for sale in the near term. They are purchased and sold frequently.

   1) Each trading security is initially recorded at cost (i.e., fair value on the acquisition date).

   b. At each balance sheet date, trading securities are **remeasured at fair value**.

   1) In the balance sheet, trading securities are reported at fair value.

   c. **Unrealized holding gains and losses** on the remeasurement of trading securities to fair value are included in **earnings** (income statement).

   1) In the income statement, unrealized and realized holding gains and losses, dividends, and interest income are included in earnings.

> **EXAMPLE**
>
> On October 1, Year 1, Maverick Co. purchased 5,000 shares of Larson Co. common stock for their fair value. Maverick classified this investment as trading securities. On March 1, Year 2, Maverick sold all of its investment in Larson for its fair value on that day. The following are the fair values per share of Larson common stock:
>
> | Date | Fair Value |
> |---|---|
> | October 1, Year 1 | $15 |
> | December 31, Year 1 | 13 |
> | March 1, Year 2 | 20 |
>
> October 1, Year 1
> Trading securities (5,000 × $15) $75,000
>   Cash $75,000
>
> December 31, Year 1 -- At each balance sheet date, trading securities are remeasured at fair value. Unrealized holding gains and losses are reported in earnings.
>
> Unrealized holding loss [5,000 × ($15 – $13)] $10,000
>   Trading securities fair value adjustment $10,000
>
> In Maverick's December 31, Year 1 balance sheet, the investment in Larson is reported in the current assets section as trading securities. It is measured at year-end fair value of $65,000 (5,000 × $13).
>
> March 1, Year 2
> Cash (5,000 × $20) $100,000
>   Trading securities ($75,000 – $10,000) $65,000
>   Gain on disposal of trading securities   35,000

    d. The accounting for **fair value option (FVO)** is the same as for trading securities, except the fair value option may be elected even if the securities were not purchased to be sold in the near term.

4. **Available-for-Sale Securities -- Fair Value Through Other Comprehensive Income (OCI)**

    a. Securities that are not classified as held-to-maturity or trading are considered available-for-sale.

        1) Each available-for-sale security is initially recorded at cost.

    b. At each balance sheet date, available-for-sale securities are **remeasured at fair value**.

        1) In the **balance sheet**, available-for-sale securities are reported at fair value.

    c. **Unrealized holding gains and losses** (net of taxes) resulting from remeasurement to fair value are reported in **other comprehensive income (OCI)**.

        1) The **statement of comprehensive income** reports unrealized holding gains and losses for the period that are included in comprehensive income.

            a) When a security classified as available-for-sale is sold, the related unrealized gains and losses that were previously recognized in OCI must be reclassified to the income statement.

            b) For example, if a gain on available-for-sale securities is realized in the current period (when the security is sold), the prior-period recognition of an unrealized holding gain must be reclassified from OCI to earnings by debiting OCI and crediting a gain.

        2) In the **income statement**, realized gains and losses, dividends, and interest income are included in earnings.

> **EXAMPLE**
>
> On April 1, Year 1, Maverick Co. purchased 1,000 shares of White Co. common stock for their fair value. Maverick classified this investment as available-for-sale securities. On May 1, Year 3, Maverick sold all of its investment in White for its fair value on that day. The following are the fair values per share of White common stock:
>
> | Date | Fair Value |
> |---|---|
> | April 1, Year 1 | $25 |
> | December 31, Year 1 | 32 |
> | December 31, Year 2 | 27 |
> | May 1, Year 3 | 31 |
>
> April 1, Year 1 Journal Entry
> Available-for-sale securities (1,000 × $25) $25,000
>   Cash $25,000
>
> December 31, Year 1 Journal Entry - At each balance sheet date, available-for-sale securities are remeasured at fair value. Unrealized holding gains and losses are included in OCI.
>
> Available-for-sale securities fair value adjustment [1,000 × ($32 – $25)] $7,000
>   Unrealized holding gain (OCI item) $7,000
>
> Presentation in Maverick's December 31, Year 1 financial statements:
> Balance sheet: Assets section -- Available-for-sale securities (1,000 × $32) $32,000
>   Equity section -- Accumulated OCI   7,000
> Statement of comprehensive income -- Unrealized holding gain (OCI)   7,000
>
> December 31, Year 2 Journal Entry
> Unrealized holding loss [1,000 × ($27 – $32)] $5,000
>   Available-for-sale securities fair value adjustment $5,000
>
> Presentation in Maverick's December 31, Year 2 financial statements:
> Balance sheet: Assets section -- Available-for-sale securities (1,000 × $27) $27,000
>   Equity section -- Accumulated OCI ($7,000 – $5,000)   2,000
> Statement of comprehensive income -- Unrealized holding loss (OCI)   5,000
>
> May 1, Year 3 Journal Entry
> Cash (1,000 × $31) $31,000
> Accumulated OCI   2,000
>   Available-for-sale securities $27,000
>   Realized gain on disposal of available-for-sale securities   6,000

NOTE: If a decline in fair value of an individual **held-to-maturity or available-for-sale** security below its amortized cost basis is **permanent**, the amortized cost basis is written down to fair value as a new cost basis. The impairment is a realized loss included in earnings.

5. **Summary of Investments in Securities -- No Significant Influence**

   a. The following table summarizes GAAP applicable when the FVO has not been elected:

Category	Held-to-maturity		Trading		Available-for-sale	
Definition	Debt that the entity has the positive ability and intent to hold to maturity		Bought and held for near-term sale		All securities not in the other two categories	
Type of security	Debt	Equity	Debt	Equity	Debt	Equity
Recognize holding G/L?	No	--	Yes	Yes	Yes	Yes
Recognize unrealized holding G/L in	--	--	Earnings	Earnings	OCI	OCI
Measured at	Amortized cost	--	Fair value	Fair value	Fair value	Fair value

Stop and review! You have completed the outline for this subunit. Study multiple-choice questions 17 through 20 beginning on page 74.

2.6 EQUITY METHOD

1. **Significant Influence**

    a. An investment in voting stock that enables the investor to exercise significant influence over the investee should be accounted for by the **equity method** (assuming no FVO election).

    b. Significant influence is presumed to exist when the investor holds between 20% and 50% of the investee's voting interests (shares of common stock).

2. **Application of the Equity Method**

    a. An equity method investment is initially recognized at cost.

    b. Under the equity method, the investor recognizes in income its **share of the investee's earnings or losses** in the periods for which they are reported by the investee. The journal entries are

Investee reported net income for the period	Investee reported net loss for the period
Investment in X Co. $XXX	Loss -- Share of X Co. losses $XXX
Revenue -- Share of X Co. earnings $XXX	Investment in X Co. $XXX

   1) An investor recognizes increases in earnings and the **investment account** for its share of the investee's net income for the period.

   2) An investor recognizes a **loss** and a **decrease in the investment account** for its share of the investee's net loss for the period.

      a) The investor's share of the investee's earnings or losses is recognized only for the portion of the year that the investment was held under the equity method.

    c. Dividends from the investee are treated as a return of an investment. They have no effect on the investor's income.

   1) The investor's share of dividends distributed by the investee increases cash and **reduces the investment**. The journal entry is

      Cash or dividend receivable $XXX
         Investment in X Co. $XXX

    d. If an investor can **no longer be presumed** to exercise significant influence (for example, due to a decrease in the level of ownership), it ceases to account for the investment using the equity method.

Stop and review! You have completed the outline for this subunit. Study multiple-choice questions 21 and 22 beginning on page 75.

2.7 BUSINESS COMBINATIONS AND CONSOLIDATED FINANCIAL STATEMENTS

1. **Definitions**

    a. A business combination is a transaction or event in which an acquirer obtains control of one or more businesses.

       1) **Control** (controlling financial interest) is the direct or indirect ability to determine the direction of management and policies of the investee. An entity is presumed to have control when it acquires **more than 50%** of the voting interests (shares of common stock) of a second entity.

       2) A **parent** is an entity that controls one or more subsidiaries.

       3) A **subsidiary** is an entity in which another entity, known as its parent, holds a controlling financial interest.

2. **Acquisition Method**
   a. A business combination must be accounted for using the acquisition method. This method involves identifying
      1) The acquirer and
      2) The acquisition date, i.e., the date on which the acquirer obtains control of the acquiree.
   b. At the acquisition date, the acquirer (parent) must recognize and measure
      1) Identifiable assets acquired,
      2) Liabilities assumed,
      3) Any noncontrolling interest, and
      4) Goodwill or a gain from a bargain purchase.
   c. **Measurement principle** -- The identifiable assets acquired, liabilities assumed, and any noncontrolling interest in the subsidiary are recognized separately from goodwill and must be measured at **acquisition-date fair value**.
   d. A **noncontrolling interest (NCI)** is the portion of equity (net assets) in a subsidiary not attributable, directly or indirectly, to the parent.
      1) At the acquisition date, it is measured at fair value.
      2) It is reported in the equity section of the consolidated balance sheet separately from the parent's shareholders' equity. This is sometimes called a minority interest.
      3) If the parent holds all the outstanding common stock of the subsidiary, no NCI is recognized.
   e. Goodwill is recognized only in a business combination. It is an intangible asset reflecting the future economic benefits arising from those assets acquired in the combination that are not individually identified and separately recognized.
      1) Goodwill has an indefinite useful life. Thus, it must not be amortized subsequent to its initial recognition and is instead periodically tested for impairment.
      2) The parent presents any goodwill recognized in its consolidated balance sheet as one amount under noncurrent assets.
      3) Internally generated goodwill must not be recognized in the financial statements.
      4) Goodwill recognized equals the excess of a) over b) below:
         a) The sum of the acquisition-date **fair value** of the consideration transferred, any NCI recognized, and any previously held equity interest in the acquiree
         b) The acquisition-date fair value of identifiable assets acquired and liabilities assumed (fair value of net assets acquired)

EXAMPLE

Entity C acquired 80% of the outstanding common stock of Entity D for $192,000. Entity D's acquisition-date fair values of identifiable assets and liabilities were $350,000 and $140,000, respectively. The acquisition-date fair value of NCI was $48,000. The goodwill is calculated as follows:

Consideration transferred		$192,000
Noncontrolling interest		48,000
Acquisition-date fair value of identifiable net assets (assets – liabilities) acquired:		
Assets	$350,000	
Liabilities	(140,000)	(210,000)
Goodwill		$ 30,000

5) If b) exceeds a) on the previous page, an ordinary **gain from a bargain purchase** must be recognized in the parent's consolidated statement of income.

EXAMPLE

In the preceding example, assume that the acquisition-date fair value of the identifiable assets acquired was $400,000 (instead of $350,000). The gain from the bargain purchase is calculated as follows:

Acquisition-date fair value of identifiable net assets (assets – liabilities) acquired:
Assets	$400,000	
Liabilities	(140,000)	$260,000
Consideration transferred		(192,000)
Noncontrolling interest		(48,000)
Gain from bargain purchase		$ 20,000

---

f. **Acquisition-related costs**, such as finder's fees, professional and consulting fees, and general administrative costs, are **expensed as incurred**.

1) Issue costs for securities are accounted for as follows:

a) Direct issue costs of equity (underwriting, legal, accounting, tax, registration, etc.) reduce additional paid-in capital.

b) **Debt issue costs** are reported in the balance sheet as deferred charges and amortized over the life of the debt using the interest method.

3. **Consolidated Financial Statements**

a. When one entity (parent) controls another (subsidiary), consolidated financial statements must be issued by the parent regardless of the percentages of ownership.

1) Consolidated reporting is required even when majority ownership is indirect, i.e., when a subsidiary holds a majority interest in another subsidiary.

b. **Consolidated financial statements** are the general-purpose financial statements of a parent with one or more subsidiaries. They present amounts for the parent and all its subsidiaries as if they were a **single economic entity**.

c. Required consolidated reporting is an example of substance over form. Even if the two entities remain legally separate, the financial statements are more meaningful to users if they see the effects of control by one over the other.

d. **Consolidated procedures**. The consolidation process begins with the parent-only and subsidiary-only adjusted trial balances (parent's and subsidiary's separate financial statements). The following steps must be performed when preparing consolidated financial statements:

1) All line items of assets, liabilities, revenues, expenses, gains, losses, and OCI items of a subsidiary are added item by item to those of the parent. These items are reported at the consolidated amounts.

2) The periodic net income or loss of a consolidated subsidiary attributable to the NCI is presented separately from the periodic net income or loss attributable to the shareholders of the parent.

3) All the equity amounts of the subsidiary are eliminated (not presented in the consolidated financial statements).

4) No investment in subsidiary account is presented in the consolidated financial statement since all the assets and liabilities of the subsidiary are reported.

5) Goodwill recognized at the acquisition date is presented separately as an intangible asset.

6) The NCI is reported separately in one line item in the equity section. It must be adjusted for its proportionate share of (a) the subsidiary's net income (increase) or net loss (decrease) for the period, (b) dividends declared by the subsidiary (decrease), and (c) items of OCI recognized by the subsidiary.

7) Intraentity balances, transactions, income, and expenses must be eliminated in full.

   a) Consolidating entities routinely conduct business with each other. The effects of these intraentity transactions must be eliminated in full during the preparation of the consolidated financial statements.

   b) Consolidated financial statements report financial position, results of operations, and cash flows as if the consolidated entities were a single economic entity. Thus, all line items in the consolidated financial statements must be presented at the amounts that would have been reported if the intraentity transactions had never occurred.

   c) After adding all the assets, liabilities, and income statement items of a parent and a subsidiary, eliminating journal entries for intraentity transactions must be recorded for proper presentation of the consolidated financial statements.

e. An example of a full set of consolidated financial statements can be found in Appendix B.

Stop and review! You have completed the outline for this subunit. Study multiple-choice questions 23 through 25 beginning on page 76.

2.8 DIFFERENT TYPES OF EXPENSES AND LIABILITIES

1. **Purchase Commitment**

   a. A commitment to acquire goods in the future is not recorded at the time of the agreement. The goods are recognized as inventory when they are received.

   b. But a **loss** is recognized on a firm's noncancelable purchase commitment if the current market price of the goods is less than the commitment price.

      1) An example of such an agreement is a **take-or-pay contract** that requires one party to purchase a certain number of goods from the other party or else pay a penalty.

   c. Material losses expected on purchase commitments are measured in the same way as inventory losses, recognized, and separately disclosed.

      1) The reason for current loss recognition is the same as that for inventory. A decrease (not an increase) in its future benefits should be recognized when it occurs even if the contract is unperformed on both sides.

      2) The entry is

      Unrealized holding loss -- earnings $XXX
        Liability -- purchase commitment $XXX

      3) The nature and the term of the contract (obligation) must be described in the notes to the financial statements.

EXAMPLE

During the year, the Lisbon Company signed a noncancelable contract to purchase 2,000 pounds of a raw material at $64 per pound during the forthcoming year. On December 31, the market price of the raw material is $52 per pound, and the selling price of the finished product is expected to decline accordingly. The financial statements prepared for the year should report a loss of $24,000 [2,000 × ($64 – $52)] in the income statement.

GAAP require recognition in the income statement of a material loss on a purchase commitment as if the inventory were already owned. Losses on firm purchase commitments are measured in the same way as inventory losses. If the cost is $128,000 and the market price is $104,000, a $24,000 loss should be disclosed.

2. **Warranty Liability**

    a. A warranty is a **written guarantee** of the integrity of a product or service. The seller also agrees to repair or replace a product, refund all or part of the price, or provide additional service.

        1) A warranty is customarily offered for a limited time, such as 2 years.
        2) It may or may not be separable.

    b. **Inseparable warranty.** Under the accrual method of accounting, if incurrence of warranty expense is probable and the amount can be reasonably estimated, a liability for warranty costs is recognized when the related revenue is recognized, i.e., on the day the product is sold. This is an example of the matching principle.

        1) This accounting treatment is sometimes called the expense warranty approach.
        2) Even if the warranty covers a period longer than the period in which the product is sold, the **entire liability** (expense) for the expected warranty costs must be recognized on the day the product is sold. The warranty liability (expense) must not be prorated over the annual periods covered by the warranty.

            Beginning warranty liability
            Warranty expense recognized in the current period
            Less: Warranty payments in the current period
            Ending warranty liability

        3) Actual payments for warranty costs reduce the amount of warranty liability recognized and do not affect warranty expense.

            a) If the warranty payments for the period are greater than the amount of warranty liability recognized, the excess is recognized as warranty expense.

EXAMPLE

In Year 1, a company began selling a product under a 2-year warranty. The estimated warranty costs are 3% of sales in the year of sale and 5% in the following year. Sales and actual warranty payments for Year 1 and Year 2 are as follows:

	Sales	Warranty Payments
Year 1	$300,000	$ 5,000
Year 2	500,000	37,000

In Year 1, warranty expense of $24,000 [$300,000 × (3% + 5%)] is recognized. The warranty liability of $19,000 ($24,000 – $5,000) is reported on the December 31, Year 1, balance sheet.

In Year 2, warranty expense of $40,000 [$500,000 × (3% + 5%)] is recognized. The warranty liability of $22,000 is reported on the December 31, Year 2, balance sheet.

Beginning warranty liability (1/1/Year 2)	$19,000
Warranty expense recognized in Year 2	40,000
Warranty payments in Year 2	(37,000)
Ending warranty liability (12/31/Year 2)	$22,000

c. **Separable warranty.** When the warranty is sold separately from the product, the **revenue is deferred** and is ordinarily recognized on the **straight-line basis** over the term of the contract.

1) This accounting treatment is sometimes called the sales warranty approach.
2) **Costs** are deferred and amortized only when they are directly related to, and vary with, the sale of the warranty. The primary example of such a cost is a commission.

   a) Furthermore, if service costs are **not incurred on a straight-line basis**, revenue recognition over the contract's term should be proportionate to the estimated service costs.

3. **Contingencies -- Recognition and Reporting**

   a. A contingency is "an existing condition, situation, or set of circumstances **involving uncertainty** as to possible gain (a gain contingency) or loss (a loss contingency) to an enterprise that will ultimately be resolved when one or more future events occur or fail to occur."
   b. A contingency may be
      1) Probable. Future events are likely to occur.
      2) Reasonably possible. The chance of occurrence is more than remote but less than probable.
      3) Remote. The chance of occurrence is slight.
   c. A **loss contingency** must be accrued (recognition of a liability and related loss contingency) when the following two conditions are met:
      1) It is **probable** that, at a balance sheet date, an asset has been impaired or a liability has been incurred.
      2) The amount of the loss can be **reasonably estimated**.
         a) The amount with the better estimate within a **range of loss** must be accrued.
         b) If no amount within that range appears to be a better estimate than any other, the **minimum** should be accrued.
         c) Disclosure of the nature of the accrual and, in some cases, the amount or the range of loss may be required to prevent the financial statements from being misleading.
   d. If at least one condition is not met but the probability of loss is at least **reasonably possible**, the nature of the contingency must be **disclosed** in the notes to the financial statements.
   e. Loss contingencies with a **remote** probability ordinarily are **not disclosed**.
   f. Gain contingencies are **recognized only when realized**. A gain contingency must be adequately disclosed in the notes.
      1) For example, an award of damages in a lawsuit is not realized if it is being appealed.

Stop and review! You have completed the outline for this subunit. Study multiple-choice questions 26 through 30 beginning on page 77.

QUESTIONS

2.1 Accounts Receivable

1. An analysis of an entity's $150,000 accounts receivable at year end resulted in a $5,000 ending balance for its allowance for uncollectible accounts and a bad debt expense of $2,000. During the past year, recoveries on bad debts previously written off were correctly recorded at $500. If the beginning balance in the allowance for uncollectible accounts was $4,700, what was the amount of accounts receivable written off as uncollectible during the year?

A. $1,200
B. $1,800
C. $2,200
D. $2,800

Answer (C) is correct.
REQUIRED: The amount of accounts receivable written off during the year.
DISCUSSION: Under the allowance method, uncollectible accounts are written off by a debit to the allowance and a credit to accounts receivable. The $500 of recovered bad debts is accounted for by a debit to accounts receivable and a credit to the allowance. The $2,000 bad debt expense is also credited to the allowance. The amount of accounts receivable written off can be calculated as follows:

Beginning allowance	$4,700
Bad debt expense	2,000
Recoveries	500
Ending allowance	(5,000)
A/R written off	$2,200

Answer (A) is incorrect. The amount of $1,200 results from subtracting the recoveries instead of adding them. Answer (B) is incorrect. The amount of $1,800 results from subtracting bad debt expense from the allowance account. Answer (D) is incorrect. The amount of $2,800 results from subtracting the recoveries and bad debt expense from the allowance account.

2. The following information applies to a manufacturing company, which has a 6-month operating cycle:

Cash sales	$100,000
Credit sales during the sixth month with net 30 days terms	150,000
Credit sale during the fifth month with special terms of net 9 months	10,000
Interest earned and accrued on an investment that matures during month 3 of the next cycle	2,000

The total of the company's trade accounts receivable at the end of the current cycle is

A. $152,000
B. $160,000
C. $260,000
D. $262,000

Answer (B) is correct.
REQUIRED: The total trade accounts receivable.
DISCUSSION: A receivable classified as current on the statement of financial position is expected to be collected within the current operating cycle or 1 year, whichever is longer. The total of the trade accounts receivable at the end of the current cycle is therefore $160,000 ($150,000 + $10,000).
Answer (A) is incorrect. The amount of $152,000 results from omitting the credit sale with special 9-month terms and including the interest receivable. Answer (C) is incorrect. The amount of $260,000 results from including cash sales. Answer (D) is incorrect. The amount of $262,000 results from including cash sales and the interest receivable.

3. A company uses the allowance method to account for uncollectible accounts receivable. After recording the estimate of uncollectible accounts expense for the current year, the company decided to write off in the current year the $10,000 account of a customer who had filed for bankruptcy. What effect does this write-off have on the company's current net income and total current assets, respectively?

	Net Income	Total Current Assets
A.	Decrease	Decrease
B.	No effect	Decrease
C.	Decrease	No effect
D.	No effect	No effect

Answer (D) is correct.
REQUIRED: The effects of writing off a receivable.
DISCUSSION: The company uses the allowance method. Thus, when a specific amount is written off, the journal entry is

Allowance for doubtful accounts	$10,000	
Accounts receivable		$10,000

The write-off of a bad debt has no effect on expenses, net income, and total current assets.
Answer (A) is incorrect. Under the allowance method, the write-off of a bad debt has no effect on either net income or total current assets. Answer (B) is incorrect. Under the allowance method, the write-off of a bad debt has no effect on total (net) current assets. Answer (C) is incorrect. Under the allowance method, the write-off of a bad debt has no effect on net income.

SU 2: Measurement, Valuation, and Disclosure: Investments and Short-Term Items

4. Based on the industry average, a corporation estimates that its bad debts should average 3% of credit sales. The balance in the allowance for uncollectible accounts at the beginning of Year 3 was $140,000. During Year 3, credit sales totaled $10,000,000, accounts of $100,000 were deemed to be uncollectible, and payment was received on a $20,000 account that had previously been written off as uncollectible. The entry to record bad debt expense at the end of Year 3 would include a credit to the allowance for uncollectible accounts of

A. $300,000
B. $260,000
C. $240,000
D. $160,000

Answer (A) is correct.
REQUIRED: The credit to the allowance for uncollectible accounts.
DISCUSSION: Bad debt expense is based on the income statement approach. It treats bad debt expense as a function of sales on account. Thus, it is projected to be $300,000 ($10,000,000 × 3%). The entry to record bad debt expense is

Bad debt expense $300,000
  Allowance for doubtful accounts $300,000

Answer (B) is incorrect. The amount of $260,000 is the sum of the beginning allowance, the accounts written off during the year, and the reestablished amount of the allowance resulting from collection of the written-off account. Answer (C) is incorrect. The amount of $240,000 is the sum of the beginning allowance and the accounts written off during the year. Answer (D) is incorrect. The amount of $160,000 is the sum of the beginning allowance and the reestablished amount of the allowance resulting from collection of the written-off account.

5. The following information has been compiled by a manufacturing company:

- Sale of company products for the period to customers with net 30-day terms amounting to $150,000.
- Sale of company products for the period to a customer, supported by a note for $25,000, with special terms of net 180 days.
- Balance of trade receivables at the end of the last period was $300,000.
- Collections of open trade receivables during the period was $200,000.
- Rental income for the period, both earned and accrued but not yet collected, from the manufacturing company's credit union for use of company facilities was $2,000.

The open trade receivables balance to be shown on the statement of financial position for the period is

A. $250,000
B. $252,000
C. $275,000
D. $277,000

Answer (A) is correct.
REQUIRED: The open trade receivables balance to be shown on the statement of financial position.
DISCUSSION: The open trade receivables balance is calculated as follows:

Previous ending balance	$300,000
Add: sales to customers (terms net 30)	150,000
Minus: collections during period	(200,000)
Open trade receivables reported	$250,000

Answer (B) is incorrect. The amount of $252,000 results from treating rental income as a trade receivable. Answer (C) is incorrect. The amount of $275,000 results from including the note receivable. Answer (D) is incorrect. The amount of $277,000 results from including the note receivable and the rental income.

2.2 Inventory -- Fundamentals

6. A retail entity maintains a markup of 25% based on cost. The entity has the following information for the current year:

Purchases of merchandise	$690,000
Freight-in on purchases	25,000
Sales	900,000
Ending inventory	80,000

Beginning inventory was

A. $40,000
B. $85,000
C. $110,000
D. $265,000

Answer (B) is correct.
REQUIRED: The beginning inventory.
DISCUSSION: Cost of goods sold for a period equals beginning inventory, plus purchases, plus freight-in, minus ending inventory. Given that sales reflect 125% of cost, cost of goods sold must equal $720,000 ($900,000 sales ÷ 1.25). Consequently, the beginning inventory must have been $85,000 ($720,000 COGS + $80,000 EI – $690,000 purchases – $25,000 freight-in).
Answer (A) is incorrect. The amount of $40,000 is based on a 25% markup on sales. Answer (C) is incorrect. The amount of $110,000 results from omitting freight-in from the computation of cost of goods available for sale. Answer (D) is incorrect. The amount of $265,000 results from using the sales figure for cost of goods sold.

Question 7 is based on the following information. An entity had the following opening and closing inventory balances during the current year:

	1/1	12/31
Finished goods	$ 90,000	$260,000
Raw materials	105,000	130,000
Work-in-progress	220,000	175,000

The following transactions and events occurred during the current year:

- $300,000 of raw materials were purchased, of which $20,000 were returned because of defects.
- $600,000 of direct labor costs were incurred.
- $750,000 of production overhead costs were incurred.

7. If the entity's raw materials inventory as of December 31 of the current year (ending inventory) was miscounted and the true figure was higher than $130,000, one effect on the year-end financial statements would be that

A. Profit is overstated.
B. Cost of goods sold is overstated.
C. Working capital is overstated.
D. Cost of goods produced is understated.

Answer (B) is correct.
REQUIRED: The effect of understating ending inventory.
DISCUSSION: If the ending inventory of raw materials is understated, raw materials used is overstated, cost of goods produced is overstated, and cost of goods sold is overstated.
Answer (A) is incorrect. If the ending inventory of raw materials is understated, cost of goods sold is overstated, and net income is understated. Answer (C) is incorrect. Working capital is higher when the balances of current assets are higher. If the raw materials inventory balance is understated, working capital will also be understated. Answer (D) is incorrect. If the ending inventory of raw materials is understated, raw materials used is overstated, and cost of goods produced is overstated.

8. A company's inventory is overstated at December 31 of this year. The result will be

A. Understated income this year.
B. Understated retained earnings this year.
C. Understated retained earnings next year.
D. Understated income next year.

Answer (D) is correct.
REQUIRED: The result of overstating ending inventory.
DISCUSSION: Cost of goods sold equals beginning finished goods, plus cost of goods manufactured for a manufacturer or purchases for a retailer, minus ending finished goods. Overstated ending inventory therefore results in understated cost of goods sold, overstated net income, and overstated retained earnings in the period of the error. When these errors reverse in the following period, beginning inventory and cost of goods sold will be overstated, and net income will be understated. Retained earnings will be correct.
Answer (A) is incorrect. Net income will be overstated this year. Answer (B) is incorrect. Retained earnings will be overstated this year. Answer (C) is incorrect. Retained earnings will be correctly stated next year.

9. The following information applies to the income statement of a company:

Gross sales	$1,000,000
Net sales	900,000
Freight-in	10,000
Ending inventory	200,000
Gross profit margin	40%

The company's cost of goods available for sale is

A. $550,000
B. $560,000
C. $740,000
D. $800,000

Answer (C) is correct.
REQUIRED: The cost of goods available for sale.
DISCUSSION: The gross profit (gross margin) method calculates ending inventory at a given time by subtracting an estimated cost of goods sold from the sum of beginning inventory and purchases (or cost of goods manufactured). The estimated cost of goods sold equals sales minus the gross profit. The gross profit equals sales multiplied by the gross profit percentage, an amount ordinarily determined on a historical basis. Given that the gross margin percentage is 40% of net sales, cost of goods sold must be 60% of net sales, or $540,000 ($900,000 × 60%). Goods available for sale equals cost of goods sold plus ending inventory ($540,000 + $200,000 = $740,000).
Answer (A) is incorrect. The amount of $550,000 results from assuming a 60% gross margin percentage and a 40% COGS rate and subtracting freight-in. Answer (B) is incorrect. The amount of $560,000 results from assuming a 60% gross margin percentage and a 40% COGS rate. Answer (D) is incorrect. The amount of $800,000 results from using gross sales rather than net sales.

2.3 Inventory -- Cost Flow Methods

10. An entity started in Year 1 with 200 scented candles on hand at a cost of $3.50 each. These candles sell for $7.00 each. The following schedule represents the purchases and sales of candles during Year 1:

Transaction Number	Quantity Purchased	Unit Cost	Quantity Sold
1	---	---	150
2	250	$3.30	---
3	---	---	100
4	200	3.10	---
5	---	---	200
6	350	3.00	---
7	---	---	300

If the entity uses periodic FIFO inventory pricing, the gross profit for Year 1 would be

A. $2,755
B. $2,805
C. $2,854
D. $2,920

Answer (B) is correct.
REQUIRED: The gross profit using periodic FIFO inventory pricing.
DISCUSSION: The FIFO method assumes that the first goods purchased are the first goods sold and that ending inventory consists of the latest purchases. Moreover, whether the inventory system is periodic or perpetual does not affect FIFO measurement. The cost of goods sold is $2,445 {beginning inventory (200 units × $3.50) + purchases [(250 units × $3.30) + (200 units × $3.10) + (350 units × $3.00)] – ending inventory (250 units × $3.00)}. Thus, the gross profit for Year 1 using FIFO is $2,805 [sales (750 units × $7.00) – cost of goods sold of $2,445].
Answer (A) is incorrect. The amount of $2,755 equals sales minus purchases. Answer (C) is incorrect. The amount of $2,854 results from using a weighted-average ending inventory and part of the cost of goods sold calculation. Answer (D) is incorrect. The amount of $2,920 results from using periodic LIFO inventory pricing.

11. The advantage of the last-in, first-out inventory method is based on the assumption that

A. The most recently incurred costs should be allocated to the cost of goods sold.
B. Costs should be charged to revenue in the order in which they are incurred.
C. Costs should be charged to cost of goods sold at average cost.
D. Current costs should be based on representative or normal conditions of efficiency and volume of operations.

Answer (A) is correct.
REQUIRED: The assumption about LIFO.
DISCUSSION: Under the LIFO method, the most recent costs of acquiring or producing inventory are expensed as part of cost of goods sold. Given inflation, this method results in the highest cost of goods.
Answer (B) is incorrect. The FIFO method charges costs to revenue in the order in which they were incurred. Answer (C) is incorrect. The LIFO method does not average costs. Answer (D) is incorrect. The LIFO method applies an inventory flow assumption, not an alternative approach to measuring the costs incurred to acquire or produce inventory.

12. The inventory method yielding the same inventory measurement and cost of goods sold whether a perpetual or periodic system is used is

A. Average cost.
B. First-in, first-out.
C. Last-in, first-out.
D. Either first-in, first-out or last-in, first-out.

Answer (B) is correct.
REQUIRED: The inventory method yielding the same inventory measurement and cost of goods sold whether a perpetual or periodic system is used.
DISCUSSION: A perpetual inventory system will result in the same dollar amount of ending inventory as a periodic inventory system assuming a FIFO cost flow. Under both perpetual and periodic systems, the same units are deemed to be in ending inventory.
Answer (A) is incorrect. The weighted-average method determines an average cost only once (at the end of the period) and is therefore applicable only to a periodic system. In contrast, the moving-average method requires determination of a new weighted-average cost after each purchase and thus applies only to a perpetual system. Answer (C) is incorrect. A perpetual inventory system may generate a dollar amount different from that of a periodic inventory system assuming a LIFO inventory cost flow. These two inventory accounting systems may result in different units in LIFO ending inventory. The periodic system determines the cost of sales only at year end, but the perpetual system determines cost of sales as sales occur. Thus, the perpetual system assumes that layers of inventory may be liquidated during a year even though inventory quantities are restored by later purchases. The periodic system does not make this assumption. Answer (D) is incorrect. The results may vary under LIFO but not FIFO depending on whether a perpetual or periodic system is used.

SU 2: Measurement, Valuation, and Disclosure: Investments and Short-Term Items

13. In a period of rising prices, which one of the following inventory methods usually provides the **best** matching of expenses against revenues?

A. Weighted average.
B. First-in, first-out.
C. Last-in, first-out.
D. Specific identification.

Answer (C) is correct.
REQUIRED: The inventory method best matching expenses against revenues in a period of rising prices.
DISCUSSION: A significant advantage of the LIFO method is its matching of current revenues with the most recent product costs. When prices are rising (which is most of the time), the most recent costs are the highest costs, resulting in higher cost of goods sold and lower net income. The lower net income means lower taxes.
Answer (A) is incorrect. The weighted-average method averages earlier (lower) costs with the latest (highest) costs. Answer (B) is incorrect. The FIFO method expenses the earliest (lowest) costs first. Answer (D) is incorrect. The specific identification method determines the actual physical flow of inventory. Unless the actual flow is last-in, first-out, specific identification results in a higher net income than the LIFO method.

2.4 Inventory Measurement in the Financial Statements -- Lower of Cost or Market

14. In accounting for inventories, generally accepted accounting principles require departure from the historical cost principle when the utility of inventory has fallen below cost. This rule is known as the "lower-of-cost-or-market" rule. The term "market" as defined here means

A. Original cost minus allowance for obsolescence.
B. Original cost plus normal profit margin.
C. Replacement cost of the inventory.
D. Original cost minus cost to dispose.

Answer (C) is correct.
REQUIRED: The meaning of the term "market."
DISCUSSION: Market is the replacement cost of the inventory as determined in the market in which the entity buys its inventory, not the market in which it sells to customers. Market is limited to a ceiling amount equal to net realizable value and a floor amount equal to net realizable value minus a normal profit margin.
Answer (A) is incorrect. The market value is not a cost. Answer (B) is incorrect. The floor amount is net realizable value minus a normal profit margin. Answer (D) is incorrect. Original cost minus cost to dispose equals net realizable value.

15. The following data apply to a unit of inventory:

Selling price	$22
Selling cost	2
Normal profit margin	5
Replacement cost	10

Using the lower of cost or market (LCM) method of measuring inventory, what is the market amount for this unit of inventory?

A. $10.00
B. $15.00
C. $17.50
D. $20.00

Answer (B) is correct.
REQUIRED: The market amount for a unit of inventory.
DISCUSSION: Under the LCM method, market is current replacement cost subject to a maximum (ceiling) equal to net realizable value and a minimum (floor) equal to net realizable value minus a normal profit margin. NRV equals selling price minus costs of completion and disposal. Thus, the maximum market amount is the $20 NRV ($22 selling price – $2 selling cost), and the minimum is $15 ($20 NRV – $5 normal profit margin). Because the minimum exceeds the $10 replacement cost, it is the market amount.
Answer (A) is incorrect. The amount of $10.00 is replacement cost, which is lower than the minimum of NRV minus a normal profit margin. Answer (C) is incorrect. The amount of $17.50 is the average of the maximum and minimum amounts. Answer (D) is incorrect. The amount of $20.00 is NRV.

16. A distribution company has determined its December 31 inventory on a FIFO basis at $200,000. Information pertaining to that inventory follows:

Estimated selling price	$204,000
Estimated cost of disposal	10,000
Normal profit margin	30,000
Current replacement cost	180,000

The company records losses that result from applying the lower-of-cost-or-market rule. At December 31, the loss that the company should recognize is

A. $0
B. $6,000
C. $14,000
D. $20,000

Answer (D) is correct.
REQUIRED: The loss resulting from applying the lower-of-cost-or-market rule.
DISCUSSION: As indicated below, the $180,000 replacement cost falls between the $194,000 ceiling and the $164,000 floor. Hence, it will be used as market in the LCM determination. Because the $180,000 market value is $20,000 lower than the $200,000 historical cost, the inventory should be valued at $180,000 and a $20,000 loss recognized.

NRV ($204,000 – $10,000)	$194,000
Replacement cost	$180,000
NRV – Normal profit ($194,000 – $30,000)	$164,000

Answer (A) is incorrect. A $20,000 loss is recognized. Answer (B) is incorrect. The amount of $6,000 results from the difference between historical cost and net realizable value (ceiling). Answer (C) is incorrect. The amount of $14,000 results from the difference between the replacement cost and the net realizable value (ceiling).

2.5 Classification of Investments

17. Investments classified as held-to-maturity are measured at

A. Fair value, with unrealized gains and losses reported in net income.
B. Fair value, with unrealized gains and losses reported in other comprehensive income (OCI).
C. Replacement cost, with no unrealized gains or losses reported.
D. Amortized cost, with no unrealized gains or losses reported.

Answer (D) is correct.
REQUIRED: The measurement of investments classified as held-to-maturity.
DISCUSSION: Assuming the fair value option has not been elected, held-to-maturity securities are reported at amortized cost, with no unrealized gains or losses reported.
Answer (A) is incorrect. Trading securities or securities for which the FVO has been elected are reported at fair value, with unrealized gains and losses reported in net income. Answer (B) is incorrect. Assuming the fair value option has not been elected, available-for-sale securities are reported at fair value, with unrealized gains and losses reported in other comprehensive income (OCI). Answer (C) is incorrect. Held-to-maturity securities are reported at amortized cost, with no unrealized gains or losses reported.

18. A company has the following investment portfolio:

	Cost	Fair Value
Trading securities:		
Q Company common stock	$140,000	$150,000
B, Inc., common stock	125,000	110,000
D, Inc., 8% bonds	225,000	240,000
Securities to be held to maturity:		
A, Inc., 9% bonds	80,000	84,000
P City municipal bonds	180,000	210,000
Available-for-sale securities:		
K Co. common stock	45,000	51,000
V, Inc., preferred stock	97,000	109,000

The total amount of these investments to be reported on the company's statement of financial position is

A. $892,000
B. $902,000
C. $920,000
D. $954,000

Answer (C) is correct.
REQUIRED: The total amount of investments.
DISCUSSION: Trading securities and available-for-sale securities are reported at their fair values at each balance sheet date. Held-to-maturity securities are reported at amortized cost. The total amount of these investments to be reported on the company's statement of financial position is therefore calculated as follows:

Trading securities:	
Q Company common stock	$150,000
B, Inc., common stock	110,000
D, Inc., 8% bonds	240,000
Securities to be held to maturity:	
A, Inc., 9% bonds	80,000
P City municipal bonds	180,000
Available-for-sale securities:	
K Co. common stock	51,000
V, Inc., preferred stock	109,000
Total	$920,000

Answer (A) is incorrect. The amount of $892,000 results from not measuring trading securities and available-for-sale securities at their fair values. Answer (B) is incorrect. The amount of $902,000 results from measuring available-for-sale securities at cost. Answer (D) is incorrect. The amount of $954,000 results from measuring held-to-maturity securities at fair value.

19. Which one of the following statements with regard to marketable securities is **incorrect**?

A. In the trading portfolio of marketable equity securities, unrealized gains and losses are recorded on the income statement.

B. In the available-for-sale portfolio of marketable equity securities, unrealized gains and losses are recorded on the income statement.

C. The held-to-maturity portfolio consists only of debt securities.

D. Securities may be transferred from the held-to-maturity to the available-for-sale portfolio.

Answer (B) is correct.
REQUIRED: The false statement about marketable securities.
DISCUSSION: Assuming the fair value option has not been elected, unrealized holding gains and losses on available-for-sale securities are reported in other comprehensive income. (But all or part of unrealized holding gains and losses on available-for-sale securities designated and qualifying as hedged items in a fair value hedge are recognized in earnings.)
Answer (A) is incorrect. Trading securities are reported at fair value, with unrealized holding gains and losses recognized in earnings. Answer (C) is incorrect. Equity securities are never classified as held-to-maturity. Answer (D) is incorrect. Securities may be transferred from any classification to any other classification, but transfers from held-to-maturity into or from trading should be rare.

20. The following information was extracted from a company's December 31 balance sheet:

	Debit Balance
Noncurrent assets:	
Available-for-sale securities (carried at fair value)	$96,450
Equity:	
Accumulated other comprehensive income (OCI)	
Unrealized gains and losses on available-for-sale securities	19,800

Historical cost of the available-for-sale securities was

A. $63,595
B. $76,650
C. $96,450
D. $116,250

Answer (D) is correct.
REQUIRED: The historical cost of the available-for-sale securities.
DISCUSSION: The existence of an equity account with a debit balance signifies that the available-for-sale securities are reported at fair value that is less than historical cost. The difference is the net unrealized loss balance. Hence, historical cost must have been $116,250 ($96,450 available-for-sale securities at fair value + $19,800 net unrealized loss).
Answer (A) is incorrect. The amount of $63,595 is a nonsense figure. Answer (B) is incorrect. The amount of $76,650 results from subtracting the unrealized loss instead of adding. Answer (C) is incorrect. The amount of $96,450 ignores the unrealized loss balance.

2.6 Equity Method

21. A company owns 10,000 shares of a corporation's stock; the corporation currently has 40,000 shares outstanding. During the year, the corporation had net income of $200,000 and paid $160,000 in dividends. At the beginning of the year, there was a balance of $150,000 in the company's equity method investment in the corporation account. At the end of the year, the balance in this account should be

A. $110,000
B. $150,000
C. $160,000
D. $240,000

Answer (C) is correct.
REQUIRED: The balance in the investment account at the end of the year.
DISCUSSION: The company holds 25% (10,000 ÷ 40,000) of the corporation's voting common stock. Under the equity method, (1) an investor recognizes its share of the investee's net income as an increase in the investment account:

Investment in the corporation ($200,000 × 25%)	$50,000	
Income -- equity-method investee		$50,000

(2) a dividend from the investee is treated as a return of an investment:

Cash ($160,000 × 25%)	$40,000	
Investment in the corporation		$40,000

Thus, at the end of the year, the balance in the investment in the corporation account is $160,000 ($150,000 + $50,000 – $40,000).
Answer (A) is incorrect. The amount of $110,000 excludes the company's share in the corporation's current-year net income. Answer (B) is incorrect. The amount of $150,000 is the beginning balance of the investment in the corporation account. Answer (D) is incorrect. The amount of $240,000 treats the dividends received from the corporation as an increase in the investment account instead of as a decrease to it.

22. A corporation acquires a 30% voting interest in another corporation. In this situation, the long-term investment is generally accounted for on the investor corporation's books using which of the following reporting methods?

A. Lower-of-cost-or-market.
B. Cost.
C. Consolidated.
D. Equity.

Answer (D) is correct.
REQUIRED: The reporting method used in the investor corporation's books.
DISCUSSION: If an investor can exercise significant influence over an investee, the investment should be accounted for by the equity method. When a corporation owns 20% or more of the voting power of the investee, the ability to exercise significant influence is presumed.
Answer (A) is incorrect. The lower-of-cost-or-market method is not generally used for equity investments. Answer (B) is incorrect. The cost basis is used when the investor cannot exercise significant influence over the investee (it has less than 20% of the voting power of the investee), and market prices are not readily available. Answer (C) is incorrect. Consolidated reporting is ordinarily required only when the investor controls the investee.

2.7 Business Combinations and Consolidated Financial Statements

23. Entity A acquires all of the voting shares of Entity B for $1,000,000. At the time of the acquisition, the net fair value of the identifiable assets acquired and liabilities assumed had a carrying amount of $900,000 and a fair value of $800,000. The amount of goodwill Entity A will record on the acquisition date is

A. $0
B. $100,000
C. $200,000
D. $300,000

Answer (C) is correct.
REQUIRED: The goodwill recorded.
DISCUSSION: Given no prior equity interest or noncontrolling interest, goodwill equals the excess of the fair value of the consideration transferred over the fair value of the net of the identifiable assets acquired and liabilities assumed. Consequently, goodwill is $200,000 ($1,000,000 – $800,000).
Answer (A) is incorrect. Goodwill must be recorded. Answer (B) is incorrect. The amount of $100,000 is the excess of the acquisition cost over the carrying amount. Answer (D) is incorrect. The amount of $300,000 equals goodwill plus the excess of the carrying amount over fair value.

24. A corporation purchased 100% of the shares of J Corporation for $600,000. Financial information for J Corporation is provided below.

	J Corporation ($000)	
	Carrying Amount	Fair Value
Cash	$ 50	$ 50
Accounts receivable	100	100
Inventory	150	100
Total current assets	300	250
Property, plant, and equipment (net)	500	600
Total assets	$800	$850
Current liabilities	$150	$150
Long-term debt	200	200
Total liabilities	350	350
Common stock	150	150
Paid-in capital	80	80
Retained earnings	220	
Total shareholders' equity	450	
Total liabilities and shareholders' equity	$800	

The amount of goodwill resulting from this purchase, if any, would be

A. $200,000
B. $150,000
C. $100,000
D. $0

Answer (C) is correct.
REQUIRED: The amount of goodwill resulting from the corporation's purchase.
DISCUSSION: Goodwill is the excess of (1) the sum of the acquisition-date fair values of (a) the consideration transferred ($600,000), (b) any noncontrolling interest in the acquiree ($0), and (c) the acquirer's previously held equity interest in the acquiree ($0) over (2) the net of the acquisition-date fair values of the identifiable assets acquired ($850,000) and liabilities assumed ($350,000). The amount of goodwill is calculated as follows:

Consideration transferred	$600,000
Acquisition-date fair value of net assets acquired ($850,000 – $350,000)	(500,000)
Goodwill	$100,000

Answer (A) is incorrect. The amount of $200,000 is the goodwill that would have been recognized if the consideration transferred was $700,000. Answer (B) is incorrect. The amount of $150,000 is based on the carrying amount of the net assets acquired instead of their fair value. Answer (D) is incorrect. The consideration transferred is greater than the fair value of the net assets acquired.

SU 2: Measurement, Valuation, and Disclosure: Investments and Short-Term Items   77

25. Entity X owns 90% of Entity Y. Early in the year, X lent Y $1,000,000. No payments have been made on the debt by year end. Proper accounting at year end in the consolidated financial statements would

A. Eliminate 100% of the receivable, the payable, and the related interest.
B. Eliminate 100% of the receivable and the payable but not any related interest.
C. Eliminate 90% of the receivable, the payable, and the related interest.
D. Eliminate 90% of the receivable and the payable but not any related interest.

Answer (A) is correct.
REQUIRED: The accounting treatment of a loan made by a parent to a subsidiary.
DISCUSSION: In a consolidated statement of financial position, reciprocal balances, such as receivables and payables, between a parent and a consolidated subsidiary should be eliminated in their entirety regardless of the portion of the subsidiary's shares held by the parent. Thus, all effects of the $1,000,000 loan should be eliminated in the preparation of the year-end consolidated statement of financial position.
Answer (B) is incorrect. The interest must be eliminated. Answer (C) is incorrect. All aspects of the transaction must be eliminated. Answer (D) is incorrect. All aspects of the transaction must be eliminated.

2.8 Different Types of Expenses and Liabilities

26. On April 1, a corporation began offering a new product for sale under a 1-year warranty. Of the 5,000 units in inventory at April 1, 3,000 had been sold by June 30. Based on its experience with similar products, the corporation estimated that the average warranty cost per unit sold would be $8. Actual warranty costs incurred from April 1 through June 30 were $7,000. At June 30, what amount should the corporation report as estimated warranty liability?

A. $9,000
B. $16,000
C. $17,000
D. $33,000

Answer (C) is correct.
REQUIRED: The estimated warranty liability.
DISCUSSION: If 3,000 units were sold at an estimated $8 per unit warranty cost, the total credits to the liability account equaled $24,000 (3,000 × $8). Given that actual warranty costs of $7,000 were debited to the account, the ending balance must have been $17,000 ($24,000 – $7,000).
Answer (A) is incorrect. The amount of $9,000 assumes 2,000 units were sold. Answer (B) is incorrect. The amount of $16,000 is the warranty cost that will be recognized when the remaining 2,000 units are sold. Answer (D) is incorrect. The amount of $33,000 assumes that 5,000 units were sold.

27. Net losses on firm purchase commitments to acquire goods for inventory result from a contract price that exceeds the current market price. If a firm expects that losses will occur when the purchase occurs, expected losses, if material,

A. Should be recognized in the accounts and separately disclosed as losses on the income statement of the period during which the decline in price takes place.
B. Should be recognized in the accounts and separately disclosed as net unrealized losses on the balance sheet at the end of the period during which the decline in price takes place.
C. Should be recognized in the accounts and separately disclosed as net unrealized losses on the balance sheet at the end of the period during which the contract is executed.
D. Should not be recognized in the accounts until the contract is executed and need not be separately disclosed in the financial statements.

Answer (A) is correct.
REQUIRED: The accounting treatment of losses arising from a firm (noncancelable) purchase commitment not yet exercised.
DISCUSSION: A loss is accrued in the income statement on goods subject to a firm purchase commitment if the market price of these goods declines below the commitment price. This loss should be measured in the same manner as inventory losses. Disclosure of the loss is also required.
Answer (B) is incorrect. The losses should be recognized in the determination of net income. Answer (C) is incorrect. The losses should be recognized in the determination of net income during the period in which the decline in price occurs. Answer (D) is incorrect. If a loss arises out of a firm, noncancelable, and unhedged commitment, it should be recognized in the current year.

28. A liability arising from a loss contingency should be recorded if the

A. Amount of the loss can be reasonably estimated.
B. Contingent future events have a reasonably possible chance of occurring.
C. Contingent future events have a reasonably possible chance of occurring and the amount of the loss can be reasonably estimated.
D. Contingent future events will probably occur and the amount of the loss can be reasonably estimated.

Answer (D) is correct.
REQUIRED: The situation when a liability should be recorded for a loss contingency.
DISCUSSION: A material contingent loss must be accrued when the following two conditions are met:

1. It is probable that, at the balance sheet date, an asset has been impaired or a liability has been incurred.
2. The amount of the loss can be reasonably estimated.

Answer (A) is incorrect. A liability arising from a loss contingency would be recorded if the contingent future events will probably occur in addition to the amount of the loss being reasonably estimated. Answer (B) is incorrect. A liability arising from a loss contingency would be recorded if the contingent future events will probably occur and also that the amount of the loss can be reasonably estimated. Answer (C) is incorrect. A liability arising from a loss contingency would be recorded if the contingent future events will probably occur, not have a reasonably possible chance of occurring.

29. Which one of the following loss contingencies would be accrued as a liability rather than disclosed in the notes to the financial statement?

A. A guarantee of the indebtedness of another.
B. A dispute over additional income taxes assessed for prior years (now in litigation).
C. A pending lawsuit with an uncertain outcome.
D. Liabilities for service or product warranties made as a regular part of business.

Answer (D) is correct.
REQUIRED: The loss contingency that would be accrued rather than disclosed.
DISCUSSION: Similarly to the guidelines for loss contingencies, a liability for future warranty costs should be accrued if (1) the incurrence of the expense is probable and (2) the amount can be reasonably estimated. Warranty liabilities are usually probable and can be reasonably estimated.
Answer (A) is incorrect. Payment on a guarantee for the indebtedness of another does not have a probable likelihood of occurrence. Answer (B) is incorrect. The likelihood of losing a dispute over additional income taxes is indeterminable. Answer (C) is incorrect. The likely outcome of the lawsuit is indeterminable.

30. A company is the plaintiff in two lawsuits. The first suit involves a competitor who has made an exact copy of one of the company's products, and the company is suing for patent infringement. The attorneys estimate a $5,000,000 award for the company; however, it is anticipated that the case will be in litigation for 2 to 3 years before final resolution. The second case also involves patent infringement; however, in this instance, the attorneys do not believe the company has a strong case. It is estimated that the company has a 50% chance of winning and the award, if any, would be in the $250,000 to $1,000,000 range. The **most** appropriate amount to be recorded as a gain contingency is

A. $0
B. $5,000,000
C. $5,125,000
D. $5,250,000

Answer (A) is correct.
REQUIRED: The most appropriate amount to be recorded as a gain contingency.
DISCUSSION: Gain contingencies are not recorded; they are recognized only when realized. A gain contingency must be adequately disclosed.

2.9 ESSAY QUESTIONS

Scenario for Essay Question 1

Company B sells one product it purchased from various suppliers. B's accounting policy is to report inventory using LIFO periodic and the lower-of-cost-or-market method applied to total inventory. Cash discounts are recorded using the gross method. At December 31, Year 5, the replacement cost of the inventory was $8 per unit, and the net realizable value was $8.80 per unit. The normal profit margin is $1.05 per unit. B reports losses from write-downs of inventory to market directly in cost of goods sold (the direct method). The trial balance at December 31, Year 5, included the following accounts:

Sales (33,000 units × $16)	$528,000
Sales discounts	7,500
Purchases	368,900
Purchase discounts	18,000
Freight-in	5,000
Freight-out	11,000

Inventory purchases during Year 5 were as follows:

	Units	Cost per Unit
Beginning inventory, January 1	8,000	$8.20
Purchases, quarter ended March 31	12,000	8.25
Purchases, quarter ended June 30	15,000	7.90
Purchases, quarter ended September 30	13,000	7.50
Purchases, quarter ended December 31	7,000	7.70
	55,000	

Question

1. Determine the correct amount for each item in the cost of goods sold calculation at year end.

    a. Beginning inventory
    b. Purchases
    c. Purchase discounts
    d. Freight-in
    e. Goods available for sale
    f. Ending inventory
    g. Cost of goods sold

Essay Question 1 — Unofficial Answers

1.
   a. The beginning inventory was $65,600 (8,000 × $8.20).
   b. Purchases is given as $368,900. Company B records purchases at gross amounts.
   c. Purchase discounts is given as $18,000. In a periodic system used in conjunction with the gross method, the amount of purchase (cash) discounts is subtracted to determine goods available for sale.
   d. Freight-in is given as $5,000. In a periodic system, freight-in is an addition to goods available for sale. Ordinarily, it is not allocated to cost of goods sold and ending inventory.
   e. Goods available for sale is the sum of beginning inventory, net purchases, and freight-in.
   f. Company B applies the LCM method to total inventory. Per-unit replacement cost ($8) is the per-unit market amount because it is less than NRV ($8.80) and greater than NRV minus a normal profit margin ($8.80 – $1.05 = $7.75). Total inventory at market is therefore $176,000 [(55,000 units purchased – 33,000 units sold) × $8]. Because the ending inventory is assumed to consist of 8,000 units from beginning inventory, 12,000 units from the first quarter layer, and 2,000 units from the second quarter layer; total inventory at cost is $180,400 [($8,000 × $8.20) + (12,000 × $8.25) + (2,000 × $7.90)]. Under the direct method, the $4,400 loss ($180,400 cost – $176,000 market) is debited to cost of goods sold and credited to inventory.
   g. Cost of goods sold equals goods available for sale minus ending inventory adjusted for the direct writedown to market.

Access the **CMA Review System** from your Gleim Personal Classroom to continue your studies with exam-emulating essay questions!

STUDY UNIT THREE
MEASUREMENT, VALUATION, AND DISCLOSURE: LONG-TERM ITEMS

(23 pages of outline)

3.1	Property, Plant, and Equipment	81
3.2	Impairment and Disposal of Long-Lived Assets	85
3.3	Intangible Assets	87
3.4	Leases	90
3.5	Income Taxes	94
3.6	Accounting for Bonds and Noncurrent Notes Payable	100
3.7	Essay Questions	115

This study unit is the **third of three** on **external financial reporting decisions**. The relative weight assigned to this major topic in Part 1 of the exam is **15%**. The three study units are

Study Unit 1: External Financial Statements and Revenue Recognition
Study Unit 2: Measurement, Valuation, and Disclosure: Investments and Short-Term Items
Study Unit 3: Measurement, Valuation, and Disclosure: Long-Term Items

If you are interested in reviewing more introductory or background material, go to www.gleim.com/CMAIntroVideos for a list of suggested third-party overviews of this topic. The following Gleim outline material is more than sufficient to help you pass the CMA exam; any additional introductory or background material is for your own personal enrichment.

3.1 PROPERTY, PLANT, AND EQUIPMENT

1. **Overview**

    a. Property, plant, and equipment (PPE), also called fixed assets, are tangible property expected to benefit the entity for more than 1 year. They are held for the production or supply of goods or services, rental to others, or administrative purposes.

2. **PPE -- Initial Measurement**

    a. PPE are initially measured at historical cost, which consists of all the costs necessarily incurred to bring the asset to the condition and location necessary for its intended use. The historical (initial) cost includes

       1) The net purchase price (minus trade discounts and rebates, plus purchase taxes and import duties) and
       2) The directly attributable costs of bringing the asset to the location and condition needed for its intended operation, such as architects' and engineers' fees, site preparation, delivery and handling, installation, assembly, and testing.

    b. Interest (borrowing costs) attributable to the acquisition, construction, or production of a PPE asset constructed for internal use is included in its initial cost.

3. **PPE -- Measurement Subsequent to Initial Recognition**

    a. The carrying amount of an item of PPE is the amount at which it is presented in the balance sheet. This amount is equal to the historical cost minus accumulated depreciation and impairment losses.

    Historical or initial cost
    Accumulated depreciation
    Less: Impairment losses
    Asset's carrying amount

b. The accounting issue related to expenditures for PPE subsequent to initial recognition is to determine whether they should be
   1) Capitalized at cost and depreciated in future periods (a capital expenditure) or
   2) Recognized as an expense as incurred (a revenue expenditure).
c. **Capital expenditures** provide additional benefits by improving the quality of services rendered by the asset, extending its useful life, or increasing its output. These expenditures are capitalized at cost.
d. **Revenue expenditures** (expenses) maintain an asset's normal service capacity. These costs are recurring, not expected to benefit future periods, and expensed as incurred.
   1) Routine, minor expenditures made to maintain the operating efficiency of PPE are ordinarily expensed as incurred.

4. **PPE -- Depreciation**
   a. **Depreciation** is the process of systematically and rationally allocating the depreciable base of a tangible capital asset over its expected useful life. The periodic depreciation expense is recognized in the income statement. Accumulated depreciation is a contra-asset account.
      1) The debit is to depreciation expense, and the credit is to accumulated depreciation. The journal entry is

         Depreciation expense $XXX
            Accumulated depreciation $XXX

   b. The asset's **depreciable base** (the amount to be allocated) is calculated as follows:

```
Depreciable base = Historical cost - Salvage value - Recognized impairment loss
```

   c. **Estimated useful life** is an estimated period over which services or economic benefits are expected to be obtained from the use of the asset.
   d. **Salvage value** (residual value) is the amount that the entity expects to obtain from disposal of the asset at the end of the asset's useful life.
   e. Land has an indefinite useful life and therefore must not be depreciated. Thus, the depreciable base of property that consists of land or a building is the depreciable base of the land or building.

EXAMPLE

Jayhawk Co. recently acquired a robot to be used in its fully automated factory for a purchase price of $850,000. Jayhawk spent another $150,000 installing and testing the robot. The company estimates that the robot will have a 5-year useful life and can be sold at the end of that time for $100,000.

The depreciable base for this asset is calculated as follows:

Purchase price	$ 850,000
Installation and testing	150,000
Historical cost	$1,000,000
Estimated salvage value	(100,000)
Depreciable base	$ 900,000

---

   f. The **depreciation method** chosen should reflect the pattern in which economic benefits (or services) from the assets are expected to be received. The chosen method allocates the cost of the asset as equitably as possible to the periods during which services (or economic benefits) are obtained from the use of the asset.

IFRS Difference

Each part of an item with a cost significant to the total cost must be depreciated separately. But an entity may separately depreciate parts that are not significant.

5. **Depreciation Methods**

   a. **Straight-line** (S-L) depreciation is the simplest method because an equal amount of depreciation is charged to each period of the asset's useful life.

      1) The easiest way to calculate straight-line depreciation is to divide the depreciable base by the estimated useful life.

   Periodic depreciation expense = Depreciable base ÷ Estimated useful life

---

EXAMPLE

If Jayhawk applies the straight-line method, depreciation expense over the life of the asset will be calculated as follows:

	Depreciable Base	Divided: Estimated Useful Life	Equals: Depreciation Expense	Accumulated Depreciation	Carrying Amount, End of Year
Year 1:	$900,000	5	$180,000	$180,000	$820,000
Year 2:	900,000	5	180,000	360,000	640,000
Year 3:	900,000	5	180,000	540,000	460,000
Year 4:	900,000	5	180,000	720,000	280,000
Year 5:	900,000	5	180,000	900,000	100,000
Total			$900,000		

The straight-line percentage for Jayhawk's new robot is 20% (100% ÷ 5-year estimated useful life).

---

      2) **Depreciation for a fractional period.** Because an asset is most likely to be acquired or disposed of in the middle of a period, the calculation often involves a fraction of a period. Time-based methods most often compute depreciation to the nearest month of a partial year. However, other conventions also are permitted.

EXAMPLE

Assume that Jayhawk purchased the robot on October 1, Year 1. Depreciation expense recognized in Year 1 is $45,000 [$180,000 depreciation expense for a full year × (3 ÷ 12)]. Annual depreciation expense recognized in Years 2 through 5 is $180,000. Depreciation expense recognized in Year 6 is $135,000 [$180,000 × (9 ÷ 12)].

---

   b. **Usage-centered activity methods** calculate depreciation as a function of an asset's use rather than the time it has been held.

      1) The **units-of-output method** allocates cost based on production. As production varies, so will the depreciation expense.

   Periodic expense = Depreciable base × (Units produced during current period / Estimated total lifetime units)

EXAMPLE

On the date of purchase, Jayhawk anticipated that the robot would produce 8,000 units of product over its 5-year life. In actuality, the robot produced the following:

Year 1	Year 2	Year 3	Year 4	Year 5	Total
2,300 units	2,000 units	1,800 units	1,200 units	700 units	8,000 units

Depreciation expense over the life of the asset will be calculated as follows:

	Depreciable Base	Times: Units-of-Production Fraction	Equals: Depreciation Expense	Accumulated Depreciation	Carrying Amount, Year End
Year 1:	$900,000	(2,300 ÷ 8,000)	$258,750	$258,750	$741,250
Year 2:	900,000	(2,000 ÷ 8,000)	225,000	483,750	516,250
Year 3:	900,000	(1,800 ÷ 8,000)	202,500	686,250	313,750
Year 4:	900,000	(1,200 ÷ 8,000)	135,000	821,250	178,750
Year 5:	900,000	(700 ÷ 8,000)	78,750	900,000	100,000
Total			$900,000		

c. **Accelerated depreciation methods** are time-based. They result in decreasing depreciation charges over the life of the asset. The two major time-based methods are declining balance and sum-of-the-years'-digits.

1) **Declining balance** determines depreciation expense by multiplying the carrying amount (not the depreciable base equal to cost minus salvage value) at the beginning of each period by some percentage (e.g., 200% or 150%) of the straight-line rate of depreciation.

```
Period depreciation expense = Carrying amount × Declining-balance percentage
```

a) The carrying amount decreases by the depreciation recognized. The result is the use of a constant rate against a declining balance.
b) Salvage value is ignored in determining the carrying amount, but the asset is not depreciated below salvage value.

EXAMPLE

If Jayhawk applies double-declining-balance (DDB) depreciation to the robot, the declining-balance percentage will be 40% (20% straight-line rate × 2). Depreciation expense over the life of the asset will be calculated as follows:

	Carrying Amount, First of Year	Times: DDB Rate	Equals: Depreciation Expense	Accumulated Depreciation	Carrying Amount, End of Year
Year 1:	$1,000,000	40%	$400,000	$400,000	$600,000
Year 2:	600,000	40%	240,000	640,000	360,000
Year 3:	360,000	40%	144,000	784,000	216,000
Year 4:	216,000	40%	86,400	870,400	129,600
Year 5:	129,600	40%	29,600*	900,000	100,000
			$900,000		

*Year 5 depreciation expense is $29,600 because the carrying amount cannot be less than salvage value.

---

2) The **sum-of-the-years'-digits (SYD)** depreciation method multiplies not the carrying amount but the constant depreciable base (cost minus salvage value) by a declining fraction. It is a declining rate, declining-charge method.

```
Periodic expense = Depreciable base × (Remaining years in useful life / Sum of all years in useful life)
```

EXAMPLE

If Jayhawk applies sum-of-the-years'-digits depreciation, the denominator of the SYD fraction is 15 (1 + 2 + 3 + 4 + 5). Depreciation expense over the life of the asset will be calculated as follows:

	Depreciable Base	SYD Fraction	Depreciation Expense	Accumulated Depreciation	Carrying Amount, Year End
Year 1:	$900,000	(5 ÷ 15)	$300,000	$300,000	$700,000
Year 2:	900,000	(4 ÷ 15)	240,000	540,000	460,000
Year 3:	900,000	(3 ÷ 15)	180,000	720,000	280,000
Year 4:	900,000	(2 ÷ 15)	120,000	840,000	160,000
Year 5:	900,000	(1 ÷ 15)	60,000	900,000	100,000
			$900,000		

---

d. **Group and composite depreciation** methods apply **straight-line** accounting to a collection of assets depreciated as if they were a single asset. The composite method applies to groups of **dissimilar assets** with varying useful lives, and the group method applies to **similar assets**. They provide an efficient way to account for large numbers of depreciable assets. They also result in the offsetting of under- and overstated depreciation estimates.

IFRS Difference

An entity may choose either the **cost model** (as under U.S. GAAP) or the **revaluation model** as its accounting policy. It must apply that policy to an entire class of PPE. A class is a grouping of assets of similar nature and use in an entity's operations, for example, land, office equipment, or motor vehicles.

An item of PPE whose fair value can be reliably measured may be carried at a **revalued amount** equal to fair value at the revaluation date (minus subsequent accumulated depreciation and impairment losses).

Revaluation is needed whenever fair value and the asset's carrying amount differ materially. Accumulated depreciation is restated proportionately or eliminated.

A revaluation increase must be recognized in other comprehensive income and accumulated in equity as **revaluation surplus**. But the increase must be recognized in profit or loss to the extent it reverses a decrease of the same asset that was recognized in profit or loss.

A revaluation decrease must be recognized in profit or loss. But the decrease must be recognized in other comprehensive income to the extent of any credit in revaluation surplus for the same asset.

IFRS Difference

Under **IAS 40**, *Investment Property*, **investment property** is property (land, building, part of a building, or both) held by the owner or by the lessee under a finance lease to earn rental income or for capital appreciation or both. Investment property may be accounted for according to (1) the **cost model** and carried at historical cost minus accumulated depreciation and impairment losses (as under U.S. GAAP) or (2) the **fair value model**. If the fair value model is chosen as the accounting policy, all of the entity's investment property must be measured at **fair value** at the end of the reporting period. A **gain or loss** arising from a change in the fair value of investment property must be recognized in profit or loss for the period in which it arises. Investment property that is accounted for according to the fair value model is not depreciated.

Stop and review! You have completed the outline for this subunit. Study multiple-choice questions 1 through 9 beginning on page 104.

3.2 IMPAIRMENT AND DISPOSAL OF LONG-LIVED ASSETS

1. **Two-Step Impairment Test**
   a. This two-step impairment test is applied to fixed assets and to intangible assets with finite useful lives.
   b. Testing for impairment occurs when events or changes in circumstances indicate that the carrying amount of the asset may not be recoverable, for example, when
      1) The market price has decreased significantly or
      2) The use or physical condition of the asset has changed significantly and adversely.
   c. The test for impairment is a **two-step test**:
      1) **Recoverability test.** The carrying amount of a long-lived asset to be held and used is not recoverable if it exceeds the sum of the **undiscounted** future cash flows expected from the use and disposition of the asset.

2) If the carrying amount is not recoverable, an impairment loss is recognized. It equals the excess of the carrying amount of the asset over its fair value.

   a) An impairment loss is recognized immediately in income from continuing operations.
   b) The journal entry to recognize the impairment loss is

   Impairment loss $XXX
       Accumulated depreciation $XXX

Determination of an Impairment Loss
1. Events or changes in circumstances indicate a possible loss
2. Carrying amount of an asset > Sum of undiscounted cash flows
3. Impairment loss = Carrying amount – Fair value

d. The carrying amount of a long-lived asset adjusted for an impairment loss is its new cost basis. A previously recognized impairment loss **must not be reversed**.

EXAMPLE

On December 31, Year 2, a machine's carrying amount after the recognition of annual depreciation expense is $160,000 ($200,000 historical cost – $40,000 accumulated depreciation). On that date, as a result of low demand for the company's products, management concludes that the carrying amount of the machine may not be recoverable. Management estimates that the undiscounted future cash flows over the remaining useful life of the machine will be $150,000. On that date, the machine's estimated fair value is $136,000.

The carrying amount of the machine exceeds the undiscounted future cash flows expected from the machine ($160,000 > $150,000). Thus, the carrying amount is deemed to not be recoverable, and the amount of impairment loss recognized is the excess of the machine's carrying amount over its fair value ($160,000 – $136,000 = $24,000).

In the Year 2 income statement, **$24,000** is recognized as an impairment loss.

The carrying amount of the machine as it is reported in the balance sheet on December 31, Year 2, is calculated as follows:

Historical (initial) cost	$200,000
Accumulated depreciation	(40,000)
Impairment losses	(24,000)
Asset's carrying amount	**$136,000**

IFRS Difference

The entity assesses at each reporting date whether an indication of impairment exists. Given such an indication, IFRS requires a **one-step impairment test**.

- The carrying amount of an asset is compared with its recoverable amount. An impairment loss is recognized equal to the excess of the carrying amount over the recoverable amount.

Determination of an Impairment Loss
1. Reporting-date assessment indicates a possible loss
2. Impairment loss = Carrying amount – Recoverable amount

The **recoverable amount** is the greater of an asset's (1) fair value minus cost to sell or (2) value in use. Value in use of the asset is the present value of its expected cash flows.

An impairment loss on an asset (besides goodwill) **may be reversed** in a subsequent period if a change in the estimates used to measure the recoverable amount has occurred. The reversal of an impairment loss is recognized immediately in profit or loss as income from continued operations.

SU 3: Measurement, Valuation, and Disclosure: Long-Term Items

2. **Disposal of Long-Lived Assets**

   a. When an item of PPE is sold, the gain or loss on disposal is the difference between the net proceeds and the carrying amount of the asset. Depreciation (if any) is recognized to the date of sale, the carrying amount is removed from the books, the proceeds are recorded, and any gain or loss is recognized.

EXAMPLE

A company sold a machine with a carrying amount of $100,000 ($180,000 historical cost – $80,000 accumulated depreciation) for $135,000 in cash. The gain on disposal recognized is $35,000 ($135,000 – $100,000). The journal entry is

Cash	$135,000	
Accumulated depreciation	80,000	
Machine		$180,000
Gain on disposal		35,000

If the machine were sold for $90,000 in cash, the loss on disposal recognized would be $10,000 ($90,000 – $100,000). The journal entry would be

Cash	$90,000	
Accumulated depreciation	80,000	
Loss on disposal	10,000	
Machine		$180,000

Stop and review! You have completed the outline for this subunit. Study multiple-choice questions 10 through 12 on page 107.

3.3 INTANGIBLE ASSETS

1. **Initial Recognition**

   a. An intangible asset is an identifiable, nonmonetary asset that lacks physical substance. Examples of intangible assets include licenses, patents, copyrights, franchises, and trademarks.

   b. **Externally acquired intangible assets** (other than goodwill) are initially recorded at acquisition cost plus any additional costs, such as legal fees.

   c. **Internally developed** intangible assets (other than goodwill) are recorded initially at the amount of the additional costs other than those for research and development (e.g., legal fees).

   d. **Research and development** (R&D) costs must be **expensed as incurred** and are thus never capitalized.

EXAMPLE

A company invested $200,000 and $300,000 in the research phase and the development phase, respectively, of an internally developed patent. In addition, the company paid $10,000 and $15,000 for patent registration fees and legal fees, respectively.

The patent will be recorded at the amount of the incidental costs of $25,000 ($10,000 patent registration fees + $15,000 legal fees). The amounts paid for research and development must be expensed as incurred and are never capitalized to the cost of the asset.

IFRS Difference

Intangible assets may be accounted for under either the cost model (as under U.S. GAAP) or the revaluation model (described on page 85 in Subunit 3.1). The revaluation model can be applied only if the intangible asset is traded in an active market.

> **IFRS Difference**
>
> Research costs must be expensed as incurred.
>
> **Development costs** may result in **recognition of an intangible asset** if the entity can demonstrate the (1) technical feasibility of completion of the asset, (2) intent to complete, (3) ability to use or sell the asset, (4) way in which it will generate probable future economic benefits, (5) availability of resources to complete and use or sell the asset, and (6) ability to measure reliably expenditures attributable to the asset.
>
> Using the data from the previous example, assume that all the criteria mentioned above were met. Under IFRS, the patent will be recorded at the amount of $325,000 ($300,000 development costs + $25,000 incidental costs). The research costs of $200,000 are expensed as incurred and are never capitalized to the cost of the asset.

2. **Intangible Assets with Finite Useful Lives**

    a. An intangible asset with a **finite useful life** (an amortized intangible asset) to the reporting entity is **amortized** over that useful life.

        1) The debit is to amortization expense, and the credit is to intangible asset. The journal entry is

            Amortization expense $XXX
                Intangible asset $XXX

    b. The **amortizable amount** equals the amount of cost initially assigned minus the residual value.

        `Amortizable amount = Historical (initial) cost - Residual value`

    c. The amortization methods are similar to the depreciation methods described on pages 83 through 84 in Subunit 3.1.
    d. The carrying amount of an intangible asset with a finite useful life equals its historical cost minus accumulated amortization and any impairment losses.
    e. The **impairment test** for an intangible asset with a finite useful life (an amortized intangible asset) is the **two-step impairment test** for long-lived assets described beginning on page 85 in Subunit 3.2.

> **IFRS Difference**
>
> An impairment loss for an asset (except goodwill) may be reversed if a change in the estimates used to measure the recoverable amount has occurred. The test for impairment of assets other than goodwill has one step: determine whether an asset's carrying amount is greater than its recoverable amount (greater of fair value minus costs to sell or value in use). The impairment test for long-lived assets is described beginning on page 85 in Subunit 3.2.

3. **Intangible Assets with Indefinite Useful Lives**

    a. An intangible asset with an **indefinite useful life** is **not amortized**. The carrying amount of an intangible asset with an indefinite useful life equals its historical cost minus any impairment losses.

        1) Goodwill is an intangible asset with an indefinite useful life. However, the accounting treatment of goodwill differs from that for other intangible assets. Thus, it is described separately in item 4. beginning on the next page.

b. **Impairment test.** An intangible asset with an indefinite useful life (a **nonamortized** intangible asset) must be reviewed for impairment at least annually. It is tested more often if events or changes in circumstances suggest that the asset may be impaired.

1) An entity may elect to perform a **qualitative assessment** to determine whether a **quantitative impairment test** is needed. The entity also may directly perform the quantitative test.

    a) **Qualitative assessment.** After the assessment of qualitative factors, the entity may determine that it is more likely than not (probability > 50%) that an indefinite-lived intangible asset is not impaired. In this case, the quantitative impairment test is not required. If potential impairment is found, the quantitative impairment test must be performed.

    b) **Quantitative impairment test.** The carrying amount of an asset is compared with its fair value. If the carrying amount exceeds the fair value, the asset is impaired, and the excess is the recognized impairment loss.

Determination of an Impairment Loss
1. Review for impairment
2. Impairment loss = Carrying amount − Fair value

2) This impairment loss is **nonreversible**, so the adjusted carrying amount is the new accounting basis.

IFRS Difference

A one-step quantitative impairment test is performed. No qualitative assessment exists.

---

4. **Goodwill**

    a. Goodwill is recognized only in a business combination. It is "an asset representing the future economic benefits arising from other assets acquired in a business combination that are not individually identified and separately recognized."

        1) The calculation of goodwill and its presentation in the financial statements are described on pages 64 and 65 in Study Unit 2, Subunit 7.

    b. **Impairment test.** Goodwill is tested for impairment at the reporting-unit level. All goodwill is assigned to the reporting units that will benefit from the business combination. It is tested for impairment each year at the same time.

    c. As in the case of an intangible asset with an indefinite useful life, an entity may elect to perform a **qualitative assessment** to determine whether the quantitative impairment test is needed.

    d. **Quantitative test.** If the qualitative assessment indicates **potential impairment**, the following two-step quantitative test is performed:

        1) The **first step** compares the fair value of the reporting unit with its carrying amount, including goodwill. If the fair value is greater than the carrying amount, no impairment loss is recognized. However, if the fair value is less than the carrying amount, the second step must be performed.

        2) The **second step** compares the implied fair value of reporting-unit goodwill with the carrying amount of that goodwill. An impairment loss is recognized for the excess of the carrying amount of reporting-unit goodwill over its implied fair value. This impairment loss is **nonreversible**.

```
Implied fair value of reporting-unit goodwill = Fair value
of reporting unit − Fair value of reporting-unit net assets
```

Determination of an Impairment Loss
1. Carrying amount of reporting unit > Its fair value
2. Estimate implied fair value of reporting-unit goodwill
3. Carrying amount of reporting-unit goodwill > Its implied fair value
4. Loss = Excess in 3. above.

5. **Patents**
    a. The **amortization period** for a patent is the **shorter** of
        1) Its **useful life** or
        2) The **legal life** remaining after acquisition or the moment the application was filed.
            a) The useful life may be substantially shorter than the legal life because of changes in consumer tastes, delays in marketing the product or service, and development of substitutes or improvements.
    b. The accounting treatment of the costs of the **legal defense of a patent** depends upon the outcome of the litigation.
        1) The costs of **successful litigation** are **capitalized** to the cost of the patent because they will benefit future periods. They are amortized over the shorter of (a) the remaining legal life or (b) the estimated useful life of the patent.
        2) The costs of **unsuccessful litigation** (damages, attorneys' fees, etc.) are **expensed** as incurred. An unsuccessful suit also may indicate that the unamortized cost of the patent has no value, or lower value, and impairment loss might be recognized.

Stop and review! You have completed the outline for this subunit. Study multiple-choice questions 13 through 16 on page 108.

3.4 LEASES

1. **Definition of a Lease**
    a. A lease is a long-term contract in which the owner of property (the lessor) allows another party (the lessee) to use the property for a stated period in exchange for a stated payment.
    b. The primary issue is whether the lease agreement transfers substantially all the benefits and risks of ownership of the asset to the lessee.
        1) If it does, the lease is classified as a **capital lease**.
        2) If it does not, the lease is classified as an **operating lease** and is accounted for as a regular long-term rental contract.
2. **Lease Classification Test**
    a. A lease agreement transfers substantially all the benefits and risks of ownership of the asset to the lessee if at least **one of the following criteria** is met:
        1) The lease provides for the transfer of ownership of the leased property.
        2) The lease contains a bargain purchase option (BPO).
            a) A bargain purchase option gives the lessee the right to purchase the leased property for a price lower than its expected fair value at the date the BPO becomes exercisable.
        3) The lease term is 75% or more of the estimated economic life of the leased property.
        4) The present value of the minimum lease payments is at least 90% of the fair value of the leased property.

3. **Operating Lease**

    a. In an **operating lease**, the lessor retains substantially all of the benefits and risks of ownership. Such a lease is a regular rental agreement.

    b. The lessee reports periodic rental expense for the amount of rent paid, but **no leased asset** or **liability is recognized**.

    1) No entry is made to record the lease. Lease payments are expensed as incurred.
    2) Rent is reported as an expense in the income statement by the lessee in accordance with the lease agreement.

        a) The lessee records the following journal entry:

        Rent expense $XXX
         Cash or rent payable $XXX

    3) If rental payments vary from a straight-line basis, e.g., if the first month is free, rent expense must be recognized over the full lease term on the straight-line basis.

    c. An operating lease is a form of off-balance-sheet financing. The lessee has the right to use the leased asset, but neither the asset nor a liability for future lease payments is recorded in its financial statements.

    1) Lessees may prefer to account for a lease as an operating lease instead of as a capital lease to avoid recognition in the financial statements of (a) a liability for future lease payments, (b) interest expense, and (c) depreciation of the leased asset.

    d. The **lessor** reports periodic rental revenue for the amount of rent received but continues to recognize and depreciate the leased asset in its financial statements.

    e. The Financial Accounting Standards Board (FASB) in the United States has issued a new lease accounting standard following the release in January 2016 of an International Financial Reporting Standard (IFRS) dealing with the same subject. The FASB's standard will take effect for public companies for fiscal years beginning after December 15, 2018. Although it had been expected that the FASB and IFRS would be identical, instead there are now two standards that, although similar in many respects, contain significant differences. Preparers will need to assess the effect of these changes on their balance sheets.

    1) The FASB standards update, ASU 2016-02, Leases (Topic 842), applies to all companies following U.S. accounting standards. As is the case with IFRS 16 (Leases), leases currently treated as off-balance-sheet operating leases will now appear on lessee companies' balance sheets. Although net assets may not be greatly affected, gross assets and gross liabilities will increase significantly for companies that currently have major leasing arrangements treated as operating leases. Details of these new statements are not covered in this volume because the provisions do not affect financial statements until 2019 (and by that time, you should have already passed the CMA exam).

4. **Capital Lease – Lessee Accounting**

    a. In a **capital lease**, the lessor transfers substantially all of the benefits and risks of ownership to the lessee. Such a lease is a purchase-and-financing agreement.

    b. At the inception of the lease, the lessee recognizes in its financial statements the **leased asset** (e.g., debit tangible asset) and a **lease liability** (e.g., credit lease obligation) at an amount equal to the **present value of the minimum lease payments**.

    Leased property $XXX
     Lease obligation $XXX

c. Minimum lease payments are the total amounts of cash that the lessee is expected to pay to the lessor over the lease term. It includes all the rental payments plus the amount of residual value (or the minimum rental payments plus the amount of BPO).

1) The minimum lease payments must be discounted (measured at present value) using the lessor's implicit rate or the lessee's incremental borrowing rate, whichever is lower.

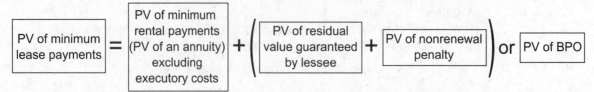

Figure 3-1

d. Each periodic lease payment made by the lessee has two components:

1) **Interest expense** recognized in the income statement and
2) The **reduction of the lease liability** recognized in the balance sheet.

```
Interest expense        $XXX
Lease obligation         XXX
    Cash                        $XXX
```

3) Interest expense is calculated using the effective-interest method. It applies the appropriate interest rate to the carrying amount of the lease obligation at the beginning of each period to calculate interest expense.

e. The leased asset is recognized in the lessee's balance sheet. Thus, the lessee must depreciate it and recognize depreciation expense in the income statement.

1) If the lease is capitalized because the lease either transfers ownership to the lessee by the end of the lease term (criterion 1) or contains a bargain purchase option (BPO) (criterion 2), the depreciation of the asset is over its **entire estimated economic life**.
2) The lessee may capitalize the lease based on the third criterion (lease term) or the fourth criterion (PV of minimum lease payments). In these cases, the asset is depreciated over the **term of the lease**.

The effect of a capital lease on lessee's financial statements		
Balance sheet	Recognition of leased asset	Recognition of a lease liability
Income statement	Depreciation of the leased asset	Interest on lease liability

5. **Capital Lease – Lessor Accounting**

a. The **lessor** removes the leased asset from its financial statements (e.g., credits leased asset) and recognizes a **receivable** (e.g., debits lease receivable) for the present value of minimum lease payments (cash) to be received.

1) Because the leased asset is removed from the lessor's books, no depreciation expense is recognized by the lessor for the leased asset.
2) Each periodic lease payment received by the lessor has two components:

   a) **Interest revenue** recognized in the income statement and
   b) The **reduction of the lease receivables** recognized in the balance sheet.

3) The lease receivable may be recorded as

   a) A debit to the gross lease receivable (undiscounted minimum lease payments) and
   b) A credit to unearned interest income (gross lease receivable minus present value of minimum lease payments).

SU 3: Measurement, Valuation, and Disclosure: Long-Term Items

- b. The lessor classifies a capital lease either as a direct financing lease or a sales-type lease.
- c. In a **direct financing lease**, the lessor's economic interest is in financing the purchase, not promoting the sale of its product. The lessor recognizes no manufacturer's or dealer's profit or loss in connection with the lease.
    1) The **fair value** of the leased property and its cost or **carrying amount** are **the same** at the inception of the lease.

Fair value of leased asset = Carrying amount of leased asset = PV of minimum lease payments

---

EXAMPLE

On January 1, Year 1, Crimson, LLC, leased a machine to Cottle, Inc. Crimson will receive three annual payments of $100,000 starting on December 31, Year 1. The title of the machine will transfer to Cottle at the end of the lease term. The lease is appropriately accounted for as a direct financing lease (the $248,690 carrying amount of the machine equals the PV of the minimum lease payments). The rate implicit in the lease is 10%. The present value factor for an ordinary annuity at 10% for three periods is 2.4869.

$$\begin{aligned} \text{PV of minimum rental payments} &= \text{PV of minimum lease payments} \\ &= \$100{,}000 \times 2.4869 \\ &= \$248{,}690 \end{aligned}$$

January 1, Year 1:

Crimson – Lessor

Gross lease payments receivable	$300,000	
Machine		$248,690
Unearned interest income		51,310

Cottle – Lessee

Machine	$248,690	
Lease liability		$248,690

December 31, Year 1:

Crimson – Lessor

Cash	$100,000	
Gross lease payments receivable		$100,000
Unearned interest income	$24,869	
Interest income		$24,869

Cottle – Lessee

Lease liability	$75,131	
Interest expense ($248,690 × 10%)	24,869	
Cash		$100,000
Depreciation expense ($248,690 ÷ 3)	$82,897	
Accumulated depreciation machine		$82,897

December 31, Year 1, Financial Statements Presentation:

Crimson – Lessor

Balance Sheet

Gross lease payments receivable ($300,000 – $100,000)	$200,000
Unearned interest income ($51,310 – $24,869)	(26,441)
Net lease receivables	$173,559

Income Statement

Interest income	$24,869

Cottle – Lessee

Balance Sheet

Machine ($248,690 – $82,897)	$165,793
Lease liability ($248,690 – $75,131)	$173,559

Income Statement

Interest expense	$24,869
Depreciation expense	$82,897

d. In a **sales-type lease**, the lessor recognizes a **manufacturer's or dealer's profit or loss**.

1) The fair value (selling price) of the leased property at the lease's inception **differs** from its cost or carrying amount.

2) The following journal entry is recorded by the lessor at the inception of a sales-type lease:

Lease payments receivable	$XXX	
Cost of goods sold	XXX	
Unearned interest income		$XXX
Sales revenue		XXX
Leased asset		XXX

    a) Sales revenue (price of the asset) is recognized (credited) for the present value of the minimum lease payments.

    b) The leased asset is removed (credited), and the cost of goods sold is recognized (debited) for the carrying amount of the leased asset.

3) Subsequent to the inception of the lease, the accounting for a direct financing lease and a sales-type lease is the same.

IFRS Difference

Under U.S. GAAP, if a lease involving land and a building contains a bargain purchase option or if the lease transfers the ownership to the lessee at the end of the lease term, the **land and building** elements are treated separately. If the lease does not meet either the transfer-of-ownership criterion or the bargain-purchase-option criterion, land and building elements are generally treated as a **single unit**, unless the land is 25% or more of the fair value of the total leased property.

Under IFRS, a capital lease is called a finance lease. In the classification of the lease as a finance (capital) lease or an operating lease, land and building elements are generally treated **separately**. The land element is normally classified as an operating lease unless title passes to the lessee at the end of the lease term. The building element is classified either as a finance lease or an operating lease based on the regular criteria.

Stop and review! You have completed the outline for this subunit. Study multiple-choice questions 17 through 22 beginning on page 109.

3.5 INCOME TAXES

1. **Objectives**

    a. The objectives of accounting for income taxes are to recognize the following:

       1) The amount of taxes currently payable or refundable
       2) Deferred tax liabilities and assets for the future tax consequences of events that have been recognized in the financial statements or tax returns

    b. To achieve these objectives, an entity uses the asset-and-liability approach to account for (1) income taxes currently payable or deductible and (2) deferred taxes.

2. **Basic Definitions**

    a. **Income tax expense or benefit** is the sum of (1) current tax expense or benefit and (2) deferred tax expense or benefit.

    b. **Current tax expense or benefit** is the amount of taxes paid or payable (or refundable) for the year as determined by applying the enacted tax law to the taxable income or excess of deductions over revenues for that year. This amount is the **income tax payable** for the period.

SU 3: Measurement, Valuation, and Disclosure: Long-Term Items

- c. **Taxable income** is the income calculated under the tax code. Taxable income equals pretax accounting income adjusted for permanent and temporary tax differences.
- d. **Deferred tax expense or benefit** is the net change during the year in an entity's deferred tax amounts.
- e. A **deferred tax liability (or asset)** records the deferred tax consequences of taxable (or deductible) temporary differences.
    1) A deferred tax liability or asset is recognized for the estimated future tax effects of temporary differences and carryforwards.
    2) A deferred tax amount is measured using the enacted tax rate(s) expected to apply when the liability or asset is expected to be settled or realized.

3. **Intraperiod Tax Allocation**
    a. Intraperiod tax allocation **is required**. Income tax expense (benefit) is allocated to
        1) Continuing operations,
        2) Discontinued operations,
        3) Other comprehensive income, and
        4) Items debited or credited directly to equity.

4. **Interperiod Tax Allocation**
    a. Amounts in the entity's income tax return for a year include the tax consequences of most items recognized in the financial statements for the same year. But significant exceptions may exist.
    b. **Temporary differences** result when the GAAP basis and the tax basis of an asset or liability differ. Differences in the two bases arise when items of income and expense are recognized in different periods under GAAP and under the tax code. The effect is that a taxable or deductible amount will occur in future years when the asset is recovered or the liability is settled.
        1) Tax consequences of some items may be recognized in **tax returns** for a year different from that in which their **financial-statement effects** are recognized. The following are examples:
            a) Different depreciation methods may be used for tax purposes and in the financial statements. Accelerated depreciation is allowed for tax purposes for certain assets, but they may be depreciated using the straight-line method in the financial statements.
            b) Expenses for warranty liability are recognized in the financial statements on the date of the sale under the accrual method of accounting. For tax purposes, warranty expenses are recognized under the cash basis when actual payments of warranty costs are made.
            c) Bad debt expense is recognized in the financial statements under the allowance method in accordance with the income-statement or balance-sheet approach. For tax purposes, bad debt expense is recognized when the debts are determined to be uncollectible using the direct write-off method.
    c. A **permanent difference** is an event that is recognized either in pretax financial income or in taxable income **but never in both**. It does not result in a deferred tax amount. The following are examples:
        1) Payments of fines or penalties are recognized as an expense in the financial statements but are never deducted in the tax return.
        2) Interest on state or municipal bonds is recognized as income in the financial statements but not in taxable income for tax purposes.
    d. When tax consequences and financial-statement effects differ, income taxes currently payable or refundable also may differ from income tax expense or benefit.
        1) The accounting for these differences is **interperiod tax allocation**.

5. **Deferred Tax Assets and Liabilities**

   a. Deferred tax assets and liabilities result from temporary differences, not permanent differences.

   b. Taxable temporary differences result in future taxable amounts and deferred tax liabilities (DTL).

   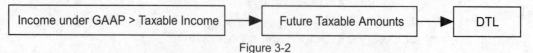

   Figure 3-2

   1) DTLs arise when **revenues or gains** are recognized under GAAP before they are included in taxable income.

      a) An example is income recognized under the equity method for financial statement purposes and at the time of distribution in taxable income.

   2) DTLs also result when **expenses or losses** are deductible for tax purposes before they are recognized under GAAP.

      a) An example is accelerated tax depreciation of property.

      $DTL = Future\ taxable\ amount \times Tax\ rate$

EXAMPLE

On January 1, Year 1, Luxor buys a piece of equipment for $100,000. It will be depreciated over its 5-year useful life on the straight-line basis for financial reporting (20% per year). The following accelerated percentages will be used for tax purposes: 59%, 16.5%, 9.5%, 8%, and 7% for years 1-5, respectively.

Year 1 excess of GAAP income over taxable income $100,000 × (59% − 20%)	$39,000
Future taxable amount in Year 2 (16.5% − 20%)	$ 3,500
Future taxable amount in Year 3 (9.5% − 20%)	10,500
Future taxable amount in Year 4 (8% − 20%)	12,000
Future taxable amount in Year 5 (7% − 20%)	13,000
Total future taxable amount	$39,000
Enacted tax rate	× 40%
Year 1 deferred tax liability	$15,600

NOTE: On December 31, Year 1, the reported amount of the equipment in the financial statements of $80,000 ($100,000 − $20,000) exceeds its tax basis of $41,000 ($100,000 − $59,000) by $39,000. This taxable temporary difference results in recognition of a deferred tax liability of $15,600 ($39,000 × 40% enacted tax rate for future years).

---

   c. Deductible temporary differences result in future deductible amounts and deferred tax assets (DTA).

   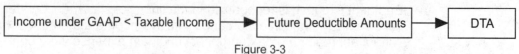

   Figure 3-3

   1) DTAs result when **revenues or gains** are included in taxable income before they are recognized under GAAP.

      a) Examples are unearned revenues such as rent and subscriptions received in advance.

   2) DTAs also result when **expenses or losses** are recognized under GAAP before they are deductible for tax purposes.

      a) Examples are bad debt expense recognized under the allowance method and warranty costs.

      $DTA = Future\ deductible\ amount \times Tax\ rate$

SU 3: Measurement, Valuation, and Disclosure: Long-Term Items

---

EXAMPLE

In Year 1, Luxor accrued $70,000 of warranty costs for financial reporting purposes. From past experience, it expects these costs to be incurred in Years 2 through 5 as follows: $5,000, $15,000, $40,000, $10,000.

Year 1 excess of taxable income over GAAP income	$70,000
Future deductible amount in Year 2	$ 5,000
Future deductible amount in Year 3	15,000
Future deductible amount in Year 4	40,000
Future deductible amount in Year 5	10,000
Total future deductible amount	$70,000
Enacted tax rate	× 40%
Year 1 deferred tax asset	$28,000

---

6. **Calculating Tax Expense or Benefit**

    a. Income tax expense or benefit reported on the income statement is the sum of the current component and the deferred component.

        1) **Current tax expense or benefit** is the amount of taxes paid or payable (or refundable) for the year based on the enacted tax law.

           *Current tax expense or benefit =
           Taxable income (or excess of deductions over revenue) × Tax rate*

        2) **Deferred tax expense or benefit** is the net change during the year in an entity's deferred tax amounts.

           Changes in DTL balances ± Changes in DTA balances

    b. Current income tax expense is recorded as follows:

Income tax expense -- current	$XXX	
Income tax payable		$XXX

    c. Deferred income tax expense or benefit is recognized for the net change during the year in the deferred tax amounts (DTL and DTA) and recorded as follows:

If the DTL balance increased during the year:			If the DTA balance increased during the year:		
Income tax expense -- deferred	$XXX		Deferred tax asset	$XXX	
Deferred tax liability		$XXX	Income tax expense -- deferred		$XXX
If the DTL balance decreased during the year:			**If the DTA balance decreased during the year:**		
Deferred tax liability	$XXX		Income tax expense -- deferred	$XXX	
Income tax expense -- deferred		$XXX	Deferred tax asset		$XXX

EXAMPLE

Lucas Company had the following deferred tax balances for the year just ended. The deferred tax asset is fully realizable. The company's taxable income was $1,000,000 for the year. The enacted tax rate is 40%.

	Beginning Balance	Ending Balance
Deferred tax asset	$ 9,000	$17,000
Deferred tax liability	13,000	23,000

Lucas calculates income tax expense for the year as follows:

- Current tax expense is $400,000 ($1,000,000 × 40%).
- Deferred tax expense is the net change in the deferred tax liability and asset balances for the year. The DTL balance increased by $10,000 ($23,000 – $13,000), and the DTA balance increased by $8,000 ($17,000 – $9,000). Thus, the net DTL increase is $2,000 ($10,000 – $8,000).

Lucas records the following entry:

Income tax expense -- current	$400,000	
Income tax expense -- deferred	2,000	
Deferred tax asset	8,000	
Income tax payable		$400,000
Deferred tax liability		10,000

7. **Operating Loss Carrybacks and Carryforwards**

    a. Entities that incur net operating losses (NOLs) have two options for obtaining the tax benefit of the loss:

        1) Carry the loss back 2 years and forward 20 years or
        2) Carry the loss forward 20 years.

    b. **Loss carryforward only.** Under this option, the entity carries the entire loss forward 20 years.

        1) A carryforward results in a **future deductible amount** requiring recognition of a deferred tax asset.
        2) The amount of net operating loss (NOL) carryforward is realized in future periods by reducing the taxable income for these periods.
        3) Upon realization, the deferred tax asset reduces the amount of income tax payable in future periods and does not affect the total amount of income tax expense recognized.

EXAMPLE

A company incurred a $90,000 net operating loss in Year 1. The company determined that it is more likely than not that the full benefit of any loss carryforward will be realized and that carrying the loss back will not result in a tax benefit. The company therefore elects to carry the loss forward only. The enacted tax rate for Year 1 is 30%, resulting in a tax benefit of $27,000 ($90,000 × 30%).

Year 1

Deferred tax asset	$27,000	
Income tax benefit from loss carryforward		$27,000

In Year 2, the company's taxable income was $240,000. The entire NOL carryforward of $90,000 is realized in Year 2. Thus, the Year 2 taxable income after realization of the NOL carryforward is $150,000 ($240,000 – $90,000). Year 2 current income tax expense is $45,000 ($150,000 × 30%). Year 2 deferred income tax expense is $27,000 (realization of deferred tax asset). The company records the following journal entry:

Year 2

Income tax expense -- current	$45,000	
Income tax expense -- deferred	27,000	
Income tax payable		$45,000
Deferred tax asset		27,000

NOTE: The total income tax expense in Year 2 is $72,000 ($45,000 + $27,000). This amount equals taxable income before realization of the NOL carryforward times the enacted tax rate ($240,000 × 30% = $72,000).

---

    c. **Loss carryback and carryforward.** Under this option, the entity files an amended tax return that carries the loss back to the second prior year, offsetting some or all of that year's tax expense.

        1) If any of the current-year loss remains after exhausting the taxable income of the second prior year, the entity files an amended return offsetting some or all of the prior year's tax expense.
        2) Both the balance sheet and income statement are affected.

    Income tax refund receivable (tax offset by carryback) $XXX
        Income tax benefit from loss carryback $XXX

        3) Carryforwards that cannot be used in the current year may be carried forward to reduce taxable income or taxes payable in a future year.

            a) Thus, if any of the current-year loss remains after the 2-year carryback, the entity is allowed to carry it forward 20 years.

EXAMPLE

Putnam Horn, Inc., incurred a $700,000 net operating loss in Year 5. The enacted tax rate is 30%, resulting in a tax benefit of $210,000 ($700,000 × 30%) available for offsetting. The company has the following historical income tax information:

	Taxable Income (Loss)		Enacted Tax Rate		Income Tax Paid
Year 1	$100,000	×	30%	=	$30,000
Year 2	300,000	×	30%	=	90,000
Year 3	200,000	×	30%	=	60,000
Year 4	100,000	×	30%	=	30,000

Putnam Horn has elected to carry the loss both back and forward. The company determined that it is more likely than not that the full benefit of any loss carryforward will be realized. The company records the following entries:

Income tax refund receivable ($60,000 + $30,000)	$90,000	
Income tax benefit from loss carryback		$90,000
Deferred tax asset ($210,000 – $90,000)	$120,000	
Income tax benefit from loss carryforward		$120,000

---

8. **Financial Statement Presentation**

   a. Deferred tax amounts must be classified as **current or noncurrent** based on the classification of the related asset or liability.

      1) Current deferred tax amounts are **netted** and presented as a single amount. Noncurrent deferred tax amounts also are offset (netted) and presented as a single amount.

   b. A valuation allowance reduces a **deferred tax asset**. It is recognized if it is **more likely than not** (probability > 50%) that some portion of the asset will not be realized. The allowance should reduce the deferred tax asset to the amount that is more likely than not to be realized.

IFRS Difference

Income tax allocation was long an American phenomenon. With respect to the International Accounting Standards Board (IASB) and its predecessor, the International Accounting Standards Committee, tax allocation has not been an important subject. IAS 12, *Income Taxes*, as originally issued in 1979, addressed the tax issue but allowed for options. The most recent international standard-setting activity involving tax allocation occurred in 2009. The goal of that project was to resolve problems in practice under IAS 12 without changing its fundamental approach and without increasing the divergence from U.S. GAAP. The project originally started as a convergence project with U.S. GAAP.

The IASB may soon consider a major review of the accounting for income taxes as part of its agenda consultation process. Part of the reason for the lesser activity by the IASC and IASB can be attributed to the fact that many countries require conformity between tax accounting and financial statement reporting. Of course, neither the U.S. GAAP nor international standards require such conformity to any degree. The result is that many members of the IASB are from countries where tax allocation is not an issue.

Stop and review! You have completed the outline for this subunit. Study multiple-choice questions 23 through 26 beginning on page 110.

3.6 ACCOUNTING FOR BONDS AND NONCURRENT NOTES PAYABLE

1. **Nature of Bonds**
   a. A bond is a formal contract to pay an amount of money (face amount) at the maturity date plus interest at the stated rate at specific intervals.

EXAMPLE

At the beginning of the year, a company issues 200 8%, 5-year, $5,000 bonds. Annual cash interest payments will be made at the end of each year. The total face amount of bonds issued is $1,000,000 (200 bonds × $5,000 face amount), and the annual interest payment is $80,000 ($1,000,000 face amount × 8% stated rate).

---

   b. The proceeds received from the investors on the day the bonds are sold equal the present value of the sum of the future cash flows expected to be received from the bonds. These proceeds equal
      1) The present value of the face amount plus
      2) The present value of the annuity of interest payments.
   c. The bonds are recognized in the financial statements as the amount of proceeds paid for them, i.e., the face amount of the bonds plus any premium or minus any discount.
      1) They are recorded as a debt in the issuer's financial statements and as an investment in the investors' financial statements.

2. **Bond Issuance**
   a. The cash proceeds from the sale of bonds can be equal to, less than, or greater than the face amount of the bonds depending on the relationship of the bonds' stated rate of interest to the market rate of interest on the date the bonds are sold.
      1) If the stated rate is equal to the market rate, the cash proceeds equal the face amount of the bonds.
      2) If the stated rate is greater than the current market rate, the cash proceeds are greater than the face amount, and the bonds are sold at a **premium**.
      3) If the stated rate is lower than the current market rate, the cash proceeds are lower than the face amount, and the bonds are sold at a **discount**.
   b. The current market rate of interest is used to discount the cash flows expected to be received by the investor (paid by the issuer) from the bonds.

EXAMPLE

The following calculation uses the data from the previous example and the following present value factors:

	At 6%	At 10%
Present value of 1 for 5 periods	0.747	0.621
Present value of ordinary annuity of 1 for 5 periods	4.212	3.791

(1) Assume that the market interest rate was 6% on the date the bonds were issued.

Present value of face amount ($1,000,000 × 0.747)	$ 747,000
Present value of cash interest ($80,000 × 4.212)	336,960
Cash proceeds from bonds issue	$1,083,960

The amount of premium is $83,960 ($1,083,960 proceeds − $1,000,000 face amount).

(2) Assume that the market interest rate was 10% on the date the bonds were issued.

Present value of face amount ($1,000,000 × 0.621)	$621,000
Present value of cash interest ($80,000 × 3.791)	303,280
Cash proceeds from bonds issue	$924,280

The amount of discount is $75,720 ($1,000,000 face amount − $924,280 proceeds).

SU 3: Measurement, Valuation, and Disclosure: Long-Term Items

3. **Amortization of Premium or Discount**

    a. Bond premium or discount must be amortized over the life of the bonds using the **effective-interest method** (the market interest rate on the date the bond was sold). Under this method, interest expense changes every period and equals the following:

    ```
    Annual interest expense =
    Carrying amount of the bond at the beginning of the period × Effective interest rate
    ```

    b. The annual interest expense consists of the cash interest paid plus the effect of amortization of premium or discount.

    1) When the bond is issued at a premium, annual interest expense equals cash interest paid minus the amount of premium amortized.
    2) When the bond is issued at a discount, annual interest expense equals cash interest paid plus the amount of discount amortized.
    3) The carrying amount of bonds as they are presented in the financial statements equals the face amount plus the premium (or minus the discount).

    EXAMPLE of Amortization of a Premium and Discount

    Using the data from the previous example, the following interest expense will be recognized by the company in the first 2 years of the bonds:

    (1) When market interest rate was 6% and bonds were issued at premium:

	A						B		A − B
Year	Beginning Carrying Amount of Bonds			Interest Expense		Cash Interest Paid	Premium Amortized	Remaining Premium	Ending Carrying Amount of Bonds
1	$1,083,960	×	6%	= $65,038	−	$80,000	= $14,962	$68,998	$1,068,998
2	1,068,998	×	6%	= 64,140	−	80,000	= 15,860	53,138	1,053,138

    (2) When market interest rate was 10% and bonds were issued at discount:

	A						B		A + B
Year	Beginning Carrying Amount of Bonds			Interest Expense		Cash Interest Paid	Discount Amortized	Remaining Discount	Ending Carrying Amount of Bonds
1	$924,280	×	10%	= $92,428	−	$80,000	= $12,428	$63,292	$936,708
2	936,708	×	10%	= 93,671	−	80,000	= 13,671	49,621	950,379

    ---

    4) At the maturity date, the discount or premium is fully amortized, and the carrying amount of the bonds equals the face amount.

4. The following are different types of bonds:

    a. Maturity Pattern

    1) A **term bond** has a single maturity date at the end of its term. The examples in this study unit are regarding a regular term bond.
    2) A **serial bond** matures in stated amounts at regular intervals.

    b. Repayment Provisions

    1) **Income bonds** pay interest contingent on the debtor's profitability.
    2) **Revenue bonds** are issued by governments and are payable from specific revenue sources.

c. Securitization

   1) **Mortgage bonds** are backed by specific assets, usually real estate.
   2) **Debentures** are backed by the borrower's general credit but not by specific collateral.
   3) **Guaranty bonds** are guaranteed by a third party, e.g., the parent of the subsidiary that issued the bonds.
   4) **Collateral trust bonds** are secured by a financial asset, such as stock or other bonds.
   5) **Equipment trust bonds** are secured by a mortgage on movable equipment, such as airplanes or railroad cars.

d. Valuation

   1) **Variable (or floating) rate bonds** pay interest that is dependent on market conditions.
   2) **Zero-coupon or deep-discount bonds** bear no stated rate of interest and thus involve no periodic cash payments; the interest component consists entirely of the bond's discount.
   3) **Commodity-backed bonds** are payable at prices related to a commodity such as gold.

e. Redemption provisions

   1) **Callable bonds** (also called redeemable bonds) may be repurchased (redeemed) by the issuer at a specified price before maturity.

      a) During a period of failing interest rates, the issuer can replace high-interest debt with low-interest debt.

   2) **Convertible bonds** may be converted into equity securities of the issuer at the option of the holder (buyer) under specified conditions. Convertible bonds generally pay a lower yield than comparable nonconvertible bonds.

5. **Noncurrent Notes Payable**

   a. Some notes require one principal payment at the end of the note's term plus periodic interest payments during the note's term (like a term bond).

EXAMPLE

An entity agrees to give, in return for merchandise, a 3-year, $100,000 note bearing 8% interest paid annually. The effective interest rate is 6%. Because the note's stated rate exceeds the effective rate, the note will be issued at a premium.

The entity records the note at the present value of (1) a single payment of $100,000 in 3 years and (2) three interest payments of $8,000 each. These payments are discounted at the effective rate (five decimal places are used for increased accuracy).

Present value of principal ($100,000 × 0.83962)	$ 83,962
Present value of interest ($8,000 × 2.67301)	21,384
Present value of note	$105,346

The entry to record the note is

Inventory	$105,346	
Premium on note payable		$ 5,346
Note payable		100,000

b. Other notes require equal periodic principal payments plus interest. Each periodic payment includes an equal amount of return of principal and an amount of interest accrued on the beginning carrying amount.

EXAMPLE

On January 1, Year 1, Shark Co. borrowed $120,000 on a 10% note payable to Bank. Three equal annual principal payments of $40,000 plus interest are paid beginning December 31, Year 1.

Year	Beginning Carrying Amount (a)	Interest Rate	Interest Payment/Expense (b)	Principal Payment (c)	Total Payment (b) + (c)	Ending Carrying Amount (a) − (c)
1	$120,000	10%	$12,000	$40,000	$52,000	$80,000
2	80,000	10%	8,000	40,000	48,000	40,000
3	40,000	10%	4,000	40,000	44,000	0

c. A third type of note requires equal periodic cash payments. Each payment includes a principal component (i.e., return of principal) and an interest component.

EXAMPLE

On January 1, Year 1, Star Co. borrowed $120,000 on a 10% note payable to Bank. Three equal annual payments of $48,254 are paid beginning December 31, Year 1.

Year	Beginning Carrying Amount (a)	Interest Rate	Interest Payment/Expense (b)	Total Payment (c)	Principal Payment (c) − (b) = (d)	Ending Carrying Amount (a) − (d)
1	$120,000	10%	$12,000	$48,254	$36,254	$83,746
2	83,746	10%	8,375	48,254	39,879	43,867
3	43,867	10%	4,387	48,254	43,867	0

NOTE: The proceeds from the note are equal to the present value of the cash payments associated with the note. The equal annual payment ($48,254) multiplied by the present value of an ordinary annuity of $1 at 10% for three periods (2.48685) equals the proceeds from the note of $120,000.

Stop and review! You have completed the outline for this subunit. Study multiple-choice questions 27 through 30 beginning on page 112.

QUESTIONS

3.1 Property, Plant, and Equipment

1. Which of the following is **not** an appropriate basis for measuring the cost of property, plant, and equipment?

A. The purchase price, freight costs, and installation costs of a productive asset should be included in the asset's cost.

B. Proceeds obtained in the process of readying land for its intended purpose, such as from the sale of cleared timber, should be recognized immediately as income.

C. The costs of improvements to equipment incurred after its acquisition should be added to the asset's cost if they increase future service potential.

D. All costs incurred in the construction of a plant building, from excavation to completion, should be considered as part of the asset's cost.

Answer (B) is correct.
REQUIRED: The basis that is inappropriate for measuring the cost of property, plant, and equipment.
DISCUSSION: Accordingly, items of property, plant, and equipment (PPE) that meet the recognition criterion are initially measured at cost. The cost includes the purchase price (minus trade discounts and rebates, plus purchase taxes) and the directly attributable costs of bringing the assets to working condition for their intended use. Directly attributable costs include site preparation, installation, initial delivery and handling, architect and equipment fees, costs of removing the assets and restoring the site, etc. Accordingly, the cost of land includes the cost of obtaining the land and readying it for its intended uses, but it is inappropriate to recognize the proceeds related to site preparation immediately in profit or loss. They should be treated as reductions in the price of the land.
Answer (A) is incorrect. The purchase price, freight costs, and installation costs of a productive asset are included in the asset's cost. Answer (C) is incorrect. Subsequent costs are added to the carrying amount of an item of PPE if it is probable that, as a result, future economic benefits will be received, and the costs are reliably measurable. Answer (D) is incorrect. All costs of construction should be included as a part of the asset's cost.

2. The board of directors of a corporation authorized the president of the corporation to pay as much as $90,000 to purchase a tract of land adjacent to the main factory. The president negotiated a price of $75,800 for the land, and legal fees for closing costs amounted to $820. A contractor cleared, filled, and graded the land for $6,800, and dug the foundation for a new building for $4,300. A prefabricated building was erected at a cost of $181,000. The building has an estimated useful life of 20 years with no residual value. The contractor's bill indicated that the cost of the parking lot and driveways was $7,060. The parking lot and the driveways will need to be replaced in 15 years. The proper amount to be recorded in the corporation's land account is

A. $76,620
B. $83,420
C. $87,720
D. $90,480

Answer (B) is correct.
REQUIRED: The amount to be recorded in the land account.
DISCUSSION: The cost of acquiring and preparing land for its expected use is capitalized. The amount to be recorded in the land account is $83,420, consisting of the $75,800 purchase price, the $820 closing costs, and the $6,800 site preparation costs.
Answer (A) is incorrect. The amount of $76,620 results from excluding the cost of clearing, grading, and filling. Answer (C) is incorrect. The amount of $87,720 results from including the cost of the building's foundation. Answer (D) is incorrect. The amount of $90,480 results from including the cost of the parking lot and driveways. This cost should be recognized in the land improvements account.

3. A corporation purchased manufacturing equipment for $100,000, with an estimated useful life of 10 years and a salvage value of $15,000. The second year's depreciation for this equipment using the double-declining balance method is

A. $8,500
B. $13,600
C. $16,000
D. $20,000

Answer (C) is correct.
REQUIRED: The second year's depreciation on the equipment.
DISCUSSION: Under the double-declining balance method, the full cost of the asset, or $100,000, is depreciated, but not below salvage value. Because the straight-line rate for a 10-year asset is 10% (100% ÷ 10), the double-declining balance rate is 20% (10% × 2). The first year's depreciation is $20,000 ($100,000 × 20%), leaving a carrying amount for the second year of $80,000 ($100,000 – $20,000). The second year's depreciation is thus $16,000 ($80,000 × 20%).
Answer (A) is incorrect. The amount of $8,500 is the first year's straight-line depreciation after improperly subtracting salvage value. Answer (B) is incorrect. The amount of $13,600 is the second year's depreciation after improperly subtracting salvage value. Answer (D) is incorrect. The amount of $20,000 is the first year's depreciation.

SU 3: Measurement, Valuation, and Disclosure: Long-Term Items

4. Which one of the following characteristics is **not** required for an asset to be properly described as property, plant, and equipment?

A. Held for use and not for investment.
B. Newly purchased.
C. Expected life of more than 1 year.
D. Tangible.

Answer (B) is correct.
REQUIRED: The item not a necessary characteristic of PPE.
DISCUSSION: These assets are known variously as property, plant, and equipment; fixed assets; or plant assets.

1. PPE are tangible. They have physical existence.
2. PPE may be either personal property (something movable, e.g., equipment) or real property (such as land or a building).
3. PPE are used in the ordinary operations of an entity and are not held primarily for investment, resale, or inclusion in another product. But they are often sold.
4. PPE are noncurrent. They are not expected to be used up within 1 year or the normal operating cycle of the business, whichever is longer.

However, an asset need not be newly purchased to be properly described as property, plant, and equipment.
Answer (A) is incorrect. PPE are held for use and not for investment. Answer (C) is incorrect. PPE are not expected to be used up within 1 year or the normal operating cycle of the business, whichever is longer. Answer (D) is incorrect. PPE are tangible.

5. Equipment bought by a company 3 years ago was charged to equipment expense in error. The cost of the equipment was $100,000, with no expected salvage value and a 10-year estimated life. The company uses the straight-line depreciation method on similar equipment. The error was discovered at the end of Year 3 prior to the issuance of the company's financial statements. After correction of the error, the correct carrying value of the equipment will be

A. $30,000
B. $70,000
C. $80,000
D. $100,000

Answer (B) is correct.
REQUIRED: The correct carrying value of the equipment.
DISCUSSION: The straight-line depreciation that should have been charged to the equipment had it been properly capitalized is $30,000 [$100,000 × (3 ÷ 10 years)]. Thus, after correction of the error, the carrying amount of the equipment will be $70,000 ($100,000 – $30,000).
Answer (A) is incorrect. The amount of $30,000 is the depreciation expense that should have been recognized over the previous 3 years. Answer (C) is incorrect. The amount of $80,000 is the equipment's correct carrying amount after 2 years. Answer (D) is incorrect. The amount of $100,000 is the full original cost of the equipment.

6. A company uses the sum-of-the-years'-digits (SYD) method of depreciation. On January 1, the company purchased a machine for $50,000. It had an estimated life of 5 years and no residual value. Depreciation for the first year would be

A. $10,000
B. $15,000
C. $16,667
D. $20,000

Answer (C) is correct.
REQUIRED: The SYD depreciation for the first year.
DISCUSSION: The SYD method multiplies a constant depreciable base (cost minus residual value) by a declining fraction. The numerator is the number of years of the useful life minus the years elapsed (5 – 0 = 5). The denominator is the sum of the digits of the years in the asset's useful life (1 + 2 + 3 + 4 + 5). The first year's depreciation expense is therefore $16,667 [$50,000 × (5 ÷ 15)].
Answer (A) is incorrect. The amount of $10,000 is the straight-line depreciation expense. Answer (B) is incorrect. The amount of $15,000 results from using the 150% declining-balance method. Answer (D) is incorrect. The amount of $20,000 results from using the double-declining balance method.

7. When a fixed plant asset with a 5-year estimated useful life is sold during the second year, how would the use of an accelerated depreciation method instead of the straight-line method affect the gain or loss on the sale of the fixed plant asset?

	Gain	Loss
A.	Increase	Increase
B.	Increase	Decrease
C.	Decrease	Increase
D.	Decrease	Decrease

Answer (B) is correct.
REQUIRED: The effect of using an accelerated depreciation method instead of straight-line.
DISCUSSION: An accelerated method reduces the carrying amount of the asset more rapidly in the early years of the useful life than does the straight-line method. Hence, the effect of an early sale is to increase the gain or decrease the loss that would have been recognized under the straight-line method.

8. An entity has owned its present facilities since 1981, and the CEO has authorized various expenditures to repair and improve the building during the current year. The building was beginning to sag, and without repair, the building would only last another 8 years. To correct the problem, the foundation was reinforced and several columns were added in the basement area at a cost of $47,200. As a result, engineers estimate that the building will have a remaining useful life of 20 years. To install a new computer local area network (LAN) and be ready for the next generation of computers, the phone lines and electrical systems were updated at a cost of $81,300. The entity's engineers estimate that these improvements should last 25 years. The offices and open work spaces were rearranged to reduce exposure to electronic emissions at a materials cost of $31,000. The purchase and installation of the computers and software for the LAN cost $102,700. The LAN hardware and software will have to be replaced in 6 years, but further rearrangement of the offices and work spaces will not be necessary. After the above improvements were completed, the entire building was painted inside and outside at a cost of $9,450.

As controller of the entity, which one of the following actions would you recommend to be in conformity with generally accepted accounting principles?

A. Treat all expenditures as expenses in the current year except the cost of rearrangement ($31,000), which should be amortized over a period not to exceed 20 years.

B. Capitalize all expenditures because they represent additions, improvements, and rearrangements.

C. Capitalize all costs with the exception of the upgrade to the phone and electrical systems and the painting because they represent maintenance expenses.

D. Capitalize all costs with the exception of the painting because it represents maintenance expense.

Answer (D) is correct.
REQUIRED: The costs to be expensed or capitalized.
DISCUSSION: Expenditures on capital assets that improve the asset's performance or extend its useful life are capitalized as part of the asset's cost. Accordingly, the building repairs are capitalized. The substitution of a better computer system is classified as an improvement, and the costs also should be capitalized. Moreover, the entity capitalizes the costs of a rearrangement of the configurations of the offices and open work spaces that (1) requires material outlays, (2) is separable from recurring expenses, and (3) provides probable future benefits. However, expenditures that merely maintain the asset at an acceptable level of productivity are expensed as they are incurred. Thus, the costs of painting the building are routine, minor outlays that should be expensed immediately.

Answer (A) is incorrect. The only costs that should be expensed are those for painting. Answer (B) is incorrect. The costs of additions, improvements, and rearrangements should be capitalized, but painting is routine maintenance. Such costs are expensed as incurred. Answer (C) is incorrect. The costs of the upgrade of the phone and electrical systems should be capitalized. They improve the performance of the asset (the building).

9. The types of assets that qualify for interest capitalization are

A. Assets that are being used in the earning activities of the reporting entity.

B. Assets that are ready for their intended use in the activities of the reporting entity.

C. Assets that are constructed for the reporting entity's own use.

D. Inventories that are manufactured in large quantities on a continuing basis.

Answer (C) is correct.
REQUIRED: The types of assets that qualify for interest capitalization.
DISCUSSION: Interest should be capitalized for (1) assets constructed or otherwise produced for an entity's own use, including those constructed or produced by others; (2) assets intended for sale or lease that are constructed or produced as discrete projects (e.g., ships); and (3) certain equity-based investments. An asset constructed for an entity's own use qualifies for capitalization of interest if (1) relevant expenditures have been made, (2) activities necessary to prepare the asset for its intended use are in progress, and (3) interest is being incurred. The investee must have activities in progress necessary to commence its planned principal operations and be expending funds to obtain qualifying assets for its operations.

Answer (A) is incorrect. Assets that are being used in earning activities do not qualify for interest capitalization. Answer (B) is incorrect. Assets that are ready for their intended use do not qualify for interest capitalization. Answer (D) is incorrect. Inventories that are manufactured in large quantities on a continuing basis do not qualify for interest capitalization.

3.2 Impairment and Disposal of Long-Lived Assets

Questions 10 and 11 are based on the following information. Blake Corporation has determined that one of its machines has experienced an impairment in value. However, the company expects to continue to use the asset for another 3 full years because no active market exists for this machine. Selected information on the impaired asset (on the date that impairment was determined to exist) is provided below.

Original cost of the machine	$22,000
Carrying amount of the machine	20,000
Undiscounted future cash flows expected to be generated by the machine	15,000
Fair value of the machine (determined by calculating the present value of the future cash flows expected to be generated by the machine)	12,000

10. After recognition of the impairment loss, Blake's carrying amount of the impaired asset will be

A. $0
B. $12,000
C. $14,000
D. $15,000

Answer (B) is correct.
REQUIRED: The carrying amount of the impaired asset after recognition of the impairment loss.
DISCUSSION: A long-lived asset (asset group) is impaired when its carrying amount is greater than its fair value. However, a loss equal to this excess is recognized for the impairment only when the carrying amount is not recoverable. The carrying amount is not recoverable when it exceeds the sum of the undiscounted cash flows expected from the use and disposition of the asset (asset group).
The asset is impaired because its carrying amount ($20,000) exceeds its fair value ($12,000). This loss ($20,000 – $12,000 = $8,000) is recognized in full because the carrying amount ($20,000) exceeds the undiscounted cash flows from the asset ($15,000). Thus, the carrying amount is reduced to $12,000.
Answer (A) is incorrect. The impairment is not total. Answer (C) is incorrect. The amount of $14,000 results from subtracting the $8,000 loss from the original cost. Answer (D) is incorrect. Impaired depreciable assets for which there is no secondary market may be measured at the present value of the discounted future cash flows expected to be generated by the asset ($12,000). This measurement differs from the undiscounted future cash flows ($15,000) used in the recoverability test.

11. What is the amount of the impairment loss to be recorded by Blake?

A. $3,000
B. $5,000
C. $7,000
D. $8,000

Answer (D) is correct.
REQUIRED: The amount of the impairment loss.
DISCUSSION: The impairment loss is the difference between the carrying amount and fair value of the asset ($20,000 – $12,000 = $8,000).
Answer (A) is incorrect. The amount of $3,000 is the difference between the discounted and undiscounted future cash flows. Answer (B) is incorrect. The amount of $5,000 is the difference between the asset's carrying amount and the undiscounted future cash flows expected to be generated. Answer (C) is incorrect. The amount of $7,000 is the difference between the asset's historical cost and the undiscounted future cash flows expected to be generated.

12. An entity purchased a machine on January 1, Year 1, for $1,000,000. The machine had an estimated useful life of 9 years and a residual value of $100,000. The entity uses straight-line depreciation. On December 31, Year 4, the machine was sold for $535,000. The gain or loss that should be recorded on the disposal of this machine is

A. $35,000 gain.
B. $65,000 loss.
C. $365,000 loss.
D. $465,000 loss.

Answer (B) is correct.
REQUIRED: The gain or loss that should be recorded on the disposal.
DISCUSSION: The accumulated depreciation was $400,000 {[($1,000,000 historical cost – $100,000 residual value) ÷ 9 years estimated useful life] × 4 years}, so the carrying amount was $600,000 ($1,000,000 – $400,000). Thus, the loss was $65,000 ($600,000 carrying amount – $535,000 sales price).
Answer (A) is incorrect. Selling price, minus carrying amount, plus residual value equals a $35,000 gain. Answer (C) is incorrect. Cost, minus selling price, minus residual value equals a $365,000 loss. Answer (D) is incorrect. Cost minus selling price equals a $465,000 loss.

3.3 Intangible Assets

13. A recognized intangible asset is amortized over its useful life

A. Unless the pattern of consumption of the economic benefits of the asset is not reliably determinable.
B. If that life is determined to be finite.
C. Unless the precise length of that life is not known.
D. If that life is indefinite but not infinite.

Answer (B) is correct.
REQUIRED: The circumstances in which a recognized intangible asset is amortized.
DISCUSSION: A recognized intangible asset is amortized over its useful life if that useful life is finite, that is, unless the useful life is determined to be indefinite. The useful life of an intangible asset is indefinite if no foreseeable limit exists on the period over which it will contribute, directly or indirectly, to the reporting entity's cash flows.
Answer (A) is incorrect. An intangible asset is amortizable if its useful life is finite. If the pattern of consumption of the economic benefits of such an intangible asset is not reliably determinable, the straight-line amortization method is applied. Answer (C) is incorrect. If the precise length of the useful life is not known, an intangible asset with a finite useful life is amortized over the best estimate of its useful life. Answer (D) is incorrect. A recognized intangible asset is not amortized if its useful life is indefinite.

14. A corporation purchased a patent at the beginning of Year 1 for $22,100 that was to be amortized over 17 years. On July 1 of Year 8, the corporation incurred legal costs of $11,400 to successfully defend the patent. The amount of amortization expense that the corporation should record for Year 8 is

A. $2,500
B. $1,971
C. $1,900
D. $1,300

Answer (C) is correct.
REQUIRED: The amount of amortization expense for Year 8.
DISCUSSION: The corporation will amortize the cost of the patent on a straight-line basis at the rate of $1,300 per year ($22,100 ÷ 17). The costs of a successful legal defense of a patent are capitalized and amortized over the shorter of the remaining legal life or the estimated useful life of the patent. Because the legal costs to defend the patent were incurred when the patent had 9.5 years of life remaining, they will be amortized at a rate of $1,200 per year ($11,400 ÷ 9.5). Because Year 8 only includes a half year's depreciation for the legal costs, total amortization expense for that year is $1,900 ($1,300 + $600).
Answer (A) is incorrect. The amount of $2,500 results from improperly including a full year's amortization of the legal costs. Answer (B) is incorrect. The amount of $1,971 results from improperly amortizing the legal costs over the life of the patent. Answer (D) is incorrect. The amount of $1,300 results from failing to include any amortization of the legal costs.

15. Which of the following costs associated with an internally developed patent should be capitalized?

	Research and Development	Patent Registration
A.	No	Yes
B.	No	No
C.	Yes	No
D.	Yes	Yes

Answer (A) is correct.
REQUIRED: The costs associated with an internally developed patent that should be capitalized.
DISCUSSION: R&D costs must be expensed as they are incurred. Legal fees and registration fees are excluded from the definition of R&D. Thus, the patent registration fees should be capitalized as a cost associated with an internally developed patent. The patent's R&D costs should have been expensed as they were incurred.
Answer (B) is incorrect. Patent registration costs should be capitalized. Answer (C) is incorrect. Patent registration costs, not R&D costs, should be capitalized. Answer (D) is incorrect. R&D costs are not capitalized.

16. On July 1, a company acquired a patent on its new manufacturing process, which streamlines its production operation. The cost of the patent was $17,000, and the company expects that the useful life of the new process will be 10 years, although the legal life of the patent is 17 years. The company is a calendar-year corporation and is preparing its December 31 Statement of Financial Position. At which amount should the patent be reported at December 31 of the year of acquisition?

A. $15,300
B. $16,000
C. $16,150
D. $16,500

Answer (C) is correct.
REQUIRED: The amount reported for the patent at December 31 of the year of acquisition.
DISCUSSION: A patent is amortized over the shorter of its useful life or legal life, so annual amortization on this patent is $1,700 ($17,000 ÷ 10 years). The depreciation expense for the year of acquisition is $850 [$1,700 × (6 ÷ 12 months)]. The patent should therefore be reported at December 31 at $16,150 ($17,000 – $850).
Answer (A) is incorrect. The amount of $15,300 results from improperly taking a full year of depreciation. Answer (B) is incorrect. The amount of $16,000 results from improperly using the legal life of the patent rather than its useful life and improperly taking a full year of depreciation. Answer (D) is incorrect. The amount of $16,500 results from improperly using the legal life of the patent rather than its useful life.

3.4 Leases

> Questions 17 and 18 are based on the following information. Neary Company has entered into a contract to lease computers from Baldwin Company starting on January 1, Year 1. Relevant information pertaining to the lease is provided below.
>
> | | |
> |---|---|
> | Lease term | 4 Years |
> | Useful life of computers | 5 Years |
> | Present value of future lease payments | $100,000 |
> | Fair value of leased asset on date of lease | 105,000 |
> | Baldwin's implicit rate | 10% |
>
> At the end of the lease term, ownership of the asset transfers from Baldwin to Neary. Neary has properly classified this lease as a capital lease on its financial statements and uses straight-line depreciation on comparable assets.

17. At January 1, Year 1, the lease would be reported on Neary's books as a(n)

A. Asset only.
B. Asset and a liability.
C. Liability only.
D. Expense and a liability.

Answer (B) is correct.
REQUIRED: The lease reported on Neary's books at January 1, Year 1.
DISCUSSION: The lease is classified as a capital lease, since the ownership of the leased asset is transferred to the lessee at the end of the lease term. The lessee must record a capital lease as an asset and as an obligation at an amount equal to the present value of the minimum lease payments.
Answer (A) is incorrect. Under a capital lease, both the leased asset and the related liability are reported in the balance sheet. Answer (C) is incorrect. Under a capital lease, both the leased asset and the related liability are reported in the balance sheet. Answer (D) is incorrect. Under a capital lease, both the leased asset and the related liability are reported in the balance sheet.

18. What is the annual depreciation expense that Neary will record on the leased computers?

A. $20,000
B. $21,000
C. $25,000
D. $26,250

Answer (A) is correct.
REQUIRED: The annual depreciation expense that Neary will record on the leased computers.
DISCUSSION: Under a capital lease, the lessee recognizes a leased asset at an amount equal to the present value of the minimum lease payments ($100,000). Since the lease provides for the transfer of ownership, Neary should depreciate the computers using the straight-line method over their estimated useful life (5 years). Annual depreciation expense on the computers is $20,000 ($100,000 ÷ 5 years).
Answer (B) is incorrect. The amount of $21,000 results from using the fair value of the computers rather than the present value of the lease payments. Answer (C) is incorrect. The amount of $25,000 results from using the term of the lease rather than the useful life of the computers. Answer (D) is incorrect. The amount of $26,250 results from using the fair value of the computers rather than the present value of the lease payments and using the term of the lease rather than the useful life of the computers.

19. If a company uses off-balance-sheet financing, assets have been acquired

A. For cash.
B. With operating leases.
C. With financing leases.
D. With a line of credit.

Answer (B) is correct.
REQUIRED: The method by which assets have been acquired using off-balance-sheet financing.
DISCUSSION: With an operating lease, no long-term liability need be reported on the face of the balance sheet.
Answer (A) is incorrect. No liability arises if the assets were paid for with cash. Answer (C) is incorrect. The long-term liability for financing leases must be reported on the face of the balance sheet. Answer (D) is incorrect. The liability associated with a line of credit is reported on the face of the balance sheet.

20. Which one of the following statements with respect to leases is **correct**?

A. An operating lease is treated like a rental contract between the lessor and lessee.
B. A lease that does not transfer ownership from the lessor to the lessee by the end of the lease is automatically an operating lease.
C. Sales and direct financing leases pertain more to lessees than lessors.
D. Unpredictability of lease revenues or expenses can transform what would otherwise be a capital lease for the lessee into an operating lease for the lessee.

Answer (A) is correct.
REQUIRED: The statement that is correct with respect to leases.
DISCUSSION: An operating lease is a transaction in which the lessee rents the right to use the lessor's assets without acquiring a substantial portion of the benefits and risks of ownership. Thus, an operating lease is treated like a rental contract between the lessor and lessee.
Answer (B) is incorrect. The transfer of ownership test is only one of four tests that are used to determined whether a lease is classified as a capital lease. Answer (C) is incorrect. Sales-type leases and direct financing leases are reported by lessors, not lessees. Answer (D) is incorrect. The degree of unpredictability of lease revenues or expenses is not a factor for the lessee in the classification of the lease as a capital or operating lease.

21. Which of the following statements about a capital lease is **false**?

A. The lessor capitalizes the net investment in the lease.
B. The lessor records the leased item as an asset.
C. The lessee records depreciation or capital cost allowance on the leased asset.
D. The lease arrangement represents a form of financing.

Answer (B) is correct.
REQUIRED: The false statement about a capital lease.
DISCUSSION: When a lease is capitalized, the lessor derecognizes the leased item and records lease payments receivable. The lessee records and depreciates the leased item.
Answer (A) is incorrect. If a lease is capitalized, the lessor recognizes a net receivable equal to the net investment in the lease: gross investment (minimum lease payments from the lessor's perspective plus unguaranteed residual value) discounted at the interest rate implicit in the lease. Answer (C) is incorrect. The lessee records depreciation on the leased asset under a capitalized lease. This process is separate from the accounting for the lease obligation. Answer (D) is incorrect. A capitalized lease is, in essence, a purchase-and-financing arrangement.

22. A corporation signed a 3-year lease for an automobile on December 1. The automobile had a list price of $17,000 and an estimated useful life of 8 years. The lease called for payments of $500 per month for 36 months. The present value of the $500 payments was $15,054 at the corporation's incremental borrowing rate and $15,496 at the lessor's implicit rate, which is known to the lessee. Based on the above information, the corporation should record the lease as a(n)

A. Capital lease.
B. Operating lease.
C. Sale-leaseback.
D. Sales-type lease.

Answer (A) is correct.
REQUIRED: The proper classification of the described lease by a corporation.
DISCUSSION: A lessee must report a lease as a capital lease if the present value of the minimum lease payments (MLP) is at least 90% of the fair value of the asset. If the lessor's implicit rate is known to the lessee, that is the appropriate rate for discounting the MLP. Dividing the present value of the MLP by the list price of the automobile yields a result > 90% ($15,496 ÷ $17,000 = 91.2%). Thus, this lease must be classified by the corporation as a capital lease.
Answer (B) is incorrect. A lease in which the present value of the minimum lease payments equals or exceeds 90% of the fair value of the asset must be classified by the lessee as a capital lease. Answer (C) is incorrect. No provision for a sale-leaseback arrangement was mentioned. Answer (D) is incorrect. Only lessors report sales-type leases.

3.5 Income Taxes

23. On a statement of financial position, all of the following should be classified as current liabilities **except**

A. Advances from customers for services to be performed.
B. Salaries payable for work performed during the previous month.
C. Deferred income taxes for differences based on depreciation methods.
D. Accounts payable for inventory items to be shipped on consignment.

Answer (C) is correct.
REQUIRED: The item not a current liability.
DISCUSSION: Deferred tax amounts are classified as current or noncurrent based on the classification of the related asset or liability (assuming such an asset or liability exists). Because depreciable assets are noncurrent, a deferred tax liability for differences based on depreciation methods is noncurrent.
Answer (A) is incorrect. Advances from customers for services to be performed are classified as unearned revenue (current liabilities). Answer (B) is incorrect. Salaries payable for work performed during the previous month are accrued as current liabilities. Answer (D) is incorrect. Trade accounts payable for inventory, whether or not to be shipped on consignment, are current liabilities.

Questions 24 and 25 are based on the following information. Lucas Company computed the following deferred tax balances for the 2 most recent years. Deferred tax assets are considered fully realizable.

	Year 1	Year 2
Current deferred tax assets	$3,000	$10,000
Noncurrent deferred tax assets	6,000	7,000
Current deferred tax liabilities	8,000	9,000
Noncurrent deferred tax liabilities	5,000	14,000

24. If Lucas calculates taxable income of $1,000,000 for Year 2 and is taxed at an effective income tax rate of 40%, how much income tax expense will be reported on Lucas's income statement for Year 2?

A. $400,000
B. $402,000
C. $404,000
D. $406,000

Answer (B) is correct.
REQUIRED: The amount of income tax expense reported.
DISCUSSION: Deferred tax expense or benefit is the net change during the year in the entity's deferred tax liabilities and assets. It is aggregated with the current tax expense or benefit to determine total income tax expense for the year. The amount of income taxes payable (current tax expense) is $400,000 ($1,000,000 × 40%). The deferred tax assets increased by $8,000 ($10,000 − $3,000 + $7,000 − $6,000) and the deferred tax liabilities increased by $10,000 ($9,000 − $8,000 + $14,000 − $5,000). Thus, Lucas's income tax expense for Year 2 is $402,000 ($400,000 current tax expense − $8,000 increase in the deferred tax assets + $10,000 increase in the deferred tax liabilities).
Answer (A) is incorrect. The current tax expense is $400,000. Answer (C) is incorrect. Improperly netting deferred tax assets and liabilities results in $404,000. Answer (D) is incorrect. Excluding the effects of noncurrent deferred tax items results in $406,000.

25. What deferred tax amounts will appear on Lucas's statement of financial position at the end of Year 2?

	Assets		Liabilities	
	Current	Noncurrent	Current	Noncurrent
A.	$0	$1,000	$5,000	$0
B.	$7,000	$1,000	$1,000	$9,000
C.	$1,000	$0	$0	$7,000
D.	$10,000	$7,000	$9,000	$14,000

Answer (C) is correct.
REQUIRED: The deferred tax amounts at the end of Year 2.
DISCUSSION: Current deferred tax amounts are netted for financial reporting purposes. Likewise, noncurrent amounts are also netted. At the end of Year 2, Lucas nets its $10,000 of current deferred tax assets and $9,000 of current deferred tax liabilities for a reported current deferred tax asset of $1,000. Similarly, the $7,000 of noncurrent deferred tax assets and $14,000 of noncurrent deferred tax liabilities are netted to produce a reported noncurrent deferred tax liability of $7,000.
Answer (A) is incorrect. Lucas should report a current deferred tax asset and a noncurrent deferred tax liability. Answer (B) is incorrect. Deferred tax assets and liabilities are netted for financial reporting purposes. Answer (D) is incorrect. Deferred tax assets and liabilities are netted for financial reporting purposes.

26. A liability that represents the accumulated difference between the income tax expense reported on the firm's books and the income tax actually paid is

A. Capital gains tax.
B. Deferred taxes.
C. Taxes payable.
D. Value-added taxes.

Answer (B) is correct.
REQUIRED: The definition of a deferred tax liability.
DISCUSSION: Deferred tax liabilities arise when temporary differences in book and taxable income result in future taxable amounts. Deferred tax assets arise when temporary differences in book and taxable income result in future deductible amounts.
Answer (A) is incorrect. Capital gains taxes arise from transactions involving capital assets. Answer (C) is incorrect. Taxes payable arise from the tax liability due within the next fiscal year or operating cycle. Answer (D) is incorrect. Value-added taxes are taxes paid on the incremental increase in value of a good at each stage of production.

3.6 Accounting for Bonds and Noncurrent Notes Payable

> Questions 27 through 30 are based on the following information. On January 1, Evangel Company issued 9% bonds in the face amount of $100,000, which mature in 5 years. The bonds were issued for $96,207 to yield 10%, resulting in a bond discount of $3,793. Evangel uses the effective interest method of amortizing bond discount. Interest is payable annually on December 31.

27. What is the amount of interest expense that should be reported on Evangel's income statement for the second year?

A. $8,779
B. $9,000
C. $9,559
D. $9,683

Answer (D) is correct.
REQUIRED: The amount of interest expense reported on Evangel's income statement for the second year.
DISCUSSION: An amortization schedule for the first 2 years of Evangel's bonds can be prepared as follows:

Year	Beginning Carrying Amount	Times: Effective Rate	Equals: Interest Expense	Minus: Cash Paid	Equals: Discount Amortized	Ending Carrying Amount
1	$96,207	10%	$9,621	$9,000	$621	$96,828
2	96,828	10%	9,683	9,000	683	97,510

Answer (A) is incorrect. The amount of $8,779 results from subtracting the cash portion of interest from the beginning carrying amount and multiplying the effective rate by the result. Answer (B) is incorrect. The amount of $9,000 is the amount of cash interest paid. Answer (C) is incorrect. The amount of $9,559 results from increasing the unamortized discount rather than reducing it.

28. What is the amount of Evangel's unamortized bond discount at the end of the first year?

A. $621
B. $2,452
C. $3,172
D. $3,793

Answer (C) is correct.
REQUIRED: The amount of Evangel's unamortized bond discount at the end of the first year.
DISCUSSION: Total interest expense for the year equals the carrying amount of the bonds times the effective rate (yield), or $9,621 ($96,207 × 10%). Subtracting the cash interest payment from this leaves the amount of discount amortized, or $621 ($9,621 – $9,000). Subtracting this amount from the previous unamortized discount ($3,793) leaves a remaining unamortized discount at the end of Year 1 of $3,172.
Answer (A) is incorrect. The amount of $621 is the amount of discount amortized. Answer (B) is incorrect. The amount of $2,452 results from reversing the face and yield rates of interest. Answer (D) is incorrect. The amount of $3,793 is the unamortized discount on January 1.

29. The net carrying amount of Evangel's bonds payable at the end of the first year is

A. $94,866
B. $95,586
C. $96,828
D. $97,548

Answer (C) is correct.
REQUIRED: The net carrying amount of Evangel's bonds payable at the end of the first year.
DISCUSSION: Total interest expense for the year equals the carrying amount of the bonds times the effective rate (yield), or $9,621 ($96,207 × 10%). Subtracting the cash interest payment from this leaves the amount of discount amortized ($9,621 – $9,000 = $621). Subtracting this amount from the previous unamortized discount ($3,793) leaves a remaining unamortized discount at the end of Year 1 of $3,172. Subtracting this amount from the face amount of the bonds ($100,000) provides a carrying amount of $96,828.
Answer (A) is incorrect. The amount of $94,866 results from reversing the face and yield rates of interest. Answer (B) is incorrect. The amount of $95,586 results from increasing the unamortized discount rather than reducing it. Answer (D) is incorrect. The amount of $97,548 results from reversing the face and yield rates of interest and from increasing the unamortized discount rather than reducing it.

30. What is the amount of interest expense that should be reported on Evangel's income statement at the end of the first year?

A. $8,659
B. $9,000
C. $9,621
D. $10,000

Answer (C) is correct.
REQUIRED: The amount of interest expense reported on Evangel's income statement at the end of the first year.
DISCUSSION: Total interest expense for the year equals the carrying amount of the bonds times the effective rate (yield), or $9,621 ($96,207 × 10%).
Answer (A) is incorrect. The amount of $8,659 results from using the stated rate rather than the yield. Answer (B) is incorrect. The amount of $9,000 is the amount of cash interest paid. Answer (D) is incorrect. The amount of $10,000 results from using the face amount of the bonds rather than the carrying amount.

Access the **CMA Review System** from your Gleim Personal Classroom to continue your studies with exam-emulating multiple-choice questions!

3.7 ESSAY QUESTIONS

Scenario for Essay Questions 1, 2, 3, 4, 5, 6

For each independent situation below, determine the effect, if any, on Company A's December 31, Year 5, financial statements. The following are the possible effects:

- Increase expenses
- Increase intangible assets
- Increase income
- Increase tangible assets
- No effect

Questions

1. During Year 3, the company recognized an impairment loss on goodwill. On December 31, Year 5, the company estimates that the fair value of goodwill is greater than its carrying amount.

2. During Year 5, the company incurred a cost of $60,000 on development activities for an internally developed intangible asset.

3. The company applies IFRS. During Year 3, the company recognized an impairment loss on an intangible asset with a useful life of 20 years. On December 31, Year 5, the company estimates that the recoverable amount of the intangible asset is greater than its carrying amount.

4. On December 31, Year 5, the company purchased for $50,000, on credit, a machine that can be used for the company's current R&D project and also for other alternative future projects.

5. The company applies IFRS and accounts for its intangible assets in accordance with the revaluation model. The company's policy is to revalue its assets at the end of each year. On December 31, Year 5, the fair value of an intangible asset that can be traded in active markets is greater than its carrying amount.

6. On December 31, Year 5, the company purchased for $55,000, on credit, a machine that can be used for the company's current R&D project only.

Essay Questions 1, 2, 3, 4, 5, 6 — Unofficial Answers

1. The impairment loss recognized is nonreversible. Thus, it has no effect on the financial statements.

2. Expenses increase because research and development costs must be expensed as incurred.

3. Under IFRS, an impairment loss for an asset (except goodwill) may be reversed if a change in the estimates used to measure the recoverable amount has occurred. The reversal of an impairment loss is recognized as an increase in current-period income.

4. Equipment having alternative future uses is capitalized (recognized as a tangible asset) and depreciated. No depreciation expense is recognized in Year 5 because the machine was purchased on the last day of the year. Thus, tangible assets increase.

5. Under IFRS, the revaluation model may be used for intangible assets if they are traded in active markets. On the date of revaluation, the asset is measured at its fair value. An increase in an intangible asset's carrying amount as a result of revaluation is recognized in other comprehensive income and has no effect on profit or loss.

6. The cost of equipment with no future uses other than in current R&D activities is recognized as an increase in R&D expenses.

Access the **CMA Review System** from your Gleim Personal Classroom to continue your studies with exam-emulating essay questions!

STUDY UNIT FOUR
COST MANAGEMENT CONCEPTS

(13 pages of outline)

4.1	Cost Management Terminology	117
4.2	Cost Behavior and Relevant Range	120
4.3	Cost Classification	123
4.4	Costing Techniques	126
4.5	Essay Questions	137

> **Cost Management**
>
> Cost management is at the heart of the field of management accounting. Thus, the CMA exam places great emphasis on this area of study. The candidate will face many questions involving numerical calculations and others requiring a knowledge of cost terminology and the implications of cost management decisions.

This study unit is the **first of four** on **cost management**. The relative weight assigned to this major topic in Part 1 of the exam is **20%**. The four study units are

  Study Unit 4: Cost Management Concepts
  Study Unit 5: Cost Accumulation Systems
  Study Unit 6: Cost Allocation Techniques
  Study Unit 7: Operational Efficiency and Business Process Performance

If you are interested in reviewing more introductory or background material, go to www.gleim.com/CMAIntroVideos for a list of suggested third-party overviews of this topic. The following Gleim outline material is more than sufficient to help you pass the CMA exam; any additional introductory or background material is for your own personal enrichment.

4.1 COST MANAGEMENT TERMINOLOGY

1. **Subdisciplines of Accounting**

    a. **Financial accounting** is concerned principally with reporting to external users, usually through a set of financial statements produced in accordance with GAAP. Financial accounting thus has a historical focus.

    b. **Management accounting** is concerned principally with reporting to internal users. The management accountant's goal is to produce reports that improve organizational decision making. Management accounting is thus future-oriented.

    c. **Cost accounting** supports both financial and management accounting. Information about the cost of resources acquired and consumed by an organization underlies effective reporting for both internal and external users.

2. **Basic Definitions**
    a. A cost is defined by the IMA in two senses:
        1) "In management accounting, a measurement in monetary terms of the amount of resources used for some purpose. The term by itself is not operational. It becomes operational when modified by a term that defines the purpose, such as acquisition cost, incremental cost, or fixed cost."
        2) "In financial accounting, the sacrifice measured by the price paid or required to be paid to acquire goods or services. The term 'cost' is often used when referring to the valuation of a good or service acquired. When 'cost' is used in this sense, a cost is an asset. When the benefits of the acquisition (the goods or services) expire, the cost becomes an expense or loss."
    b. A **cost object** is any entity to which costs can be attached.
        1) Examples are products, processes, employees, departments, and facilities.
    c. A **cost driver** is the basis used to assign costs to a cost object.
        1) Cost driver is defined by the IMA as "a measure of activity, such as direct labor hours, machine hours, beds occupied, computer time used, flight hours, miles driven, or contracts, that is a causal factor in the incurrence of cost to an entity."
        2) The key aspect of a cost driver is the existence of a direct cause-and-effect relationship between the quantity of the driver consumed and the amount of total cost. In other words, a cost driver is some event that causes costs to occur.

3. **Manufacturing vs. Nonmanufacturing**
    a. The costs of manufacturing a product can be classified as one of three types:
        1) **Direct materials** are those tangible inputs to the manufacturing process that can practically be traced to the product, e.g., sheet metal welded together for a piece of heavy equipment.
            a) In addition to the purchase price, all costs of bringing raw materials to the production line, e.g., transportation-in, are included in the cost of direct materials.
        2) **Direct labor** is the cost of human labor that can practically be traced to the product, e.g., the wages of the welder.
        3) **Manufacturing overhead** consists of all costs of manufacturing that are not direct materials or direct labor.
            a) **Indirect materials** are tangible inputs to the manufacturing process that cannot practically be traced to the product, e.g., the welding compound used to put together a piece of heavy equipment, or staples used in a stapling machine.
            b) **Indirect labor** is the cost of human labor connected with the manufacturing process that cannot practically be traced to the product, e.g., the wages of assembly line supervisors and janitorial staff.
            c) **Factory operating costs**, such as utilities, real estate taxes, insurance, depreciation on factory equipment, etc.
    b. Manufacturing costs are often grouped into the following classifications:
        1) **Prime cost** equals direct materials plus direct labor, i.e., those costs directly attributable to a product.
        2) **Conversion cost** equals direct labor plus manufacturing overhead, i.e., the costs of converting raw materials into the finished product.

c. Operating a manufacturing concern requires the incurrence of nonmanufacturing costs:

   1) **Selling (marketing) expenses** are those costs incurred in getting the product from the factory to the consumer, e.g., sales personnel salaries, advertising, and product transportation.
   2) **Administrative expenses** are those costs incurred by a company not directly related to producing or marketing the product, e.g., executive salaries, depreciation on the headquarters building, and rent on a warehouse containing inventory.

4. **Product vs. Period**

   a. One of the most important classifications a management accountant can make is whether to capitalize a cost as part of finished goods inventory or to expense it as incurred.

      1) **Product costs** (also called inventoriable costs) are capitalized as part of finished goods inventory. They eventually become a component of cost of goods sold. Such costs include direct materials and direct labor.
      2) **Period costs** are expensed as incurred, i.e., they are not capitalized in finished goods inventory and are thus excluded from cost of goods sold.

         a) The theory is that period costs are caused by the passage of time and would occur even if production was zero.

   b. This distinction is crucial because of the required treatment of manufacturing costs for external financial reporting purposes.

      1) Financial accounting

         a) For **external financial reporting**, all manufacturing costs (direct materials, direct labor, variable overhead, and fixed overhead) must be treated as product costs, and all selling and administrative (S&A) costs must be treated as period costs.

            i) This approach is called **absorption costing** (also called full costing).

      2) Management accounting

         a) For **internal reporting**, a more informative accounting treatment is often to capitalize only variable manufacturing costs as product costs, and treat all other costs (variable S&A and the fixed portion of both production and S&A expenses) as period costs.

            i) This approach is called **variable costing** (also called direct costing).

      3) The following table summarizes these two approaches:

	Absorption Costing (Required under GAAP)	Variable Costing (For Internal Reporting Only)
Product Costs (Included in Cost of Goods Sold)	Variable production costs	
	Fixed production costs	
Period Costs (Excluded from Cost of Goods Sold)		Fixed production costs
	Variable S&A expenses	
	Fixed S&A expenses	

         a) These treatments are explained more fully in item 1. in Subunit 4.4.

5. **Direct vs. Indirect**
   a. Costs can be classified by how they are assigned to cost objects.
      1) **Direct costs** are ones that can be associated with a particular cost object in an economically feasible way, i.e., they can be traced to that object.
         a) Examples are the direct materials and direct labor inputs to a manufacturing process discussed in item 3.a. on page 118.
      2) **Indirect costs** are ones that cannot be associated with a particular cost object in an economically feasible way and thus must be allocated to that object.
         a) Examples are the indirect materials and indirect labor inputs to a manufacturing process discussed in item 3.a.3) on page 118.
            i) To simplify the allocation process, indirect costs are often collected in cost pools.
         b) A **cost pool** is an account into which a variety of similar cost elements with a common cause are accumulated.
            i) It is preferable for all the costs in a cost pool to have the same cost driver.
            ii) Manufacturing overhead is a commonly used cost pool into which various untraceable costs of the manufacturing process are accumulated prior to being allocated.
      3) **Common costs** are another notable type of indirect cost. A common cost is one shared by two or more users.
         a) The key to common costs is that, since they cannot be directly traced to the users that generate the costs, they must be allocated using some systematic and rational basis.
         b) An example is depreciation or rent on the headquarters building. This is a direct cost when treating the building as a whole, but is a common cost of the departments located in the building, and thus must be allocated when treating the individual departments.

Stop and review! You have completed the outline for this subunit. Study multiple-choice questions 1 through 7 beginning on page 129.

4.2 COST BEHAVIOR AND RELEVANT RANGE

1. **Relevant Range**
   a. The relevant range defines the limits within which per-unit variable costs remain constant and fixed costs are not changeable. It is synonymous with the short run.
   b. The relevant range is established by the efficiency of a company's current manufacturing plant, its agreements with labor unions and suppliers, etc.
2. **Variable Costs**
   a. **Variable cost per unit** remains constant in the short run regardless of the level of production.

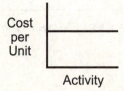

b. **Variable costs in total**, on the other hand, vary directly and proportionally with changes in volume.

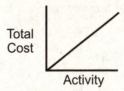

c. EXAMPLE: A company requires one unit of direct material to be used in each finished good it produces.

Number of Outputs Produced	Input Cost per Unit	Total Cost of Inputs
0	$10	$ 0
100	$10	$ 1,000
1,000	$10	$ 10,000
5,000	$10	$ 50,000
10,000	$10	$100,000

3. **Fixed Costs**

a. **Fixed costs in total** remain unchanged in the short run regardless of production level, e.g., the amount paid for an assembly line is the same even if production is halted entirely.

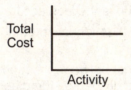

b. **Fixed cost per unit**, on the other hand, varies indirectly with the activity level.

c. EXAMPLE: The historical cost of the assembly line is settled, but its cost per unit decreases as production increases.

Number of Outputs Produced	Cost of Assembly Line	Per Unit Cost of Assembly Line
1	$1,000,000	$1,000,000
100	$1,000,000	$ 10,000
1,000	$1,000,000	$ 1,000
5,000	$1,000,000	$ 200
10,000	$1,000,000	$ 100

4. **Mixed (Semivariable) Costs**

   a. Mixed (semivariable) costs combine fixed and variable elements, e.g., rental expense on a car that carries a flat fee per month plus an additional fee for each mile driven.

   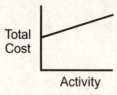

   b. EXAMPLE: The company rents a piece of machinery to make its production line more efficient. The rental is $150,000 per year plus $1 for every unit produced.

Number of Outputs Produced	Fixed Cost of Extra Machine	Variable Cost of Extra Machine	Total Cost of Extra Machine
0	$150,000	$ 0	$150,000
100	$150,000	$ 100	$150,100
1,000	$150,000	$ 1,000	$151,000
5,000	$150,000	$ 5,000	$155,000
10,000	$150,000	$10,000	$160,000

   c. Two methods of estimating mixed costs are in general use:

   1) The regression, or scattergraph, method is by far the more complex (and accurate) of the two and is beyond the scope of the CMA exam.
   2) The high-low method is the less accurate but quicker of the two methods.

   d. The first step in applying the high-low method is to isolate the variable portion of the cost.

   1) The difference in cost between the highest and lowest levels of activity for a group of periods is divided by the difference in the cost drivers (activity level) at the two levels (cost drivers are defined in item 2.c. in Subunit 4.1).

   Variable Portion of Mixed Cost Using High-Low Method

   $$\frac{\text{Cost at highest activity level} - \text{Cost at lowest activity level}}{\text{Driver at highest activity level} - \text{Driver at lowest activity level}}$$

   EXAMPLE

   A company has the following cost data:

Month	Machine Hours	Maintenance Costs
April	1,000	$2,275
May	1,600	$3,400
June	1,200	$2,650
July	800	$1,900
August	1,200	$2,650
September	1,000	$2,275

   $$\text{Variable portion} = \frac{\text{May cost} - \text{July cost}}{\text{May driver} - \text{July driver}} = \frac{\$3,400 - \$1,900}{1,600 - 800} = \frac{\$1,500}{800} = \$1.875 \text{ per machine hour}$$

   e. The fixed portion can now be calculated by inserting the appropriate values for either the high or low period in the range:

   Fixed portion = Total cost − Variable portion
   = $1,900 − (800 machine hours × $1.875 per hour)
   = $1,900 − $1,500
   = $400

   f. The firm can now use this information to project total cost at any level of activity; e.g., the expenditure of 1,300 machine hours will generate a probable total cost of $2,837.50 [$400 + (1,300 × $1.875)].

5. **Linear vs. Nonlinear Cost Functions**
   a. Four of the five costs described in this subunit are linear-cost functions; i.e., they change at a constant rate (or remain unchanged) over the short run.
   b. Fixed cost per unit, however, is an example of a nonlinear-cost function.
      1) Note that fixed cost per unit has an asymptotic character with respect to the x-axis, approaching it closely while never intersecting it (it does intersect the y-axis at the zero level of activity). The function shows a high degree of variability over its range taken as a whole (item 3.b. on page 121).
      2) Another type of nonlinear-cost function is a step-cost function, one that is constant over small ranges of output but increases by steps (discrete amounts) as levels of activity increase.

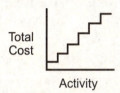

         a) Both fixed and variable costs can display step-cost characteristics. If the steps are relatively narrow, these costs are usually treated as variable. If the steps are wide, they are more akin to fixed costs.
      3) An example of a step cost would be the salary of production foremen. Operating at one shift per day might require one foreman, while two shifts would require two foremen.
6. **Relevant Range and Marginal Cost**
   a. Marginal cost is the cost incurred by a one-unit increase in the activity level of a particular cost driver.
      1) Necessarily then, marginal cost remains constant across the relevant range.
   b. Management accountants capture the concept of relevant range when they say that "All costs are variable in the long run."
      1) Investment in new, more productive equipment results in higher total fixed costs but may result in lower total and per-unit variable costs.

Stop and review! You have completed the outline for this subunit. Study multiple-choice questions 8 through 14 beginning on page 131.

4.3 COST CLASSIFICATION

1. **Controllable vs. Noncontrollable**
   a. **Controllable costs** are those that a particular manager has authority and responsibility for. **Noncontrollable costs** are those that a particular manager does not have authority over and cannot change.
   b. In other words, controllability is determined at different levels of the organization; it is not inherent in the nature of a given cost.
      1) For example, an outlay for new machinery may be controllable to the division vice president but noncontrollable to a plant manager or lower-level manager.
2. **Avoidable vs. Committed**
   a. **Avoidable costs** are those that may be eliminated by not engaging in an activity or by performing it more efficiently. An example is direct materials cost, which can be saved by ceasing production.
   b. **Committed costs** arise from holding property, plant, and equipment. Examples are insurance, real estate taxes, lease payments, and depreciation. They are by nature long-term and cannot be reduced by lowering the short-term level of production.

3. **Incremental vs. Differential**
    a. **Incremental cost** is the additional cost inherent in a given decision.
    b. **Differential cost** is the difference in total cost between two decisions.
    c. In practice, these two terms are often used interchangeably.
    d. EXAMPLE: A company must choose between introducing two new product lines.
        1) The incremental choice of the first option is the initial investment of $1.5 million; the incremental choice of the second option is the initial investment of $1.8 million.
        2) The differential cost of the two choices is $300,000.

4. **Engineered vs. Discretionary**
    a. **Engineered costs** are those having a direct, observable, quantifiable cause-and-effect relationship between the level of output and the quantity of resources consumed.
        1) Examples are direct materials and direct labor.
    b. **Discretionary costs** are those characterized by an uncertainty in the degree of causation between the level of output and the quantity of resources consumed. They tend to be the subject of a periodic (e.g., annual) outlay decision.
        1) Examples are advertising and R&D costs. Some routine maintenance costs might also fit this classification.

5. **Outlay vs. Opportunity**
    a. **Outlay costs** require actual cash disbursements. They are also called explicit, accounting, or out-of-pocket costs.
        1) An example is the tuition payment required to attend college.
    b. **Opportunity cost** is the maximum benefit forgone by using a scarce resource for a given purpose and not for the next-best alternative. It is also called implicit cost.
        1) An example is the wages foregone by attending college instead of working full-time.
    c. **Economic cost** is the sum of explicit and implicit costs.
    d. **Imputed costs** are those that should be involved in decision making even though no transaction has occurred that would be routinely recognized in the accounts. They are a type of opportunity cost.
        1) An example is the profit lost as a result of being unable to fill orders because the inventory level is too low.

6. **Relevant vs. Sunk**
    a. **Relevant costs** are those future costs that will vary depending on the action taken. All other costs are assumed to be constant and thus have no effect on (are irrelevant to) the decision.
        1) An example is tuition that must be spent to attend a fourth year of college.
    b. **Sunk costs** are costs either already paid or irrevocably committed to incur. Because they are unavoidable and will therefore not vary with the option chosen, they are not relevant to future decisions.
        1) An example is 3 years of tuition already spent. The previous 3 years of tuition make no difference in the decision to attend a fourth year.
    c. **Historical cost** is the actual (explicit) price paid for an asset. Financial accountants rely heavily on it for balance sheet reporting.
        1) Because historical cost is a sunk cost, however, management accountants often find other (implicit) costs to be more useful in decision making.

SU 4: Cost Management Concepts

7. **Joint vs. Separable**
   a. Often a manufacturing process involves processing a single input up to the point at which multiple end products become separately identifiable, called the **split-off point**.
      1) **Joint costs** are those costs incurred before the split-off point; i.e., since they are not traceable to the end products, they must be allocated.
         a) For example, the cost of a tree would be a joint cost for a lumber yard.
      2) **Separable costs** are those incurred beyond the split-off point, i.e., once separate products become identifiable.
      3) **By-products** are products of relatively small total value that are produced simultaneously from a common manufacturing process with products of greater value and quantity (joint products).
         a) For example, a lumber yard might have leftover lumber and sawdust that could be sold as by-products for a small amount.
   b. An example where joint costing is very important is petroleum refining.
      1) Costs incurred in bringing crude oil to the fractionating process are joint costs. The fractionating process is the split-off point.
      2) Once the oil has been refined into its separately identifiable end products (asphalt, diesel fuel, kerosene, etc.), all further costs are separable costs.
      3) If selling costs are lower than disposal costs, the sludge left over after the high-value products have been processed may be sold as a cheap lubricant. It is considered a by-product.

8. **Normal vs. Abnormal Spoilage**
   a. **Normal spoilage** is the spoilage that occurs under normal operating conditions. It is essentially uncontrollable in the short run.
      1) Since normal spoilage is expected under efficient operations, it is treated as a product cost; that is, it is absorbed into the cost of the good output.
   b. **Abnormal spoilage** is spoilage that is not expected to occur under normal, efficient operating conditions. The cost of abnormal spoilage should be separately identified and reported to management.
      1) Abnormal spoilage is typically treated as a period cost (a loss) because of its unusual nature.

9. **Rework, Scrap, and Waste**
   a. **Rework** consists of end products that do not meet standards of salability but can be brought to salable condition with additional effort.
      1) The decision to rework or discard is based on whether the marginal revenue to be gained from selling the reworked units exceeds the marginal cost of performing the rework.
   b. **Scrap** consists of raw material left over from the production cycle but still usable for purposes other than those for which it was originally intended.
      1) Scrap may be used for a different production process or may be sold to outside customers, usually for a nominal amount.
   c. **Waste** consists of raw material left over from the production cycle for which there is no further use.
      1) Waste is not salable at any price and must be discarded.

10. **Other Costs**
    a. **Carrying costs** are the costs of storing or holding inventory. Examples include the cost of capital, insurance, warehousing, breakage, and obsolescence.
    b. **Transferred-in costs** are those incurred in a preceding department and received in a subsequent department in a multi-departmental production setting.
    c. **Value-adding costs** are the costs of activities that cannot be eliminated without reducing the quality, responsiveness, or quantity of the output required by a customer or the organization.
11. **Manufacturing Capacity**
    a. **Normal capacity** is the long-term average level of activity that will approximate demand over a period that includes seasonal, cyclical, and trend variations. Deviations in a given year will be offset in subsequent years.
    b. **Practical capacity** is the maximum level at which output is produced efficiently. It allows for unavoidable delays in production for maintenance, holidays, etc.
    c. **Theoretical (ideal) capacity** is the maximum capacity assuming continuous operations with no holidays, downtime, etc.

Stop and review! You have completed the outline for this subunit. Study multiple-choice questions 15 through 22 beginning on page 133.

4.4 COSTING TECHNIQUES

1. **Absorption vs. Variable Costing**
    a. **Absorption costing** (sometimes called full costing or full absorption costing) treats all manufacturing costs as product costs.
        1) The inventoried cost of the product thus includes all production costs, whether variable or fixed. This technique is required for external financial reporting and for income tax purposes.
        2) **Gross margin** (also called gross profit) is the net difference between sales revenue and absorption cost of goods sold. It represents the amount available to cover selling and administrative expenses.
    b. **Variable costing** (also called direct costing) considers only variable manufacturing costs to be product costs, i.e., inventoriable (the phrase "direct costing" is considered misleading because it implies traceability).
        1) Fixed manufacturing costs are considered period costs and are thus expensed as incurred. This technique is not allowed for external financial reporting but is very useful for internal decision making. It also stops management from manipulating income by over-producing during the period.
        2) **Contribution margin** is the net of sales revenue minus all variable costs (both manufacturing and S&A). It represents the amount available to cover fixed costs.
    c. The illustration on the next page highlights the differing treatment of the four main categories of cost.
        1) The accounting for variable production costs and fixed selling and administrative expenses is identical under the two methods.
        2) The difference lies in the varying treatment of fixed production costs and variable selling and administrative expenses.

		Absorption Costing (Required for ext. rptg.)	Variable Costing (For internal reporting only)
	Sales	$100,000	$100,000
	Beg. finished goods inventory	$10,000	$10,000
Product Costs	Add: variable production costs	20,000 (a)	20,000 (a)
	Add: fixed production costs	30,000 (b)	-
	Goods available for sale	$60,000	$30,000
	Less: end. finished goods inventory	(35,000)	(25,000)
	Cost of goods sold	$(25,000)	$(5,000)
Period Costs	Less: variable S&A expenses	-	(10,000) (c)
	Gross margin (abs.) / Contribution margin (var.)	$75,000	$85,000
	Less: fixed production costs	-	(30,000) (b)
	Less: variable S&A expenses	(10,000) (c)	-
	Less: fixed S&A expenses	(20,000) (d)	(20,000) (d)
	Operating income	$45,000	$35,000

Legend	Cost Component
(a)	Variable production costs
(b)	Fixed production costs
(c)	Variable selling and administrative expenses
(d)	Fixed selling and administrative expenses

    d. Note that ending finished goods inventory will differ between the two methods due to the different treatment of fixed production costs.

        1) This leads to a difference in cost of goods sold, goods margin, and operating income.

    e. The $10,000 difference in operating income ($45,000 − $35,000) is the difference between the ending inventory values ($35,000 − $25,000).

        1) In essence, the absorption method carries 33.33% of the fixed overhead costs ($30,000 × 33.33% = $10,000) on the balance sheet as an asset because 33.33% of the month's production is still in inventory.

2. **Actual vs. Normal Costing**

    a. **Actual costing** is the most accurate method of accumulating costs in a cost accounting system. However, it is also the least timely and most volatile method.

        1) After the end of the production period, all actual costs incurred for a cost object are totaled; indirect costs are allocated.

        2) Because per-unit costs depend on the level of production in a period, large fluctuations arise from period to period. This volatility can lead to the reporting of misleading financial information.

    b. **Normal costing** charges actual direct materials and direct labor to a specific product or a production department but applies overhead on the basis of a budgeted rate. This compensates for the fluctuations in unit cost inherent in actual costing.

        1) There is usually a difference between budgeted overhead and actual overhead. If the difference is immaterial, it should be allocated to cost of goods sold. If the difference is material, it should be prorated between cost of goods sold, work-in-process, and finished goods inventories.

    c. **Extended normal costing** extends the use of normalized rates to direct material and direct labor, so that all three major input categories use normalized rates.

3. **Accumulating Manufacturing Costs**

    a. **Job-order costing** is appropriate when producing products with individual characteristics or when identifiable groupings are possible.

        1) Costs are attached to specific "jobs." Each job will result in a single, identifiable end product.

        2) Examples are any industry that generates custom-built products, such as shipbuilding or a sign shop.

b. **Process costing** is used when similar products are mass produced on a continuous basis.

1) Costs are attached to specific departments or phases of production. Examples are fence and candy manufacturing.
2) Since costs are attached to streams of products rather than individual items, process costing involves calculating an average cost for all units. The two widely used methods are weighted-average and first-in, first-out (FIFO).
3) Some units remain unfinished at the end of the period. For each department to adequately account for the costs attached to its unfinished units, the units, called work-in-process, must be restated in terms of equivalent units of production (EUP).

c. **Activity-based costing (ABC)** first assigns resource costs to activities. These activity costs are then assigned to physical goods.

1) ABC is a response to the distortions of product cost information brought about by peanut-butter costing, which is the inaccurate averaging or spreading of costs like peanut butter over products or service units that use different amounts of resources.
    a) A major cause of the problems associated with peanut-butter costing is the significant increase in indirect costs brought about by the increasing use of technology.
        i) The fixed costs associated with technology are harder to correlate to specific units of product than are the variable costs associated with direct labor.
2) The difference between traditional (that is, volume-based) costing systems and ABC can be summarized as follows:
    a) Under volume-based systems, a single pool collects all indirect costs and the total cost in the pool is then allocated to production.
    b) Under ABC, by contrast, every activity that bears on the production process has its own cost pool. The costs in each pool are assigned based on a cost driver specific to the activity.
        i) For example, with a single pool, all costs may be assigned based on a single driver, such as machine hours or direct-labor hours.
        ii) Under ABC, a dozen different cost pools might be assigned on the basis of a dozen different cost drivers. The increasing use of computers in the accounting process has made it easier to implement ABC.

d. **Life-cycle costing** emphasizes the need to price products to cover all the costs incurred over the lifespan of a product, not just the immediate costs of production.

1) Costs incurred before production, such as R&D and product design, are referred to as upstream costs.
2) Costs incurred after production, such as marketing and customer service, are called downstream costs.

4. **Standard Costing, Flexible Budgeting, and Variance Analysis**

a. **Standard costing** is a system designed to alert management when the actual costs of production differ significantly from budgeted ("standard") costs.

1) Standard costs are predetermined, attainable unit costs. A standard cost is not just an average of past costs, but an objectively determined estimate of what a cost should be. It is similar to "par" on a golf course.
2) Standard costs can be used with both job-order and process-costing systems.

3) There is usually a difference between budgeted overhead and actual overhead. If the difference is immaterial, it should be allocated to cost of goods sold. If the difference is material, it should be prorated between cost of goods sold, work-in-process, and finished goods inventories.

b. **Flexible budgeting** is the calculation of the quantity and cost of inputs that should have been consumed given the achieved level of production.

1) Flexible budgeting supplements the **static budget**, which is the company's best projection of the resource consumption and levels of output that will be achieved for an upcoming period.

c. The static and flexible budgets are compared to the actual results and the differences are calculated. These differences are referred to as variances.

1) Variance analysis enables **management by exception**, the practice of giving attention primarily to significant deviations from expectations (whether favorable or unfavorable).

5. **Target Costing**

a. Target costing is the practice of calculating the price for a product by adding the desired unit profit margin to the total unit cost. It is an adjunct concept of target pricing.

1) For example, a furniture manufacturer might want to produce a sofa that sells for $600 and has a $200 profit margin. That means the cost can be no more than $400.

2) If the new-product development team says the expected cost will be more than $400, then the product will not be manufactured because, under target costing, the product is not a "sofa" but a "$600 sofa."

Stop and review! You have completed the outline for this subunit. Study multiple-choice questions 23 through 30 beginning on page 135.

QUESTIONS

4.1 Cost Management Terminology

1. Inventoriable costs

A. Include only the prime costs of manufacturing a product.
B. Include only the conversion costs of manufacturing a product.
C. Are expensed when products become part of finished goods inventory.
D. Are regarded as assets before the products are sold.

Answer (D) is correct.
 REQUIRED: The true statement about inventoriable costs.
 DISCUSSION: Under an absorption costing system, inventoriable (product) costs include all costs necessary for good production. These include direct materials and conversion costs (direct labor and overhead). Both fixed and variable overhead is included in inventory under an absorption costing system. Inventoriable costs are treated as assets until the products are sold because they represent future economic benefits. These costs are expensed at the time of sale.
 Answer (A) is incorrect. Overhead costs as well as prime costs (direct materials and labor) are included in inventory. Answer (B) is incorrect. Materials costs are also included. Answer (C) is incorrect. Inventory costs are expensed when the goods are sold, not when they are transferred to finished goods.

2. Which one of the following **best** describes direct labor?

A. A prime cost.
B. A period cost.
C. A product cost.
D. Both a product cost and a prime cost.

Answer (D) is correct.
 REQUIRED: The best description of direct labor.
 DISCUSSION: Direct labor is both a product cost and a prime cost. Product costs are incurred to produce units of output and are deferred to future periods to the extent that output is not sold. Prime costs are defined as direct materials and direct labor.
 Answer (A) is incorrect. Direct labor is also a product cost. Answer (B) is incorrect. A period cost is expensed when incurred. Direct labor cost is inventoriable. Answer (C) is incorrect. Direct labor is also a prime cost.

3. Which of the following is a period cost rather than a product cost of a manufacturer?

A. Direct materials.
B. Variable overhead.
C. Fixed overhead.
D. Abnormal spoilage.

Answer (D) is correct.
REQUIRED: The period cost.
DISCUSSION: Materials, labor, and overhead (both fixed and variable) are examples of product costs. Abnormal spoilage is an example of a period cost. Abnormal spoilage is not inherent in a production process and should not be categorized as a product cost. Abnormal spoilage should be charged to a loss account in the period that detection of the spoilage occurs.
Answer (A) is incorrect. Direct materials are product costs. Answer (B) is incorrect. Variable overhead is a product cost. Answer (C) is incorrect. Fixed overhead is a product cost.

4. Cost drivers are

A. Activities that cause costs to increase as the activity increases.
B. Accounting techniques used to control costs.
C. Accounting measurements used to evaluate whether or not performance is proceeding according to plan.
D. A mechanical basis, such as machine hours, computer time, size of equipment, or square footage of factory, used to assign costs to activities.

Answer (A) is correct.
REQUIRED: The definition of a cost driver.
DISCUSSION: A cost driver is "a measure of activity, such as direct labor hours, machine hours, beds occupied, computer time used, flight hours, miles driven, or contracts, that is a causal factor in the incurrence of cost to an entity" (IMA). It is a basis used to assign costs to cost objects.
Answer (B) is incorrect. Cost drivers are measures of activities that cause the incurrence of costs. Answer (C) is incorrect. Cost drivers are not accounting measurements but measures of activities that cause costs. Answer (D) is incorrect. Although cost drivers may be used to assign costs, they are not necessarily mechanical. For example, a cost driver for pension benefits is employee salaries.

5. In cost terminology, conversion costs consist of

A. Direct and indirect labor.
B. Direct labor and direct materials.
C. Direct labor and factory overhead.
D. Indirect labor and variable factory overhead.

Answer (C) is correct.
REQUIRED: The components of conversion costs.
DISCUSSION: Conversion costs consist of direct labor and factory overhead. These are the costs of converting raw materials into a finished product.
Answer (A) is incorrect. All factory overhead is included in conversion costs, not just indirect labor. Answer (B) is incorrect. Direct materials are not an element of conversion costs; they are a prime cost. Answer (D) is incorrect. Direct labor is also an element of conversion costs.

6. The terms direct cost and indirect cost are commonly used in accounting. A particular cost might be considered a direct cost of a manufacturing department but an indirect cost of the product produced in the manufacturing department. Classifying a cost as either direct or indirect depends upon

A. The behavior of the cost in response to volume changes.
B. Whether the cost is expensed in the period in which it is incurred.
C. The cost object to which the cost is being related.
D. Whether an expenditure is unavoidable because it cannot be changed regardless of any action taken.

Answer (C) is correct.
REQUIRED: The factor that influences whether a cost is classified as direct or indirect.
DISCUSSION: A direct cost can be specifically associated with a single cost object in an economically feasible way. An indirect cost cannot be specifically associated with a single cost object. Thus, the specific cost object influences whether a cost is direct or indirect. For example, a cost might be directly associated with a single plant. The same cost, however, might not be directly associated with a particular department in the plant.
Answer (A) is incorrect. Behavior in response to volume changes is a factor only if the cost object is a product. Answer (B) is incorrect. The timing of an expense is not a means of classifying a cost as direct or indirect. Answer (D) is incorrect. Both direct and indirect costs can be either avoidable or unavoidable, depending upon the cost object.

7. Costs are allocated to cost objects in many ways and for many reasons. Which one of the following is a purpose of cost allocation?

A. Evaluating revenue center performance.
B. Measuring income and assets for external reporting.
C. Budgeting cash and controlling expenditures.
D. Aiding in variable costing for internal reporting.

Answer (B) is correct.
REQUIRED: The purpose of cost allocation.
DISCUSSION: Cost allocation is the process of assigning and reassigning costs to cost objects. It is used for those costs that cannot be directly associated with a specific cost object. Cost allocation is often used for purposes of measuring income and assets for external reporting purposes. Cost allocation is less meaningful for internal purposes because responsibility accounting systems emphasize controllability, a process often ignored in cost allocation.
Answer (A) is incorrect. A revenue center is evaluated on the basis of revenue generated, without regard to costs. Answer (C) is incorrect. Cost allocation is not necessary for cash budgeting and controlling expenditures. Answer (D) is incorrect. Allocations are not needed for variable costing, which concerns direct, not indirect, costs.

4.2 Cost Behavior and Relevant Range

8. The controller of a company has requested a quick estimate of the manufacturing supplies needed for the month of July when production is expected to be 470,000 units to meet the ending inventory requirements and sales of 475,000 units. The company's budget analyst has the following actual data for the last 3 months:

Month	Production in Units	Manufacturing Supplies
March	450,000	$723,060
April	540,000	853,560
May	480,000	766,560

Using these data and the high-low method to develop a cost estimating equation, the estimate of needed manufacturing supplies for July would be

A. $652,500
B. $681,500
C. $749,180
D. $752,060

Answer (D) is correct.
REQUIRED: The estimate of needed manufacturing supplies using the high-low method.
DISCUSSION: The fixed and variable portions of mixed costs may be estimated by identifying the highest and the lowest costs within the relevant range. The difference in cost divided by the difference in activity is the variable rate. Once the variable rate is found, the fixed portion is determinable. April and March provide the highest and lowest amounts. The difference in production was 90,000 units (540,000 April – 450,000 March), and the difference in the cost of supplies was $130,500 ($853,560 – $723,060). Hence, the unit variable cost was $1.45 ($130,500 ÷ 90,000 units). The total variable costs for March must have been $652,500 (450,000 units × $1.45 VC per unit), and the fixed cost must therefore have been $70,560 ($723,060 – $652,500). The probable costs for July equal $681,500 (470,000 units × $1.45 VC per unit), plus $70,560 of fixed costs, a total of $752,060.
Answer (A) is incorrect. The total variable costs for March equal $652,500. Answer (B) is incorrect. The variable portion of the total costs is $681,500. Answer (C) is incorrect. The amount of $749,180 is a nonsense answer.

9. Which of the following is the **best** example of a variable cost?

A. The corporate president's salary.
B. Cost of raw material.
C. Interest charges.
D. Property taxes.

Answer (B) is correct.
REQUIRED: The item that is a variable cost.
DISCUSSION: Variable costs vary directly with the level of production. As production increases or decreases, material cost increases or decreases, usually in a direct relationship.
Answer (A) is incorrect. The president's salary usually does not vary with production levels. Answer (C) is incorrect. Interest charges are independent of production levels. They are called "fixed" costs and are elements of overhead. Answer (D) is incorrect. Property taxes are independent of production levels. They are called "fixed" costs and are elements of overhead.

10. Which one of the following is **correct** regarding a relevant range?

A. Total variable costs will not change.
B. Total fixed costs will not change.
C. Actual fixed costs usually fall outside the relevant range.
D. The relevant range cannot be changed after being established.

Answer (B) is correct.
REQUIRED: The true statement about a relevant range.
DISCUSSION: The relevant range is the range of activity over which unit variable costs and total fixed costs are constant. The incremental cost of one additional unit of production will be equal to the variable cost.
Answer (A) is incorrect. Variable costs will change in total, but unit variable costs will be constant. Answer (C) is incorrect. Actual fixed costs should not vary greatly from budgeted fixed costs for the relevant range. Answer (D) is incorrect. The relevant range can change whenever production activity changes; the relevant range is merely an assumption used for budgeting and control purposes.

11. Which one of the following categories of cost is most likely **not** considered a component of fixed factory overhead?

A. Rent.
B. Property taxes.
C. Depreciation.
D. Power.

Answer (D) is correct.
REQUIRED: The item of cost most likely not considered a component of fixed factory overhead.
DISCUSSION: A fixed cost is one that remains unchanged within the relevant range for a given period despite fluctuations in activity. Such items as rent, property taxes, depreciation, and supervisory salaries are normally fixed costs because they do not vary with changes in production. Power costs, however, are at least partially variable because they increase as usage increases.
Answer (A) is incorrect. Rent is an example of fixed factory overhead. Answer (B) is incorrect. Property taxes are an example of fixed factory overhead. Answer (C) is incorrect. Depreciation is an example of fixed factory overhead.

12. An entity has the following cost components for 100,000 units of product for the year:

Direct materials $200,000
Direct labor 100,000
Manufacturing overhead 200,000
Selling and administrative expense 150,000

All costs are variable except for $100,000 of manufacturing overhead and $100,000 of selling and administrative expenses. The total costs to produce and sell 110,000 units for the year are

A. $650,000
B. $715,000
C. $695,000
D. $540,000

Answer (C) is correct.
REQUIRED: The flexible budget costs for producing and selling a given quantity.
DISCUSSION: Direct materials unit costs are strictly variable at $2 ($200,000 ÷ 100,000 units). Similarly, direct labor has a variable unit cost of $1 ($100,000 ÷ 100,000 units). The $200,000 of manufacturing overhead for 100,000 units is 50%. The variable unit cost is $1. Selling costs are $100,000 fixed and $50,000 variable for production of 100,000 units, and the variable unit selling expenses is $.50 ($50,000 ÷ 100,000 units). The total unit variable cost is therefore $4.50 ($2 + $1 + $1 + $.50). Fixed costs are $200,000. At a production level of 110,000 units, variable costs are $495,000 (110,000 units × $4.50). Hence, total costs are $695,000 ($495,000 + $200,000).
Answer (A) is incorrect. The cost at a production level of 100,000 units is $650,000. Answer (B) is incorrect. The amount of $715,000 assumes a variable unit cost of $6.50 with no fixed costs. Answer (D) is incorrect. Total costs are $695,000 based on a unit variable cost of $4.50 each.

13. The difference between variable costs and fixed costs is

A. Variable costs per unit fluctuate and fixed costs per unit remain constant.
B. Variable costs per unit are fixed over the relevant range and fixed costs per unit are variable.
C. Total variable costs are variable over the relevant range and fixed in the long term, while fixed costs never change.
D. Variable costs per unit change in varying increments, while fixed costs per unit change in equal increments.

Answer (B) is correct.
REQUIRED: The difference between variable and fixed costs.
DISCUSSION: Fixed costs remain unchanged within the relevant range for a given period despite fluctuations in activity, but per unit fixed costs do change as the level of activity changes. Thus, fixed costs are fixed in total but vary per unit as activity changes. Total variable costs vary directly with activity. They are fixed per unit, but vary in total.
Answer (A) is incorrect. Variable costs are fixed per unit; they do not fluctuate. Fixed costs per unit change as production changes. Answer (C) is incorrect. All costs are variable in the long term. Answer (D) is incorrect. Unit variable costs are fixed in the short term.

14. A corporation has the following information for the first quarter of its year:

	Machine Hours	Cleaning Expense
January	2,100	$ 900
February	2,600	1,200
March	1,600	800
April	2,000	1,000

Using the high-low method, what is the corporation's fixed cost?

A. $160
B. $320
C. $640
D. $1,040

Answer (A) is correct.
REQUIRED: The fixed cost using the high-low method.
DISCUSSION: Once the variable portion of a mixed cost has been determined using the high-low method (in this case, $400 cost difference ÷ 1,000 machine hours difference = $.40 per machine hour), it can be substituted in the total cost formula for one of the months to isolate the fixed portion.

Variable costs + Fixed costs = Total cost
(2,600 × $.40) + Fixed costs = $1,200
           Fixed costs = $1,200 − $1,040
           Fixed costs = $160

Answer (B) is incorrect. The fixed cost is not $320. Answer (C) is incorrect. The fixed cost is not $640. Answer (D) is incorrect. The variable cost at 2,600 machine hours is $1,040.

4.3 Cost Classification

15. Discretionary costs are costs that

A. Management decides to incur in the current period to enable the company to achieve objectives other than the filling of orders placed by customers.
B. Are likely to respond to the amount of attention devoted to them by a specified manger.
C. Are governed mainly by past decisions that established the present levels of operating and organizational capacity and that only change slowly in response to small changes in capacity.
D. Will be unaffected by current managerial decisions.

Answer (A) is correct.
REQUIRED: The definition of discretionary costs.
DISCUSSION: Discretionary costs are those that are incurred in the current period at the "discretion" of management and are not required to fill orders by customers.
Answer (B) is incorrect. Costs that are likely to respond to the amount of attention devoted to them by a specified manager are controllable costs. Answer (C) is incorrect. Costs required as a result of past decisions are committed costs. Answer (D) is incorrect. Costs unaffected by managerial decisions are costs such as committed costs and depreciation that were determined by decisions of previous periods.

16. The amount of raw materials left over from a production process or production cycle for which there is no further use is

A. Scrap.
B. Abnormal spoilage.
C. Waste.
D. Normal spoilage.

Answer (C) is correct.
REQUIRED: The raw materials left over from a production process or production cycle for which there is no further use.
DISCUSSION: Waste is the amount of raw materials left over from a production process or production cycle for which there is no further use. Waste is usually not salable at any price and must be discarded.
Answer (A) is incorrect. Scrap consists of raw materials left over from the production cycle but still usable for purposes other than those for which it was originally intended. Scrap may be sold to outside customers, usually for a nominal amount, or may be used for a different production process. Answer (B) is incorrect. Abnormal spoilage is spoilage that is not expected to occur under normal, efficient operating conditions. The cost of abnormal spoilage should be separately identified and reported to management. Abnormal spoilage is typically treated as a period cost (a loss) because of its unusual nature. Answer (D) is incorrect. Normal spoilage is the spoilage that occurs under normal operating conditions. It is essentially uncontrollable in the short run. Normal spoilage arises under efficient operations and is treated as a product cost.

17. An imputed cost is

A. The difference in total costs that results from selecting one alternative instead of another.
B. A cost that cannot be avoided because it has already been incurred.
C. A cost that does not entail any dollar outlay but is relevant to the decision-making process.
D. A cost that continues to be incurred even though there is no activity.

Answer (C) is correct.
REQUIRED: The definition of an imputed cost.
DISCUSSION: An imputed cost does not entail any dollar outlay but is relevant to the decision-making process.
Answer (A) is incorrect. The difference in total costs that results from selecting one alternative instead of another is a differential (also known as incremental or marginal) cost. Answer (B) is incorrect. A cost that cannot be avoided because it has already been incurred is a sunk cost. Answer (D) is incorrect. A cost that continues to be incurred even though there is no activity is a fixed cost.

18. The cost associated with abnormal spoilage ordinarily is charged to

A. Inventory.
B. A material variance account.
C. Manufacturing overhead.
D. A special loss account.

Answer (D) is correct.
REQUIRED: The method of accounting for abnormal spoilage.
DISCUSSION: Abnormal spoilage is usually charged to a special loss account because it is not expected to occur under normal, efficient operating conditions. Because it is unusual, it should be separately reported as a period cost.
Answer (A) is incorrect. Normal spoilage, not abnormal spoilage, costs are charged to inventory. Answer (B) is incorrect. Material variance accounts are only charged for the variances in material usage or material price, not the spoilage of product. Answer (C) is incorrect. While charging abnormal spoilage to manufacturing overhead is an occasional practice, it is not the ordinary practice.

19. Controllable costs are costs that

A. Management decides to incur in the current period to enable the company to achieve objectives other than the filling of orders placed by customers.
B. Are likely to respond to the amount of attention devoted to them by a specified manager.
C. Fluctuate in total in response to small changes in the rate of utilization of capacity.
D. Will be unaffected by current managerial decisions.

Answer (B) is correct.
REQUIRED: The definition of controllable costs.
DISCUSSION: Controllable costs can be affected by the efforts of a manager.
Answer (A) is incorrect. Costs incurred in a current period to achieve objectives other than the filling of orders by customers are known as discretionary costs. Answer (C) is incorrect. Costs that fluctuate with small changes in volume are variable costs. Answer (D) is incorrect. Costs that are unaffected by managerial decisions are costs such as committed costs and depreciation that was determined by decisions of previous periods.

20. Committed costs are

A. Costs that management decides to incur in the current period to enable the company to achieve objectives other than the filling of orders placed by customers.
B. Costs that are likely to respond to the amount of attention devoted to them by a specified manager.
C. Costs that are governed mainly by past decisions that established the present levels of operating and organizational capacity and that only change slowly in response to small changes in capacity.
D. Amortization of costs that were capitalized in previous periods.

Answer (C) is correct.
REQUIRED: The definition of committed costs.
DISCUSSION: Committed costs are those that are required as a result of past decisions.
Answer (A) is incorrect. Costs incurred in a current period to achieve objectives other than the filling of orders by customers are known as discretionary costs. Answer (B) is incorrect. Costs that are likely to respond to the amount of attention devoted to them by a specified manager are controllable costs. Answer (D) is incorrect. Amortization of costs capitalized in previous periods is depreciation.

21. A cost that bears an observable and known relationship to a quantifiable activity base is a(n)

A. Engineered cost.
B. Indirect cost.
C. Sunk cost.
D. Target cost.

Answer (A) is correct.
REQUIRED: The cost that bears an observable and known relationship to a quantifiable activity base.
DISCUSSION: A cost that bears an observable and known relationship to a quantifiable activity base is known as an engineered cost. Engineered costs have a clear relationship to output. Direct materials would be an example of an engineered cost.
Answer (B) is incorrect. An indirect cost does not have a clear relationship to output. Answer (C) is incorrect. A sunk cost is the result of a past irrevocable action; it is not important to future decisions. Answer (D) is incorrect. A target cost is the maximum allowable cost of a product and is calculated before the product is designed or produced.

22. Costs that arise from periodic budgeting decisions that have no strong input-output relationship are commonly called

A. Committed costs.
B. Discretionary costs.
C. Opportunity costs.
D. Differential costs.

Answer (B) is correct.
REQUIRED: The costs that have no strong input-output relationship.
DISCUSSION: Discretionary costs are characterized by uncertainty about the relationship between input (the costs) and the value of the related output. Advertising and research are examples. They should be contrasted with engineered costs, that is, costs having a clear input-output relationship (e.g., the cost of direct materials).
Answer (A) is incorrect. Committed costs are fixed costs arising from the possession of plant and equipment and a basic organization. These costs are affected primarily by long-run decisions as to a company's desired capacity. Answer (C) is incorrect. Opportunity cost is the return available from the next best use of a resource. Answer (D) is incorrect. Differential (incremental) costs are those that vary among decision options.

4.4 Costing Techniques

23. Which one of the following alternatives correctly classifies the business application to the appropriate costing system?

	Job Costing System	Process Costing System
A.	Wallpaper manufacturer	Oil refinery
B.	Aircraft assembly	Public accounting firm
C.	Paint manufacturer	Retail banking
D.	Print shop	Beverage manufacturer

Answer (D) is correct.
REQUIRED: The appropriate matching of business applications with costing systems.
DISCUSSION: A job costing system is used when products differ from one customer to the next, that is, when products are heterogeneous. A process costing system is used when similar products are mass produced on a continuous basis. A print shop, for example, would use a job costing system because each job will be unique. Each customer provides the specifications for the product desired. A beverage manufacturer, however, would use a process costing system because homogeneous units are produced continuously.
Answer (A) is incorrect. A wallpaper manufacturer would use a process costing system. Answer (B) is incorrect. A public accounting firm would use a job costing system. Answer (C) is incorrect. A paint manufacturer would use a process costing system.

24. Which one of the following is **least** likely to be involved in establishing standard costs for evaluation purposes?

A. Budgetary accountants.
B. Industrial engineers.
C. Top management.
D. Quality control personnel.

Answer (C) is correct.
REQUIRED: The persons least likely to be involved in the establishment of standard costs.
DISCUSSION: A standard cost is an estimate of what a cost should be under normal operating conditions based on studies by accountants and engineers. In addition, line management is usually involved in the setting of standard costs as are quality control personnel. Top management would not be involved because cost estimation is a lower level operating activity. Participation by affected employees in all control systems permits all concerned to understand both performance levels desired and the measurement criteria being applied.
Answer (A) is incorrect. Budgetary accountants are involved in the setting of standard costs. Answer (B) is incorrect. Industrial engineers are involved in the setting of standard costs. Answer (D) is incorrect. Quality control personnel are involved in the setting of standard costs.

25. In target costing,

A. The market price of the product is taken as a given.
B. Only raw materials, labor, and variable overhead cannot exceed a threshold target.
C. Only raw materials cannot exceed a threshold target.
D. Raw materials are recorded directly to cost of goods sold.

Answer (A) is correct.
REQUIRED: The true statement about target costing.
DISCUSSION: Target costing begins with a target price, which is the expected market price given the company's knowledge of its customers and competitors. Subtracting the unit target profit margin determines the long-term target cost. If this cost is lower than the full cost, the company may need to adopt comprehensive cost-cutting measures. For example, in the furniture industry, certain price points are popular with buyers: a couch might sell better at $400 than at $200 because consumers question the quality of a $200 couch and thus will not buy the lower-priced item. The result is that furniture manufacturers view $400 as the target price of a couch, and the cost must be lower.
Answer (B) is incorrect. All product cost categories are addressed by target costing. Answer (C) is incorrect. All product cost categories are addressed by target costing. Answer (D) is incorrect. The manner in which raw materials costs are accounted for is irrelevant.

26. Which one of the following considers the impact of fixed overhead costs?

A. Full absorption costing.
B. Marginal costing.
C. Direct costing.
D. Variable costing.

Answer (A) is correct.
REQUIRED: The method of costing that considers the impact of fixed overhead costs.
DISCUSSION: Full absorption costing treats fixed factory overhead costs as product costs. Thus, inventory and cost of goods sold include (absorb) fixed factory overhead.
Answer (B) is incorrect. Marginal costing considers only the incremental costs of producing an additional unit of product. In most cases marginal costs are variable costs. Answer (C) is incorrect. Direct (variable) costing treats only variable costs as product costs. Answer (D) is incorrect. Direct (variable) costing treats only variable costs as product costs.

27. An accounting system that collects financial and operating data on the basis of the underlying nature and extent of the cost drivers is

A. Direct costing.
B. Activity-based costing.
C. Cycle-time costing.
D. Variable costing.

Answer (B) is correct.
REQUIRED: The accounting system that collects data on the basis of cost drivers.
DISCUSSION: An activity-based costing (ABC) system identifies the causal relationship between the incurrence of cost and the underlying activities that cause those costs. Under an ABC system, costs are applied to products on the basis of resources consumed (drivers).
Answer (A) is incorrect. Direct costing is a system that treats fixed costs as period costs; in other words, production costs consist only of variable costs, while fixed costs are expensed as incurred. Answer (C) is incorrect. Cycle time is the period from the time a customer places an order to the time that product is delivered. Answer (D) is incorrect. Variable costing is the same as direct costing, which expenses fixed costs as incurred.

28. A standard costing system is **most** often used by a firm in conjunction with

A. Management by objectives.
B. Target (hurdle) rates of return.
C. Participative management programs.
D. Flexible budgets.

Answer (D) is correct.
REQUIRED: The manner in which a standard costing system is most often used.
DISCUSSION: A standard cost is an estimate of what a cost should be under normal operating conditions based on accounting and engineering studies. Comparing actual and standard costs permits an evaluation of the effectiveness of managerial performance. Because of the impact of fixed costs in most businesses, a standard costing system is usually not effective unless the company also has a flexible budgeting system. Flexible budgeting uses standard costs to prepare budgets for multiple activity levels.
Answer (A) is incorrect. MBO is a behavioral, communication-oriented, responsibility approach to employee self-direction. Although MBO can be used with standard costs, the two are not necessarily related. Answer (B) is incorrect. Rates of return relate to revenues as well as costs, but a standard costing system concerns costs only. Answer (C) is incorrect. Participative management stresses multidirectional communication. It has no relationship to standard costs.

29. Which of the following statements is **true** for a firm that uses variable costing?

A. The cost of a unit of product changes because of changes in number of units manufactured.
B. Profits fluctuate with sales.
C. An idle facility variation is calculated.
D. Product costs include variable administrative costs.

Answer (B) is correct.
REQUIRED: The true statement about variable costing.
DISCUSSION: In a variable costing system, only the variable costs are recorded as product costs. All fixed costs are expensed in the period incurred. Because changes in the relationship between production levels and sales levels do not cause changes in the amount of fixed manufacturing cost expensed, profits more directly follow the trends in sales.
Answer (A) is incorrect. The cost of a unit of product changing owing to a change in the number of units manufactured is a characteristic of absorption costing systems. Answer (C) is incorrect. Idle facility variation is a characteristic of absorption costing systems. Answer (D) is incorrect. Neither variable nor absorption costing includes administrative costs in inventory.

30. A difference between standard costs used for cost control and budgeted costs

A. Can exist because standard costs must be determined after the budget is completed.
B. Can exist because standard costs represent what costs should be, whereas budgeted costs represent expected actual costs.
C. Can exist because budgeted costs are historical costs, whereas standard costs are based on engineering studies.
D. Cannot exist because they should be the same amounts.

Answer (B) is correct.
REQUIRED: The true statement about the difference between standard costs and budgeted costs.
DISCUSSION: Standard costs are predetermined, attainable unit costs. Standard cost systems isolate deviations (variances) of actual from expected costs. One advantage of standard costs is that they facilitate flexible budgeting. Accordingly, standard and budgeted costs should not differ when standards are currently attainable. However, in practice, budgeted (estimated actual) costs may differ from standard costs when operating conditions are not expected to reflect those anticipated when the standards were developed.
Answer (A) is incorrect. Standard costs are determined independently of the budget. Answer (C) is incorrect. Budgeted costs are expected future costs, not historical costs. Answer (D) is incorrect. Budgeted and standard costs should in principle be the same, but in practice they will differ when standard costs are not expected to be currently attainable.

4.5 ESSAY QUESTIONS

Scenario for Essay Questions 1, 2, 3

Weng Laboratories is a relatively small company that produces widgets that started operations only a few years ago. The owner is considering expanding operations and has even considered introducing a certain amount of automation. Unfortunately, the owner of Weng Laboratories is not very knowledgeable about cost management. Production data for Weng for Year 1 and Year 2 year is as follows:

	Year 1	Year 2
Sales	$100,000	$110,000
Variable Production Costs	20,000	25,000
Fixed Production Costs	30,000	35,000
Variable S&A Expenses	15,000	20,000
Fixed S&A Expenses	20,000	25,000
Beginning Finished Goods Inventory	15,000	35,000
Ending Finished Goods Inventory	35,000 (Absorption Costing)	40,000 (Absorption Costing)
	25,000 (Variable Costing)	35,000 (Variable Costing)

Questions

1. If Weng adopts Absorption Costing, which costs are product costs and which costs are period costs? If Weng adopts Variable Costing, which costs are product costs and which costs are period costs?

2. If Weng adopts Absorption Costing, what is Operating Income for Year 1 and Year 2?

3. If Weng adopts Variable Costing, what is Operating Income for Year 1 and Year 2?

Essay Questions 1, 2, 3 — Unofficial Answers

1. Classification of costs depending on costing technique applied.

    a. Absorption Costing

    1) Product Costs
        a) Variable production costs
        b) Fixed production costs

    2) Period costs
        a) Variable S&A expenses
        b) Fixed S&A expenses

    b. Variable Costing

    1) Product costs
        a) Variable production costs

    2) Period costs
        a) Variable S&A expenses
        b) Fixed production costs
        c) Fixed S&A expenses

2. Absorption Costing

Year 1

Sales		$100,000
Beginning Finished Goods Inventory	$15,000	
Add: Variable Production Costs	20,000	
Add: Fixed Production Costs	30,000	
Goods Available for Sale	$65,000	
Less: Ending Finished Goods Inventory	(35,000)	
Cost of Goods Sold		(30,000)
Gross Margin		$70,000
Less: Variable S&A Expenses		(15,000)
Less: Fixed S&A Expenses		(20,000)
Operating Income		$35,000

Year 2

Sales		$110,000
Beginning Finished Goods Inventory	$35,000	
Add: Variable Production Costs	25,000	
Add: Fixed Production Costs	35,000	
Goods Available for Sale	$95,000	
Less: Ending Finished Goods Inventory	(40,000)	
Cost of Goods Sold		(55,000)
Gross Margin		$55,000
Less: Variable S&A Expenses		(20,000)
Less: Fixed S&A Expenses		(25,000)
Operating Income		$10,000

3. Variable Costing

   ### Year 1

Sales		$100,000
Beginning Finished Goods Inventory	$15,000	
Add: Variable Production Costs	20,000	
Goods Available for Sale	35,000	
Less: Ending Finished Goods Inventory	(25,000)	
Cost of Goods Sold		(10,000)
Less: Variable S&A Expenses		$ (15,000)
Contribution Margin		75,000
Less: Fixed Production Costs		(30,000)
Less: Fixed S&A Expenses		(20,000)
Operating Income		$ 25,000

   ### Year 2

Sales		$110,000
Beginning Finished Goods Inventory	$25,000	
Add: Variable Production Costs	25,000	
Goods Available for Sale	50,000	
Less: Ending Finished Goods Inventory	(35,000)	
Cost of Goods Sold		(15,000)
Less: Variable S&A Expenses		$ (20,000)
Contribution Margin		75,000
Less: Fixed Production Costs		(35,000)
Less: Fixed S&A Expenses		(25,000)
Operating Income		$ 15,000

Access the CMA Review System from your Gleim Personal Classroom to continue your studies with exam-emulating essay questions!

GLEIM® CMA Review Redefined™
Exceptional Coverage. Extraordinary Results.

Gleim set the standard with the **first** CMA course over 35 years ago.

It is the **most widely used** CMA review program, having trained more CMA candidates than any other course on the market.

Our innovative and guided approach is the only one of its kind.

STUDY UNIT FIVE
COST ACCUMULATION SYSTEMS

(22 pages of outline)

5.1	Job-Order Costing	141
5.2	Activity-Based Costing	144
5.3	Process Costing	152
5.4	Life-Cycle Costing	160
5.5	Essay Questions	175

This study unit is the **second of four** on **cost management**. The relative weight assigned to this major topic in Part 1 of the exam is **20%**. The four study units are

Study Unit 4: Cost Management Concepts
Study Unit 5: Cost Accumulation Systems
Study Unit 6: Cost Allocation Techniques
Study Unit 7: Operational Efficiency and Business Process Performance

If you are interested in reviewing more introductory or background material, go to www.gleim.com/CMAIntroVideos for a list of suggested third-party overviews of this topic. The following Gleim outline material is more than sufficient to help you pass the CMA exam; any additional introductory or background material is for your own personal enrichment.

5.1 JOB-ORDER COSTING

1. **Use of Job-Order Costing**

    a. Job-order costing is concerned with accumulating costs by specific job.

    1) This method is appropriate when producing products with individual characteristics (e.g., yachts), or when identifiable groupings are possible (e.g., jewelry). Units (jobs) should be dissimilar enough to warrant the special recordkeeping required by job-order costing. Products are usually custom made for a specific customer.

2. **Steps in Job-Order Costing**

    a. The first step in the process is the receipt of a sales order from a customer requesting a product or special group of products.
    b. The sales order is approved, and a production order is issued.
    c. Costs are recorded by classification, such as direct materials, direct labor, and manufacturing overhead, on a job-cost sheet (may be manual or electronic) that is specifically prepared for each job.

    1) The physical inputs required for the production process are obtained from suppliers. The journal entry to record the acquisition of inventory would be

Raw materials	$XXX
Accounts payable	$XXX

    2) Under job-order costing, direct materials and direct labor are charged based on the amounts actually applied to each job.

    a) Materials requisition forms request direct materials to be pulled from the warehouse and sent to the production line.

Work-in-process – Job 1015	$XXX
Raw materials	$XXX

b) Time tickets track the direct labor that workers expend on various jobs.

Work-in-process – Job 1015	$XXX	
Wages payable		$XXX

3) Under job-order costing, the third component, manufacturing overhead, is charged using an estimated rate.

   a) The application of an estimated overhead rate is necessary under job-order costing because the outputs are customized and the processes vary from period to period.

   b) As indirect costs are paid throughout the year, they are collected in the manufacturing overhead control account.

   i) Note that work-in-process is not affected when actual overhead costs are incurred.

   ii) The debits are made to a manufacturing overhead control account, not work-in-process.

Manufacturing overhead control	$XXX	
Property taxes payable		$XXX
Manufacturing overhead control	$XXX	
Prepaid insurance		$XXX
Manufacturing overhead control	$XXX	
Accumulated depreciation – factory equipment		$XXX

   c) Overhead costs are applied to ("absorbed" by) each job based on a predetermined overhead application rate for the year (such as $5 per direct labor hour, or machine hour, etc., or based on an activity-based costing system). If activity-based costing is used, the procedure for overhead applications is the same as above, except that multiple rates based on multiple cost drivers will be used (such as $5 per direct labor hour, plus $2 per machine hour, plus $1 per material requisition used).

   i) At the beginning of the year, an estimate is made of the total amount that will be spent for manufacturing overhead during that year.

   ii) An estimate is also made of the total quantity of allocation base, such as direct labor hours or machine hours, that will be required for manufacturing overhead during that year.

$$\text{Application Rate} = \frac{\text{Estimated Total Manufacturing Overhead}}{\text{Estimated Total Quantity of Allocation Base}}$$

   iii) The application rate is calculated by dividing the estimate of the total amount that will be spent for manufacturing overhead during that year by the estimated total amount of allocation base.

   iv) The amount applied equals the number of units of the allocation base used during the period times the application rate.

$$\text{Amount Overhead Applied} = \text{Total Quantity of Allocation Base} \times \text{Application Rate}$$

   - The credit is to manufacturing overhead applied, a contra-account for manufacturing overhead control.

Work-in-process – Job 1015	$XXX	
Manufacturing overhead applied		$XXX

   v) By tracking the amounts applied to the various jobs in a separate account, the actual amounts spent on overhead are preserved in the balance of the overhead control account.

- In addition, the firm can determine at any time how precise its estimate of overhead costs for the period was by comparing the balances in the two accounts. The closer they are (in absolute value terms), the better the estimate was.

d) At the end of the period, the overhead control and applied accounts are netted to examine any differences, which are called variances.

i) If the result is a credit, overhead was overapplied for the period. If the result is a debit, overhead was underapplied.

- If the difference is immaterial, it can be closed directly to cost of goods sold.
- If the difference is material, it should be allocated based on the relative values of work-in-process, finished goods, and cost of goods sold.

4) The amounts from the input documents are accumulated on job-cost sheets. These serve as a subsidiary ledger page for each job.

a) The total of all job-cost sheets for jobs in progress will equal the balance in the general ledger work-in-process inventory account.

b) Once the job is completed, but before it is delivered to the customer, the job-cost sheet serves as the subsidiary ledger for the finished goods inventory account.

d. When a job order is completed, all the costs are transferred to finished goods.

Finished goods $X,XXX
  Work-in-process – Job 1015 $X,XXX

e. When the output is sold, the appropriate portion of the cost is transferred to cost of goods sold.

Cost of goods sold $X,XXX
  Finished goods $X,XXX

3. **Job-Order Cost Flow Diagram**

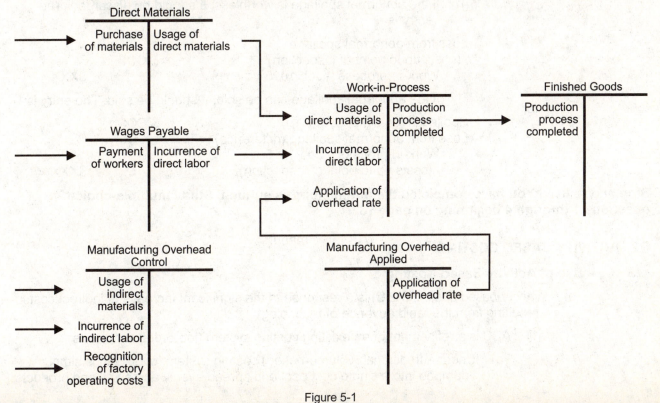

Figure 5-1

CMA candidates will be expected to understand the proper accounting procedure for normal and abnormal spoilage under both job-order costing and process costing. In job-order costing, normal spoilage is treated as a product cost while abnormal spoilage is treated as a period cost. It is important to understand not only that they are treated differently, but why. When answering questions pertaining to spoilage, pay attention to the question stem, what system is being used, and whether the product can be sold or not.

4. **Spoilage**

   a. Output that does not meet the quality standards for salability is considered spoilage.

      1) **Normal spoilage** is the amount expected in the ordinary course of production.

         a) Because management understands that good units cannot be produced without some risk of spoilage, the cost of the normal spoilage is included in the cost of the good units produced.

         b) This is accomplished by allowing the net cost of the spoilage to remain in the work-in-process account of the job that generated it.

            i) If the normal spoilage is worthless, it should be discarded. No journal entry will be made.

            ii) If the normal spoilage can be sold, its value should **not** be included in the cost of the good units produced. The entry is

            Spoiled inventory (at fair market value) $XXX
                Work-in-process – Job 1015 $XXX

      2) **Abnormal spoilage** is spoilage over and above the amount expected in the ordinary course of production.

         a) Abnormal spoilage is **not** treated as a manufacturing cost and is **not** included in the cost of the good units produced.

         b) Instead, abnormal spoilage costs are expensed in the period they occurred or the loss may be accrued. This is accomplished by charging a loss account for the net cost of the spoilage.

            i) If the abnormal spoilage is worthless, it should be discarded. The entry is

            Loss from abnormal spoilage
              (costs up to point of inspection) $XXX
                Work-in-process – Job 1015 $XXX

            ii) If the abnormal spoilage can be sold, it should be sold. The entry is

            Spoiled inventory $XXX
            Loss from abnormal spoilage (difference)   XXX
                Work-in-process – Job 1015 $XXX
                (costs up to point of inspection)

Stop and review! You have completed the outline for this subunit. Study multiple-choice questions 1 through 4 beginning on page 162.

5.2 ACTIVITY-BASED COSTING

1. **Use of Activity-Based Costing**

   a. Activity-based costing (ABC) is a response to the significant increase in indirect costs resulting from the rapid advance of technology.

      1) ABC is a refinement of an existing costing system (job-order or process).

         a) Under a traditional (volume-based) costing system, overhead is simply dumped into a single cost pool and spread evenly across all end products.

SU 5: Cost Accumulation Systems   145

        b) Under ABC, indirect costs are attached to activities that are then rationally allocated to end products.

        c) ABC may be used by manufacturing, service, or retailing entities.

2. **Traditional (Volume-Based) Costing System**

    a. The inaccurate averaging or spreading of indirect costs over products or service units that use different amounts of resources is sometimes called **peanut-butter costing**.

        1) Peanut-butter costing results in **product-cost cross-subsidization**, the condition in which the miscosting of one product causes the miscosting of other products.

        2) The peanut-butter effect of using a traditional (i.e., volume-based) costing system can be summarized as follows:

            a) Direct labor and direct materials are traced to products or service units.

            b) A single pool of indirect costs (overhead) is accumulated for a given organizational unit.

            c) Indirect costs from the pool are assigned using an allocative (rather than a tracing) procedure, such as using a single overhead rate for an entire department, e.g., $3 of overhead for every direct labor hour.

                i) The effect is an averaging of costs that may result in significant inaccuracy when products or service units do not use similar amounts of resources.

EXAMPLE of Product-Cost Cross-Subsidization

A company produces two similar products. Both products require one unit of raw material and one hour of direct labor. Raw materials costs are $14 per unit, and direct labor is $70 per hour. During the month just ended, the company produced 1,000 units of Product A and 100 units of Product B. Manufacturing overhead for the month totaled $20,000.

Using direct labor hours as the overhead allocation base, per-unit costs and profits are calculated as follows:

	Product A	Product B	Total
Raw materials	$ 14,000	$ 1,400	
Direct labor	70,000	7,000	
Overhead {$20,000 × [$70,000 ÷ ($70,000 + $7,000)]}	18,182		
Overhead {$20,000 × [$7,000 ÷ ($70,000 + $7,000)]}		1,818	
Total costs	**$102,182**	**$ 10,218**	**$112,400**
Selling price	$ 119.99	$ 119.99	
Cost per unit	(102.18)	(102.18)	
Profit per unit	**$ 17.81**	**$ 17.81**	

The company's management accountants have determined that overhead consists almost entirely of production line setup costs, and that the two products require equal setup times. Allocating overhead on this basis yields vastly different results.

	Product A	Product B	Total
Raw materials	$14,000	$ 1,400	
Direct labor	70,000	7,000	
Overhead ($20,000 × 50%)	10,000		
Overhead ($20,000 × 50%)		10,000	
Total costs	**$94,000**	**$18,400**	**$112,400**
Selling price	$119.99	$119.99	
Cost per unit	(94.00)	(184.00)	
Profit per unit	**$ 25.99**	**$ (64.01)**	

Rather than the comfortable profit the company believed it was making on both products using peanut-butter costing, it becomes clear that the company is losing money on every unit of Product B that it sells. The high-volume Product A has been heavily subsidizing the setup costs for the low-volume Product B.

b. The preceding example assumes a single component of overhead for clarity. In reality, overhead is made up of many components.

1) The peanut-butter effect of traditional overhead allocation is illustrated in the following diagram:

Overhead Allocation in a Traditional (Volume-Based) Cost Accumulation System

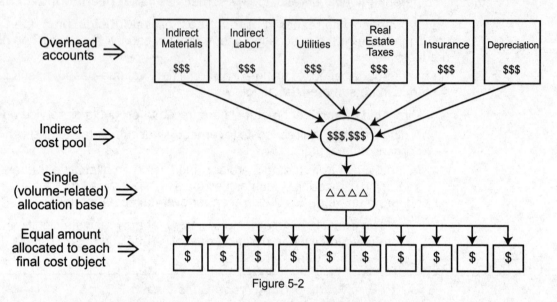

Figure 5-2

3. **Traditional-Based Systems vs. Activity-Based Systems**

   a. Traditional-based systems were appropriate when direct costs were the bulk of manufacturing costs. However, increased automation led to increased overhead. ABC was developed to address the increasing complexity of overhead costs.

      1) **Traditional-based systems**, as illustrated above, involve

         a) Accumulating costs in general ledger accounts (utilities, taxes, etc.),
         b) Using a single cost pool to combine the costs in all the related accounts,
         c) Selecting a single driver to use for the entire indirect cost pool, and
         d) Allocating the indirect cost pool to final cost objects.

      2) **Activity-based systems**, by contrast, involve

         a) Identifying organization activities that constitute overhead,
         b) Assigning the costs of resources consumed by the activities, and
         c) Assigning the costs of the activities to final cost objects, based on the activity that drives (causes) the costs.

4. **Steps in Activity-Based Costing**

   a. **Step 1 – Activity Analysis**

      1) An activity is a set of work actions undertaken within the entity, and a cost pool is established for each activity.
      2) Activities are classified in a hierarchy according to the level of the production process at which they take place.

         a) **Unit-level activities** are performed for each unit of output produced. Examples are using direct materials and using direct labor.
         b) **Batch-level activities** occur for each group of outputs produced. Examples are materials ordering, materials handling, and production line setup.

c) **Product-sustaining** (or service-sustaining) **activities** support the production of a particular product (or service), irrespective of the level of production. Examples are product design, engineering changes, and testing.

d) **Facility-sustaining activities** concern overall operations and therefore cannot be traced to products at any point in the production process. Examples are accounting, human resources, maintenance of physical plant, and safety/security arrangements.

EXAMPLE

Fabulous Foundry uses a job-order system to accumulate costs for the custom pipe fittings of all sizes that it produces. Since the 1950s, Fabulous has accumulated overhead costs in six general ledger accounts (indirect materials, indirect labor, utilities, real estate taxes, insurance, and depreciation), combined them into a single indirect cost pool, and allocated the total to its products based on machine hours.

- At the time this system was established, overhead was a relatively small percentage of the foundry's total manufacturing costs.
- With increasing reliance on robots in the production process and computers for monitoring and control, overhead is now a greater percentage of the manufacturing costs while direct labor costs have shrunk.

To obtain better data about product costs, Fabulous has decided to refine its job-order costing system by switching to activity-based costing for the allocation of overhead.

- The foundry's management accountants conducted extensive interviews with production and sales personnel to determine how the incurrence of indirect costs can be viewed as activities that consume resources.
- The accountants identified five activities and created a cost pool for each to capture the incurrence of indirect costs:

Activity	Hierarchy
Product design	Product-sustaining
Production setup	Batch-level
Machining	Unit-level
Inspection & testing	Unit-level
Customer maintenance	Facility-sustaining

---

b. **Step 2 – Assign Resource Drivers to Resource Costs**

1) Identifying resource costs in ABC is more complex than it is in volume-based overhead allocation.

a) A separate accounting system may be necessary to track resource costs separately from the general ledger.

2) Once the resources have been identified, resource drivers are designated to allocate resource costs to the activity cost pools.

a) Resource drivers (causes) are measures of the resources consumed by an activity.

EXAMPLE

Fabulous Foundry's management accountants identified the following resources used by its indirect cost processes:

Resource	Driver
Computer processing	CPU cycles
Production line	Machine hours
Materials management	Hours worked
Accounting	Hours worked
Sales & marketing	Number of orders

c. **Step 3 – Allocate Resource Costs to Activity Cost Pools**
   1) Once the resource drivers are determined, the dollar amount of resources per resource driver can be determined.
      a) One method of doing this is by dividing the total dollar amount of a resource cost by the total amount of the resource driver used by the entire entity.
   2) Costs of resources are then allocated to activity cost pools based on the amount of resource drivers used by each activity cost pool.

EXAMPLE

Fabulous Foundry's management accountants have determined that a total amount of $1,000,000 of Materials Management was used over a total of 100,000 hours worked. Fabulous's management accountants will therefore allocate $10 ($1,000,000 ÷ 100,000 hours) to each activity pool for each hour of Materials Management worked for each cost pool.

Activity	Amount Allocated
Product Design	$250,000 for 25,000 hours
Production Setup	$270,000 for 27,000 hours
Machining	$450,000 for 45,000 hours
Inspection & Testing	$30,000 for 3,000 hours
Customer Maintenance	$0 for 0 hours

---

   3) This allocation is done for each resource. This is termed first-stage allocation.
      a) Some cost activities may not be allocated resources if that cost activity did not use those resources.

d. **Step 4 – Allocate Activity Cost Pools to Final Cost Objects**
   1) The final step in enacting an ABC system is allocating the activity cost pools to final cost objects. This is termed second-stage allocation.
   2) Once the cost drivers are determined, the dollar amount of activity pool per activity driver can be determined.
      a) One method of doing this is by dividing the total dollar amount assigned to an activity cost pool by the total amount of the activity driver used by the entire entity.
   3) Costs are reassigned to final-stage (or, if intermediate cost objects are used, next-stage) cost objects on the basis of activity drivers.
      a) Activity drivers are measures of the demands made on an activity by next-stage cost objects, such as the number of parts in a product used to measure an assembly activity.

EXAMPLE

Fabulous Foundry's management accountants have designated these drivers to associate with their corresponding activities:

Activity	Driver
Product design	Number of products
Production setup	Number of setups
Machining	Number of units produced
Inspection & testing	Number of units produced
Customer maintenance	Number of orders

SU 5: Cost Accumulation Systems   149

5. **Indirect Cost Assignment Diagram**

   a. The differences between traditional overhead allocation and activity-based costing are illustrated in the following diagram:

   Indirect Cost Assignment in an Activity-Based Costing System

   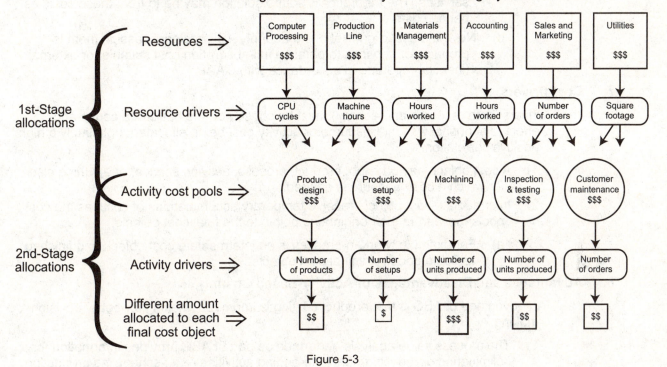

   Figure 5-3

6. **Process Value Analysis**

   a. Design of an ABC system starts with process value analysis, a comprehensive understanding of how an organization generates its output.

   1) A process value analysis involves a determination of which activities that use resources are value-adding or nonvalue-adding and how the latter may be reduced or eliminated.

      a) A **value-adding activity** contributes to customer satisfaction or meets a need of the entity. The perception is that it cannot be omitted without a loss of the quantity, quality, or responsiveness of output demanded by the entity or its customers.

      b) A **nonvalue-adding activity** does not make such a contribution. It can be eliminated, reduced, or redesigned without impairing the quantity, quality, or responsiveness of the product or service desired by customers or the entity.

   2) The linkage of product costing and continuous improvement of processes is activity-based management (ABM). It encompasses driver analysis, activity analysis, and performance measurement.

   b. Using a four-level driver-analysis model, activities are grouped, and drivers are determined for the activities.

   1) Within each grouping of activities, the cost pools for activities that can use the same driver are combined into homogeneous cost pools.

      a) In contrast, traditional systems assign costs largely on the basis of unit-level drivers.

2) A difficulty in applying ABC is that, although the first three levels of activities (unit-, batch-, and product-level) pertain to specific products or services, facility-level activities do not.

   a) Thus, facility-level costs are not accurately assignable to products or services. The theoretically sound solution may be to treat these costs as period costs.

   b) Nevertheless, organizations that apply ABC ordinarily assign them to products or services to obtain a full-absorption cost suitable for external financial reporting in accordance with GAAP.

7. **Cost Drivers**

   a. Drivers (both resource and activity) must be chosen on the basis of a cause-and-effect relationship with the resource or activity cost being allocated, not simply a high positive correlation.

      1) A cost object may be a job, product, process, activity, service, or anything else for which a cost measure is desired.

      2) Intermediate cost objects receive temporary accumulations of costs as the cost pools move from their originating points to the final cost objects.

         a) For example, work-in-process is an intermediate cost object, and finished salable goods are final cost objects.

8. **Advantages and Disadvantages of Activity-Based Costing**

   a. An advantage of ABC is that product costing is improved, making for better decision making.

      1) The process value analysis performed as part of ABC provides information for eliminating or reducing nonvalue-adding activities (e.g., scheduling production, moving components, waiting for the next operating step, inspecting output, or storing inventories).

         a) The result is therefore not only more accurate cost assignments, especially of overhead, but also better cost control and more efficient operations.

      2) The real benefits of ABC occur when a company has a high level of fixed costs and produces a wide variety of products with widely varying levels of production.

   b. Disadvantages of ABC are its cost of implementation and the increased time and effort needed to (1) maintain a separate accounting system to capture resource costs and (2) design and implement drivers and cost pools.

      1) Initial costs are quite high, and continuing costs of application can also be significant. Thus, if a company has a low level of fixed costs, there is little to no advantage in using ABC as compared to a simple overhead application method, such as a fixed amount per direct labor hour.

      2) Similarly, if a company produces a single product, there is no advantage. Also, if volume levels among various products do not vary too much, there is little advantage.

      3) ABC-derived costs of products or services may not conform with GAAP; for example, ABC may assign research costs to products but not traditional product costs such as plant depreciation, insurance, or taxes.

9. **Organizational Benefits**
    a. Organizations most likely to benefit from using ABC are those with products or services that vary significantly in volume, diversity of activities, and complexity of operations; relatively high overhead costs; or operations that have undergone major technological or design changes.
        1) Although the previous illustrations have assumed a manufacturing operation, service organizations also can use ABC and receive most of the advantages. However, service organizations may have some difficulty in implementing ABC because they tend to have relatively high facility-level costs that are difficult to assign to specific service units.
            a) Service organizations also engage in many nonuniform human activities for which information is not readily accumulated.
            b) Moreover, output measurement is more problematic in service than in manufacturing entities.
            c) Nevertheless, ABC has been adopted by various insurers, banks, railroads, and healthcare providers.
    b. Direct labor (hours or dollars) has long been the most common base for allocating overhead because of the simplicity of the calculation, but it is not always relevant.
        1) Companies now use dozens of different allocation bases depending on how activity affects overhead costs. One company reported that it used 37 different bases to allocate overhead, some of which were averages of several activities.
        2) In principle, a separate overhead account or subsidiary ledger account should be used for each type of overhead.
        3) In the past, "people were cheap and machines were expensive." This meant that direct labor was ordinarily a larger component of total production cost than overhead and was the activity that drove (caused) overhead costs.
            a) Due to the lowered cost of computers and robotics and the expansion of employee benefits ("machines are cheap and people are expensive"), overhead is more likely to be a large component of total production cost, with direct labor often a small percentage.
            b) Most overhead costs vary in proportion to product diversity and the complexity of an operation.
                i) Direct labor is not a cost driver for most overhead costs.
            c) Allocating a very large cost (overhead) using a very small cost (direct labor) as a base is irrational.
                i) A small change in direct labor on a product can make a significant difference in total production cost, an effect that may rest on an invalid assumption about the relationship of the cost and the allocation base.
        4) As previously noted, ABC is more useful when overhead costs are relatively high.
            a) Also, the more diverse a company's line of products or services or the more significant the volume differences among its products or services, the more beneficial ABC will be.

c. Companies use ABC because of its ability to solve costing problems that conventional cost accounting either creates or fails to address.

1) These problems include suboptimal pricing, poor allocation of costs, and incorrect direction by management.
2) For example, if overhead is allocated at 700% of direct labor, managers may try to reduce direct labor costs by $1 to reduce the amount of overhead allocated by $7.
   a) But the better decision may be to ignore direct labor and concentrate on such cost-cutting efforts as eliminating setups, engineering changes, and movement of materials.

Stop and review! You have completed the outline for this subunit. Study multiple-choice questions 5 through 11 beginning on page 164.

5.3 PROCESS COSTING

1. **Use of Process Costing**

    a. Process cost accounting is used to assign costs to inventoriable goods or services. It is applicable to relatively homogeneous products that are mass produced on a continuous basis (e.g., petroleum products, thread, computer monitors).

        1) Assigning an exact amount of materials, labor, and indirect costs to thousands, or even millions, of individual end products is simply not cost-effective. For this reason, process costing involves averaging the costs of production and allocating them to work-in-process and finished goods.

2. **Accumulation of Costs**

    a. The accumulation of costs under a process costing system is **by department rather than by project**. There will normally be a work-in-process inventory account for each department.

        1) This reflects the continuous, homogeneous nature of the manufacturing process.

    b. As in job-order costing, the physical inputs required for the production process are obtained from suppliers.

    Raw materials $XXX
        Accounts payable $XXX

    c. **Direct materials** actually used by the first department in the process (Department A) are added to work-in-process for that department.

    Work-in-process – Department A $XXX
        Raw materials $XXX

d. **Conversion costs**, which include direct labor and manufacturing overhead used by the first department, are added to work-in-process for that department.

1) Actual amounts are used.
2) Standard costs are applied at a later stage for purposes of variance analysis.

Work-in-process – Department A	$XXX	
Wages payable (direct and indirect labor)		$XXX
Manufacturing supplies (indirect materials)		XXX
Property taxes payable		XXX
Prepaid insurance		XXX
Accumulated depreciation – factory equipment		XXX

e. The products can move from one department to the next (from Department A to Department B).

Work-in-process – Department B	$XXX	
Work-in-process – Department A		$XXX

f. The second department (Department B) can add more direct materials and more conversion costs.

Work-in-process – Department B	$XXX	
Raw materials		$XXX
Work-in-process – Department B	$XXX	
Wages payable (direct and indirect labor)		$XXX
Manufacturing supplies (indirect materials)		XXX
Property taxes payable		XXX
Prepaid insurance		XXX
Accumulated depreciation – factory equipment		XXX

g. If a standard costing system is used, standard costs are applied before transfer from work-in-process to finished goods.

1) The differences are accumulated in a direct materials variance and a conversion costs variance account.

h. When processing is finished in the last department, all the costs are transferred to finished goods.

Finished goods	$XXX	
Work-in-process – Department B		$XXX

i. As products are sold, the costs are transferred to cost of goods sold.

Cost of goods sold	$XXX	
Finished goods		$XXX

3. **Process Costing Cost Flow Diagram**

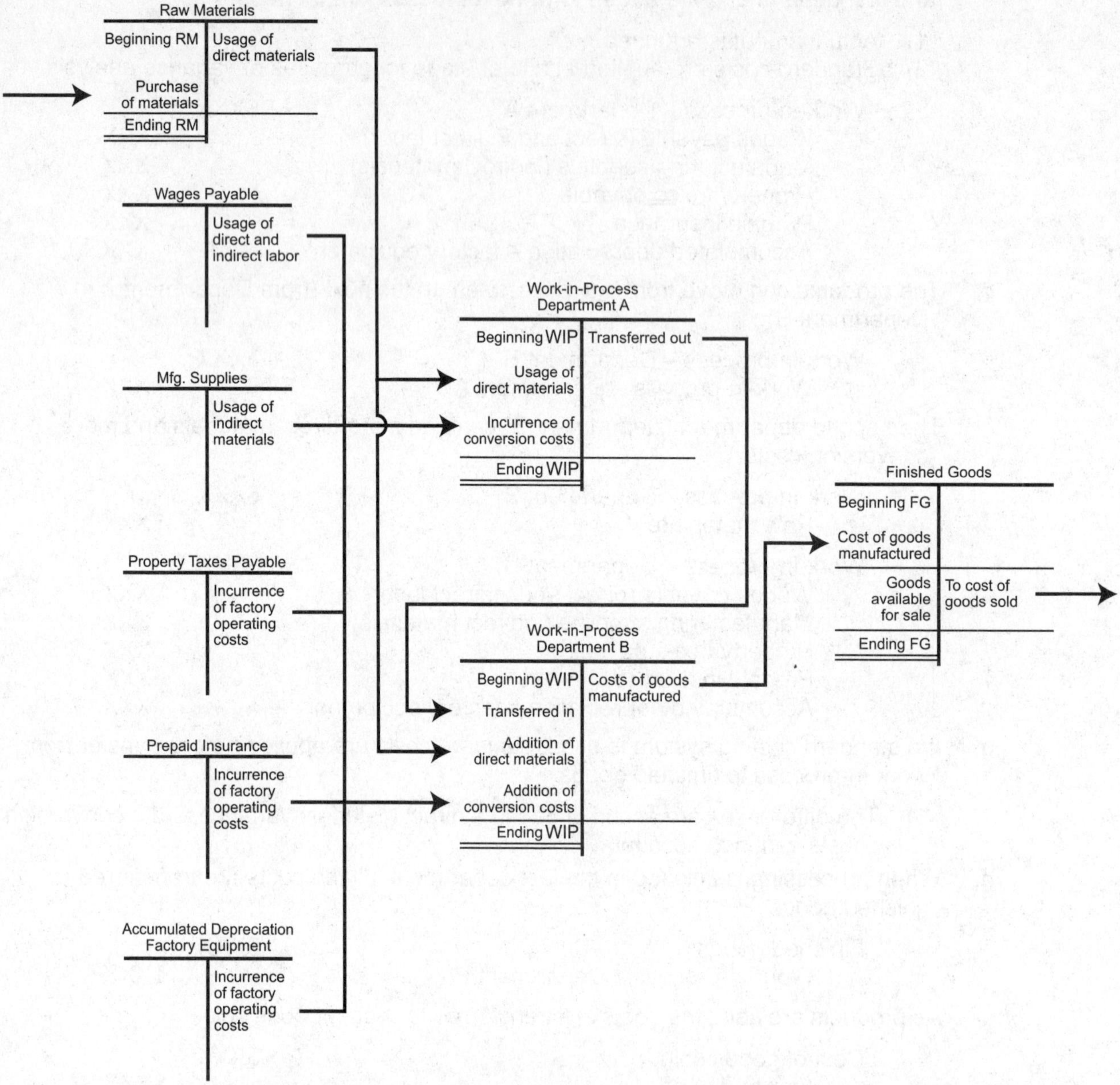

Figure 5-4

4. **Equivalent Units of Production – Basics**

   a. Some units remain unfinished at the end of the period. For each department to account adequately for costs attached to its unfinished units, the units must be restated in terms of equivalent units of production (EUP).

      1) EUP are the number of complete units that could have been produced using the inputs consumed during the period.

EXAMPLE

One thousand work-in-process units completed 80% for direct materials and 60% for conversion costs would represent 800 EUP of direct materials (1,000 × 80%) and 600 EUP of conversion costs (1,000 × 60%).

---

      2) Cost-per-unit can be calculated using EUP (cost per EUP).

b. In all EUP calculations, three populations of units must be accounted for:
   1) Units in beginning work-in-process (beginning WIP)
      a) Units in beginning WIP can be calculated as follows:

      $$\begin{array}{r} \text{Units transferred out} \\ +\ \text{Ending WIP} \\ -\ \text{Units started} \\ \hline \underline{\text{Beginning WIP}} \end{array}$$

   2) Units started and completed during the current period
      a) Units started and completed can be calculated as follows:

      $$\begin{array}{r} \text{Units transferred out} \\ -\ \text{Beginning WIP} \\ \hline \underline{\text{Units started and completed}} \end{array} \quad \text{OR} \quad \begin{array}{r} \text{Units started} \\ -\ \text{Ending WIP} \\ \hline \underline{\text{Units started and completed}} \end{array}$$

   3) Units in ending work-in-process (ending WIP)
      a) Units in ending WIP can be calculated as follows:

      $$\begin{array}{r} \text{Beginning WIP} \\ +\ \text{Units started} \\ -\ \text{Units transferred out} \\ \hline \underline{\text{Ending WIP}} \end{array}$$

      b) These units have not been completed during the period.

c. There are two methods for calculating EUP:
   1) Under the **weighted-average method**, the beginning WIP is treated as if it is started and completed during the current period.
   2) Under the **first-in, first-out (FIFO) method**, work done in the current period on units in beginning WIP are included in the calculation.
      a) For example, units in beginning WIP that are 40% complete at the beginning of the period will require an additional 60% of work in the current period for those units to be completed. The 60% of work done in the current period is included in EUP, while the 40% done in the previous period is not.

5. **Equivalent Units of Production – Materials**
   a. Materials can be added at the beginning. Refer to Section A. of the Extended Example that begins on page 157 for an illustration.
      1) Units in beginning WIP are already 100% complete with respect to direct materials; however, whether or not they produce current-period EUP depends on the method used to calculate EUP.
      2) Beginning WIP -- Weighted-average method
         a) Units in beginning WIP are treated as 100% complete and **will produce EUP in the current period** even though materials were added in the previous period.
      3) Beginning WIP -- FIFO method
         a) Units in beginning WIP **will not produce EUP in the current period** since materials were added in the previous period.
      4) Units started and completed are always 100% complete with respect to direct materials.

5) Units in ending WIP are 100% complete with respect to direct materials when materials are all added at the beginning of the production process.

   a) All materials will be treated as being added during the current period.

b. Materials can be added evenly throughout the process. Refer to Section B. of the Extended Example that begins on page 157 for an illustration.

   1) It is important to note both the method used and the completion percentage.
   2) Beginning WIP -- Weighted-average method

      a) Units in beginning WIP are treated as 100% complete and **will produce EUP in the current period** even though materials were added in the previous period.

   3) Beginning WIP -- FIFO method

      a) Since we are looking for the amount completed in the current period, we subtract the completion percentage from 100%. This will give us the percentage completed in the current period.

      b) For example, if there are 1,000 units in beginning WIP that are 30% complete with respect to materials, 70% (100% – 30%) will be completed in the current period.

         i) EUP from beginning WIP will be 700 units (1,000 units × 70%).

   4) Units started and completed are always 100% complete with respect to direct materials.
   5) Units in ending WIP will be complete based on the completion percentage.

      a) For example, if there are 1,000 units in ending WIP that are 60% complete with respect to materials, 60% were completed in the current period.

         i) EUP from ending WIP will be 600 units (1,000 units × 60%).

c. Materials added at a specific time during production:

   1) Whether or not materials are included in the current period's calculation of EUP depends on when materials would have been added and whether or not that point was reached.
   2) Beginning WIP

      a) If the point at which materials are added occurs during the current period, beginning WIP will produce EUP.

      b) If the point at which materials are added occurred during the previous period, beginning WIP will not produce EUP for the current period.

      c) For example, assume that materials are added at 50% completion. If beginning WIP is 20% complete, materials have not been added yet. All materials will be added in the current period, and the units will count 100% toward EUP.

         i) If beginning WIP is 60% complete, materials were added in the prior period and no more materials will be added in the current period. Therefore, these materials will not produce EUP in the current period.

   3) Units started and completed are always 100% complete with respect to direct materials.
   4) Ending WIP

      a) If the point at which materials are added occurred during the current period, ending WIP will produce EUP for the current period.

      b) If the point at which materials are added occurs during the next period, ending WIP will not produce EUP for the current period.

SU 5: Cost Accumulation Systems 157

c) For example, assume that materials are added at 50% completion. If ending WIP is 20% complete, materials have not been added yet. Therefore, these units will not produce EUP in the current period.

i) If ending WIP is 60% complete, materials were added during the current period and these units will produce EUP in the current period.

6. **Equivalent Units of Production – Conversion Costs**

   a. Since conversion costs are generally added throughout the process, these calculations are similar to those in item 5.b. Refer to Section C. of the Extended Example that begins below for an illustration.

   b. It is important to note both the method used and the completion percentage.

      1) Beginning WIP -- Weighted-average method

         a) Units in beginning WIP are treated as 100% complete and **will produce EUP in the current period** even though conversion costs were added in the previous period.

      2) Beginning WIP -- FIFO method

         a) Since we are looking for the amount completed in the current period, we subtract the completion percentage from 100%. This will give us the percentage completed in the current period.

         b) For example, if there are 1,000 units in beginning WIP that are 20% complete with respect to conversion costs, 80% (100% – 20%) will be completed in the current period.

            i) EUP from beginning WIP will be 800 units (1,000 units × 80%).

      3) Units started and completed are always 100% complete with respect to conversion costs.

      4) Units in ending WIP will be complete based on the completion percentage.

         a) For example, if there are 1,000 units in ending WIP that are 10% complete with respect to conversion costs, 10% were completed in the current period.

            i) EUP from ending WIP will be 100 units (1,000 units × 10%).

EXTENDED EXAMPLE

Quantity Schedule

	Units	Completed for Direct Materials	Completed for Conversion Costs
Beginning work-in-process	2,000	80%	40%
Units started during period	8,000		
Units to account for	10,000		
Units transferred to next department	9,000		
Ending work-in-process	1,000	90%	70%
Units accounted for	10,000		

In all EUP calculations, three populations of units must be accounted for:

- Beginning WIP: 2,000 (given)
- Units started and completed in the current period

  ```
    9,000 Units transferred out          8,000 Units started
  − 2,000 Beginning WIP               − 1,000 Ending WIP
    7,000 Units started and completed   7,000 Units started and completed
  ```

- Ending WIP: 1,000 (given)

– Continued on next page –

EXTENDED EXAMPLE – Continued

Section A.

EUP for direct materials – added at beginning of process:

When direct materials are added at the beginning of the process

- Under weighted-average, prior period and current period costs are both considered. Thus, direct materials costs embedded in beginning WIP, as well as those added during the period, are used in the calculation.
- Under FIFO, only current period activity is considered. Since all DM were added in the previous period, no DM costs are added in the current period.
- Under both methods, ending WIP is by definition 100% complete with respect to materials. Notice that the ending inventory is only 70% complete with respect to conversion costs.

	Weighted Average				FIFO			
Beginning WIP	2,000 units	×	100% (a)	= 2,000	2,000 units	×	0% (c)	= 0
Started and completed	7,000 units	×	100%	= 7,000	7,000 units	×	100%	= 7,000
Ending WIP	1,000 units	×	100% (b)	= 1,000	1,000 units	×	100% (d)	= 1,000
Totals	10,000			10,000	10,000			8,000

(a) Always 100% (c) Needed to complete
(b) Degree of completeness (d) Degree of completeness

One way to remember the difference between weighted average and FIFO is to consider the theoretical implications of the calculation for beginning inventory. Under weighted average, costs will be the average for two periods, so you look at the work done for both periods – in this case, 2,000 units. Under FIFO, you look at layers. Since this year's layer was zero, that is your EUP.

When direct materials are added evenly throughout the process

- Under weighted-average, the treatment of beginning WIP is the same as that when materials are added at the beginning (i.e., all units treated as started and completed in the current period).
- Under FIFO, the costs incurred in the current period for beginning WIP are only those needed to complete them.
- Under both methods, ending WIP uses the percentage of completion.

Section B.

EUP for direct materials – added throughout process:

When direct materials are added evenly throughout the process

- Under weighted-average, the treatment of beginning WIP is the same as that when materials are added at the beginning (i.e., all units treated as 100% complete and will produce EUP in the current period).
- Under FIFO, the costs incurred in the current period for beginning WIP are only those needed to complete them.
- Under both methods, ending WIP uses the percentage of completion.

Ending inventory is 90% complete, while beginning inventory is 80% complete.

	Weighted Average				FIFO			
Beginning WIP	2,000 units	×	100% (a)	= 2,000	2,000 units	×	20% (c)	= 400
Started and completed	7,000 units	×	100%	= 7,000	7,000 units	×	100%	= 7,000
Ending WIP	1,000 units	×	90% (b)	= 900	1,000 units	×	90% (d)	= 900
Totals	10,000			9,900	10,000			8,300

(a) Always 100% (c) Needed to complete
(b) Degree of completeness (d) Degree of completeness

Conversion costs by their nature are added evenly throughout the process. Based on the quantity schedule, ending inventory is 70% complete with respect to conversion costs.

– Continued on next page –

EXTENDED EXAMPLE – Continued

Section C.

EUP for conversion costs:

	Weighted Average					FIFO				
Beginning WIP	2,000 units	×	100% (a)	=	2,000	2,000 units	×	60% (c)	=	1,200
Started and completed	7,000 units	×	100%	=	7,000	7,000 units	×	100%	=	7,000
Ending WIP	1,000 units	×	70% (b)	=	700	1,000 units	×	70% (d)	=	700
Totals	10,000				**9,700**	10,000				**8,900**

(a) Always 100%   (c) Needed to complete
(b) Degree of completeness   (d) Degree of completeness

Assume that the costs to be allocated are as follows:

	Direct Materials	Conversion Costs		Total
Beginning work-in-process	$25,000	$10,000	=	$ 35,000
Added during the month	55,000	50,000	=	105,000
				$140,000

The per-unit costs under each of the two methods can now be derived.

- Under the weighted-average method, all direct materials and conversion costs are averaged in, both those incurred in the current period and those in beginning work-in-process. In other words, divide costs for both periods by all units worked on in both periods.
- Under the FIFO method, only the costs incurred in the current period are included in the calculation because only the work performed in the current period is included in EUP.

Per-unit costs – direct materials added at beginning of process:

Conversion costs are 70% complete on ending WIP.

	Weighted-average		FIFO	
Direct materials:	$\dfrac{\$25{,}000 + \$55{,}000}{10{,}000 \text{ EUP}}$	= $8.000	$\dfrac{\$55{,}000}{8{,}000 \text{ EUP}}$	= $6.875
Conversion costs:	$\dfrac{\$10{,}000 + \$50{,}000}{9{,}700 \text{ EUP}}$	= $6.186	$\dfrac{\$50{,}000}{8{,}900 \text{ EUP}}$	= $5.618
Total per-unit cost		**$14.186**		**$12.493**

Per-unit costs – direct materials added throughout process:

	Weighted-average		FIFO	
Direct materials:	$\dfrac{\$25{,}000 + \$55{,}000}{9{,}900 \text{ EUP}}$	= $8.081	$\dfrac{\$55{,}000}{8{,}300 \text{ EUP}}$	= $6.627
Conversion costs:	$\dfrac{\$10{,}000 + \$50{,}000}{9{,}700 \text{ EUP}}$	= $6.186	$\dfrac{\$50{,}000}{8{,}900 \text{ EUP}}$	= $5.618
Total per-unit cost		**$14.267**		**$12.245**

7. **Spoilage in Process Costing**

   a. As with job-order costing, the cost of a normal level of spoilage is left in cost of goods sold; abnormal spoilage is recognized separately as a loss.

   b. Recognizing the loss resulting from abnormal spoilage under process costing is a multi-step process.

   1) The manufacturer establishes inspection points, that is, the places in the production process where those goods not meeting specifications are pulled from the process. This is in contrast to job-order costing, in which a unit can be judged to be spoiled at any time.

      a) The typical arrangement is to inspect units as they are being transferred from one department to the next. This way, each department has its own amount of spoilage, calculated using its own equivalent-unit costs.

   2) The loss is equal to the number of units of abnormal spoilage multiplied by the department's equivalent-units costs, whether weighted-average or FIFO.

Loss on abnormal spoilage	$XXX	
Work-in-process – Department A		$XXX

Stop and review! You have completed the outline for this subunit. Study multiple-choice questions 12 through 27 beginning on page 166.

5.4 LIFE-CYCLE COSTING

1. **Life-Cycle Approach**

   a. A life-cycle approach to budgeting estimates a product's revenues and expenses over its entire sales life cycle beginning with research and development, proceeding through the introduction and growth stages into the maturity stage, and finally into the harvest or decline stage.

   1) Accordingly, life-cycle costing takes a long-term view of the entire cost life cycle, also known as the value chain.

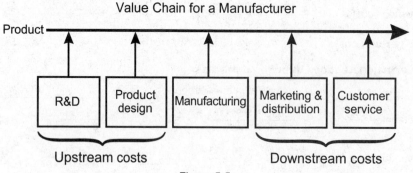

Figure 5-5

   2) This information is important for pricing decisions because revenues must cover costs incurred in each stage of the value chain, not only production.

2. **Potential Benefits**

   a. Life-cycle costing emphasizes the relationships among costs incurred at different value-chain stages, for example, the effect of reduced design costs on future customer-service costs.

      1) Because it makes a distinction between incurring costs (actually using resources) and locking in (designing in) costs, life-cycle costing highlights the potential for cost reduction activities during the upstream phase of the value chain.

      2) It is in this phase that the greatest opportunity exists to minimize downstream costs. Indeed, it has been estimated that 90% or more of costs are committed (not incurred) before production begins.

3. **Life-Cycle vs. Other Costing Methods**

   a. Traditional approaches focus on cost control (as opposed to cost reduction) during production and treat pre- and postproduction (upstream and downstream) costs as period costs that are largely ignored in determining the profitability of specific products.

      1) Other costs that traditional methods ignore are the after-purchase costs (operating, support, repair, and disposal) incurred by customers.

      2) Accordingly, whole-life cost is a concept closely associated with life-cycle cost.

         a) **Whole-life cost** equals the life-cycle cost plus after-purchase costs.

         b) Attention to the reduction of all whole-life costs through analysis and management of all value-chain activities is a powerful competitive tool because of the potential for increasing customer satisfaction.

      3) Life-cycle and whole-life cost concepts are associated with **target costing** and **target pricing**.

         a) A firm may determine that market conditions require that a product sell at a given target price.

         b) Hence, a target cost can be determined by subtracting the desired unit profit margin from the target price.

         c) The cost reduction objectives of life-cycle and whole-life cost management can therefore be determined using target costing.

      4) **Value engineering** is a means of reaching targeted cost levels.

         a) Value engineering is a systematic approach to assessing all aspects of the value chain cost buildup for a product.

            i) The purpose is to minimize costs without reducing customer satisfaction.

         b) For this purpose, distinguishing between value-adding and nonvalue-adding activities is useful.

            i) A **value-adding activity** contributes to customer value or satisfies a need of the entity. A **nonvalue-adding activity** does not make such a contribution.

            ii) Accordingly, value engineering seeks to minimize nonvalue-adding activities and their costs by reducing the cost drivers of those activities.

            iii) Value engineering also attempts to minimize the costs of value-adding activities by improving their efficiency.

4. **Internal and External Reporting Effects**

   a. For internal management accounting purposes, the costs (such as R&D) that result in marketable products represent a life-cycle investment and must be capitalized. The reporting system should also allow for capitalization and subsequent allocation of upstream costs for management accounting purposes.

   b. For external financial statement purposes, costs during the upstream phase must be expensed in the period incurred.

      1) As a result, organizations that focus on a product's life cycle must develop an accounting system consistent with GAAP for external financial reporting purposes.

      2) Essentially, life-cycle costing requires the accumulation of all costs over a product's lifetime, from inception of the idea to the abandonment of the product.

         a) These costs are then allocated to production on an expected unit-of-output basis.

      3) The internal income statement for a product will report total sales for all periods, minus all expenses to date.

         a) A risk reserve may be established as an account contra to the capitalized costs.

         b) The risk reserve consists of any deferred product costs that might not be recovered if sales are less than planned.

5. **Evaluating Management**

   a. The overall advantage of life-cycle costing is that it provides a better measure for evaluating the performance of product managers.

      1) Traditional financial statements, however, might report that certain products were extremely profitable because upstream costs were expensed in previous periods.

      2) For example, if a substantial investment is made in the development of a new product but that product quickly becomes obsolete due to new technology, how worthwhile was the investment?

      3) Life-cycle costing combines all costs and revenues for all periods to provide a better view of a product's overall performance.

Stop and review! You have completed the outline for this subunit. Study multiple-choice questions 28 through 30 beginning on page 173.

QUESTIONS

5.1 Job-Order Costing

1. A company manufactures a specialty line of T-shirts using a job-order costing system. During March, the following costs were incurred in completing job ICU2: direct materials, $13,700; direct labor, $4,800; administrative, $1,400; and selling, $5,600. Overhead was applied at the rate of $25 per machine hour, and job ICU2 required 800 machine hours. If job ICU2 resulted in 7,000 good shirts, the cost of goods sold per unit would be

A. $6.50
B. $6.30
C. $5.70
D. $5.50

Answer (D) is correct.
REQUIRED: The cost of goods sold per unit using job-order costing.
DISCUSSION: Cost of goods sold is based on the manufacturing costs incurred in production but does not include selling or general and administrative expenses. Manufacturing costs equal $38,500 [$13,700 DM + $4,800 DL + (800 hours × $25) OH]. Thus, per-unit cost is $5.50 ($38,500 ÷ 7,000 units).
Answer (A) is incorrect. The amount of $6.50 includes selling and administrative expenses. Answer (B) is incorrect. The amount of $6.30 includes selling costs. Answer (C) is incorrect. The amount of $5.70 includes administrative expenses.

SU 5: Cost Accumulation Systems

2. A company makes lenses for telescopes. Because the company will only sell lenses of the highest quality, the normal spoilage during a reporting period is 1,000 units. At the beginning of the current reporting period, the company had 2,200 units in inventory, and during the period, production was started and completed on 4,000 units. Units in inventory at the end of the current reporting period were 1,500, and the units transferred out were 3,000. During this period, the abnormal spoilage for the company's lens production was

A. 700 units.
B. 1,000 units.
C. 1,700 units.
D. 3,200 units.

Answer (A) is correct.
REQUIRED: The abnormal spoilage for the period.
DISCUSSION: The company's abnormal spoilage for the period can be calculated as follows:

Beginning inventory	2,200
Add: started and completed	4,000
Less: transferred out	(3,000)
Less: ending inventory	(1,500)
Total spoilage for period	1,700
Less: normal spoilage	(1,000)
Abnormal spoilage for period	700

Answer (B) is incorrect. The normal spoilage for the period is 1,000 units. Answer (C) is incorrect. The total spoilage for the period is 1,700 units. Answer (D) is incorrect. Failing to subtract the ending inventory to arrive at total spoilage results in 3,200 units.

3. What is the journal entry to record the purchase of materials on account?

A.	Raw materials inventory	$XXX
	Accounts payable	$XXX
B.	Accounts payable	$XXX
	Raw materials inventory	$XXX
C.	Accounts receivable	$XXX
	Accounts payable	$XXX
D.	Raw materials inventory	$XXX
	Cash	$XXX

Answer (A) is correct.
REQUIRED: The journal entry to record the purchase of materials on account.
DISCUSSION: The correct entry to record a purchase of materials on account is to increase the appropriate asset and liability accounts. Materials are charged to an inventory; the corresponding liability is accounts payable. The asset account(s) could be stores control and/or supplies or a number of other accounts. Also, subsidiary ledgers may be used to account for various individual items (a perpetual inventory system). The term "control" implies that a subsidiary ledger is being used.

Answer (B) is incorrect. The entry to record the return of materials to suppliers debits accounts payable and credits raw materials inventory. Answer (C) is incorrect. This entry reclassifies credit balances in accounts receivable as liabilities or debit balances in accounts payable as assets. Answer (D) is incorrect. This entry would record the purchase of materials for cash.

4. A calendar-year corporation had $17,000 of spoilage during April that production management characterized as abnormal. The spoilage was incurred on Job No. 532, which was sold 3 months later for $459,000. Which of the following correctly describes the impact of the spoilage on the corporation's unit manufacturing cost for Job No. 532 and on the year's operating income?

	Unit Manufacturing Cost	Operating Income
A.	Increase	No effect
B.	Increase	Decrease
C.	No effect	Decrease
D.	No effect	Not enough information to judge

Answer (C) is correct.
REQUIRED: The impact abnormal spoilage has on unit manufacturing cost and operating income.
DISCUSSION: Under job-order costing, unit manufacturing cost is unaffected by abnormal spoilage. Also, the difference between the disposal value of the spoiled goods and the value of the goods in work-in-process control must be recognized as a loss, which will decrease operating income.

Answer (A) is incorrect. Under job-order costing, the difference between the disposal value of the spoiled goods and the value of the goods in work-in-process control must be recognized as a loss. Answer (B) is incorrect. Under job-order costing, unit manufacturing cost is unaffected by abnormal spoilage. Answer (D) is incorrect. Under job-order costing, the difference between the disposal value of the spoiled goods and the value of the goods in work-in-process control must be recognized as a loss.

5.2 Activity-Based Costing

5. The series of activities in which customer usefulness is added to the product is the definition of

A. A value chain.
B. Process value analysis.
C. Integrated manufacturing.
D. Activity-based costing.

Answer (A) is correct.
REQUIRED: The series of activities in which customer usefulness is added to the product.
DISCUSSION: Value-chain analysis for assessing competitive advantage is an integral part of the strategic planning process. Value-chain analysis is a continuous process of gathering, evaluating, and communicating information for business decision making. A value chain depicts how customer value accumulates along a chain of activities that lead to an end product or service. A value chain consists of the activities required to research and develop, design, produce, market, deliver, and support its product. Extended value-chain analysis expands the view of the parties involved to include those upstream (e.g., suppliers) and downstream (e.g., customers).
Answer (B) is incorrect. Process value analysis relates to a single process. Answer (C) is incorrect. Computer-integrated manufacturing uses computers to control all aspects of manufacturing in a single location. Answer (D) is incorrect. Activity-based costing identifies the activities associated with cost incurrence and the drivers of those activities. Costs are then assigned to cost objects based on the demands they make on activities.

6. The use of activity-based costing (ABC) normally results in

A. Substantially greater unit costs for low-volume products than is reported by traditional product costing.
B. Substantially lower unit costs for low-volume products than is reported by traditional product costing.
C. Decreased setup costs being charged to low-volume products.
D. Equalizing setup costs for all product lines.

Answer (A) is correct.
REQUIRED: The true statement about ABC.
DISCUSSION: ABC differs from traditional product costing because it uses multiple allocation bases and therefore allocates overhead more accurately. The result is that ABC often charges low-volume products with more overhead than a traditional system. For example, the cost of machine setup may be the same for production runs of widely varying sizes. This relationship is reflected in an ABC system that allocates setup costs on the basis of the number of setups. However, a traditional system using an allocation base such as machine hours may underallocate setup costs to low-volume products. Many companies adopting ABC have found that they have been losing money on low-volume products because costs were actually higher than originally thought.
Answer (B) is incorrect. Low-volume products are usually charged with greater unit costs under ABC. Answer (C) is incorrect. Greater setup costs are usually charged to low-volume products under ABC. Answer (D) is incorrect. Setup costs will not be equalized unless setup time is equal for all products.

7. Because of changes that are occurring in the basic operations of many firms, all of the following represent trends in the way indirect costs are allocated **except**

A. Treating direct labor as an indirect manufacturing cost in an automated factory.
B. Using throughput time as an application base to increase awareness of the costs associated with lengthened throughput time.
C. Preferring plant-wide application rates that are applied to machine hours rather than incurring the cost of detailed allocations.
D. Using several machine cost pools to measure product costs on the basis of time in a machine center.

Answer (C) is correct.
REQUIRED: The item not a trend in the way indirect costs are being allocated.
DISCUSSION: With the automation of factories and the corresponding emphasis on activity-based costing (ABC), companies are finding new ways of allocating indirect factory overhead. One change is that plant-wide application rates are being used less often because a closer matching of costs with cost drivers provides better information to management. ABC results in a more accurate application of indirect costs because it provides more refined data. Instead of a single cost goal for a process, a department, or even an entire plant, an indirect cost pool is established for each identified activity. The related cost driver, the factor that changes the cost of the activity, also is identified.
Answer (A) is incorrect. Computerization has decreased the amount of direct labor to the point that some companies are treating direct labor as an indirect factory overhead cost. Answer (B) is incorrect. Throughput time (the rate of production over a stated time), clearly drives (influences) costs. Answer (D) is incorrect. Multiple cost pools are preferable. They permit a better matching of indirect costs with cost drivers.

SU 5: Cost Accumulation Systems

Questions 8 and 9 are based on the following information.

Zeta Company is preparing its annual profit plan. As part of its analysis of the profitability of individual products, the controller estimates the amount of overhead that should be allocated to the individual product lines from the information given in the next column:

	Wall Mirrors	Specialty Windows
Units produced	25	25
Material moves per product line	5	15
Direct labor hours per unit	200	200
Budgeted materials handling costs		$50,000

---

8. Under a costing system that allocates overhead on the basis of direct labor hours, Zeta's materials handling costs allocated to one unit of wall mirrors would be

A. $1,000
B. $500
C. $2,000
D. $5,000

Answer (A) is correct.
REQUIRED: The amount of materials handling costs allocated to one unit of wall mirrors when direct labor hours is the activity base.
DISCUSSION: If direct labor hours are used as the allocation base, the $50,000 of costs is allocated over 400 hours of direct labor. Multiplying the 25 units of each product times 200 hours results in 5,000 labor hours for each product, or a total of 10,000 hours. Dividing $50,000 by 10,000 hours results in a cost of $5 per direct labor hour. Multiplying 200 hours times $5 results in an allocation of $1,000 of overhead per unit of product.
Answer (B) is incorrect. The amount of $500 is the allocation based on number of material moves. Answer (C) is incorrect. The amount of $2,000 assumes that all the overhead is allocated to the wall mirrors. Answer (D) is incorrect. The amount of $5,000 assumes overhead of $250,000.

9. Under activity-based costing (ABC), Zeta's materials handling costs allocated to one unit of wall mirrors would be

A. $1,000
B. $500
C. $1,500
D. $2,500

Answer (B) is correct.
REQUIRED: The amount of materials handling costs allocated to one unit of wall mirrors under ABC.
DISCUSSION: An activity-based costing (ABC) system allocates overhead costs on the basis of some causal relationship between the incurrence of cost and activities. Because the moves for wall mirrors constitute 25% (5 ÷ 20) of total moves, the mirrors should absorb 25% of the total materials handling costs. Thus, $12,500 ($50,000 × 25%) is allocated to mirrors. The remaining $37,500 is allocated to specialty windows. Dividing the $12,500 by 25 units produces a cost of $500 per unit of mirrors.
Answer (A) is incorrect. The amount of $1,000 uses direct labor as the allocation basis. Answer (C) is incorrect. The amount of $1,500 is the allocation per unit of specialty windows. Answer (D) is incorrect. The amount of $2,500 is not based on the number of material moves.

10. Multiple or departmental overhead rates are considered preferable to a single or plantwide overhead rate when

A. Manufacturing is limited to a single product flowing through identical departments in a fixed sequence.
B. Various products are manufactured that do not pass through the same departments or use the same manufacturing techniques.
C. Cost drivers, such as direct labor, are the same over all processes.
D. Individual cost drivers cannot accurately be determined with respect to cause-and-effect relationships.

Answer (B) is correct.
REQUIRED: The situation in which multiple or departmental overhead rates are considered preferable.
DISCUSSION: Multiple rates are appropriate when a process differs substantially among departments or when products do not go through all departments or all processes. The trend in cost accounting is toward activity-based costing, which divides production into numerous activities and identifies the cost driver(s) most relevant to each. The result is a more accurate tracing of costs.
Answer (A) is incorrect. One rate may be cost beneficial when a single product proceeds through homogeneous processes. Answer (C) is incorrect. If cost drivers are the same for all processes, multiple rates are unnecessary. Answer (D) is incorrect. Individual cost drivers for all relationships must be known to use multiple application rates.

11. A cosmetics manufacturer has used a traditional cost accounting system to apply quality control costs uniformly to all products at a rate of 14.5% of direct labor cost. Monthly direct labor cost for makeup is $27,500. In an attempt to distribute quality control costs more equitably, the manufacturer is considering activity-based costing. The monthly data shown in the chart below have been gathered for makeup.

Activity	Cost Driver	Cost Rates	Quantity of Makeup
Incoming material inspection	Type of material	$11.50 per type	12 types
In-process inspection	Number of units	$0.14 per unit	17,500 units
Product certification	Per order	$77 per order	25 orders

The monthly quality control cost assigned to makeup using activity-based costing (ABC) is

A. $88.64 per order.
B. $525.50 lower than the cost using the traditional system.
C. $8,500.50
D. $525.50 higher than the cost using the traditional system.

Answer (D) is correct.
REQUIRED: The monthly quality control cost assigned using activity-based costing.
DISCUSSION: ABC identifies the causal relationship between the incurrence of cost and activities, determines the drivers of the activities, establishes cost pools related to the drivers and activities, and assigns costs to ultimate cost objects on the basis of the demands (resources or drivers consumed) placed on the activities by those cost objects. Hence, ABC assigns overhead costs based on multiple allocation bases or cost drivers. Under the traditional, single-base system, the amount allocated is $3,987.50 ($27,500 × 14.5%). Under ABC, the amount allocated is $4,513 [(12 × $11.50) + (17,500 × $.14) + (25 × $77)], or $525.50 more than under the traditional system.
Answer (A) is incorrect. The ABC assignment of $4,513 is at a rate of $180.52 for each of the 25 orders. Answer (B) is incorrect. ABC yields a higher allocation. Answer (C) is incorrect. The total is $4,513 on the ABC basis.

5.3 Process Costing

Questions 12 through 15 are based on the following information.

Levittown Company employs a process cost system for its manufacturing operations. All direct materials are added at the beginning of the process and conversion costs are added proportionately. Levittown's production quantity schedule for November is reproduced in the next column.

Work-in-process November 1 (60% complete as to conversion costs)	1,000
Units started during November	5,000
Total units to account for	6,000
Units completed and transferred out from beginning inventory	1,000
Units started and completed during November	3,000
Work-in-process on November 30 (20% complete as to conversion costs)	2,000
Total units accounted for	6,000

12. Using the FIFO method, Levittown's equivalent units for conversion costs for November are

A. 3,400 units.
B. 3,800 units.
C. 4,000 units.
D. 4,400 units.

Answer (B) is correct.
REQUIRED: The equivalent units for conversion costs under the FIFO method.
DISCUSSION: Given that BWIP (1,000 units) was already 60% complete, 400 [(100% − 60%) × 1,000 units] equivalent units were needed for completion. In addition, 3,000 units were started and completed during the period. The 2,000 units in EWIP equal 400 (20% × 2,000 units) equivalent units since they are 20% complete. Total equivalent units are 3,800 (400 + 3,000 + 400).
Answer (A) is incorrect. The units started and completed during November plus the 20% of work-in-process complete as to conversion costs equals 3,400 units (3,000 + 400). Answer (C) is incorrect. The number of units started and completed in November and the units completed and transferred out from BI equals 4,000 units (3,000 + 1,000). Answer (D) is incorrect. The number of units started and completed in November, plus the units completed and transferred out from BI, plus the 20% of work-in-process complete as to conversion costs equals 4,400 units (3,000 + 1,000 + 400).

13. Using the FIFO method, Levittown's equivalent units for direct materials for November are

A. 5,000 units.
B. 6,000 units.
C. 4,400 units.
D. 3,800 units.

Answer (A) is correct.
REQUIRED: The equivalent units for direct materials under the FIFO method.
DISCUSSION: The computation of equivalent units for a period using the FIFO method of process costing includes only the conversion costs and material added to the product in that period and excludes any work done in previous periods. Accordingly, FIFO equivalent units include work and material to complete BWIP, plus work and material to complete units started this period, minus work and material needed to complete EWIP. Given that all materials are added at the beginning of the process, only those units started during November would have received materials in that month. Because 5,000 units were started, the equivalent units for direct materials equal 5,000.
Answer (B) is incorrect. The total units to account for is 6,000. Answer (C) is incorrect. The number of units completed and transferred out from BI plus units started and completed in November plus 20% of work-in-process on November 30 equals 4,400 (1,000 + 3,000 + 400). Answer (D) is incorrect. The equivalent units for direct materials is not 3,800. Only those units started during November would have received materials in that month. Therefore, equivalent units for direct materials equal 5,000.

14. Using the weighted-average method, Levittown's equivalent units for direct materials for November are

A. 3,400 units.
B. 4,400 units.
C. 5,000 units.
D. 6,000 units.

Answer (D) is correct.
REQUIRED: The equivalent units for direct materials using the weighted-average method.
DISCUSSION: Under the weighted-average method, units in the beginning WIP are treated as 100% complete and will produce EUP in the current period even though materials were added in the previous period. EUP is calculated as follows:

Beginning WIP	100% × 1,000 units	1,000
Units started and completed	100% × 3,000 units	3,000
Ending WIP	100% × 2,000 units	2,000
	EUP =	6,000

Answer (A) is incorrect. Units started and completed in November plus 20% of ending work-in-process equals 3,400 units (3,000 + 400). Answer (B) is incorrect. The number of units started and completed in November plus units completed and transferred out from BI plus 20% of ending work-in-process equals 4,400 units (3,000 + 1,000 + 400). Answer (C) is incorrect. The number of units started in November is 5,000.

15. Using the weighted-average method, Levittown's equivalent units for conversion costs for November are

A. 3,400 units.
B. 3,800 units.
C. 4,000 units.
D. 4,400 units.

Answer (D) is correct.
REQUIRED: The equivalent units for conversion costs using the weighted-average method.
DISCUSSION: Under the weighted-average method, units in the beginning WIP are treated as 100% complete and will produce EUP in the current period even though conversion costs were added in the previous period. EUP is calculated as follows:

Beginning WIP	100% × 1,000 units	1,000
Units started and completed	100% × 3,000 units	3,000
Ending WIP	20% × 2,000 units	400
	EUP =	4,400

Answer (A) is incorrect. The number of 3,400 units consist of the units started and completed in November plus the 20% of work-in-process complete as to conversion costs (3,000 + 400). Answer (B) is incorrect. The number of 3,800 units equal the 400 units in BWIP needed for completion plus the units started and completed in November plus the 20% of work-in-process complete as to conversion costs (400 + 3,000 + 400). Answer (C) is incorrect. The number of 4,000 units equal the units completed and transferred out from BI plus units started and completed during November (1,000 + 3,000).

Questions 16 through 22 are based on the following information.

Kimbeth Manufacturing uses a process cost system to manufacture Dust Density Sensors for the mining industry. The following information pertains to operations for the month of May.

	Units
Beginning work-in-process inventory, May 1	16,000
Started in production during May	100,000
Completed production during May	92,000
Ending work-in-process inventory, May 31	24,000

The beginning inventory was 60% complete for materials and 20% complete for conversion costs. The ending inventory was 90% complete for materials and 40% complete for conversion costs.

Costs pertaining to the month of May are as follows:

- Beginning inventory costs are materials, $54,560; direct labor, $20,320; and overhead, $15,240.
- Costs incurred during May are materials used, $468,000; direct labor, $182,880; and overhead, $391,160.

16. Using the weighted-average method, Kimbeth's equivalent unit cost of materials for May is

A. $4.12
B. $4.50
C. $4.60
D. $5.02

Answer (C) is correct.
REQUIRED: The weighted-average equivalent unit cost for materials.
DISCUSSION: Under the weighted-average method, units in beginning WIP are treated as 100% complete and will produce EUP in the current period even though materials were added in the previous period. Because 92,000 units were completed during the period, 76,000 (92,000 – 16,000 BWIP) must have been started and completed during the year. Thus, total EUP for May is calculated as follows:

Beginning WIP	100% × 16,000 units	16,000
Units started and completed	100% × 76,000 units	76,000
Ending WIP	90% × 24,000 units	21,600
	EUP =	113,600

The total materials costs incurred during the period and accumulated in beginning work-in-process is $522,560 ($468,000 + $54,560). Thus, weighted-average unit cost is $4.60 ($522,560 ÷ 113,600 EUP).
Answer (A) is incorrect. The amount of $4.12 equals materials costs for May divided by weighted-average EUP. Answer (B) is incorrect. The amount of $4.50 is the equivalent unit cost based on the FIFO method. Answer (D) is incorrect. The amount of $5.02 is based on a FIFO calculation of equivalent units and a weighted-average calculation of costs.

17. Using the FIFO method, Kimbeth's total cost of units in the ending work-in-process inventory at May 31 is

A. $153,168
B. $154,800
C. $155,328
D. $156,960

Answer (A) is correct.
REQUIRED: The total cost of units in ending work-in-process under FIFO.
DISCUSSION: Under the FIFO method, EUP for materials equal 104,000 [(16,000 units in BWIP × 40%) + (76,000 units started and completed × 100%) + (24,000 units in EWIP × 90%)]. Consequently, the equivalent unit cost of materials is $4.50 ($468,000 total materials cost in May ÷ 104,000 EUP). EUP for materials in ending work-in-process equal 21,600 (24,000 × 90%). Thus, total FIFO materials cost is $97,200 (21,600 EUP × $4.50). Under the FIFO method, EUP for conversion costs equal 98,400 [(16,000 units in BWIP × 80%) + (76,000 units started and completed × 100%) + (24,000 units in EWIP × 40%)]. Conversion costs incurred during the current period equal $574,040 ($182,880 DL + $391,160 FOH). Therefore, the equivalent unit cost for conversion costs is $5.83 ($574,040 ÷ 98,400). EUP for conversion costs in ending work-in-process equal 9,600 (24,000 × 40%). Total conversion costs are therefore $55,968 (9,600 EUP × $5.83). Consequently, total work-in-process costs are $153,168 ($97,200 + $55,968).
Answer (B) is incorrect. The amount of $154,800 is based on a FIFO calculation for materials and a weighted-average calculation for conversion costs. Answer (C) is incorrect. The amount of $155,328 is based on a weighted-average calculation for materials and a FIFO calculation for conversion costs. Answer (D) is incorrect. The amount of $156,960 is the weighted-average cost of ending work-in-process.

18. Using the first-in, first-out (FIFO) method, Kimbeth's equivalent units of production (EUP) for materials are

A. 97,600 units.
B. 104,000 units.
C. 107,200 units.
D. 108,000 units.

Answer (B) is correct.
REQUIRED: The equivalent units of production for materials under FIFO.
DISCUSSION: Under FIFO, EUP are based solely on work performed during the current period. The EUP equals the sum of the work done on the beginning work-in-process inventory, units started and completed in the current period, and the ending work-in-process inventory. Because 92,000 units were completed during the period, 76,000 (92,000 – 16,000 in BWIP) must have been started and completed during the period. Thus, total EUP for May is calculated as follows:

Beginning WIP	[(100% – 60%) × 16,000 units]	6,400
Units started and completed	100% × 76,000 units	76,000
Ending WIP	90% × 24,000 units	21,600
	EUP =	104,000

Answer (A) is incorrect. This number of units omits the 6,400 EUP added to beginning work-in-process. Answer (C) is incorrect. This number of units assumes beginning work-in-process was 40% complete. Answer (D) is incorrect. This number of units equals the sum of the physical units in beginning work-in-process and the physical units completed.

19. Using the FIFO method, Kimbeth's equivalent units of production for conversion costs are

A. 85,600 units.
B. 88,800 units.
C. 95,200 units.
D. 98,400 units.

Answer (D) is correct.
REQUIRED: The equivalent units of production for conversion costs under FIFO.
DISCUSSION: Under FIFO, EUP are based solely on work performed during the current period. The EUP equals the sum of the work done on the beginning work-in-process inventory, units started and completed in the current period, and the ending work-in-process inventory. Because 92,000 units were completed during the period, 76,000 (92,000 – 16,000 in BWIP) must have been started and completed during the period. Thus, total EUP for May is calculated as follows:

Beginning WIP	[(100% – 20%) × 16,000 units]	12,800
Units started and completed	100% × 76,000 units	76,000
Ending WIP	40% × 24,000 units	9,600
	EUP =	98,400

Answer (A) is incorrect. This number of units omits the work done on beginning work-in-process. Answer (B) is incorrect. This number of units omits the work done on ending work-in-process. Answer (C) is incorrect. This number of units assumes the beginning work-in-process was 40% complete as to conversion costs.

20. Using the FIFO method, Kimbeth's equivalent unit cost of materials for May is

A. $4.12
B. $4.50
C. $4.60
D. $4.80

Answer (B) is correct.
REQUIRED: The equivalent unit cost of materials under FIFO.
DISCUSSION: Under the FIFO method, EUP for materials equal 104,000 [(16,000 units in BWIP × 40%) + (76,000 units started and completed × 100%) + (24,000 units in EWIP × 90%)]. Consequently, the equivalent unit cost of materials is $4.50 ($468,000 total materials cost in May ÷ 104,000 EUP).
Answer (A) is incorrect. The amount of $4.12 is based on EUP calculated under the weighted-average method. Answer (C) is incorrect. The amount of $4.60 is the weighted-average cost per equivalent unit. Answer (D) is incorrect. The amount of $4.80 omits the 6,400 EUP added to beginning work-in-process.

21. Refer to the information on the preceding page(s). Using the FIFO method, Kimbeth's equivalent unit conversion cost for May is

A. $5.65
B. $5.83
C. $6.00
D. $6.20

Answer (B) is correct.
REQUIRED: The conversion cost per equivalent unit under FIFO.
DISCUSSION: Under the FIFO method, EUP for conversion costs equal 98,400 [(16,000 units in BWIP × 80%) + (76,000 units started and completed × 100%) + (24,000 units in EWIP × 40%)]. Conversion costs incurred during the current period equal $574,040 ($182,880 DL + $391,160 FOH). Hence, the equivalent unit cost for conversion costs is $5.83 ($574,040 ÷ 98,400).
Answer (A) is incorrect. The amount of $5.65 is based on EUP calculated under the weighted-average method. Answer (C) is incorrect. The amount of $6.00 is the cost per equivalent unit calculated under the weighted-average method. Answer (D) is incorrect. The amount of $6.20 results from combining conversion costs for May with those in beginning work-in-process and dividing by 98,400 EUP.

22. Refer to the information on the preceding page(s). Using the weighted-average method, Kimbeth's equivalent unit conversion cost for May is

A. $5.65
B. $5.83
C. $6.00
D. $6.20

Answer (C) is correct.
REQUIRED: The weighted-average conversion cost per equivalent unit.
DISCUSSION: Under the weighted-average method, units in beginning WIP are treated as 100% complete and will produce EUP in the current period even though materials were added in the previous period. Because 92,000 units were completed during the period, 76,000 (92,000 – 16,000 BWIP) must have been started and completed during the year. Thus, total EUP for May is calculated as follows:

Beginning WIP	100% × 16,000 units	16,000
Units started and completed	100% × 76,000 units	76,000
Ending WIP	40% × 24,000 units	9,600
	EUP =	101,600

The sum of the conversion costs accumulated in beginning work-in-process and incurred during the period is $609,600 ($20,320 + $15,240 + $182,880 + $391,160). Thus, weighted-average unit cost is $6.00 ($609,600 ÷ 101,600 EUP).
Answer (A) is incorrect. The amount of $5.65 omits the conversion costs in beginning work-in-process. Answer (B) is incorrect. The amount of $5.83 is the equivalent unit conversion cost based on FIFO. Answer (D) is incorrect. The amount of $6.20 is based on a FIFO calculation of equivalent units and a weighted-average calculation of costs.

Questions 23 and 24 are based on the following information.

Goggle-Eyed Old Snapping Turtle, a sporting goods manufacturer, buys wood as a direct material for baseball bats. The Forming Department processes the baseball bats, and the bats are then transferred to the Finishing Department where a sealant is applied. The Forming Department began manufacturing 10,000 "Casey Sluggers" during the month of May. There was no beginning inventory.

Costs for the Forming Department for the month of May were as follows:

Direct materials	$33,000
Conversion costs	17,000
Total	$50,000

A total of 8,000 bats were completed and transferred to the Finishing Department; the remaining 2,000 bats were still in the forming process at the end of the month. All of the Forming Department's direct materials were placed in process, but, on average, only 25% of the conversion cost was applied to the ending work-in-process inventory.

23. The cost of the units transferred to Snapping Turtle's Finishing Department is

A. $50,000
B. $40,000
C. $53,000
D. $42,400

Answer (D) is correct.
REQUIRED: The cost of the units transferred to the Finishing Department.
DISCUSSION: The total equivalent units for raw materials equals 10,000 because all materials for the ending work-in-process had already been added to production. Hence, the materials cost per unit was $3.30 ($33,000 ÷ 10,000). For conversion costs, the total equivalent units equals 8,500 [8,000 completed + (2,000 in EWIP × 25%)]. Thus, the conversion cost was $2.00 per unit ($17,000 ÷ 8,500). The total cost transferred was therefore $42,400 [8,000 units × ($3.30 + $2.00)].
Answer (A) is incorrect. A portion of the total costs is still in work-in-process. Answer (B) is incorrect. The amount of $40,000 assumes that work-in-process is 100% complete as to conversion costs. Answer (C) is incorrect. The amount of $53,000 exceeds the actual costs incurred during the period. Given no beginning inventory, the amount transferred out cannot exceed the costs incurred during the period.

24. The cost of the work-in-process inventory in Snapping Turtle's Forming Department at the end of May is

A. $10,000
B. $2,500
C. $20,000
D. $7,600

Answer (D) is correct.
REQUIRED: The cost of the work-in-process inventory.
DISCUSSION: The equivalent units for raw materials would be 10,000 (8,000 + 2,000) since the work-in-process is 100% complete as to materials. Therefore, dividing the $33,000 by 10,000 units results in a unit cost for materials of $3.30. The equivalent units for conversion costs would be 8,500 units [8,000 + (2,000 units × .25)]. Dividing the $17,000 of conversion costs by 8,500 equivalent units results in a unit cost of $2 per bat. Therefore, the total cost of goods transferred out would be $5.30, consisting of $3.30 for materials and $2 for conversion costs. Multiplying $5.30 times the 8,000 bats completed results in a total transfer of $42,400. Consequently, the cost of the ending work-in-process must have been $7,600 ($50,000 total costs incurred − $42,400).
Answer (A) is incorrect. The amount of $10,000 assumes that work-in-process inventory is 100% complete as to conversion costs. Answer (B) is incorrect. The amount of $2,500 assumes that work-in-process inventory is 100% complete as to conversion costs and that 500 bats are in inventory. Answer (C) is incorrect. The amount of $20,000 assumes that work-in-process is 100% complete as to conversion costs and that 6,000 units were transferred out.

Questions 25 through 27 are based on the following information. Marlan Manufacturing produces a product that passes through two departments. The units from the molding department are completed in the assembly department. The units are completed in assembly by adding the remaining direct materials when the units are 60% complete with respect to conversion costs. Conversion costs are added proportionately in assembly. The production activity in the assembly department for the current month is presented as follows. Marlan uses the FIFO (first-in, first-out) inventory method in its process cost system.

Beginning inventory units (25% complete with respect to conversion costs)	8,000
Units transferred in from the molding department during the month	42,000
Units to account for	50,000
Units completed and transferred to finished goods inventory	38,000
Ending inventory units (40% complete with respect to conversion costs)	12,000
Units accounted for	50,000

25. The equivalent units transferred from Marlan's molding department to the assembly department for the current month are

- A. 30,000 units.
- B. 38,000 units.
- C. 40,800 units.
- D. 42,000 units.

Answer (D) is correct.
REQUIRED: The equivalent units transferred from the molding department to the assembly department.
DISCUSSION: This problem seemingly asks a technical question, but in reality was designed to test the candidate's alertness. The equivalent units transferred from the molding department are simply the total units transferred from the molding department (42,000 units).
Answer (A) is incorrect. The number of units started and completed during the period was 30,000. Answer (B) is incorrect. The number of units transferred out, not to, the assembly department was 38,000. Answer (C) is incorrect. The equivalent units for conversion costs equals 40,800.

26. The equivalent units in Marlan's assembly department for conversion costs for the current month are

- A. 34,800 units.
- B. 40,800 units.
- C. 42,800 units.
- D. 43,200 units.

Answer (B) is correct.
REQUIRED: The equivalent units for conversion costs.
DISCUSSION: Conversion costs are being added throughout the process. It is important to note both the method used and the completed percentage. During the period, 30,000 units (42,000 units transferred in − 12,000 ending WIP) were started and completed. EUP is calculated as follows:

Beginning WIP	[(100% − 25%) × 8,000 units]	6,000
Units started and completed	100% × 30,000 units	30,000
Ending WIP	40% × 12,000 units	4,800
	EUP =	40,800

Answer (A) is incorrect. The number of 34,800 units assumes the beginning inventory was 100% complete. Answer (C) is incorrect. Conversion-cost EUP based on the weighted-average method is 42,800 units. Answer (D) is incorrect. The ending inventory was 40% complete, resulting in subtracting 60%, not 40%, of the 12,000 items in ending inventory to determine work not on ending inventory.

SU 5: Cost Accumulation Systems

27. The equivalent units in Marlan's assembly department for direct materials for the current month are

A. 30,000 units.
B. 38,000 units.
C. 40,800 units.
D. 42,000 units.

Answer (B) is correct.
REQUIRED: The equivalent units in the assembly department for direct materials.
DISCUSSION: When materials are added at a specific time during production, whether or not materials are included in the current period's calculation of EUP depends on when materials would have been added, and whether or not that point was reached. In this scenario, direct materials are added when the products are 60% complete with respect to conversion costs. Thus, 30,000 units (38,000 units transferred out – 8,000 beginning WIP) were started and completed, and EUP is calculated as follows:

Beginning WIP	100% × 8,000 units	8,000
Units started and completed	100% × 30,000 units	30,000
Ending WIP	0% × 12,000 units	0
	EUP =	38,000

Answer (A) is incorrect. The number of 30,000 units ignores the 8,000 units in process at the beginning of the period. Answer (C) is incorrect. Equivalent units for conversion costs, not direct materials, is 40,800. Answer (D) is incorrect. The 42,000 units were transferred in during the month. Not all received an input of direct materials.

5.4 Life-Cycle Costing

28. Life-cycle costing

A. Is sometimes used as a basis for cost planning and product pricing.
B. Includes only manufacturing costs incurred over the life of the product.
C. Includes only manufacturing cost, selling expense, and distribution expense.
D. Emphasizes cost savings opportunities during the manufacturing cycle.

Answer (A) is correct.
REQUIRED: The true statement about life-cycle costing.
DISCUSSION: Life-cycle costing estimates a product's revenues and expenses over its expected life cycle. This approach is especially useful when revenues and related costs do not occur in the same periods. It emphasizes the need to price products to cover all costs, not just those for production. Hence, costs are determined for all value-chain categories: upstream (R&D, design), manufacturing, and downstream (marketing, distribution, and customer service). The result is to highlight upstream and downstream costs in the cost planning process that often receive insufficient attention.
Answer (B) is incorrect. The life-cycle model includes the upstream (R&D and design) and downstream (marketing, distribution, and customer service) elements of the value chain as well as manufacturing costs. Answer (C) is incorrect. The life-cycle model includes the upstream (R&D and design) and downstream (marketing, distribution, and customer service) elements of the value chain as well as manufacturing costs. Answer (D) is incorrect. Life-cycle costing emphasizes the significance of locked-in costs, target costing, and value engineering for pricing and cost control. Thus, cost savings at all stages of the life cycle are important.

29. Target pricing

A. Is more effective when applied to mature, long-established products.

B. Considers short-term variable costs and excludes fixed costs.

C. Is often used when costs are difficult to control.

D. Is a pricing strategy used to create competitive advantage.

Answer (D) is correct.
REQUIRED: The definition of target pricing.
DISCUSSION: Target pricing and costing may result in a competitive advantage because it is a customer-oriented approach that focuses on what products can be sold at what prices. It is also advantageous because it emphasizes control of costs prior to their being locked in during the early links in the value chain. The company sets a target price for a potential product reflecting what it believes consumers will pay and competitors will do. After subtracting the desired profit margin, the long-run target cost is known. If current costs are too high to allow an acceptable profit, cost-cutting measures are implemented or the product is abandoned. The assumption is that the target price is a constraint.
 Answer (A) is incorrect. Target pricing is used on products that have not yet been developed. Answer (B) is incorrect. Target pricing considers all costs in the value chain. Answer (C) is incorrect. Target pricing can be used in any situation, but it is most likely to succeed when costs can be well controlled.

30. A company has been asked to evaluate the profitability of a product that it manufactured and sold from Year 7 through Year 10. The product had a one-year warranty from date of sale. The following information appears in the financial records:

Research, development, and design cost Yr 5 & Yr 6	Manufacturing and distribution costs Yr 7 - Yr 10	Warranty costs Yr 7 - Yr 10	Warranty cost Yr 11
$5,000,000	$7,000,000	$200,000	$100,000

The life-cycle cost for this product is

A. $10,000,000

B. $12,000,000

C. $12,200,000

D. $12,300,000

Answer (D) is correct.
REQUIRED: The cost of a product calculated on a life-cycle basis.
DISCUSSION: Life-cycle costing takes into account costs incurred at all stages of the value-chain, not just manufacturing. The life-cycle cost for this product is thus $12,300,000 ($5,000,000 + $7,000,000 + $200,000 + $100,000).
 Answer (A) is incorrect. The amount of $10,000,000 is not supported by the information given. Answer (B) is incorrect. The amount of $12,000,000 improperly excludes future warranty costs. Answer (C) is incorrect. The amount of $12,200,000 improperly excludes the $100,000 of warranty costs for Year 11.

Access the CMA Review System from your Gleim Personal Classroom to continue your studies with exam-emulating multiple-choice questions!

5.5 ESSAY QUESTIONS

Scenario for Essay Questions 1, 2, 3

Kristina Company, which manufactures quality paint sold at premium prices, uses a single production department. Production begins with the blending of various chemicals, which are added at the beginning of the process, and ends with the canning of the paint. Canning occurs when the mixture reaches the 90% stage of completion. The gallon cans are then transferred to the Shipping Department for crating and shipment. Labor and overhead are added continuously throughout the process. Factory overhead is applied on the basis of direct labor hours at the rate of $3.00 per hour.

Prior to May, when a change in the process was implemented, work-in-process inventories were insignificant. The change in the process enables greater production but results in material amounts of work-in-process for the first time. The company has always used the weighted-average method to determine equivalent production and unit costs. Now, production management is considering changing from the weighted-average method to the first-in, first-out method.

The following data relate to actual production during the month of May:

Costs for May

Work-in-process inventory, May 1 (4,000 gallons 25% complete):	
Direct materials – chemicals	$ 45,600
Direct labor ($10 per hour)	6,250
Factory overhead	1,875
May costs added	
Direct materials – chemicals	228,400
Direct materials – cans	7,000
Direct labor ($10 per hour)	35,000
Factory overhead	10,500

Units for May

	Gallons
Work-in-process inventory, May 1 (25% complete)	4,000
Sent to Shipping Department	20,000
Started in May	21,000
Work-in-process inventory, May 31 (80% complete)	5,000

Questions

1. Prepare a schedule of equivalent units for each cost element for the month of May using the
   a. Weighted-average method
   b. First-in, first-out method

2. Calculate the cost (to the nearest cent) per equivalent unit for each cost element for the month of May using the
   a. Weighted-average method
   b. First-in, first-out method

3. Discuss the advantages and disadvantages of using the weighted-average method versus the first-in, first-out method, and explain under what circumstances each method should be used.

Essay Questions 1, 2, 3 — Unofficial Answers

1. a. **Weighted-Average Method**

    Direct Materials – Chemicals
    Chemicals are added at the beginning so units in beginning WIP are treated as 100% complete and will produce EUP in the current period. During May, 16,000 units (21,000 units started – 5,000 ending WIP) were started and completed. EUP is calculated as follows:

Beginning WIP	100% × 4,000 units	4,000
Units started and completed	100% × 16,000 units	16,000
Ending WIP	100% × 5,000 units	5,000
	EUP =	25,000

    Direct Material - Cans
    Canning occurs when the mixture reaches the 90% stage of production. Whether or not the materials are included in this period's calculation of EUP depends on when materials would have been added and whether or not that point was reached. During May, 16,000 units (20,000 units transferred out – 4,000 beginning WIP) were started and completed. EUP is calculated as follows:

Beginning WIP	100% × 4,000 units	4,000
Units started and completed	100% × 16,000 units	16,000
Ending WIP	0% × 5,000 units	0
	EUP =	20,000

    Conversion Costs
    Conversion costs are added throughout the process. Units in beginning WIP are treated as 100% complete and produce EUP in the current period. During May, 16,000 units (21,000 units started – 5,000 ending WIP) were started and completed. EUP is calculated as follows:

Beginning WIP	100% × 4,000 units	4,000
Units started and completed	100% × 16,000 units	16,000
Ending WIP	80% × 5,000 units	4,000
	EUP =	24,000

    b. **First-in, First-out Method**

    Direct Materials – Chemicals
    Chemicals are added at the beginning so units in beginning WIP will not produce EUP in the current period. During May, 16,000 units (20,000 units transferred out – 4,000 beginning WIP) were started and completed. EUP is calculated as follows:

Beginning WIP	0% × 4,000 units	0
Units started and completed	100% × 16,000 units	16,000
Ending WIP	100% × 5,000 units	5,000
	EUP =	21,000

    Direct Materials – Cans
    Canning occurs when the mixture reaches the 90% stage of production. Whether or not the materials are included in this period's calculation of EUP depends on when materials would have been added and whether or not that point was reached. During May, 16,000 units (21,000 units started – 5,000 ending WIP) were started and completed. EUP is calculated as follows:

Beginning WIP	100% × 4,000 units	4,000
Units started and completed	100% × 16,000 units	16,000
Ending WIP	0% × 5,000 units	0
	EUP =	20,000

Conversion Costs

Conversion costs are added throughout the process, and we are looking for the amount completed during the current period. During May, 16,000 units (20,000 units transferred out – 4,000 beginning WIP) were started and completed. EUP is calculated as follows:

Beginning WIP	[(100% – 25%) × 4,000 units]	3,000
Units started and completed	100% × 16,000 units	16,000
Ending WIP	80% × 5,000 units	4,000
	EUP =	23,000

The equivalent units for each cost element, using the first-in, first-out method, are presented below.

	Direct Materials Chemicals	Cans	Conversion
Transferred to Shipping from 5/1 work-in-process (4,000 at 25%)			
Chemicals (0%)	0		
Cans (100%)		4,000	
Conversion costs (75%)			3,000
Current production transferred to Shipping (100%)	16,000	16,000	16,000
5/31 work-in-process (5,000 at 80%)			
Chemicals (100%)	5,000		
Cans (0%)		0	
Conversion costs (80%)			4,000
Equivalent units	21,000	20,000	23,000

2. a. **Cost per EUP**

Weighted-Average Method

	Direct Materials Chemicals	Cans	Conversion*
Work-in-process at 5/1	$ 45,600	$ 0	$ 8,125
Plus: May costs incurred	228,400	7,000	45,500
Total costs	$274,000	$ 7,000	$53,625
Divided by: EUP	÷ 25,000	÷20,000	÷24,000
Weighted-average unit costs	$ 10.96	$ .35	$ 2.23

*Conversion cost = Direct labor + Factory overhead

b. <u>First-in, First-out, Method</u>

	Direct Materials Chemicals	Cans	Conversion
May costs incurred	$228,400	$ 7,000	$45,500
Divided by: EUP	÷ 21,000	÷20,000	÷23,000
FIFO unit costs	$ 10.88	$ .35	$ 1.98

3. The weighted-average method is easier to use, as the calculations are simpler. This method tends to obscure current period costs, as the cost per equivalent unit includes both current costs and prior costs that were in the beginning inventory. This method is most appropriate when conversion costs, inventory levels, and raw material prices are stable.

The first-in, first-out method is based on the work done in the current period only. This method is most appropriate when conversion costs, inventory levels, or raw material prices fluctuate. In addition, this method should be used when accuracy in current equivalent unit costs is important or when a standard cost system is used.

Access the **CMA Review System** from your Gleim Personal Classroom to continue your studies with exam-emulating essay questions!

Notes

STUDY UNIT SIX
COST ALLOCATION TECHNIQUES

(21 pages of outline)

6.1	Absorption and Variable Costing -- Theory	179
6.2	Absorption and Variable Costing -- Calculations	185
6.3	Joint Product and By-Product Costing	185
6.4	Overhead Allocation and Normal Costing -- Theory	189
6.5	Overhead Allocation and Normal Costing -- Calculations	195
6.6	Allocating Service Department Costs -- Theory	195
6.7	Allocating Service Department Costs -- Calculations	199
6.8	Essay Questions	211

This study unit is the **third of four** on **cost management**. The relative weight assigned to this major topic in Part 1 of the exam is **20%**. The four study units are

Study Unit 4: Cost Management Concepts
Study Unit 5: Cost Accumulation Systems
Study Unit 6: Cost Allocation Techniques
Study Unit 7: Operational Efficiency and Business Process Performance

If you are interested in reviewing more introductory or background material, go to www.gleim.com/CMAIntroVideos for a list of suggested third-party overviews of this topic. The following Gleim outline material is more than sufficient to help you pass the CMA exam; any additional introductory or background material is for your own personal enrichment.

6.1 ABSORPTION AND VARIABLE COSTING -- THEORY

1. **Two Ways of Treating Fixed Production Costs**

    a. For internal purposes, decision making is improved by treating fixed overhead as a period cost so that only costs that are variable in the short run are included in the cost of the product.

    1) Fixed overhead costs are considered as period costs and are deducted in the period in which they are incurred.

    2) This practice is termed **variable,** or **direct, costing**. Variable costing is the preferred term because it concisely describes what is happening – namely that product costs are based only on variable costs.

    b. For external reporting purposes, the cost of a product must include **all** the costs of manufacturing it: direct labor, direct materials, and all factory overhead (both fixed and variable).

    1) This method is commonly known as **absorption, full,** or **full absorption costing**.

2. **Absorption Costing**

    a. Under absorption costing, the fixed portion of manufacturing overhead is "absorbed" into the cost of each unit of product.

    1) Product cost thus includes all manufacturing costs, both fixed and variable.

    2) Absorption-basis cost of goods sold is subtracted from sales to arrive at gross margin.

    3) Total selling and administrative (S&A) expenses (i.e., both fixed and variable) are then subtracted from gross margin to arrive at operating income.

    b. This method is required for external reporting purposes and for tax purposes.

3. **Variable Costing**
   a. This method is more appropriate for internal reporting.
      1) Product cost includes only the variable portion of manufacturing costs.
      2) Variable-basis cost of goods sold and the variable portion of S&A expenses are subtracted from sales to arrive at **contribution margin**.
         a) This figure (sales – total variable costs) is an important element of the variable costing income statement because it is the amount available for covering fixed costs (both manufacturing and S&A).
         b) For this reason, some accountants call the method contribution margin reporting.
      3) The term "direct costing" is somewhat misleading. It suggests traceability, which is not what is meant in this context. "Variable costing" is more suitable.
      4) Contribution margin is an important metric internally but is generally considered irrelevant to outside financial statement users.

4. **Justification for Variable Costing**
   a. Under variable costing, fixed overhead cost is considered a cost of maintaining capacity, not a cost of production.
      1) To illustrate, a company has a fixed rental expense of $10,000 per month on its factory building. That cost will be $10,000 regardless of whether there is any production.
         a) If the company produces zero units, the cost will be $10,000; if the company produces 10,000 units, the cost will be $10,000.
      2) Therefore, the $10,000 is not viewed as a cost of production and is not added to the cost of the inventories produced. The $10,000 was a cost of maintaining a certain level of production capacity.
   b. To emphasize, variable costing is used only for internal decision-making purposes; it is not permitted for external financial reporting or for tax calculation.
      1) The main advantage of the variable costing method is that income cannot be manipulated by management action, whereas management can manipulate income when using the absorption method (explained in item 7. beginning on page 183).
   c. EXAMPLE: During its first month in business, a firm produced 100 units and sold 80 while incurring the following costs:

Direct materials	$1,000
Direct labor	2,000
Variable overhead	1,500
Manufacturing costs used in variable costing	**$4,500**
Fixed overhead	3,000
Manufacturing costs used in absorption costing	**$7,500**

   1) The impact on the financial statements from using one method over the other can be seen in these calculations:

	Absorption Basis	Variable Basis
Manufacturing costs	$7,500	$4,500
Divided by: units produced	÷ 100	÷ 100
Per-unit cost	$ 75	$ 45
Times: ending inventory	× 20	× 20
Value of ending inventory	**$1,500**	**$ 900**

SU 6: Cost Allocation Techniques   181

2) The $600 difference ($1,500 − $900) in inventory value represents the fixed overhead that is charged to the absorption basis inventory. Because 20% of the units produced are still in inventory, 20% of the $3,000 of fixed costs, or $600, is still in inventory. Under the variable basis, all fixed costs are expended.

3) The per-unit selling price of the finished goods was $100, and the company incurred $200 of variable selling and administrative expenses and $600 of fixed selling and administrative expenses.

d. The following are partial income statements prepared using the two methods:

		Absorption Costing (Required under GAAP)	Variable Costing (For Internal Reporting Only)
	Sales	$ 8,000	$ 8,000
	Beginning finished goods inventory	$ 0	$ 0
Product Costs	Plus: variable production costs	4,500 (a)	4,500 (a)
	Plus: fixed production costs	3,000 (b)	
	Goods available for sale	$7,500	$4,500
	Less: ending finished goods inventory	(1,500)	(900)
	Cost of goods sold	$(6,000)	$(3,600)
	Less: variable S&A expenses		(200) (c)
	Gross margin (abs.) / Contribution margin (var.)	$ 2,000	$ 4,200
Period Costs	Less: fixed production costs		(3,000) (b)
	Less: variable S&A expenses	(200) (c)	
	Less: fixed S&A expenses	(600) (d)	(600) (d)
	Operating income	$ 1,200	$ 600

1) The $600 difference in operating income ($1,200 − $600) is the difference between the two ending inventory values ($1,500 − $900).

a) In essence, the absorption method carries 20% of the fixed overhead costs ($3,000 × 20% = $600) on the balance sheet as an asset because 20% of the month's production (100 available − 80 sold = 20 on hand) is still in inventory.

2) This calculation is for illustrative purposes only. The difference in operating income is exactly the difference in ending inventory only when beginning inventory is $0.

5. **Impact on Operating Income**

a. As production and sales levels change, the two methods have varying impacts on operating income.

1) When everything produced during a period is sold that period, the two methods report the same operating income.

a) Total fixed costs budgeted for the period are charged to sales revenue in the period under both methods.

2) When production and sales are not equal for a period, the two methods report different operating income.

b. When production exceeds sales, ending inventory expands.

1) Under absorption costing, some fixed costs are embedded in ending inventory whereas, under variable costing, all costs have been expensed.

2) **Therefore, when production exceeds sales, operating income is higher under absorption costing than it would be under variable costing.**

c. When production is less than sales, ending inventory contracts.

1) Under absorption costing, fixed costs embedded in beginning inventory get expensed whereas, under variable costing, only the current period's fixed costs are expenses.

2) **Therefore, when production is less than sales, operating income is higher under variable costing than it would be under absorption costing.**

d. Many companies prefer variable costing for internal reporting because of the perverse incentive inherent in absorption costing.

  1) Whenever production exceeds sales, fewer fixed costs are expensed under the absorption basis, and operating income always increases.
  2) A production manager can thus **increase absorption-basis operating income merely by increasing production**, whether there is any customer demand for the additional product or not.

     a) The company must also deal with the increased carrying costs resulting from swelling inventory levels.

  3) This practice, called producing for inventory, can be effectively discouraged by using variable costing for performance reporting and consequent bonus calculation.

EXTENDED EXAMPLE of Absorption and Variable Operating Income

A company has the following sales and cost data:

	Year 1	Year 2	Year 3
Production in units	40,000	50,000	0
Sales in units	30,000	30,000	30,000
Ending inventory in units (FIFO)	10,000	30,000	0

Unit sales price	$1.00
Unit variable cost	$0.50
Fixed manufacturing costs	$4,000 per year
Variable S&A expenses	$0.03 per unit
Fixed S&A expenses	$1,000 per year

Compare the 3-year income statements prepared under the two methods:

Absorption Costing (Required for external reporting)

	Year 1	Year 2	Year 3
Sales	$30,000	$30,000	$30,000
Beginning inventory	$ 0	$ 6,000	$17,500
Variable mfg. costs	20,000	25,000	0
Fixed mfg. costs	4,000	4,000	4,000
Goods available for sale	$24,000	$35,000	$21,500
Less: ending inventory*	(6,000)	(17,500)	0
Absorption COGS	$18,000	$17,500	$21,500
Gross margin	$12,000	$12,500	$ 8,500
Variable S&A expenses	(900)	(900)	(900)
Fixed S&A expenses	(1,000)	(1,000)	(1,000)
Operating income	$10,100	$10,600	$ 6,600

Variable Costing (For internal reporting only)

	Year 1	Year 2	Year 3
Sales	$30,000	$30,000	$30,000
Beginning inventory	$ 0	$ 5,000	$15,000
Variable mfg. costs	20,000	25,000	0
Goods avail. for sale	$20,000	$30,000	$15,000
Less: ending inventory	(5,000)	(15,000)	0
Variable COGS	$15,000	$15,000	$15,000
Variable S&A exps.	(900)	(900)	(900)
Contribution margin	$14,100	$14,100	$14,100
Fixed mfg. costs	(4,000)	(4,000)	(4,000)
Fixed S&A expenses	(1,000)	(1,000)	(1,000)
Operating income	$ 9,100	$ 9,100	$ 9,100

Note that, assuming zero inventory at the beginning of Year 1 and at the end of Year 3, the total operating income for the 3-year period is the same under either costing method.

	Absorption Costing	Variable Costing
Year 1	$10,100	$ 9,100
Year 2	10,600	9,100
Year 3	6,600	9,100
3-Year Total	$27,300	$27,300

-- Continued on the next page --

> **EXTENDED EXAMPLE -- Continued**
>
> Absorption costing shows a higher operating income than variable costing in Years 1 and 2 because fixed overhead has been capitalized and does not get expensed until Year 3. Variable costing, on the other hand, treats fixed overhead as an expense of the period in which the cost is incurred. In Year 2, despite the same cash flow, there is a $1,500 difference between the final operating income figures. There is an even greater difference in Year 3.
>
> If fixed costs increase relative to variable costs, the differences become more dramatic (here, 50% of the selling price is variable manufacturing cost, and fixed overhead is no more than 20% of the variable manufacturing cost).
>
> From an internal point of view, a manager can manipulate absorption income by changing production levels. But, with variable costing, a manager cannot manipulate simply by changing production levels.
>
> Note that, under the absorption method, management was able to show higher incomes in Years 1 and 2 by overproducing. If the manager was being given a bonus for a higher level of income, (s)he could obtain the bonus by producing more units than could be sold. As a result, some fixed costs would be added to the balance sheet as inventories. Thus, the income statement and balance sheet both look good, despite the fact that the production manager has done a bad thing: (S)he has produced excessive inventories, that require the company to incur storage and financing costs. Spoilage may also be a result.
>
> Ending inventory is calculated on the weighted-average basis. The use of FIFO would result in slightly different numbers in Year 2 under the absorption method, but the impact would be the same.

6. **Summary of Effects on Income and Ending Inventory**

    a. The value of ending inventory is **never** higher under variable costing than it is under absorption costing because fixed manufacturing costs are not included in inventory under variable costing.

    b. Income and inventory levels will differ whenever sales and production differ.

    1) Income will be higher or lower under variable costing depending upon whether inventories are increased during the period or liquidated.
    2) If inventories increase during a period, the variable costing method will show a lower income because all fixed costs are being subtracted on the income statement, while under the absorption method, some fixed costs are being capitalized as inventories.
    3) Variable costing will show a higher income in periods when inventories decline because the absorption method forces the subtraction of current period fixed costs included in inventory sold, plus some fixed costs incurred (and capitalized) in prior periods.

    c. Under variable costing, profits always move in the same direction as sales volume. Profits reported under absorption costing behave erratically and sometimes move in the opposite direction from sales trends.

    d. In the long run, the two methods will report the same total profits if sales equal production. The inequalities between production and sales are usually minor over an extended period.

7. **Benefits of Variable Costing**

    a. Although the use of variable costing for financial statements is prohibited, most agree about its superiority for internal reporting. It is far better suited than absorption costing to the needs of management.

    1) Management requires a knowledge of cost behavior under various operating conditions. For planning and control, management is more concerned with treating fixed and variable costs separately than with calculating full costs.
    2) Full costs are usually of dubious value because they contain arbitrary allocations of fixed cost.

    b. Under the variable costing method, a production manager cannot manipulate income levels by overproducing. Given the same cost structure every year, the income levels will be based on sales, not the level of production.

c. Under variable costing, the cost data for profit planning and decision making are readily available from accounting records and statements. Reference to auxiliary records and supplementary analyses is not necessary.

   1) For example, cost-volume-profit relationships and the effects of changes in sales volume on net income can easily be computed from the income statement prepared under the variable costing concept, but not from the conventional absorption cost income statement based on the same data.

d. Profits and losses reported under variable costing have a relationship to sales revenue and are not affected by inventory or production variations.

e. Absorption cost income statements may show decreases in profits when sales are rising and increases in profits when sales are decreasing, which may be confusing to management. Attempts at explanation by means of volume variances often compound rather than clarify the confusion.

f. When variable costing is used, the favorable margin between selling prices and variable cost should provide a constant reminder of profits forgone because of lack of sales volume. A favorable margin justifies a higher production level.

g. The full impact of fixed costs on net income, partially hidden in inventory values under absorption costing, is emphasized by the presentation of costs on an income statement prepared under variable costing.

h. Proponents of variable costing maintain that fixed factory overhead is more closely correlated to capacity to produce than to the production of individual units.

8. **Further Aspects of Variable Costing**

   a. Variable costing is also preferred over absorption costing for studies of relative profitability of products, territories, and other segments of a business. It concentrates on the contribution that each segment makes to the recovery of fixed costs that will not be altered by decisions to make and sell. Under variable costing procedures,

      1) The marginal income concept leads to better pricing decisions, which are a principal advantage of variable costing.
      2) The impact of fixed costs on net income is emphasized by showing the total amount of such costs separately in financial reports.
      3) Out-of-pocket expenditures required to manufacture products conform closely with the valuation of inventory.
      4) The relationship between profit and the major factors of selling price, sales mix, sales volume, and variable manufacturing and nonmanufacturing costs is measured in terms of a single index of profitability.

         a) This profitability index, expressed as a positive amount or as a ratio, facilitates the analysis of cost-volume-profit relationships, compares the effects of two or more contemplated courses of action, and aids in answering many questions that arise in profit planning.

      5) Inventory changes have no effect on the breakeven computations.
      6) Marginal income figures facilitate appraisal of products, territories, and other business segments without having the results hidden or obscured by allocated joint fixed costs.
      7) Questions regarding whether a particular part should be made or bought can be more effectively answered if only variable costs are used.

         a) Management must consider whether to charge the product being made with variable costs only or to charge a percentage of fixed costs as well.
         b) Management must also consider whether the making of the part will require additional fixed costs and a decrease in normal production.

SU 6: Cost Allocation Techniques 185

8) Disinvestment decisions are facilitated because whether a product or department is recouping its variable costs can be determined.

a) If the variable costs are being covered, operating a department at an apparent loss may be profitable.

9) Management is better able to judge the differences between departments if certain fixed costs are omitted from the statements instead of being allocated arbitrarily.

10) Cost figures are guided by the sales figures.

a) Under variable costing, cost of goods sold will vary directly with sales volume, and the influence of production on gross profit is avoided.

b) Variable costing also eliminates the possible difficulties of having to explain over- or underapplied factory overhead to higher management.

Stop and review! You have completed the outline for this subunit. Study multiple-choice questions 1 through 4 beginning on page 199.

6.2 ABSORPTION AND VARIABLE COSTING -- CALCULATIONS

 Management accountants are expected to know the theory and how to complete detailed calculations for the topics covered in this study unit. To provide a more focused approach to studying, Gleim has broken up the theoretical questions and computational questions of the different cost allocation techniques into separate subunits. CMA candidates should expect a mix of both theory and computational questions on the CMA exam.

Some of the questions concerning absorption and variable costing that a candidate will encounter on the CMA exam focus on the detailed calculations required under the two methods. This subunit consists entirely of such questions. Please review Subunit 6.1 before attempting to answer the questions in this subunit.

Stop and review! You have completed the outline for this subunit. Study multiple-choice questions 5 through 8 beginning on page 200.

6.3 JOINT PRODUCT AND BY-PRODUCT COSTING

1. **Joint Processing and the Split-Off Point**

   a. When two or more separate products are produced by a common manufacturing process from a common input, the outputs from the process are joint products.

   b. **Joint (common) costs** are those costs incurred up to the point where the products become separately identifiable, called the split-off point.

   1) Joint costs include direct materials, direct labor, and manufacturing overhead. Because they are not separately identifiable, they must be allocated to the individual joint products.

   2) EXAMPLE: Crude oil can be refined into multiple salable products. All costs incurred in getting the crude oil to the distilling tower are joint costs.

   c. Because joint costs cannot be traced to individual products, they must be allocated. The methods available for this allocation can be classified in two conceptual groupings.

   1) The physical-measure-based approach employs a physical measure, such as volume, weight, or a linear measure.

2) Market-based approaches assign a proportionate amount of the total cost to each product on a monetary basis.

    a) Sales-value at split-off method
    b) Estimated net realizable value (NRV) method
    c) Constant-gross-margin percentage NRV method

d. At the split-off point, the joint products acquire separate identities. Costs incurred after split-off are separable costs.

1) **Separable costs** can be identified with a particular joint product and allocated to a specific unit of output.
2) EXAMPLE: Once crude oil has been distilled into asphalt, fuel oil, diesel fuel, kerosene, and gasoline, costs incurred in further refining and distributing these individual products are separable costs.

2. **Physical-Measure-Based Approach**

   a. The **physical-unit method** allocates joint production costs to each product based on their relative proportions of the measure selected.

   1) EXAMPLE: A refinery processes 1,000 barrels of crude oil and incurs $100,000 of processing costs. The process results in the following outputs. Under the physical unit method, the joint costs up to split-off are allocated as follows:

Asphalt	$100,000 × (300 barrels ÷ 1,000 barrels) =	$ 30,000
Fuel oil	$100,000 × (300 barrels ÷ 1,000 barrels) =	30,000
Diesel fuel	$100,000 × (200 barrels ÷ 1,000 barrels) =	20,000
Kerosene	$100,000 × (100 barrels ÷ 1,000 barrels) =	10,000
Gasoline	$100,000 × (100 barrels ÷ 1,000 barrels) =	10,000
Joint costs allocated		$100,000

   b. The physical-unit method's simplicity makes it appealing, but it does not match costs with the individual products' revenue-generating potential.

   1) Basically, there is almost no situation where the physical-unit method is beneficial. Its advantage is that it is easy to use.
   2) However, its limitations are that it treats low-value products that are large in size as if they were valuable. As a result, a large, low-value product might always show a loss, whereas small, high-value products will always show a profit.

3. **Market-Based Approaches**

   a. These allocations are performed using the entire production run for an accounting period, not units sold. This is because the joint costs were incurred on all the units produced, not just those sold.

   b. The **sales-value at split-off method** is based on the relative sales values of the separate products at split-off.

   1) EXAMPLE: The refinery estimates that the five outputs can sell for the following prices at split-off:

Asphalt	300 barrels at $ 60/barrel =	$ 18,000
Fuel oil	300 barrels at $180/barrel =	54,000
Diesel fuel	200 barrels at $160/barrel =	32,000
Kerosene	100 barrels at $ 80/barrel =	8,000
Gasoline	100 barrels at $180/barrel =	18,000
Total sales value at split-off		$130,000

The total expected sales value for the entire production run at split-off is thus $130,000. Multiply the total joint costs to be allocated by the proportion of the total expected sales of each product:

Asphalt	$100,000 × ($18,000 ÷ $130,000) =	$ 13,846
Fuel oil	$100,000 × ($54,000 ÷ $130,000) =	41,539
Diesel fuel	$100,000 × ($32,000 ÷ $130,000) =	24,615
Kerosene	$100,000 × ($ 8,000 ÷ $130,000) =	6,154
Gasoline	$100,000 × ($18,000 ÷ $130,000) =	13,846
Joint costs allocated		$100,000

c. The **estimated net realizable value (NRV)** method also allocates joint costs based on the relative market values of the products.

1) The significant difference is that, under the estimated NRV method, all separable costs necessary to make the product salable are subtracted before the allocation is made.

2) EXAMPLE: The refinery estimates final sales prices as follows:

Asphalt	300 barrels at $ 70/barrel =	$21,000
Fuel oil	300 barrels at $200/barrel =	60,000
Diesel fuel	200 barrels at $180/barrel =	36,000
Kerosene	100 barrels at $ 90/barrel =	9,000
Gasoline	100 barrels at $190/barrel =	19,000

From these amounts, separable costs are subtracted (these costs are given):

Asphalt	$21,000 – $1,000 =	$ 20,000
Fuel oil	$60,000 – $1,000 =	59,000
Diesel fuel	$36,000 – $1,000 =	35,000
Kerosene	$ 9,000 – $2,000 =	7,000
Gasoline	$19,000 – $2,000 =	17,000
Total net realizable value		$138,000

Multiply the total joint costs to be allocated by the proportion of the final expected sales of each product:

Asphalt	$100,000 × ($20,000 ÷ $138,000) =	$ 14,493
Fuel oil	$100,000 × ($59,000 ÷ $138,000) =	42,754
Diesel fuel	$100,000 × ($35,000 ÷ $138,000) =	25,362
Kerosene	$100,000 × ($ 7,000 ÷ $138,000) =	5,072
Gasoline	$100,000 × ($17,000 ÷ $138,000) =	12,319
Joint costs allocated		$100,000

d. The **constant-gross-margin percentage NRV** method is based on allocating joint costs so that the gross-margin percentage is the same for every product.

1) The three steps under this method are

a) Determine the overall gross-margin percentage.

b) Subtract the appropriate gross margin from the final sales value of each product to calculate total costs for that product.

c) Subtract the separable costs to arrive at the joint cost amount.

2) EXAMPLE: The refinery uses the same calculation of expected final sales price as under the estimated NRV method:

Asphalt	300 barrels at $ 70/barrel =	$ 21,000
Fuel oil	300 barrels at $200/barrel =	60,000
Diesel fuel	200 barrels at $180/barrel =	36,000
Kerosene	100 barrels at $ 90/barrel =	9,000
Gasoline	100 barrels at $190/barrel =	19,000
Total of final sales prices		$145,000

The final sales value for the entire production run is thus $145,000. From this total, the joint costs and total separable costs are deducted to arrive at a total gross margin for all products:

$145,000 − $100,000 − $7,000 = $38,000

The gross margin percentage can then be derived:

$38,000 ÷ $145,000 = 26.21%

Deduct gross margin from each product to arrive at a cost of goods sold:

Asphalt	$21,000 − ($21,000 × 26.21%) =	$15,497
Fuel oil	$60,000 − ($60,000 × 26.21%) =	44,276
Diesel fuel	$36,000 − ($36,000 × 26.21%) =	26,565
Kerosene	$ 9,000 − ($ 9,000 × 26.21%) =	6,641
Gasoline	$19,000 − ($19,000 × 26.21%) =	14,021

Deduct the separable costs from each product to arrive at the allocated joint costs:

Asphalt	$15,497 − $1,000 =	$ 14,497
Fuel oil	$44,276 − $1,000 =	43,276
Diesel fuel	$26,565 − $1,000 =	25,565
Kerosene	$ 6,641 − $2,000 =	4,641
Gasoline	$14,021 − $2,000 =	12,021
Joint costs allocated		$100,000

e. The three market-based approaches are far superior to the physical-measure-based approach, although they do require more work and more recordkeeping. However, they produce more usable results.

4. **Accounting for By-Products**

   a. By-products are one or more products of relatively small total value that are produced simultaneously from a common manufacturing process with products of greater value and quantity.

   b. The first question that must be answered in regard to by-products is: Do the benefits of further processing and bringing them to market exceed the costs?

Selling price − Additional processing costs − Selling costs = Net realizable value

   1) If the net realizable value is zero or negative, the by-products should be discarded as scrap.

   c. If the by-products are material, they are capitalized in a separate inventory account, as in this example:

Finished goods inventory − Asphalt (allocated costs)	$XX,XXX
Finished goods inventory − Fuel oil (allocated costs)	XX,XXX
Finished goods inventory − Diesel fuel (allocated costs)	XX,XXX
Finished goods inventory − Kerosene (allocated costs)	XX,XXX
Finished goods inventory − Gasoline (allocated costs)	XX,XXX
By-product inventory − Sludge (estimated net realizable value)	X,XXX
Work-in-process (total manufacturing costs for period)	$XXX,XXX

SU 6: Cost Allocation Techniques   189

- 1) The amount capitalized is the entire estimated net realizable value of the by-products generated during the period.
    - a) This treatment is justifiable when a ready market for the by-products is available.
- 2) By proportionally reducing the amounts capitalized for the major finished goods, this treatment of by-product inventory effectively reduces cost of goods sold. Thus, when the by-products are sold, the income statement effects have already been recognized.

    Cash $X,XXX
       By-product inventory – Sludge $X,XXX

- d. If the by-products are immaterial, they are not recognized until the time of sale.
    - 1) The amount of miscellaneous revenue (or reduction to cost of goods sold) reported is the actual proceeds from the sale of the by-products.

    Cash $X,XXX
       Cost of goods sold/Miscellaneous revenue $X,XXX

- e. Regardless of the timing of their recognition in the accounts, by-products usually do not receive an allocation of joint costs because the cost of this accounting treatment ordinarily exceeds the benefit.

5. **Sell-or-Process-Further Decisions**
    - a. The decision to sell or process further is made based on whether the incremental revenue to be gained by further processing exceeds the incremental cost thereof.
        - 1) The joint cost of the product is irrelevant because it is a sunk cost.

Stop and review! You have completed the outline for this subunit. Study multiple-choice questions 9 through 13 beginning on page 202.

6.4 OVERHEAD ALLOCATION AND NORMAL COSTING -- THEORY

1. **Components of Manufacturing Overhead**
    - a. Manufacturing overhead consists of all costs of manufacturing that are not direct materials or direct labor.
    - b. Indirect materials are tangible inputs to the manufacturing process that cannot practicably be traced to the product, e.g., the welding compound used to put together a piece of heavy equipment.
    - c. Indirect labor is the cost of human labor connected with the manufacturing process that cannot practicably be traced to the product, e.g., the wages of assembly line supervisors and janitorial staff.
    - d. Factory operating costs, such as utilities, real estate taxes, insurance, depreciation on factory equipment, etc.
        - 1) Overhead thus consists of all costs of manufacturing that are not direct materials or direct labor.

2. **Variable and Fixed Components**
    - a. Unlike direct materials and direct labor, which are purely variable costs, overhead contains both variable and fixed components.
        - 1) Variable overhead costs include indirect materials, indirect labor, utilities, and depreciation expense under any method that ties depreciation to the level of output.
            - a) The time frame for planning variable overhead is the short run, i.e., the period within which per-unit variable costs remain constant and therefore predictable.

2) Fixed overhead costs include real estate taxes, insurance, and depreciation expense under any method that is not tied to the level of output.

   a) The time frame for planning fixed overhead is the long run. Such cost elements as real estate taxes and depreciation are determined by capital expenditures, i.e., those that by their nature span multiple years.

b. Estimated overhead for the year is accumulated in two indirect cost pools (one for variable costs and one for fixed), which will then be allocated to production using an approximate allocation base for each.

c. EXAMPLE: A manufacturer is preparing its budget for the upcoming year and has compiled the following estimates of total costs:

Cost Element	Estimated Variable Overhead	Estimated Fixed Overhead
Indirect materials	$ 80,000	
Indirect labor	46,000	
Utilities	155,000	
Real estate taxes		$ 81,000
Insurance		54,000
Straight-line depreciation		240,000
Totals	$281,000	$375,000

3. **Selecting an Allocation Base**

   a. The crucial quality of an allocation base is that it be a cost driver of the costs in the pool to be allocated.

      1) Recall that a cost driver should capture a cause-and-effect relationship between the level of the driver and the level of the cost being allocated.

   b. In labor-intensive industries, direct labor hours or cost is an appropriate driver. In capital-intensive industries, machine hours is more appropriate. Still other bases may be used in an ABC system.

      1) It is therefore possible that variable and fixed overhead will employ the same allocation base.

      2) Overhead is usually not allocated on the basis of units produced because of the lack of a cause-and-effect relationship.

   c. EXAMPLE: The variable elements of overhead vary directly with the level of production, so the company has chosen to use units of output as the allocation base for variable overhead. The fixed elements of overhead are related directly to the level of productive capacity, such as factory space and amount of machinery, so the company has decided that it will use machine hours as the allocation base for fixed overhead.

4. **Calculating the Application Rate**

   a. Once appropriate allocation bases have been selected, the predetermined overhead application rates are calculated.

      1) The estimates made of the total amounts of overhead will be the numerators.

      2) Estimates are then made of the total quantity of each allocation base that will be expended; these will be the denominators.

      3) The quotients are the application rates for that budget period.

b. Estimates of the total quantity of each allocation base can be based off different capacity levels.

1) **Normal capacity** is the long-term average level of activity that will approximate demand over a period that includes seasonal, cyclical, and trend variations. Deviations in a given year will be offset in subsequent years.
2) **Practical capacity** is the maximum level at which output is produced efficiently. It allows for unavoidable delays in production for maintenance, holidays, etc. Practical capacity is based on realistic, attainable levels of production and input efficiency and is the most appropriate denominator level to use in selecting an overhead application rate.
3) **Theoretical (ideal) capacity** is the maximum capacity assuming continuous operations with no holidays, downtime, etc.

c. EXAMPLE: The company's best projection for the upcoming year is that 1,110,000 units will be produced and 57,000 machine hours will be expended. The overhead allocation rates can thus be calculated as follows:

Variable overhead application rate: $281,000 ÷ 1,110,000 units of output = $0.253 per unit
Fixed overhead application rate: $375,000 ÷ 57,000 machine hours = $6.579 per hour

d. A significant conceptual challenge is understanding the need to apply fixed overhead using an allocation base rather than simply to recognize one-twelfth of the estimated total every month.

1) Since fixed costs are by their nature unchanging within the relevant range, using an allocation base at first appears to unnecessarily complicate the bookkeeping process. But, one way or another, fixed costs must be covered by selling products to customers.
2) The advantage of applying fixed overhead at a predetermined rate is that an allocation base, even if only indirectly, reflects the level of productive activity.
   a) If production is way down or way up in a particular month, using an allocation base will result in a fixed overhead production-volume variance, also called the denominator-level variance (discussed in more detail in Study Unit 10, Subunit 6).
   b) The existence of a production-volume/denominator-level variance alerts management to the fact that fixed costs are being spread among fewer or more units, respectively, than anticipated.

e. Under activity-based costing, individual overhead costs are assigned based on the level of an associated activity rather than lumped in a single (or double) pool (discussed further in Study Unit 5, Subunit 2).

5. **Departmental vs. Plantwide Rates**

a. All the examples of overhead application so far have employed a single plantwide rate. This method has the benefit of simplicity.

1) However, some production departments may be labor-intensive while others are machine-intensive. In these cases, the use of a single driver for applying overhead to every phase of the production results in the miscosting of products.
2) A more accurate method is the use of departmental rates.

b. EXAMPLE: A company is preparing its overhead budget for the coming year and has selected direct labor hours as the allocation base.

	Budgeted Overhead		Allocation Base		Overhead Application Rate
Department A	$ 60,000				
Department B	40,000				
Total process	$100,000	÷	20,000	=	$5.00 per direct labor hour

A study by the company's management accountants reveals that Department A heavily employs direct labor while Department B is far more automated.

- Of the total direct labor hours budgeted for the year, 15,000 are projected for Department A and only 5,000 for Department B.
- At the same time, Department A is projected to consume 8,000 machine hours while Department B is projected to use 16,000.

Instead of applying a single plantwide application rate, then, a more accurate allocation can be obtained by using a different allocation base for each production department.

	Budgeted Overhead		Allocation Base		Overhead Application Rate
Department A	$60,000	÷	15,000	=	$4.00 per direct labor hour
Department B	$40,000	÷	16,000	=	$2.50 per machine hour

c. When indirect costs represent a large proportion of total production costs, activity-based costing, which uses cost pools for all costs (not just overhead), may be the most appropriate cost accumulation system.

6. **Time Frame for Calculating Application Rates**

   a. Calculating new overhead application rates each month can result in misleading unit costs. Thus, overhead rates are normally calculated no more often than annually.

      1) This is because, during months of low production, per-unit overhead charges will skyrocket. This leads to higher product costs during months of lower production and to distortions in the financial statements.
      2) The following example illustrates this phenomenon.

EXTENDED EXAMPLE of Unit-Cost Distribution

A manufacturing firm divides its reporting year into 3 budget periods. The company is expecting the following units of production and sales during the upcoming year. Note that production is expected to fluctuate but sales are expected to be even:

	Jan-Apr	May-Aug	Sep-Dec	Totals
Production	10,000	6,000	8,000	24,000
Sales	7,000	7,000	7,000	21,000

Variable overhead costs are calculated at $1 per unit:

	Jan-Apr	May-Aug	Sep-Dec	Totals
Variable overhead cost	$10,000	$ 6,000	$ 8,000	$24,000
Fixed overhead cost	20,000	20,000	20,000	60,000
Total overhead cost	$30,000	$26,000	$28,000	$84,000

For simplicity, a single overhead application rate is used in this example:

	Jan-Apr	May-Aug	Sep-Dec
Estimated total overhead / Estimated production	$30,000 / 10,000 = $3.00	$26,000 / 6,000 = $4.33	$28,000 / 8,000 = $3.50

– Continued on next page –

SU 6: Cost Allocation Techniques

EXTENDED EXAMPLE of Unit-Cost Distribution -- Continued

These fluctuations in the applied overhead rate will lead to fluctuations in unit cost:

	Jan-Apr	May-Aug	Sep-Dec
Direct materials	$ 3.00	$ 3.00	$ 3.00
Direct labor	4.00	4.00	4.00
Manufacturing overhead	3.00	4.33	3.50
Total unit cost	**$10.00**	**$11.33**	**$10.50**

The comparative income statements make clear the distorting effect:

	Jan-Apr	May-Aug	Sep-Dec	Totals
Sales:				
Produced in Jan-Apr	7,000	3,000		
Produced in May-Aug		4,000	2,000	
Produced in Sep-Dec			5,000	
Expected unit sales	7,000	7,000	7,000	
Expected selling price	× $12	× $12	× $12	
Total expected sales	$84,000	$84,000	$84,000	$252,000
Cost of goods sold:				
From Jan-Apr	$70,000	$30,000		
From May-Aug		45,333	$22,667	
From Sep-Dec			52,500	
Total expected COGS	$70,000	$75,333	$75,167	$220,500
Gross margin	**$14,000**	**$ 8,667**	**$ 8,833**	**$ 31,500**

Large fluctuations in gross margin are reported during a period when there was no change at all in the company's underlying cost structure, and sales were the same throughout.

---

b. To prevent these distortions in the financial statements, **normal costing** derives a single overhead application rate by looking at the entire year.

EXTENDED EXAMPLE of Normal Costing

Instead of using a different overhead application rate for each budget period, the company uses a single average figure for the entire year.

- The company expects to produce 24,000 units during the year, for an average of 8,000 units per budget period.
- Dividing the fixed overhead of $20,000 for each budget period by 8,000 units yields a fixed overhead application rate of $2.50.
- The new total overhead application rate per unit is thus $3.50 ($1.00 variable cost + $2.50 fixed cost), and the new per-unit cost for all 3 budget periods is $10.50 ($3.00 direct materials + $4.00 direct labor + $3.50 overhead application rate).

The revised income statements prepared using a normalized overhead rate reveal the smoothing effect on gross margin:

	Jan-Apr	May-Aug	Sep-Dec	Totals
Sales:				
Produced in Jan-Apr	7,000	3,000		
Produced in May-Aug		4,000	2,000	
Produced in Sep-Dec			5,000	
Expected unit sales	7,000	7,000	7,000	
Expected selling price	× $12	× $12	× $12	
Total expected sales	$84,000	$84,000	$84,000	$252,000
Cost of goods sold:				
From Jan-Apr	$73,500	$31,500		
From May-Aug		42,000	$21,000	
From Sep-Dec			52,500	
Total expected COGS	$73,500	$73,500	$73,500	$220,500
Gross margin	**$10,500**	**$10,500**	**$10,500**	**$ 31,500**

c. **Extended normal costing** applies a normalized rate to direct costs as well as to manufacturing overhead.

1) The following table summarizes the use of rates in the three costing methods described:

	Actual Costing	Normal Costing	Extended Normal Costing
Direct Materials	Actual	Actual	Budgeted
Direct Labor	Actual	Actual	Budgeted
Manufacturing Overhead	Actual	Budgeted	Budgeted

7. **Recording Actual Overhead Costs**

   a. During the budget period, actual overhead costs are accumulated in the control accounts as they are incurred.

   b. EXAMPLE: At the end of October, the company recorded the following journal entries to recognize actual overhead costs incurred during the month:

   ```
   Variable overhead control                                 $22,050
       Raw materials (withdrawals for indirect materials)           $ 6,059
       Wages payable (indirect labor)                                 4,120
       Utilities payable (bill from utility provider)                11,871

   Fixed overhead control                                    $31,250
       Real estate taxes ($81,000 ÷ 12 months)                      $ 6,750
       Insurance expense ($54,000 ÷ 12 months)                        4,500
       Depreciation expense ($240,000 ÷ 12 months)                   20,000
   ```

8. **Allocating Overhead to Work-in-Process**

   a. At the end of the period, overhead is applied to work-in-process based on the actual level of the driver (e.g., actual machine hours × application rate).

   b. EXAMPLE: During October, the company produced 91,000 units and expended 4,000 machine hours. The journal entry to apply overhead for October is as follows:

   ```
   Work-in-process                                           $49,339
       Variable overhead applied (91,000 units × $0.253)            $23,023
       Fixed overhead applied (4,000 hours × $6.579)                 26,316
   ```

9. **Over- and Underapplied Overhead**

   a. Inevitably, the overhead amounts applied throughout the year will vary from the amount actually incurred, which is only determinable once the job is complete. This variance is called over- or underapplied overhead.

   1) Overapplied overhead (a credit balance in overhead applied) results when product costs are overstated because the

      a) Activity level was higher than expected or
      b) Actual overhead costs were lower than expected.

   2) Underapplied overhead (a debit balance in overhead applied) results when product costs are understated because the

      a) Activity level was lower than expected or
      b) Actual overhead costs were higher than expected.

b. If the amount of over- or under-applied overhead is considered **immaterial**, it can be closed directly to cost of goods sold.

1) EXAMPLE:

If overapplied:
Variable overhead applied (balance)	$23,023	
Cost of goods sold (difference)		$ 973
Variable overhead control (balance)		22,050

If underapplied:
Fixed overhead applied (balance)	$26,316	
Cost of goods sold (difference)	4,934	
Fixed overhead control (balance)		$31,250

c. If the amount of over- or under-applied overhead is considered **material**, it should be allocated based on the relative values of work-in-process, finished goods, and cost of goods sold.

1) EXAMPLE: Work-in-process, finished goods, and cost of goods sold bear a 20:20:60 cost relationship.

If overapplied:
Variable overhead applied (balance)	$23,023	
Work-in-process (overapplied amount × allocation %)		$ 195
Finished goods (overapplied amount × allocation %)		195
Cost of goods sold (overapplied amount × allocation %)		583
Variable overhead control (balance)		22,050

If underapplied:
Fixed overhead applied (balance)	$26,316	
Work-in-process (underapplied amount × allocation %)	987	
Finished goods (underapplied amount × allocation %)	987	
Cost of goods sold (underapplied amount × allocation %)	2,960	
Fixed overhead control (balance)		$31,250

2) The most accurate method of allocating over- or under-applied overhead is based on the relative amounts of overhead in work-in-process, finished goods, and cost of goods sold.

Stop and review! You have completed the outline for this subunit. Study multiple-choice questions 14 through 17 on page 204.

6.5 OVERHEAD ALLOCATION AND NORMAL COSTING -- CALCULATIONS

Some of the questions concerning overhead allocation and normal costing that a candidate will encounter on the CMA exam focus on the detailed calculations required. This subunit consists entirely of such questions. Please review Subunit 6.4 before attempting to answer the questions in this subunit.

Stop and review! You have completed the outline for this subunit. Study multiple-choice questions 18 through 21 beginning on page 205.

6.6 ALLOCATING SERVICE DEPARTMENT COSTS -- THEORY

1. **Reasons for Allocation**

    a. Service (support) department costs are considered part of overhead (indirect costs). Thus, they cannot feasibly be traced to cost objects and must be allocated to the operating departments that use the services.

    1) When service departments also render services to each other, their costs may be allocated to each other before allocation to operating departments.

b. Four criteria are used to allocate costs:

1) **Cause and effect** should be used if possible because of its objectivity and acceptance by operating management.
2) **Benefits received** is the most frequently used alternative when a cause-and-effect relationship cannot be determined.
   a) However, it requires an assumption about the benefits of costs, for example, that advertising that promotes the company but not specific products was responsible for increased sales by the various divisions.
3) **Fairness** is sometimes mentioned in government contracts but appears to be more of a goal than an objective allocation base.
4) **Ability to bear** (based on profits) is usually unacceptable because of its dysfunctional effect on managerial motivation.

c. The three methods of service department allocation in general use are the direct method, the step-down method, and the reciprocal method.

1) With the direct and reciprocal methods, the order of allocation is irrelevant.
2) However, under the step-down method, some service department cost is allocated to other service departments before allocation to the operating departments.
   a) These first allocations change the proportions of the total constituted by each department.

2. Direct Method

a. The direct method is the simplest. Under the direct method, service department costs are allocated directly to the producing departments without regard for services rendered by service departments to each other.

1) Service department costs are allocated to production departments based on an allocation base appropriate to each service department's function.

b. EXAMPLE: A company has the following service department costs and allocation bases:

Service Department	Costs to Be Allocated	Allocation Base
Information Technology	$120,000	CPU cycles
Custodial Services	40,000	Floor space
Total	**$160,000**	

The production departments have the following preallocation costs and allocation base amounts:

Production Department	Preallocation Costs	CPU Cycles Used	%	Floor Space in Sq. Ft.	%
Milling	$300,000	60,000,000	62.5%	56,000	70.0%
Finishing	200,000	36,000,000	37.5%	24,000	30.0%
Totals	**$500,000**	**96,000,000**	**100.0%**	**80,000**	**100.0%**

The direct method allocates the service department costs to the production departments as follows:

	Service Departments		Production Departments		
	Information Technology	Custodial Services	Milling	Finishing	Total
Totals before allocation	$120,000	$40,000	$300,000	$200,000	$660,000
Allocate IT (62.5%, 37.5%)	(120,000)	–	75,000	45,000	0
Allocate Custodial (70.0%, 30.0%)	–	(40,000)	28,000	12,000	0
Totals after allocation	**$ 0**	**$ 0**	**$403,000**	**$257,000**	**$660,000**

SU 6: Cost Allocation Techniques 197

3. **Step (Step-Down) Method**
   a. Under the step, or step-down method, some of the costs of services rendered by service departments are allocated to each other.
      1) This method derives its name from the procedure involved. The service departments are allocated in order, from the one that provides the most service to other service departments down to the one that provides the least.
   b. EXAMPLE: The services that each service department provides the other must be ascertained:

	Provided by IT		Provided by CS	
Service Department	CPU Cycles Used	%	Floor Space in Sq. Ft.	%
Information Technology	196,000,000	98.0%	20,000	80.0%
Custodial Services	4,000,000	2.0%	5,000	20.0%
Totals	200,000,000	100.0%	25,000	100.0%

   Looking only at reciprocal service department activity, custodial services provides 80% of its services to information technology, but IT only provides 2% of its services to custodial. Thus, custodial will be allocated first.

   The next step is to determine the relative proportions of the three departments that will receive the first allocation (the second allocation will only be distributed to the two production departments, whose allocation bases were determined under the direct method on the preceding page).

Allocate Custodial Services:	Floor Space in Sq. Ft.	%	Amount to Be Allocated	Departmental Allocations
To Milling	56,000	56.0%	$40,000	$22,400
To Finishing	24,000	24.0%	40,000	9,600
To Information Technology	20,000	20.0%	40,000	8,000
Totals	100,000	100.0%		$40,000

   The step-down allocation is performed as follows:

	Service Departments		Production Departments		
	Custodial Services	Information Technology	Milling	Finishing	Total
Totals before allocation	$40,000	$120,000	$300,000	$200,000	$660,000
Allocate Custodial	(40,000)	8,000	22,400	9,600	0
Totals after first allocation	$0	$128,000	$322,400	$209,600	$660,000

Allocate IT:	CPU Cycles Used	%	Amount to Be Allocated	Departmental Allocations
To Milling	60,000,000	62.5%	$128,000	$80,000
To Finishing	36,000,000	37.5%	128,000	48,000
Totals	96,000,000	100.0%		$128,000

		Production Departments		
	Information Technology	Milling	Finishing	Total
Totals after first allocation	$128,000	$322,400	$209,600	$660,000
Allocate IT	(128,000)	80,000	48,000	0
Totals after second allocation	$0	$402,400	$257,600	$660,000

4. **Reciprocal Method**
   a. The reciprocal method is the most complex and the most theoretically sound of the three methods. It is also known as the simultaneous solution method, cross allocation method, matrix allocation method, or double distribution method.
      1) Under the reciprocal method, services rendered by all service departments to each other are recognized.

b. EXAMPLE: The reciprocal method requires calculating the allocation base amounts for information technology; i.e., the service department that was not allocated to the other service department under the step method.

Allocate Information Technology:	CPU Cycles Used	%
To Milling	60,000,000	60.0%
To Finishing	36,000,000	36.0%
To Custodial Services	4,000,000	4.0%
Totals	**100,000,000**	**100.0%**

Use linear algebra to calculate fully reciprocated information technology costs (FRITC) and fully reciprocated custodial services costs (FRCSC):

FRITC = Preallocation IT costs + (FRCSC × Portion of custodial effort used by IT)
= $120,000 + (FRCSC × 20%)

FRCSC = Preallocation custodial costs + (FRITC × Portion of IT effort used by custodial)
= $40,000 + (FRITC × 4%)

These algebraic equations can be solved simultaneously.

FRITC = $120,000 + (FRCSC × 20%)
= $120,000 + {[$40,000 + (FRITC × 4%)] × 20%}
= $120,000 + [($40,000 + .04FRITC) × .2]
= $120,000 + $8,000 + .008FRITC
.992FRITC = $128,000
FRITC = $129,032

FRCSC = $40,000 + (FRITC × 4%)
= $40,000 + ($129,032 × .04)
= $40,000 + $5,161
= $45,161

The reciprocal allocation is performed as follows:

	Service Departments		Production Departments		
	Custodial Services	Information Technology	Milling	Finishing	Total
Totals before allocation	$40,000	$120,000	$300,000	$200,000	$ 660,000
Allocate Custodial Services (20.0%, 56.0%, 24.0%)	(45,161)	9,032	25,290	10,839	0
Allocate Information Technology (4.0%, 60.0%, 36.0%)	5,161	(129,032)	77,419	46,452	0
Totals after allocation	**$ 0**	**$ 0**	**$402,709**	**$257,291**	**$ 660,000**

5. **Single-Rate vs. Dual-Rate Allocation**

   a. The examples presented employed a single rate to allocate the costs of each support department. Some firms find that employing dual-rate allocation provides more useful information.

   b. EXAMPLE: The company has decided to allocate the IT department's costs using a dual-rate method, one rate for the costs of IT's investment in hardware and software (fixed) and another rate for the costs of services provided (variable).

   - The IT department has determined that $40,000 of its total allocable costs are associated with variable costs. These will henceforth be allocated using technician and programmer hours.
   - The company's technicians and programmers worked a total of 1,600 hours on projects for the Milling and Finishing Departments during the period. Variable IT costs will thus be applied at the rate of $25 per hour ($40,000 ÷ 1,600).
   - The remaining $80,000 of allocable IT costs are associated with the department's investment in fixed plant. These costs will continue to be allocated using CPU cycles.

- Since the company's central computers consumed a total of 96 million CPU cycles doing processing for the Milling and Finishing Departments during the period, fixed IT costs will be applied at the rate of $0.00083 per cycle ($80,000 ÷ 96,000,000).

The dual-rate allocations will be made as follows:

Allocate to Milling:	Driver Units Consumed		Application Rate		Totals
Variable IT costs	640 hours	×	$25.00	=	$16,000
Fixed IT costs	60,000,000 cycles	×	$0.00083	=	50,000
Total					$66,000

Allocate to Finishing:	Driver Units Consumed		Application Rate		Totals
Variable IT costs	960 hours	×	$25.00	=	$24,000
Fixed IT costs	36,000,000 cycles	×	$0.00083	=	30,000
Total					$54,000

1) The total amount of IT department costs has been allocated ($66,000 + $54,000 = $120,000).

c. The dual-rate method can be used to refine a system currently using a single rate under any of the other methods (direct, step-down, reciprocal).

Stop and review! You have completed the outline for this subunit. Study multiple-choice questions 22 through 25 beginning on page 206.

6.7 ALLOCATING SERVICE DEPARTMENT COSTS -- CALCULATIONS

Some of the questions concerning service department allocation costing that a candidate will encounter on the CMA exam focus on the detailed calculations required. This subunit consists entirely of such questions. Please review Subunit 6.6 before attempting to answer the questions in this subunit.

Stop and review! You have completed the outline for this subunit. Study multiple-choice questions 26 through 30 beginning on page 208.

QUESTIONS

6.1 Absorption and Variable Costing -- Theory

1. Which method of inventory costing treats direct manufacturing costs and manufacturing overhead costs, both variable and fixed, as inventoriable costs?

A. Direct costing.
B. Variable costing.
C. Absorption costing.
D. Conversion costing.

Answer (C) is correct.
REQUIRED: The method of inventory costing that treats direct manufacturing costs and all manufacturing overhead as inventoriable.
DISCUSSION: Absorption (full) costing considers all manufacturing costs to be inventoriable as product costs. These costs include variable and fixed manufacturing costs, whether direct or indirect. The alternative to absorption is known as variable (direct) costing.
Answer (A) is incorrect. Variable (direct) costing does not inventory fixed overhead. Answer (B) is incorrect. Variable (direct) costing does not inventory fixed overhead. Answer (D) is incorrect. Conversion costs include direct labor and overhead but not direct materials.

2. The costing method that is properly classified for both external and internal reporting purposes is

	External Reporting	Internal Reporting
A. Activity-based costing	No	Yes
B. Job-order costing	No	Yes
C. Variable costing	No	Yes
D. Process costing	No	No

Answer (C) is correct.
REQUIRED: The costing method that is properly classified for both internal and external reporting purposes.
DISCUSSION: Activity-based costing, job-order costing, process costing, and standard costing can all be used for both internal and external purposes. Variable costing is not acceptable under GAAP for external reporting purposes.
Answer (A) is incorrect. ABC is appropriate for external as well as internal purposes. Answer (B) is incorrect. Job-order costing is acceptable for external reporting purposes. Answer (D) is incorrect. Process costing is acceptable for external reporting purposes.

3. Which one of the following statements is **true** regarding absorption costing and variable costing?

A. Overhead costs are treated in the same manner under both costing methods.
B. If finished goods inventory increases, absorption costing results in higher income.
C. Variable manufacturing costs are lower under variable costing.
D. Gross margins are the same under both costing methods.

Answer (B) is correct.
REQUIRED: The true statement regarding absorption costing and variable costing.
DISCUSSION: Under variable costing, inventories are charged only with the variable costs of production. Fixed manufacturing costs are expensed as period costs. Absorption costing charges to inventory all costs of production. If finished goods inventory increases, absorption costing results in higher income because it capitalizes some fixed costs that would have been expensed under variable costing. When inventory declines, variable costing results in higher income because some fixed costs capitalized under the absorption method in prior periods are expensed in the current period.
Answer (A) is incorrect. Fixed overhead is treated differently under the two methods. Answer (C) is incorrect. Variable costs are the same under either method. Answer (D) is incorrect. Gross margins will be different. Fixed factory overhead is expensed under variable costing and capitalized under the absorption method.

4. Absorption costing and variable costing are two different methods of assigning costs to units produced. Of the four cost items listed below, identify the one that is **not** correctly accounted for as a product cost.

	Part of Product Cost Under	
	Absorption Costing	Variable Costing
A. Manufacturing supplies	Yes	Yes
B. Insurance on factory	Yes	No
C. Direct labor cost	Yes	Yes
D. Packaging and shipping costs	Yes	Yes

Answer (D) is correct.
REQUIRED: The cost not correctly accounted for.
DISCUSSION: Under absorption costing, all manufacturing costs, both fixed and variable, are treated as product costs. Under variable costing, only variable costs of manufacturing are inventoried as product costs. Fixed manufacturing costs are expensed as period costs. Packaging and shipping costs are not product costs under either method because they are incurred after the goods have been manufactured. Instead, they are included in selling and administrative expenses for the period.
Answer (A) is incorrect. Manufacturing supplies are variable costs inventoried under both methods. Answer (B) is incorrect. Factory insurance is a fixed manufacturing cost inventoried under absorption costing but written off as a period cost under variable costing. Answer (C) is incorrect. Direct labor cost is a product cost under both methods.

6.2 Absorption and Variable Costing -- Calculations

Questions 5 and 6 are based on the following information. At the end of its fiscal year, Jubal Manufacturing recorded the data below:

Prime cost	$800,000
Variable manufacturing overhead	100,000
Fixed manufacturing overhead	160,000
Variable selling and other expenses	80,000
Fixed selling and other expenses	40,000

5. If Jubal uses variable costing, the inventoriable costs for the fiscal year are

A. $800,000
B. $900,000
C. $980,000
D. $1,060,000

Answer (B) is correct.
REQUIRED: The inventoriable costs using the variable costing method.
DISCUSSION: The only costs capitalized are the variable costs of manufacturing. Prime costs (direct materials and direct labor) are variable.

Prime costs (direct materials and direct labor)	$800,000
Variable manufacturing overhead	100,000
Total inventoriable costs	$900,000

Answer (A) is incorrect. The amount of $800,000 equals only the prime costs. Answer (C) is incorrect. The amount of $980,000 includes the variable selling and other expenses. Answer (D) is incorrect. The amount of $1,060,000 equals inventoriable costs under absorption costing.

SU 6: Cost Allocation Techniques

6. Using absorption (full) costing, Jubal's inventoriable costs are

A. $800,000
B. $900,000
C. $1,060,000
D. $1,180,000

Answer (C) is correct.
REQUIRED: The inventoriable costs using the absorption costing method.
DISCUSSION: The absorption method is required for financial statements prepared according to GAAP. It charges all costs of production to inventories. The prime costs of $800,000, variable manufacturing overhead of $100,000, and the fixed manufacturing overhead of $160,000 are included. They total $1,060,000.
Answer (A) is incorrect. The amount of $800,000 equals only prime costs. Answer (B) is incorrect. The amount of $900,000 equals inventoriable costs under variable costing. Answer (D) is incorrect. The amount of $1,180,000 includes the fixed and variable selling and other expenses.

Questions 7 and 8 are based on the following information. Osawa, Inc., planned and actually manufactured 200,000 units of its single product during its first year of operations. Variable manufacturing costs were $30 per unit of product. Planned and actual fixed manufacturing costs were $600,000, and selling and administrative costs totaled $400,000. Osawa sold 120,000 units of product at a selling price of $40 per unit.

---

7. Osawa's operating income for the year using variable costing is

A. $200,000
B. $440,000
C. $800,000
D. $600,000

Answer (A) is correct.
REQUIRED: The operating income under variable costing.
DISCUSSION: The contribution margin from manufacturing (sales – variable costs) is $10 ($40 – $30) per unit sold, or $1,200,000 (120,000 units × $10). The fixed costs of manufacturing ($600,000) and selling and administrative costs ($400,000) are deducted from the contribution margin to arrive at an operating income of $200,000.
Answer (B) is incorrect. The amount of $440,000 is the operating income under absorption costing. Answer (C) is incorrect. The amount of $800,000 is the operating income if fixed costs of manufacturing are not deducted. Answer (D) is incorrect. The amount of $600,000 is the operating income that results from capitalizing 40% of both fixed manufacturing costs and selling and administrative costs.

8. Osawa's operating income using absorption (full) costing is

A. $200,000
B. $440,000
C. $600,000
D. $840,000

Answer (B) is correct.
REQUIRED: The operating income under absorption costing.
DISCUSSION: Absorption costing net income is computed as follows:

Sales (120,000 units × $40)		$4,800,000
Variable production costs		
(200,000 units × $30)	$6,000,000	
Fixed production costs	600,000	
Total production costs	$6,600,000	
Ending inventory (80,000 units × $33)	(2,640,000)	
Cost of goods sold		(3,960,000)
Gross profit		$ 840,000
Selling and administrative expenses		(400,000)
Operating income		$ 440,000

Answer (A) is incorrect. The amount of $200,000 is the operating income under variable costing. Answer (C) is incorrect. The amount of $600,000 is the operating income that results from capitalizing $240,000 fixed manufacturing costs and $160,000 of selling and administrative costs (the $160,000 is incorrect as all selling and administrative costs should be expensed). Answer (D) is incorrect. The amount of $840,000 is the gross profit under absorption costing, i.e., before selling and administrative expenses.

6.3 Joint Product and By-Product Costing

Questions 9 through 13 are based on the following information.

Atlas Foods produces the following three supplemental food products simultaneously through a refining process costing $93,000.

The joint products, Alfa and Betters, have a final selling price of $4 per pound and $10 per pound, respectively, after additional processing costs of $2 per pound of each product are incurred after the split-off point. Morefeed, a by-product, is sold at the split-off point for $3 per pound.

Alfa	10,000 pounds of Alfa, a popular but relatively rare grain supplement having a caloric value of 4,400 calories per pound	
Betters	5,000 pounds of Betters, a flavoring material high in carbohydrates with a caloric value of 11,200 calories per pound	
Morefeed	1,000 pounds of Morefeed, used as a cattle feed supplement with a caloric value of 1,000 calories per pound	

9. Assuming Atlas Foods inventories Morefeed, the by-product, the joint cost to be allocated to Alfa using the net realizable value method is

A. $3,000
B. $30,000
C. $31,000
D. $60,000

Answer (B) is correct.
REQUIRED: The joint cost allocated to Alfa based on net realizable values if the by-product is inventoried.
DISCUSSION: The NRV at split-off for each of the joint products must be determined. Given that Alfa has a $4 selling price and an additional $2 of processing costs, the value at the split-off is $2 per pound. The total value at split-off for 10,000 pounds is $20,000. Betters has a $10 selling price and an additional $2 of processing costs. Thus, the value at split-off is $8 per pound. The total value of 5,000 pounds of Betters is therefore $40,000. The 1,000 pounds of Morefeed has a split-off value of $3 per pound, or $3,000. Assuming that Morefeed (a by-product) is inventoried (recognized in the accounts when produced) and treated as a reduction of joint costs, the allocable joint cost is $90,000 ($93,000 – $3,000). (NOTE: Several other methods of accounting for by-products are possible.) The total net realizable value of the main products is $60,000 ($20,000 Alfa + $40,000 Betters). The allocation to Alfa is $30,000 [($20,000 ÷ $60,000) × $90,000].
Answer (A) is incorrect. The amount of $3,000 is the value of the by-product. Answer (C) is incorrect. The amount of $31,000 fails to adjust the joint processing cost for the value of the by-product. Answer (D) is incorrect. The amount of $60,000 is the amount allocated to Betters.

10. Assuming Atlas Foods inventories Morefeed, the by-product, the joint cost to be allocated to Alfa, using the physical quantity method is

A. $3,000
B. $30,000
C. $31,000
D. $60,000

Answer (D) is correct.
REQUIRED: The joint cost allocated to Alfa based on the physical quantity method if the by-product is inventoried.
DISCUSSION: Joint cost is $93,000 and Morefeed has a split-off value of $3,000 (1,000 pounds × $3 split-off value per pound). Assuming the latter amount is treated as a reduction in joint cost, the allocable joint cost is $90,000. The total physical quantity (volume) of the two joint products is 15,000 pounds (10,000 Alfa + 5,000 Betters). Hence, $60,000 of the net joint costs [(10,000 ÷ 15,000) × $90,000] should be allocated to Alfa.
Answer (A) is incorrect. The figure of $3,000 is the value of the by-product. Answer (B) is incorrect. The figure of $30,000 is based on the net realizable value method. Answer (C) is incorrect. The figure of $31,000 is based on the net realizable value method and fails to adjust the joint processing cost for the value of the by-product.

11. Assuming Atlas Foods inventories Morefeed, the by-product, the joint cost to be allocated to Betters using the weighted-quantity method based on caloric value per pound is

A. $39,208
B. $39,600
C. $40,920
D. $50,400

Answer (D) is correct.
REQUIRED: The joint cost allocated to Betters based on weighted quantities if the by-product is inventoried.
DISCUSSION: Joint cost is $93,000 and Morefeed has a split-off value of $3,000 (1,000 pounds × $3 split-off value per pound). Assuming the latter amount is treated as a reduction in joint cost, the allocable joint cost is $90,000. The caloric value of Alfa is 44,000,000 (4,400 × 10,000 pounds), the caloric value of Betters is 56,000,000 (11,200 × 5,000 pounds), and the total is 100,000,000. Of this total volume, Alfa makes up 44% and Betters 56%. Thus, $50,400 ($90,000 × 56%) should be allocated to Betters.
Answer (A) is incorrect. The figure of $39,208 is the amount allocated to Alfa if the 1,000,000 calories attributable to Morefeed is included in the computation. Answer (B) is incorrect. The figure of $39,600 is the allocation to Alfa. Answer (C) is incorrect. The figure of $40,920 is the allocation to Alfa if the sales value of the by-product is not treated as a reduction of joint cost.

12. Assuming Atlas Foods inventories Morefeed, the by-product, and that it incurs no additional processing costs for Alfa and Betters, the joint cost to be allocated to Alfa using the gross market value method is

A. $36,000
B. $40,000
C. $41,333
D. $50,000

Answer (B) is correct.
REQUIRED: The joint cost allocated to Alfa using the gross market value method if the by-product is inventoried.
DISCUSSION: The gross market value of Alfa is $40,000 (10,000 pounds × $4), Betters has a total gross value of $50,000 (5,000 pounds × $10), and Morefeed has a split-off value of $3,000. If the value of Morefeed is inventoried and treated as a reduction in joint cost, the allocable joint cost is $90,000 ($93,000 – $3,000). The total gross value of the two main products is $90,000 ($40,000 + $50,000). Of this total value, $40,000 should be allocated to Alfa [($40,000 ÷ $90,000) × $90,000].
Answer (A) is incorrect. The amount of $36,000 is based on 40%, not 4/9. Answer (C) is incorrect. The amount of $41,333 fails to adjust the joint cost by the value of the by-product. Answer (D) is incorrect. The amount of $50,000 is the joint cost allocated to Betters.

13. Assuming Atlas Foods does not inventory Morefeed, the by-product, the joint cost to be allocated to Betters using the net realizable value method is

A. $30,000
B. $31,000
C. $52,080
D. $62,000

Answer (D) is correct.
REQUIRED: The joint cost allocated to Betters based on net realizable values if the by-product is not inventoried.
DISCUSSION: The NRV of Alfa is $20,000 [10,000 pounds × ($4 selling price – $2 additional processing costs)], and the NRV of Betters is $40,000 [5,000 pounds × ($10 selling price – $2 additional processing costs)]. If the joint cost is not adjusted for the value of the by-production, the amount allocated to Betters is $62,000 {[$40,000 ÷ ($20,000 + $40,000)] × $93,000}.
Answer (A) is incorrect. The amount of $30,000 is the amount allocated to Alfa when the by-product is inventoried. Answer (B) is incorrect. The amount of $31,000 is the amount allocated to Alfa when the by-product is not inventoried. Answer (C) is incorrect. The amount of $52,080 assumes that a weighting method using caloric value is used.

6.4 Overhead Allocation and Normal Costing -- Theory

14. Units of production is an appropriate overhead allocation base when

A. Several well-differentiated products are manufactured.
B. Direct labor costs are low.
C. Direct material costs are large relative to direct labor costs incurred.
D. Only one product is manufactured.

Answer (D) is correct.
REQUIRED: The situation in which units of production is an appropriate overhead allocation base.
DISCUSSION: Allocating overhead on the basis of the number of units produced is usually not appropriate. Costs should be allocated on the basis of some plausible relationship between the cost object and the incurrence of the cost, preferably cause and effect. The fixed portion of overhead costs is incurred regardless of the level of production. When multiple products are involved, the number of units of production may bear no relationship to the incurrence of the allocated cost. If overhead is correlated with machine hours but different products require different quantities of that input, the result may be an illogical allocation. However, if a firm manufactures only one product, this allocation method may be acceptable because all costs are to be charged to the single product.
Answer (A) is incorrect. The number of units of production may have no logical relationship to overhead when several different products are made. Answer (B) is incorrect. A low level of direct labor costs means that fixed overhead is substantial, and an appropriate cost driver should be used to make the allocation. Answer (C) is incorrect. The allocation should be made on the basis of the appropriate cost drivers without regard to the relationship between direct materials and labor costs.

15. The appropriate method for the disposition of underapplied or overapplied overhead of a manufacturer

A. Is to cost of goods sold only.
B. Is to finished goods inventory only.
C. Is apportioned to cost of goods sold and finished goods inventory.
D. Depends on the significance of the amount.

Answer (D) is correct.
REQUIRED: The appropriate treatment of underapplied or overapplied overhead at the end of a period.
DISCUSSION: Overapplied or underapplied overhead should be disposed of at the end of an accounting period by transferring the balance either to cost of goods sold (if the amount is not material) or to cost of goods sold, finished goods inventory, and work-in-process inventory. Theoretically, the allocation is preferred, but, because the amount is usually immaterial, the entire balance is often transferred directly to cost of goods sold. Thus, the entry depends upon the significance of the amount.

16. In determining next year's overhead application rates, a company desires to focus on manufacturing capacity rather than output demand for its products. To derive a realistic application rate, the denominator activity level should be based on

A. Practical capacity.
B. Maximum capacity.
C. Normal capacity.
D. Master-budget (expected annual) capacity.

Answer (A) is correct.
REQUIRED: The proper denominator level of activity for selecting an overhead application rate.
DISCUSSION: Practical capacity is based on realistic, attainable levels of production and input efficiency and is the most appropriate denominator level to use in selecting an overhead application rate.
Answer (B) is incorrect. Using maximum capacity assumes no downtime, an unrealistic assumption in any case. Answer (C) is incorrect. Normal capacity may be lower than the equipment is capable of with proper maintenance and attention to efficiency. Answer (D) is incorrect. Master-budget (expected) capacity cannot be determined until the application base is selected.

17. Generally, individual departmental rates rather than a plantwide rate for applying manufacturing overhead are used if

A. A company wants to adopt a standard cost system.
B. A company's manufacturing operations are all highly automated.
C. Manufacturing overhead is the largest cost component of its product cost.
D. The manufactured products differ in the resources consumed from the individual departments in the plant.

Answer (D) is correct.
REQUIRED: The circumstance in which individual departmental overhead application rates are used.
DISCUSSION: Overhead is usually assigned to products based on a predetermined rate or rates. The activity base for overhead allocation should have a high degree of correlation with the incurrence of overhead. Given only one cost driver, one overhead application rate is sufficient. If products differ in the resources consumed in individual departments, multiple rates are preferable.
Answer (A) is incorrect. A standard cost system can be based on individual or multiple application rates. Answer (B) is incorrect. Whether production is machine intensive affects the nature but not necessarily the number of cost drivers. Answer (C) is incorrect. A single plant-wide application rate is acceptable, even with high overhead, if all overhead is highly correlated with a single application base.

6.5 Overhead Allocation and Normal Costing -- Calculations

18. A company uses a job costing system and applies overhead to products on the basis of direct labor cost. Job No. 75, the only job in process on January 1, had the following costs assigned as of that date: direct materials, $40,000; direct labor, $80,000; and factory overhead, $120,000. The following selected costs were incurred during the year:

Traceable to jobs:	
Direct materials	$178,000
Direct labor	345,000
Total	$523,000

Not traceable to jobs:	
Factory materials and supplies	$ 46,000
Indirect labor	235,000
Plant maintenance	73,000
Depreciation on factory equipment	29,000
Other factory costs	76,000
Total	$459,000

The company's profit plan for the year included budgeted direct labor of $320,000 and overhead of $448,000. Assuming no work-in-process on December 31, the company's overhead for the year was

A. $11,000 overapplied.
B. $24,000 overapplied.
C. $11,000 underapplied.
D. $24,000 underapplied.

Answer (B) is correct.
REQUIRED: The extent to which overhead was under- or overapplied.
DISCUSSION: The company applies overhead to products on the basis of direct labor cost. The rate is 1.4 ($448,000 budgeted OH ÷ $320,000 budgeted DL cost). Thus, $483,000 ($345,000 actual DL cost × 1.4) of overhead was applied, of which $24,000 ($483,000 – $459,000 actual OH) was overapplied.
Answer (A) is incorrect. The amount of $11,000 equals the difference between budgeted and actual overhead. Answer (C) is incorrect. The amount of $11,000 equals the difference between budgeted and actual overhead. Answer (D) is incorrect. The overhead was overapplied.

19. A manufacturer allocates overhead to jobs in process using direct labor costs, direct materials costs, and machine hours. The overhead application rates for the current year are

100% of direct labor
20% of direct materials
$117 per machine hour

A particular production run incurred the following costs:

Direct labor, $8,000
Direct materials, $2,000
A total of 140 machine hours were required for the production run.

What is the total cost charged to the production run?

A. $18,000
B. $18,400
C. $34,780
D. None of the answers are true.

Answer (C) is correct.
REQUIRED: The total cost for a production run given overhead application rates.
DISCUSSION: The total cost charged to the production run is calculated as follows:

Direct labor			$ 8,000
Direct materials			2,000
Manufacturing overhead:			
$8,000 of direct labor × 100%	=	$ 8,000	
$2,000 of direct materials × 20%	=	400	
140 machine hours × $117	=	16,380	24,780
Total charged to production			$34,780

Answer (A) is incorrect. The amount of $18,000 includes only $8,000 for overhead (based on 100% of direct labor). Answer (B) is incorrect. The amount of $18,400 includes only $8,400 for overhead (based on 100% of direct labor and 20% of direct materials). Answer (D) is incorrect. Total cost is $34,780.

20. A review of the year-end accounting records of a company discloses the following information:

Raw materials	$ 80,000
Work-in-process	128,000
Finished goods	272,000
Cost of goods sold	1,120,000

The company's underapplied overhead equals $133,000. On the basis of this information, cost of goods sold is **most** appropriately reported as

A. $987,000
B. $1,213,100
C. $1,218,000
D. $1,253,000

Answer (C) is correct.
REQUIRED: The reported year-end balance of cost of goods sold.
DISCUSSION: Given the amounts involved, $133,000 is material; thus, over- or underapplied overhead should be allocated to all work-in-process, finished goods, and cost of goods sold. The proportion of the total of these three accounts represented by cost of goods sold is 73.68% [$1,120,000 ÷ ($128,000 + $272,000 + $1,120,000)]. The amount of underapplied overhead assigned to cost of goods sold is thus $98,000 ($133,000 × 73.68%), making the total reported amount of cost of goods sold $1,218,000 ($1,120,000 + $98,000).
Answer (A) is incorrect. The amount of $987,000 results from improperly subtracting the entire amount of underapplied overhead from the balance of cost of goods sold instead of allocating it across three inventory accounts. Answer (B) is incorrect. The amount of $1,213,100 improperly includes raw materials in the allocation base for underapplied overhead. Answer (D) is incorrect. The amount of $1,253,000 results from improperly allocating the entire amount of underapplied overhead to cost of goods sold.

21. A company applies factory overhead based upon machine hours. At the beginning of the year, the company budgeted factory overhead at $250,000 and estimated that 100,000 machine hours would be used to make 50,000 units of product. During the year, the company produced 48,000 units using 97,000 machine hours. Actual overhead for the year was $252,000. Under a standard cost system, the amount of factory overhead applied during the year was

A. $240,000
B. $242,500
C. $250,000
D. $252,000

Answer (A) is correct.
REQUIRED: The amount of applied factory overhead given relevant information.
DISCUSSION: The company's application rate for overhead is $2.50 per machine hour ($250,000 budgeted total ÷ 100,000 estimated machine hours), and each unit of output is estimated to require 2 machine hours (100,000 estimated machine hours ÷ 50,000 units budgeted output). Under a standard cost system, the amount of overhead applied during the year was therefore $240,000 (48,000 units actual output × $2.50 per machine hour application rate × 2 machine hours standard per unit).
Answer (B) is incorrect. The amount of $242,500 results from improperly multiplying by 48,500 units of product (half the number of machine hours). Answer (C) is incorrect. The amount of $250,000 results from improperly multiplying by the 50,000 budgeted units of product instead of by the 48,000 actual units. Answer (D) is incorrect. The amount of $252,000 was the actual overhead incurred.

6.6 Allocating Service Department Costs -- Theory

22. In allocating factory service department costs to producing departments, which one of the following items would **most** likely be used as an activity base?

A. Units of product sold.
B. Salary of service department employees.
C. Units of electric power consumed.
D. Direct materials usage.

Answer (C) is correct.
REQUIRED: The item most likely used as an activity base when allocating factory service department costs.
DISCUSSION: Service department costs are considered part of factory overhead and should be allocated to the production departments that use the services. A basis reflecting cause and effect should be used to allocate service department costs. For example, the number of kilowatt hours used by each producing department is probably the best allocation base for electricity costs.
Answer (A) is incorrect. Making allocations on the basis of units sold may not meet the cause-and-effect criterion. Answer (B) is incorrect. The salary of service department employees is the cost allocated, not a basis of allocation. Answer (D) is incorrect. Making allocations on the basis of materials usage may not meet the cause-and-effect criterion.

SU 6: Cost Allocation Techniques   207

23. The two **most** appropriate factors for budgeting manufacturing overhead expenses would be

A. Machine hours and production volume.
B. Management judgment and contribution margin.
C. Management judgment and production volume.
D. Management judgment and sales dollars.

Answer (C) is correct.
REQUIRED: The two most important factors for budgeting manufacturing overhead expenses.
DISCUSSION: The most important factor in budgeting manufacturing overhead is production volume. Many overhead items have variable costs, and those that are fixed with a relevant range of output may increase if production exceeds that range. The other essential consideration is management's judgment with respect to the nature and amount of costs to be incurred and expectations for production volume. Because overhead is applied based on predetermined rates, accurate judgment is important.
Answer (A) is incorrect. Machine hours may not be the appropriate activity base. Moreover, some overhead is fixed regardless of the activity base. Answer (B) is incorrect. The contribution margin can be calculated only after variable costs and sales prices are determined. Some overhead is variable. Answer (D) is incorrect. Sales volume (or dollars) is less significant because overhead is based on production volume.

24. When allocating service department costs to production departments, the method that does **not** consider different cost behavior patterns is the

A. Step method.
B. Reciprocal method.
C. Direct method.
D. Single-rate method.

Answer (D) is correct.
REQUIRED: The method of service department cost allocation that does not consider cost behavior patterns.
DISCUSSION: The single-rate method combines fixed and variable costs. However, dual rates are preferable because they allow variable costs to be allocated on a different basis from fixed costs.
Answer (A) is incorrect. The step method can be used on a single- or dual-rate basis. Answer (B) is incorrect. The reciprocal method can be used on a single- or dual-rate basis. Answer (C) is incorrect. The direct method can be used on a single- or dual-rate basis.

25. Allocation of service department costs to the production departments is necessary to

A. Control costs.
B. Coordinate production activity.
C. Determine overhead rates.
D. Maximize efficiency.

Answer (C) is correct.
REQUIRED: The reason service department costs are allocated to production departments.
DISCUSSION: Service department costs are indirect costs allocated to production departments to better determine overhead rates when the measurement of full (absorption) costs is desired. Overhead should be charged to production on some equitable basis to provide information useful for such purposes as allocation of resources, pricing, measurement of profits, and cost reimbursement.
Answer (A) is incorrect. Costs can be controlled by the service departments without allocation. However, allocation encourages cost control by the production departments. If the costs are allocated, managers have an incentive not to use services indiscriminately. Answer (B) is incorrect. Allocation does not affect the coordination of production activity. Answer (D) is incorrect. Allocation of costs has no effect on the efficiency of the provision of services when the department that receives the allocation has no control over the costs being controlled.

6.7 Allocating Service Department Costs -- Calculations

Questions 26 through 30 are based on the following information. The managers of Rochester Manufacturing are discussing ways to allocate the cost of service departments, such as Quality Control and Maintenance, to the production departments. To aid them in this discussion, the controller has provided the following information:

	Quality Control	Maintenance	Machining	Assembly	Total
Budgeted overhead costs before allocation	$350,000	$200,000	$400,000	$300,000	$1,250,000
Budgeted machine hours	--	--	50,000	--	50,000
Budgeted direct labor hours	--	--	--	25,000	25,000
Budgeted hours of service:					
Quality Control	--	7,000	21,000	7,000	35,000
Maintenance	10,000	--	18,000	12,000	40,000

26. If Rochester uses the step-down method of allocating service costs beginning with quality control, the maintenance costs allocated to the assembly department would be

A. $70,000
B. $108,000
C. $162,000
D. $200,000

Answer (B) is correct.
REQUIRED: The maintenance costs allocated to the Assembly Department if the step-down method is applied beginning with quality control costs.
DISCUSSION: The step-down method allocates service costs to both service and production departments but does not involve reciprocal allocations among service departments. Accordingly, Quality Control will receive no allocation of maintenance costs. The first step is to allocate quality control costs to the Maintenance Department. Maintenance is expected to use 20% (7,000 ÷ 35,000) of the available quality control hours and will be allocated $70,000 ($350,000 × 20%) of quality control costs. Thus, total allocable maintenance costs equal $270,000 ($70,000 + $200,000). The Assembly Department is estimated to use 40% (12,000 ÷ 30,000) of the available maintenance hours. Consequently, it will be allocated maintenance costs of $108,000 ($270,000 × 40%).
Answer (A) is incorrect. The Assembly Department will be allocated maintenance costs of $108,000. Answer (C) is incorrect. The Assembly Department will be allocated maintenance costs of $108,000. Answer (D) is incorrect. The Assembly Department will be allocated maintenance costs of $108,000.

27. If Rochester uses the direct method of allocating service department costs, the total service costs allocated to the assembly department would be

A. $80,000
B. $87,500
C. $120,000
D. $167,500

Answer (D) is correct.
REQUIRED: The total service costs allocated to the Assembly Department using the direct method.
DISCUSSION: Under the direct method, service department costs are allocated directly to the production departments, with no allocation to other service departments. The total budgeted hours of service by the Quality Control Department to the two production departments is 28,000 (21,000 + 7,000). Given that the Assembly Department is expected to use 25% (7,000 ÷ 28,000) of the total hours budgeted for the production departments, it will absorb 25% of total quality control costs ($350,000 × 25% = $87,500). The total budgeted hours of service by the Maintenance Department to the production departments is 30,000 (18,000 + 12,000). The Assembly Department is expected to use 40% (12,000 ÷ 30,000) of the total maintenance hours budgeted for the production departments. Thus, the Assembly Department will be allocated 40% of the $200,000 of maintenance costs, or $80,000. The total service department costs allocated to the Assembly Department is $167,500 ($87,500 + $80,000).
Answer (A) is incorrect. The total of the service department costs allocated to the Assembly Department is $167,500. Answer (B) is incorrect. The Assembly Department is allocated the service department costs totaling $167,500. Answer (C) is incorrect. The total of the service department costs allocated to the Assembly Department is $167,500.

28. Using the direct method, the total amount of overhead allocated to each machine hour at Rochester would be

A. $2.40
B. $5.25
C. $8.00
D. $15.65

Answer (D) is correct.
REQUIRED: The total overhead allocated to each machine hour.
DISCUSSION: Machining uses 75% (21,000 ÷ 28,000) of the total quality control hours and 60% (18,000 ÷ 30,000) of the total maintenance hours budgeted for the production departments. Under the direct method, it will therefore be allocated $262,500 ($350,000 × 75%) of quality control costs and $120,000 ($200,000 × 60%) of maintenance costs. In addition, Machining is expected to incur another $400,000 of overhead costs. Thus, the total estimated Machining overhead is $782,500 ($262,500 + $120,000 + $400,000), and the overhead cost per machine hour is $15.65 ($782,500 ÷ 50,000 hours).
Answer (A) is incorrect. The overhead cost per machine hour is $15.65. Answer (B) is incorrect. The overhead cost per machine hour is $15.65. Answer (C) is incorrect. The overhead cost per machine hour is $15.65.

29. If Rochester uses the reciprocal method of allocating service costs, the total amount of quality control costs (rounded to the nearest dollar) to be allocated to the other departments would be

A. $284,211
B. $336,842
C. $350,000
D. $421,053

Answer (D) is correct.
REQUIRED: The total quality control costs to be allocated to the other departments using the reciprocal method.
DISCUSSION: The reciprocal method involves mutual allocations of service costs among service departments. For this purpose, a system of simultaneous equations is necessary. The total costs for the Quality Control Department consist of $350,000 plus 25% (10,000 hours ÷ 40,000 hours) of maintenance costs. The total costs for the Maintenance Department equal $200,000 plus 20% (7,000 hours ÷ 35,000 hours) of quality control costs. These relationships can be expressed by the following equations:

$$Q = \$350{,}000 + .25M$$
$$M = \$200{,}000 + .2Q$$

To solve for Q, the second equation can be substituted into the first as follows:

$$Q = \$350{,}000 + .25(\$200{,}000 + .2Q)$$
$$Q = \$350{,}000 + \$50{,}000 + .05Q$$
$$.95Q = \$400{,}000$$
$$Q = \$421{,}053$$

Answer (A) is incorrect. The total quality control costs to be allocated equal $421,053. Answer (B) is incorrect. The total quality control costs to be allocated equal $421,053. Answer (C) is incorrect. The total quality control costs to be allocated equal $421,053.

30. If Rochester decides not to allocate service costs to the production departments, the overhead allocated to each direct labor hour in the Assembly Department would be

A. $3.20
B. $3.50
C. $12.00
D. $16.00

Answer (C) is correct.
REQUIRED: The overhead cost per direct labor hour in the Assembly Department if no service costs are allocated to production departments.
DISCUSSION: With no allocation of service department costs, the only overhead applicable to the Assembly Department is the $300,000 budgeted for that department. Hence, the overhead cost applied per direct labor hour will be $12 ($300,000 budgeted overhead ÷ 25,000 hours).
Answer (A) is incorrect. The overhead cost applied per direct labor hour will be $12. Answer (B) is incorrect. The overhead cost applied per direct labor hour will be $12. Answer (D) is incorrect. The overhead cost applied per direct labor hour will be $12.

Access the **CMA Review System** from your Gleim Personal Classroom to continue your studies with exam-emulating multiple-choice questions!

6.8 ESSAY QUESTIONS

Scenario for Essay Questions 1, 2, 3

The Daniels Tool & Die Corporation has been in existence for a little over 3 years, and sales have been increasing each year. A job-order cost system is used. Factory overhead is applied to jobs based on direct labor hours, utilizing the absorption (full) costing method. Overapplied or underapplied overhead is treated as an adjustment to cost of goods sold. The company's income statements for the last 2 years are presented below.

Daniels Tool & Die Corporation
Year 3-Year 4 Comparative Income Statements

	Year 3	Year 4
Sales	$840,000	$1,015,000
Cost of goods sold:		
Finished goods, 1/1	$ 25,000	$ 18,000
Cost of goods manufactured	548,000	657,600
Total available	$573,000	$ 675,600
Finished goods, 12/31	18,000	14,000
Cost of goods sold before overhead adjustment	$555,000	$ 661,600
Underapplied factory overhead	36,000	14,400
Cost of goods sold	$591,000	$ 676,000
Gross profit	$249,000	$ 339,000
Selling expenses	$ 82,000	$ 95,000
Administrative expenses	70,000	75,000
Total operating expenses	$152,000	$ 170,000
Operating income	$ 97,000	$ 169,000

Daniels Tool & Die Corporation
Inventory Balances

	1/1/Year 3	12/31/Year 3	12/31/Year 4
Raw material	$22,000	$30,000	$10,000
Work-in-process costs	$40,000	$48,000	$64,000
Direct labor hours	1,335	1,600	2,100
Finished goods costs	$25,000	$18,000	$14,000
Direct labor hours	1,450	1,050	820

Daniels used the same predetermined overhead rate in applying overhead to production orders in both Year 3 and Year 4. The rate was based on the following estimates:

Fixed factory overhead	$ 25,000
Variable factory overhead	$155,000
Direct labor hours	25,000
Direct labor costs	$150,000

In Year 3 and Year 4, actual direct labor hours expended were 20,000 and 23,000, respectively. Raw materials put into production were $292,000 in Year 3 and $370,000 in Year 4. Actual fixed overhead was $37,400 for Year 4 and $42,300 for Year 3, and the planned direct labor rate was the direct labor rate achieved.

For both years, all of the reported administrative costs were fixed, while the variable portion of the reported selling expenses result from a commission of 5% of sales revenue.

Questions

1. For the year ended December 31, Year 4, prepare a revised income statement utilizing the variable (direct) costing method. Be sure to include contribution margin.

2. Prepare a numerical reconciliation of the difference in operating income between Daniels' Year 4 income statement prepared on the basis of absorption costing and the revised Year 4 income statement prepared on the basis of variable costing.

3. Describe both the advantages and disadvantages of using variable costing.

Essay Questions 1, 2, 3 — Unofficial Answers

1.

Daniels Tool & Die Corporation
Variable Costing Income Statement
For the Year Ended December 31, Year 4

Sales		$1,015,000
Finished goods, 1/1/Year 4 ($18,000 − $1,050 fixed overhead)	$ 16,950	
Work-in-process, 1/1/Year 4 ($48,000 − $1,600 fixed overhead)	46,400	
Manufacturing costs incurred*	650,600	
Total available	$713,950	
Work-in-process, 12/31/Year 4 ($64,000 − $2,100 fixed overhead)	(61,900)	
Finished goods, 12/31/Year 4 ($14,000 − $820 fixed overhead)	(13,180)	
Variable manufacturing cost of goods sold	$638,870	
Variable selling expenses ($1,015,000 × .05)	50,750	
Total variable costs		(689,620)
Contribution margin		$ 325,380
Fixed factory overhead (given)	$ 37,400	
Fixed selling expenses ($95,000 − $50,750)	44,250	
Fixed administrative expenses (all)	75,000	
Total fixed costs		(156,650)
Operating income		$ 168,730

*Raw materials	$370,000	(same as under absorption method)
Direct labor	138,000	(23,000 hours × $6.00 [same as under absorption method])
Variable overhead	142,600	(23,000 hours × $6.20 [same as under absorption method])
Mfg. costs incurred	$650,600	

*(The $6.00 direct labor rate, which is the same as under the absorption method, is calculated by dividing the $150,000 of budgeted direct labor by the 25,000 budgeted hours. The variable overhead rate is $6.20 ($155,000 ÷ 25,000).

2. The difference in the operating income of $270 is caused by the different treatment of fixed manufacturing overhead. Under absorption costing, fixed overhead costs are assigned to inventory and are not expensed until the goods are sold. Under variable costing, these costs are treated as expenses in the period incurred. Since the direct labor hours in the work-in-process and finished goods inventories had a net increase of 270 hours, the absorption costing operating profit is higher because the fixed factory overhead associated with the increased labor hours in inventory is not expensed under absorption costing.

	1/1/Year 4 Inventories	12/31/Year 4 Inventories	Difference
Work-in-process	1,600	2,100	500
Finished goods	1,050	820	(230)
Total	2,650	2,920	270

Supporting Calculations

Calculation of variable finished goods inventory at 1/1/87.

Absorption finished goods inventory	$18,000
Less fixed overhead (1,050 hours × $1)	1,050
Variable finished goods inventory	$16,950

Calculation of variable work-in-process inventory at 1/1/87.

Absorption work-in-process inventory	$48,000
Less fixed overhead (1,600 hours × $1)	1,600
Variable work-in-process inventory	$46,400

Calculation of variable manufacturing costs incurred during 1987.

Direct materials	$370,000
Direct labor (23,000 hours × $6)	138,000
Variable overhead (23,000 hours × $6.20)	142,600
Variable manufacturing costs	$650,600

The direct labor rate is ($150,000 ÷ 25,000)	$6.00
The variable overhead rate is ($155,000 ÷ 25,000)	$6.20

Calculation of variable work-in-process inventory at 12/31/87.

Absorption work-in-process inventory	$64,000
Less fixed overhead (2,100 hours × $1)	2,100
Variable work-in-process inventory	$61,900

Calculation of variable finished goods inventory at 12/31/87.

Absorption work-in-process inventory	$14,000
Less fixed overhead (820 hours × $1)	820
Variable work-in-process inventory	$13,180

Calculation of variable selling expenses.

Sales $1,015,000 × 5%	$50,750

Calculation of fixed selling expenses.

Total selling expenses	$95,000
Less variable selling expenses	50,750
Fixed selling expenses	$44,250

3. The advantages of using variable costing follow:

   a. The fixed manufacturing costs are reported at incurred values, not at absorbed values, which increases the likelihood of better control over fixed costs.

   b. Profits are directly influenced by changes in sales volume and not by changes in inventory levels.

   c. Contribution margin by product line, territory, department, or division is emphasized.

   The disadvantages of using variable costing follow:

   d. Variable costing is not acceptable for tax reporting, for SEC reporting, nor for external financial reporting; therefore, companies need to keep two sets of records.

   e. Costs other than variable costs, i.e., fixed costs and total production costs, may be ignored when making decisions, especially long-term decisions.

   f. With the movement toward a fully automated factory, fixed factory overhead may be a significant portion of production costs. To ignore these significant costs in inventory valuation may not be acceptable.

GLEIM® CMA Review Redefined™
Exceptional Coverage. Extraordinary Results.

Why is GLEIM® the #1 CMA Prep Course?

- **Gleim Mega Test Bank:** The largest exam-emulating question and essay bank on the market

- **Gleim Instruct:** Over 40 hours of video lectures by professional educators

- **No-Hassle Guarantee:** True Access Until You Pass®

800.874.5346

gleim.com/**cma**

STUDY UNIT SEVEN
OPERATIONAL EFFICIENCY AND BUSINESS PROCESS PERFORMANCE

(22 pages of outline)

7.1	Just-in-Time Inventory and Lean Operation	215
7.2	Enterprise Resource Planning and Outsourcing	218
7.3	Theory of Constraints and Throughput Costing	221
7.4	Capacity Management	225
7.5	Value-Chain Analysis	227
7.6	Other Process Improvement Tools	230
7.7	Essay Questions	245

This study unit is the **last of four** on **cost management**. The relative weight assigned to this major topic in Part 1 of the exam is **20%**. The four study units are

Study Unit 4: Cost Management Concepts
Study Unit 5: Cost Accumulation Systems
Study Unit 6: Cost Allocation Techniques
Study Unit 7: Operational Efficiency and Business Process Performance

If you are interested in reviewing more introductory or background material, go to www.gleim.com/CMAIntroVideos for a list of suggested third-party overviews of this topic. The following Gleim outline material is more than sufficient to help you pass the CMA exam; any additional introductory or background material is for your own personal enrichment.

7.1 JUST-IN-TIME INVENTORY AND LEAN OPERATION

1. **Overview**

    a. Modern inventory planning favors the **just-in-time (JIT)** model. Many companies have traditionally built parts and components for subsequent operations on a preset schedule. Such a schedule provides a cushion of inventory so that the next operation will always have parts to work with–a just-in-case method.

    1) In contrast, JIT limits output to the demand of the subsequent operation. Reductions in inventory levels result in less money invested in idle assets; reduction of storage space requirements; and lower inventory taxes, pilferage, and obsolescence risks.

    b. JIT is a reaction to the trends of global competition and rapid technological progress that have resulted in shorter product life cycles and greater consumer demand for product diversity.

    1) High inventory levels often mask production problems because defective parts can be overlooked when plenty of good parts are available. If only enough parts are made for the subsequent operation, however, any defects will immediately halt production.

    2) The focus of quality control under JIT shifts from the discovery of defective parts to the prevention of quality problems, so zero machine breakdowns (achieved through preventive maintenance) and zero defects are ultimate goals. Higher quality and lower inventory go together.

    c. **Lean operation** is often used as a synonym for JIT.

    1) Lean implies a demand-driven (i.e., pull) system, a focus on waste reduction, and a commitment to low- or zero-defect production.

2. **Role of Kanban**

The Japanese term "kanban" and JIT are often confused. For the purpose of this exam, CMA candidates will be required to understand the benefits of implementing just-in-time (JIT) systems and how kanban is used in the process.

   a. JIT is a total system of purchasing, production, and inventory control. **Kanban** is one of the many elements in the JIT system and was developed by the Toyota Motor Corporation (kanban is not characteristic of Japanese industry as a whole).
   b. Kanban means ticket. Tickets (also described as cards or markers) control the flow of production or parts so that they are produced or obtained in the needed amounts at the needed times. A basic kanban system includes
      1) A withdrawal kanban that states the quantity that a later process should withdraw from its predecessor;
      2) A production kanban that states the output of the preceding process; and
      3) A vendor kanban that tells a vendor what, how much, where, and when to deliver.
   c. Kanban is essentially a visual workflow management system.
      1) When a worker sees a kanban, the card or ticket acts as authorization to release inventory to the next step. Work cannot move to the next stage until a kanban indicates the next stage is ready for it.
   d. U.S. companies have not been comfortable with controlling production using tickets on the production floor. **Computerized information systems** have been used for many years, and U.S. companies have been reluctant to give up their computers in favor of the essentially manual kanban system. Instead, U.S. companies have integrated their existing complex computerized planning systems with the JIT system.

3. **Objectives**
   a. Higher productivity, reduced order costs as well as carrying costs, faster and cheaper setups, shorter manufacturing cycle times, better due date performance, improved quality, and more flexible processes are objectives of JIT methods.
      1) The ultimate goal is increased competitiveness and higher profits.

4. **Features**
   a. JIT is a **pull system**; i.e., items are pulled through production by current demand, not pushed through by anticipated demand.
      1) One operation produces only what is needed by the next operation, and components and raw materials arrive just in time to be used.
   b. Demand-driven production allows **inventory levels to be minimized**. Counting, handling, and storing inventory are viewed as nonvalue-added.
      1) Indeed, carrying inventory is regarded as a symptom of correctable problems, such as poor quality, long cycle times, and lack of coordination with suppliers.

c. The **dependability of suppliers** is crucial.

1) Organizations that adopt JIT systems therefore develop close relationships with a few carefully chosen suppliers who are extensively involved in the buyer's processes.

a) Buyer-supplier relationships are further facilitated by electronic data interchange (EDI), a technology that allows the supplier access to the buyer's online inventory management system. Thus, electronic messages replace paper documents (purchase orders and sales invoices), and the production schedules and deliveries of the parties can be more readily coordinated.

5. **Effects on Operations**

a. One consequence of the lower inventory levels associated with a JIT (lean) system is elimination of the need for certain internal controls.

1) Frequent receipt of deliveries from suppliers often means less need for a sophisticated inventory control system and for control personnel.

b. JIT also may eliminate central receiving areas, hard copy receiving reports, and storage areas.

c. Manufacturing cycle time and setup time are also reduced.

1) As a result, on-time delivery performance and response to changes in markets are enhanced, and production of customized goods in small lots becomes feasible.

d. The quality of parts provided by suppliers is verified by use of statistical controls rather than inspection of incoming goods.

1) Storage, counting, and inspecting are eliminated in an effort to perform only value-adding work.

6. **Implementing JIT**

a. To implement a JIT inventory or lean production system, the factory is reorganized around what are called **manufacturing cells**.

1) In a conventional plant layout, each department or function operates specialized machines that perform one task. All work moves from department to department.

2) In a cellular layout, each cell is a miniature manufacturing plant. Cells are sets of machines, often grouped in semicircles, that produce a given product or product family.

b. Each worker in a cell must be able to operate all machines and, possibly, to perform support tasks, such as setup activities, preventive maintenance, movement of work-in-process within the cell, and quality inspection.

1) In such a pull system, workers might often be idle if they are not multi-skilled.

c. A cellular organization requires workers to operate as effective teams, so employee empowerment is crucial in a JIT inventory or lean production system.

1) Greater participation by employees is needed to achieve the objectives of continuous improvement and zero defects, so they may, for example, have the power to stop production to correct a problem, be consulted about changes in processes, or become involved in hiring co-workers. Thus, managers in such a system usually play more of a facilitating than a support role.

Stop and review! You have completed the outline for this subunit. Study multiple-choice questions 1 through 7 beginning on page 237.

7.2 ENTERPRISE RESOURCE PLANNING AND OUTSOURCING

1. **Overview**
   a. Short-range (tactical or operational) plans must be converted into specific production targets for finished goods. The raw materials going into the creation of these end products must be carefully scheduled for delivery.
      1) The yearly/quarterly/monthly numbers and styles of finished goods called for in the demand forecasts included in the operational plans must be turned into specific dates for completion and availability for shipment to the customer. This is the task of the **master production schedule (MPS)**.
   b. A **materials requirements planning (MRP)** system enables a company to efficiently fulfill the requirements of the MPS by coordinating both the manufacture of component parts for finished goods and the arrival of the raw materials necessary to create the intermediate components.
      1) As computers were introduced into manufacturing, it was common for firms to have a production scheduling system and an inventory control system. MRP joins the two into a single application.
      2) The three overriding goals of MRP are the arrival of the right part, in the right quantity, at the right time.
   c. MRP is a push system; i.e., the demand for raw materials is driven by the forecasted demand for the final product, which can be programmed into the computer.
      1) For example, an automobile manufacturer need only tell the computer how many autos of each type are to be manufactured.
   d. MRP, in effect, creates schedules of when items of inventory will be needed in the production departments.
      1) If parts are not in stock, the system automatically generates a purchase order on the proper date (considering lead times) so that deliveries will arrive on time.
      2) The timing of deliveries is vital to avoid both production delays and a pileup of raw materials inventory that must be stored.
   e. The MRP system consults the **bill of materials** (BOM), a record of which (and how many) subassemblies go into the finished product. The system then generates a complete list of every part and component needed.

EXAMPLE of MRP

A manufacturer has the following bill of materials for its main product AA115:

Subunit	Quantity
CM12	1
PR75	5

The bill of materials for the component subunits is as follows:

Subunit	Contains	Quantity
CM12	TT413	2
	XH511	3
PR75	LQ992	1

Current inventory quantities are as follows:

Subunit	On Hand
CM12	25
PR75	35
LQ992	50
TT413	30
XH511	40

-- Continued on next page --

EXAMPLE of MRP -- Continued

The company has 20 units of finished AA115 in inventory and wishes to maintain this level throughout the year. Production of 40 units is scheduled for the upcoming month. The quantities of the principal subunits that must be produced are calculated below:

Subunit	Quantity per Finished Product		Production Run		Quantity Needed		Quantity On Hand		To Be Built
CM12	1	×	40	=	40	−	25	=	15
PR75	5	×	40	=	200	−	35	=	165

The parts that must be ordered from vendors can thus be calculated as follows:

Subunit	Components	Component Quantity		Subunits To Be Built		Quantity Needed		Quantity On Hand		To Be Purchased
CM12	TT413	2	×	15	=	30	−	30	=	0
	XH511	3	×	15	=	45	−	40	=	5
PR75	LQ992	1	×	165	=	165	−	50	=	115

The lead times required are

CM12	2 weeks
TT413	1 week
XH511	2 weeks
PR75	3 weeks
LQ992	1 week
AA115	1 week

Product	Action	Weeks					
		1	2	3	4	5	6
AA115	Due Date						40
	Place Order					40	
PR75	Due Date					165	
	Place Order		165				
LQ992	Due Date		115				
	Place Order	115					
CM12	Due Date					15	
	Place Order			15			
TT413	Due Date			0			
	Place Order		0				
XH511	Due Date			5			
	Place Order	5					

 f. When items of inventory will be needed is determined by their lead time and the lead times of other component items or procedures. **Lead time** is the amount of time between when a process starts and when it is completed.

  1) Once it is known how many of a final product is necessary, the lead times of all the included components and processes can be used to create a schedule outlining when certain items and components must be ordered or produced so that the final product will be completed on time.

 g. Some benefits of MRP are

  1) Reduced idle time
  2) Lower setup costs
  3) Lower inventory carrying costs
  4) Increased flexibility in responding to market changes

2. **Manufacturing Resource Planning (MRP II)**

   a. MRP II is a closed-loop manufacturing system that integrates all facets of a manufacturing business, including production, sales, inventories, schedules, and cash flows.

      1) The same system is used for both the financial reporting and managing operations (both use the same transactions and numbers).
      2) Because manufacturing resource planning encompasses materials requirements planning, MRP is a component of an MRP II system.

3. **Enterprise Resource Planning (ERP)**

   a. ERP is a software platform that is used to plan and keep records of resources, including

      1) Finances,
      2) Labor capabilities and capacity,
      3) Materials, and
      4) Property.

   b. MRP is a common function contained in ERP.

      1) Although ERP and MRP are similar, they are not interchangeable since ERP includes functions not included in MRP.
      2) An ERP system would allow a company to determine what hiring decisions might need to be made or whether a company should invest in new capital assets.

         a) A company that merely needed to maintain inventory and materials levels would only need to implement a MRP system.

4. **Outsourcing**

   a. Outsourcing is the management or day-to-day execution of an entire business function by a third-party service provider. Outsourced services may be provided on or off premises, in the same country, or in a separate country.

      1) Outsourcing enables a company to focus on its core business rather than having to be concerned with marginal activities. For example, payroll preparation is often outsourced because a company does not want to maintain a full-time staff to perform what is only a weekly or monthly activity.

   b. Business process outsourcing is the outsourcing of back office and front office functions typically performed by white-collar and clerical workers. Examples of these functions include data processing, accounting, human resources, and medical coding and transcription.

      1) **Insourcing** is the transfer of an outsourced function to an internal department of a company to be managed entirely by company employees. The term has also been used to describe a foreign company's locating of facilities in a host country where it employs local workers.
      2) **Cosourcing** is performance of a business function by both internal staff and external resources, such as consultants or outsourcing vendors, who have specialized knowledge of the business function.

   c. Benefits of outsourcing include reliable service, reduced costs, avoidance of the risk of obsolescence, and access to technology. Disadvantages include dependence on an outside party and loss of control over a necessary function.

Stop and review! You have completed the outline for this subunit. Study multiple-choice questions 8 through 11 beginning on page 238.

7.3 THEORY OF CONSTRAINTS AND THROUGHPUT COSTING

1. **Overview**

   a. The theory of constraints (TOC), devised by Israeli physicist and business consultant Eliyahu Goldratt, is a system to improve human thinking about problems. It has been greatly extended to include manufacturing operations.

   b. The basic premise of TOC as applied to business is that improving any process is best done not by trying to maximize efficiency in every part of the process, but by focusing on the slowest part of the process.

   c. The slowest part of the process is called the **constraint**.

      1) Constraints cause backup in the process because other processes need to "wait" for the constraint to finish before the next process can be completed.
      2) Increasing the efficiency of processes that are not constraints merely creates backup in the system.

   d. The **steps in a TOC analysis** are as follows (they are described in more detail under items 2. through 6.):

      1) Identify the constraint.
      2) Determine the most profitable product mix given the constraint.
      3) Maximize the flow through the constraint.
      4) Increase capacity at the constraint.
      5) Redesign the manufacturing process for greater flexibility and speed.

2. **Step 1 -- Identify the Constraint**

   a. The bottleneck operation can usually be identified as the one where work-in-process backs up the most.

   b. A more sophisticated approach is to analyze available resources (number and skill level of employees, inventory levels, time spent in other phases of the process) and determine which phase has negative slack time, i.e., the phase without enough resources to keep up with input.

3. **Step 2 -- Determine the Most Profitable Product Mix Given the Constraint**

   a. A basic principle of TOC analysis is that short-term profit maximization requires maximizing the contribution margin through the constraint, called the **throughput margin** or throughput contribution.

      1) TOC thus helps managers to recognize that the product they should produce the most of is not necessarily the one with the highest contribution margin per unit, but the one with the highest throughput margin per unit; i.e., managers must make the most profitable use of the bottleneck operation.

   b. **Throughput costing**, sometimes called **supervariable costing**, recognizes only direct materials costs as being truly variable and thus relevant to the calculation of throughput margin. All other manufacturing costs are ignored because they are considered fixed in the short run.

      1) Even direct labor is considered a fixed cost, which makes sense considering that many companies have union contracts or paternalistic policies that involve employing laborers, or at least paying them, even when no work is available.

   Throughput margin = Sales − Direct materials

2) **EXAMPLE:** During its first month in business, a firm produced 100 units and sold 80 while incurring the following costs:

Direct materials	$1,000
Manufacturing costs used in supervariable costing	**$1,000**
Direct labor	2,000
Variable overhead	1,500
Manufacturing costs used in variable costing	**$4,500**
Fixed overhead	3,000
Manufacturing costs used in absorption costing	**$7,500**

c. The different costing methods can result in drastically different costs per unit, which can affect the value of ending inventory.

1) **EXAMPLE:**

Cost per unit:
Absorption ($7,500 ÷ 100 units)	$75
Variable ($4,500 ÷ 100 units)	45
Supervariable ($1,000 ÷ 100 units)	10

Ending inventory:
Absorption ($75 × 20 units)	$1,500
Variable ($45 × 20 units)	900
Supervariable ($10 × 20 units)	200

a) Note that, because throughput costing capitalizes so few costs as product costs, ending inventory and cost of goods sold are lower than under variable costing and much lower than under absorption costing.

2) Below is a comparison of the calculation of operating income under two of the methods.

a) The units were sold at a price of $100 each.

b) The company incurred $200 of variable selling and administrative expenses and $600 of fixed selling and administrative expenses.

c) Note the drastic reduction in operating income resulting from the treatment of so many costs as period costs under throughput costing.

Variable Costing			Supervariable Costing		
Sales		$8,000	Sales		$8,000
Beginning inventory	$ 0		Beginning inventory	$ 0	
Variable manufacturing costs	4,500		Direct materials costs	1,000	
Goods available for sale	$4,500		Goods available for sale	$1,000	
Less: ending inventory	(900)		Less: ending inventory	(200)	
Variable cost of goods sold		(3,600)	**Supervariable cost of goods sold**		(800)
Variable S&A expenses		(200)			
Contribution margin		$4,200	**Throughput margin**		$7,200
			Direct labor		(2,000)
			Variable overhead		(1,500)
			Variable S&A expenses		(200)
Fixed overhead		(3,000)	Fixed overhead		(3,000)
Fixed S&A expenses		(600)	Fixed S&A expenses		(600)
Operating income		$ 600	**Operating loss**		$ (100)

SU 7: Operational Efficiency and Business Process Performance

- d. To determine the most profitable use of the bottleneck operation, a manager next calculates the throughput margin per unit of time spent in the constraint.
    1) Profitability is maximized by keeping the bottleneck operation busy with the product with the highest throughput margin per unit of time.
- e. When there are multiple products, the crucial factor in determining the optimal product mix is not which product is the most profitable in terms of absolute throughput margin, but which one has the highest **throughput margin per hour**.
    1) EXAMPLE: Under the current setup, the unit spends 5 hours in the manufacturing process.

Price	$100
Less: materials cost	(10)
Throughput margin	$ 90
Divided by: constraint time	÷ 5
Throughput margin per hour	**$ 18**

- f. To derive the most profitable product mix given finite resources, customer demand must be taken into account.
    1) The available time in the bottleneck operation is first devoted to the product with the highest throughput margin per hour, then to the other products in descending order until the company is unable to meet additional demand.
    2) EXAMPLE: A firm sells 3 products, A, B, and C, with throughput margins per hour of $18, $15, and $12, respectively. Product A spends 5 hours in the bottleneck, Product B spends 5 hours in the bottleneck, and Product C spends 4 hours in the bottleneck. The firm has determined it can sell 10 units of A, 8 units of B, and 6 units of C. The firm has a total of 100 hours available.

	Highest TM: A	2nd Highest TM: B	3rd Highest TM: C
Hours available	100	50	10
Hours needed to fill demand:			
Demand in units	10	8	6
Hours per unit in bottleneck	× 5 (50)	5 (40)	4 (24)
Hours remaining	50	10	(14)

        The firm will forgo some sales of Product C to focus on products that are more profitable.

4. **Step 3 -- Maximize the Flow Through the Constraint**
    a. Production flow through a constraint is managed using the **drum-buffer-rope (DBR)** system.
        1) The drum (i.e., the beat to which a production process marches) is the bottleneck operation. The constraint sets the pace for the entire process.
        2) The buffer is a minimal amount of work-in-process input to the drum that is maintained to ensure that it is always in operation.
        3) The rope is the sequence of activities preceding and including the bottleneck operation that must be coordinated to avoid inventory buildup.

5. **Step 4 -- Increase Capacity at the Constraint**
    a. In the short run, TOC encourages a manager to make the best use of the bottleneck operation. The medium-term step for improving the process is to increase the bottleneck operation's capacity.

6. **Step 5 -- Redesign the Manufacturing Process for Greater Flexibility and Speed**

    a. The long-term solution is to reengineer the entire process. The firm should take advantage of new technology, product lines requiring too much effort should be dropped, and remaining products should be redesigned to ease the manufacturing process.

        1) Value engineering is useful for this purpose because it explicitly balances product cost and the needs of potential customers (product functions).

EXTENDED EXAMPLE of a TOC Calculation

Step 1 -- Identify the Constraint

A company makes three products: an airborne radar unit, a seagoing sonar unit, and a ground sonar unit. Under the current setup, the hours spent by each product in the two phases of the manufacturing process are as follows:

Product	Assembly	Testing
Airborne Radar	3	4
Seagoing Sonar	8	10
Ground Sonar	5	5

The company has 150 hours available every month for testing. Under the current setup, therefore, the testing phase is the constraint.

Step 2 -- Determine the Most Profitable Product Mix Given the Constraint

The company calculates the throughput margin on each product and divides by the hours spent in testing:

	Radar	Seagoing Sonar	Ground Sonar
Price	$200,000	$600,000	$300,000
Less: materials costs	(100,000)	(400,000)	(250,000)
Throughput margin	$100,000	$200,000	$ 50,000
Divided by: constraint time	÷ 4	÷ 10	÷ 5
Throughput margin per hour	**$ 25,000**	**$ 20,000**	**$ 10,000**

To derive the most profitable product mix given finite resources, customer demand must be taken into account. The company has determined that it can sell 12 units of radar, 6 units of seagoing sonar, and 22 units of ground sonar per month.

The available time in the bottleneck operation is first devoted to the product with the highest throughput margin (TM), then in descending order until the company is unable to meet demand.

In the calculation below, the hours remaining after assignment to each product are the hours that can be devoted to the next product.

	Highest TM: Radar	2nd Highest TM: Seagoing Sonar	Lowest TM: Ground Sonar
Hours available	150	102	42
Hours needed to fulfill demand:			
Demand in units	12	6	22
Hours per unit in bottleneck	× 4 (48)	× 10 (60)	× 5 (110)
Hours remaining	102	42	(68)

Applying the principles of TOC, the company will forgo some sales of the ground sonar in favor of products that are more profitable given the current constraint.

-- Continued on the next page --

SU 7: Operational Efficiency and Business Process Performance

> **EXTENDED EXAMPLE of a TOC Calculation -- Continued**
>
> **Step 3 -- Maximize the Flow Through the Bottleneck Operation**
>
> The company will apply a drum-buffer-rope system to ensure that the bottleneck operation stays busy on high-TM products while keeping work-in-process inventory to a minimum.
>
> **Step 4 -- Increase Capacity at the Bottleneck Operation**
>
> The company will hire and train more employees for the testing department.
>
> **Step 5 -- Redesign the Manufacturing Process for Greater Flexibility and Speed**
>
> The company will examine its markets and new manufacturing technology to determine which products it wants to continue selling, whether to add new ones, and whether to retool the production line.

Stop and review! You have completed the outline for this subunit. Study multiple-choice questions 12 through 17 beginning on page 240.

7.4 CAPACITY MANAGEMENT

1. **Capacity Planning**

    a. Capacity planning is an element of strategic planning that is closely related to capital budgeting. The IMA's Statement on Management Accounting *Measuring the Cost of Capacity* (issued in March 1996) states that maximizing the value created within an organization starts with understanding the nature and capabilities of all of the company's resources. According to that statement, effective capacity cost management requires

        - In the short run, optimizing capital decisions and the effective and flexible use of investments that have already been made
        - Maximizing the value delivered to customers
        - Helping minimize requirements for future investment
        - Supporting effective matching of a firm's resources with current and future market opportunities
        - Closing any gap between market demands and a firm's capabilities
            - At times, the firm may have excess capabilities; at others, shortages may exist. These capabilities may be physical, human, technological, or financial.
        - Eliminating waste in the short, intermediate, and long run
        - Providing useful costing information on current process costs versus those proposed in current or future investment proposals
        - Supporting the establishment of capacity usage measurements that identify the cost of capacity and its impact on business cycles and overall company performance
        - Identifying the capacity required to meet strategic and operational objectives and to estimate current available capacity
        - Detailing the opportunity cost of unused capacity and suggesting ways to account for that cost
        - Supporting change efforts by providing predecision information and analysis on the potential resource and cost implications of a planned change
        - Creating a common language for, and understanding of, capacity cost management
        - Thus, capacity should be defined from several different perspectives. Managing the cost of that capacity starts when a product or process is first envisioned. It continues through the subsequent disposal of resources downstream.

b. Capacity planning is part of the capital budgeting process.

1) Estimating capacity levels for future periods allows for the acquisition of more capacity when needed or disposal of capacity that is not expected to be utilized.

c. Capacity level influences product costing, pricing decisions, and financial statements.

1) Excess capacity has a cost. Having excess capacity means that a company will either have to charge higher prices for its products or report lower income on its financial statements.

d. Similarly, producing at full capacity can have a cost in the form of opportunity costs. A company that could generate additional sales if it had more capacity needs to address whether the acquisition of additional capacity is warranted.

2. **Capacity Levels**

a. **Theoretical capacity** is the optimal level of output that can be completed with zero downtime and zero waste.

1) Budgeting and planning based on theoretical capacity is not recommended because it is not reasonable to assume zero downtime (i.e., no maintenance) and zero waste.

b. **Practical capacity** is the highest level of output that can reasonably be attained taking into account both planned and unplanned downtime (e.g., set-up costs, maintenance, breakdowns, etc.) and expected waste.

1) Budgeting and planning based on practical capacity aligns the allocation of fixed costs with normal production activity. Any variance can be a signal for a change in demand for the product, an issue with production, etc.

c. **Normal capacity** is the average level of output that can be completed over a period of time.

3. **Capacity Expansion**

a. According to business strategy theorist Michael E. Porter, determining whether to expand capacity is a major strategic decision because of the capital required, the difficulty of forming accurate expectations, and the long timeframe of the lead times and the commitment. The key forecasting problems are long-term demand and behavior of competitors. The key strategic issue is avoidance of industry overcapacity.

1) Capacity expansion is also referred to as market penetration because it involves increasing the amount of an existing product in an existing market.

b. Undercapacity in a profitable industry tends to be a short-term issue. Profits ordinarily lure additional investors. Overcapacity tends to be a long-term problem because firms are more likely to compete intensely rather than reverse their expansion.

c. The formal capital budgeting process entails predicting future cash flows related to the expansion project, discounting them at an appropriate interest rate, and determining whether the net present value is positive. This process permits comparison with other uses of the firm's resources.

1) The apparent simplicity of this process is deceptive because it depends upon, among many other things, which expansion method is chosen, developments in technology, and profitability. The latter factor in turn depends on such uncertainties as total long-term demand and the expansion plans of rival firms.

d. Porter's model of the decision process for capacity expansion has the following interrelated steps:

1) The firm must identify the options in relation to their size, type, degree of vertical integration (if any), and possible response by competitors.
2) The second step is to forecast demand, input costs, and technology developments. The firm must be aware that its technology may become obsolete or that future design changes to allow expansion may or may not be possible. Moreover, the expansion itself may put upward pressure on input prices.
3) The next step is analysis of competitors to determine when each will expand. The difficulty is that forecasting their behavior depends on knowing their expectations. Another difficulty is that each competitor's actions potentially affect all other competitors' actions, with the industry leader being most influential.
4) Using the foregoing information, the firm predicts total industry capacity and firms' market shares. These estimates, together with the expected demand, permit the firm to predict prices and cash flows.
5) The final step is testing for inconsistencies.

e. The extent of uncertainty about future demand is a crucial variable in determining the nature of industry expansion. For example, if uncertainty is great, firms willing to take greater risks because of their large cash resources or strategic stake in the industry will act first. Other firms will await events.

1) When demand uncertainty is low, firms will tend to adopt a strategy of preemption, usually with strong market signals, to forestall competitors' expansion plans. Excess preemption leads to excess industry capacity because firms overestimate their competitive strengths, misunderstand market signals, or fail to accurately assess competitors' intentions.

Stop and review! You have completed the outline for this subunit. Study multiple-choice question 18 on page 241.

7.5 VALUE-CHAIN ANALYSIS

1. **Value and Customers' Perceptions**

    a. To remain on the market, a product must provide value to the customer and a profit to the seller.

    1) Customers assign value to a product. The producer can affect the customer's perception of value by differentiating the product and lowering its price.
    2) The producer's profit is the difference between its costs and the price it charges for the product. Thus, by keeping costs low, the producer has more flexibility in pricing.

    b. The relationship of these three aspects of value creation can be graphically depicted as follows:

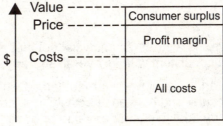

Figure 7-1

2. **Value-Added and Nonvalue-Added Activities**

   a. A value-added activity increases the value of a product or service to the customer. Examples include assembling the product and shipping it to the customer.

   b. A nonvalue-added activity does not increase the value of a product or service to the customer even if this activity is necessary. Examples include inspection for testing and inventory storage costs.

3. **The Value Chain**

   a. The value chain is a model for depicting the way in which every function in a company adds value to the final product.

      1) The IMA's Statement on Management Accounting (SMA) *Value Chain Analysis for Assessing Competitive Advantage* (issued in March 1996) says, "The value chain approach for assessing competitive advantage is an integral part of the strategic planning process."

   b. A value chain depicts how costs and customer value accumulate along a chain of activities that lead to an end product or service.

      1) A value chain consists of the internal processes or activities a company performs: R&D, design, production, marketing, distribution, and customer service.

   c. Another view is that the value chain consists of all of the value-creating activities leading to the ultimate end-use product delivered into the final consumers' hands.

      1) In other words, a value chain is a firm's overall chain of value-creating (value-added) processes.

   d. Primary activities deal with the product directly. Support activities lend aid to the primary activity functions. The value chain can be graphically depicted as follows:

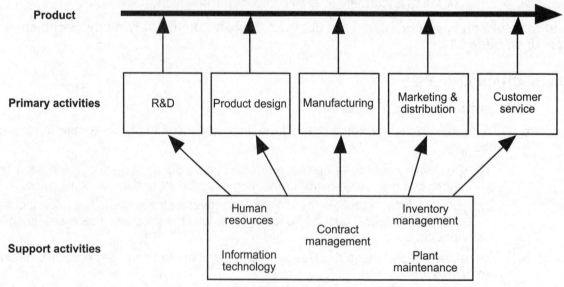

Figure 7-2

4. **Value-Chain Analysis**

   a. Value-chain analysis is a strategic analysis tool that allows a firm to focus on those activities that are consistent with its overall strategy.

      1) Value-chain analysis allows a firm to decide which parts of the value chain it wants to occupy and how each activity then contributes to the firm's competitive advantage by adding customer value or by reducing costs.

b. Because the value chain identifies and connects the organization's strategic activities, value-chain analysis improves the firm's knowledge of its relations with customers, suppliers, and competitors. It also facilitates the strategic determination of the phase(s) of the industry's value chain in which the firm should operate.

1) The first step in a value-chain analysis is to identify the firm's value-creating activities.

2) The second step is to determine how each value-creating activity can produce a competitive advantage for the firm. This step has multiple substeps.

   a) Identify the firm's competitive advantage (e.g., cost reduction, product differentiation) so that the firm's position in the industry's value chain can be clarified.

   b) Identify the ways in which the firm's value-creating activities can generate additional customer value.

   c) Identify activities that are candidates for cost reduction or, in the case of non-core competencies, outsourcing.

   d) Identify value-adding ways in which the firm's remaining activities can be linked.

c. Value-chain analysis is a team effort. Management accountants need to collaborate with engineering, production, marketing, distribution, and customer service professionals to focus on the strengths, weaknesses, opportunities, and threats identified in the value-chain analysis results.

1) Value-chain analysis offers an excellent opportunity to integrate strategic planning and management accounting to guide the firm to survival and growth.

5. **The Supply Chain**

a. The supply chain is the flow of materials and services from their original sources to final consumers. Moreover, it usually encompasses more than one firm.

1) Firms seeking to improve performance and reduce costs must analyze all phases of the supply chain as well as the value chain. Thus, a firm must reduce the cost of, and increase the value added by, its purchasing function.

b. Purchasing is the management function that concerns the acquisition process. It includes choice of vendors, contract negotiation, the decision whether to purchase centrally or locally, and value analysis. The process is initiated by purchase requisitions issued by the production control function.

1) Purchase requisitions ultimately result from insourcing vs. outsourcing (make vs. buy) decisions made when production processes were designed.

2) The choice of vendors depends on price, quality, delivery performance, shipping costs, credit terms, and service. Purchasers with a competitive orientation and considerable economic power may be able to extract very favorable terms from vendors.

3) Purchasers with a cooperative orientation adopt a longer-term approach: supply-chain coordination. The purchaser and the vendor are viewed as committed to a partnership involving joint efforts to improve quality.

   a) For example, in the case of a major manufacturer and one of its suppliers, this orientation may include the purchaser's willingness to help develop the vendor's managerial, technical, and productive capacities. Thus, it tends to result in minimizing the number of vendors.

c. Supply-chain analysis and coordination should extend to all parties in the chain, from initial sources of materials to retailers.

1) Coordination has special relevance to inventory management. By sharing information among all parties, demand uncertainty is reduced at each level, with consequent decreases of inventory at each level, minimization of stockouts, and avoidance of overproduction and rush orders.
2) For example, such cooperation counteracts what has been called the **bullwhip or backlash effect**. This phenomenon occurs when demand variability increases at each level of the supply chain.
3) Retailers face only customer demand variability, but the manufacturer must cope with retailer demand variability that is greater than customer demand variability because retailers' purchases vary with additional factors, such as batching of orders and trade promotions.
4) Similarly, the variability of manufacturer demands on suppliers may be greater than the variability of retailer demands on manufacturers.

d. Value-chain and supply-chain analysis should be used to meet customer requirements for better performance regarding such critical success factors as

1) Cost reduction,
2) Efficiency,
3) Continuous improvement of quality to meet customer needs and wants,
4) Minimization or elimination of defects,
5) Faster product development and customer response times, and
6) Constant innovation.

6. **Value Engineering**

a. Value engineering is a means of reaching targeted cost levels. It is a systematic approach to assessing all aspects of the value chain cost buildup for a product. The purpose is to minimize costs without sacrificing customer satisfaction.

1) Value engineering requires distinguishing between cost incurrence and **locked-in costs**.

b. Cost incurrence is the actual use of resources, but locked-in (designed-in) costs will result in use of resources in the future as a result of past decisions. Thus, value engineering emphasizes controlling costs at the design stage, that is, before they are locked in.

c. Life-cycle costing is sometimes used as a basis for cost planning and product pricing. Life-cycle costing estimates a product's revenues and expenses over its expected life cycle. The result is to highlight upstream and downstream costs in the cost-planning process that often receive insufficient attention. Emphasis is on the need to price products to cover all costs, not just production costs.

Stop and review! You have completed the outline for this subunit. Study multiple-choice questions 19 through 23 beginning on page 242.

7.6 OTHER PROCESS IMPROVEMENT TOOLS

1. **Process Analysis**

a. Process analysis is a means of linking a firm's internal processes to its overall strategy.

b. Types of Processes

1) Continuous, such as candy bars produced by machinery
2) Batch, such as beer brewing
3) Hybrid, in which both continuous and batch processes are used
4) Make-to-stock, such as automobile assembly
5) Make-to-order, such as deli sandwich making

c. Process Interdependence

1) The degree of interdependence among the stages in a process is referred to as "tightness."
2) A tight process is one in which a breakdown in one stage brings the succeeding stages to a halt. This is characteristic of continuous processes that do not have buffer work-in-process inventories.
3) A loose process is one in which subsequent stages can continue working after a breakdown in a previous stage. This is characteristic of batch processes and any others with extensive work-in-process inventories.

d. Bottlenecks

1) Very few processes run at precisely the same speed in every stage.
2) One part of the process is almost always the slowest, referred to as the "bottleneck." If capacity is added at that point, the bottleneck simply shifts to the next slowest operation.
   a) The theory of constraints (discussed in Subunit 7.3) was developed to deal with this challenge.
3) The bottleneck issue only arises when demand for the firm's product is sufficient to absorb all of the output. When a production line is running at less than full capacity, bottlenecks can be avoided.

2. **Process Value Analysis**

a. **Process value analysis** is a comprehensive understanding of how an organization generates its output. It involves a determination of which activities that use resources are value-adding or nonvalue-adding and how the latter may be reduced or eliminated.

1) This linkage of product costing and continuous improvement of processes is **activity-based management (ABM)**. ABM redirects and improves the use of resources to increase the value created for customers and other stakeholders.
   a) ABM encompasses activity analysis, cost driver analysis, and quality performance measurement.
2) A **continuous improvement process (CIP)** is an ongoing effort to improve products, services, or processes.
   a) These efforts can lead to "incremental" improvement over time or "breakthrough" improvement all at once.
   b) Delivery (customer valued) processes are constantly evaluated and improved in light of their efficiency, effectiveness, and flexibility.
   c) The purpose of CIP is the identification, reduction, and elimination of suboptimal processes to improve efficiency.
3) **Kaizen** is the Japanese word for the continuous pursuit of improvement in every aspect of organizational operations.
   a) For example, a budget prepared on the Kaizen principle projects costs based on future improvements. The possibility of such improvements must be determined, and the cost of implementation and the savings therefrom must be estimated.

b) Key features of Kaizen include the following:

i) Improvements are based on many small changes rather than the radical changes that might arise from research and development.

ii) Ideas come from the workers themselves, so they are less likely to be radically different and therefore are easier to implement.

iii) Small improvements are less likely to require major capital investment than major process changes.

iv) The ideas come from the talents of the existing workforce, as opposed to using research, consultants, or equipment–any of which could be expensive.

v) All employees, including management, should continually seek ways to improve their own performance.

vi) Workers are encouraged to take ownership of their work and can help reinforce teamwork, thereby improving worker motivation.

c) The key features of Kaizen are the more tactical elements of CIP. The more strategic elements include deciding how to increase the value of the delivery process output to the customer (effectiveness) and how much flexibility is valuable in the process to meet changing needs.

b. An **activity analysis** determines what is done, by whom, at what cost in time and other resources, and the value added by each activity.

1) A value-added activity is necessary to remain in business. For example, a manufacturer would deem the conversion of raw materials into salable products a value-added activity.

a) Such an activity may be mandated (e.g., a regulatory requirement) or discretionary. The latter produces some changes not otherwise achievable that enables other activities to occur.

2) A value-added cost is incurred to perform a value-added activity without waste. Most types of direct labor would be considered value-added cost because the costs are being incurred to directly produce the product.

3) A nonvalue-added activity is unnecessary and should be eliminated. The act of generating nonsalable final products is a nonvalue-added activity.

a) An example of a nonvalue-added activity is where inventory has to be moved long distances from one work station to another in a production process. Similarly, inventory that has to wait in line before being processed is a waste. This is why just-in-time inventory systems have proved popular: JIT eliminates much of the waste in a production process.

4) A nonvalue-added cost is caused by a nonvalue-added activity or inefficient performance of a value-added activity. The costs of raw materials and direct labor expended on products that fail inspection would be considered nonvalue-added costs.

a) Thus, managing the causes of cost results in elimination of unnecessary activities as well as greater efficiency of activities.

c. Financial and nonfinancial **measures of activity performance** address efficiency, quality, and time. The purpose is to assess how well activities meet customer demands.

1) To satisfy customer needs and wants, activities should be efficient (a favorable input-to-output ratio) so that customers are willing to pay the prices charged.

2) Activities should produce defect-free output (high quality), and that output should be produced in a timely manner (with less resource usage and in response to customer requirements).

d. The selection of value-added activities in each place of the value chain reflects the firm's determination of its competitive advantage and its choice of competitive strategy.

1) For example, different design strategies require different activities and costs. A firm might choose to be the low-cost producer of an undifferentiated product rather than compete on the basis of superior product quality.

e. One aspect of process analysis is the management of time. Product development time is a crucial factor in the competitive equation. A company that is first in the market with a new product has obvious advantages.

1) Reducing development time is also important because product life cycles are becoming shorter.
2) Companies need to respond quickly and flexibly to new technology, changes in consumer tastes, and competitive challenges.

3. **Business Process Reengineering (BPR)**

a. BPR is a complete rethinking of how business functions are performed to provide value to customers, that is, radical innovation instead of mere improvement, and a disregard for current jobs, hierarchies, and reporting relationships.

1) Technological advances have increased the popularity of business process reengineering.

b. A process is how something is accomplished in a firm. It is a set of activities directed toward the same objective. Reengineering is process innovation and core process redesign. Instead of improving existing procedures, it finds new ways of doing things. Thus, reengineering should be contrasted with process improvement, which consists of incremental but constant changes that improve efficiency.

1) Accordingly, BPR techniques eliminate many traditional controls. They exploit modern technology to improve productivity and decrease the number of clerical workers. Thus, the emphasis is on developing controls that are automated and self-correcting and require minimal human intervention.

c. The emphasis therefore shifts to monitoring internal control so management can determine when an operation may be out of control and corrective action is needed.

1) Most BPR techniques also assume that humans will be motivated to work actively in improving operations when they are full participants in the process.

d. Part of the BPR process involves looking at possible alternatives and determining the cost of those possible alternatives compared to the costs of maintaining the same processes.

1) To do this, the management accountant must determine

a) The cost to reengineer the process, and
b) The expected savings.

2) Some desirable alternatives may actually increase total costs.

a) For example, more expensive materials could lead to higher product quality. While this will increase total costs, it may be necessary to maintain/increase market share.
b) In situations like these, the management accountant would determine the savings attributed to possible alternatives compared to maintaining the same processes.

3) After determining the cost and savings of BRP, the company must look at all of its goals and needs to determine if overall, they should invest in a possible alternative.

EXAMPLE

It currently takes 3 people working for 10 hours each at a rate of $15 per hour to produce 10 units of Product P. For $350, the company has the option of purchasing a machine that will allow the same 3 people to produce 10 units of Product P in 5 hours.

It currently costs $450 (3 people × 10 hours × $15 per hour) to produce 10 units of Product P. If the company purchases the machine, it will cost $225 (3 people × 5 hours × $15 per hour) to produce 10 units of Product P for an annual saving of $225 ($450 − $225). Since this company will achieve these savings each year, the company should probably purchase the machine.

---

4. **Benchmarking**

   a. The IMA's Statement on Management Accounting (SMA) *Effective Benchmarking*, issued in July 1995, describes techniques for improving the effectiveness of benchmarking, which is a means of helping companies with productivity management and business process reengineering.

      1) "Benchmarking involves continuously evaluating the practices of best-in-class organizations and adapting company processes to incorporate the best of these practices." It "analyzes and measures the key outputs of a business process or function against the best and also identifies the underlying key actions and root causes that contribute to the performance difference."

      2) Benchmarking is an ongoing process that entails quantitative and qualitative measurement of the difference between the company's performance of an activity and the performance by the best in the world. The benchmark organization need not be a competitor.

   b. The first phase in the benchmarking process is to select and prioritize benchmarking projects.

      1) An organization must understand its critical success factors and business environment to identify key business processes and drivers and to develop parameters defining what processes to benchmark.

      2) The criteria for selecting what to benchmark relate to the reasons for the existence of a process and its importance to the entity's mission, values, and strategy. These reasons relate in large part to satisfaction of end users or customer needs.

   c. The next phase is to organize benchmarking teams.

      1) A team organization is appropriate because it permits an equitable division of labor, participation by those responsible for implementing changes, and inclusion of a variety of functional expertise and work experience.

      2) Team members should have knowledge of the function to be benchmarked, respected positions in the company, good communication skills, teaming skills, motivation to innovate and to support cross-functional problem solving, and project management skills.

   d. The benchmarking team must thoroughly investigate and document internal processes.

      1) The organization should be seen as a series of processes, not as a fixed structure. A process is "a network of related and independent activities linked by the outputs they exchange." One way to determine the primary characteristics of a process is to trace the path a request for a product or service takes through the organization.

SU 7: Operational Efficiency and Business Process Performance

2) The benchmarking team must also develop a family of measures that are true indicators of process performance and a process taxonomy, that is, a set of process elements, measures, and phrases that describes the process to be benchmarked.

e. Researching and identifying best-in-class performance is often the most difficult phase.

1) The critical steps are setting up databases, choosing information-gathering methods (internal sources, external public domain sources, and original research are the possible approaches), formatting questionnaires (lists of questions prepared in advance), and selecting benchmarking partners.

f. The data analysis phase entails identifying performance gaps, understanding the reasons they exist, and prioritizing the key activities that will facilitate the behavioral and process changes needed to implement the benchmarking study's recommendations.

1) Sophisticated statistical analysis and other methods may be needed when the study involves many variables, testing of assumptions, or presentation of quantified results.

g. Leadership is most important in the implementation phase of the benchmarking process because the team must be able to justify its recommendations.

1) Moreover, the process improvement teams must manage the implementation of approved changes.

5. **Balanced Scorecard**

a. The balanced scorecard approach employs multiple measures of performance to permit a determination as to whether the organization is achieving certain objectives at the expense of others that may be equally or more important.

1) For example, an improvement in operating results at the expense of new product development would be apparent using this approach.

b. The scorecard is a goal congruence tool that informs managers about the nonfinancial factors that top management believes to be important.

1) As mentioned previously, measures may be financial or nonfinancial, internal or external, and short term or long term.

c. The balanced scorecard facilitates best practice analysis.

1) Best practice analysis is a method of accomplishing a business function or process that is considered to be superior to all other known methods. A lesson learned from one area of a business can be passed on to another area of the business or between businesses.

2) Thus, the whole concept of benchmarking is aimed at identifying best practices.

d. A typical scorecard includes measures in four categories:

1) Financial
2) Customer
3) Learning, growth, and innovation
4) Internal business processes

6. **Costs of Quality**

a. The IMA's Statement on Management Accounting *Managing Quality Improvements*, issued in 1993, describes four categories of costs of quality: prevention, appraisal, internal failure, and external failure. The organization should attempt to minimize its total cost of quality.

b. Conformance costs include prevention and appraisal, which are both financial measures of internal performance.

1) **Prevention** attempts to avoid defective output. These costs include preventive maintenance, employee training, review of equipment design, and evaluation of suppliers. Providing quality training to employees should reduce all types of quality costs.
2) **Appraisal** encompasses such activities as statistical quality control programs, inspection, and testing.

c. Nonconformance costs include costs of internal failure (a financial measure of internal performance) and external failure costs (a financial measure of customer satisfaction).

1) **Internal failure** costs occur when defective products are detected before shipment.
    a) Examples are scrap, rework, tooling changes, downtime, redesign of products or processes, lost output, reinspection and retesting, expediting of operations after delays, lost learning opportunities, and searching for and correcting problems.
2) The costs of **external failure** or lost opportunity include lost profits from a decline in market share as dissatisfied customers make no repeat purchases, return products for refunds, cancel orders, and communicate their dissatisfaction to others.
    a) Thus, external failure costs are incurred for customer service complaints; rejection, return, repair, or recall of products or services; warranty obligations; products liability claims; and customer losses.
        i) Given the wide variety of causes of external failure, the best solution is to provide all employees with training about the importance of providing quality to customers.
    b) Environmental costs are also external failure costs, e.g., fines for nonadherence to environmental law and loss of customer goodwill.
        i) To minimize environmental damage and its resulting costs, the International Organization for Standardization has issued ISO 14000 standards to promote the reduction of environmental damage by an organization's products, services, and operations and to develop environmental auditing and performance evaluation systems.

7. **Efficient accounting processes**

    a. Improving accounting processes can increase a company's ability to minimize the costs of these processes while also maximizing their usefulness.
    b. Four important areas where companies can optimize their accounting processes include

        1) Accounts payable,
        2) Cash cycle,
        3) Closing and reconciliation processes, and
        4) Data analysis.

Stop and review! You have completed the outline for this subunit. Study multiple-choice questions 24 through 30 beginning on page 243.

QUESTIONS

7.1 Just-in-Time Inventory and Lean Operation

1. The effectiveness of a JIT system is often facilitated by the elimination of some common forms of internal control. The elimination of which internal control is usually acceptable with a JIT system?

A. Preparation of hard copy receiving reports.
B. Voucher approval prior to paying accounts payable.
C. Two signatures required on large checks.
D. Locked doors on production areas.

Answer (A) is correct.
REQUIRED: The internal control that is not necessary with a JIT system.
DISCUSSION: Receiving departments are often eliminated with a JIT system so receiving reports are not needed. Also, the quantity received should be exactly equal to immediate production needs.
Answer (B) is incorrect. Voucher approval prior to paying accounts payable is a control that should not be affected by adoption of a JIT system. Answer (C) is incorrect. Two signatures required on large checks is a control that should not be affected by adoption of a JIT system. Answer (D) is incorrect. Locked doors on production areas is a control that should not be affected by adoption of a JIT system.

2. Just-in-time manufacturing practices are based in part on the belief that

A. High inventory levels provide greater flexibility in production scheduling.
B. Attempting to reduce inventory to a consistently low level can lead to "panic" situations.
C. Goods should be "pulled" through the production process, not "pushed."
D. Beefed-up internal control in the central warehouse can greatly enhance productivity in the production areas.

Answer (C) is correct.
REQUIRED: The concept that is part of the philosophy of just-in-time manufacturing.
DISCUSSION: Just-in-time (JIT) manufacturing is a pull system; items are pulled through production by current demand, not pushed through by anticipated demand as in traditional manufacturing setups.
Answer (A) is incorrect. Under the JIT philosophy, high inventory levels often mask production problems. Answer (B) is incorrect. Attempting to reduce inventory to a consistently low level is a core objective of JIT. Answer (D) is incorrect. Under JIT, central warehouses are often eliminated.

3. If a worker encounters a production kanban at his or her workstation, the worker should

A. Issue a purchase requisition.
B. Begin manufacturing the requested item.
C. Initiate a purchase order with the supplier of the requested item.
D. Confirm the amount of the item requested and present the kanban to the production supervisor.

Answer (B) is correct.
REQUIRED: The action a worker should take upon being presented with a production kanban.
DISCUSSION: In a kanban inventory control system, a production kanban is an indication to a worker to begin producing the item referred to on the kanban.
Answer (A) is incorrect. Release of an item to a subsequent stage in production is initiated with a production kanban. Answer (C) is incorrect. A purchase from a supplier is indicated by a vendor kanban. Answer (D) is incorrect. Under a kanban system, a worker is authorized to take action upon being presented with a kanban; involving the production supervisor only slows down the process.

4. A firm that is deploying just-in-time manufacturing for the first time will

A. Establish contracts with many suppliers since an interruption in supply is extremely disruptive of the production process.
B. Establish contracts with a few carefully chosen suppliers since an interruption in supply is extremely disruptive of the production process.
C. Maintain a carefully calibrated safety stock since interruptions in supply are inevitable.
D. Acquire considerable computer processing capability to manage the demands of the data-dependent kanban inventory management system.

Answer (B) is correct.
REQUIRED: The aspect of employing just-in-time (JIT) inventory management.
DISCUSSION: In a JIT system, the suppliers' dependability is crucial. Organizations that adopt JIT systems develop close relationships with a few carefully chosen suppliers who are extensively involved in the buyer's processes.
Answer (A) is incorrect. In a JIT system, the suppliers' dependability is crucial. Organizations that adopt JIT systems develop close relationships with a few carefully chosen suppliers who are extensively involved in the buyer's processes. Answer (C) is incorrect. The use of safety stock is considered a nonvalue-adding activity under a JIT system, and interruptions in supply are not considered inevitable. Answer (D) is incorrect. A JIT system does not necessarily require the employment of kanban inventory management. Also, kanban is essentially a manual system.

5. Which of the following internal controls is **not** one typically eliminated when a just-in-time inventory system is introduced?

   A. Sophisticated inventory tracking system.
   B. Central receiving dock.
   C. Statistical methods for quality assurance.
   D. Hard copy receiving report.

Answer (C) is correct.
REQUIRED: The internal control that is not one typically eliminated when a just-in-time (JIT) inventory system is introduced.
DISCUSSION: Under a JIT system, the quality of parts provided by suppliers is verified by use of statistical controls rather than inspection of incoming goods. Storage, counting, and inspection are eliminated in an effort to perform only value-adding work.
Answer (A) is incorrect. Frequent receipt of deliveries from suppliers often means less need for a sophisticated inventory control system and for control personnel. Answer (B) is incorrect. Under JIT, a central receiving area and central warehouse are not needed because deliveries are made by suppliers directly to the area of production. Answer (D) is incorrect. With the elimination of central receiving areas and central warehouses that typically accompanies the institution of a JIT system, hard copy receiving reports are unnecessary.

6. The physical reconfiguration of equipment that often accompanies the institution of a just-in-time manufacturing regime is described as the creation of

   A. Cells.
   B. Kanbans.
   C. Electronic Data Interchange.
   D. Tickets.

Answer (A) is correct.
REQUIRED: The term referring to the result of equipment reconfiguration that often accompanies just-in-time manufacturing.
DISCUSSION: Plant layout in a JIT-lean production environment is not arranged by functional department or process but by manufacturing cells (work cells). Cells are sets of machines, often group in semicircles, that produce a given product or product type.
Answer (B) is incorrect. While a kanban system is sometimes part of a JIT arrangement, the term does not refer to the physical rearrangement of machinery. Answer (C) is incorrect. While electronic data interchange (EDI) facilitates the vendor relations that make JIT possible, the term does not refer to the physical rearrangement of machinery. Answer (D) is incorrect. Ticket is the meaning of the Japanese term kanban, which does not refer to the physical rearrangement of machinery.

7. Which of the following terms is **not** connected with the employment of just-in-time (JIT) manufacturing?

   A. Cells.
   B. Kanban.
   C. Lean production.
   D. Safety stock.

Answer (D) is correct.
REQUIRED: The term that is not connected with just-in-time manufacturing.
DISCUSSION: Safety stock involves always keeping enough raw materials on hand to overcome the effects of an interruption in supply. In a JIT system, manufacturers are completely dependent upon the reliability of their suppliers in delivering raw materials as they are needed. Keeping safety stock undercuts the entire philosophy of JIT.
Answer (A) is incorrect. Cells are the configurations of manufacturing equipment that facilitate JIT and lean production. Answer (B) is incorrect. Kanban is a Japanese system for inventory control that is often implemented as part of JIT manufacturing. Answer (C) is incorrect. Lean production is often part of a JIT manufacturing system.

7.2 Enterprise Resource Planning and Outsourcing

8. In contrast to just-in-time manufacturing, materials requirements planning is a

   A. Push system.
   B. Pull system.
   C. Automated system.
   D. Manual system.

Answer (A) is correct.
REQUIRED: The description of materials requirements planning (MRP) that stands in contrast to just-in-time manufacturing.
DISCUSSION: MRP is a push system, that is, the demand for raw materials is driven by the forecasted demand for the final product, which can be programmed into the computer. This is in contrast with just-in-time manufacturing, which is a pull system, meaning items are pulled through production by current demand, not pushed through by anticipated demand.
Answer (B) is incorrect. Just-in-time manufacturing is a pull system. Answer (C) is incorrect. Both systems may be automated. Answer (D) is incorrect. Neither system need be manual.

9. Materials requirements planning (MRP) sometimes results in

A. Longer idle periods.
B. Less flexibility in responding to customers.
C. Increased inventory carrying costs.
D. Decreased setup costs.

Answer (D) is correct.
REQUIRED: The result of implementing a materials requirements planning (MRP) system.
DISCUSSION: Among the benefits of MRP are reduced idle time, lower setup costs, lower inventory carrying costs, and increased flexibility in responding to market changes.
Answer (A) is incorrect. MRP often results in reduced idle time. Answer (B) is incorrect. MRP often results in increased flexibility in responding to market changes. Answer (C) is incorrect. MRP often results in lower inventory carrying costs.

10. A company uses material requirements planning (MRP) and manufactures a product with the following product structure tree.

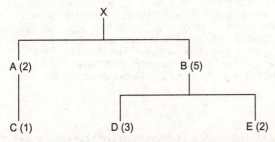

The company has just received an order for 100 units of X, the finished product. The company has 20 units of X, 100 units of B, and 50 units of E in inventory. How many units of E must the company purchase in order to fill the order?

A. 1,000
B. 950
C. 800
D. 550

Answer (D) is correct.
REQUIRED: The subunits required by a bill of materials in an MRP system.
DISCUSSION: The company already has 20 units of the finished product in inventory so 80 will need to be manufactured to fill this order. The amount of Subunit B that must be purchased is [(80 × 5) − 100 on hand] = 300. The amount of Subunit E that must be purchased is therefore [(300 × 2) − 50 on hand] = 550.
Answer (A) is incorrect. Failing to consider the units already in inventory results in 1,000. Answer (B) is incorrect. Failing to consider the 20 units of X and the 100 units of B results in 950. Answer (C) is incorrect. Failing to consider the 100 units of B and the 50 units of E already in inventory results in 800.

11. One reason to outsource is so a firm can focus on its

A. Customers.
B. Suppliers.
C. Undifferentiated activities.
D. Core competencies.

Answer (D) is correct.
REQUIRED: The reason for a firm to consider outsourcing.
DISCUSSION: Firms may gain a competitive advantage by outsourcing those activities which can be performed more efficiently, and thus at lower cost, by outside providers. Doing this allows the company to expend its effort on those activities which it performs comparatively well, referred to as its core competencies.
Answer (A) is incorrect. To stay in business, a firm must focus on its customers whether it outsources or not. Answer (B) is incorrect. Focusing on suppliers is not a strategy for gaining a competitive advantage. Answer (C) is incorrect. Undifferentiated activities is not a meaningful term in this context.

7.3 Theory of Constraints and Throughput Costing

12. A company manufactures three products at its highly automated factory. The products are very popular, with demand far exceeding the company's ability to supply the marketplace. To maximize profit, management should focus on each product's

A. Gross margin.
B. Segment margin.
C. Contribution margin ratio.
D. Contribution margin per machine hour.

Answer (D) is correct.
REQUIRED: The measure used to determine the profit maximizing output.
DISCUSSION: When demand far exceeds a company's ability to supply the marketplace, management will want to maximize its profits per unit of scarce resource. If the scarce resource is raw materials, the products that provide the greatest contribution margin per unit of raw materials are the products to emphasize. If machine hours are the constraint, profits are maximized by emphasizing the contribution margin per machine hour.
Answer (A) is incorrect. Focusing on high gross margin products does not maximize profits if those products require an excessive amount of resources. Answer (B) is incorrect. The company can sell as much of each product as it can produce. Thus, sales are limited by production constraints, e.g., machine hours. The company should therefore seek to maximize its return per unit of the constraint. Answer (C) is incorrect. The contribution margin ratio is only important as it translates to dollars. A high margin on a low sales volume will not be profitable.

13. A manufacturer produces a single product that sells for $150 per unit. The product is processed through the Cutting and Finishing Departments. Additional data for these departments are as follows:

	Cutting	Finishing
Annual capacity (36,000 direct labor hours available in each department)	180,000 units	135,000 units
Current production rate (annualized)	108,000 units	108,000 units
Fixed manufacturing overhead	$1,296,000	$1,944,000
Fixed selling and administrative expense	864,000	1,296,000
Direct materials cost per unit	45	15

The current production rate is the budgeted rate for the entire year. Direct labor employees earn $20 per hour, and the company has a "no layoff" period in effect. What is the amount of the throughput contribution per unit as computed using the theory of constraints?

A. $90.00
B. $76.67
C. $46.67
D. $26.67

Answer (A) is correct.
REQUIRED: The amount of throughput contribution per unit.
DISCUSSION: Throughput costing, sometimes called supervariable costing, recognizes only direct materials costs as being truly variable and thus relevant to the calculation of throughput margin (throughput contribution). All other manufacturing costs are ignored because they are considered fixed in the short turn. For the manufacturer's single product, the throughput margin is therefore $90 ($150 selling price – $45 direct materials in Cutting – $15 direct materials in Finishing).
Answer (B) is incorrect. Labor, overhead, and selling and administrative costs are not considered in the calculation of throughput contribution. Answer (C) is incorrect. Labor, overhead, and selling and administrative costs are not considered in the calculation of throughput contribution. Answer (D) is incorrect. Labor, overhead, and selling and administrative costs are not considered in the calculation of throughput contribution.

14. Three of the basic measurements used by the theory of constraints (TOC) are

A. Gross margin (or gross profit), return on assets, and total sales.
B. Number of constraints (or subordinates), number of nonconstraints, and operating leverage.
C. Throughput (or throughput contribution), inventory (or investments), and operational expense.
D. Fixed manufacturing overhead per unit, fixed general overhead per unit, and unit gross margin (or gross profit).

Answer (C) is correct.
REQUIRED: The relevant measurements in TOC analysis.
DISCUSSION: Theory of constraints (TOC) analysis describes three basic measurements: throughput contribution (sales – direct materials), investments (raw materials; work-in-process; finished goods; R&D costs; and property, plant, and equipment), and operating costs (all costs except direct materials).
Answer (A) is incorrect. Gross margin, return on assets, and total sales are used in analyzing a firm's profitability; they are not measurements used in TOC analysis. Answer (B) is incorrect. Although the number of constraints/nonconstraints is important under the TOC, these numbers are not basic measurements used in TOC analysis. Operating leverage concerns contribution margin, which is not a basic measurement under TOC. Answer (D) is incorrect. These measurements are used under absorption (full) costing, not in TOC analysis.

SU 7: Operational Efficiency and Business Process Performance

15. A manufacturer can sell its single product for $660. Below are the cost data for the product:

Direct materials	$170
Direct labor	225
Manufacturing overhead	90

The relevant margin amount when beginning a theory of constraints (TOC) analysis is

A. $490
B. $345
C. $265
D. $175

Answer (A) is correct.
REQUIRED: The relevant margin amount when beginning a theory of constraints (TOC) analysis.
DISCUSSION: A theory of constraints (TOC) analysis proceeds from the assumption that only direct materials costs are truly variable in the short run. This is called throughput, or supervariable, costing. The relevant margin amount is throughput margin, which equals price minus direct materials. Thus, the relevant margin amount for this manufacturer is $490 ($660 – $170).
Answer (B) is incorrect. The amount of $345 results from subtracting conversion cost, rather than throughput cost, from selling price. Answer (C) is incorrect. The amount of $265 results from subtracting prime cost, rather than throughput cost, from selling price. Answer (D) is incorrect. The amount of $175 results from subtracting all manufacturing costs, rather than only throughput cost, from selling price.

16. Under throughput costing, the only cost considered to be truly variable in the short run is

A. Direct materials.
B. Direct labor.
C. Manufacturing overhead.
D. All manufacturing costs are considered variable.

Answer (A) is correct.
REQUIRED: The variable cost under throughput costing.
DISCUSSION: Throughput costing, also called supervariable costing, recognizes only direct materials costs as being truly variable and thus relevant to the calculation of throughput margin.
Answer (B) is incorrect. Under throughput costing, direct labor is considered fixed because of labor contracts and employment levels. Answer (C) is incorrect. Under throughput costing, overhead is considered fixed in the short run. Answer (D) is incorrect. Under throughput costing, only direct materials costs are considered variable in the short run.

17. The immediate goal of a theory of constraints (TOC) analysis is to

A. Maximize the efficiency of the entire production process.
B. Minimize direct materials cost.
C. Maximize contribution margin through the constraint.
D. Smooth production flow to eliminate backup in the system.

Answer (C) is correct.
REQUIRED: The immediate goal of a theory of constraints analysis.
DISCUSSION: A basic principle of TOC analysis is that short-term profit maximization requires maximizing the contribution margin through the constraint, called the throughput margin or throughput contribution.
Answer (A) is incorrect. Under the principles of TOC, maximizing the efficiency of processes that have excess capacity merely creates backup in the system. Answer (B) is incorrect. Holding down direct materials costs, while an important part of improving contribution margin, is not part of a TOC analysis. Answer (D) is incorrect. While eliminating backup is a goal of a TOC analysis, it is not done by simply "smoothing" production flow because this could mean slowing down the entire process to match the bottleneck.

7.4 Capacity Management

18. Capacity expansion is also referred to as

A. Market penetration.
B. Market development.
C. Product development.
D. Diversification.

Answer (A) is correct.
REQUIRED: The term used for capacity expansion.
DISCUSSION: Market penetration is growth of existing products or development of existing markets. It occurs in mature firms within an industry.
Answer (B) is incorrect. Market development seeks new markets for current products. Answer (C) is incorrect. Product development is launching new products in existing markets. Answer (D) is incorrect. Diversification is launching new products for new markets.

7.5 Value-Chain Analysis

19. Process value analysis is a key component of activity-based management that links product costing and

A. Reduction of the number of cost pools.
B. Continuous improvement.
C. Accumulation of heterogeneous cost pools.
D. Overhead rates based on broad averages.

Answer (B) is correct.
REQUIRED: The element of process value analysis.
DISCUSSION: Design of an ABC system starts with process value analysis, a comprehensive understanding of how an organization generates its output. It involves a determination of which activities that use resources are value-adding or nonvalue-adding and how the latter may be reduced or eliminated. This linkage of product costing and continuous improvement of processes is activity-based management (ABM). It encompasses driver analysis, activity analysis, and performance measurement.
Answer (A) is incorrect. ABC tends to increase the number of cost pools and drivers used. Answer (C) is incorrect. ABC's philosophy is to accumulate homogeneous cost pools. Thus, the cost elements in a pool should be consumed by cost objects in proportion to the same driver. Homogenizing cost pools minimizes broad averaging of costs that have different drivers. Answer (D) is incorrect. ABC's philosophy is to accumulate homogeneous cost pools. Thus, the cost elements in a pool should be consumed by cost objects in proportion to the same driver. Homogenizing cost pools minimizes broad averaging of costs that have different drivers.

20. A systematic approach to reaching targeted cost levels during value chain analysis is known as

A. Value engineering.
B. Life-cycle costing.
C. Process value analysis.
D. Activity analysis.

Answer (A) is correct.
REQUIRED: The term referring to a systematic approach to reaching targeted cost levels during value chain analysis.
DISCUSSION: Value engineering is a means of reaching targeted cost levels. It is a systematic approach to assessing all aspects of the value chain cost buildup for a product.
Answer (B) is incorrect. Life-cycle costing is a basis for cost planning and product pricing. Answer (C) is incorrect. Process value analysis is a way of understanding how a company generates its output. Answer (D) is incorrect. Activity analysis determines what is done, by whom, at what cost in time and other resources, and the value added by each activity.

21. An entity develops computer programs to meet customers' special requirements. How should the entity categorize payments to employees who develop these programs?

	Direct Costs	Value-Adding Costs
A.	Yes	Yes
B.	Yes	No
C.	No	No
D.	No	Yes

Answer (A) is correct.
REQUIRED: The proper categorization of employee costs.
DISCUSSION: Direct costs may be defined as those that can be specifically associated with a single cost object and can be assigned to it in an economically feasible manner. Wages paid to labor that can be identified with a specific finished good are direct costs. Value-adding costs may be defined as the costs of activities that cannot be eliminated without reducing the quality, responsiveness, or quantity of the output required by a customer or by an organization. Clearly, the amounts paid to programmers add value to computer programs.
Answer (B) is incorrect. The activities performed by programmers add value to computer programs. Therefore, the payments to employees who develop these programs is considered a value-adding cost. Answer (C) is incorrect. Payments to programmers are both direct costs and value-adding costs of computer programs. Answer (D) is incorrect. Wages paid to labor that can be identified with a specific finished good are direct costs. Therefore, payments to employees who develop computer programs is a direct cost.

22. The term referring to the excess of the price of a good over its cost is

A. Consumer surplus.
B. Profit margin.
C. Contribution margin.
D. Value-added transfer.

Answer (B) is correct.
REQUIRED: The term referring to the excess of the price of a good over its cost.
DISCUSSION: To remain in the market, a product must provide value to the customer and a profit to the seller. The producer's profit (profit margin) is the difference between its costs and the price it charges for the product.
Answer (A) is incorrect. Consumer surplus is the excess of the value a consumer places on a good over the price (s)he pays for it. Answer (C) is incorrect. Contribution margin is the excess of the sales price over variable costs. Answer (D) is incorrect. Value-added transfer is not a meaningful term in this context.

23. Which of the following is **not** a component of the value chain?

A. Primary activities.
B. Secondary activities.
C. Support activities.
D. The product.

Answer (B) is correct.
REQUIRED: The items not a component of the value chain.
DISCUSSION: The value chain is a model for depicting the way in which every function in a company adds value to the final product. Primary activities deal with the product directly. Support activities lend aid to the primary activity functions.
Answer (A) is incorrect. In value-chain analysis, primary activities are those that deal with the product directly. Answer (C) is incorrect. In value-chain analysis, support activities lend aid to the primary activity functions. Answer (D) is incorrect. The product is the ultimate reason for having a value chain.

7.6 Other Process Improvement Tools

24. Which of the following statements regarding benchmarking is **false**?

A. Benchmarking involves continuously evaluating the practices of best-in-class organization and adapting company processes to incorporate the best of these practices.
B. Benchmarking, in practice, usually involves a company forming benchmarking teams.
C. Benchmarking is an ongoing process that entails quantitative and qualitative measurement of the difference between the company's performance of an activity and the performance by the best in the world or the best in the industry.
D. The benchmarking organization against which a firm is comparing itself must be a direct competitor.

Answer (D) is correct.
REQUIRED: The false statement about benchmarking.
DISCUSSION: Benchmarking is an ongoing process that entails quantitative and qualitative measurement of the difference between the company's performance of an activity and the performance by a best-in-class organization. The benchmarking organization against which a firm is comparing itself need not be a direct competitor. The important consideration is that the benchmarking organization be an outstanding performer in its industry.
Answer (A) is incorrect. This is a true statement about benchmarking. Answer (B) is incorrect. This is a true statement about benchmarking. Answer (C) is incorrect. This is a true statement about benchmarking.

25. Which of the following statements is **false** with respect to best practices analysis?

A. The balanced scorecard facilitates best practice analysis.
B. Best practice analysis is a way or method of accomplishing a business function or process that is considered to be superior to all other known methods.
C. Best practices analysis assumes that a lesson learned from one area of a business can be passed on to another area of the business or between businesses.
D. The concept of benchmarking is incompatible with best practices analysis.

Answer (D) is correct.
REQUIRED: The false statement about best practices analysis.
DISCUSSION: Best practice analysis is a method of accomplishing a business function or process that is considered to be superior to all other known methods. The balanced scorecard facilitates best practice analysis. A lesson learned from one area of a business can be passed on to another area of the business or between businesses. The whole concept of benchmarking is aimed at identifying best practices.
Answer (A) is incorrect. The balanced scorecard facilitates best practice analysis. Answer (B) is incorrect. The best practice analysis is a method of accomplishing a business function or process that is considered to be superior to all other known methods. Answer (C) is incorrect. A lesson learned in one area of a business can be passed on to another area of the business or between businesses.

26. The cost of scrap, rework, and tooling changes in a product quality cost system is categorized as a(n)

A. Training cost.
B. External failure cost.
C. Internal failure cost.
D. Prevention cost.

Answer (C) is correct.
REQUIRED: The categorization of the cost of scrap, rework, and tooling changes in a product quality cost system.
DISCUSSION: According to IMA's *Management Accounting Glossary*, internal failure costs are incurred when detection of defective products occurs before shipment. Examples of internal failure costs are scrap, rework, tooling changes, and downtime.
Answer (A) is incorrect. Training costs are prevention costs. Answer (B) is incorrect. The costs of external failure, such as warranty expense, product liability, and customer ill will, arise when problems are discovered after products have been shipped. Answer (D) is incorrect. Prevention costs are incurred to avoid defective output. Examples include preventive maintenance, employee training, review of equipment design, and evaluation of suppliers.

27. The four categories of costs associated with product quality costs are

A. External failure, internal failure, prevention, and carrying.
B. External failure, internal failure, prevention, and appraisal.
C. External failure, internal failure, training, and appraisal.
D. Warranty, product liability, training, and appraisal.

Answer (B) is correct.
REQUIRED: The categories of product quality costs.
DISCUSSION: IMA's *Management Accounting Glossary* lists four categories of quality costs: prevention, appraisal, internal failure, and external failure (lost opportunity). Costs of prevention include attempts to avoid defective output, including employee training, review of equipment design, preventive maintenance, and evaluation of suppliers. Appraisal costs include quality control programs, inspection, and testing. Internal failure costs are incurred when detection of defective products occurs before shipment, including scrap, rework, tooling changes, and downtime. External failure costs are incurred after the product has been shipped, including the costs associated with warranties, product liability, and customer ill will.
Answer (A) is incorrect. Carrying cost is not one of the elements of quality costs. Answer (C) is incorrect. Training costs are not a category of quality costs. Answer (D) is incorrect. Warranty, product liability, and training are not cost categories identified by IMA's *Management Accounting Glossary*.

28. The cost of statistical quality control in a product quality cost system is categorized as a(n)

A. Internal failure cost.
B. Training cost.
C. External failure cost.
D. Appraisal cost.

Answer (D) is correct.
REQUIRED: The cost category that includes statistical quality control.
DISCUSSION: The following are the four categories of quality costs: prevention, appraisal, internal failure, and external failure (lost opportunity). Appraisal costs include quality control programs, inspection, and testing. However, some authorities regard statistical quality and process control as preventive activities because they not only detect faulty work but also allow for adjustment of processes to avoid future defects.
Answer (A) is incorrect. Internal failure costs arise after poor quality has been found; statistical quality control is designed to detect quality problems. Answer (B) is incorrect. Statistical quality control is not a training cost. Answer (C) is incorrect. External failure costs are incurred after the product has been shipped, including the costs associated with warranties, product liability, and customer ill will.

29. Which of the following is **not** a type of process?

A. Make-to-stock.
B. Make-to-order.
C. Buffer.
D. Hybrid.

Answer (C) is correct.
REQUIRED: The term not referring to a type of process.
DISCUSSION: A buffer in the context of process analysis is a quantity of work-in-process inventory that allows some stage(s) of the overall process to continue operating when an earlier stage breaks down.
Answer (A) is incorrect. Make-to-stock is a type of process, exemplified by automobile assembly. Answer (B) is incorrect. Make-to-order is a type of process, exemplified by deli sandwich making. Answer (D) is incorrect. A hybrid process is one in which both continuous and batch processes are used.

30. Listed below are selected line items from the Cost of Quality Report for last month.

Category	Amount
Rework	$ 725
Equipment maintenance	1,154
Product testing	786
Product repair	695

What is the total prevention and appraisal cost for last month?

A. $786
B. $1,154
C. $1,940
D. $2,665

Answer (C) is correct.
REQUIRED: The total prevention and appraisal costs.
DISCUSSION: The costs of prevention and appraisal are conformance costs that serve as financial measures of internal performance. Prevention costs are incurred to prevent defective output. These costs include preventive maintenance, employee training, review of equipment design, and evaluation of suppliers. Appraisal costs are incurred to detect nonconforming output. They embrace such activities as statistical quality control programs, inspection, and testing. The equipment maintenance cost of $1,154 is a prevention cost. The product testing cost of $786 is an appraisal cost. Their sum is $1,940.
Answer (A) is incorrect. The appraisal cost is $786. Answer (B) is incorrect. The prevention cost is $1,154. Answer (D) is incorrect. The amount of $2,665 includes rework, an internal failure cost.

7.7 ESSAY QUESTIONS

Scenario for Essay Questions 1, 2, 3

The management at Megafilters, Inc., has been discussing the possible implementation of a just-in-time (JIT) production system at its Illinois plant, where oil filters and air filters for heavy construction equipment and large, off-the-road vehicles are manufactured. The Metal Stamping Department at the Illinois plant has already instituted a JIT system for controlling raw materials inventory, but the remainder of the plant is still discussing how to proceed with the implementation of this concept. Some of the other department managers have grown increasingly cautious about the JIT process after hearing about the problems that have arisen in the Metal Stamping Department.

Robert Goertz, manager of the Illinois plant, is a strong proponent of the JIT production system and recently made the following statement at a meeting of all departmental managers: "Just-in-time is often referred to as a management philosophy of doing business rather than a technique for improving efficiency of the plant floor. We will all have to make many changes in the way we think about our employees, our suppliers, and our customers if we are going to be successful in using just-in-time procedures. Rather than dwelling on some of the negative things you have heard from the Metal Stamping Department, I want each of you to prepare a list of things we can do to make a smooth transition to the just-in-time philosophy of management for the rest of the plant."

Questions

1. The just-in-time (JIT) management philosophy emphasizes objectives for the general improvement of a production system. Describe several important objectives of this philosophy.

2. Discuss several actions that Megafilters can take to ease the transition to a just-in-time (JIT) production system at the Illinois plant.

3. In order for the just-in-time (JIT) production system to be successful, Megafilters must establish appropriate relationships with its vendors, employees, and customers. Describe each of these three relationships.

Essay Questions 1, 2, 3 — Unofficial Answers

1. The objectives for the general improvement of a production system as emphasized in the just-in-time (JIT) management philosophy include

    a. Flowing product continuously through the plant and minimizing the investment in raw materials, work-in-process, and finished goods inventories

    b. Making production operations in the plant more efficient by redesigning work stations, simplifying the environment, and reducing both set-up and lead times

    c. Increasing the attention to quality control, reducing obsolescence and waste, and identifying non-value-added cost drivers (i.e., nonproductive labor, insurance, taxes) that can be eliminated

2. Megafilters, Inc., can take the following actions to ease the transition to a just-in-time (JIT) production system at the Illinois plant:

    a. Communicate to employees, customers, and vendors the corporate objectives and plans for implementing the JIT production system.

    b. Elicit employee participation in implementing the JIT system and train employees on the necessary tools (i.e., computers).

    c. Chart the production-process flows through the plant and develop statistical measurement and control procedures. Simplify processing and identify and alleviate cost drivers, non-value-added activities, and waste.

    d. Obtain competitive bids and JIT proposals from several vendors for each material, selecting the few who will reduce lead times, increase the quality of raw materials, and comply with strict delivery schedules.

3. Megafilters, Inc., must establish the following appropriate relationships in order to successfully implement the just-in-time (JIT) production system:

    a. Vendors

        1) Reduce the number of vendors to those who will be highly dependable and reliable.

        2) Commit the vendor to high quality standards by shifting responsibility for production problems to the suppliers (i.e., defective parts).

    b. Employees

        1) Develop trust and communication with the employees to obtain team participation in the initial plan and elicit feedback in the future.

        2) Increase the employees' responsibility to assist in improving operations and quality while reducing cost drivers.

        3) Treat employees as partners in the process, eliciting their commitment.

    c. Customers

        1) Develop trust and communication for including the customers' participation in the initial plan and eliciting feedback in the future.

        2) Ensure that Megafilters is fulfilling the customers' needs and demands.

        3) Build a team spirit through assurances that the company will meet the customers' demands at a competitive price. Employ the customer as a partner in the process (i.e., wait together for delayed deliveries, in order to keep costs at a minimum).

Access the **CMA Review System** from your Gleim Personal Classroom to continue your studies with exam-emulating essay questions!

STUDY UNIT EIGHT
ANALYSIS AND FORECASTING TECHNIQUES

(27 pages of outline)

8.1	Correlation and Regression	247
8.2	Learning Curve Analysis	251
8.3	Expected Value	253
8.4	Sensitivity Analysis	256
8.5	Strategic Management	258
8.6	The Balanced Scorecard	265
8.7	Strategic Planning	270
8.8	Essay Question	283

This study unit is the **first of two** on **planning, budgeting, and forecasting**. The relative weight assigned to this major topic in Part 1 of the exam is **30%**. The two study units are

Study Unit 8: Analysis and Forecasting Techniques
Study Unit 9: Budgeting -- Concepts, Methodologies, and Preparation

If you are interested in reviewing more introductory or background material, go to www.gleim.com/CMAIntroVideos for a list of suggested third-party overviews of this topic. The following Gleim outline material is more than sufficient to help you pass the CMA exam; any additional introductory or background material is for your own personal enrichment.

8.1 CORRELATION AND REGRESSION

1. **Forecasting Methods**

    a. Forecasts are the basis for business plans and budgets. Forecasts are used to project product demand, inventory levels, cash flow, etc.

    1) **Qualitative methods** of forecasting rely on the manager's experience and intuition.
    2) **Quantitative methods** use mathematical models and graphs.

        a) When some factor in the organization's environment is plotted on the x axis, the technique is causal relationship forecasting.
        b) When time periods are plotted on the x axis, the technique is time-series analysis.

2. **Correlation Analysis**

    a. Correlation analysis is the foundation of any quantitative method of forecasting.

    1) Correlation is the strength of the linear relationship between two variables, expressed mathematically in terms of the coefficient of correlation (r). It can be graphically depicted by plotting the values for the variables on a graph in the form of a scatter diagram.

        a) The value of r ranges from 1 (perfect direct relationship) to –1 (perfect inverse relationship). The more the scatter pattern resembles a straight line, the greater the absolute value of r.

b) **Perfect direct relationship (r = 1)**

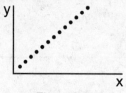

Figure 8-1

c) **Perfect inverse relationship (r = –1)**

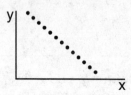

Figure 8-2

d) **Strong direct relationship (r = 0.7)**

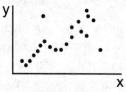

Figure 8-3

e) **No linear relationship (r = 0)**

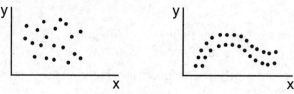

Figure 8-4

  i) Note from the right-hand graph of the pair above that a coefficient of correlation of zero does not mean there is no relationship at all between the two variables, only that the relationship they may have cannot be expressed as a linear equation.

2) The **coefficient of determination (r^2)**, or the coefficient of correlation squared, is a measure of how good the fit between the two variables is.

  a) Mathematically, the coefficient of determination is the proportion of the total variation in the dependent variable that is accounted for by the independent variable.

  b) EXAMPLE: A car dealership determines that new car sales are a function of disposable income with a coefficient of correlation of .8. This is equivalent to stating that 64% ($.8^2$) of the variation of new car sales from the average can be explained by changes in disposable income.

3. **Regression Analysis**

 CMA candidates should be able to demonstrate an understanding of the measures associated with simple regression as well as calculate the result of the equation. They should also be able to identify when it is appropriate to use multiple regression. Therefore, candidates should memorize and fully understand the formulas for both simple and multiple regression analysis.

a. Regression analysis, also called least-squares analysis, is the process of deriving the linear equation that describes the relationship between two variables with a nonzero coefficient of correlation.

1) **Simple regression** is used when there is one independent variable.

   a) The simple regression equation is the algebraic formula for a straight line:

   $$y = a + bx$$

   Where: y = the dependent variable
   a = the y intercept
   b = the slope of the regression line
   x = the independent variable

   b) The best straight line that fits a set of data points is derived using calculus to minimize the sum of the squares of the vertical distances of each point to the line (hence the name least-squares method).

   c) EXAMPLE: A firm has collected observations on advertising expenditures and annual sales.

Advertising ($000s)	Sales ($000,000s)
71	26.3
31	13.9
50	19.8
60	22.9
35	15.1

   i) Solving with the least-squares method reveals that expected sales equal $4.2 million plus 311.741 times the advertising expenditure.

   $$y = \$4,200,000 + 311.741x$$

   ii) The observations are graphed as follows:

   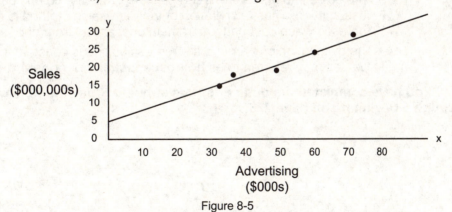

   Figure 8-5

   iii) The firm can now project the amount it will have to spend on advertising to generate $32,000,000 in sales.

   $$\begin{aligned} y &= \$4,200,000 + 311.741x \\ \$32,000,000 &= \$4,200,000 + 311.741x \\ 311.741x &= \$27,800,000 \\ x &= \$89,177 \end{aligned}$$

2) Regression analysis is particularly valuable for budgeting and cost accounting purposes.

   a) Regression analysis is almost a necessity for computing the fixed and variable portions of mixed costs for flexible budgeting. The y-axis intercept is the fixed portion and the slope of the regression line is the variable portion.

3) **Regression does not determine causality.**

   a) Although x and y move together, the apparent relationship may be caused by some other factor. For instance, car wash sales volume and sunny weather are strongly correlated, but car wash sales do not cause sunny weather.

4) **Multiple regression** is used when there is more than one independent variable.

   a) The example on the previous page relating advertising to sales is clearly unrealistic. Sales are dependent upon more than just advertising expenditures.

   b) Multiple regression allows a firm to identify many factors (independent variables), and to weight each one according to its influence on the overall outcome.

   $$y = a + b_1x_1 + b_2x_2 + b_3x_3 + b_4x_4 + etc.$$

5) **Assumptions** of the linear regression model.

   a) The linear relationship established for x and y is only valid across the **relevant range**. The user must identify the relevant range and ensure that (s)he does not project the relationship beyond it.

      i) A negative y intercept in the simple regression equation usually indicates that it is outside the relevant range.

   b) Regression analysis assumes that **past relationships** can be validly projected into the future. Economists call this the ceteris paribus assumption. Thus, a limitation of the regression method is that it can only be used when cost patterns remain unchanged from prior periods.

   c) The distribution of y around the regression line is constant for different values of x, referred to as **homoscedasticity** or **constant variance**.

Stop and review! You have completed the outline for this subunit. Study multiple-choice questions 1 through 6 beginning on page 273.

8.2 LEARNING CURVE ANALYSIS

1. **Learning Curves**

    a. Learning curve analysis reflects the increased rate at which people perform tasks as they gain experience.

    1) The time required to perform a given task becomes progressively shorter during the early stages of production.

    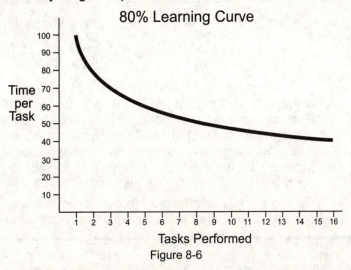

    Figure 8-6

    2) The curve is usually expressed as a percentage of reduced time each time cumulative production doubles.

        a) When determining whether cumulative production doubles, it is important to look at units produced as well as batch numbers.

        b) EXAMPLE: A firm produces units in batches of 100 and experiences an 80% learning curve.

Batch	Cumulative Units Produced	Doubling
1	100	
2	200	1st doubling from 100 to 200
3	300	
4	400	2nd doubling from 200 to 400
5	500	
6	600	
7	700	
8	800	3rd doubling from 400 to 800

3) In practice, the most common percentage used is 80%. However, on the exam, be prepared to see a variety of percentages.

   a) The following table illustrates this phenomenon for a product whose first unit takes 100 minutes to produce:

Batch	Cumulative Units Produced	70% Cumulative Average Time per Unit	80% Cumulative Average Time per Unit	90% Cumulative Average Time per Unit
1 (Unit 1)	1	100	100	100
2 (Unit 2)	2	70 (100 × 70%)	80 (100 × 80%)	90 (100 × 90%)
3 (Units 3-4)	4	49 (70 × 70%)	64 (80 × 80%)	81 (90 × 90%)
4 (Units 5-8)	8	34.3 (49 × 70%)	51.2 (64 × 80%)	72.9 (81 × 90%)
5 (Units 9-16)	16	24.01 (34.3 × 70%)	40.96 (51.2 × 80%)	65.61 (72.9 × 90%)

   b) The time listed in the cumulative average time per unit column is an average of all the units produced up to that point. Note that with an 80% learning curve upon completion of the final batch (units 9 – 16), the average had come down to 40.96 minutes per unit. For it to reach this level from the 51.2 minutes it had reached at the end of the fourth batch (units 5 – 8), the average of the units in the fifth batch alone must have been 30.72 minutes [(40.96 minutes × 2) – 51.2 minutes].

   c) With more sophisticated quantitative techniques, a more accurate average can be calculated of the units within each "batch."

CMA candidates need to be alert as to the nature of the question being asked. Sometimes the question might ask, "What is the average time per unit after two units?" From the table above, with an 80% learning curve, you can see that the answer is 80. Alternatively, sometimes the question asks, "What is the time to produce the second unit?" The answer would be 60. Since the first unit took 100 minutes and the average for the two units is 80 minutes (a total of 160), then the second unit must have taken only 60 minutes.

2. **Application**

   a. **Two methods** of applying learning curve analysis are in common use.

      1) The **cumulative average-time learning model** projects the reduction in the cumulative average time it takes to complete a certain number of tasks.

      2) The **incremental unit-time learning model** projects the reduction in the incremental time it takes to complete the last task.

      3) EXAMPLE: A firm determines that 100 minutes of labor are required to complete one unit of product. Assuming an 80% learning curve, the following table illustrates the difference between the two methods.

Learning Curve 80% at Each Doubling		Cumulative Average-Time Model		Incremental Unit-Time Model	
(A) Unit Produced	(B) Cumulative Average Time per Unit	(A) × (B) Cumulative Total Time	Time Spent on Most Recent Unit	Σ (B) Incremental Unit Total Time	Σ (B) / (A) Average Time Spent on Most Recent Unit
1	100.00	100.00	100.00	100.00	100.00
2	80.00	160.00	60.00	180.00	90.00
3	70.21	210.63	50.63	250.21	83.40
4	64.00	256.00	45.37	314.21	78.55

      a) CMA candidates will not need to know how to calculate units within a batch. You should know how to calculate the learning curves for 1, 2, and 4 unit(s) produced.

   4) The difference between the two methods is clear in the way each calculates total time. Most CMA questions have historically used the cumulative-average-time method, and it is often called the "traditional" learning curve model.

3. **Limitations**

   a. The limitation of the learning curve in practice is the difficulty in knowing the shape of the learning curve.

      1) There is no question that the learning curve effect exists, but companies typically do not know what percentage they should use in calculations until after it is too late to use the information effectively. As a result, many companies simply assume an 80% learning curve and make decisions based on those results.

Stop and review! You have completed the outline for this subunit. Study multiple-choice questions 7 through 11 beginning on page 275.

8.3 EXPECTED VALUE

1. **Expected Value**

   a. Expected value is a means of associating a dollar amount with each of the possible outcomes of a probability distribution.

      1) The outcome yielding the highest expected monetary value (which may or may not be the most likely one) is the optimal alternative.

         a) The **decision** alternative is under the manager's control.

         b) The **state of nature** is the future event whose outcome the manager is attempting to predict.

         c) The **payoff** is the financial result of the combination of the manager's decision and the actual state of nature.

      2) The expected value of an event is calculated by multiplying the probability of each outcome by its payoff and summing the products.

         a) EXAMPLE: An investor is considering the purchase of two identically priced pieces of property. The value of the properties will change if a road, currently planned by the state, is built.

            i) The following are estimates that road construction will occur:

Future State of Nature (SN)	Event	Probability
SN 1	No road is ever built.	.1
SN 2	A road is built this year.	.2
SN 3	A road is built more than 1 year from now.	.7

            ii) The following are estimates of the values of the properties under each of the three possible events:

Property	SN 1	SN 2	SN 3
Bivens Tract	$10,000	$40,000	$35,000
Newnan Tract	$20,000	$50,000	$30,000

            iii) The expected value of each property is determined by multiplying the probability of each state of nature by the value under that state of nature and adding all of the products.

		Expected Value
Bivens Tract:	.1($10,000) + .2($40,000) + .7($35,000) =	**$33,500**
Newnan Tract:	.1($20,000) + .2($50,000) + .7($30,000) =	**$33,000**

            Thus, Bivens Tract is the better investment.

            iv) A calculation such as this is often referred to as a payoff table.

3) The difficult aspect of constructing a payoff table is the determination of all possible outcomes of decisions and their probabilities. Thus, a probability distribution must be established.

   a) The assigned probabilities may reflect prior experience with similar decisions, the results of research, or highly subjective estimates.

4) It is important to capture all values when constructing a payoff table. Otherwise, results may be inaccurate.

   a) For example, unsold items may be sold for scrap or may require storage costs.
   b) Failure to account for these and other factors will skew results.
   c) EXAMPLE: A vendor can order 10, 20, or 30 hats.

      i) The probabilities of demand are as follows:

Demand	Probability
10	60%
20	30%
30	10%

      ii) Each hat can be sold for $5. Unsold hats can be sold as scrap for $1.

      iii) The expected profit or loss if the ability to sell unsold hats as scrap is included when calculating the payoff table is as follows:

	States of Nature			Expected Value
Decision	Demand = 10	Demand = 20	Demand = 30	Totals
10 hats	$50	$ 50	$ 50	$50
20 hats	$60	$100	$100	$76
30 hats	$70	$110	$150	$90

         $50 = [.6 × $50] + [.3 × $ 50] + [.1 × $ 50]
         $76 = [.6 × $60] + [.3 × $100] + [.1 × $100]
         $90 = [.6 × $70] + [.3 × $110] + [.1 × $150]

      iv) The expected profit or loss if the ability to sell unsold hats as scrap is **not** included when calculating the payoff table is as follows:

	States of Nature			Expected Value
Decision	Demand = 10	Demand = 20	Demand = 30	Totals
10 hats	$50	$ 50	$ 50	$50
20 hats	$50	$100	$100	$70
30 hats	$50	$100	$150	$75

         $50 = [.6 × $50] + [.3 × $ 50] + [.1 × $ 50]
         $70 = [.6 × $50] + [.3 × $100] + [.1 × $100]
         $75 = [.6 × $50] + [.3 × $100] + [.1 × $150]

      v) In this example, failing to include the option to sell unsold hats for $1 results in much more similar expected values across the different decisions.

      vi) Even though the result is the same, the goal is to provide the most accurate and useful information for decision-making purposes.

5) The expected value criterion is likely to be adopted by a decision maker who is risk neutral. However, other circumstances may cause the decision maker to be risk averse or even risk seeking.

   a) EXAMPLE: A dealer in luxury yachts may order 0, 1, or 2 yachts for this season's inventory.

      i) The dealer projects demand for the season as follows:

Demand	Probability
0 yachts	10%
1 yacht	50%
2 yachts	40%

      ii) The cost of carrying each excess yacht is $50,000, and the gain for each yacht sold is $200,000. The profit or loss resulting from each combination of decision and outcome is thus as follows:

	States of Nature			Expected Value
Decision	Demand = 0	Demand = 1	Demand = 2	Totals
Stock 0 yachts	$ 0	$ 0	$ 0	$ 0
Stock 1 yacht	(50,000)	200,000	200,000	175,000
Stock 2 yachts	(100,000)	150,000	400,000	225,000

         $175,000 = [.1 × -$ 50,000] + [.5 × $200,000] + [.4 × $200,000]
         $225,000 = [.1 × -$100,000] + [.5 × $150,000] + [.4 × $400,000]

   b) In this example, a risk-averse decision maker may not wish to accept the risk of losing $100,000 by ordering two yachts.

6) The benefit of expected value analysis is that it allows a manager to apply scientific management techniques to applications that would otherwise be guesswork.

   a) Although exact probabilities may not be known, the use of expected value analysis forces managers to evaluate decisions in a more organized manner. At the least, managers are forced to think of all of the possibilities that could happen with each decision.

7) A criticism of expected value is that it is based on repetitive trials, whereas in reality, most business decisions involve only one trial.

   a) EXAMPLE: A company wishes to launch a communications satellite.

      i) The probability of launch failure is .2, and the value of the satellite if the launch fails is $0. The probability of a successful launch is .8, and the value of the satellite would then be $25,000,000. The expected value is calculated as follows:

         .2($0) + .8($25,000,000) = $20,000,000

      ii) But $20,000,000 is not a possible value for a single satellite; either it flies for $25,000,000 or it crashes for $0.

2. **Perfect Information**

   a. Perfect information is the certain knowledge of which state of nature will occur.

      1) The **expected value of perfect information (EVPI)** is the additional expected value that could be obtained if a decision maker knew ahead of time which state of nature would occur.

         a) EXAMPLE: The yacht dealer on the previous page would maximize profits if (s)he were able to determine exactly what all potential customers intended to do for the season.

            i) Since the yacht dealer has perfect information, the values used in the payoff table are based on the known demand; i.e., if demand will be 0 yachts, the dealer knows this and purchases 0 yachts, if demand will be 1 yacht, the dealer knows this and only purchases 1 yacht, etc.

	States of Nature			Expected Value with Perfect Information
Decision	Demand = 0	Demand = 1	Demand = 2	Totals
Stock 0 yachts	$ 0	$ 0	$ 0	$ 0
Stock 1 yacht	(50,000)	200,000	200,000	100,000
Stock 2 yachts	(100,000)	150,000	400,000	160,000
				$260,000

            ii) The profit that could be obtained with this perfect knowledge of the market is calculated as follows:

               $260,000 = (.1 × $0) + (.5 × $200,000) + (.4 × $400,000)

            iii) The difference between this amount and the best choice without perfect information is the EVPI.

Expected value with perfect information	$260,000
Expected value without perfect information	(225,000)
Expected value of perfect information (EVPI)	$ 35,000

            iv) The dealer is therefore not willing to pay more than $35,000 for perfect information about future demand.

      2) The maximum anyone should be willing to pay for perfect information is the expected value of perfect information.

Stop and review! You have completed the outline for this subunit. Study multiple-choice questions 12 through 14 beginning on page 276.

8.4 SENSITIVITY ANALYSIS

1. Sensitivity analysis reveals how sensitive expected value calculations are to the accuracy of the initial estimates.

   a. Sensitivity analysis is thus useful in determining whether expending additional resources to obtain better forecasts is justified.

      1) If a change in the probabilities assigned to the various states of nature results in large changes in the expected values, the decision maker is justified in expending more effort to make better predictions about the outcomes.

      2) The benefit of sensitivity analysis is that managers can see the effect of changed assumptions on the final objective.

SU 8: Analysis and Forecasting Techniques

a) For example, in a capital budgeting situation, a proposed investment might promise a return of $10,000 per year and a rate of return of 15%. But that $10,000 is based on an estimate. What management needs to know is how acceptable would the investment be if the return was only $6,000 per year.

b. EXAMPLE: The yacht dealer in the expected value computation illustrated on the previous page is testing different combinations of probabilities. All three of the scenarios depicted here yield the same decision (stock two yachts for the season):

Decision Alternatives	States of Nature	Payoff	Original		First Alternative		Second Alternative	
			Probability	Expected Value	Probability	Expected Value	Probability	Expected Value
Stock 0 Yachts	Demand = 0	$ 0	0.1	$ 0	0.5	$ 0	0.333	$ 0
	Demand = 1	0	0.5	0	0.1	0	0.333	0
	Demand = 2	0	0.4	0	0.4	0	0.333	0
				$ 0		$ 0		$ 0
Stock 1 Yacht	Demand = 0	(50,000)	0.1	(5,000)	0.5	(25,000)	0.333	(16,650)
	Demand = 1	200,000	0.5	100,000	0.1	20,000	0.333	66,600
	Demand = 2	200,000	0.4	80,000	0.4	80,000	0.333	66,600
				$175,000		$ 75,000		$116,550
Stock 2 Yachts	Demand = 0	(100,000)	0.1	(10,000)	0.5	(50,000)	0.333	(33,300)
	Demand = 1	150,000	0.5	75,000	0.1	15,000	0.333	49,950
	Demand = 2	400,000	0.4	160,000	0.4	160,000	0.333	133,200
				$225,000		$125,000		$149,850

1) However, the following combination indicates that only one yacht should be stocked:

Decision Alternatives	States of Nature	Payoff	Third Alternative	
			Probability	Expected Value
Stock 0 Yachts	Demand = 0	$ 0	0.1	$ 0
	Demand = 1	0	0.8	0
	Demand = 2	0	0.1	0
				$ 0
Stock 1 Yacht	Demand = 0	(50,000)	0.1	(5,000)
	Demand = 1	200,000	0.8	160,000
	Demand = 2	200,000	0.1	20,000
				$175,000
Stock 2 Yachts	Demand = 0	(100,000)	0.1	(10,000)
	Demand = 1	150,000	0.8	120,000
	Demand = 2	400,000	0.1	40,000
				$150,000

2) Clearly, the more accurately the dealer is able to anticipate demand, the more profit (s)he will make. In this case, the dealer considers it worthwhile to expend further resources gathering more data about market conditions for yachts.

c. A trial-and-error method inherent in sensitivity analysis is obviously greatly facilitated by the use of computer software.

d. A major use of sensitivity analysis is in capital budgeting, where small changes in prevailing interest rates or payoff amounts can make a very great difference in the profitability of a project.

Stop and review! You have completed the outline for this subunit. Study multiple-choice questions 15 through 18 beginning on page 277.

8.5 STRATEGIC MANAGEMENT

1. **Strategic Management**

    a. Strategic management sets overall objectives for an entity and guides the process of reaching those objectives. It is the responsibility of upper management.

        1) Strategic planning is the design and implementation of the specific steps and processes necessary to reach the overall objectives.

    b. Strategic management and strategic planning are thus closely linked. By their nature, strategic management and strategic planning have a long-term planning horizon.

2. **Steps in the Strategic Management Process**

    a. Strategic management is a five-stage process:

        1) The board of directors drafts the organization's mission statement.
        2) The organization performs a situational analysis, also called a SWOT analysis.
        3) Based on the results of the situational analysis, upper management develops a group of strategies describing how the mission will be achieved.
        4) Strategic plans are implemented through the execution of component plans at each level of the entity.
        5) Strategic controls and feedback are used to monitor progress, isolate problems, and take corrective action. Over the long term, feedback is the basis for adjusting the original mission and objectives.

Strategic Management

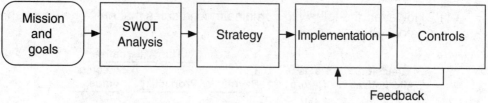

Figure 8-7

    b. The **mission statement** summarizes the entity's reason for existing. It provides the framework for formulation of the company's strategies.

        1) Missions tend to be most effective when they consist of a single sentence.

            a) For example, the mission of Starbucks Coffee Company is "to inspire and nurture the human spirit – one person, one cup and one neighborhood at a time."

        2) Missions tend to be stated in general terms. Setting specific objectives in the mission statement can limit an entity's ability to respond to a changing marketplace.

        3) A mission statement and a vision statement serve different purposes for a company but are sometimes confused with each other. A mission statement describes what a company wants to achieve now, while a **vision statement** outlines what a company wants to achieve in the future.

            a) The mission statement concentrates on the present; it defines the customers and critical processes, and it explains the desired level of performance.

            b) The vision statement focuses on the future; it is a source of inspiration and motivation. It often describes not just the future of the organization, but the future of the industry or society in which the organization operates. It answers the question, "Where do we want to be in the future?"

c) A mission statement describes how a company will achieve its vision. It defines the entity's purpose and primary objectives and answers the question, "What do we do, and what makes us different?"

c. The **situational analysis** is most often called a SWOT analysis because it identifies the entity's strengths, weaknesses, opportunities, and threats.

1) **Strengths and weaknesses** are usually identified by considering the entity's capabilities and resources (its internal environment).

a) What the entity does particularly well or has in greater abundance are its core competencies. But many entities may have the same core competencies (cutting-edge IT, efficient distribution, etc.).

b) An entity gains a competitive advantage in the marketplace by developing one or more distinctive competencies, i.e., competencies that are unlike those of its competitors.

2) **Opportunities and threats** exist in the entity's external environment. They are identified by considering

a) Macroenvironment factors (economic, demographic, political, legal, social, cultural, and technical) and

b) Microenvironment factors (suppliers, customers, distributors, competitors, and other competitive factors in the industry).

d. Based on the results of the situational analysis, upper management develops a **group of strategies** describing how the mission will be achieved. The strategies answer such questions as

1) "Which lines of business will we be in?"
2) "How do we penetrate and compete in the international marketplace?"
3) "How will this line of business reach its objectives that contribute to achievement of the overall entity's mission?"
4) "How do we perform each strategic business unit's basic processes (materials handling, assembly, shipping, human resources, customer relations, etc.) as efficiently as possible?"

e. **Implementing** the chosen strategies involves every employee at every level of the entity. Incentive systems and employee performance evaluations must be designed so that they encourage employees to focus their efforts on achieving the entity's objectives.

1) This approach requires communication among senior managers, who devise strategies; middle managers, who supervise and evaluate employees; and human resources managers, who must approve evaluation and compensation plans.

f. As plans are executed at each organizational level, **strategic controls and feedback** allow management to determine the degree of progress toward the stated objectives.

1) For controls to be effective, standards against which performance can be measured must be established. Then, the results of actual performance must be measured against the standards and reported to the appropriate managers. If performance is unsatisfactory, managers take corrective action.

2) Results are sent to higher-level management for continual refinement of the strategies.

3. **Porter's Five Competitive Forces**

    a. Business theorist Michael E. Porter has developed a model of the structure of industries and competition. It includes an analysis of the five competitive forces that determine long-term profitability as measured by long-term return on investment.

    1) This analysis includes an evaluation of the basic economic and technical characteristics that determine the strength of each force and the attractiveness of the industry. The competitive forces are depicted in the diagram below and discussed in detail on the following pages.

Porter's Five Competitive Forces

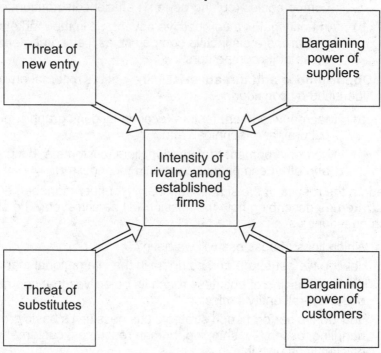

Figure 8-8

    b. **Rivalry among existing firms** will be intense when an industry contains many strong competitors. Price-cutting, large advertising budgets, and frequent introduction of new products are typical. The intensity of rivalry and the threat of entry vary with the following factors:

    1) The stage of the industry life cycle, e.g., rapid growth, growth, maturity, decline, or rapid decline

        a) Thus, growth is preferable to decline. In a declining or even a stable industry, a firm's growth must come from winning other firms' customers, thereby strengthening competition.

    2) The distinctions among products (product differentiation) and the costs of switching from one competitor's product to another

        a) Less differentiation tends to heighten competition based on price, with price cutting leading to lower profits. But high costs of switching suppliers weaken competition.

    3) Whether fixed costs are high in relation to variable costs

        a) High fixed costs indicate that rivalry will be intense. The greater the cost to generate a given amount of sales revenues, the greater the investment intensity and the need to operate at or near capacity. Hence, price cutting to sustain demand is typical.

4) Capacity expansion

   a) If the size of the expansion must be large to achieve economies of scale, competition will be more intense. The need for large-scale expansion to achieve production efficiency may result in an excess of industry capacity over demand.

c. The prospects of long-term profitability depend on the industry's **barriers to entry**.

   1) Factors that increase the threat of entry are the following:

      a) Economies of scale (and learning curve effects) are not significant.
      b) Brand identity of existing products is weak.
      c) Costs of switching suppliers are low.
      d) Existing firms do not have the cost advantages of vertical integration.
      e) Product differences are few.
      f) Access to existing suppliers is not blocked, and distribution channels are willing to accept new products.
      g) Capital requirements are low.
      h) Exit barriers are low.
      i) The government's policy is to encourage new entrants.

   2) The most favorable industry condition is one in which entry barriers are high and exit barriers are low.

      a) When the threat of new entrants is minimal and exit is not difficult, returns are high, and risk is reduced in the event of poor performance.
      b) Low entry barriers keep long-term profitability low because new firms can enter the industry, increasing competition and lowering prices and the market shares of existing firms.

d. The **threat of substitutes** limits price increases and profit margins. The greater the threat, the less attractive the industry is to potential entrants.

   1) Substitutes are types (not brands) of goods and services that have the same purposes, for example, plastic and metal or minivans and SUVs. Hence, a change in the price of one such product (service) causes a change in the demand for its substitutes.

   2) Structural considerations affecting the threat of substitutes are

      a) Relative prices,
      b) Costs of switching to a substitute, and
      c) Customers' inclination to use a substitute.

e. As the **threat of buyers' bargaining power** increases, the appeal of an industry to potential entrants decreases. Buyers seek lower prices, better quality, and more services. Moreover, they use their purchasing power to obtain better terms, possibly through a bidding process. Thus, buyers affect competition.

   1) Buyers' bargaining power varies with the following factors:

      a) When purchasing power is concentrated in a few buyers or when buyers are well organized, their bargaining power is greater. This effect is reinforced when sellers are in a capital-intensive industry.
      b) High (low) switching costs decrease (increase) buyers' bargaining power.
      c) The threat of backward (upstream) vertical integration, that is, the acquisition of a supply capacity, increases buyers' bargaining power.

d) Buyers are most likely to bargain aggressively when their profit margins are low and a supplier's product accounts for a substantial amount of their costs.

e) Buyers are in a stronger position when the supplier's product is undifferentiated.

f) The more important the supplier's product is to buyers, the less bargaining power they have.

f. As the **threat of suppliers' bargaining power** increases, the appeal of an industry to potential entrants decreases. Accordingly, suppliers affect competition through pricing and the manipulation of the quantity supplied.

1) Suppliers' bargaining power is greater when

a) Switching costs are substantial.
b) Prices of substitutes are high.
c) They can threaten forward (downstream) vertical integration.
d) They provide something that is a significant input to the value added by the buyer.
e) Their industry is concentrated, or they are organized.

2) Buyers' best responses are to develop favorable, mutually beneficial relationships with suppliers or to diversify their sources of supply.

4. **Generic Competitive Analysis (Strategies) Model**

a. Strategies with a Broad Competitive Scope

1) **Cost leadership** is the generic strategy of entities that seek competitive advantage through lower costs and that have a broad competitive scope.

2) **Differentiation** is the generic strategy of entities that seek competitive advantage through providing a unique product and that have a broad competitive scope.

b. Strategies with a Narrow Competitive Scope

1) **Cost focus** is the generic strategy of entities that seek competitive advantage through lower costs and that have a narrow competitive scope (a regional or smaller market).

2) **Focused differentiation** is the generic strategy of entities that seek competitive advantage through providing a unique product and that have a narrow competitive scope (a regional or smaller market).

	Competitive Advantage	
Competitive Scope	Low Cost	Product Uniqueness
Broad (Industry-wide)	Cost Leadership Strategy	Differentiation Strategy
Narrow (Market segment)	Focused Strategy: Cost	Focused Strategy: Differentiation

Figure 8-9

5. **Five Operations Strategies**
    a. A **cost strategy** is successful when the entity is the low-cost producer. However, the product (e.g., a commodity) tends to be undifferentiated in these cases, the market is often very large, and the competition tends to be intense because of the possibility of high-volume sales.
    b. A **quality strategy** involves competition based on product quality or process quality. Product quality relates to design, for example, the difference between a luxury car and a subcompact. Process quality concerns the degree of freedom from defects.
    c. A **delivery strategy** may permit an entity to charge a higher price when the product is consistently delivered rapidly and on time. An example company is UPS.
    d. A **flexibility strategy** involves offering many different products. This strategy also may reflect an ability to shift rapidly from one product line to another. An example company is a publisher that can write, edit, print, and distribute a book within days to exploit the public's short-term interest in a sensational event.
    e. A **service strategy** seeks to gain a competitive advantage and maximize customer value by providing services, especially post-purchase services such as warranties on automobiles and home appliances.
6. **The Growth-Share Matrix**
    a. Since a large firm may be viewed as a portfolio of investments in the form of strategic business units (SBUs), techniques of portfolio analysis have been developed to aid management in making decisions about resource allocation, new business startups and acquisitions, downsizing, and divestitures.
    b. One of the models most frequently used for competitive analysis was created by the Boston Consulting Group (BCG). This model, the growth-share matrix, has two variables. The market growth rate (MGR) is on the vertical axis, and the firm's relative market share (RMS) is on the horizontal axis.

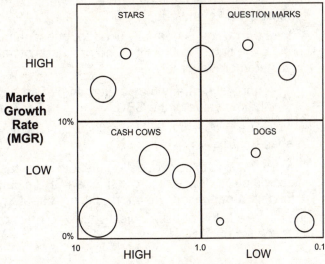

Figure 8-10

1) The annual MGR is stated in constant units of the currency used in the measurement. It reflects the maturity and attractiveness of the market and the relative need for cash to finance expansion.
2) The RMS reflects the SBU's competitive position in the market segment. It equals the SBU's absolute market share divided by that of its leading competitor.

3) The growth-share matrix has four quadrants. The firm's SBUs are commonly represented in their appropriate quadrants by circles. The size of a circle is directly proportional to the SBU's sales volume.

   a) **Dogs** (low RMS, low MGR) are weak competitors in low-growth markets. Their net cash flow (plus or minus) is modest.
   b) **Question marks** (low RMS, high MGR) are weak competitors and poor cash generators in high-growth markets. They need large amounts of cash not only to finance growth and compete in the market, but also to increase RMS. If RMS increases significantly, a question mark may become a star. If not, it becomes a dog.
   c) **Cash cows** (high RMS, low MGR) are strong competitors and cash generators. A cash cow ordinarily enjoys high profit margins and economies of scale. Financing for expansion is not needed, so the SBU's excess cash can be used for investments in other SBUs. However, marketing and R&D expenses should not necessarily be slashed excessively. Maximizing net cash inflow might precipitate a premature decline from cash cow to dog.
   d) **Stars** (high RMS, high MGR) are strong competitors in high growth markets. Such an SBU is profitable but needs large amounts of cash for expansion, R&D, and meeting competitors' attacks. Net cash flow (plus or minus) is modest.

4) A portfolio of SBUs should not have too many dogs and question marks or too few cash cows and stars.

5) Each SBU should have objectives, a strategy should be formulated to achieve those objectives, and a budget should be allocated.

   a) A **hold strategy** is used for strong cash cows.
   b) A **build strategy** is necessary for a question mark with the potential to be a star.
   c) A **harvest strategy** maximizes short-term net cash inflow. Harvesting means zero-budgeting R&D, reducing marketing costs, not replacing facilities, etc. This strategy is used for weak cash cows and possibly question marks and dogs.
   d) A **divest strategy** is normally used for question marks and dogs that reduce the firm's profitability. The proceeds of sale or liquidation are then invested more favorably.

      i) A harvest strategy may undermine a future divestiture by decreasing the fair value of the SBU.

6) The life cycle of a successful SBU is reflected by its movement within the growth-share matrix.

   a) The progression is from question mark to star, cash cow, and dog. Accordingly, a firm should consider an SBU's current status and its probable progression when formulating a strategy.

7) A serious mistake is to not tailor objectives (e.g., rates of return or growth) to the circumstances of each SBU.

SU 8: Analysis and Forecasting Techniques

8) Cash cows should not be underfunded because premature decline is risked. However, overfunding cash cows means less investment in SBUs with greater growth prospects.

　　a) A large investment in a dog with little likelihood of a turnaround is also a typical mistake.

　　b) A firm should not have too many question marks. Results are excess risk and underfunded SBUs.

9) According to Kotler, managers need to be aware of the limitations inherent in the use of a matrix (*Principles of Marketing*, 14th edition). Managers may find it difficult to measure market share and growth or even define SBUs. Thus, BCG's growth-share matrix may have limited strategic value.

Stop and review! You have completed the outline for this subunit. Study multiple-choice questions 19 through 22 beginning on page 279.

8.6 THE BALANCED SCORECARD

1. **Key Performance Indicators (KPIs)**

　　a. The trend in performance evaluation is the balanced scorecard approach to managing the implementation of the firm's strategy.

　　　　1) The balanced scorecard is an accounting report that connects the firm's critical success factors to measurements of its performance.

　　b. Key performance indicators (KPIs) are specific, measurable financial and nonfinancial elements of a firm's performance that are vital to its competitive advantage.

　　　　1) Multiple measures of performance permit a determination as to whether a manager is achieving certain objectives at the expense of others that may be equally or more important. For example, an improvement in operating results at the expense of new product development would be apparent using a balanced scorecard approach.

　　c. The balanced scorecard is a goal congruence tool that informs managers about the nonfinancial factors that top management believes to be important.

　　　　1) Measures on the balanced scorecard may be financial or nonfinancial, internal or external, and short term or long term.

　　　　2) The balanced scorecard facilitates best practice analysis. Best practice analysis determines a method of carrying on a business function or process that is considered to be superior to all other known methods. A lesson learned from one area of a business can be passed on to another area of the business or between businesses.

2. **SWOT Analysis**

　　a. A firm identifies its KPIs by means of a SWOT analysis that addresses internal factors (its strengths and weaknesses) and external factors (its opportunities and threats).

　　　　1) The firm's greatest strengths are its core competencies, which are functions the company performs especially well. These are the basis for its competitive advantages and strategy.

　　b. Strengths and weaknesses are internal resources or a lack thereof, for example, technologically advanced products, a broad product mix, capable management, leadership in R&D, modern production facilities, and a strong marketing organization.

c. **Opportunities and threats** arise from such externalities as government regulation, advances in technology, and demographic changes. They may be reflected in such competitive conditions as

   1) Raising or lowering of barriers to entry into the firm's industry by competitors
   2) Changes in the intensity of rivalry within the industry, for example, because of overcapacity or high exit barriers
   3) The relative availability of substitutes for the firm's products or services
   4) Bargaining power of customers, which tends to be greater when switching costs are low and products are not highly differentiated
   5) Bargaining power of suppliers, which tends to be higher when suppliers are few

d. The SWOT analysis tends to highlight the basic factors of cost, quality, and the speed of product development and delivery.

3. **PEST Analysis**

   a. A PEST analysis is an analysis of certain factors in the external environment of an organization, which can affect its activities and performances.

      1) It is used to identify KPIs.

   b. PEST analysis includes

      1) **P**olitical factors,
      2) **E**conomic factors,
      3) **S**ocial factors, and
      4) **T**echnological factors.

   c. PEST analysis may also include environmental, legal, and ethical considerations, among others.

4. **Measures**

   a. Once the firm has identified its KPIs, it must establish specific measures for each KPI that are both relevant to the success of the firm and can be reliably stated.

      1) Thus, the balanced scorecard varies with the strategy adopted by the firm.
      2) For example, product differentiation or cost leadership either in a broad market or a narrowly focused market (a focus strategy). These measures provide a basis for implementing the firm's competitive strategy.

   b. The scorecard should include lagging indicators (such as output and financial measures) and leading indicators (such as many types of nonfinancial measures).

      1) The latter should be used only if they are predictors of ultimate financial performance.

   c. The scorecard should permit a determination of whether certain objectives are being achieved at the expense of others.

      1) For example, reduced spending on customer service may improve short-term financial results at a significant cost that is revealed by a long-term decline in customer satisfaction measures.

   d. By providing measures that are **nonfinancial as well as financial**, long term as well as short term, and internal as well as external, the balanced scorecard de-emphasizes short term financial results and focuses attention on KPIs.

   e. An effective balanced scorecard requires a vast amount of data of many different types.

      1) For this reason, an enterprise resource planning (ERP) system is almost a necessity. An ERP integrates information systems across the organization by creating one database linking all of the firm's applications.

SU 8: Analysis and Forecasting Techniques

5. **Possible KPIs and Measures**
    a. A typical balanced scorecard classifies objectives into one of four perspectives on the business.
    b. **Financial**

KPI	Measure
Sales	New Product Sales
FV of Firm's Stock	Price/Earnings Ratio
Profits	Return on Investment
Liquidity	Quick Ratio

    1) Other measures may include sales, projected sales, accuracy of sales projections, stock prices, operating earnings, earnings trend, revenue growth, gross margin percentage, cost reductions, residual income, cash flow coverage and trends, turnover (assets, receivables, and inventory), and interest coverage.

    c. **Customer Satisfaction**

KPI	Financial Measure	Nonfinancial Measure
Customer Satisfaction	Trends in dollar amounts of returns	Market share
Dealer and Distributor Relationships	Trends in dollar amounts of discounts taken	Lead time
Marketing and Selling Performance	Trends in dollar amounts of sales	Market research results
Prompt Delivery	Trend in delivery expenses	On-time delivery rate
Quality	Dollar amount of defects	Rate of defects

    1) Other financial measures may include dollar amount of sales, dollar amount of returns, and warranty expense.
    2) Other nonfinancial measures may include unit sales, trends in unit sales, trend in market share, number of returns, rate of returns, customer retention rate, number of defects, number of warranty claims, rate of warranty claims, survey results, coverage and strength of distribution channels, training of marketing people, service response time, and service effectiveness.

    d. **Internal Business Processes**

KPI	Financial Measure	Nonfinancial Measure
Quality	Scrap costs	Rate of scrap and rework
Productivity	Change in company revenue/change in company costs	Units produced per machine hour
Flexibility of Response to Changing Conditions	Cost to re-purpose machine for new use	Time to repurpose machine for new use
Operating Readiness	Set-up costs	Downtime
Safety	Dollar amount of injury claims	Number of injury claims

    1) Other financial measures may include such things as quality costs and level of inventory carrying costs.
    2) Other nonfinancial measures may include new products marketed, technological capabilities, survey results, field service reports, vendor defect rate, cycle time, labor and machine efficiency, setup time, scheduling effectiveness, capacity usage, maintenance, and accidents and their results.

e. **Learning and Growth**

KPI	Financial Measure	Nonfinancial Measure
Development of New Products	R&D costs	Number of new patents applied for
Promptness of Their Introduction	Lost revenue (from slow introduction of new product to market)	Length of time to bring a product to market
Human Resource Development	Recruiting costs	Personnel turnover
Morale	Orientation/team-building costs	Personnel complaints
Competence of Work Force	Training/retraining costs	Hours of training

1) Other financial measures may include financial and operating results.
2) Other nonfinancial measures may include number of design changes and copyrights registered, R&D personnel qualifications, actual versus planned shipping dates, skill set levels attained, personnel survey results, organizational learning, and industry leadership.

6. **Development**

    a. The active support and participation of senior management are essential.

    1) This involvement will in turn ensure the cooperation of lower-level managers in the identification of objectives, appropriate measures, targeted results, and methods of achieving the results.

    b. The scorecard should contain measures at the detail level that permit everyone to understand how his or her efforts affect the firm's results.

    1) The scorecard and the strategy it represents must be communicated to all managers and used as a basis for compensation decisions.

7. **Functionality**

    a. Each objective is associated with one or more measures that permit the organization to gauge progress toward the objective.

    1) In order for the balanced scorecard to be useful, the organization must be able to identify a cause-and-effect relationship between an action that could be taken (or avoided) and an effect on a KPI.

        a) For example, if the organization increases its R&D budget, then the organization can increase the number of new patents applied for.

    2) Achievement of the objectives in each perspective makes it possible to achieve the objectives in the next higher perspective.
    3) This chaining of objectives and perspectives embodies the implementation of a **strategy map**.

b. To achieve its objectives, the organization must establish the following:
1) Relevant criteria to measure outcomes.
   a) This requires the use of **lagging indicators** which measure the results of actions.
2) Relevant performance drivers
   a) This requires the use of **leading indicators** which are used to determine how an outcome can be met.
c. When measuring results and planning actions to take, the organization must stay focused on the cost-effectiveness of any action taken (or not taken).
1) Achieving goals should not become ends unto themselves.
   a) Achievement of goals should be linked to the bottom line.
d. The following are problems in implementation of the balanced scorecard approach:
1) Using too many measures, with a consequent loss of focus on KPIs
2) Failing to evaluate personnel on nonfinancial as well as financial measures
3) Including measures that will not have long-term financial benefits
4) Not understanding that subjective measures (such as customer satisfaction) are imprecise
5) Trying to achieve improvements in all areas at all times
6) Not being aware that the hypothesized connection between nonfinancial measures and ultimate financial success may not continue to be true

EXAMPLE of a Balanced Scorecard

OBJECTIVES	PERFORMANCE MEASURES	TARGETS	INITIATIVES
PERSPECTIVE: Financial			
Increase sales	Gross revenues	Increase 15%	• Expand into new markets • Improve same-store sales
PERSPECTIVE: Customer Satisfaction			
Reduce returns	Number of returns	Decrease 10%	• Reduce number of defects • Determine customer needs prior to sale
PERSPECTIVE: Internal Business Processes			
Reduce scrap	Costs of scrap	Decrease 5%	• Employee training • Seek higher quality materials
PERSPECTIVE: Learning and Growth			
Reduce personal turnover	Length of time employed	Increase 50%	• Improve hiring practices • Reevaluate compensation plan

Stop and review! You have completed the outline for this subunit. Study multiple-choice questions 23 through 26 beginning on page 280.

8.7 STRATEGIC PLANNING

1. **Planning**
   a. Planning is the determination of what is to be done and of how, when, where, and by whom it is to be done. Plans serve to direct the activities that all organizational members must undertake and successfully perform to move the organization from where it is to where it wants to be (accomplishment of its objectives).
      1) However, no transactions occur during the planning cycle that must be recorded in the general ledger.
   b. Planning must be completed before undertaking any other managerial function.
      1) Forecasting is the basis of planning because it projects the future.
   c. Planning establishes the means to reach organizational ends (objectives).
      1) This means-end relationship extends throughout the organizational hierarchy and ties together the parts of the organization so that the various means all focus on the same end.
      2) One organizational level's ends provide the next higher level's means.

> **EXAMPLE**
>
> Management by objectives (MBO) identifies relationships between an individual's job objectives (ends) and the immediate superior's objectives (ends). Thus, the subordinate can understand how his or her job is the means by which the superior's job is accomplished. This will be discussed in more detail later in this subunit.

2. **The Planning Process**
   a. Long-range (strategic) planning includes **strategic budgeting**. It has a horizon of 1 to 10 years or more. Such planning is difficult because of uncertainty about future events and conditions.
      1) Thus, strategic plans tend to be general and exclude operational detail.
      2) An entity must complete its strategic plan before any specific budgeting can begin. The strategic plan states the means by which an entity expects to achieve its stated mission.
   b. Strategic planning embodies the concerns of senior management. It is based on a strategic analysis that includes the following:
      1) Identifying and specifying organizational objectives.
      2) Evaluating the strengths (competitive advantages) and weaknesses of the organization and its competitors.
      3) Assessing risk levels.
      4) Identifying and forecasting the effects of external (environmental) factors relevant to the organization. For example, market trends, changes in technology, international competition, and social change may provide opportunities, impose limitations, or represent threats.
         a) Forecasting is the basis of planning because it projects the future. A variety of quantitative methods are used in forecasting.
      5) Deriving the best strategy for reaching the objectives, given the organization's strengths and weaknesses and the relevant future trends.
      6) Capital budgeting, a planning process for choosing and financing long-term projects and programs.
      7) Capacity planning, an element of planning closely related to capital budgeting that includes, among other things, consideration of business combinations or divestitures.

SU 8: Analysis and Forecasting Techniques   271

   c. Strategic plans are translated into measurable and achievable intermediate and operational plans. Thus, intermediate and operational plans must be consistent with, and contribute to achieving, strategic objectives.

3. **Premises**

   a. Premises are the underlying assumptions about the expected environment in which the strategic plan will be carried out. Thus, the next step in planning is premising, or the generation of planning assumptions. Premises should be limited to those crucial to the success of the plans.

   b. Managers should ask, "What internal and external factors would influence the actions planned for this organization (division, department, program)?" Premises must be considered at all levels of the organization.

      1) Thus, capital budgeting plans should be premised on assumptions (forecasts) about economic cycles, price movements, etc.

      2) The inventory department's plans might be premised on stability of parts prices or on forecasts that prices will rise.

EXAMPLES

- The general economy will suffer an 11% decline next year.
- Our closest competitor's new model will provide greater competition for potential sales.
- Union negotiations will result in a general wage increase of 8%.
- Over the next 5 years, the cost of our raw materials will increase by 30%.
- The elasticity of demand for the company's products is 1.2.

---

4. **Organizational Objectives**

   a. Organizations may have multiple objectives that are contradictory.

      1) The objective of maximizing profit and the objective of growth could be mutually exclusive within a given year. Maximizing short-term profit might hamper or preclude future growth.

      2) Conflict among an organization's objectives is common.

   b. Objectives vary with the organization's type and stage of development.

5. **Management Objectives**

   a. The primary task of management is to carry on operations effectively and efficiently.

      1) **Effectiveness** is the degree to which the objective is accomplished. **Efficiency** is maximizing the output for a given quantity of input.

      2) Effectiveness is sometimes called "doing the right things," and efficiency is known as "doing things right."

         a) Trade-offs are frequently made between efficiency and effectiveness.

   b. Objectives should be clearly and specifically stated, communicated to all concerned parties, and accepted by those affected.

6. **Means-End Hierarchy**

    a. Objectives should be established at the top and retranslated in more specific terms as they are communicated downward in the means-end hierarchy.

    EXAMPLE

    - An entity has a socioeconomic purpose, such as providing food.
    - The entity's mission is the accomplishment of its socioeconomic purpose through the production of breakfast cereal.
    - The entity develops long-range or strategic objectives with regard to profitability, growth, or survival.
    - A more specific overall objective might be to provide investors with an adequate return on their investment.
    - Divisional objectives can be developed, e.g., to increase the sales of a certain kind of cereal.
    - Departmental objectives are developed, e.g., to reduce waste in the packaging department.
    - Low-level managers and supervisors then develop personal performance and development objectives.
    ---

7. **Policies, Procedures, and Rules**

    a. After premises and objectives are formulated, the next step in the planning process is the development of policies, procedures, and rules. These elements are necessary at all levels of the organization and overlap both in definition and in practice.

    1) Intermediate and operational plans are translated into policies, procedures, and rules, which are standing plans for repetitive situations.

    b. Policies and procedures provide **feedforward control** because they anticipate and prevent problems and provide guidance on how an activity should be performed to best ensure that an objective is achieved.

    1) **Policies** are general statements that guide thinking and action in decision making. Policies may be explicitly published by, or implied by the actions of, management.

        a) A strong organizational culture means that the organization's key values are intensely held and widely shared. In this case, the need for formal written policies is minimized.

    2) **Procedures** are specific directives that define how work is to be done.
    3) **Rules** are specific, detailed guides that restrict behavior.

8. **Management by Objectives (MBO)**

    a. MBO is a behavioral, communications-oriented, responsibility approach to management and employee self-direction. It is a comprehensive management approach and therefore is relevant to planning and control.

    b. MBO is based on the philosophy that employees

    1) Want to work hard if they know what is expected
    2) Like to understand what their jobs actually entail
    3) Are capable of self-direction and self-motivation

    c. MBO requires

    1) Senior management participation and commitment to the program. These managers must

        a) Determine the overall direction and objectives for the organization
        b) Communicate these effectively in operational or measurable terms
        c) Coordinate subordinates' objectives with overall objectives
        d) Follow up at the end of the MBO cycle period to reward performance and review problems

2) Integration of objectives for all subunits into a compatible, balanced system directed toward accomplishment of the overall objectives.
3) Provisions for regular periodic reporting of performance toward attainment of the objectives.
4) Free and honest communication between supervisor and subordinate.
5) A commitment to taking the ideas of subordinates seriously on the part of supervisors.
6) An organizational climate that encourages mutual trust and respect.

d. Steps necessary to implement an MBO program include establishing objectives and action plans (the planning steps) and periodic review and final appraisal (the control steps).

Stop and review! You have completed the outline for this subunit. Study multiple-choice questions 27 through 30 beginning on page 281.

QUESTIONS

8.1 Correlation and Regression

1. A company is an automobile replacement parts dealer in a large metropolitan community. The company is preparing its sales forecast for the coming year. Data regarding both the company's and industry sales of replacement parts as well as both the used and new automobile sales in the community for the last 10 years have been accumulated. If the company wants to determine whether its sales of replacement parts are dependent upon the industry sales of replacement parts or upon the sales of used and new automobiles, the company should employ

A. Simulation techniques.
B. Correlation and regression analysis.
C. Statistical sampling.
D. Time series analysis.

Answer (B) is correct.
REQUIRED: The technique to determine the variable to which sales are related.
DISCUSSION: Correlation and regression analysis can be used to determine whether a relationship exists among two or more variables. The degree of that relationship is assessed by means of correlation analysis. Thus, regressing sales (the dependent variable) on both sales of replacement parts and sales of automobiles (independent variables) determines the extent of the dependence.
Answer (A) is incorrect. Simulation is a means of experimenting with logical or mathematical models using a computer. Answer (C) is incorrect. Statistical sampling is a means of choosing and analyzing a sample to estimate population characteristics. Answer (D) is incorrect. Time series or trend analysis regresses the dependent variable on time (the independent variable).

2. A company has accumulated data for the last 24 months in order to determine if there is an independent variable that could be used to estimate shipping costs. Three possible independent variables being considered are packages shipped, miles shipped, and pounds shipped. The quantitative technique that should be used to determine whether any of these independent variables might provide a good estimate for shipping costs is

A. Flexible budgeting.
B. Linear programming.
C. Linear regression.
D. Variable costing.

Answer (C) is correct.
REQUIRED: The quantitative technique that should be used to determine whether any of those independent variables might provide a good estimate for shipping costs.
DISCUSSION: Regression analysis, also called least-squares analysis, is the process of deriving the linear equation that describes the relationship between two (or more) variables with a nonzero coefficient of correlation.
Answer (A) is incorrect. Flexible budgeting is the calculation of the quantity and cost of inputs that should have been consumed given the achieved level of production. Answer (B) is incorrect. Linear programming is a mathematical technique used to optimize a linear function subject to certain constraints. Answer (D) is incorrect. Variable costing is a costing technique that treats only variable manufacturing costs as product costs.

3. In the standard regression equation $y = a + bx$, the letter b is **best** described as a(n)

A. Independent variable.
B. Dependent variable.
C. Constant coefficient.
D. Variable coefficient.

Answer (D) is correct.
REQUIRED: The meaning of the letter b in the standard regression equation.
DISCUSSION: In the standard regression equation, b represents the variable coefficient. For example, in a cost determination regression, y equals total costs, b is the variable cost per unit, x is the number of units produced, and a is fixed cost.
Answer (A) is incorrect. The independent variable is x. Answer (B) is incorrect. The dependent variable is y. Answer (C) is incorrect. The constant coefficient is a.

4. The correlation coefficient that indicates the weakest linear association between two variables is

A. –0.73
B. –0.11
C. 0.12
D. 0.35

Answer (B) is correct.
REQUIRED: The correlation coefficient that indicates the weakest linear association between two variables.
DISCUSSION: The correlation coefficient can vary from –1 to +1. A –1 relationship indicates a perfect negative correlation, and a +1 relationship indicates a perfect positive correlation. A zero correlation coefficient would indicate no linear association between the variables. Thus, the correlation coefficient that is nearest to zero indicates the weakest linear association. Of the options given in the question, the correlation coefficient that is nearest to zero is –0.11.
Answer (A) is incorrect. This figure signifies a strong negative correlation. Answer (C) is incorrect. This figure indicates a slightly stronger correlation than the weakest linear association. Answer (D) is incorrect. This figure indicates a considerably stronger correlation.

5. Correlation is a term frequently used in conjunction with regression analysis and is measured by the value of the coefficient of correlation, r. The **best** explanation of the value r is that it

A. Is always positive.
B. Interprets variances in terms of the independent variable.
C. Ranges in size from negative infinity to positive infinity.
D. Is a measure of the relative relationship between two variables.

Answer (D) is correct.
REQUIRED: The best explanation of the coefficient of correlation (r).
DISCUSSION: The coefficient of correlation (r) measures the strength of the linear relationship between the dependent and independent variables. The magnitude of r is independent of the scales of measurement of x and y. The coefficient lies between –1.0 and +1.0. A value of zero indicates no linear relationship between the x and y variables. A value of +1.0 indicates a perfectly direct relationship, and a value of –1.0 indicates a perfectly inverse relationship.
Answer (A) is incorrect. The coefficient is negative if the relationship between the variables is inverse. Answer (B) is incorrect. The coefficient relates the two variables to each other. Answer (C) is incorrect. The size of the coefficient varies between –1.0 and +1.0.

6. All of the following are assumptions underlying the validity of linear regression output **except**

A. The errors are normally distributed.
B. The mean of the errors is zero.
C. Certainty.
D. The standard deviation of the errors is constant.

Answer (C) is correct.
REQUIRED: The assumption that does not underlie linear regression.
DISCUSSION: Linear regression is based on several assumptions; for example, that there is no change in the environment, that errors in the values of the dependent variables are normally distributed with a mean of zero, that the standard deviation of these errors is constant, that the values of the dependent variables are statistically independent of each other, and that the independent variables are not correlated with each other. However, regression is only a means of predicting the future; it cannot provide certainty.

8.2 Learning Curve Analysis

7. An entity is preparing a bid for a special project requiring the production of 35,000 units. The engineering personnel have advised that the units can be produced in groups with the first group consisting of 1,000 units. A review of prior experience indicates that the direct labor time needed per unit will be progressively smaller by a constant percentage rate as experience is gained in the production process. The quantitative method that would **best** estimate the entity's total cost for the project is

A. Linear programming.
B. Dynamic programming.
C. Learning curve analysis.
D. Time series analysis.

Answer (C) is correct.
REQUIRED: The quantitative method for estimating the decline in direct labor costs as production increases.
DISCUSSION: Learning curves reflect the increased rate at which people perform tasks as they gain experience. Thus, the time required to perform a given task becomes progressively shorter. Ordinarily, the learning curve is expressed as a percentage of reduced time to complete a task for each doubling of cumulative production.
Answer (A) is incorrect. Linear programming is an optimizing model used to determine a minimum or maximum, e.g., of a cost or revenue function, given certain constraints on resources. Answer (B) is incorrect. Dynamic programming is an approach to solving problems, not a particular algorithm. It divides a large mathematical model into smaller, more manageable pieces in such a way that, once the smaller problems have been solved, the result is the optimal solution to the overall model. Answer (D) is incorrect. Time series analysis applies to data gathered at successive moments in time. It is a forecasting technique in which the dependent variable is regressed on time.

8. The average labor cost per unit for the first batch produced by a new process is $120. The cumulative average labor cost after the second batch is $72 per product. Using a batch size of 100 and assuming the learning curve continues, the total labor cost of four batches will be

A. $4,320
B. $10,368
C. $2,592
D. $17,280

Answer (D) is correct.
REQUIRED: The total labor cost assuming the learning curve continues.
DISCUSSION: The learning curve reflects the increased rate at which people perform tasks as they gain experience. The time required to perform a given task becomes progressively shorter. Ordinarily, the curve is expressed in a percentage of reduced time to complete a task for each doubling of cumulative production. One common assumption in a learning curve model is that the cumulative average time (and labor cost) per unit is reduced by a certain percentage each time production doubles. Given a $120 cost per unit for the first 100 units and a $72 cost per unit when cumulative production doubled to 200 units, the learning curve percentage must be 60% ($72 ÷ $120). If production is again doubled to 400 units (four batches), the average unit labor cost should be $43.20 ($72 × 60%). Hence, total labor cost for 400 units is estimated to be $17,280 (400 units × $43.20).
Answer (A) is incorrect. The cost of the items in the fourth batch equals $4,320. Answer (B) is incorrect. The amount of $10,368 is based on the assumption that the cumulative average unit labor cost is reduced by the learning curve percentage with each batch, not each doubling of output. Answer (C) is incorrect. The amount of $2,592 represents the labor cost of 100 units at the unit rate expected after another doubling of production to eight batches.

9. A corporation manufactures specialty components for the electronics industry in a highly labor intensive environment. A manufacturer has asked the corporation to bid on a component that the corporation made for the manufacturer last month. The previous order was for 80 units and required 120 hours of direct labor to manufacture. The manufacturer would now like 240 additional components. The corporation experiences an 80% learning curve on all of its jobs. The number of direct labor hours needed for the corporation to complete the 240 additional components is

A. 360.0
B. 187.2
C. 307.2
D. 256.0

Answer (B) is correct.
REQUIRED: The number of labor hours needed to complete 240 additional components.
DISCUSSION: One common assumption made in a learning curve model is that the cumulative average time per unit is reduced by a certain percentage each time production doubles. An 80% learning curve results in the following performance for the lots shown:

Units	Cumulative Average Hours
80	1.5 hours (120 ÷ 80)
160	1.2 hours (1.5 × .8)
320	.96 hours (1.2 × .8)

Thus, to produce 320 units, total production time will be 307.2 hours (320 × .96). The total time for the last 240 units will be 187.2 hours (307.2 − 120).
Answer (A) is incorrect. Assuming no learning curve effect results in 360 hours. Answer (C) is incorrect. The total time for completing 320 units is 307.2 hours. Answer (D) is incorrect. The figure of 256 hours is a nonsense answer.

10. It is estimated that a particular manufacturing job is subject to an 80% learning curve. The first unit required 50 labor hours to complete. What is the cumulative average time per unit after completing four units?

A. 50.0 hours.
B. 40.0 hours.
C. 32.0 hours.
D. 30.0 hours.

Answer (C) is correct.
REQUIRED: The cumulative average completion time per unit after the completion of four units.
DISCUSSION: Learning curve models reflect the increased rate at which people perform tasks as they gain experience. One common assumption is that the cumulative average time per unit is reduced by a certain percentage when production doubles during the early stages of production. An 80% learning curve indicates that a doubling of production reduces the time required by 20%. For example, if the first unit requires 50 hours, the cumulative average completion time is 40 hours (80% × 50 hours) for two units and 32 hours (80% × 40 hours) for four units.
Answer (A) is incorrect. The time for the first unit is 50 hours. Answer (B) is incorrect. The cumulative average completion time for two units is 40 hours. Answer (D) is incorrect. The time necessary to complete the second unit is 30 hours.

11. A manufacturing company required 800 direct labor hours to produce the first lot of four units of a new motor. Management believes that a 90% learning curve will be experienced over four lots of production. How many direct labor hours will be required to manufacture the next 12 units?

A. 1,792
B. 1,944
C. 2,016
D. 2,160

Answer (A) is correct.
REQUIRED: The direct labor hours required to manufacture the next 12 units.
DISCUSSION: With a 90% learning curve, the cumulative production times would be as follows:

Batch	Units	Average Time	Cumulative Time
1	1-4	800	800
2	5-8	720 (800 × 90%)	1,440
3	9-16	648 (720 × 90%)	2,592

Subtracting the 800 hours spent on the first batch from the cumulative time for three batches leaves 1,792 hours for the last three groups of units (12 units).
Answer (B) is incorrect. A 90% learning curve produces an incremental production time of 1,792. Answer (C) is incorrect. A 90% learning curve produces an incremental production time of 1,792. Answer (D) is incorrect. A 90% learning curve produces an incremental production time of 1,792.

8.3 Expected Value

12. A distributor of video discs is developing its budgeted cost of goods sold for next year. The distributor has developed the following range of sales estimates and associated probabilities for the year:

Sales Estimate	Probability
$ 60,000	25%
85,000	40
100,000	35

The distributor's cost of goods sold averages 80% of sales. What is the expected value of the distributor's budgeted cost of goods sold?

A. $85,000
B. $84,000
C. $68,000
D. $67,200

Answer (D) is correct.
REQUIRED: The expected value of cost of goods sold.
DISCUSSION: The expected value is calculated by weighting each sales estimate by the probability of its occurrence. Consequently, the expected value of sales is $84,000 [($60,000 × .25) + ($85,000 × .40) + ($100,000 × .35)]. Cost of goods sold is therefore $67,200 ($84,000 × .80).
Answer (A) is incorrect. The amount of $85,000 is the sales estimate with the highest probability. Answer (B) is incorrect. The amount of $84,000 is the expected value of sales. Answer (C) is incorrect. The amount of $68,000 is 80% of the sales estimate with the highest probability.

SU 8: Analysis and Forecasting Techniques 277

13. The expected value of perfect information is the

A. Same as the expected profit under certainty.
B. Sum of the conditional profit (loss) for the best event of each act times the probability of each event occurring.
C. Difference between the expected profit under certainty and the expected opportunity loss.
D. Difference between the expected profit under certainty and the expected monetary value of the best act under uncertainty.

Answer (D) is correct.
REQUIRED: The true statement about the expected value of perfect information.
DISCUSSION: Perfect information permits certainty that a future state of nature will occur. The expected value of perfect information determines the maximum amount a decision maker is willing to pay for information. It is the difference between the expected value without perfect information, that is, the expected value of the best action under uncertainty and the expected value under certainty. Under certainty, a decision maker knows in each case which state of nature will occur and can act accordingly.
Answer (A) is incorrect. The expected value of perfect information is the difference between the expected profit under certainty and the profit from the best decision under uncertainty. Answer (B) is incorrect. The expected value of perfect information is the excess of the total conditional profits under certainty over the profit from the best decision under uncertainty. Answer (C) is incorrect. There is no expected opportunity loss under conditions of certainty.

14. The expected monetary value of an act is the

A. Sum of the conditional profit (loss) for each event.
B. Sum of the conditional profit (loss) for each event times the probability of each event's occurrence.
C. Conditional profit (loss) for the best event times the probability of each event's occurrence.
D. Revenue minus the costs for the act.

Answer (B) is correct.
REQUIRED: The definition of the expected monetary value of an act.
DISCUSSION: Expected value analysis estimates future monetary value based on forecasts and their related probabilities of occurrence. The expected value under uncertainty is found by multiplying the probability of each outcome (event) by its payoff (conditional profit or loss) and summing the products.
Answer (A) is incorrect. The conditional profit or loss must be weighted by the probability of each event's occurrence. Answer (C) is incorrect. The best event will not occur every time; less desirable events will also occur and must enter into the calculation. Answer (D) is incorrect. Each event must be weighted by the probability of its occurrence.

8.4 Sensitivity Analysis

15. A widely used approach that managers use to recognize uncertainty about individual items and to obtain an immediate financial estimate of the consequences of possible prediction errors is

A. Expected value analysis.
B. Learning curve analysis.
C. Sensitivity analysis.
D. Regression analysis.

Answer (C) is correct.
REQUIRED: The approach that gives an immediate financial estimate of the consequences of possible prediction errors.
DISCUSSION: Sensitivity analysis determines how a result varies with changes in a given variable or parameter in a mathematical decision model. For example, in a present value analysis, a manager might first calculate the net present value or internal rate of return assuming that a new asset has a 10-year life. The NPV or IRR can then be recalculated using a 5-year life to determine how sensitive the result is to the change in the assumption.
Answer (A) is incorrect. Expected value is the probabilistically weighted average of the outcomes of an action. Answer (B) is incorrect. Learning curve analysis quantifies how labor costs decline as employees learn their jobs through repetition. Answer (D) is incorrect. Regression, or least squares, analysis determines the average change in the dependent variable given a unit change in one or more independent variables.

16. Through the use of decision models, managers thoroughly analyze many alternatives and decide on the best alternative for the company. Often, the actual results achieved from a particular decision are not what was expected when the decision was made. In addition, an alternative that was not selected would have actually been the best decision for the company. The appropriate technique to analyze the alternatives by using expected inputs and altering them before a decision is made is

A. Expected value analysis.
B. Linear programming.
C. Program Evaluation Review Technique (PERT).
D. Sensitivity analysis.

Answer (D) is correct.
REQUIRED: The technique that involves altering expected inputs during the decision process.
DISCUSSION: Sensitivity modeling can be used to determine the outcome of a variety of decisions. A trial-and-error method may be adopted, usually in a computer model, to calculate the sensitivity of the solution (variability of outcomes) to changes in a variable.
Answer (A) is incorrect. Expected value analysis is used to determine an anticipated return or cost based upon probabilities of events and their related outcomes. Answer (B) is incorrect. Linear programming optimizes a function given certain constraints. Answer (C) is incorrect. PERT is a network technique used to plan and control large projects.

Questions 17 and 18 are based on the following information. A beverage stand can sell either soft drinks or coffee on any given day. If the stand sells soft drinks and the weather is hot, it will make $2,500; if the weather is cold, the profit will be $1,000. If the stand sells coffee and the weather is hot, it will make $1,900; if the weather is cold, the profit will be $2,000. The probability of cold weather on a given day at this time is 60%.

---

17. The expected payoff for selling coffee is

A. $1,360
B. $2,200
C. $3,900
D. $1,960

Answer (D) is correct.
REQUIRED: The expected payoff for selling coffee.
DISCUSSION: The expected payoff calculation for coffee is

Expected payoff = Prob. hot (Payoff hot) + Prob. cold (Payoff cold)
= .4($1,900) + .6($2,000)
= $1,960

Answer (A) is incorrect. The least the company can make by selling coffee is $1,900. Answer (B) is incorrect. The most the company can make by selling coffee is $2,000. Answer (C) is incorrect. The most the company can make by selling coffee is $2,000.

18. The expected payoff if the vendor has perfect information is

A. $3,900
B. $2,200
C. $1,360
D. $1,960

Answer (B) is correct.
REQUIRED: The expected payoff if the vendor has perfect information.
DISCUSSION: The vendor would like to sell coffee on cold days ($2,000) and soft drinks on hot days ($2,500). Hot days are expected 40% of the time. Hence, the probability is 40% of making $2,500 by selling soft drinks. The chance of making $2,000 by selling coffee is 60%. The payoff equation is:

Exp. payoff with perf. info. = Prob. hot (Payoff soft drinks) + Prob. cold (Payoff coffee)
= .4($2,500) + .6($2,000)
= $2,200

Answer (A) is incorrect. The most the vendor can make is $2,500 per day. Answer (C) is incorrect. The least the vendor could make by having perfect information is $2,000 on cold days. Answer (D) is incorrect. The least the vendor could make by having perfect information is $2,000 on cold days.

8.5 Strategic Management

19. A firm's statement of broad objectives or mission statement should accomplish all of the following **except**

A. Outlining strategies for technological development, market expansion, and product differentiation.
B. Defining the purpose of the company.
C. Providing an overall guide to those in high-level, decision-making positions.
D. Stating the moral and ethical principles that guide the actions of the firm.

Answer (A) is correct.
REQUIRED: The purpose not achieved by a mission statement.
DISCUSSION: The determination of organizational objectives is the first step in the planning process. A mission statement is a formal, written document that defines the organization's purpose in society, for example, to produce and distribute certain goods of high quality in a manner beneficial to the public, employees, shareholders, and other constituencies. Thus, a mission statement does not announce specific operating plans. It does not describe strategies for technological development, market expansion, or product differentiation because these are tasks for operating management.
Answer (B) is incorrect. A mission statement defines the purpose of the company (some writers differentiate between purpose and mission). Answer (C) is incorrect. Broad objectives provide guidance to those in high-level positions who are responsible for long-range planning. Answer (D) is incorrect. Mission statements increasingly are concerned with ethical principles.

20. Intensity of rivalry among existing firms in an industry increases when

I. Products are relatively undifferentiated
II. Consumer switching costs are low

A. I only.
B. II only.
C. Both I and II.
D. Neither I nor II.

Answer (C) is correct.
REQUIRED: The condition(s), if any, that increase(s) the intensity of rivalry in an industry.
DISCUSSION: The degree of product differentiation and the costs of switching from one competitor's product to another increase the intensity of rivalry and competition in an industry. Less differentiation tends to heighten competition based on price, with price cutting leading to lower profits. Low costs of switching products also increase competition.
Answer (A) is incorrect. Low consumer switching costs also increase rivalry. Answer (B) is incorrect. A low degree of product differentiation also increases rivalry. Answer (D) is incorrect. Both low consumer switching costs and a low degree of product differentiation increase rivalry.

21. Michael E. Porter's competitive strategies model includes an analysis of the competitive forces that determine the attractiveness of an industry. These forces include

I. The stage of the industry life cycle
II. Threats of, and barriers to, entry
III. Threat of substitutes
IV. The threat of suppliers' bargaining power

A. I and II only.
B. I and III only.
C. II, III, and IV only.
D. I, II, III, and IV.

Answer (C) is correct.
REQUIRED: The competitive forces in the Porter model.
DISCUSSION: Michael E. Porter has developed a model of the structure of industries and competition. It includes an analysis of the five competitive forces that determine long-term profitability measured by long-term return on investment. This analysis results in an evaluation of the attractiveness of an industry. The five forces are (1) the degree of rivalry among existing firms; (2) threats of, and barriers to, entry; (3) the threat of substitute products or services; (4) the threat of buyers' bargaining power; and (5) the threat of suppliers' bargaining power.
Answer (A) is incorrect. The stage of the industry life cycle is one of many variables that affect the degree of rivalry among existing firms and the threat of entry. Thus, it is not one of the basic competitive forces. Answer (B) is incorrect. The stage of the industry life cycle is one of many variables that affect the degree of rivalry among existing firms and the threat of entry. Thus, it is not one of the basic competitive forces. Answer (D) is incorrect. The stage of the industry life cycle is one of many variables that affect the degree of rivalry among existing firms and the threat of entry. Thus, it is not one of the basic competitive forces.

22. In a product's life cycle, the first symptom of the decline stage is a decline in the

A. Firm's inventory levels.
B. Product's sales.
C. Product's production cost.
D. Product's prices.

Answer (B) is correct.
REQUIRED: The initial symptom of the decline stage in a product's life cycle.
DISCUSSION: The first symptom of the decline stage of a product's life cycle triggers such other effects as price cutting, narrowing of the product line, and reduction in promotion budgets.
Answer (A) is incorrect. A decline in the firm's purchases, resulting in a decline in the firm's inventory levels, is not the first symptom. It will occur only when production declines as a result of a drop in sales. Answer (C) is incorrect. A decline in production costs may be due to many factors, e.g., new plant technology or the increased availability of raw materials. Moreover, production costs may decrease in any stage of a product's life cycle and not specifically in the decline stage. Answer (D) is incorrect. A change in prices is a marketing decision. It is an action that may be taken in the maturity stage to compete in the market. Moreover, a decrease in the product's prices is a response to a permanent decline in sales.

8.6 The Balanced Scorecard

23. The balanced scorecard provides an action plan for achieving competitive success by focusing management attention on critical success factors. Which one of the following is **not** one of the perspectives on the business into which critical success factors are commonly grouped in the balanced scorecard?

A. Competitor business strategies.
B. Financial performance.
C. Internal business processes.
D. Employee innovation and learning.

Answer (A) is correct.
REQUIRED: The item not a perspective on the business as used on a balanced scorecard.
DISCUSSION: A typical balanced scorecard classifies critical success factors and measures into one of four perspectives on the business: financial, customer satisfaction, internal business processes, and learning and growth.
Answer (B) is incorrect. Financial performance measures are among the tools used in a typical balanced scorecard. Answer (C) is incorrect. A typical balanced scorecard contains critical success factors and measures focused on internal business processes. Answer (D) is incorrect. Employee innovation and learning is one of the perspectives on the business commonly used in a balanced scorecard.

24. Using the balanced scorecard approach, an organization evaluates managerial performance based on

A. A single ultimate measure of operating results, such as residual income.
B. Multiple financial and nonfinancial measures.
C. Multiple nonfinancial measures only.
D. Multiple financial measures only.

Answer (B) is correct.
REQUIRED: The nature of the balanced scorecard approach.
DISCUSSION: The trend in managerial performance evaluation is the balanced scorecard approach. Multiple measures of performance permit a determination as to whether a manager is achieving certain objectives at the expense of others that may be equally or more important. These measures may be financial or nonfinancial and usually include items in four categories: profitability; customer satisfaction; innovation; and efficiency, quality, and time.
Answer (A) is incorrect. The balanced scorecard approach uses multiple measures. Answer (C) is incorrect. The balanced scorecard approach uses financial and nonfinancial measures. Answer (D) is incorrect. The balanced scorecard approach uses financial and nonfinancial measures.

25. On a balanced scorecard, which of the following would **not** be an example of a customer satisfaction measure?

A. Market share.
B. Economic value added.
C. Response time.
D. Customer retention.

Answer (B) is correct.
REQUIRED: The measure that is not an element of customer satisfaction on a balanced scorecard.
DISCUSSION: Customer satisfaction measures include market share, retention, response time, delivery performance, number of defects, and lead time. Economic value added, or EVA, is a profitability measure.
Answer (A) is incorrect. Market share is a customer satisfaction measure. Answer (C) is incorrect. Response time is a customer satisfaction measure. Answer (D) is incorrect. Customer retention is a customer satisfaction measure.

26. On a balanced scorecard, which is more of an internal process measure than an external-based measure?

A. Cycle time.
B. Profitability.
C. Customer satisfaction.
D. Market share.

Answer (A) is correct.
REQUIRED: The measure that is more internal-process related on a balanced scorecard.
DISCUSSION: Cycle time is the manufacturing time to complete an order. Thus, cycle time is strictly related to internal processes. Profitability is a combination of internal and external considerations. Customer satisfaction and market share are related to how customers perceive a product and how competitors react.
Answer (B) is incorrect. Profitability is a measure that includes external considerations. Answer (C) is incorrect. Customer satisfaction is a measure that includes external considerations. Answer (D) is incorrect. Market share is a measure that includes external considerations.

8.7 Strategic Planning

27. What is strategic planning?

A. It establishes the general direction of the organization.
B. It establishes the resources that the plan will require.
C. It establishes the budget for the organization.
D. It consists of decisions to use parts of the organization's resources in specified ways.

Answer (A) is correct.
REQUIRED: The definition of strategic planning.
DISCUSSION: Strategic planning establishes the general direction of an organization. It embodies the concerns of senior management and is based specifically on (1) identifying and specifying organizational objectives; (2) evaluating the organization's strengths and weaknesses; (3) assessing risk levels; (4) identifying and forecasting the effect of external (environmental) factors relevant to the organization; (5) deriving the best strategy for reaching the objectives, given the organization's strengths and weaknesses and the relevant future trends; and (6) analyzing and reviewing the capital budgeting process and capacity planning.
Answer (B) is incorrect. Establishing the resources the strategic plan will require is merely one phase of strategic planning. Answer (C) is incorrect. Establishing the budget for the organization cannot take place until the strategic plan is complete. Answer (D) is incorrect. Decisions to use parts of the organization's resources in specified ways defines operational planning.

28. Which one of the following management considerations is usually addressed first in strategic planning?

A. Outsourcing.
B. Overall objectives of the firm.
C. Organizational structure.
D. Recent annual budgets.

Answer (B) is correct.
REQUIRED: The management consideration usually addressed first in strategic planning.
DISCUSSION: Strategic planning is the process of setting overall organizational objectives and drafting strategic plans. Setting ultimate objectives for the firm is a necessary prelude to developing strategies for achieving those objectives. Plans and budgets are then needed to implement those strategies.
Answer (A) is incorrect. Outsourcing is an operating decision of a more short-term nature. Answer (C) is incorrect. Organizational structure, although important in strategic planning, is based upon the firm's overall objectives. Answer (D) is incorrect. Recent annual budgets are a basis for short-term planning.

29. Strategy is a broad term that usually means the selection of overall objectives. Strategic analysis ordinarily **excludes** the

A. Trends that will affect the entity's markets.
B. Target product mix and production schedule to be maintained during the year.
C. Forms of organizational structure that would best serve the entity.
D. Best ways to invest in research, design, production, distribution, marketing, and administrative activities.

Answer (B) is correct.
REQUIRED: The item ordinarily excluded from the process of strategic analysis.
DISCUSSION: Strategic analysis is the process of long-range planning. Such tasks as setting the target product mix and production schedule for the current year are short-term activities.
Answer (A) is incorrect. Strategic analysis includes examining marketing trends. Answer (C) is incorrect. Strategic analysis evaluates organizational structure. Answer (D) is incorrect. Strategic analysis includes evaluation of the best ways to invest in research, design, etc.

30. Strategic planning, as practiced by most modern organizations, includes all of the following **except**

A. Top-level management participation.
B. A long-term focus.
C. Strategies that will help in achieving long-range goals.
D. Analysis of the current month's actual variances from budget.

Answer (D) is correct.
REQUIRED: The item not an element of strategic planning.
DISCUSSION: Strategic planning is the process of setting overall organizational objectives. It is a long-term process aimed at determining the future course of the organization. Analysis of the current month's budget variances is a short-term activity.
Answer (A) is incorrect. Top-level management participation is an element of strategic planning. Answer (B) is incorrect. A long-term focus is an element of strategic planning. Answer (C) is incorrect. Strategies that will help in achieving long-range goals are elements of strategic planning.

Access the CMA Review System from your Gleim Personal Classroom to continue your studies with exam-emulating multiple-choice questions!

8.8 ESSAY QUESTION

Scenario for Essay Question 1

Video Recreation, Inc., (VRI) is a supplier of video games and equipment, such as large-screen televisions and DVD players. The company has recently concluded a major contract with Sunview Hotels to supply games for the hotel video lounges. Under this contract, a total of 4,000 games will be delivered to Sunview Hotels throughout the western United States, and all of the games will have a warranty period of 1 year for both parts and labor. The number of service calls required to repair these games during the first year after installation is estimated as follows:

Number of Service Calls	Probability
400	.1
700	.3
900	.4
1,200	.2

VRI's Customer Service Department has developed three alternatives for providing the warranty service to Sunview. These three plans are presented below.

Plan 1: VRI would contract with local firms to perform the repair services. It is estimated that six such vendors would be needed to cover the appropriate areas and that each of these vendors would charge an annual fee of $15,000 to have personnel available and to stock the appropriate parts. In addition to the annual fee, VRI would be billed $250 for each service call and would be billed for parts used at cost plus a 10% surcharge.

Plan 2: VRI would allow the management of each hotel to arrange for repair service when needed and then would reimburse the hotel for the expenses incurred. It is estimated that 60% of the service calls would be for hotels located in urban areas where the charge for a service call would average $450. At the remaining hotels, the charges would be $350. In addition to these service charges, parts would be billed at cost.

Plan 3: VRI would hire its own personnel to perform repair services and to do preventive maintenance. Nine employees located in the appropriate geographical areas would be required to fulfill these responsibilities, and their average salary would be $24,000 annually. The fringe benefit expense for these employees would amount to 35% of their wages. Each employee would be scheduled to make an average of 200 preventive maintenance calls during the year; each of these calls would require $15 worth of parts. Because of this preventive maintenance, it is estimated that the expected number of hotel calls for repair service would decline 30%, and the cost of parts required for each repair service call would be reduced by 20%.

VRI's Accounting Department has reviewed the historical data on the repair costs for equipment installations similar to those proposed for Sunview Hotels and found that the cost of parts required for each repair occurred in the following proportions:

Parts Cost per Repair	Proportion
$30	15%
$40	15%
$60	45%
$90	25%

Question

1. Video Recreation, Inc., wishes to select the least costly alternative to fulfill its warranty obligations to Sunview Hotels. Recommend which of the three plans presented above should be adopted by VRI. Support your recommendation with appropriate calculations and analysis.

Essay Question 1 — Unofficial Answers

1. Video Recreation, Inc., should adopt Plan 3 as the least costly alternative. Calculations for all three plans are as follows:

Expected Number of Service Calls

Number of Service Calls	×	Probability	=	Expected Calls
400		.1		40
700		.3		210
900		.4		360
1,200		.2		240
		1.0		850

Expected Value of Parts Costs

Parts Cost per Repair	×	Proportion	=	Expected Cost
$30		.15		$ 4.50
40		.15		6.00
60		.45		27.00
90		.25		22.50
		1.00		$60.00

Plan 1
Vendor fees (6 × $15,000)	$ 90,000
Service calls (850 × $250)	212,500
Parts (850 × $60 × 1.1)	56,100
Estimated total cost	$358,600

Plan 2
Urban service calls (850 × $450 × .6)	$229,500
Rural service calls (850 × $350 × .4)	119,000
Parts (850 × $60)	51,000
Estimated total cost	$399,500

Plan 3
Employee salaries (9 × $24,000)	$216,000
Fringe benefits ($216,000 × .35)	75,600
Preventive maintenance parts (200 × 9 × $15)	27,000
Repair parts (850 × .7) × ($60 × .8)	28,560
Estimated total cost	$347,160

Access the CMA Review System from your Gleim Personal Classroom to continue your studies with exam-emulating essay questions!

STUDY UNIT NINE
BUDGETING -- CONCEPTS, METHODOLOGIES, AND PREPARATION

(33 pages of outline)

9.1	Roles of Budgets and the Budgeting Process	285
9.2	Budgeting and Standard Costs	292
9.3	The Master Budget	293
9.4	Budget Methodologies	296
9.5	Operating Budget Calculations -- Production and Direct Materials	300
9.6	Operating Budget Calculations -- Others	301
9.7	Projecting Cash Collections	306
9.8	The Cash Budget	306
9.9	Sales Forecasts and Pro Forma Financial Statements	308
9.10	Essay Questions	332

Planning, Budgeting, and Forecasting

A budget is a realistic plan for the future that is expressed in quantitative terms. A budget is many tools in one: It is a planning tool, a control tool, a communication tool, and a motivational tool. As such, the area of budgeting, as tested on the CMA exam, is a composite of theory and calculations. Some of the calculations have many steps, making budgeting problems among the most-missed questions on the exam. Alternatively, budgeting should not be viewed as a difficult area; the concepts are easy, but you need to pay close attention to detail as you work numerical questions.

This study unit is the **second of two** on **planning, budgeting, and forecasting**. The relative weight assigned to this major topic in Part 1 of the exam is **30%**. The two study units are

Study Unit 8: Analysis and Forecasting Techniques
Study Unit 9: Budgeting -- Concepts, Methodologies, and Preparation

If you are interested in reviewing more introductory or background material, go to www.gleim.com/CMAIntroVideos for a list of suggested third-party overviews of this topic. The following Gleim outline material is more than sufficient to help you pass the CMA exam; any additional introductory or background material is for your own personal enrichment.

9.1 ROLES OF BUDGETS AND THE BUDGETING PROCESS

1. **The Budget as a Tool**

    a. The budget is a **planning** tool.

    1) A budget is a written plan for the future that forces management to evaluate the assumptions and the objectives identified in the budgetary process.
    2) Companies that prepare budgets anticipate problems before they occur.

        a) EXAMPLE: If a company runs out of critical raw material, it may have to shut down. At best, it will incur extremely high freight costs to have the needed materials rushed in. The company with a budget will have anticipated the shortage and planned around it.

    3) A firm that has no goals may not always make the best decisions. A firm with a goal in the form of a budget will be able to plan.

b. The budget is a **control** tool.
   1) A budget helps a firm control costs by setting cost guidelines.
   2) Guidelines reveal the efficient or inefficient use of company resources.
   3) A manager is less apt to spend money for things that are not needed if (s)he knows that all costs will be compared with the budget.
      a) (S)he will be accountable if controllable costs exceed budgeted amounts.
   4) Budgets can also reveal the progress of highly effective managers. Consequently, employees should not view budgets negatively. A budget is just as likely to provide a boost to a manager's career as it is to be detrimental.
   5) Managers can also use a budget as a personal self-evaluation tool.
   6) Budgetary slack (overestimation of expenses), however, must be avoided if a budget is to have its desired effects. The natural tendency of a manager is to negotiate for a less stringent measure of performance so as to avoid unfavorable variances from expectations.
   7) For the budgetary process to serve effectively as a control function, it must be integrated with the accounting system and the organizational structure. Such integration enhances control by transmitting data and assigning variances to the proper organizational subunits.

c. The budget is a **motivational** tool.
   1) A budget helps motivate employees to do a good job.
      a) Employees are particularly motivated if they help prepare the budget.
      b) A manager who is asked to prepare a budget for his or her department will work hard to stay within the budget.
   2) A budget must be seen as realistic by employees before it can become a good motivational tool.
   3) Unfortunately, the budget is not always viewed in a positive manner. Some managers view a budget as a restriction.
   4) Employees are more apt to have a positive feeling toward a budget if some degree of flexibility is allowed.

d. The budget is a means of **communication**.
   1) A budget can help tell employees what goals the firm is attempting to accomplish.
   2) A budget functions as an aid to planning, coordination, and control. Thus, a budget helps management allocate resources efficiently and ensure that subunit objectives are consistent with those of other subunits and of the organization.
      a) For the budget to function in these roles, senior management must be involved with the process. This involvement does not extend to dictating exact numerical contents of the budget because senior management lacks detailed knowledge of daily operations.
   3) If the firm does not have an overall budget, each department might think the firm has different goals.
   4) For example, the sales department may want to keep as much inventory as possible so that no sales will be lost, but the company treasurer may want to keep the inventory as low as possible in order to conserve cash reserves. If the budget specifies the amount of inventory, all employees can work toward the same objectives.

2. **The Budget as a Formal Quantification of Management's Plans**
    a. Corporations have goals for market share, profitability, growth, dividend payout, etc. Not-for-profit organizations also have goals, such as increased number of free meals served, lowered recidivism rate among offenders, etc.
        1) These goals cannot be achieved without careful planning about the allocation of resources and the expected results.
    b. A budget lays out in specific terms an organization's expectations about the consumption of resources and the resulting outcomes.
    c. An organizational budget requires a significant commitment of internal resources. The most important factor in ensuring its success is for senior managers to demonstrate that they take the project seriously and consider it vital to the organization's future.

3. **Budgeting's Role in the Overall Planning and Evaluation Process**
    a. **Planning** is the process by which an organization sets specific goals for itself and sets about pursuing those goals. Planning is an organization's response to the saying "If you don't know where you're going, any path will take you there."
        1) The starting point for any organization's planning process is the formulation of its **mission statement**. The mission statement, formulated by the board and senior management, embodies the organization's reason for existing.
            a) EXAMPLE: Increase shareholder value by providing global telecommunications services.
        2) Next, the organization draws up its **strategic plan** containing the means by which the firm expects to fulfill its stated mission.
            a) To a great extent, the strategy is made up of **long-term objectives**, a set of specific, measurable goals.
            b) EXAMPLE: Hold a 35% market share of U.S. cell phone users within 5 years.
        3) Once the long-term objectives are in place, the **priorities** of the organization will be clear.
            a) Awareness of priorities is crucial for the **allocation of limited resources**.
            b) EXAMPLE: How many cell towers, each of which require the outlay of construction and maintenance costs, will provide the optimum amount of coverage.
        4) **Short-term objectives** flow directly from the priorities.
            a) EXAMPLE: Determine the appropriate number of cell towers needed and where they can feasibly be placed in the Metro Atlanta region.
            b) The planning process coordinates the efficient allocation of organizational resources.
    b. To **evaluate progress** toward success in each of these stages, quantification is necessary. This is the role of the various types of budgets.
        1) Not all quantification is in monetary terms. To extend the previous example, although cell towers obviously have a dollar cost, they must be simply counted as well.
        2) **Comparing actual results to the budget** allows the organization as a whole to evaluate its performance and managers to do the same on an individual level.
            a) The budget is therefore a strategic control.

4. **Participation in the Budget Process**

    a. Participation in the budget preparation process is up and down the organization.

        1) The budget process begins with the mission statement formulated by the **board of directors**.
        2) **Senior management** translates the mission statement into a strategic plan with measurable, realizable goals.
        3) A **budget committee/department** composed of top management is formed to draft the budget calendar and budget manual. The budget committee/department also reviews and approves the departmental budgets submitted by operating managers.
            a) A budget director's primary responsibility is to compile the budget and manage the budget process.
        4) **Middle and lower management** receive their budget instructions, draw up their departmental budgets in conformity with the guidelines, and submit them to the budget committee.

    b. **Top-down (authoritative) budgeting** is imposed by upper management and therefore has less of a chance of acceptance by those on whom the budget is imposed.

        1) This approach has the advantage of ensuring consistency across functional areas. It is also far less complex and time-consuming than coordinating input from middle and lower levels.

    c. **Bottom-up (participative) budgeting** is characterized by general guidance from the highest levels of management, followed by extensive input from middle and lower management. Because of this level of participation within the company, there is usually a greater chance of acceptance.

        1) Disadvantages of participative standards setting include its time and money costs. In addition, the quality of participation is affected by the goals, values, beliefs, and expectations of those involved.

	Advantages	**Disadvantages**
Top-down budgeting	• Ensures consistency across all functional areas • Is far less complex and time-consuming than coordinating input from the middle and lower levels	• An imposed budget is much less likely to promote a sense of commitment
Bottom-up budgeting	• Encourages employees to have a sense of ownership of the output of the process, resulting in acceptance of, and commitment to, objectives expressed in the budget • Enables employees to relate performance to rewards or penalties • Provides a broader information base (middle- and lower-level managers often are far better informed about operational realities than senior managers)	• Higher costs in time and money • Quality of participation is affected by the objectives, values, beliefs, and expectations of those involved • Creation of budgetary slack

    d. Participation in developing a budget may result in a **padding** of the budget, also known as budgetary slack.

        1) **Budgetary slack** is the excess of resources budgeted over the resources necessary to achieve organizational goals. This must be avoided if a budget is to have its desired effects.
            a) The natural tendency of a manager is to negotiate for a less stringent measure of performance so as to avoid unfavorable variances from expectations.

SU 9: Budgeting -- Concepts, Methodologies, and Preparation

2) Management may create slack by overestimating costs and underestimating revenues.

   a) A firm may decrease slack by emphasizing the consideration of all variables, holding in-depth reviews during budget development, and allowing for flexibility in making additional budget changes.

   b) A manager who expects his or her request to be reduced may inflate the amount.

   c) If a budget is to be used as a performance evaluator, a manager asked for an estimate may provide one that is easily attained.

3) The existence of slack can have both positive and negative effects on the budgeting process. The existence of slack can reduce the planning benefits of a budget, since the budget may not be entirely accurate.

   a) For example, a cash budget might show that $500,000 needs to be borrowed this month, whereas that amount is not really needed because managers were just being cautious.

   b) Alternatively, the lack of slack may discourage managers from implementing new programs or might cause managers to avoid routine maintenance when the budget does not show funds available in a particular period.

5. **Time Frames for Budgets**

   a. Each phase of the organization's planning cycle has its own budget with an appropriate **time frame**.

      1) **Strategic** plans and budgets most concern senior managers and have time frames of up to 10 years or more.

      2) **Intermediate** plans and budgets most concern middle managers and have time frames of up to 2 years.

      3) **Operational** plans and budgets most concern lower-level managers and generally have time frames of 1 month to 1 year.

6. **Budgeting's Role in Formulating and Controlling Short-term Objectives**

   a. A company's goal of increasing market share, making a steady dividend payout, etc., can only be achieved through the completion of incremental steps.

   b. The budget lays out the specific revenue targets and expense limitations for each functional area and department of the organization on a month-by-month basis.

      1) A budget cannot simply be a lump-sum total for a year. Incremental goals must be achieved each month or week. This is especially true in seasonal businesses, such as agricultural supply.

7. **Role of Budgets in Measuring Performance against Established Goals**

   a. One of the most important reasons for adopting a budget is to provide guideposts for the assessment of success or failure on the part of individual managers and functional areas.

   b. As the fiscal year progresses, revenues, expenses, and other metrics can be compared to the budget to determine where organizational performance is meeting, lagging, or exceeding expectations.

8. **The Role of Budgets in Monitoring and Controlling Expenditures**

   a. The initial budget is a planning tool. To monitor how actual performance compares with the budget, budget reports are produced periodically during the year.

      1) The difference between actual performance and a budgeted amount is called a **variance**. Analysis of variances reveals the efficient or inefficient use of company resources (Study Unit 10, "Cost and Variance Measures").

9. **Role of Budgeting Process in Facilitating Communication among Organizational Units and Enhancing Coordination of Organizational Activities**

    a. On a detailed level, the budget informs employees at all levels what objectives the firm is attempting to accomplish.

        1) If the firm does not have an overall budget, each department tends to pursue its own objectives without regard to what is good for the firm as a whole. Thus, a budget promotes goal congruence.

    b. The concrete nature of a budget facilitates coordination of the activities of a firm. An example is the purchasing of raw materials.

        1) Materials are needed prior to production, but the proper quantity to buy cannot be determined until the projected level of output is established.

            a) Thus, a production budget (in units) is a prerequisite to the preparation of a materials purchases budget.

        2) Similarly, a direct labor budget is based on how many units are to be produced and how fast the workers are.

            a) Labor standards are also complex in that they must consider the impact of the learning curve on productivity.

10. **Characteristics of a Successful Budgeting Process**

    a. **Sufficient lead time.** For a budget to be useful, it must be finalized when the fiscal year begins. This often calls for months of preparation, since the overall goals and baseline assumptions must be announced before functional areas and individual departments can begin formulating their numbers.

        1) The preparation of a complete organizational budget usually takes several months. A firm with a calendar year end may start the budget process in September, anticipating its completion by the first of December.

        2) The **budget planning calendar** is the schedule of activities for the development and adoption of the budget. It includes a list of dates indicating when specific information is to be provided to others by each information source.

            a) Because all of the individual departmental budgets are based on forecasts prepared by others and the budgets of other departments, it is essential to have a planning calendar to integrate the entire process.

        3) The budget department is responsible for compiling the budget and managing the budget process. However, the budget director and department are not responsible for actually developing the estimates on which the budget is based.

    b. **Budget manual.** Everyone involved in preparing the budget at all levels must be educated on the detailed procedures for preparing and submitting their part of the overall budget.

        1) Because of the number of component departments, budgets must be prepared in a standard format.

            a) In addition, all concerned must be informed of the ultimate goals that are being pursued and the baseline assumptions that have been laid down. A budget may, for example, begin with a blanket mandate to raise revenues by 6.5% or to cut expenses across all departments by 2%.

        2) Distribution instructions are vital because of the interdependencies of a master budget.

            a) One department's budget may be dependent on another's, and functional areas must be aggregated from their constituent department budgets. The distribution instructions coordinate these interdependencies.

c. **Buy-in at all levels.** Participative budgeting has a much greater chance of acceptance by those affected and thus of achieving ultimate success than does a budget that is imposed from above.

   1) The support of top management is crucial to the budgeting efforts. This is because the single most important factor in ensuring the success of a budget process is for senior management to demonstrate that it takes the project seriously and considers it vital to the organization's future.

11. **Effects of External Factors on the Budgeting Process**

    a. Decisions about a firm's strategy, and in turn about its budget, are dependent upon **general economic conditions** and their expected trends as well as the availability of financial resources.

       1) For instance, if the economy is entering a period of lower demand, a manufacturer will not project increased sales. If costs are not changeable, the company may budget losses for the short term to hold on to market share.

    b. **Industry situation** includes the company's current market share, governmental regulatory measures, the labor market, and the activities of competitors.

       1) For instance, if input costs are rising in a firm's industry, the budget must reflect that reality; profit margins and cash flows will not be the same as in prior years. Also, a company in or near bankruptcy will face a different financial situation than would the market leader.

12. **The Concept of Controllability**

    a. Controllability is a key concept in the use of budgets and other standards to evaluate performance. Controllability is the extent to which a manager can influence activities and related revenues and costs.

    b. Controllable costs are those that are under the discretion of a particular manager. Noncontrollable costs are those to which another level of the organization has committed, removing the manager's discretion.

    c. Controllability can be difficult to isolate because few costs or revenues are under the sole influence of one manager. Also, separating the effects of current management's decisions from those of former management is difficult.

       1) If responsibility exceeds the extent to which a manager can influence an activity, the result may be reduced morale, a decline in managerial effort, and poor performance.

       2) The principle of controllability must be kept in mind when the budget is used as the basis for managerial evaluation.

13. **Revisions to the Budget**

    a. Often an organization will find that the assumptions under which the budget was prepared undergo significant change during the year. A policy must be in place to accommodate revisions to the budget resulting from these changes.

       1) Accommodation of change is a key characteristic of successful budgeting. If such a policy is not in place, managers can come to believe they are being held to a budget that is no longer possible to achieve, and morale can suffer.

    b. Information gained during the year as actual results and variances are reported can be used to help the company take corrective action. These steps make up a control loop:

       1) Establishing standards of performance (the budget)
       2) Measuring actual performance
       3) Analyzing and comparing performance with standards
       4) Devising and implementing corrective actions
       5) Reviewing and revising the standards

Stop and review! You have completed the outline for this subunit. Study multiple-choice questions 1 through 6 beginning on page 318.

9.2 BUDGETING AND STANDARD COSTS

1. **The Use of Cost Standards**
   a. Standard costs are **predetermined expectations** about how much a unit of input, a unit of output, or a given activity should cost.
      1) The use of standard costs in budgeting allows the standard-cost system to alert management when the actual costs of production differ significantly from the standard.
   b. A standard cost is not just an average of past costs but an objectively determined estimate of what a cost should be. Standards may be based on accounting, engineering, or statistical quality control studies.
      1) Because of the impact of fixed costs in most businesses, a standard costing system is usually not effective unless the company also has a flexible budgeting system.

2. **Developing Standards**
   a. **Activity analysis** identifies, describes, and evaluates the activities that go into producing a particular output. Determining the resources and steps that go into the production process aids in the development of standard costs.
      1) Each operation requires its own unique set of inputs and preparations. Activity analysis describes what these inputs are and who performs these preparations.
         a) Inputs include the amounts and kinds of equipment, facilities, materials, and labor. Engineering analysis, cost accounting, time-and-motion study, and other approaches may be useful.
      2) **Historical data** may be used to set standards by firms that lack the resources to engage in the complex task of activity analysis.
   b. For **direct materials**, there is often a direct relationship between unit price and quality. In establishing its cost standards, a manufacturer must decide whether it will use an input that is
      1) Cheaper per unit but will ultimately result in using more because of low quality or
      2) More expensive per unit but will ultimately result in using less because of lower waste and spoilage.
   c. For **direct labor**, the complexity of the production process and the restrictions on pay scales imposed by union agreements have the most impact on formulating cost standards. Human resources also must be consulted to help project the costs of benefits.
   d. Standards can be set using the top-down (authoritative) approach or the bottom-up (participative) approach.
      1) A form of the bottom-up approach that involves line managers and their supervisors, accountants, engineers, and other interested employees before standards are accepted by top management is also called the team development approach.

3. **Theoretical vs. Practical Standards**

    a. **Ideal (theoretical) standards** are standard costs that are set for production under optimal conditions. For this reason, they are also called perfection or maximum efficiency standards.

    1) They are based on the work of the most skilled workers with no allowance for waste, spoilage, machine breakdowns, or other downtime.
    2) Often called "tight" standards, they can have positive behavioral implications if workers are motivated to strive for excellence. However, they are not widely used because they can have negative behavioral effects if the standards are perceived as impossible to attain.
    3) Ideal standards have been adopted by some companies that apply continuous improvement and other total quality management principles.
    4) Ideal standards are ordinarily replaced by currently attainable standards for cash budgeting, product costing, and budgeting departmental performance. Otherwise, accurate financial planning will be impossible.

    b. **Currently attainable (practical) standards** are defined as the performance that is expected to be achieved by reasonably well-trained workers with an allowance for normal spoilage, waste, and downtime.

    1) An alternative interpretation is that practical standards represent possible but difficult-to-attain results.

Stop and review! You have completed the outline for this subunit. Study multiple-choice questions 7 through 9 beginning on page 319.

9.3 THE MASTER BUDGET

 This study unit provides a brief overview of the master budget process. CMA candidates are expected to be able to prepare budgets based on relevant information. Take care to know the budget cycle and, especially, the order in which each budget is prepared.

1. **Annual Profit Plan**

    a. The master budget, also called the comprehensive budget or annual profit plan, encompasses the organization's operating and financial plans for a specified period (ordinarily a year or single operating cycle).
    b. The importance of carefully drafting the budget calendar is explained in this subunit. The information contained in the lower-numbered budgets feeds the higher-numbered budgets.

    1) For example, the production budget cannot be prepared until after the sales budget. The direct materials budget and the direct labor budget cannot be prepared until after the production budget has been completed.

2. **Operating Budget**

    a. In the operating budget, the emphasis is on obtaining and using current resources.

        1) Sales budget
        2) Production budget
        3) Direct materials budget
        4) Direct labor budget
        5) Manufacturing overhead budget
        6) Ending finished goods inventory budget
        7) Cost of goods sold budget
        8) Nonmanufacturing budget

            a) Research and development budget
            b) Design budget
            c) Marketing budget
            d) Distribution budget
            e) Customer service budget
            f) Administrative budget

        9) Pro forma income statement

3. **Financial Budget**

    a. In the financial budget, the emphasis is on obtaining the funds needed to purchase operating assets. It contains the

        1) Capital budget (completed before operating budget is begun)
        2) Projected cash disbursement schedule
        3) Projected cash collection schedule
        4) Cash budget
        5) Pro forma balance sheet
        6) Pro forma statement of cash flows

4. **Sales Budget**

    a. The sales budget is the first budget prepared because sales volume affects production and purchasing levels, operating expenses, and cash flows.

        1) Thus, expectations about sales drive the entire budget process.

    b. Once a firm can estimate sales, the next step is to decide how much to produce or purchase.

        1) Sales are usually budgeted by product or department. The sales budget also establishes targets for sales personnel.
        2) Sales credit policies can have a large effect on the sales budget.

5. **Production Budgets**

    a. Production budgets (for manufacturing firms) are based on sales in units (not dollars) plus or minus desired inventory buildup or reduction.

        1) They are prepared for each department and each item. Production budgets are usually stated in units instead of dollars.

SU 9: Budgeting -- Concepts, Methodologies, and Preparation

    b. When the production budget has been completed, it is used to prepare three additional budgets:

        1) Raw materials purchases, which is similar to the purchases budget of a merchandising firm

        2) Direct labor budget, which includes hours, wage rates, and total dollars

        3) Factory overhead budget, which is similar to a department expenses budget

6. **Purchases Budget**

    a. The purchases budget can follow after projected sales have been set. It is prepared on a monthly or even a weekly basis.

        1) Purchases can be planned so that stockouts are avoided. Inventory should be at an appropriate level to avoid unnecessary carrying costs.

        2) Attempts should be made to determine potential purchasing terms.

7. **Expense Budgets**

    a. Expense budgets are prepared by department heads using the sales budget as a basis.

        1) Expense budgets are based on prior years' costs and adjusted for anticipated changes in prices, wages, and sales volume estimates.

8. **Capital Budget**

    a. Equipment purchases (capital expenditures) are technically not part of the operating budget, but they must be incorporated into the preparation of the cash budget and pro forma financial statements.

    b. Capital budgets may be prepared more than a year in advance to allow sufficient time to

        1) Plan financing of major expenditures for equipment or buildings or

        2) Receive custom orders of specialized equipment, buildings, etc.

9. **Cash Budget**

    a. The cash budget is usually the last to be prepared and is also probably the most important part of a company's budget program.

        1) Almost all organizations, regardless of size, prepare a cash budget. It is particularly important for organizations operating in seasonal industries.

        2) An organization must have adequate cash at all times. Even with plenty of other assets, an organization with a temporary shortage of cash can be driven into bankruptcy. Proper planning can keep an entity from financial embarrassment.

    b. A cash budget details projected cash receipts and disbursements. It cannot be prepared until the other budgets have been completed.

        1) Cash budgeting facilitates loans and other financing. A bank is more likely to lend money to a firm if the money will not be needed immediately.

c. Below is an example of a cash budget for a company that had budgeted sales of $9,000 for January, $9,700 for February, and $13,950 for March.

Cash Budget
For Quarter Ending March 31

	January	February	March	Total
Beginning cash balance	$ 80	$ 20	$ 1,957	$ 80
Receipts:				
Collection from sales*	6,800	9,350	11,825	27,975
Total cash available	$6,880	$9,370	$13,782	$28,055
Payments:				
Purchases**	$3,150	$2,760	$ 3,960	$ 9,870
Sales salaries	1,350	1,455	2,093	4,898
Supplies	360	388	558	1,306
Utilities	120	110	100	330
Administrative salaries	1,800	1,800	1,800	5,400
Advertising	80	80	80	240
Equipment purchases	0	820	3,000	3,820
Total payments	$6,860	$7,413	$11,591	$25,864
Ending balance	$ 20	$1,957	$ 2,191	$ 2,191

* Sales are 50% cash sales and 50% on credit (net 30 days). Thus, 50% of each month's sales are collected in the month of the sale and 50% are collected in the following month. For example, the February collections were calculated as follows:

50% of January sales	$4,500
50% of February sales	4,850
	$9,350

** Purchases are on terms of net 30 days. Thus, purchases are paid for in the month following the purchase. The amount paid in February ($2,760) was the total purchases for January.

Stop and review! You have completed the outline for this subunit. Study multiple-choice questions 10 through 14 beginning on page 320.

9.4 BUDGET METHODOLOGIES

CMA candidates must know how to both apply and select a specific budgeting method. They may also be required to explain a specific action, such as why a method should be selected. All topics are eligible to be tested on the multiple-choice section, the essay section, or both.

1. **Project Budget**

    a. A project budget consists of all the costs expected to attach to a particular project, such as the design of a new airliner or the building of a single ship.

      1) While the project is obviously part of the company's overall line of business, the costs and profits associated with it are significant enough to be tracked separately.

    b. A project will typically use resources from many parts of the organization, e.g., design, engineering, production, marketing, accounting, and human resources.

      1) All of these aspects of the project budget must align with those of the firm's master budget.

c. EXAMPLE of a project budget:

Function	1st Quarter	2nd Quarter	3rd Quarter	4th Quarter	Totals
Design	$ 800,000	$ 200,000	$ --	$ --	$1,000,000
Engineering	500,000	1,200,000	400,000	--	2,100,000
Production	--	2,100,000	1,500,000	1,500,000	5,100,000
Marketing	--	100,000	200,000	200,000	500,000
Accounting	100,000	100,000	100,000	100,000	400,000
Human Resources	20,000	20,000	20,000	20,000	80,000
Totals	$1,420,000	$3,720,000	$2,220,000	$1,820,000	$9,180,000

2. **Activity-Based Budgeting**

a. Activity-based budgeting applies activity-based costing principles (Study Unit 5, Subunit 2) to budgeting. Its greatest effect is on the application of indirect costs.

1) A traditional budgeting system involves lumping all indirect costs into a single pool and allocating them to products based on a (usually arbitrary) driver such as volume or machine hours.

2) EXAMPLE: A manufacturer produces two valves, a simple one and a complex one. It has budgeted production costs for the upcoming year using a volume-based budgeting system:

Cost Category	Simple Valve 50,000 Total	Per Unit	Complex Valve 10,000 Total	Per Unit	Total
Direct materials	$ 450,000	$ 9.00	$270,000	$27.00	$ 720,000
Direct labor	240,000	4.80	78,000	7.80	318,000
Total direct costs	$ 690,000	$13.80	$348,000	$34.80	$1,038,000
Allocated indirect costs	720,000	14.40	234,000	23.40	954,000
Total manufacturing costs	$1,410,000	$28.20	$582,000	$58.20	$1,992,000

b. Activity-based budgeting involves defining the activities that drive indirect costs.

1) A cost pool is established for each activity, and a cost driver is identified for each pool.

a) The key to successful activity-based budgeting is selecting a driver for each pool that has a direct cause-and-effect relationship with the level of activity in that pool.

2) The budgeted cost for each pool is determined by multiplying the demand for the activity by the estimated cost of a unit of the activity.

3) EXAMPLE: The manufacturer has designed an indirect-cost assignment system based on the following pools and drivers:

Indirect cost pool	Driver
Product design	Engineering hours
Production setup	Number of batches
Machining	Machine hours
Inspection & testing	Number of valves
Customer maintenance	Salesperson hours

c. Since activity-based budgeting employs multiple indirect cost pools, it provides far greater detail regarding indirect costs than traditional functional or spending-category budgeting (which only employs a single pool).

1) EXAMPLE: Note that while the amounts of indirect costs assigned to the two products are different, indirect costs in total are (necessarily) the same as under the traditional system:

Cost Category	Estimated Driver Level	Cost per Unit of Driver	Simple Valve 50,000 Total	Per Unit	Complex Valve 10,000 Total	Per Unit	Total
Direct materials			$ 450,000	$ 9.00	$270,000	$27.00	$ 720,000
Direct labor			240,000	4.80	78,000	7.80	318,000
Total direct costs			**$ 690,000**	**$13.80**	**$348,000**	**$34.80**	**$1,038,000**
Indirect cost assignment:							
Product design:							
Simple valve	1,000 ×	$23.75 =	$ 23,750	$ 0.48			$ 90,250
Complex valve	2,800 ×	23.75 =			$ 66,500	$ 6.65	
Production setup:							
Simple valve	200 ×	21.00 =	4,200	0.08			4,620
Complex valve	20 ×	21.00 =			420	0.04	
Machining:							
Simple valve	2,000 ×	3.25 =	6,500	0.13			68,250
Complex valve	19,000 ×	3.25 =			61,750	6.18	
Inspection & testing:							
Simple valve	50,000 ×	12.50 =	625,000	12.50			750,000
Complex valve	10,000 ×	12.50 =			125,000	12.50	
Customer maintenance:							
Simple valve	1,500 ×	17.60 =	26,400	0.53			40,480
Complex valve	800 ×	17.60 =			14,080	1.41	
Total indirect costs			**$ 685,850**	**$13.72**	**$267,750**	**$26.78**	**$ 953,600**
Total manufacturing costs			**$1,375,850**	**$27.52**	**$615,750**	**$61.58**	**$1,991,600**

3. **Zero-Based Budgeting**

a. Zero-based budgeting (ZBB) is a budget and planning process in which each manager must justify his or her department's entire budget every budget cycle.

1) The concept originated in the U.S. Department of Agriculture in the early 1960s but was abandoned. Texas Instruments Corporation began using it in the late 1960s and early 1970s, as did the state of Georgia under Governor Jimmy Carter. Carter also tried to introduce the concept into the federal budget system when he served as president (1977–1980).

b. ZBB differs from the traditional concept of **incremental budgeting**, in which the current year's budget is simply adjusted to allow for changes planned for the coming year.

1) The managerial advantage of incremental budgeting is that the manager has to put forth less effort to justify changes in the budget.

c. Under ZBB, a manager must build the budget every year from a base of zero. All expenditures must be justified regardless of variance from previous years.

1) The objective is to encourage periodic reexamination of all costs in the hope that some can be reduced or eliminated.

d. ZBB begins with the deepest budgetary units of the entity.
1) It requires determination of objectives, operations, and costs for each activity and the alternative means of carrying out that activity.
2) Different levels of service (work effort) are evaluated for each activity, measures of work and performance are established, and activities are ranked according to their importance to the entity.
3) For each budgetary unit, a decision package is prepared that describes various levels of service that may be provided, including at least one level of service lower than the current one.
    a) Accordingly, ZBB requires managers to justify each expenditure for each budget period and to review each cost component from a cost-benefit perspective.
e. The major limitation of ZBB is that it requires more time and effort to prepare than a traditional budget.

4. **Continuous (Rolling) Budgeting**
    a. A continuous (rolling) budget is one that is revised on a regular (continuous) basis.
        1) Typically, a company continuously extends such a budget for an additional month or quarter in accordance with new data as the current month or quarter ends.
        2) For example, if the budget cycle is 1 year, a budget for the next quarter will be available continuously as each quarter ends.
    b. EXAMPLE of rolling budget:

Product Line	Fiscal Year 1				Four Quarter Totals
	1st Quarter	2nd Quarter	3rd Quarter	4th Quarter	
Feed	$ 12,000	$ 10,000	$ 10,000	$ 14,000	$ 46,000
Animal health	2,000	1,200	800	1,000	5,000
Fertilizer	80,000	75,000	20,000	10,000	185,000
Crop protectants	74,000	76,000	41,000	11,000	202,000
Petroleum	120,000	20,000	14,000	100,000	254,000
Farm supplies	15,000	45,000	55,000	20,000	135,000
Totals	$303,000	$227,200	$140,800	$156,000	$827,000

Product Line	Fiscal Year 1			Fiscal Year 2	Four Quarter Totals
	2nd Quarter	3rd Quarter	4th Quarter	1st Quarter	
Feed	$ 10,000	$ 10,000	$ 14,000	$ 9,000	$ 43,000
Animal health	1,200	800	1,000	2,200	5,200
Fertilizer	75,000	20,000	10,000	90,000	195,000
Crop protectants	76,000	41,000	11,000	90,000	218,000
Petroleum	20,000	14,000	100,000	85,000	219,000
Farm supplies	45,000	55,000	20,000	10,000	130,000
Totals	$227,200	$140,800	$156,000	$286,200	$810,200

   c. The principal advantage of a rolling budget is that it requires managers to always be thinking ahead.
        1) The disadvantage is the amount of time managers must constantly spend on budget preparation.

Stop and review! You have completed the outline for this subunit. Study multiple-choice questions 15 through 19 beginning on page 322.

9.5 OPERATING BUDGET CALCULATIONS -- PRODUCTION AND DIRECT MATERIALS

1. **Sales Budget**

    a. The sales budget, also called the revenue budget, is the starting point for the massive cycle that produces the annual profit plan (i.e., the master budget).

    b. The sales budget is an outgrowth of the sales forecast. The sales forecast distills recent sales trends, overall conditions in the economy and industry, market research, activities of competitors, and credit and pricing policies.

    1) For example,

        a) The company may determine that demand is highly elastic for its mature products and that growth will come only from new product introductions and from cost savings on existing products.

        b) At the same time, the company determines that a tight monetary policy on the Fed's part must cause the firm to tighten its credit standards.

        c) Simultaneously, a competitor that the firm knows is a low-cost producer is also considering moving into the markets that the budgeting company is considering.

    2) All of these factors must be taken into account when forming expectations about product sales for the coming budget cycle.

    c. The sales budget must specify both projected unit sales and dollar revenues.

    d. EXAMPLE of a sales budget: The demand for this firm's product is elastic, so the price cut in the third month is expected to boost sales.

	April	May	June	2nd Quarter Totals	Ref.
Projected sales in units	1,000	1,200	1,800	4,000	SB1
Selling price	× $400	× $400	× $380		
Projected total sales	$400,000	$480,000	$684,000	$1,564,000	SB2

2. **Production Budget**

    a. The production budget follows directly from the sales budget. To minimize finished goods carrying costs and obsolescence, the levels of production are dependent upon the projections contained in the sales budget.

    1) The production budget is concerned with **units only**. Product pricing is not a consideration since the goal is purely to plan output and inventory levels and the necessary manufacturing activity.

    b. EXAMPLE of a production budget:

	Source	April	May	June	2nd Quarter Totals	Ref.
Projected sales in units	SB1	1,000	1,200	1,800		
Add: Desired ending inventory (10% of next month's sales)		120	180	200		
Total needed		1,120	1,380	2,000		
Less: Beginning inventory		(100)	(120)	(180)		
Units to be produced		1,020	1,260	1,820	4,100	PB

3. **Direct Materials Budget**

    a. The direct materials budget follows directly from the production budget. It is concerned with both units and input prices.

    1) To minimize raw materials carrying costs and obsolescence, the purchasing of inputs is tied closely to the projections contained in the production budget.

b. EXAMPLES of two direct materials budgets: Note that in the third month,
1) The process is expected to experience improved efficiency with regard to Raw Material A.
2) A price break on Raw Material B is expected.

Raw Material A	Source	April	May	June	2nd Quarter Totals	Ref.
Units to be produced	PB	1,020	1,260	1,820		
Raw material per finished product		× 4	× 4	× 3		DMB1
Total units needed for production		4,080	5,040	5,460		
Raw material cost per unit		× $12	× $12	× $12		DMB2
Cost of units used in production		$48,960	$60,480	$65,520	$174,960	DMB3
Add: Desired units in ending inventory (20% of next month's need)		1,008	1,092	1,600		
Total needs		5,088	6,132	7,060		
Less: Beginning inventory		(400)	(1,008)	(1,092)		
Raw material to be purchased		4,688	5,124	5,968		
Raw material cost per unit		× $12	× $12	× $12		
Cost of raw material to be purchased		**$56,256**	**$61,488**	**$71,616**		DMB4

Raw Material B	Source	April	May	June	2nd Quarter Totals	Ref.
Units to be produced	PB	1,020	1,260	1,820		
Raw material per finished product		× 2	× 2	× 2		DMB5
Total units needed for production		2,040	2,520	3,640		
Raw material cost per unit		× $10	× $10	× $8		DMB6
Cost of units used in production		$20,400	$25,200	$29,120	$74,720	DMB7
Add: Desired units in ending inventory (20% of next month's need)		504	728	900		
Total needs		2,544	3,248	4,540		
Less: Beginning inventory		(200)	(504)	(728)		
Raw material to be purchased		2,344	2,744	3,812		
Raw material cost per unit		× $10	× $10	× $8		
Cost of raw material to be purchased		**$23,440**	**$27,440**	**$30,496**		DMB8

Stop and review! You have completed the outline for this subunit. Study multiple-choice questions 20 through 23 beginning on page 323.

9.6 OPERATING BUDGET CALCULATIONS -- OTHERS

1. **Direct Labor Budget**

   a. The direct labor budget depends on wage rates, amounts and types of production, numbers and skill levels of employees to be hired, etc.

   b. EXAMPLE of a direct labor budget: No new efficiencies are expected, and the wage rate is set by contract with the union.

	Source	April	May	June	2nd Quarter Totals	Ref.
Units to be produced	PB	1,020	1,260	1,820		
Direct labor hours per unit		× 2	× 2	× 2		DLB1
Projected total direct labor hours		2,040	2,520	3,640		DLB2
Direct labor cost per hour		× $18.64	× $18.64	× $18.64		
Total projected direct labor cost*		**$38,026**	**$46,973**	**$67,850**	**$152,849**	DLB3

*NOTE: For the remaining calculations, please round to the nearest whole number.

2. **Employee Fringe Benefits**

   a. The **cost of fringe benefits** must be derived once the cost of wages has been determined.

   b. EXAMPLE of an employee fringe benefit projection:

	Source	April	May	June	2nd Quarter Totals	Ref.
Projected direct labor wages	DLB3	$38,026	$46,973	$67,850	$152,849	
Employer FICA match (7.65%)		2,909	3,593	5,191	11,693	
Health insurance (12.1%)		4,601	5,684	8,210	18,495	
Life insurance (5%)		1,901	2,349	3,393	7,643	
Pension matching (4%)		1,521	1,879	2,714	6,114	
Total projected direct labor cost		**$48,958**	**$60,478**	**$87,358**	**$196,794**	**DLB4**

   c. The full per-hour cost of labor can now be determined. This will be used in determining the costs embedded in units remaining in ending finished goods inventory.

   1) Since a first-in, first-out (FIFO) assumption is used for all inventories and only units produced in June are expected to remain at the end of June, the calculation is only necessary for June's data.

Total projected direct labor cost	÷	Total projected direct labor hours	=	Full direct labor cost per hour	Ref.
$87,358	÷	3,640	=	$24	DLB5

   d. Whether employee fringes are included in direct labor costs or treated as overhead, the effect on cost of goods sold is the same. Both ways include the amounts in variable manufacturing costs.

3. **Variable Overhead**

   a. The manufacturing overhead budget reflects the nature of overhead as a mixed cost, i.e., one that has a variable component and a fixed component.

   b. Variable overhead contains those elements that vary with the level of production.

   1) Indirect materials
   2) Some indirect labor
   3) Variable factory operating costs (e.g., electricity)

   c. EXAMPLE of a variable overhead budget: Note that variable overhead will be applied to finished goods on the basis of direct labor hours.

Variable overhead	Source	April	May	June	2nd Quarter Totals	Ref.
Projected total direct labor hours	DLB2	2,040	2,520	3,640		
Variable OH rate per direct labor hour		× $2	× $2	× $2		MOB1
Projected variable overhead		**$4,080**	**$5,040**	**$7,280**	**$16,400**	**MOB2**

4. **Fixed Overhead**

   a. Fixed overhead contains those elements that remain the same regardless of the level of production.

   1) Real estate taxes
   2) Insurance
   3) Depreciation

b. EXAMPLE of a fixed overhead budget: Note that fixed overhead will be applied based on the number of units produced.

Fixed overhead	Source	April	May	June	2nd Quarter Totals	Ref.
Projected fixed overhead		**$9,000**	**$9,000**	**$9,000**	**$27,000**	**MOB3**
Projected unit production	PB	÷ 1,020	÷ 1,260	÷ 1,820		
Fixed OH applied per unit		$ 8.82	$ 7.14	$ 4.95		**MOB4**

5. **Ending Finished Goods Inventory Budget**

   a. The ending finished goods inventory budget can be prepared now that the components of finished goods cost have been projected.

      1) The end result will have a direct impact on the pro forma balance sheet. The higher the amount of costs capitalized in finished goods, the higher will be the firm's projected asset balance at year end.

   b. EXAMPLE of a unit-cost calculation: Since a first-in, first-out (FIFO) assumption is used for all inventories and only units produced in June are expected to remain at the end of June, this calculation uses June's data.

	Source	Qty.	Source	Input cost	Cost per finished unit
Production costs in ending inventory:					
Direct materials -- raw material A	DMB1	3	DMB2	$12.00	$ 36.00
Direct materials -- raw material B	DMB5	2	DMB6	8.00	16.00
Direct labor	DLB1	2	DLB5	24.00	48.00
Variable overhead	DLB1	2	MOB1	2.00	4.00
Fixed overhead	--	1	MOB4	4.95	4.95
Finished goods cost					$108.95

   c. Now the total amount of cost embedded in ending inventory can be derived.

Total FIFO cost per finished unit	×	Projected units at June 30	=	Projected ending inventory	Ref.
$108.95	×	200	=	**$21,790**	**EFGIB**

6. **Cost of Goods Sold Budget**

   a. The cost of goods sold budget combines the results of the projections for the three major inputs (materials, labor, overhead).

      1) The end result will have a direct impact on the pro forma income statement. Cost of goods sold is the single largest reduction to revenues for a manufacturer.

   b. EXAMPLE of a cost of goods sold budget for the quarter:

	Source			Ref.
Beginning finished goods inventory			$ 16,200	
Manufacturing costs:				
Direct materials used -- A	DMB3	$174,960		
Direct materials used -- B	DMB7	74,720		
Direct labor employed	DLB4	196,794		
Variable overhead	MOB2	16,400		
Fixed overhead	MOB3	27,000		
Cost of goods manufactured			489,874	
Cost of goods available for sale			$506,074	
Ending finished goods inventory	EFGIB		(21,790)	
Cost of goods sold			**$484,284**	**CGSB**

c. Budgeted gross margin, the amount left over from sales revenue after the cost of the product, can now be calculated:

	Source	
Sales	SB2	$1,564,000
Cost of goods sold	CGSB	(484,284)
Gross margin		**$1,079,716**

1) The calculation of gross margin is required for external financial reporting. Cost of goods sold for this purpose must be derived using absorption (full) costing, i.e., by including all manufacturing costs, both variable and fixed.

2) For internal reporting, variable (direct) costing, which includes only variable costs in cost of goods sold, is more useful than absorption costing.

7. **Variable Costing and Contribution Margin**

   a. Contribution margin is the amount left over from sales after subtracting variable costs.

      1) Contribution margin is the amount available for "contributing" to the covering of fixed costs and providing a profit (a more detailed discussion of absorption and variable costing can be found in Study Unit 6, Subunit 1).

      2) Although it is impermissible for external financial reporting, contribution margin is more useful to management accountants because it more accurately reveals the change in profitability resulting from a given change in output.

   b. Cost of goods sold calculated on a variable-costing basis includes **only** those costs that vary directly with the level of production. The amount of sales left over after subtracting variable-basis cost of goods sold is contribution margin.

      1) Absorption costing (required for external reporting) includes certain amounts in cost of goods sold that do not vary directly with the level of production, such as fixed overhead costs.

      2) Because costs are accumulated so differently, inventory amounts as well as cost of goods sold are different under variable costing from what they are under absorption costing.

   c. The breakeven point is the level of production at which operating income equals zero, i.e., the level at which all fixed costs plus those variable costs incurred to that point have been covered.

      1) Every sales dollar beyond breakeven provides operating profit.

      $$\text{Breakeven point} = \frac{\text{Total fixed costs}}{\text{Contribution margin per unit}}$$

      2) EXAMPLE: A manufacturer has budgeted total fixed costs of $1,240,000 and a budgeted contribution margin of $6.80 per unit. The breakeven point for the budget period is 182,353 units ($1,240,000 ÷ $6.80).

      NOTE: Breakeven analysis, also called cost-volume-profit analysis, is tested in Part 2 of the CMA exam.

8. **Nonmanufacturing Budget**

   a. The nonmanufacturing budget consists of the individual budgets for R&D, design, marketing, distribution, customer service, and administrative costs.

      1) The development of separate R&D, design, marketing, distribution, customer service, and administrative budgets reflects a value chain approach.

      2) An alternative is to prepare a single selling and administrative budget for nonproduction costs.

b. The variable and fixed portions of selling and administrative costs must be treated separately.

1) Some S&A costs vary directly and proportionately with the level of sales. As more product is sold, sales representatives must travel more miles and serve more customers.
2) Other S&A expenses, such as sales support staff, are fixed; they must be paid no matter the level of sales.
3) As the variable portion of S&A costs increases, contribution margin, i.e., the amount available for covering fixed costs, is decreased.

c. EXAMPLE of a nonmanufacturing costs budget: Note the separate treatment of the variable and fixed portions.

	Source	April	May	June	2nd Quarter Totals	Ref.
Variable nonmanufacturing costs:						
Projected sales in units	SB1	1,000	1,200	1,800		
Variable S&A expenses ($3 per unit sold)		× $3	× $3	× $3		
Total variable nonmanufacturing costs		$ 3,000	$ 3,600	$ 5,400	$ 12,000	
Fixed nonmanufacturing costs:						
Research and development		$ 8,000	$ 8,000	$ 8,000	$ 24,000	
Design		4,000	4,000	4,000	12,000	
Marketing		7,000	7,000	7,000	21,000	
Distribution		10,000	10,000	10,000	30,000	
Customer service		11,000	11,000	11,000	33,000	
Administrative		50,000	50,000	50,000	150,000	
Total fixed nonmanufacturing costs		$90,000	$90,000	$90,000	$270,000	
Total nonmanufacturing costs		**$93,000**	**$93,600**	**$95,400**	**$282,000**	**NMB**

d. Note that management can make tradeoffs among elements of selling and administrative expenses that can affect contribution margin.

1) For example, use of fixed advertising expense will increase contribution margin, while the same sales level might be reached using variable sales commissions, a method that would reduce contribution margin.

9. **Pro Forma Operating Income**

a. If the projected level of operating income is insufficient, the various components of the operating budget can be adjusted.

1) EXAMPLE of pro forma operating income:

	Source	
Sales	SB2	$1,564,000
Cost of goods sold	CGSB	(484,284)
Gross margin		$1,079,716
Nonmanufacturing costs	NMB	(282,000)
Operating income		**$ 797,716**

Stop and review! You have completed the outline for this subunit. Study multiple-choice questions 24 through 27 beginning on page 324.

9.7 PROJECTING CASH COLLECTIONS

1. **Capital Budget**

   a. Outside the annual financial budget cycle is the preparation of the capital budget, which often must be approved by the board of directors.

      1) The capital budget concerns financing of major expenditures for long-term assets and must therefore have a multi-year perspective. Productive machinery must be acquired to enable the company to achieve its projected levels of output.

   b. A procedure for ranking projects according to their risk and return characteristics is necessary because every organization has finite resources.

   NOTE: These procedures (net present value, internal rate of return, payback method, etc.) are tested in Part 2 of the CMA exam.

   c. The capital budget has a direct impact on the cash budget and the pro forma financial statements.

      1) Principal and interest on debt acquired to finance capital purchases require regular cash outflows. The acquired debt also appears in the liabilities section of the pro forma balance sheet.

      2) At the same time, the output produced by the new productive assets generates regular cash inflows. In addition, the new assets themselves appear in the assets section of the pro forma balance sheet.

2. **Cash Collections Schedule**

   a. The projected cash collections schedule is used to estimate the inflows of cash from customer payments.

      1) EXAMPLE of a cash collections schedule: Note the assumption that 5% of sales will prove to be uncollectible.

	Source	April	May	June	Ref.
Projected February sales		$180,000			
Projected March sales		$220,000			
Projected sales	SB2	$400,000	$480,000	$684,000	
Cash collections from sales:					
From 2nd prior month sales (30%)		54,000	66,000	120,000	
From prior month sales (50%)		110,000	200,000	240,000	
From current month sales (15%)		60,000	72,000	102,600	
Total cash collections from sales		**$224,000**	**$338,000**	**$462,600**	PCCS

Stop and review! You have completed the outline for this subunit. Study multiple-choice questions 28 through 32 beginning on page 326.

9.8 THE CASH BUDGET

1. **Cash Budget as Lynchpin of Budget Process**

   a. The cash budget is the part of the financial budget cycle that ties together all the schedules from the operating budget.

      1) A cash budget projects cash receipts and disbursements for planning and control purposes. Hence, it helps prevent not only cash emergencies but also excessive idle cash.

b. A cash budget is vital because an organization must have adequate cash at all times. Almost all organizations, regardless of size, prepare a cash budget. Even with plenty of other assets, an organization with a temporary shortage of cash can be driven into bankruptcy.

1) Proper planning can keep an entity from financial embarrassment. Thus, cash budgets are prepared not only for annual and quarterly periods but also for monthly and weekly periods.

   a) They are particularly important for organizations operating in seasonal industries.
   b) The factors needed to prepare a cash forecast include all other elements of the budget preparation process, plus consideration of collection policies, bad debt estimates, changes in the economy, and anticipation of non-routine transactions.
   c) Factors should be considered for short-term and long-term cash forecasting (i.e., nonroutine property purchases and sales).

2) Credit and purchasing policies have a direct impact on the cash budget.

   a) Loose credit policies toward customers' credit result in delayed cash receipts.
   b) Taking advantage of purchase discounts results in accelerated cash outlays.

2. **Cash Disbursements Schedule**

   a. First, a projected cash disbursements schedule for raw materials is prepared.

      1) EXAMPLE of a raw materials cash disbursements schedule:

	Source	April	May	June	Ref.
March raw materials purchases -- A		$45,000			
March raw materials purchases -- B		$17,000			
Projected raw materials cost -- A	DMB4	$56,256	$61,488	$71,616	
Cash payments for purchases of A:					
For prior month purchases (40%)		18,000	22,502	24,595	
For current month purchases (60%)		33,754	36,893	42,970	
Total cash disbursements for A		$51,754	$59,395	$67,565	PCDS1
Projected raw materials cost -- B	DMB8	$23,440	$27,440	$30,496	
Cash payments for purchases of B:					
For prior month purchases (40%)		6,800	9,376	10,976	
For current month purchases (60%)		14,064	16,464	18,298	
Total cash disbursements for B		$20,864	$25,840	$29,274	PCDS2

3. **Cash Budget Preparation**

   a. The cash budget combines the results of the operating budget with the cash collection and disbursement schedules to produce a comprehensive picture of where the company's cash flows are expected to come from and where they are expected to go.

      1) The completed cash budget can be used to plan outside financing activities. For example, if the budget shows a cash deficit at some future date, the firm can plan ahead to borrow the necessary funds or sell stock.
      2) Dividend policy can also be planned using the cash budget. Dividend payment dates should correspond to a time when the firm has excess cash.

b. **EXAMPLE** of a cash budget: The bottom section deals with the anticipated handling of the inevitable temporary excesses and deficiencies of cash.

	Source	April	May	June
Beginning cash balance		$ 50,000	$100,000	$130,767
Cash collections from sales	PCCS	224,000	338,000	462,600
Cash available for disbursement		$274,000	$438,000	$593,367
Cash disbursements:				
For raw material A	PCDS1	$ 51,754	$ 59,395	$ 67,565
For raw material B	PCDS2	20,864	25,840	29,274
For direct labor	DLB4	48,958	60,478	87,358
For variable overhead	MOB2	4,080	5,040	7,280
For fixed overhead	MOB3	9,000	9,000	9,000
For nonmanufacturing costs	NMB	93,000	93,600	95,400
For equipment purchases	Cap. Budg.	0	0	30,000
Total disbursements		$227,656	$253,353	$325,877
Surplus of cash available over disbursements		$ 46,344	$184,647	$267,490
Desired ending cash balance		(100,000)	(100,000)	(100,000)
Surplus (deficiency) of cash		**$ (53,656)**	**$ 84,647**	**$167,490**
Financing:				
Borrowings		$ 53,656	$ 0	$ 0
Repayments:				
Principal		0	(53,656)	0
Interest		0	(224)	0
Net financing		$ 53,656	$ (53,880)	$ 0
Ending cash balance		**$100,000**	**$130,767**	**$267,490**

Stop and review! You have completed the outline for this subunit. Study multiple-choice questions 33 and 34 on page 328.

9.9 SALES FORECASTS AND PRO FORMA FINANCIAL STATEMENTS

1. **Sales Forecasts**

    a. The sales forecast starts by looking back at historical trends and seeks to determine a pattern so that next year's sales can be predicted.

    b. One of the most effective ways to do this is to plot sales on a graph and use regression analysis (covered in Study Unit 8, Subunit 1) to forecast next year's sales.

    1) For example, MoeCo had the following sales for Years 1-5:

Year	Sales (in millions)
1	$1,146
2	$1,318
3	$1,214
4	$1,362
5	$1,589
6	--

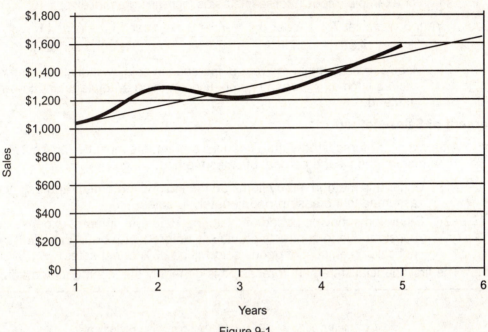

Figure 9-1

c. Using this information, a preliminary forecast for Year 6 sales can be developed.

1) Using either the regression analysis or sales per year, the average annual growth rate (AAGR) in sales can be determined.

Growth rate (GR) = (Ending value − Beginning value) ÷ Beginning value

AAGR = (GR_1 + GR_2 + GR_3 + . . . GR_x) ÷ Number of periods

2) For example, using the 5 years of sales data, MoeCo's AAGR equals

($1,318 − $1,146) ÷ $1,146 =	15.0%
($1,214 − $1,318) ÷ $1,318 =	-7.9%
($1,362 − $1,214) ÷ $1,214 =	12.1%
($1,589 − $1,362) ÷ $1,362 =	16.7%
	35.9%
Divided by Number of Periods	÷ 4
AAGR	9.0%

d. Based on other factors, MoeCo may choose to revise its initial AAGR up or down.

1) Other factors may include macroeconomic factors, production capabilities, competitors' production capabilities, new product introductions, markets opening or closing, inflation, advertising, promotional discounts, etc.

2) For example, since MoeCo plans to cut its sales budget by 25% for Year 6, MoeCo anticipates that sales for Year 6 will rise by only 7.8%, not 9.0%.

e. Managers will also forecast sales many years into the future in order to plan more effectively.

1) For example, MoeCo forecasts sales increasing as follows:

Year 6	Year 7	Year 8	Year 9	Year 10	Year 11
7.8%	7.8%	7.8%	7.0%	7.0%	6.5%

2) MoeCo forecasts that the rate of increase in sales will decline after Year 8 due to factors such as increased competition in the marketplace and lower customer demand.

2. **Percent of Sales Method**

    a. After sales are forecasted, future financial statements must be forecasted. The most common method is the percent of sales method.

    1) Under this method, many items on the income statement and balance sheets are assumed to increase proportionately to sales.

    2) Other items may be based off historical data (i.e., interest expense may remain constant due to contracts previously entered into) or be based off forecasted net sales (i.e., cost of goods sold will be 60% of net sales).

    b. The first financial statement forecasted is generally the income statement.

EXAMPLE

LisaCo's Actual Year 5 and Projected Year 6 Income Statement
(millions of dollars)

	Actual Year 5	Forecast Basis	Year 6 Forecast
Sales	$4,000	1.11 × Year 6 sales	$4,440
Cost of goods sold	(3,200)	80% of net sales	(3,552)
Gross margin	$ 800		$ 888
Selling and administrative expenses	(300)	1.11 × Year 6 sales	(333)
Operating income	$ 500		$ 555
Other revenue	200	Same as last year	200
Earnings before interest and taxes (EBIT)	$ 700		$ 755
Interest	(100)	Same as last year	(100)
Earnings before taxes (EBT)	$ 600		$ 655
Taxes (40%)	(240)		(262)
Net income	$ 360		$ 393

Notes

- Sales and selling and administrative expenses are expected to increase by 11% in the next year.
- Cost of goods sold is expected to remain at 80% of net sales.
- Other revenue and interest expense are expected to remain constant.

---

3. **Pro Forma Statement of Income**

    a. **Pro forma** is a Latin phrase meaning "according to form." It can be loosely translated to mean "as if." Financial statements are referred to as pro forma when they reflect projected, rather than actual, results.

    1) The pro forma income statement is used to decide whether the budgeted activities will result in an acceptable level of income. If the initial pro forma income shows a loss or an unacceptable level of income, adjustments can be made to the component parts of the master budget.

    2) Other strategic objectives can also be observed from the pro forma income statement, such as a target gross margin percentage and the interest coverage ratio (times interest earned). The adequacy of earnings per share can also be observed from the pro forma income statement.

b. EXAMPLE of a pro forma income statement:

Manufacturing Company
Pro Forma Statement of Income
2nd Quarter

Sales		$1,564,000
Beginning finished goods inventory	$ 16,200	
Add: Cost of goods manufactured	489,874	
Goods available for sale	$506,074	
Less: Ending finished goods inventory	(21,790)	
Cost of goods sold		(484,284)
Gross margin		$1,079,716
Less: Selling and administrative expenses		(282,000)
Operating income		$ 797,716
Add: Other revenues and gains		15,000
Less: Other expenses and losses		(10,000)
Earnings before interest and taxes		$ 802,716
Less: Interest expense		(224)
Earnings before income taxes		$ 802,492
Less: Income taxes (40%)		(320,997)
Net income		**$ 481,495**
Basic earnings per share for 2nd quarter (5,000,000 common shares issued and outstanding)		**$0.096**

1) Revenue and cost assumptions can be changed and their effects on pro forma net income observed.

a) EXAMPLE: The company has projected gross margin to be 69% of sales ($1,079,716 ÷ $1,564,000). If gross margin is changed to 75% of sales ($1,564,000 × .75 = $1,173,000), the pro forma income statement will reflect a different bottom line.

Manufacturing Company
Pro Forma Statement of Income
2nd Quarter

Sales	$1,564,000
Cost of goods sold	(391,000)
Gross margin	$1,173,000
Less: Selling and administrative expenses	(282,000)
Operating income	$ 891,000
Add: Other revenues and gains	15,000
Less: Other expenses and losses	(10,000)
Earnings Before interest and taxes	$ 896,000
Less: Interest expense	(224)
Earnings before income taxes	$ 895,776
Less: Income taxes (40%)	(358,310)
Net income	**$ 537,466**
Basic earnings per share for 2nd quarter (5,000,000 common shares issued and outstanding)	**$0.107**

4. **Pro Forma Balance Sheet**
    a. The pro forma balance sheet is prepared using the cash and capital budgets and the pro forma income statement.
        1) The pro forma balance sheet is the beginning-of-the-period balance sheet updated for projected changes in cash, receivables, payables, inventory, etc.
        2) If the balance sheet indicates that a contractual agreement may be violated, the budgeting process must be repeated.
            a) For example, some loan agreements require that owners' equity be maintained at some percentage of total debt or that current assets be maintained at a given multiple of current liabilities.

5. **Pro Forma Statement of Cash Flows**
    a. The pro forma statement of cash flows is normally the last statement prepared.
    b. The pro forma statement of cash flows classifies cash receipts and disbursements depending on whether they are from operating, investing, or financing activities.
        1) The direct presentation reports the major classes of gross cash operating receipts and payments and the difference between them.
        2) The indirect presentation reconciles net income with net operating cash flow. Under GAAP, this reconciliation must be disclosed, regardless of which presentation is chosen.
            a) The reconciliation requires balance sheet data, such as the changes in accounts receivable, accounts payable, and inventory, as well as net income.
    c. All the pro forma statements are interrelated (articulated), e.g., the pro forma cash flow statement will include anticipated borrowing. The interest on this borrowing will appear in the pro forma income statement.

6. **Financial Projections and Ratio Analysis**
    a. Pro forma financial statements are of interest to parties outside the organization as well as inside.
        1) Banks and stock analysts in particular want to know what the firm believes its results will be.
    b. Projections help the bank assess whether the company anticipates satisfying the requirements of debt covenants.
        1) Typically, a firm's financing agreement with its bank requires that its debt ratio remain below a certain threshold and that its coverage ratios remain above a threshold.
            a) The debt ratio is the portion of the firm's capital structure that consists of debt, i.e., total liabilities divided by total assets.
            b) The most common coverage ratio is times interest earned, i.e., earnings before interest and taxes divided by interest expense.
        2) Projection of satisfactory levels of these ratios provide the bank some assurance that the firm will remain solvent for the foreseeable future.

c. Earnings per share (EPS) is probably the most heavily relied-upon performance measure used by investors.

1) EPS states the amount of current-period earnings that can be associated with a single share of a corporation's common stock.

   a) EPS is only calculated for common stock because common shareholders are the residual owners of a corporation.

2) Of the two versions of EPS required for external financial reporting (basic and diluted), only basic is needed on Part 1 of the CMA exam.

Basic Earnings per Share (EPS)

$$\frac{Net\ income\ -\ Preferred\ dividend}{Weighted\text{-}average\ number\ of\ common\ shares\ outstanding}$$

   a) The claims of preferred shareholders must be satisfied before those of the residual owners. Thus, amounts associated with preferred stock are not available to the common shareholders and must be removed from the numerator.

   b) The number of shares outstanding is weighted by the number of months the shares are outstanding.

COMPREHENSIVE EXAMPLE of Pro Forma Financial Statement Preparation
from CMA exam

Jefferson Binders, Inc., is a manufacturer of notebooks with a comprehensive annual budgeting process that ends with the preparation of pro forma financial statements. All underlying budget schedules have been completed for the year ending December 31, Year 2, and selected data from these schedules are presented below.

To facilitate the budgeting process, Jefferson accumulates all raw materials, direct labor, manufacturing overhead (with the exception of depreciation), selling, and administrative costs in an account called expenses payable. The company's income tax rate is 40%, and income tax expense is classified as current income taxes payable.

Unit Sales	Unit Price	Total Revenue
9,500,000	$5.50	$52,250,000

Production Units	Unit Cost	Total Manufacturing Cost
9,640,000	$4.75	$45,790,000

Raw Materials	Quantity	Cost	Total Purchases
Ring Assembly	9,600,000	$.80	$7,680,000
Cover (2 per unit)	18,800,000	$.30	$5,640,000

Production Hours	Direct Labor Cost per Hour	Total Direct Labor Cost
2,410,000	$9.00	$21,690,000

Variable overhead	$ 5,790,000
Supervisory salaries	1,250,000
Depreciation	724,000
Other fixed costs	2,840,000
Total manufacturing overhead	$10,604,000
Selling expense	$1,875,000
Administrative expense	3,080,000
Total S&A expense	$4,955,000

Additional information:
- The majority of sales are on account.
- Each finished binder requires 15 minutes of direct labor time.
- Manufacturing overhead will be applied at the rate of $4.40 per direct labor hour ($10,604,000 ÷ 2,410,000 hours).
- Each semi-annual mortgage payment consists of interest plus an even principal reduction of $100,000. Interest payments for Year 2 are $250,000.

-- Continued on next page --

COMPREHENSIVE EXAMPLE -- Continued

Jefferson has prepared the following pro forma statement of cash receipts and disbursements for the year ending December 31, Year 2, and pro forma statement of financial position as of December 31, Year 1. Jefferson uses the accrual basis of accounting.

Jefferson Binders, Inc.
Pro Forma Statement of Cash Receipts and Disbursements
For the Year Ending December 31, Year 2
($000 omitted)

Cash balance 1/1/Year 2 (estimated)	$ 565
Cash receipts:	
Cash sales	5,300
Collection of accounts receivable	46,600
Proceeds from sale of additional common stock (20,000 shares)	420
Total cash available	$52,885
Total cash available	
Cash disbursements:	
Raw materials	$13,380
Direct labor	21,640
Manufacturing overhead	9,650
Selling and administrative expense	4,980
Income taxes	860
Purchase of equipment	1,200
Cash dividends	320
Mortgage payment	450
Total disbursements	$52,480
Projected cash balance 12/31/Year 2	$ 405

Jefferson Binders, Inc.
Pro Forma Statement of Financial Position
as of December 31, Year 1
($000 omitted)

Assets

Cash	$ 565
Accounts receivable	825
Raw materials inventory*	301
Finished goods inventory**	608
Total current assets	$ 2,299
Land	$ 1,757
Property, plant, and equipment	12,400
Less: Accumulated depreciation	2,960
Total long-term assets	$11,197
Total assets	$13,496

Liabilities and Equity

Expenses payable	$ 690
Mortgage payable	200
Income taxes payable	356
Total current liabilities	$ 1,246
Long-term mortgage payable	$ 2,700
Total liabilities	$ 3,946
Common stock (500,000 shares authorized, 300,000 shares outstanding, $10 par value)	$ 3,000
Paid-in capital in excess of par	5,400
Retained earnings	1,150
Total equity	$ 9,550
Total liabilities and equity	$13,496

*65,000 ring assemblies at $.80 each
830,000 covers at $.30 each
**128,000 units at $4.75 each

Jefferson's pro forma statement of income for Year 2 is prepared as follows:

Jefferson Binders, Inc.
Pro Forma Statement of Income
For the Year Ending December 31, Year 2

Sales		$52,250,000
Cost of goods sold (9,500 units × $4.75)		(45,125,000)
Gross margin		$ 7,125,000
S&A expenses		(4,955,000)
Operating income		$ 2,170,000
Interest expense		(250,000)
Earnings before taxes		$ 1,920,000
Income tax expense (40%)		(768,000)
Net income		$ 1,152,000

For the pro forma statement of financial position for Year 2, current assets are calculated as follows:

Cash		$ 405,000
Accounts receivable		
Beginning balance		$ 825,000
Net increase for the year:		
Total sales	$52,250,000	
Less: Collections on credit sales	(46,600,000)	
Less: Cash sales	(5,300,000)	350,000
Ending balance		$ 1,175,000

-- Continued on next page --

COMPREHENSIVE EXAMPLE -- Continued

Raw materials inventory			
Beginning balance			$ 301,000
Purchases:			
Ring assemblies	$ 7,680,000		
Covers	5,640,000		13,320,000
Used in production:			
Ring assemblies (9,640 × $0.80)	$ 7,712,000		
Covers (9,640 × 2 × $0.30)	5,784,000		(13,496,000)
Ending balance			$ 125,000
Finished goods inventory			
Beginning balance			$ 608,000
Completed (9,640 units × $4.75)			45,790,000
Goods available for sale			$46,398,000
Cost of goods sold (9,500 units × $4.75)			(45,125,000)
Ending balance			$ 1,273,000

Noncurrent assets are calculated as follows:

	Property, Plant, and Equipment	Accumulated Depreciation
Beginning balances	$12,400,000	$ 2,960,000
Activity for year	1,200,000	724,000
Ending balances	$13,600,000	$ 3,684,000

Liabilities are calculated as follows:

Expenses payable			
Beginning balance			$ 690,000
Increases:			
Materials purchases		$13,320,000	
Direct labor		21,690,000	
Manufacturing overhead:			
Total for year	$10,604,000		
Less: Depreciation	(724,000)	9,880,000	
Selling and administrative		4,955,000	49,845,000
Decreases:			
Materials purchases		$13,380,000	
Direct labor		21,640,000	
Manufacturing overhead		9,650,000	
Selling and administrative		4,980,000	(49,650,000)
Ending balance			$ 885,000
Income taxes payable			
Beginning balance			$ 356,000
Add: Current period expense			768,000
Less: Disbursements			(860,000)
Ending balance			$ 264,000
Mortgage payable			
Beginning balance			$ 2,700,000
Less: Reclassified as current liability			(200,000)
Ending balance			$ 2,500,000

-- Continued on next page --

COMPREHENSIVE EXAMPLE -- Continued

Stockholders' equity is calculated as follows:

<u>Common stock</u>
Beginning balance	$ 3,000,000
Issuance of new shares (20,000 × $10 par value)	200,000
Ending balance	$ 3,200,000

<u>Paid-in capital in excess of par</u>
Beginning balance	$ 5,400,000
Issuance of new shares ($420,000 – $200,000)	220,000
Ending balance	$ 5,620,000

<u>Retained earnings</u>
Beginning balance	$ 1,150,000
Add: Net income	1,152,000
Less: Dividends	(320,000)
Ending balance	$ 1,982,000

Jefferson can now prepare its pro forma statement of financial position for Year 2:

Jefferson Binders, Inc.
Pro Forma Statement of Financial Position
As of December 31, Year 2

Current assets			**Liabilities**	
Cash		$ 405,000	Expenses payable	$ 885,000
Accounts receivable		1,175,000	Mortgage payable -- current	200,000
Raw materials inventory		125,000	Income taxes payable	264,000
Finished goods inventory		1,273,000	Mortgage payable -- noncurrent	2,500,000
Total current assets		$ 2,978,000	Total liabilities	$ 3,849,000
Noncurrent assets			**Stockholders' equity**	
Land		$ 1,757,000	Common stock	$ 3,200,000
Net prop., plant, and equipment:			Paid-in capital in excess of par	5,620,000
At historical cost	$13,600,000		Retained earnings	1,982,000
Less: Accum. deprec.	(3,684,000)	9,916,000	Total stockholders' equity	$10,802,000
Total noncurrent assets		$11,673,000		
			Total liabilities and	
Total assets		$14,651,000	stockholders' equity	$14,651,000

Jefferson can now prepare its pro forma statement of cash flows for Year 2 using the indirect method of presentation for cash flows from operating activities:

Jefferson Binders, Inc.
Pro Forma Statement of Cash Flows
For the Year Ending December 31, Year 2

Cash flows from operating activities:		
Net income		$1,152,000
Adjustments to reconcile net income:		
Depreciation expense	$724,000	
Decrease in raw materials inventory	176,000	
Increase in finished goods inventory	(665,000)	
Increase in accounts receivable	(350,000)	
Increase in expenses payable	195,000	
Decrease in income taxes payable	(92,000)	
Net cash used in operating activities		(12,000)
Cash flows from investing activities:		
Purchase of equipment		(1,200,000)
Cash flows from financing activities:		
Reduction in mortgage principal	$(200,000)	
Issuance of common stock -- par value	200,000	
Issuance of common stock -- addl. PIC	220,000	
Dividends distributed	(320,000)	
Net cash used in financing activities		(100,000)
Net decrease in cash		$ (160,000)
Beginning balance		565,000
Ending balance		$ 405,000

SU 9: Budgeting -- Concepts, Methodologies, and Preparation

7. **Graphical Depiction**

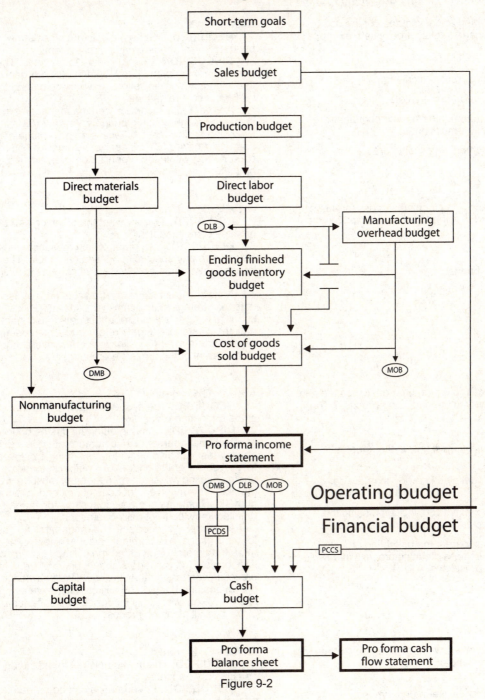

Figure 9-2

PCDS = projected cash disbursements schedule

PCCS = projected cash collection schedule

Stop and review! You have completed the outline for this subunit. Study multiple-choice questions 35 through 38 beginning on page 329.

QUESTIONS

9.1 Roles of Budgets and the Budgeting Process

1. All of the following are advantages of the use of budgets in a management control system **except** that budgets

- A. Force management planning.
- B. Provide performance criteria.
- C. Promote communication and coordination within the organization.
- D. Limit unauthorized expenditures.

Answer (D) is correct.
REQUIRED: The item that is not an advantage of the use of budgets in a management control system.
DISCUSSION: Budgets serve many roles. They force management to plan ahead, communicate organizational goals throughout the organization, and provide criteria for future performance evaluations.
Answer (A) is incorrect. Forcing management planning is an advantage of using budgets. Answer (B) is incorrect. Providing performance criteria is an advantage of using budgets. Answer (C) is incorrect. Promoting communication and coordination within the organization is an advantage of using budgets.

2. In the budgeting and planning process for a firm, which one of the following should be completed first?

- A. Sales budget.
- B. Financial budget.
- C. Cost management plan.
- D. Strategic plan.

Answer (D) is correct.
REQUIRED: The phase of the planning and budgeting process completed first.
DISCUSSION: An organization must complete its strategic plan before any specific budgeting can begin. The strategic plan lays out the means by which a firm expects to fulfill its stated mission.
Answer (A) is incorrect. The sales budget cannot be started until the strategic plan is finished. Answer (B) is incorrect. The financial budget is a cluster of budgets that cannot be started until the cluster of budgets referred to as the operating budget is finished. Answer (C) is incorrect. A cost management plan is independent of the firm's stated budget.

3. Which one of the following **best** describes the role of top management in the budgeting process? Top management

- A. Should be involved only in the approval process.
- B. Lacks the detailed knowledge of the daily operations and should limit their involvement.
- C. Needs to be involved, including using the budget process to communicate goals.
- D. Needs to separate the budgeting process and the business planning process into two separate processes.

Answer (C) is correct.
REQUIRED: The best description of top management's role in the budgeting process.
DISCUSSION: Among other things, the budget is a tool by which management can communicate goals to lower-level employees. It is also a tool for motivating employees to reach those goals. For the budget to function in these communication and motivating roles, top management must be involved in the process. This involvement does not extend to dictating the exact numerical contents of the budget since top management lacks a detailed knowledge of daily operations.
Answer (A) is incorrect. Top managers can use the budget for motivational and communication purposes; they should do more than merely sign off on the finished document. Answer (B) is incorrect. Top managers should be involved in the budget process even though they lack detailed knowledge of daily operations; the budget can still communicate company objectives and goals. Answer (D) is incorrect. The budget process is a part of the overall planning process.

4. Which one of the following is **not** an advantage of a participatory budgeting process?

- A. Coordination between departments.
- B. Communication between departments.
- C. Goal congruence.
- D. Control of uncertainties.

Answer (D) is correct.
REQUIRED: The item that is not an advantage of a participatory budgeting process.
DISCUSSION: Uncertainties can be prepared for, but they cannot be subjected to human control through any budget process.
Answer (A) is incorrect. Participatory budgeting involves extensive coordination between departments. Answer (B) is incorrect. Participatory budgeting involves extensive communication between departments. Answer (C) is incorrect. Goal congruence is one of the advantages of participatory budgeting.

SU 9: Budgeting -- Concepts, Methodologies, and Preparation

5. In developing the budget for the next year, which one of the following approaches would produce the greatest amount of positive motivation and goal congruence?

A. Permit the divisional manager to develop the goal for the division that in the manager's view will generate the greatest amount of profits.
B. Have senior management develop the overall goals and permit the divisional manager to determine how these goals will be met.
C. Have the divisional and senior management jointly develop goals and objectives while constructing the corporation's overall plan of operation.
D. Have the divisional and senior management jointly develop goals and the divisional manager develop the implementation plan.

Answer (D) is correct.
REQUIRED: The item that would produce the greatest amount of positive motivation and goal congruence.
DISCUSSION: Joint development of goals is more conducive to motivation, as is allowing divisional managers to develop the implementation plan. Goal congruence is enhanced when senior management is involved in the budgeting process along with division managers.
Answer (A) is incorrect. Using division managers to develop their goals does nothing for goal congruence. Answer (B) is incorrect. Having senior management set goals would not be as conducive to motivation as would having input from divisions. Answer (C) is incorrect. Senior management may not be in a position to develop an implementation plan.

6. Which one of the following statements concerning approaches for the budget development process is **correct**?

A. The top-down approach to budgeting will ensure adherence to strategic organizational goals.
B. To prevent ambiguity, once departmental budgeted goals have been developed, they should remain fixed even if the sales forecast upon which they are based proves to be wrong in the middle of the fiscal year.
C. With the information technology available, the role of budgets as an organizational communication device has declined.
D. Since department managers have the most detailed knowledge about organizational operations, they should use this information as the building blocks of the operating budget.

Answer (D) is correct.
REQUIRED: The correct statement concerning the budget development process.
DISCUSSION: Since department managers have the most detailed knowledge about organizational operations, they should use this information as the building blocks of the operating budget.
Answer (A) is incorrect. In the top-down approach, the budget is developed by upper management. Upper management can therefore develop the budget with the strategic organizational goals in mind. Answer (B) is incorrect. Any budget should be adapted to changing circumstances. Answer (C) is incorrect. Information technology makes budgeting easier, not less relevant as a means of organizational communication.

9.2 Budgeting and Standard Costs

7. A corporation is developing standards for the next year. Currently, one of the material components is being purchased for $36.45 per unit. It is expected that the component's cost will increase by approximately 10% next year and that the price could range from $38.75 to $44.18 per unit, depending on the quantity purchased. The appropriate standard for the material component for next year should be set at the

A. Current actual cost plus the forecasted 10% price increase.
B. Lowest purchase price in the anticipated range to keep pressure on purchasing to always buy in the lowest price range.
C. Highest price in the anticipated range to ensure that there are only favorable purchase price variances.
D. Price agreed upon by the purchasing manager and the appropriate level of company management.

Answer (D) is correct.
REQUIRED: The appropriate standard for the material component for next year.
DISCUSSION: Standard prices are designed for internal performance measurement. Standards should be attainable, but not so easily as to not provide motivation. Management should decide its objectives and set a standard that will achieve that objective when the standard is met. For example, the lowest price might not be selected if the company is using a JIT system, for which the primary objective is the minimization of inventories.
Answer (A) is incorrect. The actual cost could be more or less depending in the quantity purchased. Answer (B) is incorrect. The lowest price may not always be in the company's best interests if the quantity required to obtain the lowest price would lead to much higher carrying costs. Answer (C) is incorrect. Standards should be set tightly enough to provide motivation to purchasing management.

8. After performing a thorough study of a firm's operations, an independent consultant determined that the firm's labor standards were probably too tight. Which one of the following facts would be inconsistent with the consultant's conclusion?

A. A review of performance reports revealed the presence of many unfavorable efficiency variances.
B. The firm's budgeting process was well-defined and based on a bottom-up philosophy.
C. Management noted that minimal incentive bonuses have been paid in recent periods.
D. Production supervisors found several significant fluctuations in manufacturing volume, with short-term increases on output being followed by rapid, sustained declines.

Answer (B) is correct.
REQUIRED: The fact inconsistent with the conclusion that the firm's labor standards were probably too tight.
DISCUSSION: It is highly unlikely that workers familiar with their own processes would set too-tight standards.
Answer (A) is incorrect. Many unfavorable efficiency variances would be an indicator of too-tight standards. Answer (C) is incorrect. The widespread failure for expected bonuses to be earned would be an indicator of too-tight standards. Answer (D) is incorrect. The situation described is indicative of rush jobs being too common, which is a result of poor production planning, not tight labor standards.

9. A manufacturer's factory manager had lost her patience. Six months ago, she appointed a team from the production and service departments to finalize the allocation of costs and setting of standard costs. They were still feuding, so she hired a large consulting firm to resolve the matter.

All of the following are potential consequences of having the standards set by the consulting firm **except** that

A. The consulting firm may not fully understand the manufacturer's manufacturing process, resulting in suboptimal performance.
B. Employees could react negatively since they did not participate in setting the standards.
C. There could be dissatisfaction if the standards contain costs that are not controllable by the unit held responsible.
D. The standards may appear to lack management support.

Answer (D) is correct.
REQUIRED: What is not a potential consequence of having standards set by a consulting firm.
DISCUSSION: Of the choices listed, this one is not a potential consequence of having an outside consultant set standards. Since management did the hiring, the consultant's work product would naturally appear to have management support.
Answer (A) is incorrect. The consulting firm may not fully understand the manufacturer's manufacturing process, resulting in suboptimal performance. Answer (B) is incorrect. Employees could react negatively since they did not participate in setting the standards. Answer (C) is incorrect. There could be dissatisfaction if the standards contain costs that are not controllable by the unit held responsible.

9.3 The Master Budget

10. While an operating budget is a key element in planning and control, it is **not** likely to

A. Establish a commitment of company resources.
B. Set out long-range, strategic concepts.
C. Integrate organizational activities.
D. Provide subsidiary planning information.

Answer (B) is correct.
REQUIRED: What a budget is not likely to do.
DISCUSSION: Operating budgets seldom set out long-range strategic concepts because they usually deal with the quantitative allocation of people and resources. Strategic concepts are overall goals for the organization and are almost always stated in words.
Answer (A) is incorrect. Budgets do commit company resources in that the allotment of scarce resources is the primary purpose of a budget. Answer (C) is incorrect. Budgets do integrate organizational activities. Failure of a budget to integrate activities will result in the budgeting of more or less materials and resources than are available to the organization. Answer (D) is incorrect. Subsidiary plans can be made directly from overall budgets.

11. In preparing a corporate master budget, which one of the following is **most** likely to be prepared last?

A. Sales budget.
B. Cash budget.
C. Production budget.
D. Cost of goods sold budget.

Answer (B) is correct.
REQUIRED: The last step in the typical corporate master budget.
DISCUSSION: The cash budget is the lynchpin of the financial budget. It combines the results of the operating budget with the cash collection and disbursement schedules to produce a comprehensive picture of where the company's cash flows are expected to come from and where they are expected to go. All the other budgets listed feed the cash budget in one way or another.
Answer (A) is incorrect. The sales budget precedes the cash budget. Answer (C) is incorrect. The production budget is the second step in the master budget, immediately following the sales budget. Answer (D) is incorrect. The cost of goods sold budget is completed well before the cash budget in the budgeting process.

12. A company uses a comprehensive planning and budgeting system. The proper order for the company to prepare certain budget schedules would be

A. Cost of goods sold, balance sheet, income statement, and statement of cash flows.
B. Income statement, balance sheet, statement of cash flows, and cost of goods sold.
C. Statement of cash flows, cost of goods sold, income statement, and balance sheet.
D. Cost of goods sold, income statement, balance sheet, and statement of cash flows.

Answer (D) is correct.
REQUIRED: The proper order in which budget schedules should be prepared.
DISCUSSION: The pro forma cost of goods sold must be prepared before the pro forma income statement because it is a component of the income statement. Also, the income statement must be prepared before the pro forma balance sheet because net income is a necessary part of preparing the stockholders' equity section of the balance sheet. In turn, the income statement and the balance sheet are necessary for estimating cash flows. If the statement of cash flows is prepared using the indirect method, balance sheet data, e.g., the changes in accounts receivable, inventory, and accounts payable, must be available to determine the adjustments needed to reconcile net income to net cash flow.
Answer (A) is incorrect. The balance sheet should not precede the income statement. Answer (B) is incorrect. The income statement cannot precede cost of goods sold. Answer (C) is incorrect. The statement of cash flows cannot precede the cost of goods sold. The latter is an input of the former.

13. The foundation of a profit plan is the

A. Capital budget.
B. Sales forecast.
C. Cost and expense budget.
D. Production plan.

Answer (B) is correct.
REQUIRED: The basis for a profit plan (budget).
DISCUSSION: The starting point for the annual budget is the sales forecast. All other aspects of the budget, including production, costs, and inventory levels, rely on projected sales figures.
Answer (A) is incorrect. A capital budget is only concerned with capital expenditures and cannot be prepared until it is known whether new equipment or facilities will be needed to service the expected sales for the upcoming period. Answer (C) is incorrect. This aspect of the budget cannot be prepared until sales have been estimated. Answer (D) is incorrect. Sales must be estimated before a production plan can be prepared.

14. Which one of the following schedules would be the last item to be prepared in the normal budget preparation process?

A. Direct labor budget.
B. Cash budget.
C. Cost of goods sold budget.
D. Manufacturing overhead budget.

Answer (B) is correct.
REQUIRED: The last item prepared in the normal budget preparation process.
DISCUSSION: The budget process begins with the sales budget, proceeds to the production and expense budgets, and eventually the cash budget. The cash budget cannot be prepared until the end of the process because all other budgets provide inputs to the cash budget.
Answer (A) is incorrect. A direct labor budget must be prepared before the cash budget. Answer (C) is incorrect. A cost of goods sold budget must be prepared before the cash budget. Answer (D) is incorrect. A manufacturing overhead budget must be prepared before the cash budget.

9.4 Budget Methodologies

15. Which one of the following is **not** an advantage of activity-based budgeting?

A. Better identification of resource needs.
B. Linking of costs to outputs.
C. Identification of budgetary slack.
D. Reduction of planning uncertainty.

Answer (D) is correct.
REQUIRED: The factor not an advantage of activity-based budgeting.
DISCUSSION: Although activity-based budgeting provides greater detail than other budgeting methods, it does not necessarily reduce planning uncertainty.
Answer (A) is incorrect. Because activity-based budgeting employs multiple cost pools, it better identifies resource needs compared to other budgeting methods. Answer (B) is incorrect. Because activity-based budgeting employs multiple cost pools and assigns a specific cost driver to each pool, it has the advantage of linking costs to outputs with greater detail compared to other budgeting methods. Answer (C) is incorrect. Because activity-based budgeting employs multiple cost pools and assigns a specific cost driver to each pool, it can more precisely estimate costs, and therefore increase the identification of budgetary slack.

16. An advantage of incremental budgeting when compared with zero-based budgeting is that incremental budgeting

A. Encourages adopting new projects quickly.
B. Accepts the existing base as being satisfactory.
C. Eliminates functions and duties that have outlived their usefulness.
D. Eliminates the need to review all functions periodically to obtain optimum use of resources.

Answer (B) is correct.
REQUIRED: The advantage of incremental budgeting compared with zero-based budgeting (ZBB).
DISCUSSION: Incremental budgeting simply adjusts the current year's budget to allow for changes planned for the coming year; a manager is not asked to justify the base portion of the budget. ZBB, however, requires a manager to justify the entire budget for each year. Incremental budgeting offers to managers the advantage of requiring less managerial effort to justify changes in the budget.
Answer (A) is incorrect. Both types of budgets treat new projects in the same manner. Answer (C) is incorrect. Reexamining functions and duties that may have outlived their usefulness is an advantage of ZBB. Answer (D) is incorrect. Periodic review of functions is essential regardless of the budgetary system used.

17. The type of budget that is available on a continuous basis for a specified future period -- by adding a month, quarter, or year in the future as the month, quarter, or year just ended is dropped -- is called a(n)

A. Rolling budget.
B. Kaizen budget.
C. Activity-based budget.
D. Flexible budget.

Answer (A) is correct.
REQUIRED: The budget type that involves continually adding new periods and dropping old ones.
DISCUSSION: A continuous (rolling) budget is one that is revised on a regular (continuous) basis. Typically, a company continuously extends such a budget for an additional month or quarter in accordance with new data as the current month or quarter ends. For example, if the budget cycle is 1 year, a budget for the next 12 months will be available continuously as each month ends. The principal advantage of a rolling budget is that it requires managers always to be thinking ahead.
Answer (B) is incorrect. A kaizen budget is one that assumes the continuous improvement of products and processes. Answer (C) is incorrect. An activity-based budget is one that applies activity-based costing principles to budgeting. Answer (D) is incorrect. A flexible budget consists of a series of budgets prepared for many levels of activity.

18. The use of the master budget throughout the year as a constant comparison with actual results signifies that the master budget is also a

A. Flexible budget.
B. Capital budget.
C. Zero-base budget.
D. Static budget.

Answer (D) is correct.
REQUIRED: The type of budget that is used throughout the year for comparison with actual results.
DISCUSSION: If an unchanged master budget is used continuously throughout the year for comparison with actual results, it must be a static budget, that is, one prepared for just one level of activity.
Answer (A) is incorrect. A flexible budget can be used in conjunction with standard costs to provide budgets for different activity levels. Answer (B) is incorrect. A capital budget concerns only long-term investments. Answer (C) is incorrect. A zero-base budget is one that requires its preparer to fully justify every item in the budget for each period.

SU 9: Budgeting -- Concepts, Methodologies, and Preparation

19. Which one of the following budgeting methodologies would be **most** appropriate for a firm facing a significant level of uncertainty in unit sales volumes for next year?

A. Top-down budgeting.
B. Life-cycle budgeting.
C. Static budgeting.
D. Flexible budgeting.

Answer (D) is correct.
REQUIRED: The budgeting methodology most appropriate for a firm facing significant uncertainty about unit sales volumes.
DISCUSSION: With flexible budgeting, the firm prepares a series of budgets for many levels of sales and production. At the end of the period, management can compare actual sales performance with the appropriate budgeted level in the flexible budget.
Answer (A) is incorrect. Top-down budgeting entails imposition of a budget by top management on lower-level employees. It is the antithesis of participatory budgeting. Answer (B) is incorrect. Life-cycle budgeting estimates a product's revenues and costs for each link in the value chain from R&D and design to production, marketing, distribution, and customer service. The product life cycle ends when customer service is withdrawn. Answer (C) is incorrect. A static budget is for only one level of activity.

9.5 Operating Budget Calculations -- Production and Direct Materials

Questions 20 and 21 are based on the following information.

Daffy Tunes manufactures a toy rabbit with moving parts and a built-in voice box. Projected sales in units for the next 5 months are as follows:

Month	Projected Sales in Units
January	30,000
February	36,000
March	33,000
April	40,000
May	29,000

Each rabbit requires basic materials that Daffy purchases from a single supplier at $3.50 per rabbit. Voice boxes are purchased from another supplier at $1.00 each. Assembly labor cost is $2.00 per rabbit, and variable overhead cost is $.50 per rabbit. Fixed manufacturing overhead applicable to rabbit production is $12,000 per month. Daffy's policy is to manufacture 1.5 times the coming month's projected sales every other month, starting with January (i.e., odd-numbered months) for February sales, and to manufacture 0.5 times the coming month's projected sales in alternate months (i.e., even-numbered months). This allows Daffy to allocate limited manufacturing resources to other products as needed during the even-numbered months.

20. Daffy Tunes' unit production budget for toy rabbits for January is

A. 45,000 units.
B. 16,500 units.
C. 54,000 units.
D. 14,500 units.

Answer (C) is correct.
REQUIRED: The unit production budget for January.
DISCUSSION: The production budget for January is 54,000 units (36,000 projected February sales × 1.5).
Answer (A) is incorrect. The figure of 45,000 is based on January sales. Answer (B) is incorrect. Budgeted production for February is 16,500 units. Answer (D) is incorrect. Budgeted production for April is 14,500 units.

21. Daffy Tunes' dollar production budget for toy rabbits for February is

A. $327,000
B. $390,000
C. $113,500
D. $127,500

Answer (D) is correct.
REQUIRED: The dollar production budget for February.
DISCUSSION: The units to be produced in February equal 50% of March sales, or 16,500 units (33,000 × .5). The unit variable cost is $7.00 ($3.50 + $1.00 + $2.00 + $.50), so total variable costs are $115,500 (16,500 × $7). Thus, the dollar production budget for February is $127,500 ($115,500 variable + $12,000 fixed).
Answer (A) is incorrect. The amount of $327,000 is based on January sales. Answer (B) is incorrect. The production budget for January is $390,000. Answer (C) is incorrect. The production budget for April is $113,500.

Questions 22 and 23 are based on the following information.

Rokat Corporation is a manufacturer of tables sold to schools, restaurants, hotels, and other institutions. The table tops are manufactured by Rokat, but the table legs are purchased from an outside supplier. The Assembly Department takes a manufactured table top and attaches the four purchased table legs. It takes 20 minutes of labor to assemble a table. The company follows a policy of producing enough tables to ensure that 40% of next month's sales are in the finished goods inventory. Rokat also purchases sufficient direct materials inventory to ensure that direct materials inventory is 60% of the following month's scheduled production.

Rokat's sales budget in units for the next quarter is as follows:

July	2,300
August	2,500
September	2,100

Rokat's ending inventories in units for June 30 are

Finished goods	1,900
Direct materials (legs)	4,000

22. The number of tables to be produced by Rokat during August is

A. 1,400 tables.
B. 2,340 tables.
C. 1,440 tables.
D. 1,900 tables.

Answer (B) is correct.
REQUIRED: The number of tables to be produced.
DISCUSSION: The company will need 2,500 finished units for August sales. In addition, 840 units (2,100 September unit sales × 40%) should be in inventory at the end of August. August sales plus the desired ending inventory equals 3,340 units. Of these units, 40% of August's sales, or 1,000 units, should be available from beginning inventory. Consequently, production in August should be 2,340 units.
Answer (A) is incorrect. The number of tables to be produced in July is 1,400. Answer (C) is incorrect. The figure of 1,440 tables is based on July's beginning inventory. Answer (D) is incorrect. July's beginning inventory equals 1,900 tables.

23. Assume Rokat's required production for August and September is 1,600 and 1,800 units, respectively, and the July 31 direct materials inventory is 4,200 units. The number of table legs to be purchased in August is

A. 6,520 legs.
B. 9,400 legs.
C. 2,200 legs.
D. 6,400 legs.

Answer (A) is correct.
REQUIRED: The number of table legs to be purchased.
DISCUSSION: Some of the legs needed for August's production are already included in the 4,200 units in direct materials. Legs needed for August are 6,400 (1,600 × 4), but there are already 4,200 legs in the July 31 direct materials inventory. Therefore, 2,200 legs should be purchased for August production. Rokat needs 4,320 legs (1,800 × 4 × 60%) for September production. Thus, the total amount of legs to be purchased is 6,520 (2,200 + 4,320).
Answer (B) is incorrect. The figure of 9,400 legs is based on an ending inventory of 100% of September's production. Answer (C) is incorrect. Failing to consider the legs needed for the ending inventory results in 2,200 legs. Answer (D) is incorrect. The amount needed for August production is 6,400 legs.

9.6 Operating Budget Calculations -- Others

24. Which one of the following statements regarding selling and administrative budgets is **most** accurate?

A. Selling and administrative budgets are usually optional.
B. Selling and administrative budgets are fixed in nature.
C. Selling and administrative budgets are difficult to allocate by month and are best presented as one number for the entire year.
D. Selling and administrative budgets need to be detailed in order that the key assumptions can be better understood.

Answer (D) is correct.
REQUIRED: The most accurate statement about selling and administrative budgets.
DISCUSSION: Sales and administrative budgets are prepared after the sales budget. Like the other budgets, they constitute prospective information based on the preparer's assumptions about conditions expected to exist and actions expected to be taken.
Answer (A) is incorrect. Selling and administrative budgets are no more optional than any other component of the master budget. Answer (B) is incorrect. Selling and administrative budgets have both variable and fixed components. Answer (C) is incorrect. Selling and administrative budgets should be prepared on the same basis as the remainder of the budget, typically on at least a monthly basis.

SU 9: Budgeting -- Concepts, Methodologies, and Preparation

Question 25 is based on the following information.

Rokat Corporation is a manufacturer of tables sold to schools, restaurants, hotels, and other institutions. The table tops are manufactured by Rokat, but the table legs are purchased from an outside supplier. The Assembly Department takes a manufactured table top and attaches the four purchased table legs. It takes 20 minutes of labor to assemble a table. The company follows a policy of producing enough tables to ensure that 40% of next month's sales are in the finished goods inventory. Rokat also purchases sufficient direct materials inventory to ensure that direct materials inventory is 60% of the following month's scheduled production.

Rokat's sales budget in units for the next quarter is as follows:

July	2,300
August	2,500
September	2,100

Rokat's ending inventories in units for June 30 are

Finished goods	1,900
Direct materials (legs)	4,000

---

25. Assume that Rokat Corporation will produce 1,800 units in the month of September. How many employees will be required for the Assembly Department? (Fractional employees are acceptable since employees can be hired on a part-time basis. Assume a 40-hour week and a 4-week month.)

A. 15 employees.
B. 3.75 employees.
C. 60 employees.
D. 600 employees.

Answer (B) is correct.
REQUIRED: The number of employees required.
DISCUSSION: Each unit requires 20 minutes of assembly time, or 1/3 of an hour. The assembly of 1,800 units will therefore require 600 hours of labor (1,800 × 1/3). At 40 hours per week for 4 weeks, each employee will work 160 hours during the month. Thus, 3.75 employees (600 ÷ 160) are needed.
Answer (A) is incorrect. This number of employees assumes production occurs in a single 40-hour week. Answer (C) is incorrect. This number of employees assumes that each leg requires 20 minutes to assemble and that production occurs in a single 40-hour week. Answer (D) is incorrect. This number of employees is the number of hours needed, not the number of employees.

Question 26 is based on the following information.

Jordan Auto has developed the following production plan:

Month	Units
January	10,000
February	8,000
March	9,000
April	12,000

Each unit contains 3 pounds of direct materials. The desired direct materials ending inventory each month is 120% of the next month's production, plus 500 pounds. (The beginning inventory meets this requirement.) Jordan has developed the following direct labor standards for production of these units:

	Department 1	Department 2
Hours per unit	2.0	0.5
Hourly rate	$7.25	$12.00

---

26. Jordan Auto's total budgeted direct labor dollars for February usage should be

A. $164,000
B. $174,250
C. $184,500
D. $221,400

Answer (A) is correct.
REQUIRED: The total budgeted direct labor dollars for February.
DISCUSSION: The standard unit labor cost is $20.50 [($7.25 × 2 hours in Department 1) + ($12 × .5 hour in Department 2)], so the total budgeted direct labor dollars for February equal $164,000 (8,000 units × $20.50).
Answer (B) is incorrect. The amount of $174,250 is for 500 more units than budgeted usage. Answer (C) is incorrect. The amount for March is $184,500. Answer (D) is incorrect. The amount of $221,400 is for 120% of budgeted March production.

27. For the month of December, a bottling company expects to sell 12,500 cases of water at $24.80 per case and 33,100 cases of cola at $32.00 per case. Sales personnel receive 6% commission on each case of water and 8% commission on each case of cola. In order to receive a commission on a product, the sales personnel team must meet the individual product revenue quota. The sales quota for water is $500,000, and the sales quota for cola is $1,000,000. The sales commission that should be budgeted for December is

- A. $4,736
- B. $82,152
- C. $84,736
- D. $103,336

Answer (C) is correct.
REQUIRED: The budgeted sales commissions for the month.
DISCUSSION: The sale of 12,500 cases of water at $24.80 per case produces revenue of $310,000, an amount that does not qualify for commissions. The sale of 33,100 cases of cola at $32 per case produces revenue of $1,059,200. This amount is greater than the minimum and therefore qualifies for a commission of $84,736 ($1,059,200 × 8%). This calculation assumes that commissions are paid on all sales if the revenue quota is met.
Answer (A) is incorrect. The commission on $59,200 of cola sales is $4,736. Answer (B) is incorrect. The amount of $82,152 equals 6% of all sales. Answer (D) is incorrect. The amount of $103,336 assumes that a commission of $18,600 is paid on water.

9.7 Projecting Cash Collections

28. Which one of the following is the **best** characteristic concerning the capital budget? The capital budget is a(n)

- A. Plan to ensure that there are sufficient funds available for the operating needs of the company.
- B. Exercise that sets the long-range goals of the company including the consideration of external influences caused by others in the market.
- C. Plan that results in the cash requirements during the operating cycle.
- D. Plan that assesses the long-term needs of the company for plant and equipment purchases.

Answer (D) is correct.
REQUIRED: The true statement about the capital budget.
DISCUSSION: Capital budgeting is the process of planning expenditures for long-lived assets. It involves choosing among investment proposals using a ranking procedure. Evaluations are based on various measures involving the rate of ROI.
Answer (A) is incorrect. Capital budgeting involves long-term investment needs, not immediate operating needs. Answer (B) is incorrect. Establishing long-term goals in the context of relevant factors in the firm's environment is strategic planning. Answer (C) is incorrect. Cash budgeting determines operating cash flows. Capital budgeting evaluates the rate of return on specific investment alternatives.

29. Which one of the following items would have to be included for a company preparing a schedule of cash receipts and disbursements for calendar Year 1?

- A. A purchase order issued in December Year 1 for items to be delivered in February Year 2.
- B. Dividends declared in November Year 1 to be paid in January Year 2 to shareholders of record as of December Year 1.
- C. The amount of uncollectible customer accounts for Year 1.
- D. The borrowing of funds from a bank on a note payable taken out in June Year 1 with an agreement to pay the principal and interest in June Year 2.

Answer (D) is correct.
REQUIRED: The item included in a cash budget for Year 1.
DISCUSSION: A schedule of cash receipts and disbursements (cash budget) should include all cash inflows and outflows during the period without regard to the accrual accounting treatment of the transactions. Hence, it should include all checks written and all sources of cash, including borrowings. A borrowing from a bank in June Year 1 should appear as a cash receipt for Year 1.
Answer (A) is incorrect. The cash disbursement presumably will not occur until Year 2. Answer (B) is incorrect. The cash flow will not occur until dividends are paid in Year 2. Answer (C) is incorrect. Bad debt expense is a noncash item.

30. A company has developed the following sales projections for the calendar year.

May	$100,000
June	120,000
July	140,000
August	160,000
September	150,000
October	130,000

Normal cash collection experience has been that 50% of sales are collected during the month of sale and 45% in the month following sale. The remaining 5% of sales is never collected. The company's budgeted cash collections for the third calendar quarter are

A. $427,500
B. $422,500
C. $414,000
D. $450,000

Answer (C) is correct.
REQUIRED: The budgeted cash collections for the third quarter.
DISCUSSION: If 50% of sales are collected in the month of sale and 45% in the next month, with the balance uncollectible, collections during the third quarter will be based on sales during June, July, August, and September. As calculated below, total budgeted collections are $414,000.

June:	$120,000 × 45%	=	$ 54,000
July:	140,000 × (50% + 45%)	=	133,000
August:	160,000 × (50% + 45%)	=	152,000
September:	150,000 × 50%	=	75,000
Total			$414,000

Answer (A) is incorrect. The total cash expected to be collected from third calendar quarter sales is $427,500. Answer (B) is incorrect. The budgeted cash collections for August through October, not the third calendar quarter, is $422,500. Answer (D) is incorrect. The total budgeted sales for the third calendar quarter is $450,000.

31. The cash receipts budget includes

A. Funded depreciation.
B. Operating supplies.
C. Extinguishment of debt.
D. Loan proceeds.

Answer (D) is correct.
REQUIRED: The item included in a cash receipts budget.
DISCUSSION: A cash budget may be prepared monthly or even weekly to facilitate cash planning and control. The purpose is to anticipate cash needs while minimizing the amount of idle cash. The cash receipts section of the budget includes all sources of cash. One such source is the proceeds of loans.
Answer (A) is incorrect. Funded depreciation involves cash outlays. Answer (B) is incorrect. Purchases of supplies involves cash outlays. Answer (C) is incorrect. The extinguishment of debt involves cash outlays.

32. A corporation anticipates the following sales during the last 6 months of the year:

July	$460,000
August	500,000
September	525,000
October	500,000
November	480,000
December	450,000

20% of the corporation's sales are for cash. The balance is subject to the collection pattern shown below.

Percentage of balance collected in the month of sale	40%
Percentage of balance collected in the month following sale	30%
Percentage of balance collected in the second month following sale	25%
Percentage of balance uncollectible	5%

What is the planned net accounts receivable balance as of December 31?

A. $279,300
B. $294,000
C. $360,000
D. $367,500

Answer (B) is correct.
REQUIRED: The ending balance in receivables given cash collection information.
DISCUSSION: December 31 receivables will consist of portions of credit sales from November ($480,000 × 80% = $384,000) and December ($450,000 × 80% = $360,000). The collections on these sales can be calculated as follows:

	Credit Sales	Collections			
		November	December	January	February
November	$384,000	$153,600	$115,200	$ 96,000	
December	360,000		144,000	108,000	$90,000
				$204,000	$90,000

The corporation's December 31 balance in accounts receivable is therefore $294,000 ($204,000 + $90,000).
Answer (A) is incorrect. The amount of $279,300 results from subtracting the bad debts from the net receivables. Answer (C) is incorrect. The amount of $360,000 results from including an extra month in receivables that has already been collected. Answer (D) is incorrect. The amount of $367,500 is based on total sales rather than credit sales.

9.8 The Cash Budget

Questions 33 and 34 are based on the following information.

Karmee Company has been accumulating operating data in order to prepare an annual profit plan. Details regarding Karmee's sales for the first 6 months of the coming year are as follows:

Estimated Monthly Sales		Type of Monthly Sale	
January	$600,000	Cash sales	20%
February	650,000	Credit sales	80%
March	700,000		
April	625,000		
May	720,000		
June	800,000		

Collection Pattern for Credit Sales	
Month of sale	30%
One month following sale	40%
Second month following sale	25%

Karmee's cost of goods sold averages 40% of the sales value. Karmee's objective is to maintain a target inventory equal to 30% of the next month's sales in units. Purchases of merchandise for resale are paid for in the month following the sale.

The variable operating expenses (other than cost of goods sold) for Karmee are 10% of sales and are paid for in the month following the sale. The annual fixed operating expenses are presented below. All of these are incurred uniformly throughout the year and paid monthly except for insurance and property taxes. Insurance is paid quarterly in January, April, July, and October. Property taxes are paid twice a year in April and October.

Annual Fixed Operating Costs	
Advertising	$ 720,000
Depreciation	420,000
Insurance	180,000
Property taxes	240,000
Salaries	1,080,000

---

33. The purchase of merchandise that Karmee Company will need to make during February will be

A. $254,000
B. $260,000
C. $266,000
D. $338,000

Answer (C) is correct.
REQUIRED: The purchase of merchandise for February.
DISCUSSION: Purchases equal cost of goods sold, plus ending inventory, minus beginning inventory. Estimated cost of goods sold for February equals $260,000 ($650,000 sales × 40%). Ending inventory is given as 30% of sales in units. Stated at cost, this amount equals $84,000 ($700,000 March sales × 30% × 40%). Furthermore, beginning inventory is $78,000 ($260,000 COGS for February × 30%). Thus, purchases equal $266,000 ($260,000 + $84,000 − $78,000).
Answer (A) is incorrect. The amount of $254,000 reverses the treatment of the change in inventory. Answer (B) is incorrect. February COGS is $260,000. Answer (D) is incorrect. The sum of COGS and beginning inventory equals $338,000.

34. The total cash disbursements that Karmee Company will make for the operating expenses (expenses other than the cost of goods sold) during the month of April will be

A. $255,000
B. $290,000
C. $385,000
D. $420,000

Answer (C) is correct.
REQUIRED: The total cash disbursements for operating expenses during April.
DISCUSSION: Cash disbursements for variable operating expenses in April (excluding cost of goods sold) equal $70,000 ($700,000 March sales × 10%). Cash disbursements for fixed operating expenses (excluding depreciation, a noncash expense) include advertising ($720,000 ÷ 12 = $60,000), salaries ($1,080,000 ÷ 12 = $90,000), insurance ($180,000 ÷ 4 = $45,000), and property taxes ($240,000 ÷ 2 = $120,000). Hence, cash payments for April operating expenses are $385,000 ($70,000 + $60,000 + $90,000 + $45,000 + $120,000).
Answer (A) is incorrect. The amount of $255,000 excludes variable selling expenses and advertising. Answer (B) is incorrect. The amount of $290,000 includes depreciation but excludes variable selling expenses and advertising. Answer (D) is incorrect. The amount of $420,000 includes depreciation.

9.9 Sales Forecasts and Pro Forma Financial Statements

Questions 35 and 36 are based on the following information. Super Drive, a computer disk storage and back-up company, uses accrual accounting. The company's Statement of Financial Position for the year ended November 30 is as follows:

Super Drive
Statement of Financial Position
as of November 30

Assets		Liabilities and Stockholders' Equity	
Cash	$ 52,000	Accounts payable	$ 175,000
Accounts receivable, net	150,000	Common stock	900,000
Inventory	315,000	Retained earnings	442,000
Property, plant, and equipment	1,000,000	Total liabilities and stockholders' equity	$1,517,000
Total assets	$1,517,000		

Additional information regarding Super Drive's operations include the following:

- Sales are budgeted at $520,000 for December and $500,000 for January of the next year.
- Collections are expected to be 60% in the month of sale and 40% in the month following the sale.
- Eighty percent of the disk drive components are purchased in the month prior to the month of sale, and 20% are purchased in the month of sale. Purchased components are 40% of the cost of goods sold.
- Payment for the components is made in the month following the purchase.
- Cost of goods sold is 80% of sales.

35. Super Drive's projected balance in accounts payable on December 31 is

A. $161,280
B. $326,400
C. $166,400
D. $416,000

Answer (A) is correct.
REQUIRED: The projected balance in accounts payable on December 31.
DISCUSSION: Payments are made in the month following purchase. The balance in accounts payable on November 30 is $175,000; this amount will be paid in December. The account is credited for purchases of a portion of components to be used for sales in December (20% of December components) and for sales in January (80% of January components). Cost of goods sold is 80% of sales, and components are 40% of cost of goods sold. Thus, December component needs are $166,400 ($520,000 sales × 80% × 40%), and January component needs are $160,000 ($500,000 sales × 80% × 40%). The December purchases of December component needs equal $33,280 ($166,400 × 20%). December purchases of January component needs are $128,000 ($160,000 × 80%). Hence, the total of December purchases (ending balance in accounts payable) equals $161,280 ($33,280 + $128,000).
Answer (B) is incorrect. The sum of the component needs for December and January equals $326,400. Answer (C) is incorrect. December component needs equals $166,400. Answer (D) is incorrect. Cost of sales for December equals $416,000.

36. Super Drive's projected gross profit for the month ending December 31 is

A. $416,000
B. $104,000
C. $134,000
D. $536,000

Answer (B) is correct.
REQUIRED: The projected gross profit for December.
DISCUSSION: Given that cost of goods sold is 80% of sales, gross profit is 20% of sales. Consequently, pro forma gross profit is $104,000 ($520,000 × 20%).
Answer (A) is incorrect. Cost of goods sold is $416,000 (80% of sales). Answer (C) is incorrect. The amount of $134,000 equals 20% of the sum of November receivables and December sales. Answer (D) is incorrect. Gross profit cannot be greater than sales.

Questions 37 and 38 are based on the following information. Kelly Company is a retail sporting goods store that uses accrual accounting for its records. Facts regarding Kelly's operations are as follows:

- Sales are budgeted at $220,000 for December Year 1 and $200,000 for January Year 2.
- Collections are expected to be 60% in the month of sale and 38% in the month following the sale.
- Gross margin is 25% of sales.
- A total of 80% of the merchandise held for resale is purchased in the month prior to the month of sale and 20% is purchased in the month of sale. Payment for merchandise is made in the month following the purchase.
- Other expected monthly expenses to be paid in cash are $22,600.
- Annual depreciation is $216,000.

Below is Kelly Company's statement of financial position at November 30, Year 1.

Assets		Liabilities and Stockholders' Equity	
Cash	$ 22,000	Accounts payable	$ 162,000
Accounts receivable (net of $4,000 allowance for uncollectible accounts)	76,000	Common stock	800,000
Inventory	132,000	Retained earnings	138,000
Property, plant, and equipment (net of $680,000 accumulated depreciation)	870,000	Total liabilities and stockholders' equity	$1,100,000
Total assets	$1,100,000		

37. Kelly's pro forma income (loss) before income taxes for December Year 1 is

A. $32,400
B. $28,000
C. $10,000
D. $9,000

Answer (C) is correct.
REQUIRED: The pro forma income (loss) before taxes for the month.
DISCUSSION: Sales are budgeted at $220,000. Given that cost of goods sold is 75% of sales, or $165,000, gross profit is $55,000. Deduct cash expenses of $22,600, depreciation of $18,000 ($216,000 ÷ 12), and bad debt expense of $4,400 ($220,000 × .02). This leaves an income of $10,000.
Answer (A) is incorrect. The amount of $32,400 does not reflect depreciation or bad debt expense. Answer (B) is incorrect. The amount of $28,000 does not consider depreciation. Answer (D) is incorrect. The amount of $9,000 is the result of a subtraction error.

38. Kelly's projected balance in accounts payable on December 31, Year 1, is

A. $162,000
B. $204,000
C. $153,000
D. Some amount other than those given.

Answer (C) is correct.
REQUIRED: The projected balance in accounts payable at the end of the month.
DISCUSSION: The balance is equal to the purchases made during December since all purchases are paid for in the month following purchase. Purchases for December is given as 20% of December's sales and 80% of January's sales. Thus, of the $220,000 of merchandise sold during December, 20%, or $44,000, would have been purchased during the month. January's sales are expected to be $200,000, so 80% of that amount, or $160,000, would have been purchased during December. December purchases are thus estimated as $204,000 at the company's selling prices. The merchandise costs only 75% of the marked selling prices, however. Therefore, the balance in the purchases account at month-end is projected to be $153,000 ($204,000 × 75%).
Answer (A) is incorrect. The accounts payable balance on November 30 is $162,000. Answer (B) is incorrect. Estimated purchases in December at the company's selling prices equals $204,000. Answer (D) is incorrect. The correct amount is given in one of the other answer choices.

Access the **CMA Review System** from your Gleim Personal Classroom to continue your studies with exam-emulating multiple-choice questions!

9.10 ESSAY QUESTIONS

Scenario for Essay Questions 1, 2

Watson Corporation manufactures and sells extended keyboard units. Robin Halter, budget analyst, coordinated the preparation of the annual budget for the year ending August 31, Year 7. The budget was based on the prior year's activity. The pro forma statements of income and cost of goods sold are presented below.

Watson Corporation
Pro Forma Statement of Income
For the Year Ending August 31, Year 7
($000 omitted)

Net sales		$25,550
Cost of goods sold		16,565
Gross profit		$ 8,985
Operating expenses:		
Marketing	$3,200	
General and administrative	2,000	5,200
Income from operations		$ 3,785

Watson Corporation
Pro Forma Statement of Cost of Goods Sold
For the Year Ending August 31, Year 7
($000 omitted)

Direct materials:		
Materials inventory, 9/1/Year 6	$ 1,200	
Materials purchased	11,400	
Materials available for use	$12,600	
Materials inventory, 8/31/Year 7	1,480	
Direct materials consumed		$11,120
Direct labor		980
Factory overhead:		
Indirect materials	$ 1,112	
General factory overhead	2,800	3,912
Cost of goods manufactured		$16,012
Finished goods inventory, 9/1/Year 6		930
Cost of goods available for sale		$16,942
Finished goods inventory, 8/31/Year 7		377
Cost of goods sold		$16,565

On December 10, Year 6, Halter met with Walter Collins, vice president of finance, to discuss the results. After their discussion, Collins directed Halter to reflect the following changes to the budget assumptions in revised pro forma statements:

- The estimated production in units for the fiscal year should be revised from 140,000 to 145,000 units with the balance of production being scheduled in equal segments over the last 9 months of the year. The actual first quarter's production was 25,000 units.
- The planned inventory for finished goods of 3,300 units at the end of the fiscal year remains unchanged and will be valued at the average manufacturing cost for the year. The finished goods inventory of 9,300 units on September 1, Year 6, and dropped to 9,000 units by November 30, Year 6.

- Due to a new labor agreement, the labor rate will increase 8% effective June 1, Year 7, the beginning of the fourth quarter, instead of the previously anticipated effective date of September 1, Year 7, the beginning of the next fiscal year.
- The assumptions remain unchanged for direct materials inventory at 16,000 units for the beginning inventory and 18,500 units for the ending inventory. Direct materials inventory is valued on a first-in, first-out basis. During the first quarter, direct materials for 27,500 units of output were purchased for $2,200,000. Although direct materials will be purchased evenly for the last 9 months, the cost of the direct materials will increase by 5% on March 1, Year 7, the beginning of the third quarter.
- Indirect material costs will continue to be 10% of the cost of direct materials.
- One-half of general factory overhead and all of the marketing and general and administrative expenses are fixed.

Questions

1. Based on the revised data presented, calculate Watson Corporation's projected sales for the year ending August 31, Year 7, in

    a. Number of units to be sold
    b. Dollar volume of net sales

2. Prepare the pro forma statement of cost of goods sold for the year ending August 31, Year 7.

Essay Questions 1, 2 — Unofficial Answers

1. a. Based on the revised data presented, Watson Corporation's projected unit sales for the year ending August 31, Year 7, are calculated as follows:

Finished goods beginning inventory	9,300
Add: planned production	145,000
Units available for sale	154,300
Less: finished goods ending inventory	(3,300)
Units to be sold	151,000

   b. Based on the revised data presented, Watson Corporation's projected dollar volume of net sales for the year ending August 31, Year 7, is $26,425,000 calculated as follows:

   Selling price per unit = Original projected sales dollars ÷ Original projected unit sales
   = $25,550,000 ÷ (9,300 + 140,000 − 3,300) units
   = $175 per unit

   Dollar volume of projected net sales = 151,000 units × $175 per unit
   = $26,425,000

2. Based on the revised data presented, Watson Company's pro forma statement of costs of goods sold for the year ending August 31, Year 7, is presented below. Supporting calculations are on the next page.

   Watson Corporation
   Pro Forma Statement of Cost of Goods Sold
   For the Year Ending August 31, Year 7

Direct materials:		
Materials inventory, 9/1/Year 6		$ 1,200,000
Materials purchased[1]		12,120,000
Materials available for use		$13,320,000
Materials inventory, 8/31/Year 7[2]		1,554,000
Direct materials consumed		$11,766,000
Direct labor[3]		1,037,400
Factory overhead:		
Indirect material[4]	$1,176,600	
General factory overhead[5]	2,850,000	
Factory overhead applied		4,026,600
Cost of goods manufactured		$16,830,000
Add: finished goods inventory, 9/1/Year 6		930,000
Cost of goods available for sale		$17,760,000
Less: finished goods inventory, 8/31/Year 7[6]		383,028
Cost of goods sold		$17,376,972

Supporting Calculations

[1] Materials purchased:

1st quarter:	27,500 units at $80 per unit	=	$ 2,200,000
2nd quarter:	40,000 units at $80 per unit*	=	3,200,000
3rd quarter:	40,000 units at $84 per unit**	=	3,360,000
4th quarter:	40,000 units at $84 per unit	=	3,360,000
Total			$12,120,000

   *$2,200,000 ÷ 27,500 units
 **$80.00 × 1.05

145,000 planned production + 18,500 beginning inventory −
16,000 ending inventory = 147,500 total to be purchased
147,500 − 27,500 purchased in first quarter = 120,000
120,000 ÷ 3 remaining quarters = 40,000 per quarter

[2] Materials inventory, 8/31/Year 7:
   18,500 units at $84 per unit   = $ 1,554,000

[3] Direct labor:

1st quarter:	25,000 units at $7 per unit*	=	$ 175,000
2nd quarter:	40,000 units at $7 per unit	=	280,000
3rd quarter:	40,000 units at $7 per unit	=	280,000
4th quarter:	40,000 units at $7.56 per unit**	=	302,400
Total			$ 1,037,400

   *$980,000 ÷ 140,000 units
 **$7.00 × 1.08

[4] Indirect materials:
   $11,766,000 × .10   = $ 1,176,600

[5] General factory overhead:

Variable: 145,000 units × ($1,400,000 ÷ 140,000 units)	=	$ 1,450,000
Fixed: $2,800,000 ÷ 2	=	1,400,000
Total		$ 2,850,000

[6] Finished goods inventory, 8/31/Year 7:
   3,300 units × ($16,830,000 ÷ 145,000 units)   = $ 383,028

Access the CMA Review System from your Gleim Personal Classroom to continue your studies with exam-emulating essay questions!

Notes

STUDY UNIT TEN
COST AND VARIANCE MEASURES

(22 pages of outline)

10.1	Variance Analysis Overview	337
10.2	Static and Flexible Budget Variances	341
10.3	Direct Materials Variances	344
10.4	Direct Labor Variances	346
10.5	Mix and Yield Variances	348
10.6	Overhead Variances	349
10.7	Comprehensive Example	353
10.8	Sales Variances	356
10.9	Essay Questions	373

Performance Management

Performance reporting is a major topic on the CMA exam. Factors to be analyzed for control and performance evaluation include revenues, costs, profits, and investment in assets. Variance analysis based on flexible budgets and standard costs is heavily tested, as is responsibility accounting for revenue, cost, contribution, and profit centers. The balanced scorecard and quality considerations are included in this coverage (both of which were covered in Study Unit 7 and are not repeated in this study unit).

This study unit is the **first of two** on **performance management**. The relative weight assigned to this major topic in Part 1 of the exam is **20%**. The two study units are

Study Unit 10: Cost and Variance Measures
Study Unit 11: Responsibility Accounting and Performance Measures

If you are interested in reviewing more introductory or background material, go to www.gleim.com/CMAIntroVideos for a list of suggested third-party overviews of this topic. The following Gleim outline material is more than sufficient to help you pass the CMA exam; any additional introductory or background material is for your own personal enrichment.

10.1 VARIANCE ANALYSIS OVERVIEW

1. **Uses of a Budget**

    a. A budget communicates to employees the organization's operational and strategic objectives. The budget quantifies the operational steps that ultimately lead to the achievement of strategic objectives.

    b. A performance evaluation system must be used to monitor progress toward the budget's objectives.

    c. Feedback should be timely so that managers can take corrective action.

2. **Variance Analysis**

    a. Variance analysis is the basis of any performance evaluation system using a budget. Variances are the differences between the amounts budgeted and the amounts actually incurred (or earned in the case of revenues).

    1) Whether a variance is favorable or unfavorable depends on how it affects income. A favorable variance increases income, and an unfavorable variance decreases income.

2) On the revenue side,
   a) A **favorable variance** occurs when actual revenues are greater than budgeted revenues.
   b) An **unfavorable variance** occurs when actual revenues are less than budgeted revenues.
3) On the cost side,
   a) A **favorable variance** occurs when actual costs are less than budgeted costs.
   b) An **unfavorable variance** occurs when actual costs are greater than budgeted costs.
4) EXAMPLE: Under efficient conditions, a worker should complete one unit of product per hour. If workers are normally paid $6 per hour, the standard labor cost per unit is $6 per unit.
   a) If the actual per-unit amounts for a 1-week period were 1.1 hours at $6.25 per hour, or $6.88 per unit, the variance is $.88 per unit.
   b) The variance is unfavorable because the actual cost exceeded the standard cost.

b. The significance of variances depends not only on their amount but also on their direction, frequency, and trend.
   1) Persistent variances may indicate that standards need to be reevaluated.

c. Variance analysis is an important tool for the management accountant.
   1) Variance analysis enables **management by exception**, the practice of giving attention primarily to significant deviations from expectations (whether favorable or unfavorable).
      a) The primary reason for calculating variances is to notify management whenever an unusual event has occurred.
      b) Concentrating on operations that are not performing within expected limits is likely to yield the best ratio of benefits to costs.

3. **Assignment of Responsibility**

   a. A crucial part of variance analysis is the **assignment of responsibility**. The performance measures on which managers are judged should be directly related to the factors that drive the element being measured, e.g., cost drivers and revenue drivers.
   b. The goal is to assign responsibility for variances to those most likely to have information that will enable management to find solutions. A manager who does not control an activity may nevertheless be the individual who is best informed about it.
      1) The constructive approach is to promote learning and continuous improvement in manufacturing operations, not to assign blame. However, variance analysis may be useful in evaluating managers' performance.

4. **Overview of Variances**

   a. The variances on the following page are covered in greater detail throughout this study unit. CMA candidates should be prepared to calculate and understand these variances.

b. **Static Budget Variance**

1) The beginning of variance analysis is the static budget variance.
2) The static budget variance measures the difference between the static (master) budget amount and the actual results. It is the total variance to be explained.

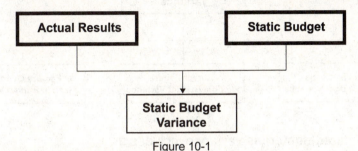

Figure 10-1

c. **Flexible Budget Variance and Sales-Volume Variance**

1) The static budget variance consists of a flexible budget variance and a sales volume variance.

   a) The **flexible budget variance** is the difference between the actual results and the budgeted amount for the actual activity level. It may be analyzed in terms of variances related to selling prices, input costs, and input quantities.

      i) A **flexible budget** consists of the costs that should have been incurred given the actual level of production.

         • The actual level of production is based on the actual output while still using the standard level of inputs (e.g., direct labor hours, machine hours, etc.).

      ii) **Standard costs** should be established for direct materials, direct labor, and overhead. These standards can then be used to calculate variances.

   b) The **sales-volume variance** is the difference between the flexible budget and static budget amounts if selling prices and costs are constant.

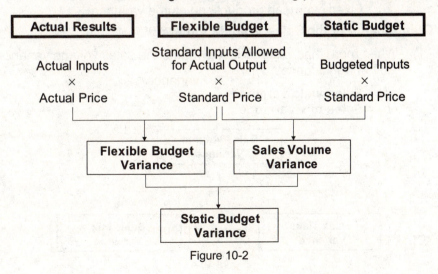

Figure 10-2

d. **Components of the Flexible Budget Variance**

1) The flexible budget variance consists of the following variances:

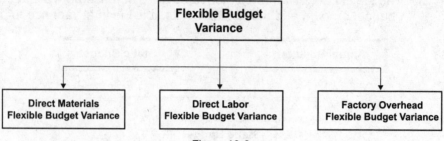

Figure 10-3

2) A **direct materials variance** includes a

   a) Price variance
   b) Quantity or usage variance (an efficiency variance for direct materials)

   i) When a product has more than one input, the following variances can be calculated:
   - Materials mix variance
   - Materials yield variance

3) A **direct labor variance** includes a(n)

   a) Rate variance (a price variance for direct labor)
   b) Efficiency variance

   i) When labor rates vary, the following variances can be calculated:
   - Labor mix variance
   - Labor yield variance

4) **Factory overhead variances** have variable and fixed components. A four-way analysis includes two variable and two fixed components:

   a) Variable overhead spending variance
   b) Variable overhead efficiency variance
   c) Fixed overhead spending variance (also known as a budget variance)
   d) Fixed overhead production-volume variance

e. **Components of the Sales-Volume Variance**

1) When more than one product is made, the sales volume variance consists of the following variances:

   a) **Sales yield variance**
   b) **Sales mix variance**

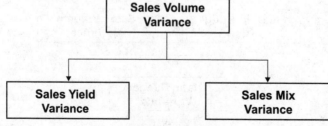

Figure 10-4

NOTE: Each of the variances introduced above will be examined in detail in subsequent subunits.

Stop and review! You have completed the outline for this subunit. Study multiple-choice questions 1 and 2 on page 359.

10.2 STATIC AND FLEXIBLE BUDGET VARIANCES

1. **The Static Budget Variance**

    a. The static budget and actual results of the period are required to calculate the static budget variance.

    b. A **static budget** is prepared before the budget period begins and is not changed. It is based only on the output planned at the beginning of the budget period.

    1) The static budget reflects management's best estimates of, for example, sales, production, input prices, labor and overhead costs, and selling and administrative costs.

    c. **Standard prices (SP)** are determined for the underlying cost drivers. They are budgeted unit costs established to improve productivity and efficiency.

    1) A **cost driver** is used to assign costs to a cost object. It is a measure of activity, such as direct labor hours or machine hours, that has a cause-and-effect relationship with total cost.

    2) A standard price is not an average of past costs but an objectively determined estimate of what a cost should be. It may be based on accounting, engineering, or statistical quality control studies.

        a) A standard price can be compared to "par" on a golf course.

    3) Standard prices must be kept **current** to provide relevant information.

        a) If prices have changed considerably for a particular material, a variance is always reported if the standard price is not changed. Much of the usefulness of standard prices is lost if a large variance is always expected.

    d. The **standard quantity** is an objectively determined estimate of the quantity expected to be produced.

    1) **Ideal standards** are standard costs under optimal conditions. They are based on the work of the most skilled workers with no allowance for waste, spoilage, machine breakdowns, or other downtime.

        a) These **tight standards** are not in wide use because they are difficult to attain.

    2) **Practical standards** are defined as the performance that is reasonably expected to be achieved with an allowance for normal spoilage, waste, and downtime.

        a) Practical standards represent possible but difficult-to-attain results; thus, practical standards are useful in determining standard quantity.

It is important to note that on the CMA exam, you may encounter slightly different names for the terms used in this outline. As a CMA candidate, it is important to be able to understand and apply variance analysis regardless of the terminology used.

Standard Price	Standard Quantity
Standard Cost	Standard Materials
Budgeted Price	Budgeted Quantity
Budgeted Cost	Budgeted Materials

e. Once all standard prices and standard quantities are determined, the static budget can be calculated.

   Static budget = (Standard quantity × Standard price) = (SQ × SP)

f. The **actual results** are prepared after the budget period ends.
   1) The actual results reflect the revenues actually earned and the costs actually incurred.
   2) The drivers are therefore adjusted to the actual amounts.

   Actual results = (Actual quantity × Actual price) = (AQ × AP)

g. The **static budget variance** is the difference between the static budget and the actual results for the period.
   1) The static budget variance provides useful information, but it does not explain the cause of the variance.

   Static budget variance = Actual results − Static budget = (AQ × AP) − (SQ × SP)

h. EXAMPLE: At the end of the current period, ChowDown, Inc., a pet food manufacturer, prepared the following analysis of the static budget variance:

	AQ × AP Actual Results	Static Budget Variances	SQ × SP Static Budget
Units sold	16,500	1,500	18,000
Revenue	$1,947,000	$213,000 U	$2,160,000
Variable costs:			
Direct materials	750,750	160,500 F	911,250
Direct labor	321,750	24,750 U	297,000
Variable manufacturing overhead	214,500	41,700 U	172,800
Total variable costs	$1,287,000	$ 94,050 F	$1,381,050
Contribution margin	660,000	118,950 U	778,950
Fixed overhead	429,000	21,000 F	450,000
Operating income	$ 231,000	$ 97,950 U	$ 328,950

Total Static Budget Variance
$ 97,950 U

   1) Interpretation of the static budget variance can sometimes be misleading. For example, the above $160,500 variance on direct materials is labeled as favorable because actual cost was less than standard. However, if the variance was mostly the result of production being lower than planned, the manager responsible did not do anything wonderful to generate the favorable variance. In fact, he may have been the cause of production delays, which led to the use of fewer materials.
   2) A flexible budget using standard costs helps management determine how much of the static budget variance arose from inaccurate forecasts of output sold and variations in the effectiveness and efficiency of actual output.

2. **Flexible Budget and Sales-Volume Variances**

   a. Flexible budget variances and sales-volume variances are based on flexible budgets.
   b. A **flexible budget** adjusts for changes in the volume of activity. It can be adapted to any level of production. Budgeted revenues and costs are based on the actual quantities and standard costs.

   ```
   Flexible budget = (Actual quantity × Standard price) = (AQ × SP)
   ```

   c. **Flexible budget variances** result from variations in the efficiency and effectiveness of producing actual output. They are the differences between actual results and flexible budget amounts.

   ```
   Flexible budget variance = Actual results - Flexible budget
                            = (AQ × AP) - (AQ × SP)
                            = AQ × (AP - SP)
   ```

   d. **Sales-volume variances** result from inaccurate forecasts of output sold. They are the differences between flexible budget amounts and static budget amounts.

   ```
   Sales-volume variance = Flexible budget - Static budget
                         = (AQ × SP) - (SQ × SP)
                         = SP × (AQ - SQ)
   ```

   The questions in this study unit use formulas written in different ways. For example, the flexible budget variance can be written in the following formats: AQ × (AP − SP), AQ × (SP − AP), (AP − SP) × AQ, or (SP − AP) × AQ. In each case, the absolute value is derived. The effect on income is then determined to decide whether the variance is favorable or unfavorable. Understanding the variances and understanding what each question is looking for will help you avoid becoming confused by the formulas being presented in different formats.

   e. EXAMPLE: At the end of the current period, ChowDown, Inc., prepared the following analysis of the flexible budget variance:

	AQ × AP Actual Results (AR)	AR − FB Flexible Budget Variances	AQ × SP Flexible Budget (FB)	FB − SB Sales Volume Variances	SQ × SP Static Budget (SB)
Units sold	16,500		16,500	1,500	18,000
Revenue	$1,947,000	$33,000 U	$1,980,000	$180,000 U	$2,160,000
Variable costs:					
Direct materials	750,750	84,563 F	835,313	75,937 F	911,250
Direct labor	321,750	49,500 U	272,250	24,750 F	297,000
Variable nonmanufacturing overhead	214,500	56,100 U	158,400	14,400 F	172,800
Total variable costs	$1,287,000	$21,037	$1,265,963	$115,087	$1,381,050
Contribution margin	660,000	54,037	714,037	64,913	778,950
Fixed overhead	429,000	21,000 F	450,000	0	450,000
Operating income	$ 231,000	$33,037	$ 264,037	$ 64,913	$ 328,950

   Total Flexible Budget Variance $33,037 U   Total Sales Volume Variance $64,913 U

   Total Static Budget Variance $97,950 U

Stop and review! You have completed the outline for this subunit. Study multiple-choice questions 3 through 10 beginning on page 359.

10.3 DIRECT MATERIALS VARIANCES

 CMA candidates must be able to calculate and analyze variances. They must be able to identify causes and recommend corrective actions. Typically, a favorable variance is seen as desirable while an unfavorable one is undesirable, but this is not always the case. When taking the exam, it is easy to see a favorable variance and determine that this is desirable; however, as a CMA candidate, you will need to analyze the variances and determine their causes. You must be able to evaluate if they are desirable or not and recommend a course of action.

1. The **direct materials flexible budget variance** has price and quantity (efficiency) components. These two sources of the total variance can be isolated.

    a. Part of the total variance is attributed to using more or less materials than planned (the quantity component).
    b. Part is attributed to the price of materials being different than what was planned (the price component).

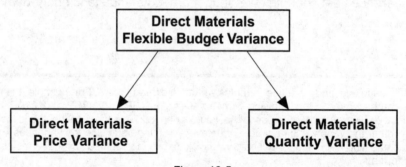

Figure 10-5

2. **Direct Materials Price Variance**

    a. The direct materials price variance equals the actual quantity of total input times the difference between the standard price and the actual price.

    $$\left(\begin{array}{c} \text{Actual} \\ \text{units} \\ \text{produced} \end{array} \times \begin{array}{c} \text{Actual} \\ \text{materials} \\ \text{per unit} \end{array} \right) \times \left(\begin{array}{c} \text{Actual} \\ \text{price} \end{array} - \begin{array}{c} \text{Standard} \\ \text{price} \end{array} \right)$$

    b. The price variance may be isolated at the time of purchase or when materials are transferred to work-in-process.

        1) A **purchase price variance** is a nonmanufacturing variance. It measures the difference between (a) the amount paid for **all** units of materials purchased during a specific period and (b) the amount expected to be paid. This formula can be used to calculate variances at the earliest time possible, which is at the time goods are purchased.

    c. Once a variance has been calculated, the next step is to analyze the reasons for the variance. In general, a favorable variance is desirable and an unfavorable variance is undesirable. But that is not always true.

        1) An **unfavorable direct materials price variance** means that the actual price paid for materials is higher than the estimated standard price. This is usually undesirable.

            a) The purchasing function may be responsible under the assumption that it bought materials that cost too much. Thus, an unfavorable variance is not the fault of the production departments.
            b) However, the unfavorable variance may simply indicate that prices in the industry have risen, and standard prices should be updated.

2) A **favorable direct materials price variance** may mean that the purchasing function performed well by finding a lower-cost source for the materials.

   a) However, the favorable variance may simply indicate that prices in the industry have fallen, and standard prices should be updated.

   b) Another possibility is that the lower price may be attributable to lower-quality materials. An analysis must be made to determine whether the lower quality materials result in a lower quality product or the use of excessive quantities in production. In these cases, the purchasing function is at fault.

3) This variance is generally considered the responsibility of the purchasing manager and purchasing department.

3. **Direct Materials Quantity Variance**

   a. The direct materials quantity variance (an efficiency or usage variance) equals the budgeted price times the difference between the actual quantity of total input and the budgeted quantity of total input.

   $$\text{Standard price} \times \left[\left(\text{Actual units produced} \times \text{Actual materials per unit} \right) - \left(\text{Actual units produced} \times \text{Standard materials per unit} \right) \right]$$

   1) When calculating the quantity variance, the standard quantity equals actual units produced times the standard materials per unit. This equals the materials that should have been used given the actual level of production.

   2) The actual cost of the materials is ignored because the variance isolates the effect that would have occurred given no price variance.

   b. Once a variance has been calculated, the next step is to analyze the reasons for the variance. In general, a favorable variance is desirable and an unfavorable variance is undesirable. But that is not always true.

   1) An **unfavorable materials quantity variance** is usually blamed on the excessive use of materials by the production departments. It also may indicate theft of materials or other waste or shrinkage.

      a) However, the excessive use might be attributable to using lower-quality materials that were purchased at a lower price.

      b) An alternative explanation is that excessive usage may have been caused by using unskilled (and lower cost) labor. Thus, a favorable labor rate variance may have contributed to an unfavorable materials quantity variance.

   2) A **favorable materials quantity variance** may indicate that workers have been unusually efficient, for example, by reducing normal spoilage.

      a) However, the reduced usage may indicate that they are producing lower-quality products with less than the standard quantity of materials.

      b) Accordingly, a favorable variance is not always desirable. It may be as bad as, or worse than, an unfavorable variance. It may suggest that costs have been reduced at the expense of product quality.

   3) This variance is generally considered the responsibility of the production manager and production department.

4. **EXAMPLE:** ChowDown, Inc., estimated output for the period of 18,000 units. However, actual output was 16,500 units. Standard direct materials per unit were estimated at 7.5, but the actual usage was 6.5 per unit. The standard price was budgeted at $6.75, but the actual price was $7.00. The direct materials variances are calculated as follows:

Direct Materials Variance	Units	×	Materials per Unit	=	Quantity of Total Input	×	Price	=	Total
Static budget direct materials	18,000		7.5		135,000		$6.75		$911,250
Flexible budget direct materials	16,500		7.5		123,750		$6.75		$835,313
Actual direct materials	16,500		6.5		107,250		$7.00		$750,750

Direct materials price variance	107,250 × ($7.00 − $6.75)	$ 26,813 U	
Direct materials quantity variance	$6.75 × (107,250 − 123,750)	111,375 F	
Direct materials flexible budget variance		$ 84,562 F	($1 rounding difference)

5. **Service Organizations**

   a. In a service organization, the direct materials variances are usually immaterial compared with the direct labor variances. The reason is that only a relatively small investment is made in direct materials because these organizations tend to be labor intensive.

Stop and review! You have completed the outline for this subunit. Study multiple-choice questions 11 through 18 beginning on page 362.

10.4 DIRECT LABOR VARIANCES

1. The direct labor variance is similar to the direct materials variance. The total direct labor flexible budget variance consists of the rate (price) variance and the efficiency (quantity) variance.

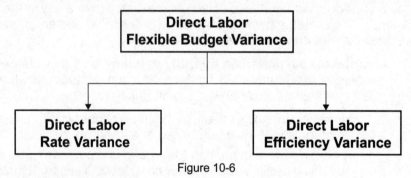

Figure 10-6

2. **Direct Labor Rate Variance**

   a. This variance equals the actual quantity of total input times the difference between the actual price and the standard price.

   $$\left(\begin{array}{c} \text{Actual} \\ \text{units} \\ \text{produced} \end{array} \times \begin{array}{c} \text{Actual} \\ \text{labor hours} \\ \text{per unit} \end{array} \right) \times \left(\begin{array}{c} \text{Actual} \\ \text{price} \end{array} - \begin{array}{c} \text{Standard} \\ \text{price} \end{array} \right)$$

   b. Once a variance has been calculated, the next step is to analyze the reasons for the variance. In general, a favorable variance is desirable and an unfavorable variance is undesirable. But that is not always true.

   1) An **unfavorable labor rate variance** is usually caused by assigning skilled workers to a production process when the standard price calculation assumed that unskilled (lower paid) workers could complete the job.

      a) However, the greater efficiency of skilled workers might result in a favorable labor efficiency variance to offset the unfavorable labor rate variance.

SU 10: Cost and Variance Measures

  b) Another explanation for an unfavorable labor rate variance is that a new union contract resulted in a higher wage to workers, in which case the standard prices should be updated.
 2) A **favorable labor rate variance** is usually caused by assigning workers with less skill to a job. This may be desirable when they are qualified for the job.
  a) However, the favorable rate variance may be offset by an unfavorable efficiency variance or lower quality products.
3. **Direct Labor Efficiency Variance**
 a. This variance equals the standard price times the difference between the actual quantity of total input and the standard quantity of total input.

$$\text{Standard price} \times \left[\left(\begin{array}{c}\text{Actual}\\\text{units}\\\text{produced}\end{array} \times \begin{array}{c}\text{Actual}\\\text{labor hours}\\\text{per unit}\end{array} \right) - \left(\begin{array}{c}\text{Actual}\\\text{units}\\\text{produced}\end{array} \times \begin{array}{c}\text{Standard}\\\text{labor hours}\\\text{per unit}\end{array} \right) \right]$$

 b. Once a variance has been calculated, the next step is to analyze the reasons for the variance. In general, a favorable variance is desirable and an unfavorable variance is undesirable. But that is not always true.
 1) An **unfavorable labor efficiency variance** means that workers are spending too much time on a production process, which is normally undesirable.
  a) However, it may be caused by using workers with less skill than anticipated, in which case the labor rate variance may be favorable.
  b) Another explanation is the use of low-quality materials that require extra time in the production process, in which case, the material price variance may be favorable.
 2) A **favorable labor efficiency variance** is almost always desirable. It means that employees are working efficiently and have been able to complete production in fewer hours than anticipated.
  a) It is considered a production department efficiency.
4. EXAMPLE: ChowDown, Inc., estimated output for the period of 18,000 units. However, actual output was 16,500 units. Standard direct labor was estimated at 3 hours per unit, but the actual usage was 3.25 hours per unit. The standard price was $5.50, but the actual price was $6.00. The direct labor variances are calculated as follows:

Direct Materials Variance	Units	×	Labor Hours per Unit	=	Quantity of Total Input	×	Price	=	Total
Static budget direct materials	18,000		3		54,000		$5.50		$297,000
Flexible budget direct materials	16,500		3		49,500		$5.50		$272,250
Actual direct materials	16,500		3.25		53,625		$6.00		$321,750
Direct labor rate variance	53,625 × ($6.00 − $5.50)				$26,813 U				
Direct labor efficiency variance	$5.50 × (53,625 − 49,500)				22,688 U				
Direct labor flexible budget variance					$49,501 U		($1 rounding difference)		

5. **Service Organizations**
 a. In a service organization, the direct labor variances are usually more relevant than the direct materials variances. A relatively large investment is made in direct labor and only a minor investment in direct materials.

Stop and review! You have completed the outline for this subunit. Study multiple-choice questions 19 through 25 beginning on page 364.

10.5 MIX AND YIELD VARIANCES

1. In some production processes, inputs are **substitutable**; for example, a baker of pecan pies may use pecans from Florida instead of Georgia or higher-skilled labor instead of lower-skilled labor.

    a. Given substitutable inputs, the quantity variance for direct materials consists of the **materials mix variance** and the **materials yield variance**.

        1) A favorable (unfavorable) materials mix variance means that more (less) lower-priced materials were used than budgeted.
        2) A favorable (unfavorable) materials yield variance means that less (more) materials than budgeted were used to produce the output.

    b. Given substitutable inputs, the efficiency variance for direct labor consists of the **labor mix variance** and the **labor yield variance**.

        1) A favorable (unfavorable) labor mix variance means that low-paid employees worked more (less) hours and higher-paid employees worked less (more) hours than budgeted.
        2) A favorable (unfavorable) labor yield variance means less (more) hours than budgeted were used to produce the output.

    c. The sum of the mix and yield variance is the efficiency variance.

2. To calculate these variances, the entity must determine the weighted-average standard price (a) using the standard mix of inputs at standard prices **(SMSP)** and (b) using the actual mix of inputs at standard prices **(AMSP)**.

    a. EXAMPLE: A retail store budgets its employee hours for the upcoming month and calculates its weighted-average standard price of wages using the standard mix (SMSP) as follows:

	Budgeted Hours (SM)		Standard Wage (SP)		Subtotals
Managers	200	×	$22	=	$ 4,400
Sales associates	800	×	14	=	11,200
Warehouse	600	×	8	=	4,800
Totals	1,600				$20,400

    SMSP = $20,400 ÷ 1,600 hours = $12.75 per hour

    After month end, the store employs the actual hours worked to calculate the weighted-average standard price using the actual mix (AMSP) as follows:

	Actual Hours (AM)		Standard Wage (SP)		Subtotals
Managers	220	×	$22	=	$ 4,840
Sales associates	800	×	14	=	11,200
Warehouse	480	×	8	=	3,840
Totals	1,500				$19,880

    AMSP = $19,880 ÷ 1,500 hours = $13.2533 per hour

SU 10: Cost and Variance Measures

3. The **mix variance** measures the relative use of higher-priced and lower-priced inputs in the production process based on standard input prices and **actual total quantity (ATQ)** of inputs. It isolates the effect of using the actual mix instead of the standard mix.

    $$Mix\ variance = ATQ \times (SMSP - AMSP)$$

    a. EXAMPLE: The store calculates its labor mix variance as follows:

    Labor mix variance = ATQ × (SMSP − AMSP)
    = 1,500 hours × ($12.75 − $13.2533)
    = 1,500 hours × −$0.5033
    = $755 unfavorable

    This variance was unfavorable because higher-paid managers worked more hours and lower-paid warehouse employees worked fewer hours than budgeted.

4. The **yield variance** isolates the effect of the difference between the ATQ of inputs and the **STQ (standard total quantity)**. The calculation is based on standard input prices and the standard mix.

    $$Yield\ variance = (STQ - ATQ) \times SMSP$$

    a. EXAMPLE: The store calculates its labor yield variance as follows:

    Labor yield variance = (STQ − ATQ) × SMSP
    = (1,600 hours − 1,500 hours) × $12.75
    = 100 hours × $12.75
    = $1,275 favorable

    The variance was favorable because fewer hours than budgeted were used to produce the output.

    The sum of the mix and yield variances is the efficiency variance ($755 U + $1,275 F = $520 F).

5. The same formulas can be applied to the mix and yield variances for direct materials.

Stop and review! You have completed the outline for this subunit. Study multiple-choice question 26 on page 367.

10.6 OVERHEAD VARIANCES

1. The total overhead variance consists of four variances. Two are calculated for variable overhead and two for fixed overhead.

2. **Variable Overhead**

    a. The total **variable overhead variance** is the flexible-budget variance. It is the difference between actual variable overhead and the amount applied based on the budgeted application rate and the standard input allowed for the actual output.

    $$\text{Actual variable overhead} - \left[\text{Budgeted application rate} \times \left(\text{Standard cost driven per unit} \times \text{Actual units} \right) \right]$$

b. It includes the following:

1) The **spending variance** is the difference between (a) actual variable overhead and (b) the product of the budgeted application rate and the actual amount of the allocation base.

$$\left(\begin{array}{c}\text{Actual} \\ \text{allocation} \\ \text{base}\end{array} \times \begin{array}{c}\text{Actual} \\ \text{application} \\ \text{rate}\end{array}\right) - \left(\begin{array}{c}\text{Actual} \\ \text{allocation} \\ \text{base}\end{array} \times \begin{array}{c}\text{Budgeted} \\ \text{application} \\ \text{rate}\end{array}\right)$$

$$\begin{array}{c}\text{Actual} \\ \text{allocation} \\ \text{base}\end{array} \times \left(\begin{array}{c}\text{Actual} \\ \text{application} \\ \text{rate}\end{array} - \begin{array}{c}\text{Budgeted} \\ \text{application} \\ \text{rate}\end{array}\right)$$

a) The variable overhead spending variance is favorable or unfavorable if production spending is less or more, respectively, than the standard.

2) The **efficiency variance** is the budgeted application rate times the difference between (a) the actual allocation base and (b) the standard cost driven per unit allowed for the actual quantity.

$$\begin{array}{c}\text{Budgeted} \\ \text{application} \\ \text{rate}\end{array} \times \left[\begin{array}{c}\text{Actual} \\ \text{allocation} \\ \text{base}\end{array} - \left(\begin{array}{c}\text{Standard} \\ \text{cost driven} \\ \text{per unit}\end{array} \times \begin{array}{c}\text{Actual} \\ \text{units}\end{array}\right)\right]$$

a) Variable overhead applied equals the flexible-budget amount for the actual output level. The reason is that unit variable costs are assumed to be constant within the relevant range.

b) If variable overhead is applied on the basis of output, not inputs, no efficiency variance arises.

c) The variable overhead efficiency variance is related to the labor efficiency variance if overhead is applied to production on the basis of direct labor hours. For example, if the labor efficiency variance is unfavorable, the overhead efficiency variance also is unfavorable because they are based on the same number of input hours.

Variable Overhead Variances

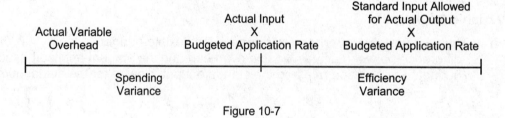

Figure 10-7

3) **EXAMPLE:** ChowDown, Inc., estimated output for the period of 18,000 units. However, actual output was 16,500 units. Standard processing time is 1.2 machine hours per unit. But actual usage was 1.3 machine hours per unit. The standard application rate was $8.00 per machine hour, but the actual rate was $10.00 per machine hour. The variable overhead variances are calculated as follows:

Variable Overhead Variances	Units	×	Cost Driver per Unit	=	Allocation Base	×	Application Rate	=	Total
Static budget variable overhead	18,000		1.2		21,600		$ 8.00		$172,800
Flexible budget variance overhead	16,500		1.2		19,800		$ 8.00		$158,400
Actual variable overhead	16,500		1.3		21,450		$10.00		$214,500

Variable overhead spending variance	21,450 × ($10.00 − $8.00)	$42,900 U
Variable overhead efficiency variance	$8.00 × (21,450 − 19,800)	13,200 U
Total variable overhead variances		$56,100 U

3. **Fixed Overhead**

   a. The **total fixed overhead variance** is the difference between (1) actual fixed overhead and (2) the product of the budgeted application rate and the standard input allowed for the actual output.

   $$\text{Actual fixed overhead} - \left[\text{Budgeted application rate} \times \left(\text{Standard cost driver per unit} \times \text{Actual units}\right)\right]$$

   b. It includes the following:

      1) The **spending variance** (budget variance) is the difference between (a) actual fixed overhead and (b) the amount budgeted.

         Actual fixed overhead − Budgeted fixed overhead

         a) This variance is the same as the fixed overhead flexible-budget variance. The reason is that the static budget lump-sum of fixed overhead is also the flexible budget amount over the relevant range of output. Moreover, the efficiency of production does not affect the fixed overhead variances.

         b) Thus, an efficiency variance is calculated for variable, but not fixed, overhead.

         c) The fixed overhead variance is simply attributable to more or less spending by the production function. Whether the difference is justified should be investigated.

      2) The **production-volume variance** (idle capacity variance or denominator-level variance) is the difference between (a) budgeted fixed overhead and (b) the product of the budgeted application rate and the standard input allowed for the actual output.

      $$\text{Budgeted fixed overhead} - \left[\text{Budgeted application rate} \times \left(\text{Standard cost driver per unit} \times \text{Actual units}\right)\right]$$

         a) This variance results when production capacity differs from capacity usage. A favorable (unfavorable) variance occurs when overhead applied is more (less) than budgeted fixed costs. For example, the variance is favorable when actual production exceeds planned production.

b) The production-volume variance is typically not the fault of the production function. The sales staff often is blamed, or rewarded, for a volume variance. If sales are greater than expected, production increases, and the variance may be favorable. An unfavorable volume variance may be caused by low sales (the fault of the sales staff) or by a production shutdown, perhaps due to a labor strike, power failure, or natural disaster. In these cases, the variance is attributable to actions of the general administration of the entity or to uncontrollable external factors.

Fixed Overhead Variances

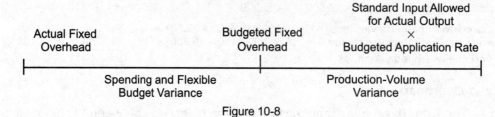

Figure 10-8

3) EXAMPLE: ChowDown, Inc., estimates output for the period of 18,000 units. However, actual output was 16,500 units. Fixed overhead is applied at $25 per unit sold. But actual cost per unit was $26. The fixed overhead variances are calculated below:

Fixed Overhead Variances	Units	×	Cost Driver per Unit	×	Application Rate	=	Total
Static and flexible budget fixed overhead	18,000		1		$25.00		$450,000
Applied fixed overhead	16,500		1		$25.00		$412,500
Actual fixed overhead	16,500		1		$26.00		$429,000

Fixed overhead spending variance	$429,000 − 450,000	$21,000 F
Fixed overhead production-volume variance	$450,000 − [$25 × (1 × 16,500)]	37,500 U

NOTE: The production-volume variance is unfavorable because it indicates that fixed overhead was underallocated to actual output. The variance is the amount of fixed overhead incurred for unused production capacity.

4. **Analysis of Overhead Variances**

   a. **Four-way overhead variance analysis** includes all four components of the total overhead variance.

Four-Way Analysis	Spending Variance	Efficiency Variance	Production-Volume Variance
Variable OH	$42,900 U	$13,200 U	--
Fixed OH	$21,000 F	--	$37,500 U

   b. **Three-way overhead variance analysis** combines the variable and fixed spending variances and reports the other two variances separately.

Three-Way Analysis	Spending Variance	Efficiency Variance	Production-Volume Variance
Total OH	$21,900 U	$13,200 U	$37,500 U

c. **Two-way overhead variance analysis** combines the spending and efficiency variances into one flexible-budget variance and reports the production-volume variance separately.

Two-Way Analysis	Flexible-Budget Variance	Production-Volume Variance
Total OH	$35,100 U	$37,500 U

1) The flexible-budget variance in two-way analysis also is called the **controllable variance**. It is the portion of the total variance not attributable to the production-volume variance.

Stop and review! You have completed the outline for this subunit. Study multiple-choice questions 27 through 33 beginning on page 367.

10.7 COMPREHENSIVE EXAMPLE

As a CMA candidate, you will be expected to know and understand the different variance formulas. Take the time to memorize them but also to understand them. We have provided a summary below, and it may be useful to create notecards for these formulas to aid in retention. When you arrive at the exam, you will first be presented with a tutorial before your time for the exam begins. However, since you are using Gleim Online and CMA Test Prep, you will already be familiar with the information provided in the tutorial. Take these few minutes to write any formulas or variances you can recall on your scrap paper. (Don't forget to pay attention to the time, as once the time for the tutorial is up, your exam will begin.) This way, when you are presented with questions requiring you to calculate variances, you will be able to look at your scrap paper rather than trying to recall from memory during a time when you are stressed. This will help you keep the formulas straight and manage your time on the exam.

1. **Summary of Variance Formulas**

   a. **Direct Materials Variances**

      1) Flexible budget direct materials variances consist of a price variance and a quantity variance:

         a) Direct materials **price variance**

         $$\left(\text{Actual units produced} \times \text{Actual materials per unit} \right) \times \left(\text{Actual price} - \text{Standard price} \right)$$

         b) Direct materials **quantity variance**

         $$\text{Standard price} \times \left[\left(\text{Actual units produced} \times \text{Actual materials per unit} \right) - \left(\text{Actual units produced} \times \text{Standard materials per unit} \right) \right]$$

         c) A favorable materials quantity variance indicates the use of less than the standard quantity of materials. A favorable quantity variance may therefore result from unusual efficiency or the production of lower quality products. An unfavorable materials quantity variance is usually caused by waste, shrinkage, or theft.

   b. **Direct Labor Variances**

      1) Flexible budget direct labor variance consists of a price (rate) variance and a quantity (efficiency) variance:

         a) Direct labor **rate variance**

         $$\left(\text{Actual units produced} \times \text{Actual labor hours per unit} \right) \times \left(\text{Actual price} - \text{Standard price} \right)$$

b) Direct labor **efficiency variance**

$$\text{Standard price} \times \left[\left(\begin{array}{c}\text{Actual} \\ \text{units} \\ \text{produced}\end{array} \times \begin{array}{c}\text{Actual} \\ \text{labor hours} \\ \text{per unit}\end{array} \right) - \left(\begin{array}{c}\text{Actual} \\ \text{units} \\ \text{produced}\end{array} \times \begin{array}{c}\text{Standard} \\ \text{labor hours} \\ \text{per unit}\end{array} \right) \right]$$

c) A favorable labor efficiency variance indicates the use of less than the standard number of labor hours. A favorable variance may therefore result from unusual efficiency or the production of lower quality products. An unfavorable labor efficiency variance may be caused by production delays resulting from materials shortages, inferior materials, or excessive work breaks.

c. The quantity variance for materials and the efficiency variance for labor can be further subdivided into **mix and yield variances**:

1) Mix variance = ATQ × (SMSP − AMSP)
2) Yield variance = (STQ − ATQ) × SMSP

d. A manufacturer's total **overhead variance** consists of variable and fixed portions.

1) The **variable overhead variance** consists of a spending variance and an efficiency variance.
2) The **fixed overhead variance** consists of a spending variance and a production-volume variance.

2. At the end of the current period, the following analysis of the flexible budget variance was prepared:

	Actual Amounts	Standard Amounts
Units	7,000	6,000
Selling Price	$65.00	$63.00
Materials Per Unit	1.50	2
Materials Price	$7.00	$6.00
Labor Hours Per Unit	3.50	3
Labor Price	$5.50	$5.00
Machine Hours Per Unit	2.00	1.50
VOH Application Rate	$4/Machine Hour	$3/Machine Hour
FOH Application Rate	$8/Machine Hour	$7.50/Machine Hour

	AQ × AP Actual Results (AR)	AR − FB Flexible Budget Variances	AQ × SP Flexible Budget (FB)	FB − SB Sales Volume Variances	SQ × SP Static Budget (SB)
Units sold	7,000		7,000	1,000	6,000
Revenue	$455,000	$14,000 F	$441,000	$63,000 F	$378,000
Variable costs:					
Direct materials	73,500	10,500 F	84,000	9,000 F	72,000
Direct labor	134,750	29,750 U	105,000	15,000 U	90,000
Variable nonmanufacturing overhead	56,000	24,500 U	31,500	9,000 U	27,000
Total variable costs	$264,250	$43,750	$220,500	$31,500	$189,000
Contribution margin	190,750	29,750	220,500	31,500	189,000
Fixed overhead	112,000	44,500 U	67,500	0	67,500
Operating income	$ 78,750	$74,250	$153,000	$31,500	$121,500

Total Flexible Budget Variance
$74,250 U

Total Sales Volume Variance
$31,500 F

Total Static Budget Variance
$42,750 U

Variances

MATERIALS VARIANCES

Price Variance
```
= (Actual Units  ×  Actual Materials/Unit)  ×  (Actual Price  −  Std Price)
= (7,000        ×  1.50)                   ×  ($7.00        −  $6.00)
= 10,500        ×  $1.00
= $10,500 U
```

Quantity Variance
```
= Std Price  ×  [(Actual Units  ×  Actual Materials/Unit)  −  (Actual Units  ×  Std Materials/Unit)]
= $6.00      ×  [(7,000         ×  1.50)                   −  (7,000        ×  2.00)]
= $6.00      ×  (10,500         −  14,000)
= $21,000 F
```

Direct Materials Price Variance $10,500 U
Direct Materials Quantity Variance $21,000 F
Direct Materials Flexible Budget Variance $10,500 F

LABOR VARIANCES

Rate Variance
```
= (Actual Units  ×  Actual Labor Hrs/Unit)  ×  (Actual Price  −  Std Price)
= (7,000         ×  3.50)                   ×  ($5.50        −  $5.00)
= 24,500         ×  $0.50
= $12,250 U
```

Efficiency Variance
```
= Std Price  ×  [(Actual Units  ×  Actual Labor Hrs/Unit)  −  (Actual Units  ×  Std Labor Hrs/Unit)]
= $5.00      ×  [(7,000         ×  3.50)                   −  (7,000        ×  3.00)]
= $5.00      ×  (24,500         −  21,000)
= $17,500 U
```

Direct Labor Rate Variance $12,250 U
Direct Labor Efficiency Variance $17,500 U
Direct Labor Flexible Budget Variance $29,750 U

VARIABLE OVERHEAD VARIANCES

Spending Variance
```
= Actual Allocation Base  ×  (Actual Application Rate  −  Budgeted Application Rate)
= 14,000                  ×  ($4.00                    −  $3.00)
= $14,000 U
```

Efficiency Variance
```
= Budgeted Application Rate  ×  [Actual Allocation Base  −  (Std Cost Driver/Unit  ×  Actual Units)]
= $3.00                      ×  [14,000                  −  (1.50*                 ×  7,000)]
= $3.00                      ×  (14,000                  −  10,500)
= $10,500 U
```

*The standard cost driver/unit is the standard input allowed for actual output. In this example, it is the $3 per machine hour (standard input) ÷ 2 machine hours per unit (actual output).

1.5 = $3 per machine hour ÷ 2 machine hours per unit

Variable Overhead Spending Variance $14,000 U
Variable Overhead Efficiency Variance $10,500 U
Variable Overhead Flexible Budget Variance $24,500 U

FIXED OVERHEAD VARIANCES
Spending Variance
= Actual Fixed Overhead − Budgeted Fixed Overhead
= $112,000 − 67,500
= $44,500 U

Production Volume Variance
= Budgeted Fixed Overhead − [Budgeted Application Rate × (Std Cost Driver/Unit × Actual Units)]
= $67,500 − [$7.50 × (1.50 × 7,000)]
= $67,500 − ($7.50 × 10,500)
= $11,250 F

	Actual Output at Actual Input and Cost	Actual Output at Standard Input and Cost	Variance
Materials	$ 73,500	$ 84,000	$10,500 F
Labor	134,750	105,000	29,750 U
Variable overhead	56,000	31,500	24,500 U
Fixed overhead	112,000	67,500	44,500 U
	376,250	288,000	
Net unfavorable variance		88,250	88,250 U
	$376,250	$376,250	

Stop and review! You have completed the outline for this subunit. Study multiple-choice questions 34 through 37 beginning on page 370.

10.8 SALES VARIANCES

1. **Single Product Sales Variances**

   a. Variance analysis is useful for evaluating not only the production function but also the selling function.

      1) If sales differ from the amount budgeted, the difference could be attributable to either the **sales price variance** or the **sales volume variance** (sum of the sales quantity and mix variances).
      2) The analysis of these variances concentrates on **contribution margins** because fixed costs are assumed to be constant.

   b. EXAMPLE: A firm has budgeted sales of 10,000 units of its sole product at $17 per unit. Variable costs are expected to be $10 per unit, and fixed costs are budgeted at $50,000. The following compares budgeted and actual results:

	Budget Computation	Budget Amount	Actual Computation	Actual Amount
Sales	10,000 units × $17 per unit	$170,000	11,000 units × $16 per unit	$176,000
Variable costs	10,000 units × $10 per unit	(100,000)	11,000 units × $10 per unit	(110,000)
Contribution margin		$ 70,000		$ 66,000
Fixed costs		(50,000)		(50,000)
Operating income		$ 20,000		$ 16,000
Unit contribution margin (UCM)	$70,000 ÷ 10,000 units	$7	$66,000 ÷ 11,000 units	$6

   1) Although sales were greater than budgeted, the actual contribution margin (ACM) is less than the standard contribution margin (SCM). The discrepancy can be analyzed in terms of the sales price variance and the sales volume variance.

   c. For a single product, the **sales price variance** is the change in the contribution margin attributable solely to the change in selling price (holding quantity constant).

$$Sales\ price\ variance = (AP - SP) \times AQ$$
$$= (\$16 - \$17) \times 11,000$$
$$= \$11,000\ U$$

d. For a single product, the **sales volume variance** is the change in the contribution margin attributable solely to the difference between the actual and standard unit sales.

```
Sales volume variance = (AQ - SQ) × SCM
                     = (11,000 - 10,000) × $7
                     = $7,000 F
```

1) For a single product, the sales mix variance is zero.

e. The sales price variance ($11,000 U) plus the sales volume variance ($7,000 F) equals the total change in the contribution margin ($4,000 U).

f. A similar analysis may be done for **cost of goods sold**.

1) The average production cost per unit is used instead of the average unit selling price, but the quantities for unit production are the same.
2) Accordingly, the overall variation in gross profit is the sum of the variation in revenue plus the variation in cost of goods sold.

2. **Multiproduct Sales Variances**

a. For two or more products, the multiproduct sales variances reflect not only the change in total unit sales but also the change in the sales mix.

1) The **multiproduct sales price variance** may be calculated as in the single-product case for each product. The results are then added.

a) An alternative is to multiply the actual total units sold times the difference between the following:

i) The weighted-average price based on actual units sold at actual unit prices
ii) The weighted-average price based on actual units sold at standard prices

2) The **multiproduct sales volume variance** may be calculated as in the single-product case for each product. The results are then added.

a) An alternative is to determine the difference between the following:

i) Actual total unit sales times the standard weighted-average UCM for the actual mix
ii) Standard total unit sales times the standard weighted-average UCM for the standard mix

3) The multiproduct sales volume variance consists of the sales quantity and sales mix variances.

a) The **sales quantity variance** is the difference between (1) the standard contribution margin based on actual unit sales and (2) the standard contribution margin based on standard unit sales.

i) One way to calculate this variance is to multiply the standard UCM (SUCM) for each product times the difference between (a) its standard percentage of actual total unit sales and (b) the standard unit sales of the product. The results for each product are then added together. The equation to calculate this variance for each product is

```
Sales quantity variance = SUCM × [(Total AQ × Standard mix %) - Standard unit sales]
```

- An alternative is to multiply the standard weighted-average UCM based on the standard mix times the difference between (1) total actual unit sales and (2) the total standard unit sales.

b) The **sales mix variance** is the difference between (1) the standard contribution margin for the actual mix and actual total unit sales and (2) the standard contribution margin for the standard mix and actual total unit sales.

  i) One way to calculate this variance is to multiply the SUCM for each product times the difference between (a) actual unit sales of the product and (b) its standard percentage of actual total unit sales. The results for each product are then added together. The equation to calculate this variance for each product is

```
Sales mix variance = SUCM × [AQ − (Total AQ × Standard mix %)]
```

- An alternative is to multiply total actual unit sales times the difference between (1) the standard weighted-average UCM for the standard mix and (2) the standard weighted-average UCM for the actual mix.

4) **Comprehensive example:**

	Plastic	Metal	Total
Standard selling price per unit	$6.00	$10.00	
Standard variable cost per unit	3.00	7.50	
Standard contribution margin per unit	$3.00	$ 2.50	
Standard unit sales	300	200	500
Standard mix percentage	60%	40%	100%
Actual units sold	260	260	520
Actual selling price per unit	$6.00	$9.50	

a) As shown below (000 omitted), the **total contribution margin variance** was $100 unfavorable ($130 unfavorable sales price variance − $30 favorable sales volume variance).

Sales price variance:
  Plastic 260 × ($6.00 − $6.00) $ 0
  Metal 260 × ($10 − $9.50)   (130) $130 unfavorable
Sales volume variance:
  Plastic (260 − 300) × $3.00 $(120)
  Metal (260 − 200) × $2.50   150 $ 30 favorable
Total contribution margin variance $100 unfavorable

b) The sales volume variance consists of the following:

Sales quantity variance:
  Plastic [(520 × .6) − 300] × $3.00 $ 36
  Metal [(520 × .4) − 200] × $2.50   20 $ 56 favorable
Sales mix variance:
  Plastic [260 − (520 × .6)] × $3.00 $(156)
  Metal [260 − (520 × .4)] × $2.50   130 $ 26 unfavorable
Sales volume variance $ 30 favorable

Stop and review! You have completed the outline for this subunit. Study multiple-choice questions 38 through 40 beginning on page 371.

QUESTIONS

10.1 Variance Analysis Overview

1. The purpose of identifying manufacturing variances and assigning their responsibility to a person/department should be to

A. Use the knowledge about the variances to promote learning and continuous improvement in the manufacturing operations.

B. Trace the variances to finished goods so that the inventory can be properly valued at year-end.

C. Determine the proper cost of the products produced so that selling prices can be adjusted accordingly.

D. Pinpoint fault for operating problems in the organization.

Answer (A) is correct.
REQUIRED: The purpose of identifying and assigning responsibility for manufacturing variances.
DISCUSSION: The purpose of identifying and assigning responsibility for variances is to determine who is likely to have information that will enable management to find solutions. The constructive approach is to promote learning and continuous improvement in manufacturing operations, not to assign blame. However, information about variances may be useful in evaluating managers' performance.
Answer (B) is incorrect. Depending on a cost-benefit determination, variances either are adjustments of cost of goods sold or are allocated among the inventory accounts and cost of goods sold. Moreover, the accounting issues are distinct from supervisory considerations. Answer (C) is incorrect. Selling prices are based on much more than the cost of production; for instance, competitive pressure is also a consideration. Answer (D) is incorrect. By itself, pinpointing fault is not an appropriate objective. Continuous improvement is the ultimate objective.

2. A difference between standard costs used for cost control and the budgeted costs of the same manufacturing effort can exist because

A. Standard costs represent what costs should be, whereas budgeted costs are expected actual costs.

B. Budgeted costs are historical costs, whereas standard costs are based on engineering studies.

C. Budgeted costs include some slack, whereas standard costs do not.

D. Standard costs include some slack, whereas budgeted costs do not.

Answer (A) is correct.
REQUIRED: The difference between standard costs and budgeted costs.
DISCUSSION: In the long run, these costs should be the same. In the short run, however, they may differ because standard costs represent what costs should be, whereas budgeted costs are expected actual costs. Budgeted costs may vary widely from standard costs in certain months, but, for an annual budget period, the amounts should be similar.
Answer (B) is incorrect. Standard costs are not necessarily determined by engineering studies. Answer (C) is incorrect. Standard costs are usually based on currently attainable standards applicable when a process is under control. They are set without regard to variances or slack. Answer (D) is incorrect. Budgeted costs include expected deviations from the standards.

10.2 Static and Flexible Budget Variances

3. The corporation expected to sell 150,000 board games during the month of November, and the corporation's master budget contained the following data related to the sale and production of these games:

Revenue	$2,400,000
Cost of goods sold:	
Direct materials	675,000
Direct labor	300,000
Variable overhead	450,000
Contribution margin	$ 975,000
Fixed overhead	250,000
Fixed selling and administration	500,000
Operating income	$ 225,000

Actual sales during November were 180,000 games. Using a flexible budget, the corporation expects the operating income for the month of November to be

A. $225,000

B. $270,000

C. $420,000

D. $510,000

Answer (C) is correct.
REQUIRED: The expected operating income based on a flexible budget at a given production level.
DISCUSSION: Revenue of $2,400,000 reflects a unit selling price of $16 ($2,400,000 ÷ 150,000 games). The contribution margin is $975,000, or $6.50 per game ($975,000 ÷ 150,000 games). Increasing sales will result in an increased contribution margin of $195,000 (30,000 games × $6.50). Since fixed costs are, by their nature, unchanging across the relevant range, net income will increase to $420,000 ($225,000 originally reported + $195,000).
Answer (A) is incorrect. The net income before the increase in sales is $225,000. Answer (B) is incorrect. Net income was originally $1.50 per game. The $270,000 figure simply extrapolates that amount to sales of 180,000 games. Answer (D) is incorrect. Treating variable overhead as a fixed cost results in $510,000. Variable overhead is a $3 component ($450,000 ÷ 150,000 units) of unit variable cost.

4. A major disadvantage of a static budget is that

A. It is more difficult to develop than a flexible budget.
B. It is made for only one level of activity.
C. Variances tend to be smaller than when flexible budgeting is used.
D. Variances are more difficult to compute than when flexible budgeting is used.

Answer (B) is correct.
REQUIRED: A major disadvantage of the static budget.
DISCUSSION: Static budgets are prepared based on the best estimates for output to be produced and costs to be incurred before the period begins. If there are any variations in conditions actually experienced, the static budget is unhelpful for diagnosing specific problem areas since it only reflects one level of activity. Answer (A) is incorrect. A static budget is easier to prepare than a flexible budget. Answer (C) is incorrect. The size of the variances encountered is not a function of the budgeting system used. Answer (D) is incorrect. Variances are no harder to compute under static budgeting than under flexible budgeting.

5. A manufacturing firm planned to manufacture and sell 100,000 units of product during the year at a variable cost per unit of $4.00 and a fixed cost per unit of $2.00. The firm fell short of its goal and only manufactured 80,000 units at a total incurred cost of $515,000. The firm's manufacturing cost variance was

A. $85,000 favorable.
B. $35,000 unfavorable.
C. $5,000 favorable.
D. $5,000 unfavorable.

Answer (C) is correct.
REQUIRED: The manufacturing cost variance.
DISCUSSION: The firm planned to produce 100,000 units at $6 each ($4 variable + $2 fixed cost), or a total of $600,000, consisting of $400,000 of variable costs and $200,000 of fixed costs. Total production was only 80,000 units at a total cost of $515,000. The flexible budget for a production level of 80,000 units includes variable costs of $320,000 (80,000 units × $4). Fixed costs would remain at $200,000. Thus, the total flexible budget costs are $520,000. Given that actual costs were only $515,000, the variance is $5,000 favorable.
Answer (A) is incorrect. The amount of $85,000 favorable is based on a production level of 100,000 units. Answer (B) is incorrect. The variance is favorable. Answer (D) is incorrect. The variance is favorable.

6. The difference between the actual amounts and the flexible budget amounts for the actual output achieved is the

A. Production volume variance.
B. Flexible budget variance.
C. Sales volume variance.
D. Standard cost variance.

Answer (B) is correct.
REQUIRED: The term for the difference between the actual amounts and the flexible budget amounts.
DISCUSSION: A flexible budget is prepared at the end of the budget period when the actual results are available. A flexible budget reflects the revenues that should have been earned and costs that should have been incurred given the achieved levels of production and sales. The difference between the flexible budget and actual figures is known as the flexible budget variance.
Answer (A) is incorrect. The production volume variance equals under- or overapplied fixed overhead. Answer (C) is incorrect. The sales volume variance is the difference between the flexible budget amount and the static budget amount. Answer (D) is incorrect. A standard cost variance is not necessarily based on a flexible budget.

7. The company's master budget shows straight-line depreciation on factory equipment of $258,000. The master budget was prepared at an annual production volume of 103,200 units of product. This production volume is expected to occur uniformly throughout the year. During September, the company produced 8,170 units of product, and the accounts reflected actual depreciation on factory machinery of $20,500. The company controls manufacturing costs with a flexible budget. The flexible budget amount for depreciation on factory machinery for September would be

A. $19,475
B. $20,425
C. $20,500
D. $21,500

Answer (D) is correct.
REQUIRED: The amount of depreciation expense shown on the flexible budget for the month.
DISCUSSION: Since depreciation is a fixed cost, that cost will be the same each month regardless of production. Therefore, the budget for September would show depreciation of $21,500 ($258,000 annual depreciation × 1/12).
Answer (A) is incorrect. Depreciation is a fixed cost that will be the same each month regardless of production. The budget for September would show depreciation of $21,500 ($258,000 × 1/12). Answer (B) is incorrect. The amount of $20,425 is based on the units-of-production method. Answer (C) is incorrect. The amount shown in the accounts is $20,500.

SU 10: Cost and Variance Measures

8. A static budget

A. Drops the current month or quarter and adds a future month or a future quarter as the current month or quarter is completed.

B. Presents a statement of expectations for a period but does not present a firm commitment.

C. Presents the plan for only one level of activity and does not adjust to changes in the level of activity.

D. Presents the plan for a range of activity so that the plan can be adjusted for changes in activity.

Answer (C) is correct.
REQUIRED: The definition of a static budget.
DISCUSSION: A static budget plans for only one level of activity and does not provide for changed levels of activity.
Answer (A) is incorrect. Budgets dropping the current month or quarter and adding a future month or quarter as the current month or quarter is completed are known as continuous budgets. Answer (B) is incorrect. A statement of expectations for a period without a firm commitment is a forecast. Answer (D) is incorrect. A budget planning for a range of activities so the plan can be adjusted for a change in activity level is known as a flexible budget.

9. When preparing a performance report for a cost center using flexible budgeting techniques, the planned cost column should be based on the

A. Budgeted amount in the original budget prepared before the beginning of the year.

B. Actual amount for the same period in the preceding year.

C. Budget adjusted to the actual level of activity for the period being reported.

D. Budget adjusted to the planned level of activity for the period being reported.

Answer (C) is correct.
REQUIRED: The basis for the planned cost column in a flexible budget performance report.
DISCUSSION: If a report is to be used for performance evaluation, the planned cost column should be based on the actual level of activity for the period. The ability to adjust amounts for varying activity levels is the primary advantage of flexible budgeting.
Answer (A) is incorrect. The static budget amount is not useful for comparison purposes. The budget for the actual activity level achieved is more important. Answer (B) is incorrect. Prior-year figures are not useful if activity levels are different. Answer (D) is incorrect. A budget based on planned activity level is not as meaningful as one based on actual activity level.

10. Based on past experience, a company has developed the following budget formula for estimating its shipping expenses. The company's shipments average 12 lbs. per shipment:

Shipping costs = $16,000 + ($0.50 × lbs. shipped)

The planned activity and actual activity regarding orders and shipments for the current month are given in the following schedule:

	Plan	Actual
Sales orders	800	780
Shipments	800	820
Units shipped	8,000	9,000
Sales	$120,000	$144,000
Total pounds shipped	9,600	12,300

The actual shipping costs for the month amounted to $21,000. The appropriate monthly flexible budget allowance for shipping costs for the purpose of performance evaluation would be

A. $20,680
B. $20,920
C. $20,800
D. $22,150

Answer (D) is correct.
REQUIRED: The appropriate budgeted amount for shipping costs when 12,300 pounds are shipped.
DISCUSSION: The flexible budget formula is

Shipping costs = $16,000 + ($.50 × lbs. shipped)

Therefore, to determine the flexible budget amount, multiply the actual pounds shipped (12,300) times the standard cost ($.50) to arrive at a total expected variable cost of $6,150. Adding the variable cost to $16,000 of fixed cost produces a budget total of $22,150.
Answer (A) is incorrect. The amount of $20,680 is based on the actual number of sales orders, rather than on pounds shipped. Answer (B) is incorrect. The amount of $20,920 is based on the number of shipments, not the number of pounds shipped. Answer (C) is incorrect. The amount of $20,800 is based on planned pounds shipped of 9,600, not actual pounds shipped of 12,300.

10.3 Direct Materials Variances

> Questions 11 through 13 are based on the following information. ChemKing uses a standard costing system in the manufacture of its single product. The 35,000 units of direct materials in inventory were purchased for $105,000, and two units of direct materials are required to produce one unit of final product. In November, the company produced 12,000 units of product. The standard allowed for materials was $60,000, and the unfavorable quantity variance was $2,500.

11. ChemKing's standard price for one unit of direct materials is

A. $2.00
B. $2.50
C. $3.00
D. $5.00

Answer (B) is correct.
REQUIRED: The standard price for one unit of direct materials.
DISCUSSION: Given that the company produced 12,000 units with a total standard cost for direct materials of $60,000, the standard cost must be $5.00 ($60,000 ÷ 12,000 units) per unit of finished product. Because each unit of finished product requires two units of direct materials, the standard unit cost for direct materials must be $2.50.
Answer (A) is incorrect. The unit standard cost is $2.50. Answer (C) is incorrect. The actual cost per unit of direct materials is $3. Answer (D) is incorrect. The total standard cost of direct materials for each unit of finished product is $5.

12. ChemKing's units of direct materials used to produce November output totaled

A. 12,000 units.
B. 12,500 units.
C. 23,000 units.
D. 25,000 units.

Answer (D) is correct.
REQUIRED: The number of units of direct materials used to produce November output.
DISCUSSION: The company produced 12,000 units of output, each of which required two units of direct materials. Thus, the standard input allowed for direct materials was 24,000 units at a standard cost of $2.50 each [$60,000 ÷ (12,000 units of output × 2 units of direct materials)]. An unfavorable quantity variance signifies that the actual quantity used was greater than the standard input allowed. The direct materials quantity variance equals the standard price per unit times the difference between actual and standard quantities. Consequently, because 1,000 ($2,500 U ÷ $2.50) additional units were used, the actual total quantity must have been 25,000 units (24,000 standard + 1,000).
Answer (A) is incorrect. The number of units of finished product is 12,000. Answer (B) is incorrect. Assuming that each unit of finished product includes only one unit of direct materials results in 12,500 units. Answer (C) is incorrect. Assuming a favorable quantity variance results in 23,000 units.

13. ChemKing's direct materials price variance for the units used in November was

A. $2,500 unfavorable.
B. $11,000 unfavorable.
C. $12,500 unfavorable.
D. $3,500 unfavorable.

Answer (C) is correct.
REQUIRED: The direct materials price variance for the units used in November.
DISCUSSION: The standard price was $2.50 [$60,000 ÷ (12,000 units of output × 2 units of direct materials)]. An unfavorable quantity variance of $2,500 means that 1,000 ($2,500 U ÷ $2.50) additional units were used, resulting in an actual total quantity of 25,000 units [(12,000 units of output × 2 units of direct materials) + 1,000]. Actual price was $3.00 ($105,000 total cost ÷ 35,000 units purchased). Consequently, the direct materials price variance is $12,500 unfavorable {AQ × (AP − SP) = [25,000 units × ($3.00 − $2.50)]}.
Answer (A) is incorrect. The direct materials quantity variance is $2,500 unfavorable. Answer (B) is incorrect. The price variance is $12,500, or $.50 per unit. Answer (D) is incorrect. The price variance is $12,500, or $.50 per unit.

SU 10: Cost and Variance Measures 363

14. A favorable materials price variance coupled with an unfavorable materials usage variance **most** likely results from

A. Machine efficiency problems.
B. Product mix production changes.
C. The purchase and use of higher-than-standard quality materials.
D. The purchase of lower than standard quality materials.

Answer (D) is correct.
REQUIRED: The cause of a favorable materials price variance coupled with an unfavorable materials usage variance.
DISCUSSION: A favorable materials price variance is the result of paying less than the standard price for materials. An unfavorable materials usage variance is the result of using an excessive quantity of materials. If a purchasing manager were to buy substandard materials to achieve a favorable price variance, an unfavorable quantity variance could result from using an excessive amount of poor quality materials.
Answer (A) is incorrect. Machine efficiency problems do not explain the price variance. Answer (B) is incorrect. A change in product mix does not explain the price variance. Answer (C) is incorrect. Materials of higher-than-standard quality are more likely to cause an unfavorable price variance and a favorable quantity variance.

15. A manufacturer planned to produce 5,000 units of its single product during November. The standard specifications for one unit include ten pounds of materials at $.50 per pound. Actual production in November was 5,200 units. The accountant computed a favorable materials purchase price variance of $580 and an unfavorable materials quantity variance of $320. Based on these variances, one could conclude that

A. More materials were purchased than were used.
B. More materials were used than were purchased.
C. The actual cost of materials was less than the standard cost.
D. The actual usage of materials was less than the standard allowed.

Answer (C) is correct.
REQUIRED: The implication of a favorable materials price variance or an unfavorable materials quantity variance.
DISCUSSION: A favorable price variance indicates that the materials were purchased at a price less than standard. The unfavorable quantity variance indicates that the quantity of materials used for actual production exceeded the standard quantity for the good units produced.
Answer (A) is incorrect. The quantity of materials purchased cannot be determined from the information given. Answer (B) is incorrect. The quantity of materials purchased cannot be determined from the information given. Answer (D) is incorrect. The actual usage was greater than standard.

16. A company planned to produce 3,000 units of its single product, Titactium, during November. The standard specifications for one unit of Titactium include 6 pounds of materials at $.30 per pound. Actual production in November was 3,100 units of Titactium. The accountant computed a favorable direct materials purchase price variance of $380 and an unfavorable direct materials quantity variance of $120. Based on these variances, one could conclude that

A. More materials were purchased than were used.
B. More materials were used than were purchased.
C. The actual cost of materials was less than the standard cost.
D. The actual usage of materials was less than the standard allowed.

Answer (C) is correct.
REQUIRED: The meaning of a favorable direct materials purchase price variance and an unfavorable direct materials quantity variance.
DISCUSSION: The direct materials purchase price variance may be isolated at the time of purchase or at the time of transfer to production. It equals the actual quantity of materials purchased or transferred times the difference between the standard and actual unit prices. Hence, a favorable direct materials purchase price variance means that materials were purchased at a price less than the standard price.
Answer (A) is incorrect. No variance relates quantity purchased to quantity used. Answer (B) is incorrect. No variance relates quantity purchased to quantity used. Answer (D) is incorrect. The unfavorable quantity variance indicates that more materials were used than allowed by the standards. The direct materials quantity variance equals the standard unit price times the difference between the standard quantity allowed for the actual output and the actual quantity used.

17. Price variances and efficiency variances can be key to the performance measurement within a company. In evaluating the performance within a company, a materials efficiency variance can be caused by all of the following **except** the

A. Performance of the workers using the material.
B. Actions of the purchasing department.
C. Design of the product.
D. Sales volume of the product.

Answer (D) is correct.
 REQUIRED: The item not a cause of a materials efficiency variance.
 DISCUSSION: An unfavorable materials quantity or usage (efficiency) variance can be caused by a number of factors, including waste, shrinkage, theft, poor performance by production workers, nonskilled workers, or the purchase of below-standard-quality materials by the purchasing department. Changes in product design can also affect the quantity of materials used. Sales volume of the product should not be a contributing factor to a materials efficiency variance.
 Answer (A) is incorrect. Worker performance is a possible cause of a materials efficiency variance. Answer (B) is incorrect. Purchasing department actions are possible causes of a materials efficiency variance. Answer (C) is incorrect. Product design is a possible cause of a materials efficiency variance.

18. A company uses a standard cost system. The standard for each finished unit of product allows for 3 pounds of plastic at $0.72 per pound. During December, the company bought 4,500 pounds of plastic at $0.75 per pound, and used 4,100 pounds in the production of 1,300 finished units of product. What is the materials purchase price variance for the month of December?

A. $117 unfavorable.
B. $123 unfavorable.
C. $135 unfavorable.
D. $150 unfavorable.

Answer (C) is correct.
 REQUIRED: The materials purchase price variance.
 DISCUSSION: The materials purchase price variance equals the quantity purchased multiplied by the difference between the standard price and the actual price, or $135 unfavorable [4,500 lbs. × ($.75 – $.72)].
 Answer (A) is incorrect. The variance of $117 unfavorable is based on the standard input for 1,300 units. Answer (B) is incorrect. The variance of $123 unfavorable is based on the actual quantity used. Answer (D) is incorrect. The variance of $150 unfavorable is based on the assumption that 5,000 lbs. were purchased.

10.4 Direct Labor Variances

19. Under a standard cost system, direct labor price variances are usually **not** attributable to

A. Union contracts approved before the budgeting cycle.
B. Labor rate predictions.
C. The use of a single average standard rate.
D. The assignment of different skill levels of workers than planned.

Answer (A) is correct.
 REQUIRED: The factor that usually does not affect the direct labor price variance.
 DISCUSSION: The direct labor price (rate) variance is the actual hours worked times the difference between the standard rate and the actual rate paid. This difference may be attributable to (1) a change in labor rates since the establishment of the standards, (2) using a single average standard rate despite different rates earned among different employees, (3) assigning higher-paid workers to jobs estimated to require lower-paid workers (or vice versa), or (4) paying hourly rates, but basing standards on piecework rates (or vice versa). The difference should not be caused by a union contract approved before the budgeting cycle because such rates would have been incorporated into the standards.
 Answer (B) is incorrect. Predictions about labor rates may have been inaccurate. Answer (C) is incorrect. Using a single average standard rate may lead to variances if some workers are paid more than others and the proportions of hours worked differ from estimates. Answer (D) is incorrect. Assigning higher paid (and higher skilled) workers to jobs not requiring such skills leads to an unfavorable variance.

Questions 20 through 22 are based on the following information. Jackson Industries employs a standard cost system in which direct materials inventory is carried at standard cost. Jackson has established the following standards for the prime costs of one unit of product.

	Standard Quantity	Standard Price	Standard Cost
Direct materials	5 pounds	$ 3.60/pound	$18.00
Direct labor	1.25 hours	$12.00/hour	15.00
			$33.00

During May, Jackson purchased 125,000 pounds of direct materials at a total cost of $475,000. The total factory wages for May were $364,000, 90% of which were for direct labor. Jackson manufactured 22,000 units of product during May using 108,000 pounds of direct materials and 28,000 direct labor hours.

20. Jackson's direct materials usage (quantity) variance for May is

A. $7,200 unfavorable.
B. $7,600 favorable.
C. $5,850 unfavorable.
D. $7,200 favorable.

Answer (D) is correct.
REQUIRED: The direct materials usage (quantity) variance.
DISCUSSION: This variance equals the standard unit cost times the difference between the actual quantity used and the standard quantity for good production. Consequently, the variance is $7,200 favorable {[(5 pounds × 22,000 units) – 108,000 pounds used] × $3.60}.
Answer (A) is incorrect. The variance is favorable. Answer (B) is incorrect. The variance is calculated by multiplying the quantity difference times the standard unit cost of $3.60, not the actual unit cost. Answer (C) is incorrect. The variance is favorable. Actual usage was less than the standard.

21. Jackson's direct labor price (rate) variance for May is

A. $8,400 favorable.
B. $7,200 unfavorable.
C. $8,400 unfavorable.
D. $6,000 unfavorable.

Answer (A) is correct.
REQUIRED: The direct labor rate variance.
DISCUSSION: The direct labor rate variance equals the actual quantity of hours worked times the difference between the standard and actual labor rates. Total direct labor cost was $327,600 ($364,000 × 90%), and the actual unit direct labor cost was $11.70 ($327,600 ÷ 28,000 hours). Thus, the variance is $8,400 favorable [28,000 hours × ($12.00 – $11.70)].
Answer (B) is incorrect. The variance is favorable. The actual labor rate was less than the standard rate. Answer (C) is incorrect. The variance is favorable. The actual labor rate was less than the standard rate. Answer (D) is incorrect. The labor efficiency variance is $6,000, not the labor rate variance.

22. Jackson's direct labor usage (efficiency) variance for May is

A. $5,850 favorable.
B. $6,000 unfavorable.
C. $5,850 unfavorable.
D. $6,000 favorable.

Answer (B) is correct.
REQUIRED: The direct labor usage (efficiency) variance.
DISCUSSION: The direct labor efficiency variance equals the standard unit cost times the difference between actual hours and standard hours. Accordingly, the variance is $6,000 unfavorable {[28,000 hours – (1.25 hours × 22,000 units)] × $12}.
Answer (A) is incorrect. The variance is unfavorable. More hours were worked than allowed by the standards. Answer (C) is incorrect. The labor efficiency variance is calculated using the standard labor rate, not the actual labor rate. Answer (D) is incorrect. The variance is unfavorable.

23. The static budget for the month of May was for 9,000 units with direct materials at $15 per unit. Direct labor was budgeted at 45 minutes per unit for a total of $81,000. Actual output for the month was 8,500 units with $127,500 in direct materials and $77,775 in direct labor expense. The direct labor standard of 45 minutes was maintained throughout the month. Variance analysis of the performance for the month of May shows a(n)

A. Favorable direct materials usage variance of $7,500.
B. Favorable direct labor efficiency variance of $1,275.
C. Unfavorable direct labor efficiency variance of $1,275.
D. Unfavorable direct labor price variance of $1,275.

Answer (D) is correct.
REQUIRED: The result of variance analysis based on a flexible budget for direct labor and materials.
DISCUSSION: Because direct labor for 9,000 units was budgeted at $81,000, the unit direct labor cost is $9. Thus, the direct labor budget for 8,500 units is $76,500, and the total direct labor variance is $1,275 ($77,775 − $76,500). Because the actual cost is greater than the budgeted amounts, the $1,275 variance is unfavorable. Given that the actual time per unit (45 minutes) was the same as that budgeted, no direct labor efficiency variance was incurred. Hence, the entire $1,275 unfavorable variance must be attributable to the direct labor rate (or price) variance.
Answer (A) is incorrect. The amount of $7,500 equals the difference between the static budget output (9,000 units) and the flexible budget output (8,500 units), multiplied by the budgeted unit cost of direct materials ($15). This amount is not a direct materials usage variance [(Actual quantity of input − Standard quantity of input) × Standard price of input]. Answer (B) is incorrect. No direct labor efficiency variance occurred. Budgeted hours were identical to actual hours for 8,500 units. Answer (C) is incorrect. No direct labor efficiency variance occurred. Budgeted hours were identical to actual hours for 8,500 units.

24. An unfavorable direct labor efficiency variance could be caused by a(n)

A. Unfavorable variable overhead spending variance.
B. Unfavorable direct materials usage variance.
C. Unfavorable fixed overhead volume variance.
D. Favorable variable overhead spending variance.

Answer (B) is correct.
REQUIRED: The possible cause of an unfavorable direct labor efficiency variance.
DISCUSSION: An unfavorable direct labor efficiency variance indicates that actual hours exceeded standard hours. Too many hours may have been used because of inefficiency on the part of employees, excessive coffee breaks, machine down-time, inadequate materials, or materials of poor quality that required excessive rework. An unfavorable direct materials usage variance might be related to an unfavorable labor efficiency variance. Working on a greater quantity of direct materials may require more direct labor time.
Answer (A) is incorrect. The variable overhead spending variance may be affected by, but does not affect, a direct labor efficiency variance. It equals the difference between actual variable overhead, which includes indirect but not direct labor, and the variable overhead applied based on the standard rate and the actual activity level, which may or may not be measured in direct labor hours. Thus, the effect of an unfavorable direct labor efficiency variance is to decrease an unfavorable variable overhead spending variance or to increase a favorable variable overhead spending variance. Answer (C) is incorrect. The fixed overhead volume variance does not affect, and is not affected by, a direct labor efficiency variance. It equals the difference between budgeted fixed overhead and the fixed overhead applied based on the standard rate and the standard input (e.g., direct labor) allowed for the actual output. Answer (D) is incorrect. The variable overhead spending variance may be affected by, but does not affect, a direct labor efficiency variance. It equals the difference between actual variable overhead, which includes indirect but not direct labor, and the variable overhead applied based on the standard rate and the actual activity level, which may or may not be measured in direct labor hours. Thus, the effect of an unfavorable direct labor efficiency variance is to decrease an unfavorable variable overhead spending variance or to increase a favorable variable overhead spending variance.

SU 10: Cost and Variance Measures

25. A manager prepared the following table by which to analyze labor costs for the month:

Actual Hours at Actual Rate	Actual Hours at Standard Rate	Standard Hours at Standard Rate
$10,000	$9,800	$8,820

What variance was $980?

A. Labor efficiency variance.
B. Labor rate variance.
C. Volume variance.
D. Labor spending variance.

Answer (A) is correct.
REQUIRED: The variance that equaled the specified amount.
DISCUSSION: The labor efficiency variance is $980 ($9,800 – $8,820). It is the difference between actual and standard hours multiplied by the standard labor rate.
Answer (B) is incorrect. The labor rate variance is $200. It is the difference between the actual and standard rates time the actual hours. Answer (C) is incorrect. The volume variance is the difference between budgeted fixed overhead and the amount applied based on the standard input allowed for the actual output. Answer (D) is incorrect. The term "spending variance" is usually applied to overhead variances.

10.5 Mix and Yield Variances

26. The efficiency variance for either direct labor or materials can be divided into

A. Spending variance and yield variance.
B. Yield variance and price variance.
C. Volume variance and mix variance.
D. Yield variance and mix variance.

Answer (D) is correct.
REQUIRED: The components into which a direct labor or materials efficiency variance can be divided.
DISCUSSION: A direct labor or materials efficiency variance is calculated by multiplying the difference between standard and actual usage times the standard cost per unit of input. The efficiency variances can be divided into yield and mix variances. Mix and yield variances are calculated only when the production process involves combining several materials or classes of labor in varying proportions (when substitutions are allowable in combining resources).
Answer (A) is incorrect. A spending variance is not the same as an efficiency variance. Answer (B) is incorrect. A price variance is not the same as an efficiency variance. Answer (C) is incorrect. A volume variance is based on fixed costs, and an efficiency variance is based on variable costs.

10.6 Overhead Variances

27. A manufacturer has an estimated practical capacity of 90,000 machine hours, and each unit requires two machine hours. The following data apply to a recent accounting period:

Actual variable overhead	$240,000
Actual fixed overhead	$442,000
Actual machine hours worked	88,000
Actual finished units produced	42,000
Budgeted variable overhead at 90,000 machine hours	$200,000
Budgeted fixed overhead	$450,000

Of the following factors, the manufacturer's production volume variance is **most** likely to have been caused by

A. A wage hike granted to a production supervisor.
B. A newly imposed initiative to reduce finished goods inventory levels.
C. Acceptance of an unexpected sales order.
D. Temporary employment of workers with lower skill levels than originally anticipated.

Answer (B) is correct.
REQUIRED: The most likely cause of a production volume overhead variance.
DISCUSSION: Fixed overhead was budgeted based on a practical capacity of 90,000 machine hours. Because the standard hours allowed for actual output was 84,000 hours (42,000 units × 2 hours per unit), fixed overhead was underapplied, and an unfavorable production-volume variance resulted. The only one of the four actions that would result in fewer machine hours than were budgeted being consumed is the initiative to reduce finished goods inventory levels.
Answer (A) is incorrect. A wage hike to a production supervisor is a variable cost and would thus affect the variable, not the fixed, variance. Answer (C) is incorrect. An unexpected sales order would result in more machine hours than were budgeted, not fewer. In other words, an unexpected order would result in a variable volume variance. Answer (D) is incorrect. Worker wages are a variable cost and would thus affect the variable, not the fixed, overhead variance.

28. Which one of the following variances is of **least** significance from a behavioral control perspective?

A. Unfavorable direct materials quantity variance amounting to 20% of the quantity allowed for the output attained.

B. Unfavorable direct labor efficiency variance amounting to 10% more than the budgeted hours for the output attained.

C. Favorable direct labor rate variance resulting from an inability to hire experienced workers to replace retiring workers.

D. Fixed overhead volume variance resulting from management's decision midway through the fiscal year to reduce its budgeted output by 20%.

Answer (D) is correct.
REQUIRED: The variance of least significance from a behavioral control perspective.
DISCUSSION: Most variances are of significance to someone who is responsible for that variance. However, a fixed overhead volume variance is often not the responsibility of anyone other than top management. The fixed overhead volume variance equals the difference between budgeted fixed overhead and the amount applied (standard input allowed for the actual output × standard rate). It can be caused by economic downturns, labor strife, bad weather, or a change in planned output. Thus, a fixed overhead volume variance resulting from a top management decision to reduce output has fewer behavioral implications than other variances.
Answer (A) is incorrect. An unfavorable direct materials quantity variance affects production management and possibly the purchasing function. It may indicate an inefficient use of materials or the use of poor quality materials. Answer (B) is incorrect. An unfavorable direct labor efficiency variance reflects upon production workers who have used too many hours. Answer (C) is incorrect. A favorable direct labor rate variance related to hiring is a concern of the human resources function. The favorable rate variance might be more than offset by an unfavorable direct labor efficiency variance or a direct materials quantity variance (if waste occurred).

29. Variable overhead is applied on the basis of standard direct labor hours. If, for a given period, the direct labor efficiency variance is unfavorable, the variable overhead efficiency variance will be

A. Favorable.
B. Unfavorable.
C. Zero.
D. The same amount as the direct labor efficiency variance.

Answer (B) is correct.
REQUIRED: The effect on the variable overhead efficiency variance.
DISCUSSION: If variable overhead is applied to production on the basis of direct labor hours, both the variable overhead efficiency variance and the direct labor efficiency variance will be calculated on the basis of the same number of hours. If the direct labor efficiency variance is unfavorable, the overhead efficiency variance will also be unfavorable because both variances are based on the difference between standard and actual direct labor hours worked.
Answer (A) is incorrect. Both efficiency variances are based on the same number of hours worked. Thus, if one is unfavorable, the other will also be unfavorable. Answer (C) is incorrect. Both efficiency variances are based on the same number of hours worked. Thus, if one is unfavorable, the other will also be unfavorable. Answer (D) is incorrect. The amount of the variances will be different depending on the amount of the costs anticipated and actually paid.

30. A manufacturer uses a standard cost system with overhead applied based upon direct labor hours. The manufacturing budget for the production of 5,000 units for the month of May included the following information:

Direct labor
10,000 hours at $15 per hour $150,000
Variable overhead   30,000
Fixed overhead   80,000

During May, 6,000 units were produced and the fixed overhead budget variance was $2,000 favorable. Fixed overhead during May was

A. Underapplied by $2,000.
B. Underapplied by $16,000.
C. Overapplied by $16,000.
D. Overapplied by $18,000.

Answer (D) is correct.
REQUIRED: The amount of overapplied overhead given relevant information.
DISCUSSION: First, the actual production level for the month was 6,000 units of output. Second, the standard number of labor hours consumed per unit of output is 2 (10,000 budgeted direct labor hours ÷ 5,000 budgeted units output). Third, since fixed overhead for the month was budgeted at $80,000 and it is to be applied in proportion to 10,000 budgeted direct labor hours, the application rate is $8 per direct labor hour ($80,000 ÷ 10,000). Thus, the amount of fixed overhead applied for the month was $96,000 = (6,000 × $8 × 2). The fixed overhead budget variance was $2,000 favorable, which means the actual fixed overhead incurred for the month was $78,000 ($80,000 − $2,000). Thus, fixed overhead was overapplied by $18,000 ($96,000 − $78,000).
Answer (A) is incorrect. Misinterpreting the $2,000 favorable budget (spending) variance results in $2,000 underapplied. Answer (B) is incorrect. Reversing the proper order of subtraction results in $16,000 underapplied. Answer (C) is incorrect. The production-volume variance is $16,000 overapplied.

SU 10: Cost and Variance Measures

31. The fixed overhead volume variance is the

A. Measure of the lost profits from the lack of sales volume.
B. Amount of the underapplied or overapplied fixed overhead costs.
C. Potential cost reduction that can be achieved from better cost control.
D. Measure of production inefficiency.

Answer (B) is correct.
REQUIRED: The definition of fixed overhead volume variance.
DISCUSSION: The fixed overhead volume variance is the difference between budgeted fixed costs and actual overhead applied, which equals the budgeted fixed overhead rate times the standard input allowed for the actual output. It is solely a measure of capacity usage and does not signify that fixed costs were more or less than budgeted.
Answer (A) is incorrect. The fixed overhead volume variance concerns the application of fixed cost to product and does not encompass revenue or sales concepts in any way. Answer (C) is incorrect. The fixed overhead volume variance is calculated on the assumption that fixed costs are constant. Answer (D) is incorrect. The volume variance concerns output levels rather than the efficiency of production.

32. The production volume variance is due to

A. Inefficient or efficient use of direct labor hours.
B. Efficient or inefficient use of variable overhead.
C. Difference from the planned level of the base used for overhead allocation and the actual level achieved.
D. Excessive application of direct labor hours over the standard amounts for the output level actually achieved.

Answer (C) is correct.
REQUIRED: The cause of the production volume variance.
DISCUSSION: The production volume variance (also called an idle capacity variance) is a component of the total overhead variance. It is the difference between budgeted fixed costs and the product of the standard fixed cost per unit of input times the standard units of input allowed for the actual output. Thus, the production volume variance equals under- or overapplied fixed overhead. This variance results when actual activity differs from the activity base used to calculate the fixed overhead application rate.
Answer (A) is incorrect. The direct labor efficiency variance relates to inefficient or efficient use of direct labor hours. Answer (B) is incorrect. The variable overhead efficiency variance relates to efficient or inefficient use of variable overhead. Answer (D) is incorrect. The volume variance is related to overhead application, not direct labor.

33. If overhead is applied on the basis of units of output, the variable overhead efficiency variance will be

A. Zero.
B. Favorable, if output exceeds the budgeted level.
C. Unfavorable, if output is less than the budgeted level.
D. A function of the direct labor efficiency variance.

Answer (A) is correct.
REQUIRED: The effect on the variable overhead efficiency variance.
DISCUSSION: The variable overhead efficiency variance equals the product of the variable overhead application rate and the difference between the standard input for the actual output and the actual input. Hence, the variance will be zero if variable overhead is applied on the basis of units of output because the difference between actual and standard input cannot be recognized.
Answer (B) is incorrect. The variance will be zero. Answer (C) is incorrect. The variance will be zero. Answer (D) is incorrect. The correlation between the variable overhead and direct labor efficiency variances occurs only when overhead is applied on the basis of direct labor.

10.7 Comprehensive Example

Questions 34 through 37 are based on the following information.

Ardmore Enterprises uses a standard cost system in its small appliance division. The standard cost of manufacturing one unit of Zeb is as follows:

Direct materials -- 60 pounds at $1.50 per pound	$ 90
Direct labor -- 3 hours at $12 per hour	36
Overhead -- 3 hours at $8 per hour	24
Total standard cost per unit	$150

The budgeted variable overhead rate is $3 per direct labor hour, and the budgeted fixed overhead is $27,000 per month. During May, Ardmore produced 1,650 units of Zeb compared with a normal capacity of 1,800 units. The actual cost per unit was as follows:

Direct materials (purchased and used) -- 58 pounds at $1.65 per pound	$ 95.70
Direct labor -- 3.1 hours at $12 per hour	37.20
Overhead -- $39,930 per 1,650 units	24.20
Total actual cost per unit	$157.10

34. Ardmore's total direct materials quantity variance for May is

A. $14,355 favorable.
B. $14,355 unfavorable.
C. $4,950 favorable.
D. $4,950 unfavorable.

Answer (C) is correct.
REQUIRED: The direct materials quantity variance.
DISCUSSION: The direct materials quantity variance equals the difference between the standard and actual quantities times the standard price. Hence, the favorable direct materials quantity variance is $4,950 [1,650 units × (60 standard pounds – 58 actual pounds) × $1.50 standard].
Answer (A) is incorrect. The amount of the direct materials price variance is $14,355. Answer (B) is incorrect. The amount of the direct materials price variance is $14,355. Answer (D) is incorrect. A favorable variance exists. The standard amount for the actual output exceeded the actual amount.

35. Ardmore's direct materials price variance for May is

A. $14,355 unfavorable.
B. $14,850 unfavorable.
C. $14,355 favorable.
D. $14,850 favorable.

Answer (A) is correct.
REQUIRED: The direct materials price variance.
DISCUSSION: The direct materials price variance equals the actual quantity used times the difference between the standard and actual price per unit. Thus, the unfavorable direct materials price variance is $14,355 [1,650 units × 58 actual pounds × ($1.50 standard price – $1.65 actual price)].
Answer (B) is incorrect. The variance of $14,850 is based on the standard unit quantity, not the actual quantity. Answer (C) is incorrect. The price variance is unfavorable. The actual price is greater than the standard price. Answer (D) is incorrect. The variance of $14,850 is based on the standard unit quantity, not the actual quantity.

36. Ardmore's direct labor rate variance for May is

A. $1,920 favorable.
B. $0
C. $4,950 unfavorable.
D. $4,950 favorable.

Answer (B) is correct.
REQUIRED: The direct labor rate variance.
DISCUSSION: The direct labor rate variance equals the actual hours used times the difference between the standard and actual rates. Consequently, the direct labor rate variance is zero [1,650 units × 3.1 actual hours × ($12 per hour standard rate – $12 per hour actual rate)].
Answer (A) is incorrect. The amount of the flexible budget overhead variance is $1,920. Answer (C) is incorrect. The amount of the direct materials quantity variance is $4,950. Answer (D) is incorrect. The amount of the direct materials quantity variance is $4,950.

37. Ardmore's flexible budget overhead variance for May is

A. $3,270 unfavorable.
B. $3,270 favorable.
C. $1,920 unfavorable.
D. $1,920 favorable.

Answer (D) is correct.
REQUIRED: The flexible budget overhead variance.
DISCUSSION: The flexible budget overhead variance is the difference between actual overhead costs and the flexible budget amount for the actual output. Standard total fixed costs at any level of production are $27,000. Standard variable overhead is $9 per unit (3 labor hours × $3). Thus, total standard variable overhead is $14,850 for the actual output (1,650 units × $9), and the total flexible budget amount is $41,850 ($27,000 FOH + $14,850 VOH). Accordingly, the favorable flexible budget variance is $1,920 favorable ($41,850 flexible budget amount − $39,930 actual amount).
Answer (A) is incorrect. The flexible budget amount for an output of 1,800 units is $3,270. Answer (B) is incorrect. The flexible budget amount for an output of 1,800 units is $3,270. Answer (C) is incorrect. A favorable variance exists. Actual overhead is less than the standard overhead at the actual production level.

10.8 Sales Variances

38. In analyzing company operations, the controller of the corporation found a $250,000 favorable flexible-budget revenue variance. The variance was calculated by comparing the actual results with the flexible budget. This variance can be wholly explained by

A. The total flexible budget variance.
B. The total sales volume variance.
C. The total static budget variance.
D. Changes in unit selling prices.

Answer (D) is correct.
REQUIRED: The cause of a favorable flexible-budget revenue variance.
DISCUSSION: Variance analysis can be used to judge the effectiveness of selling departments. If a firm's sales differ from the amount budgeted, the difference may be attributable to either the sales price variance or the sales volume (quantity) variance. Changes in unit selling prices may account for the entire variance if the actual quantity sold is equal to the quantity budgeted. None of the revenue variance is attributed to the sales volume variance because no such variance exists when a flexible budget is used. The flexible budget is based on the level of sales at actual volume.
Answer (A) is incorrect. The total flexible budget variance includes items other than revenue. Answer (B) is incorrect. The sales volume variance represents the change in contribution margin caused by a difference between actual and budgeted units sold. However, given a flexible budget, there is no difference between budgeted and actual units sold. By definition, a flexible budget's volume is identical to actual volume. Answer (C) is incorrect. The total static budget variance includes many items other than revenue.

39. The variance that arises solely because the quantity actually sold differs from the quantity budgeted to be sold is

A. Static budget variance.
B. Master budget increment.
C. Sales mix variance.
D. Sales volume variance.

Answer (D) is correct.
REQUIRED: The variance that arises solely when actual sales differ from budgeted sales.
DISCUSSION: If a firm's sales differ from the amount budgeted, the difference could be attributable either to the sales price variance or the sales volume variance. The sales volume variance is the change in contribution margin caused by the difference between the actual and budgeted sales volumes.
Answer (A) is incorrect. A static budget variance is the difference between actual costs or revenues and those budgeted on a static budget. Answer (B) is incorrect. A master budget increment is an increase in a budgeted figure on the firm's master budget. Answer (C) is incorrect. The sales mix variance is caused when a company's actual sales mix is different from the budgeted sales mix.

Question 40 is based on the following information.

Folsom Fashions sells a line of women's dresses. Folsom's performance report for November follows.

The company uses a flexible budget to analyze its performance and to measure the effect on operating income of the various factors affecting the difference between budgeted and actual operating income.

	Actual	Budget
Dresses sold	5,000	6,000
Sales	$235,000	$300,000
Variable costs	(145,000)	(180,000)
Contribution margin (CM)	90,000	120,000
Fixed costs	(84,000)	(80,000)
Operating income	$ 6,000	$ 40,000

40. The retailer's sales price variance for November is

   A. $30,000 unfavorable.
   B. $18,000 unfavorable.
   C. $20,000 unfavorable.
   D. $15,000 unfavorable.

Answer (D) is correct.
 REQUIRED: The amount of the sales price variance for the month.
 DISCUSSION: The sales price variance is the actual number of units sold (5,000), times the difference between budgeted selling price ($300,000 ÷ 6,000) and actual selling price ($235,000 ÷ 5,000).

$$(\$50 - \$47) \times 5,000 = \$15,000 \ U$$

Answer (A) is incorrect. The difference between the actual and budgeted contribution margins is $30,000. Answer (B) is incorrect. The difference between actual and budgeted unit sales times the actual unit CM equals $18,000. Answer (C) is incorrect. The sales quantity variance is $20,000.

Access the **CMA Review System** from your Gleim Personal Classroom to continue your studies with exam-emulating multiple-choice questions!

10.9 ESSAY QUESTIONS

Scenario for Essay Questions 1, 2

The LAR Chemical Co. manufactures a wide variety of chemical compounds and liquids for industrial uses. The standard mix for producing a single batch of 500 gallons of one liquid is as follows:

Liquid Chemical	Quantity (in gallons)	Cost (per gallon)	Total Cost
Maxan	100	2.00	$200
Salex	300	.75	225
Cralyn	225	1.00	225
	625		$650

There is a 20% loss in liquid volume during processing due to evaporation. The finished liquid is put into 10 gallon bottles for sale. Thus, the standard material cost for a 10-gallon bottle is $13.00.

The actual quantities of materials and the respective cost of the materials placed in production during November were as follows:

Liquid Chemical	Quantity (in gallons)	Total Cost
Maxan	8,480	$17,384
Salex	25,200	17,640
Cralyn	18,540	16,686
	52,220	$51,710

A total of 4,000 bottles (40,000 gallons) were produced during November.

Questions

1. Calculate the total materials variance for the liquid product for the month of November and then further analyze the total variance into
   a. Materials price variance
   b. Materials mix variance
   c. Materials yield variance

2. Explain how LAR Chemical Co. could use each of the three materials variances–price, mix, and yield–to help control the cost to manufacture this liquid compound.

Essay Questions 1, 2 — Unofficial Answers

1. Total direct materials variance:

Static budget (SQ × SP): 4,000 bottles × $13.00 =	$52,000	
Less: Actual cost	(51,710)	
Static budget variance	$ 290	F

   a. Materials price variance

Chemical	Actual Quantity		Standard Price		Totals
Maxan	8,480 gallons	×	$2.00	=	$16,960
Salex	25,200 gallons	×	.75	=	18,900
Cralyn	18,540 gallons	×	1.00	=	18,540
	Total AQ × SP				$54,400
	Less: Actual cost				(51,710)
	Price variance				$ 2,690 F

   b. Materials mix variance

   $$\frac{\text{Standard weighted-average input cost per batch}}{\text{Standard input gallons per batch}} = \frac{\$650}{625} = \$1.04 \text{ per input gallon}$$

Actual gallons × standard cost (calculated in a.)	$54,400.00
Less actual quantity × standard weighted-average cost per input gallon (standard proportion) (52,220 × $1.04)	54,308.80
Mix variance	$ 91.20 U

   c. Materials yield variance

Expected quantity[1]	50,000	gallons
Less: Actual quantity	(52,220)	gallons
Variance in input quantity	(2,220)	gallons
Times: Standard weighted-average cost per input	× $1.04	per gallon
Yield variance	$2,308.80	U

   [1] Every batch experiences a 20% loss in inputs due to evaporation. To generate 40,000 gallons of output, therefore, 50,000 gallons must be consumed.

2. Before management can control costs, they need to know which costs are out of line, within whose area of responsibility has the variance appeared, what the cause of the variance is, and who has the responsibility to correct the cause. Variances help management to answer these issues. Specifically, the variances indicate where management should begin its investigation:

   a. Price variation – the information to identify the causes of the price variance usually can be obtained in the purchasing department. A review of purchasing procedures and records would disclose whether the variances were caused by permanent changes in prices, poor purchasing practices, or poor production scheduling requiring incurrence of extra costs to expedite shipments. The information obtained will identify the department responsible for the extra cost and provide clues to improve the control.

   b. Mix and yield variances – the information to identify the cause of these variances can be obtained in production. A review of material records and handling procedure would disclose whether the mix variance was caused by the use of wrong proportions, entering excess materials into the process because of carelessness, or adjustment of the mix to accommodate off-standard material quality. Yield variance would often be explained by the same information. Nonstandard proportions would result in nonstandard yields and excess material inputs. The information obtained would identify the department responsible and provide clues to improve control.

STUDY UNIT ELEVEN
RESPONSIBILITY ACCOUNTING AND PERFORMANCE MEASURES

(13 pages of outline)

11.1	Responsibility Centers	375
11.2	Performance Measures -- Cost, Revenue, and Profit Centers	377
11.3	Performance Measures -- Investment Centers	379
11.4	Comparing Performance Measures for Investment Centers	381
11.5	Allocating Common Costs	382
11.6	Transfer Pricing	384
11.7	Essay Questions	397

This study unit is the **second of two** on **performance management**. The relative weight assigned to this major topic in Part 1 of the exam is **20%**. The two study units are

Study Unit 10: Cost and Variance Measures

Study Unit 11: Responsibility Accounting and Performance Measures

If you are interested in reviewing more introductory or background material, go to www.gleim.com/CMAIntroVideos for a list of suggested third-party overviews of this topic. The following Gleim outline material is more than sufficient to help you pass the CMA exam; any additional introductory or background material is for your own personal enrichment.

11.1 RESPONSIBILITY CENTERS

1. **Decision Making and Decentralization**

    a. The primary distinction between centralized and decentralized organizations is in the degree of freedom of decision making by managers at many levels.

    1) In a centralized organization, decision making is consolidated so that activities throughout the organization may be more effectively coordinated from the top.

    2) In a decentralized organization, decision making is at as low a level as possible. The premise is that the local manager can make more informed decisions than a manager farther from the decision.

2. **Responsibility Centers**

    a. A decentralized organization is divided into **responsibility centers** (also called **strategic business units**, or SBUs) to facilitate local decision making.

    1) Four types of responsibility centers are generally recognized.

    b. A **cost center**, e.g., a maintenance department, is responsible for costs only.

    1) Cost drivers are the relevant performance measures.

    2) A disadvantage of a cost center is the potential for cost shifting, for example, replacement of variable costs for which a manager is responsible with fixed costs for which (s)he is not.

        a) Another disadvantage is that long-term issues may be disregarded when the emphasis is on, for example, annual cost amounts.

        b) Yet another issue is allocation of service department costs to cost centers.

    3) Service centers exist primarily and sometimes solely to provide specialized support to other organizational subunits. They are usually operated as cost centers.

c. A **revenue center**, e.g., a sales department, is responsible for revenues only.

   1) Revenue drivers are the relevant performance measures. They are factors that influence unit sales, such as changes in prices and products, customer service, marketing efforts, and delivery terms.

d. A **profit center**, e.g., an appliance department in a retail store, is responsible for both revenues and expenses.

e. An **investment center**, e.g., a branch office, is responsible for revenues, expenses, and invested capital.

   1) The advantage of an investment center is that it permits an evaluation of performance that can be compared with that of other responsibility centers or other potential investments on a return on investment basis, i.e., on the basis of the effectiveness of asset usage.

3. **Performance Measures and Manager Motivation**

   a. Each responsibility center is structured such that a logical group of operations is under the direction of a single manager.

      1) Measures are designed for every responsibility center to monitor performance.

   b. **Controllability.** The performance measures on which the manager's incentive package are based must be, as far as practicable, under the manager's direct responsibility and authority.

      1) "Controllable" factors can be thought of as those factors that a manager can influence in a given time period.

         a) Inevitably, some costs, especially common costs such as the costs of central administrative functions, cannot be traced to particular activities or responsibility centers.

         b) The challenges associated with allocating common costs fully and fairly are discussed in Subunit 11.5.

      2) Controllable cost is not synonymous with variable cost. Often this classification is particular to the level of the organization.

         a) For instance, the fixed cost of depreciation may not be a controllable cost of the manager of a revenue center but is controllable by the division vice president to which that manager reports.

   c. **Goal congruence.** These performance measures must be designed such that the manager's pursuit of them ties directly to accomplishment of the organization's overall goals.

      1) Suboptimization results when segments of the organization pursue goals that are in that segment's own best interests rather than those of the organization as a whole.

   d. Along with the responsibility, a manager must be granted sufficient authority to control those factors on which his or her incentive package is based.

Stop and review! You have completed the outline for this subunit. Study multiple-choice questions 1 through 6 beginning on page 388.

11.2 PERFORMANCE MEASURES -- COST, REVENUE, AND PROFIT CENTERS

1. **Cost Centers and Revenue Centers**

    a. Since managers of cost and revenue centers can influence only one type of factor, variance analysis (Study Unit 10) is the most appropriate performance measurement technique for these responsibility centers.

    b. To be effective, a performance measure should be based on a cause-and-effect relationship between the outcome being measured and a driver that is under the manager's control.

    1) An appropriate performance measure for a cost or revenue center might not even be financial. Examples might include number of invoices processed per hour or percentage of customer shipments correctly filled.

2. **Profit Centers**

    a. The contribution margin approach to reporting (in contrast to the financial reporting approach) is extremely useful in performance measurement for profit centers.

    1) The contribution margin approach isolates the effects of variable and fixed costs and thus highlights the effects of a manager's choices.

    2) In addition to contribution margin and operating income, this approach can also be used to calculate multiple intermediate measures, as shown below:

    Contribution Margin Income Statement

Sales		$150,000
Variable production costs		(40,000)
Manufacturing contribution margin		$110,000
Variable S&A expenses		(20,000)
Contribution margin		$ 90,000
Controllable fixed costs:		
Fixed production costs	$30,000	
Fixed S&A expenses	25,000	(55,000)
Short-run performance margin		$ 35,000
Traceable fixed costs:		
Depreciation	$10,000	
Insurance	5,000	(15,000)
Segment margin		$ 20,000
Allocated common costs		(10,000)
Segment operating income		$ 10,000

3. **Segment Reporting**

    a. A segment is a product line, geographical area, or other meaningful subunit of the organization.

    1) As the examples on the following page illustrate, contribution margin reporting is extremely useful for manager decision making.

    b. **Product profitability analysis** allows management to determine whether a product is providing any coverage of fixed costs.

1) **EXAMPLE:** At first glance, a dairy operation appears to be comfortably profitable.

Sales	$540,000
Variable costs	312,000
Contribution margin	**$228,000**
Other traceable costs:	
Marketing	116,000
R&D	18,000
Product line margin	**$ 94,000**
Fixed costs	24,000
Operating income	**$ 70,000**

A product profitability analysis shows an entirely different picture. Two product lines are losing money, and one is not even covering its own variable costs.

	Milk	Cream	Cottage Cheese	Total
Sales	$300,000	$ 60,000	$180,000	$540,000
Variable costs	110,000	62,000	140,000	312,000
Contribution margin	**$190,000**	**$ (2,000)**	**$ 40,000**	**$228,000**
Other traceable costs:				
Marketing	66,000	10,000	40,000	116,000
R&D	8,000	4,000	6,000	18,000
Product line margin	**$116,000**	**$(16,000)**	**$ (6,000)**	**$ 94,000**
Fixed costs				24,000
Operating income				**$ 70,000**

c. **Area office profitability analysis** performs the same function on the segment level.

1) **EXAMPLE:** A geographic profitability analysis for a company that provides research services allows management to see which branch offices are the most profitable.

	Cartagena	Riyadh	Mumbai	Osaka	Total
Sales	$1,200,000	$800,000	$2,000,000	$4,600,000	$8,600,000
Variable costs of sales	800,000	460,000	1,400,000	3,200,000	5,860,000
Other variable costs	256,000	176,000	320,000	544,000	1,296,000
Contribution margin	**$ 144,000**	**$164,000**	**$ 280,000**	**$ 856,000**	**$1,444,000**
Traceable fixed costs	150,000	100,000	160,000	220,000	630,000
Area office margin	**$ (6,000)**	**$ 64,000**	**$ 120,000**	**$ 636,000**	**$ 814,000**
Nontraceable fixed costs					200,000
Operating income					**$ 614,000**

d. **Customer profitability analysis** enables a firm to make decisions about whether to continue servicing a given customer.

1) **EXAMPLE:** At first, it might appear that the two unprofitable customers should be dropped.

	Gonzales	Abdullah	Patel	Kawanishi	Total
Sales	$10,000	$40,000	$62,000	$22,000	$134,000
Cost of goods sold	7,200	26,000	41,000	18,100	92,300
Other relevant costs	1,000	2,200	4,400	4,100	11,700
Customer margin	**$ 1,800**	**$11,800**	**$16,600**	**$ (200)**	**$ 30,000**
Allocated fixed costs	2,000	6,000	8,800	4,000	20,800
Operating income	**$ (200)**	**$ 5,800**	**$ 7,800**	**$(4,200)**	**$ 9,200**

Dropping Kawanishi makes sense. However, Gonzales is contributing to the coverage of fixed costs, costs that would have to be shifted to the other customers if Gonzales were dropped.

Stop and review! You have completed the outline for this subunit. Study multiple-choice questions 7 through 11 beginning on page 389.

11.3 PERFORMANCE MEASURES -- INVESTMENT CENTERS

1. **Purpose**
   a. Performance measures for investment centers reveal how efficiently the manager is deploying capital to produce income for the organization.
   b. Thus, most performance measures relate the center's resources (balance sheet) to its income (income statement).

2. **Return on Investment (ROI)**
   a. ROI is one of the two most widely used performance measures for an investment center.

   $$ROI = \frac{Business\ unit\ profit}{Assets\ of\ business\ unit}$$

   b. EXAMPLE: The ROI calculations for the branch offices displayed in item 3.c.1) on the previous page are shown here:

	Cartagena	Riyadh	Mumbai	Osaka
Business unit profit	$ (6,000)	$ 64,000	$ 120,000	$ 636,000
Total assets	121,000	825,000	1,015,000	9,900,000
Return on investment (ROI)	**(5.0%)**	**7.8%**	**11.8%**	**6.4%**

   Even though the managers of the Osaka branch generated by far the largest contribution, they were not as efficient in the deployment of the resources at their disposal as were the managers of the Riyadh or Mumbai branches.

   1) This example illustrates the principle that the appraisal of individual performance must consider more factors than simple dollars.

   c. A major problem with the application of ROI is that an investment center with a high ROI may not accept a profitable investment even though the investment's return is higher than the center's target ROI.

   1) EXAMPLE: An investment center has an 8% ROI, and its investors expect 2%. If the decision makers look only at current ROI, they will reject a project earning 6%, even though that return exceeds the target.

3. **Residual Income**
   a. Residual income is a variation of ROI that measures performance in dollar terms rather than as a percentage return.

   $$Residual\ income = Business\ unit\ profit - (Assets\ of\ business\ unit \times Required\ rate\ of\ return)$$

   1) Income means operating income unless otherwise noted.
   2) Residual income is a significant refinement of the ROI concept because it forces business unit managers to consider the opportunity cost of capital.

b. EXAMPLE: The residual income calculations for the branch offices displayed in item 2.b. on the previous page are shown here:

	Cartagena		Riyadh	
Business unit profit		$ (6,000)		$ 64,000
Total assets	$121,000		$825,000	
Times: Target rate of return	× 6.0%		× 6.0%	
Opportunity cost of capital		(7,260)		(49,500)
Residual income		**$(13,260)**		**$ 14,500**

	Mumbai		Osaka	
Business unit profit		$120,000		$636,000
Total assets	$1,015,000		$9,900,000	
Times: Target rate of return	× 6.0%		× 6.0%	
Opportunity cost of capital		(60,900)		(594,000)
Residual income		**$ 59,100**		**$ 42,000**

  1) This calculation reveals that, by employing the most resources, the Osaka branch has by far the highest threshold to clear for profitability.

4. **Comparability Issues with Investment Center Performance Measures**

   a. Alternative income measurements include business unit profit, business unit profit adjusted for price level changes, cash flow, and earnings before interest and taxes (EBIT).
   b. Invested capital may be defined in various ways, for example, as
      1) Total assets available
      2) Total assets employed, which excludes assets that are idle, such as vacant land
      3) Working capital plus other assets, which excludes current liabilities (i.e., capital provided by short-term creditors)
         a) This investment base assumes that the manager controls short-term credit.
   c. Different attributes of financial information will also affect the elements of the investment base.
      1) Historical cost
      2) Replacement cost
      3) Market value
      4) Present value
   d. The comparability of performance measures may be affected by differences in the accounting policies used by different business units.
      1) For example, policies regarding depreciation, decisions to capitalize or expense, inventory flow assumptions, and revenue recognition can lead to comparability issues for performance measures.
      2) These differences may be heightened for the business units of a multinational enterprise.
   e. Issues other than accounting policy may also affect comparability.
      1) Differences in the tax systems in the jurisdictions where business units operate
      2) The presence of extraordinary items of profit or loss
      3) Allocation of common costs
      4) The varying availability of resources

Stop and review! You have completed the outline for this subunit. Study multiple-choice questions 12 through 16 beginning on page 391.

11.4 COMPARING PERFORMANCE MEASURES FOR INVESTMENT CENTERS

1. **ROI vs. Residual Income**
   a. Residual income is often considered preferable to ROI because it deals in absolute dollars rather than percentages.
      1) A manager with a 10% ROI would be reluctant to invest in a project with only an 8% return because his or her average overall return would decline. This would be detrimental to the company as a whole if the cost of capital were only 5%.
      2) However, under the residual income method, the manager would invest in any project with a return greater than the cost of capital or the hurdle rate that (s)he has been assigned.
      3) Thus, overall, the company would be better off even though the individual manager's ROI declined.

2. **Revenue and Expense Recognition Policies**
   a. A company's revenue and expense recognition policies may affect the measurement of income and thus reduce comparability among business units.
      1) For example, a company that uses last-in, first-out (LIFO) for inventory valuation will often show lower inventories and higher costs than a company that uses the first-in, first-out (FIFO) methodology. As a result, the LIFO company could appear to have a lower rate of return than if it had used the FIFO method.
      2) Other ratios would also be impacted, such as inventory turnover and asset turnover.
   b. Thus, when comparing companies or units on the basis of either ROI or residual income, the analyst must be sure that both companies or units are using the same accounting policies in the determination of income.
   c. The sharing of assets by subunits within an organization may also affect measures of return.
      1) For instance, assets normally appear on the books of only one division, even though another division might have access to those assets. Therefore, the division that shares its assets with another division may find that it has a lower rate of return than the division that has access to the use of the assets.
   d. Similarly, a company or division that uses straight-line depreciation on its plant assets will have lower expenses in the early years of an asset's life than if an accelerated method were being used. Thus, the straight-line division would appear to be more profitable than the division using the accelerated method.
      1) Of course, the accelerated method may be preferred by top management because it results in a tax savings, but the implication of the ROI measure might be that the straight-line division is more profitable.
   e. International operations may not always be comparable to domestic divisions, since the complication of changes in foreign-currency exchange rates might make income comparisons difficult. Also, transfer pricing is complicated in the international arena, since differences in tax rates between countries may have a role in the selection of the transfer prices selected.
      1) For example, a company will set a transfer price at a level that will limit the profits in high-tax countries and shift that profit to the low-tax country.
      2) Similarly, high profits in a foreign country might not always be transferable to the home country; thus, to say that the foreign subsidiary is more profitable is meaningless if that profit cannot be enjoyed by the parent company.

Stop and review! You have completed the outline for this subunit. Study multiple-choice questions 17 through 19 beginning on page 392.

11.5 ALLOCATING COMMON COSTS

1. **Issues**
   a. Common costs are the costs of products, activities, facilities, services, or operations shared by two or more cost objects.
      1) The difficulty with common costs is that they are **indirect costs** whose allocation may be arbitrary.
   b. A direct cause-and-effect relationship between a common cost and the actions of the cost object to which it is allocated is desirable.
      1) Such a relationship promotes acceptance of the allocation by managers who perceive the fairness of the procedure, but identification of cause and effect may not be feasible.
   c. An alternative allocation criterion is the benefit received.
      1) For example, advertising costs that do not relate to particular products may increase sales of all products.
      2) Allocation based on the increase in sales by organizational subunits is likely to be accepted as equitable despite the absence of clear cause-and-effect relationships.
   d. Allocating costs to foster competition may also be appropriate.
      1) Care must be taken to ensure this competition is healthy for organizational dynamics.

2. **Headquarters Costs**
   a. A persistent problem in large organizations is the treatment of the costs of headquarters and other central support costs. Such costs are frequently allocated.
      1) The allocation reminds managers that support costs exist and that the managers would incur these costs if their operations were independent. The allocation also reminds managers that profit center earnings must cover some amount of support costs.
   b. Research has shown that central support costs are allocated to departments or divisions for the following reasons:
      1) The allocation reminds managers that support costs exist and that the managers would incur these costs if their operations were independent.
      2) The allocation reminds managers that profit center earnings must cover some amount of support costs.
      3) Departments or divisions should be motivated to use central support services appropriately.
      4) Managers who must bear the costs of central support services that they do not control may be encouraged to exert pressure on those who do. Thus, they may be able to restrain such costs indirectly.
         a) However, department or division managers pressuring central managers is not a healthy organizational dynamic.

3. **Effects of Arbitrary Allocations**
   a. Managers' morale may suffer when allocations depress operating results.
   b. Dysfunctional conflict may arise among managers when costs controlled by one are allocated to others.
   c. Resentment may result if cost allocation is perceived to be arbitrary or unfair.
      1) For example, an allocation on an ability-to-bear basis, such as operating income, penalizes successful managers and rewards underachievers and may therefore have a demotivating effect.

SU 11: Responsibility Accounting and Performance Measures 383

4. **Allocation Alternatives**

   a. If allocation is based on actual sales or contribution margin, responsibility centers that increase their sales (or contribution margin) will be charged with increased overhead.

   b. If central administrative or other fixed costs are not allocated, responsibility centers might reach their revenue (or contribution margin) goals without covering all fixed costs (which is necessary to operate in the long run).

   c. Allocation of overhead, however, is motivationally negative; central administrative or other fixed costs may appear noncontrollable and be unproductive.

   d. A much preferred alternative is to budget a certain amount of contribution margin earned by each responsibility center to the central administration based on negotiation.

      1) The intended result is for each unit to see itself as contributing to the success of the overall entity rather than carrying the weight (cost) of central administration.

      2) Central administration can then make the decision whether to expand, divest, or close responsibility centers.

5. **Calculations**

   a. Two specific approaches to common cost allocation are in general use.

      1) Under the **stand-alone method**, the common cost is allocated to each cost object on a proportionate basis.

      2) Under the **incremental method**, the cost objects are sorted in descending order by total traceable cost, and the common cost is allocated up to the amount of each.

EXAMPLE of Common Cost Allocation

The proportionate costs of servicing three customers are presented in the table below. The common cost of providing service to these customers is $8,000.

	Cost of Servicing	%
Luciano	$ 7,000	70%
Ratzinger	2,000	20%
Wojtyla	1,000	10%
Total	$10,000	100%

Stand-Alone Method

	Total Cost to Be Allocated		Allocation %		Allocated Cost
Luciano	$8,000	×	70%	=	$5,600
Ratzinger	8,000	×	20%	=	1,600
Wojtyla	8,000	×	10%	=	800
Total			100%		$8,000

Incremental Method

	Traceable Cost	Allocated Cost	Remaining Unallocated
To be allocated			$8,000
Luciano	$ 7,000	$7,000	1,000
Ratzinger	2,000	1,000	0
Wojtyla	1,000	0	
Total	$10,000	$8,000	

Stop and review! You have completed the outline for this subunit. Study multiple-choice questions 20 through 23 beginning on page 393.

11.6 TRANSFER PRICING

1. **Purpose**
   a. Transfer prices are the amounts charged by one segment of an organization for goods and services it provides to another segment of the same organization.
      1) The principal challenge is determining a price that motivates both the selling and the buying manager to pursue organizational goal congruence.
   b. In a decentralized system, each responsibility center theoretically may be completely separate.
      1) Thus, Division A should charge the same price to Division B as would be charged to an outside buyer.
      2) The reason for decentralization is to motivate managers, and the best interests of Division A may not be served by giving a special discount to Division B if the goods can be sold at the regular price to outside buyers. However, having A sell at a special price to B may be to the company's advantage.

2. **Transfer Pricing Schemes**
   a. Four basic methods of transfer price setting are in common use: variable cost, full cost, market price, and negotiated price.
   b. **Variable Cost**
      1) By allowing the buyer to purchase at the selling division's variable cost, unused production capacity will be utilized (this method should only be used when the selling division has excess capacity).
      2) However, there is no incentive for the selling division, since it will be producing the products at a loss (even though the company as a whole will benefit from the arrangement).
         a) In practice, companies who wish to follow this philosophy actually adopt a negotiation policy wherein the transfer price will be something greater than variable costs but less than full costs. At least the seller would have a positive contribution margin if the price is set slightly above variable costs.
      3) The advantage of using variable costs is that the buyer is motivated to solve the company's excess capacity problem, even though that excess capacity is not in the buyer's division.
   c. **Full Cost**
      1) Full (absorption) cost includes materials, labor, and full allocation of manufacturing overhead.
      2) The use of full (absorption) cost ensures that the selling division will not incur a loss and provides more incentive to the buying division to buy internally than does use of market price.
         a) However, there is no motivation for the seller to control production costs since all costs can be passed along to the buying division.
   d. **Market Price**
      1) A market price is the best transfer price to use in many situations. For example, if the selling division is operating at full capacity and can sell all of its output at the market price, then there is no justification to use a lower price as the transfer price for intracompany transfers.
      2) Alternatively, if the selling division is not producing at full capacity, the use of market prices for internal transfers is not justified. A lower price might be more motivational to either the buyer or the seller.

e. **Negotiation**

1) A negotiated price may result when organizational subunits are free to determine the prices at which they buy and sell internally. Hence, a transfer price may simply reflect the best bargain that the parties can strike between themselves.
2) The transfer price need not be based directly on particular market or cost information.
3) A negotiated price may be especially appropriate when market prices are subject to rapid fluctuation.

3. **Choice of Transfer Pricing Policy**

   a. The choice of a transfer pricing policy (which type of transfer price to use) is normally decided by top management at the corporate level. The decision typically includes consideration of multiple factors.
   b. Goal congruence factors
      1) The transfer price should promote the goals of the company as a whole.
   c. Segmental performance factors
      1) The segment making the transfer should be allowed to recover its incremental cost plus its opportunity cost of the transfer. The opportunity cost is the benefit forgone by not selling to an outsider.
         a) For this purpose, the transfer should be at market price.
         b) The selling manager should not lose income by selling within the company.
      2) Properly allocating revenues and expenses through appropriate transfer pricing also facilitates evaluation of the performance of the various segments.
   d. Negotiation factors
      1) If the purchasing segment could purchase the product or service outside the company, it should be permitted to negotiate the transfer price.
      2) The purchasing manager should not have to incur greater costs by purchasing within the company.
   e. Capacity factors
      1) If Division A has excess capacity, it should be used for producing products for Division B. If Division A is operating at full capacity and selling its products at the full market price, profitable work should not be abandoned to produce for Division B.
   f. Cost structure factors
      1) If Division A has excess capacity and an opportunity arises to sell to Division B at a price in excess of the variable cost, the work should be performed for Division B because a contribution to cover the fixed costs will result.
   g. Tax factors
      1) A wide range of tax issues on the interstate and international levels may arise, e.g., income taxes, sales taxes, value-added taxes, inventory and payroll taxes, and other governmental charges.
      2) In the international context, exchange rate fluctuations, threats of expropriation, and limits on transfers of profits outside the host country are additional concerns.
         a) Thus, because the best transfer price may be a low one because of the existence of tariffs or a high one because of the existence of foreign exchange controls, the effect may be to skew the performance statistics of management.

b) The high transfer price may result in foreign management appearing to show a lower return on investment than domestic management, but the ratio differences may be negated by the fact that a different transfer pricing formula is used.

Transfer Price Decision Tree

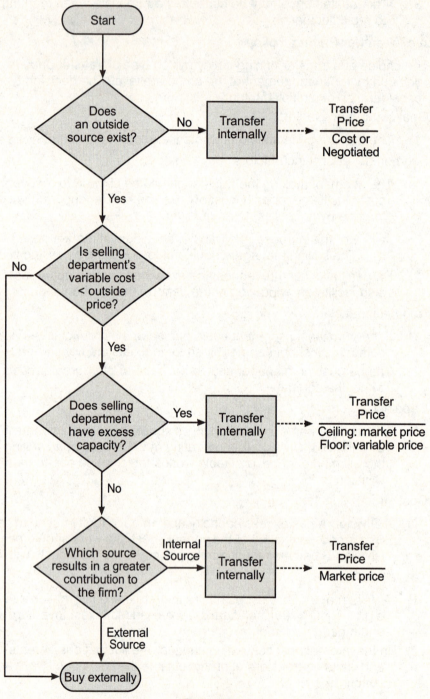

Figure 11-1

h. EXAMPLE: Division A produces a small part at a cost of $6 per unit. The regular selling price is $10 per unit. If Division B can use the part in its production, the cost to the company (as a whole) will be $6.

   1) Division B has another supplier who will sell the item to B at $9.50 per part. Division B wants to buy the $9.50 part from the outside supplier instead of the $10 part from Division A, but making the part for $6 is in the company's best interest.

      a) What amount should Division A charge Division B?

   2) The answer is complicated by many factors. For example, if Division A has excess capacity, B should be charged a lower price. If it is operating at full capacity, B should be charged $10.

   3) Also consider what portion of Division A's costs is fixed. For example, if a competitor offered to sell the part to B at $5 each, can Division A advantageously sell to B at a price lower than $5? If Division A's $6 total cost is composed of $4 of variable costs and $2 of fixed costs, it is beneficial for all concerned for A to sell to B at a price less than $5. Even at a price of $4.01, the parts would be providing a contribution margin to cover some of A's fixed costs.

4. **Dual Pricing**

   a. Under dual pricing, the selling and buying units record the transfer at different prices.

      1) For example, the seller could record the transfer to another segment as a sale at the usual market price that would be paid by an outsider. The buyer, however, would record a purchase at the variable cost of production.

      2) Each segment's reported performance is improved by the use of a dual-pricing scheme.

      3) The firm as a whole would benefit because variable costs would be used for decision-making purposes. In a sense, variable costs would be the relevant price for decision-making purposes, but the regular market price would be used for evaluation of production divisions.

   b. However, under a dual-pricing system, the profit for the company will be less than the sum of the profits of the individual segments. In effect, the seller is given a corporate subsidy.

      1) The dual-pricing system is rarely used because the incentive to control costs is reduced.

      2) The seller is assured of a high price, and the buyer is assured of an artificially low price. Thus, neither manager must exert much effort to show a profit on segmental performance reports.

      3) Also, an elimination entry must be recorded at the end of the period to reconcile the fact that sales were recorded at an amount different from the corresponding purchases.

Stop and review! You have completed the outline for this subunit. Study multiple-choice questions 24 through 30 beginning on page 394.

QUESTIONS

11.1 Responsibility Centers

1. A corporation uses an accounting system that charges costs to the manager who has been delegated the authority to make the decisions incurring the costs. For example, if the sales manager accepts a rush order that will result in higher-than-normal manufacturing costs, these additional costs are charged to the sales manager because the authority to accept or decline the rush order was given to the sales manager. This type of accounting system is known as

- A. Responsibility accounting.
- B. Functional accounting.
- C. Reciprocal allocation.
- D. Transfer price accounting.

Answer (A) is correct.
REQUIRED: The system in which additional costs are charged to the manager with authority for their incurrence.
DISCUSSION: In a responsibility accounting system, managerial performance should be evaluated only on the basis of those factors directly regulated (or at least capable of being significantly influenced) by the manager. For this purpose, operations are organized into responsibility centers. Costs are classified as controllable and noncontrollable, which implies that some revenues and costs can be changed through effective management. If a manager has authority to incur costs, a responsibility accounting system will charge them to the manager's responsibility center. However, controllability is not an absolute basis for establishment of responsibility. More than one manager may be able to influence a cost, and responsibility may be assigned on the basis of knowledge about the incurrence of a cost rather than the ability to control it.
Answer (B) is incorrect. Functional accounting allocates costs to functions regardless of responsibility. Answer (C) is incorrect. Reciprocal allocation is a means of allocating service department costs. Answer (D) is incorrect. Transfer price accounting is a means of charging one department for products acquired from another department in the same organization.

2. The basic purpose of a responsibility accounting system is

- A. Budgeting.
- B. Motivation.
- C. Authority.
- D. Variance analysis.

Answer (B) is correct.
REQUIRED: The basic purpose of a responsibility accounting system.
DISCUSSION: The basic purpose of a responsibility accounting system is to motivate management to perform in a manner consistent with overall company objectives. The assignment of responsibility implies that some revenues and costs can be changed through effective management. The system should have certain controls that provide for feedback reports indicating deviations from expectations. Higher-level management may focus on those deviations for either reinforcement or correction.
Answer (A) is incorrect. Budgeting is an element of a responsibility accounting system, not the basic purpose. Answer (C) is incorrect. Authority is an element of a responsibility accounting system, not the basic purpose. Answer (D) is incorrect. Analysis of variances is an element of a responsibility accounting system, not the basic purpose.

3. A successful responsibility accounting reporting system is dependent upon

- A. The correct allocation of controllable variable costs.
- B. Identification of the management level at which all costs are controllable.
- C. The proper delegation of responsibility and authority.
- D. A reasonable separation of costs into their fixed and variable components since fixed costs are not controllable and must be eliminated from the responsibility report.

Answer (C) is correct.
REQUIRED: The factor upon which a successful responsibility accounting system is dependent.
DISCUSSION: Managerial performance should ideally be evaluated only on the basis of those factors controllable by the manager. Managers may control revenues, costs, and/or investments in resources. However, controllability is not an absolute. More than one manager may be able to influence a cost, and managers may be accountable for some costs they do not control. In practice, given the difficulties of determining the locus of controllability, responsibility may be assigned on the basis of knowledge about the incurrence of a cost rather than the ability to control it. Accordingly, a successful system is dependent upon the proper delegation of responsibility and the commensurate authority.
Answer (A) is incorrect. Fixed costs may also be controllable, and some costs not controllable may need to be assigned. Answer (B) is incorrect. Knowledge about the incurrence of a cost rather than controllability may in practice be an appropriate basis for delegation of responsibility. Answer (D) is incorrect. Fixed costs can be controllable.

4. In responsibility accounting, a center's performance is measured by controllable costs. Controllable costs are **best** described as including

A. Direct material and direct labor only.
B. Only those costs that the manager can influence in the current time period.
C. Only discretionary costs.
D. Those costs about which the manager is knowledgeable and informed.

Answer (B) is correct.
REQUIRED: The elements of controllable costs.
DISCUSSION: Control is the process of making certain that plans are achieving the desired objectives. A controllable cost is one that is influenced by a specific responsible manager at a given level of production within a given time span. For example, fixed costs are often not controllable in the short run.
Answer (A) is incorrect. Many overhead costs are also controllable. Answer (C) is incorrect. Controllable costs need not be discretionary. Discretionary costs are characterized by uncertainty about the relationship between input and the value of the related output; they may or may not be controllable. Answer (D) is incorrect. Controllable costs are those over which a manager has control; the manager may be informed or know about costs that (s)he cannot directly regulate or influence.

5. A segment of an organization is referred to as a service center if it has

A. Responsibility for developing markets and selling the output of the organization.
B. Responsibility for combining the raw materials, direct labor, and other factors of production into a final output.
C. Authority to make decisions affecting the major determinants of profit including the power to choose its markets and sources of supply.
D. Authority to provide specialized support to other units within the organization.

Answer (D) is correct.
REQUIRED: The definition of a service center.
DISCUSSION: A service center exists primarily and sometimes solely to provide specialized support to other units within the organization. Service centers are usually operated as cost centers.
Answer (A) is incorrect. A service center has no responsibility for developing markets or selling. Answer (B) is incorrect. A production center is engaged in manufacturing. Answer (C) is incorrect. A profit center can choose its markets and sources of supply.

6. The **least** complex segment or area of responsibility for which costs are allocated is a(n)

A. Profit center.
B. Investment center.
C. Contribution center.
D. Cost center.

Answer (D) is correct.
REQUIRED: The least complex segment or area of responsibility for which costs are allocated.
DISCUSSION: A cost center is a responsibility center that is accountable only for costs. The cost center is the least complex type of segment because it has no responsibility for revenues or investments.
Answer (A) is incorrect. A profit center is a segment responsible for both revenues and costs. A profit center has the authority to make decisions concerning markets and sources of supply. Answer (B) is incorrect. An investment center is a responsibility center that is accountable for revenues (markets), costs (sources of supply), and invested capital. Answer (C) is incorrect. A contribution center is responsible for revenues and variable costs, but not invested capital.

11.2 Performance Measures -- Cost, Revenue, and Profit Centers

7. The segment margin of the Wire Division of a manufacturer should **not** include

A. Net sales of the Wire Division.
B. Fixed selling expenses of the Wire Division.
C. Variable selling expenses of the Wire Division.
D. The Wire Division's fair share of the salary of the manufacturer's president.

Answer (D) is correct.
REQUIRED: The item not included in a statement showing segment margin.
DISCUSSION: Segment margin is the contribution margin for a segment of a business minus fixed costs. It is a measure of long-run profitability. Thus, an allocation of the corporate officers' salaries should not be included in segment margin because they are neither variable costs nor fixed costs that can be rationally allocated to the segment. Other items that are often not allocated include corporate income taxes, interest, company-wide R&D expenses, and central administration costs.
Answer (A) is incorrect. Sales of the division would appear on the statement. Answer (B) is incorrect. The division's fixed selling expenses are separable fixed costs. Answer (C) is incorrect. Variable costs of the division are included.

8. When using a contribution margin format for internal reporting purposes, the major distinction between segment manager performance and segment performance is

A. Unallocated fixed costs.
B. Direct variable costs of producing the product.
C. Direct fixed costs controllable by the segment manager.
D. Direct fixed costs controllable by others.

Answer (D) is correct.
REQUIRED: The major distinction between segment manager performance and segment performance.
DISCUSSION: The performance of the segment is judged on all costs assigned to it, but the segment manager is only judged on costs that he or she can control. Some fixed costs are imposed on segments by the organization's upper management, and they are thus beyond the segment manager's control. These direct costs controllable by others make up the difference between segment manager performance and segment performance.
Answer (A) is incorrect. Unallocated fixed costs do not affect either performance measure. Answer (B) is incorrect. Direct variable costs affect both performance measures. Answer (C) is incorrect. Direct fixed costs controllable by the segment manager affect both performance measures.

9. Which of the following techniques would be **best** for evaluating the management performance of a department that is operated as a cost center?

A. Return on assets ratio.
B. Return on investment ratio.
C. Payback method.
D. Variance analysis.

Answer (D) is correct.
REQUIRED: The best method for evaluating a cost center.
DISCUSSION: A cost center is a responsibility center that is responsible for costs only. Of the alternatives given, variance analysis is the only one that can be used in a cost center. Variance analysis involves comparing actual costs with predicted or standard costs.
Answer (A) is incorrect. Return on assets cannot be computed for a cost center. The manager is not responsible for revenue (return) or the assets available. Answer (B) is incorrect. Return on investment cannot be computed for a cost center. The manager is not responsible for revenue (return) or the assets available. Answer (C) is incorrect. The payback method is a means of evaluating alternative investment proposals.

10. An entity's income statement for profit center No. 12 for August includes

Contribution margin	$84,000
Manager's salary	24,000
Depreciation on accommodations	9,600
Allocated corporate expenses	6,000

The profit center's manager is **most** likely able to control which of the following?

A. $84,000
B. $68,400
C. $60,000
D. $44,400

Answer (A) is correct.
REQUIRED: The amount most likely subject to the control of the profit center's manager.
DISCUSSION: A profit center is a segment of a company responsible for both revenues and expenses. A profit center has the authority to make decisions concerning markets (revenues) and sources of supplies (costs). However, the profit center's manager does not control his or her salary, investment and the resulting costs (e.g., depreciation of plant assets), or expenses incurred at the corporate level. Consequently, profit center No. 12 is most likely to control the $84,000 contribution margin (sales – variable costs) but not the other items in the summarized income statement.
Answer (B) is incorrect. The profit center manager does not control depreciation on accommodations ($9,600) or the allocated corporate expenses ($6,000). Answer (C) is incorrect. The profit center manager does not control his or her $24,000 salary. Answer (D) is incorrect. The profit center's manager does not control the listed period expenses and therefore does not control the profit center's income.

11. Ordinarily, the **most** appropriate basis on which to evaluate the performance of a division manager is the division's

A. Contribution margin.
B. Net revenue minus controllable division costs.
C. Gross profit.
D. Net income minus the division's fixed costs.

Answer (B) is correct.
REQUIRED: The most appropriate basis on which to evaluate the performance of a division manager.
DISCUSSION: Managerial performance should be evaluated on the basis of those factors controllable by the manager. Managers may control revenues, costs, and/or investment in resources. A well-designed responsibility accounting system establishes responsibility centers within the organization.
Answer (A) is incorrect. Contribution margin ignores the fixed costs of production; managers may control some fixed costs. Answer (C) is incorrect. Not everything included in the calculation of gross profit is controllable by the manager. Answer (D) is incorrect. Net income is computed after deducting fixed costs.

11.3 Performance Measures -- Investment Centers

12. The imputed interest rate used in the residual income approach to performance evaluation can **best** be described as the

A. Average lending rate for the year being evaluated.
B. Historical weighted-average cost of capital for the company.
C. Target return on investment set by the company's management.
D. Average return on investments for the company over the last several years.

Answer (C) is correct.
REQUIRED: The true statement about the imputed interest rate used in the residual income approach to performance evaluation.
DISCUSSION: Residual income is the excess of the return on an investment over a targeted amount equal to an imputed interest charge on invested capital. The rate used is ordinarily set as a target return by management but is often equal to the weighted average cost of capital. Some enterprises prefer to measure managerial performance in terms of the amount of residual income rather than the percentage ROI because the firm will benefit from expansion as long as residual income is earned.
Answer (A) is incorrect. The cost of equity capital must also be incorporated into the imputed interest rate. Answer (B) is incorrect. The current weighted-average cost of capital must be used. Answer (D) is incorrect. The rate should be based on cost of capital, not investment returns of preceding years.

13. A firm earning a profit can increase its return on investment by

A. Increasing sales revenue and operating expenses by the same dollar amount.
B. Decreasing sales revenues and operating expenses by the same percentage.
C. Increasing investment and operating expenses by the same dollar amount.
D. Increasing sales revenues and operating expenses by the same percentage.

Answer (D) is correct.
REQUIRED: The means by which a profitable company can increase its return on investment (ROI).
DISCUSSION: ROI equals income divided by invested capital. If a company is already profitable, increasing sales and expenses by the same percentage will increase ROI. For example, if a company has sales of $100 and expenses of $80, its net income is $20. Given invested capital of $100, ROI is 20% ($20 ÷ $100). If sales and expenses both increase 10% to $110 and $88, respectively, net income increases to $22. ROI will then be 22% ($22 ÷ $100).
Answer (A) is incorrect. Increasing sales and expenses by the same dollar amount will not change income or ROI. Answer (B) is incorrect. Decreasing revenues and expenses by the same percentage will reduce income and lower ROI. Answer (C) is incorrect. Increasing investment and operating expenses by the same dollar amount will lower ROI. The higher investment increases the denominator, and the increased expenses reduce the numerator.

14. Which one of the following statements pertaining to the return on investment (ROI) as a performance measurement is **false**?

A. When the average age of assets differs substantially across segments of a business, the use of ROI may not be appropriate.
B. ROI relies on financial measures that are capable of being independently verified, while other forms of performance measures are subject to manipulation.
C. The use of ROI may lead managers to reject capital investment projects that can be justified by using discounted cash flow models.
D. The use of ROI can make it undesirable for a skillful manager to take on troubleshooting assignments such as those involving turning around unprofitable divisions.

Answer (B) is correct.
REQUIRED: The false statement about ROI as a performance measurement.
DISCUSSION: Return on investment is the key performance measure in an investment center. ROI is a rate computed by dividing a segment's income by the invested capital. ROI is therefore subject to the numerous possible manipulations of the income and investment amounts. For example, a manager may choose not to invest in a project that will yield less than the desired rate of return, or (s)he may defer necessary expenses.
Answer (A) is incorrect. ROI can be misleading when the quality of the investment base differs among segments. Answer (C) is incorrect. Managers may reject projects that are profitable (a return greater than the cost of capital) but would decrease ROI. For example, the managers of a segment with a 15% ROI may not want to invest in a new project with a 10% ROI, even though the cost of capital might be only 8%. Answer (D) is incorrect. The use of ROI does not reflect the relative difficulty of tasks undertaken by managers.

15. Listed below is selected financial information for the Western Division of a corporation for last year.

Account	Amount (thousands)
Average working capital	$ 625
General and administrative expenses	75
Net sales	4,000
Average plant and equipment	1,775
Cost of goods sold	3,525

If the corporation treats the Western Division as an investment center for performance measurement purposes, what is the before-tax return on investment (ROI) for last year?

A. 34.78%
B. 22.54%
C. 19.79%
D. 16.67%

Answer (D) is correct.
REQUIRED: The before-tax ROI for an investment center.
DISCUSSION: An investment center is responsible for revenues, expenses, and invested capital. Given average plant and equipment of $1,775 and average working capital of $625, the net investment is $2,400. Before-tax profit is $400 ($4,000 sales – $3,525 cost of goods sold – $75 general expenses). If before-tax ROI equals before-tax profit divided by net investment, the answer is 16.67% ($400 ÷ $2,400).
Answer (A) is incorrect. This percentage results from subtracting working capital from plant and equipment in calculating the net investment. Answer (B) is incorrect. This percentage fails to include average working capital in the total for the net investment. Answer (C) is incorrect. This percentage results from not subtracting general and administrative expenses in the calculation of before-tax profit.

16. Which one of the following items would most likely **not** be incorporated into the calculation of a division's investment base when using the residual income approach for performance measurement and evaluation?

A. Fixed assets employed in division operations.
B. Land being held by the division as a site for a new plant.
C. Division inventories when division management exercises control over the inventory levels.
D. Division accounts payable when division management exercises control over the amount of short-term credit used.

Answer (B) is correct.
REQUIRED: The item most likely not incorporated into the calculation of a division's investment base.
DISCUSSION: An evaluation of an investment center is based upon the return on the investment base. These assets include plant and equipment, inventories, and receivables. Most likely, however, an asset, such as land, that is being held by the division as a site for a new plant would not be included in the investment base because it is not currently being used in operations. Total assets in use rather than total assets available is preferable when the investment center has been forced to carry idle assets.
Answer (A) is incorrect. Fixed operating assets are controlled by the division manager and contribute to profits. Answer (C) is incorrect. Inventories are operating assets that contribute to profits and are controlled by the division manager. Answer (D) is incorrect. The level of accounts payable is an operating decision that should be considered in the evaluation of the division manager.

11.4 Comparing Performance Measures for Investment Centers

17. A computer service center had the following operating statistics for the month:

Sales	$450,000
Operating income	25,000
Net profit after taxes	8,000
Total assets	500,000
Shareholders' equity	200,000
Cost of capital	6%

Based on the above information, which one of the following statements is **true**? The computer service center has a

A. Return on investment of 4%.
B. Residual income of $(5,000).
C. Return on investment of 1.6%.
D. Residual income of $(22,000).

Answer (B) is correct.
REQUIRED: The true statement about the company's performance.
DISCUSSION: Return on investment is commonly calculated by dividing pretax income by total assets available. Residual income is the excess of the return on investment over a targeted amount equal to an imputed interest charge on invested capital. The rate used is ordinarily the weighted-average cost of capital. Some companies measure managerial performance in terms of the amount of residual income rather than the percentage return on investment. Because the computer service center has assets of $500,000 and a cost of capital of 6%, it must earn $30,000 on those assets to cover the cost of capital. Given that operating income was only $25,000, it had a negative residual income of $5,000.
Answer (A) is incorrect. Although the firm's return on equity investment was 4%, its return on all funds invested was 5% ($25,000 pretax operating income ÷ $500,000). Answer (C) is incorrect. ROI is commonly based on before-tax income. Answer (D) is incorrect. The amount of $(22,000) equals the difference between net profit after taxes and targeted income.

18. Managerial performance can be measured in many different ways, including return on investment (ROI) and residual income. A good reason for using residual income instead of ROI is that

A. Residual income can be computed without regard to identifying an investment base.
B. Goal congruence is more likely to be promoted by using residual income.
C. Residual income is well understood and often used in the financial press.
D. ROI does not take into consideration both the investment turnover ratio and return-on-sales percentage.

Answer (B) is correct.
REQUIRED: The good reason for using the residual income method instead of ROI.
DISCUSSION: Residual income is a significant refinement of the return on investment concept because it forces business unit managers to consider the opportunity cost of capital. The rate used is usually the weighted-average cost of capital. Residual income may be preferable to ROI because a business unit will benefit from expansion as long as residual income is earned. Using only ROI, managers might be tempted to reject expansion that would lower ROI, even though residual income would increase. Thus, the residual income method promotes the congruence of a manager's goals with those of the overall firm. Actions that tend to benefit the company will also tend to improve the measure of the manager's performance.
Answer (A) is incorrect. An investment base is needed to calculate residual income. Answer (C) is incorrect. ROI and residual income calculations generally require the use of unpublished financial information. Answer (D) is incorrect. Both measures consider the same items.

19. Residual income is a better measure for performance evaluation of an investment center manager than return on investment because

A. The problems associated with measuring the asset base are eliminated.
B. Desirable investment decisions will not be neglected by high-return divisions.
C. Only the gross book value of assets needs to be calculated.
D. The arguments about the implicit cost of interest are eliminated.

Answer (B) is correct.
REQUIRED: The reason residual income is a better measure of performance evaluation than return on investment.
DISCUSSION: Residual income is the excess of the amount of the ROI over a targeted amount equal to an imputed interest charge on invested capital. The advantage of using residual income rather than percentage ROI is that the former emphasizes maximizing a dollar amount instead of a percentage. Managers of divisions with a high ROI are encouraged to accept projects with returns exceeding the cost of capital even if those projects reduce the department's ROI.
Answer (A) is incorrect. The methods use the same asset base. Answer (C) is incorrect. The methods use the same asset base. Answer (D) is incorrect. Use of the residual income method requires a knowledge of the cost of capital; thus, arguments about the implicit cost of interest may escalate with use of the residual income method.

11.5 Allocating Common Costs

20. Which one of the following companies is likely to experience dysfunctional motivation on the part of its managers due to its allocation methods?

A. To allocate depreciation of forklifts used by workers at its central warehouse, Company A uses predetermined amounts calculated on the basis of the long-term average use of the services provided.
B. Company B uses the sales revenue of its various divisions to allocate costs connected with the upkeep of its headquarters building. It also uses ROI to evaluate the divisional performances.
C. Company C does not allow its service departments to pass on their cost overruns to the production departments.
D. Company D's MIS is operated out of headquarters and serves its various divisions. The allocation of the MIS-related costs to its divisions is limited to costs the divisions will incur if they were to outsource their MIS needs.

Answer (B) is correct.
REQUIRED: The company most likely to experience dysfunctional motivation on the part of its managers.
DISCUSSION: Managerial performance ordinarily should be evaluated only on the basis of those factors controllable by the manager. If a manager is allocated costs that (s)he cannot control, dysfunctional motivation can result. In the case of allocations, a cause-and-effect basis should be used. Allocating the costs of upkeep on a headquarters building on the basis of sales revenue is arbitrary because cost may have no relationship to divisional sales revenues. Consequently, divisional ROI is reduced by a cost over which a division manager has no control. Furthermore, the divisions with the greatest sales are penalized by receiving the greatest allocation.
Answer (A) is incorrect. Allocating depreciation on the basis of long-term average use is a reasonable basis of allocation. This basis is controllable by the division managers and reflects a causal relationship. Answer (C) is incorrect. A service department's cost overruns may not be attributable to any activities of production departments. Answer (D) is incorrect. Market-based allocations of costs of services are reasonable applications of the cause-and-effect principle.

21. Managers are **most** likely to accept allocations of common costs based on

A. Cause and effect.
B. Ability to bear.
C. Fairness.
D. Benefits received.

Answer (A) is correct.
REQUIRED: The criterion most likely to result in acceptable allocations of common costs.
DISCUSSION: The difficulty with common costs is that they are indirect costs whose allocation may be arbitrary. A direct cause-and-effect relationship between a common cost and the actions of the cost object to which it is allocated is desirable. Such a relationship promotes acceptance of the allocation by managers who perceive the fairness of the procedure, but identification of cause and effect may not be feasible.
Answer (B) is incorrect. Allocation using an ability-to-bear criterion punishes successful managers and rewards underachievers. Answer (C) is incorrect. Fairness is an objective rather than a criterion. Moreover, fairness may be interpreted differently by different managers. Answer (D) is incorrect. The benefits-received criterion is preferable when a cause-effect relationship cannot be feasibly identified.

22. Common costs are

A. Direct costs.
B. Current costs.
C. Controllable costs.
D. Indirect costs.

Answer (D) is correct.
REQUIRED: The nature of common costs.
DISCUSSION: Common costs are the cost of products, activities, facilities, services, or operations shared by two or more cost objects. They are indirect costs because they cannot be traced to a particular cost object in an economically feasible manner. Hence, they must be allocated.
Answer (A) is incorrect. Direct costs can be traced to a particular cost object in an economically feasible manner. Answer (B) is incorrect. Current cost is an attribute used to measure assets. Answer (C) is incorrect. Controllable costs can be influenced by a particular manager.

23. A large corporation allocates the costs of its headquarters staff to its decentralized divisions. The **best** reason for this allocation is to

A. More accurately measure divisional operating results.
B. Improve divisional management's morale.
C. Remind divisional managers that common costs exist.
D. Discourage any use of central support services.

Answer (C) is correct.
REQUIRED: The best reason for allocating headquarters costs.
DISCUSSION: The allocation reminds managers that support costs exist and that the managers would incur these costs if their operations were independent. The allocation also reminds managers that profit center earnings must cover some amount of support costs.
Answer (A) is incorrect. An arbitrary allocation may skew operating results. Answer (B) is incorrect. The allocation may create resentment and conflict. Answer (D) is incorrect. Efficient use of central support services should be encouraged.

11.6 Transfer Pricing

Questions 24 through 26 are based on the following information.

Parkside, Inc., has several divisions that operate as decentralized profit centers. Parkside's Entertainment Division manufactures video arcade equipment using the products of two of Parkside's other divisions. The Plastics Division manufactures plastic components, one type that is made exclusively for the Entertainment Division, while other less complex components are sold to outside markets. The products of the Video Cards Division are sold in a competitive market; however, one video card model is also used by the Entertainment Division.

The actual costs per unit used by the Entertainment Division are presented below.

	Plastic Components	Video Cards
Direct material	$1.25	$2.40
Direct labor	2.35	3.00
Variable overhead	1.00	1.50
Fixed overhead	.40	2.25
Total cost	$5.00	$9.15

The Plastics Division sells its commercial products at full cost plus a 25% markup and believes the proprietary plastic component made for the Entertainment Division would sell for $6.25 per unit on the open market. The market price of the video card used by the Entertainment Division is $10.98 per unit.

24. A per-unit transfer price from the Video Cards Division to the Entertainment Division at full cost, $9.15, would

A. Allow evaluation of both divisions on a competitive basis.
B. Satisfy the Video Cards Division's profit desire by allowing recovery of opportunity costs.
C. Provide no profit incentive for the Video Cards Division to control or reduce costs.
D. Encourage the Entertainment Division to purchase video cards from an outside source.

Answer (C) is correct.
REQUIRED: The negative effect of a full-cost transfer price.
DISCUSSION: The use of full (absorption) cost ensures that the selling division will not incur a loss and provides more incentive to the buying division to buy internally than does use of market price. However, there is no motivation for the seller to control production cost since all costs can be passed along to the buying division.
Answer (A) is incorrect. Evaluating the seller is difficult if it can pass along all costs to the buyer. Answer (B) is incorrect. Transfers at full cost do not allow for a seller's profit. Answer (D) is incorrect. A full-cost transfer is favorable to the buyer. It is lower than the market price.

25. Assume that the Entertainment Division is able to purchase a large quantity of video cards from an outside source at $8.70 per unit. The Video Cards Division, having excess capacity, agrees to lower its transfer price to $8.70 per unit. This action would

A. Optimize the profit goals of the Entertainment Division while subverting the profit goals of Parkside, Inc.
B. Allow evaluation of both divisions on the same basis.
C. Subvert the profit goals of the Video Cards Division while optimizing the profit goals of the Entertainment Division.
D. Optimize the overall profit goals of Parkside, Inc.

Answer (D) is correct.
REQUIRED: The impact of lowering the transfer price to match an outside seller's price.
DISCUSSION: If the selling division has excess capacity, it should lower its transfer price to match the outside offer. This decision optimizes the profits of the company as a whole by allowing for use of capacity that would otherwise be idle.
Answer (A) is incorrect. This action is congruent with the goals of Parkside. The use of idle capacity enhances profits. Answer (B) is incorrect. The transfer is at a loss (relative to full cost) to the selling division, although the company as a whole will benefit. Answer (C) is incorrect. The buying division is indifferent as to whether to purchase internally or externally.

26. Assume that the Plastics Division has excess capacity and it has negotiated a transfer price of $5.60 per plastic component with the Entertainment Division. This price will

A. Cause the Plastics Division to reduce the number of commercial plastic components it manufactures.
B. Motivate both divisions as estimated profits are shared.
C. Encourage the Entertainment Division to seek an outside source for plastic components.
D. Demotivate the Plastics Division causing mediocre performance.

Answer (B) is correct.
REQUIRED: The effect of using a negotiated transfer price that is greater than full cost but less than market price.
DISCUSSION: Given that the seller has excess capacity, transfers within the company entail no opportunity cost. Accordingly, the transfer at the negotiated price will improve the performance measures of the selling division. Purchasing internally at below the market price also benefits the buying division, so the motivational purpose of transfer pricing is achieved. The goal congruence purpose is also achieved because the internal transaction benefits the company.
Answer (A) is incorrect. This arrangement creates no disincentive for the selling division. It will make a profit on every unit transferred. Answer (C) is incorrect. The market price charged by outside sources is higher than the negotiated price. Answer (D) is incorrect. Given idle capacity, selling at any amount in excess of variable cost should motivate the selling division.

27. A limitation of transfer prices based on actual cost is that they

A. Charge inefficiencies to the department that is transferring the goods.
B. Can lead to suboptimal decisions for the company as a whole.
C. Must be adjusted by some markup.
D. Lack clarity and administrative convenience.

Answer (B) is correct.
REQUIRED: The limitation of transfer prices based on actual cost.
DISCUSSION: The optimal transfer price of a selling division should be set at a point that will have the most desirable economic effect on the firm as a whole while at the same time continuing to motivate the management of every division to perform efficiently. Setting the transfer price based on actual costs rather than standard costs would give the selling division little incentive to control costs.
Answer (A) is incorrect. Inefficiencies are charged to the buying department. Answer (C) is incorrect. By definition, cost-based transfer prices are not adjusted by some markup. Answer (D) is incorrect. Cost-based transfer prices provide the advantages of clarity and administrative convenience.

28. An appropriate transfer price between two divisions of a manufacturer can be determined from the following data:

Fabricating Division:
- Market price of subassembly $50
- Variable cost of subassembly $20
- Excess capacity (in units)   1,000

Assembling Division:
- Number of units needed   900

What is the natural bargaining range for the two divisions?

A. Between $20 and $50.
B. Between $50 and $70.
C. Any amount less than $50.
D. $50 is the only acceptable price.

Answer (A) is correct.
REQUIRED: The natural bargaining range for the transfer price.
DISCUSSION: An ideal transfer price should permit each division to operate independently and achieve its goals while functioning in the overall best interest of the firm. The production capacity of the selling division is always a consideration in setting transfer price. If Fabricating had no excess capacity, it would charge Assembling the regular market price. However, since Fabricating has excess capacity of 1,000 units, negotiation is possible because any transfer price greater than the variable cost of $20 would absorb some of the fixed costs and result in increased divisional profits. Thus, any price between $20 and $50 is acceptable to Fabricating. Any price under $50 is acceptable to Assembling because that is the price that would be paid to an outside supplier.
Answer (B) is incorrect. Assembling would not pay more than the market price of $50. Answer (C) is incorrect. Fabricating will not be willing to accept less than its variable cost of $20. Answer (D) is incorrect. Fabricating should be willing to accept any price between $20 and $50.

29. The **most** fundamental responsibility center affected by the use of market-based transfer prices is a(n)

A. Production center.
B. Investment center.
C. Cost center.
D. Profit center.

Answer (D) is correct.
REQUIRED: The most fundamental responsibility center affected by the use of market-based transfer prices.
DISCUSSION: Transfer prices are often used by profit centers and investment centers. Profit centers are the more fundamental of these two centers because investment centers are responsible not only for revenues and costs but also for invested capital.
Answer (A) is incorrect. A production center may be a cost center, a profit center, or even an investment center. Transfer prices are not used in a cost center. Transfer prices are used to compute profitability, but a cost center is responsible only for cost control. Answer (B) is incorrect. An investment center is not as fundamental as a profit center. Answer (C) is incorrect. Transfer prices are not used in a cost center.

30. In theory, the optimal method for establishing a transfer price is

A. Flexible budget cost.
B. Incremental cost.
C. Budgeted cost with or without a markup.
D. Market price.

Answer (D) is correct.
REQUIRED: The optimal method for establishing a transfer price.
DISCUSSION: Transfer prices should promote congruence of subunit goals with those of the organization, subunit autonomy, and managerial effort. Although no rule exists for determining the transfer price that meets these criteria in all situations, a starting point is to calculate the sum of the additional outlay costs and the opportunity cost to the supplier. Given no idle capacity and a competitive external market (all goods transferred internally can be sold externally), the sum of the outlay and opportunity costs will be the market price.
Answer (A) is incorrect. Using flexible budget cost as a transfer price provides no motivation to the seller to control costs and no reward for selling internally when an external market exists. Answer (B) is incorrect. Using incremental cost as a transfer price provides no motivation to the seller to control costs and no reward for selling internally when an external market exists. Answer (C) is incorrect. Market price is preferable to a budgeted or actual cost with or without a markup (unless the markup equals the profit earned by selling externally).

Access the **CMA Review System** from your Gleim Personal Classroom to continue your studies with exam-emulating multiple-choice questions!

11.7 ESSAY QUESTIONS

Scenario for Essay Questions 1, 2, 3, 4

Ajax Consolidated has several divisions; however, only two divisions transfer products to other divisions. The Mining Division refines toldine, which is then transferred to the Metals Division. The toldine is processed into an alloy by the Metals Division and is sold to customers at a price of $150 per unit. The Mining Division is currently required by Ajax to transfer its total yearly output of 400,000 units of toldine to the Metals Division at total manufacturing cost plus 10%. Unlimited quantities of toldine can be purchased and sold on the open market at $90 per unit. While the Mining Division could sell all the toldine it produces at $90 per unit on the open market, it would have to incur a variable selling cost of $5 per unit.

Brian Jones, manager of the Mining Division, is unhappy with having to transfer the entire output of toldine to the Metals Division at 110 percent of cost. In a meeting with the management of Ajax, he said, "Why should my division be required to sell toldine to the Metals Division at less than market price? For the year just ended, Metals' contribution margin was over $19 million on sales of 400,000 units while Mining's contribution was just over $5 million on the transfer of the same number of units. My division is subsidizing the profitability of the Metals Division. We should be allowed to charge the market price for toldine when transferring to the Metals Division."

Presented below is the detailed unit cost structure for both the Mining and Metals Divisions for the fiscal year ended May 31.

Cost Structure Per Unit

	Mining Division	Metals Division
Transfer price from Mining Division	--	$ 66
Direct material	$12	6
Direct labor	16	20
Manufacturing overhead	32[1]	25[2]
Total cost per unit	$60	$117

[1] Manufacturing overhead cost in the Mining Division is 25% fixed and 75% variable.
[2] Manufacturing overhead cost in the Metals Division is 60% fixed and 40% variable.

Questions

1. Explain why transfer prices based on cost are not appropriate as a divisional performance measure.

2. Using the market price as the transfer price, determine the contribution margin for both the Mining Division and the Metals Division for the year ended May 31.

3. If Ajax Consolidated were to institute the use of negotiated transfer prices and allow divisions to buy and sell on the open market, determine the price range for toldine that would be acceptable to both the Mining Division and the Metals Division. Explain your answer.

4. Identify which one of the three types of transfer prices -- cost-based, market-based, or negotiated -- is most likely to elicit desirable management behavior at Ajax Consolidated and thus benefit overall operations. Explain your answer.

Essay Questions 1, 2, 3, 4 — Unofficial Answers

1. Among the reasons transfer prices based on cost are not appropriate as a divisional performance measure are because they

   a. Provide little incentive for the selling division to control manufacturing costs as all costs incurred will be recovered

   b. Often lead to suboptimal decisions for the company as a whole

2. Using the market price as the transfer price, the contribution margin for both the Mining Division and the Metals Division for the year ended May 31 is calculated below.

   Ajax Consolidated Calculation of
   Divisional Contribution Margin
   For the Year Ended May 31

	Mining Division	Metals Division
Selling price	$ 90	$ 150
Less: Variable costs		
Direct material	12	6
Direct labor	16	20
Manufacturing overhead	$24^{(1)}$	$10^{(2)}$
Transfer price		90
Unit contribution margin	$ 38	$ 24
Volume	× 400,000	× 400,000
Total contribution margin	$15,200,000	$ 9,600,000

   $^{(1)}$ Variable overhead: $32 × 75% = $24
   $^{(2)}$ Variable overhead: $25 × 40% = $10

   NOTE: The $5 variable selling cost that the Mining Division would incur for sales on the open market should not be included as this is an internal transfer.

3. If the use of a negotiated transfer price was instituted by Ajax Consolidated, which also permitted the divisions to buy and sell on the open market, the price range for toldine that would be acceptable to both divisions would be determined as follows:

   a. The Mining Division would like to sell to the Metals Division for the same price it can obtain on the outside market, $90 per unit. However, Mining would be willing to sell the toldine for $85 per unit as the $5 variable selling cost would be avoided.

   b. The Metals Division would like to continue paying the bargain price of $66 per unit. However, if Mining does not sell to Metals, Metals would be forced to pay $90 on the open market. Therefore, Metals would be satisfied to receive a price concession from Mining equal to the costs that Mining would avoid by selling internally. Therefore, a negotiated transfer price for toldine between $85 and $90 would benefit both divisions and the company as a whole.

4. A negotiated transfer price is the most likely to elicit desirable management behavior as it will

   a. Encourage the management of the Mining Division to be more conscious of cost control

   b. Benefit the Metals Division by providing toldine at less cost than its competitors

   c. Provide a more realistic measure of divisional performance

---

Access the **CMA Review System** from your Gleim Personal Classroom
to continue your studies with exam-emulating essay questions!

STUDY UNIT TWELVE
INTERNAL CONTROLS -- CORPORATE GOVERNANCE

(27 pages of outline)

12.1	Corporate Governance and Legal Aspects of Internal Control	399
12.2	Risk and Internal Control	408
12.3	Internal Auditing	419
12.4	Essay Questions	435

Internal Controls

Management accountants are expected to have a thorough understanding of the risks inherent to, and the internal controls within, a business. Internal controls have always been a good idea in a well-run business, but with the passage of the Foreign Corrupt Practices Act in 1977, an effective internal control system became a legal requirement. The Sarbanes-Oxley Act of 2002 further enhanced the legal requirements for internal controls.

This study unit is the **first of two** on **internal controls**. The relative weight assigned to this major topic in Part 1 of the exam is **15%**. The two study units are

Study Unit 12: Internal Controls -- Corporate Governance
Study Unit 13: Internal Controls -- Controls and Security Measures

If you are interested in reviewing more introductory or background material, go to www.gleim.com/CMAIntroVideos for a list of suggested third-party overviews of this topic. The following Gleim outline material is more than sufficient to help you pass the CMA exam; any additional introductory or background material is for your own personal enrichment.

12.1 CORPORATE GOVERNANCE AND LEGAL ASPECTS OF INTERNAL CONTROL

1. **Definition of Corporate Governance**
    a. **Governance** is the combination of people, policies, procedures, and processes (including internal control) that help ensure that an entity effectively and efficiently directs its activities toward meeting the objectives of its stakeholders.
        1) Stakeholders are persons or entities who are affected by the activities of the entity. Among others, these include shareholders, employees, suppliers, customers, neighbors of the entity's facilities, and government regulators.
    b. Corporate governance can be either internal or external.
        1) Corporate charters and bylaws, boards of directors, and internal audit functions are internal.
        2) Laws, regulations, and the government regulators who enforce them are external.

2. **Governance Practices**
    a. Governance practices reflect the organization's unique culture and largely depend on it for effectiveness.
        1) The organizational culture
            a) Sets values, objectives, and strategies;
            b) Defines roles and behaviors;
            c) Measures performance; and
            d) Specifies accountability.
        2) Thus, the culture determines the degree of sensitivity to social responsibility.

b. Governance practices may use various legal forms, structures, strategies, and procedures. They ensure that the organization

1) Complies with society's legal and regulatory rules;
2) Satisfies the generally accepted business norms, ethical principles, and social expectations of society;
3) Provides overall benefit to society and enhances the interests of the specific stakeholders in both the long and short term; and
4) Reports fully and truthfully to its stakeholders, including the public, to ensure accountability for its decisions, actions, and performances.

c. Governance applies to all organizational activities. Thus, its processes provide overall direction for risk management activities.

1) Internal control activities are in turn a key element of risk management. They implement the organization's risk management strategies.

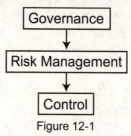
Figure 12-1

3. **Governance in Corporations**

a. Unlike a sole proprietorship or a general partnership, a corporation is a legal entity created under authority of a **state statute** to carry out the purposes permitted by that statute and the articles of incorporation.

1) The corporation ordinarily is treated as a **legal person** with rights and obligations separate from its owners and managers.

b. Corporations are governed by **shareholders** (owners) who elect a board of directors and approve fundamental changes in the corporate structure.

1) **Directors** establish corporate policies, adapt bylaws, and elect or appoint corporate **officers** who carry out the policies in the day-to-day management of the organization.

c. Incorporation may be in any state. **Articles of incorporation** must be filed with the secretary of state or another designated official. The articles must include the following:

1) Corporation's name (must differ from the name of any corporation authorized to do business in the state)
2) Number of authorized shares of stock
3) Street address of the corporation's initial registered office
4) Name of the registered agent at that office
5) Name and address of each incorporator

d. **Bylaws** govern the internal structure and operation of the corporation.

1) Initial bylaws are adopted by the incorporators or the board.
2) They may contain any provision for managing the business and regulating the entity's affairs that does not conflict with the law or the articles.

4. **Corporate Governance Process**

    a. Governance has two major components: strategic direction and oversight.

        1) Strategic direction determines

            a) The business model,
            b) Overall objectives,
            c) The approach to risk taking (including the risk appetite), and
            d) The limits of organizational conduct.

        2) Oversight is the governance component with which internal auditing is most concerned. It is also the component to which risk management and control activities are most likely to be applied. The elements of oversight are

            a) Risk management activities performed by senior management and risk owners and
            b) Internal and external assurance activities.

    b. The **board** is the source of overall direction to, and the authority of, management. It also has the ultimate responsibility for oversight.

        1) Another responsibility is to identify stakeholders, whether directly involved with the business (employees, customers, and suppliers), indirectly involved (investors), or having influence over the business (regulators and competitors).

        2) The board must determine the expectations of stakeholders and the outcomes that are unacceptable.

    c. **Management** performs day-to-day governance functions and determines

        1) What specific risks are to be managed,
        2) Who will be **risk owners** (managers responsible for specific day-to-day risks), and
        3) How specific risks will be managed.

    d. The functions of risk owners include

        1) Evaluating the adequacy of the design of risk management activities and the organization's ability to carry them out as designed;
        2) Determining whether risk management activities are operating as designed;
        3) Establishing monitoring activities; and
        4) Ensuring that information to be reported to senior management and the board is accurate, timely, and available.

    e. A **risk committee** may be created that

        1) Identifies key risks,
        2) Connects them to risk management processes,
        3) Delegates them to risk owners, and
        4) Considers whether tolerance levels delegated to risk owners are consistent with the organization's risk appetite.

    f. Governance expectations, including tolerance levels, must be periodically reevaluated by the board and senior management. The result may be changes in risk management activities.

5. **Audit Approaches**

    a. Essentially, there are four different audit approaches:

        1) The substantive procedures approach
        2) The balance sheet approach
        3) The systems-based approach
        4) The risk-based approach

b. The **substantive procedures approach** is also referred to as the vouching approach or the direct verification approach. In this approach, audit resources are targeted on testing large volumes of transactions and account balances without any particular focus on specified areas of the financial statements.
c. Under the **balance sheet approach**, substantive procedures are focused on balance sheet accounts, with only limited procedures being carried out on income statement/ profit and loss accounts. The justification for this approach is the notion that if the relevant management assertions for all balance sheet accounts are tested and verified, then the income figure reported for the accounting period will not be materially misstated.
d. The **systems-based approach** requires auditors to assess the effectiveness of the internal controls and then to direct substantive procedures primarily to those areas where it is considered that systems objectives will not be met. Reduced testing is carried out in those areas where it is considered systems objectives will be met.
e. With the **risk-based approach**, audit resources are directed towards those areas of the financial statements that may contain misstatements (either by error or omission) as a consequence of the risks faced by the business.

   1) Auditors are required to make risk assessments of material misstatements at the financial statement and assertion levels, based on an appropriate understanding of the entity and its environment, including internal controls.

      a) This is known as the "top down" approach to identifying risks. The word "top" refers to the day-to-day operations of the entity and the environment in which it operates; "down" refers to the financial statements of the entity.

   2) This approach requires auditors to identify the key day-to-day risks faced by a business, consider the impact these risks could have on the financial statements, and plan their audit procedures accordingly.

f. There are four types of audit options (audit reports) that an external auditor may give on a set of financial statements.

   1) **Unqualified opinion:** Often called a clean opinion, an unqualified opinion is an audit report issued when an auditor determines that the financial records are free of any misrepresentations. An unqualified opinion indicates that the statements have been maintained in accordance with generally accepted accounting principles (GAAP). This is the best type of report a business can receive and is the most commonly issued report. The auditor signs and dates the document, including his or her address.

   2) **Qualified opinion:** In situations when a company's financial records have not been maintained in accordance with GAAP but no misrepresentations are identified, an auditor will issue a qualified opinion. The writing of a qualified opinion is similar to that of an unqualified opinion. A qualified opinion, however, will include an additional paragraph that highlights the reason why the audit report is not unqualified.

   3) **Adverse opinion:** The worst type of financial report that can be issued to a business is an adverse opinion. This indicates that the firm's financial records do not conform to GAAP.

   4) **Disclaimer of opinion:** On some occasions, an auditor is unable to complete an accurate audit report. This may occur for a variety of reasons, such as an absence of appropriate financial records. When this happens, the auditor issues a disclaimer of opinion, stating that an opinion of the firm's financial status could not be determined. It is issued when the scope of the audit is not sufficient to permit formation of an opinion or when the auditor is not independent.

SU 12: Internal Controls -- Corporate Governance

6. **Foreign Corrupt Practices Act**

   a. The Foreign Corrupt Practices Act (FCPA), enacted in 1977, had its origin in the Watergate investigations. The FCPA is designed to prevent secret payments of corporate funds for purposes that Congress has determined to be contrary to public policy, such as bribery of foreign officials.

      1) The Act amends the Securities Exchange Act of 1934 to prohibit a domestic concern, including any person acting on its behalf, whether or not doing business overseas and whether or not registered with the SEC, from offering or authorizing corrupt payments to any

         a) Foreign official
         b) Foreign political party or official thereof
         c) Candidate for political office in a foreign country

      2) Only political payments to foreign government officials are prohibited. Payments to foreign business owners or corporate officers are not addressed by the FCPA.

      3) Corrupt payments are payments for the purpose of inducing the recipient to act or refrain from acting so that the domestic concern might obtain or retain business.

         a) The FCPA prohibits a mere offer or promise of a bribe, even if it is not consummated.
         b) The FCPA prohibits payment of anything of value. De minimis gifts and tokens of hospitality are acceptable.
         c) Payments are prohibited if the person making them knew or should have known that some or all of them would be used to influence a governmental official.

      4) Foreign officials do not include clerical or ministerial employees.

         a) EXAMPLE: Payments made to a clerk to expedite the processing of goods through customs may not be prohibited by the act.
         b) Such payments are not prohibited as long as the recipient has no discretion in carrying out a governmental function.
         c) Payments that are allowed under the written law of the foreign country are also not prohibited.

      5) Regardless of whether they have foreign operations, all public companies must make and keep books, records, and accounts in reasonable detail that accurately and fairly reflect transactions and dispositions of assets.

      6) All public companies registered under the 1934 Act must devise and maintain a system of internal accounting control sufficient to provide reasonable assurance that

         a) Transactions are executed in accordance with management's general or specific authorization.
         b) Transactions are recorded as necessary to

            i) Permit preparation of financial statements in conformity with generally accepted accounting principles (GAAP) or any other criteria applicable to such statements and
            ii) Maintain accountability for assets.

         c) Access to assets is permitted only in accordance with management's general or specific authorization.
         d) The recorded accountability for assets is compared with the existing assets at reasonable intervals, and appropriate action is taken with respect to any differences.

7) The penalties for an individual for each criminal violation of the corrupt practices provisions are a fine of up to $100,000 or imprisonment for up to 5 years, or both. A corporation may be assessed a fine of up to $2,000,000 for violation of the same section.

   a) Fines imposed upon individuals may not be paid directly or indirectly by an employer.

8) The implications of the Foreign Corrupt Practices Act of 1977 extend well beyond its anti-bribery provisions.

   a) All American businesses and business people are involved. Management is particularly affected. The responsibility for internal control is not new, but the potential for civil and criminal liabilities represents an added burden.

   b) The impact of the law and the threat its ambiguities pose may alter business operations. Management might decide to abandon direct selling operations in foreign countries in favor of the use of foreign agents in hopes that this might lessen their "reason to know."

9) A written code of ethics and conduct is a necessity. This code should be communicated and monitored by internal auditors for compliance.

   a) The code might include an explanation of the Foreign Corrupt Practices Act and its penalties. A firm may require written representations from employees that they have read and understood the provisions of the code.

   b) Written representations regarding compliance might also be requested at future times. Foreign agents should be made aware of the prohibitions of indirect payments.

7. **Sarbanes-Oxley Act**

   a. The Sarbanes-Oxley Act of 2002 was a response to numerous financial reporting scandals involving large public companies. The act contains provisions that impose new responsibilities on public companies and their auditors. The act applies to issuers of publicly traded securities subject to federal securities laws.

   1) The act requires that each member of the audit committee, including at least one who is a financial expert, be an independent member of the issuer's board of directors. An independent director is not affiliated with, and receives no compensation (other than for service on the board) from, the issuer.

      a) The audit committee must be directly responsible for appointing, compensating, and overseeing the work of the public accounting firm employed by the issuer. In addition, this audit firm must report directly to the audit committee, not to management.

   2) Prohibited nonaudit services. Section 201 of the act lists several activities that cannot be performed on behalf of audit clients. Item 10. on page 406 has a detailed explanation.

   3) An accounting firm may perform non-audit services (e.g., tax services) for an audit client only if the activity is approved in advance by the audit committee of the client.

   4) Audit partner rotation. Section 203 of the act requires the lead auditor and the reviewing partner to be rotated off the audit so that the same individual is not supervising a client's audit for an extended period of time. Item 11. on page 406 has a detailed explanation.

      a) The lead audit partner cannot perform audit services for more than 5 consecutive fiscal years of the audit client.

5) Corporate responsibility of a public company. Section 302 requires periodic statutory financial reports to include certain certifications. Item 12. on page 407 has a detailed explanation.
6) Internal control report. Section 404 of the act requires management to establish and document internal control procedures and to include in the annual report a report on the company's internal control over financial reporting.

   a) This report is to include

      i) A statement of management's responsibility for internal control;
      ii) Management's assessment of the effectiveness of internal control as of the end of the most recent fiscal year;
      iii) Identification of the framework used to evaluate the effectiveness of internal control (such as the report of the Committee of Sponsoring Organizations);
      iv) A statement about whether significant changes in controls were made after their evaluation, including any corrective actions; and
      v) A statement that the external auditor has issued an attestation report on management's assessment.

         - Because of this requirement, two audit opinions are expressed: one on internal control and one on the financial statements.

   b) The external auditor must attest to and report on management's assessment.

      i) The auditor must evaluate whether the structure and procedures

         - Include records accurately and fairly reflecting the firm's transactions and
         - Provide reasonable assurance that transactions are recorded so as to permit statements to be prepared in accordance with GAAP.

      ii) The auditor's report also must describe any material weaknesses in internal controls.
      iii) The evaluation is not to be the subject of a separate engagement but be in conjunction with the audit of the financial statements.

8. **The Public Company Accounting Oversight Board (PCAOB)**

   a. The PCAOB was vested with the authority to promulgate standards for the practice of auditing. PCAOB Auditing Standard 2 (issued in 2004) required that an audit of internal control be integrated with the audit of the financial statements. Although auditors are allowed to issue separate reports on the audits of financial statements and internal controls, in practice they are most often combined into a single report.

      1) In 2007, Auditing Standard 2 was superseded by PCAOB Auditing Standard 5, which had similar requirements.

   b. **Auditing Standard No. 5**

      1) Standard No. 5 is principles-based. It is designed to increase the likelihood that material weaknesses in internal control will be found before they result in material misstatement of a company's financial statements and, at the same time, eliminate procedures that are unnecessary.
      2) The final standard also focuses the auditor on the procedures necessary to perform a high-quality audit tailored to the company's facts and circumstances. The new standard is more risk-based and scalable, which will better meet the needs of investors, public companies, and auditors alike.

3) The new auditing standard, by focusing the auditor's attention on those matters that are most important to effective internal control, presents another significant opportunity to strengthen the financial reporting process.

9. **Fraud vs. Error**

    a. Fraud differs from error because it is intentional. It typically involves pressures or incentives to engage in wrongdoing and a perceived opportunity to do so.

        1) Examples are fraudulent financial reporting and misappropriation of assets.

    b. Internal controls are designed to, among other things, prevent fraud. However, because of the concealment aspects of fraudulent activity (e.g., collusion or falsification of documents), the controls cannot give absolute assurance that material fraud will be prevented or detected.

10. **Sarbanes-Oxley Section 201. SERVICES OUTSIDE THE SCOPE OF PRACTICE OF AUDITORS**

    (a) PROHIBITED ACTIVITIES - *Section 10A of the Securities Exchange Act of 1934 is amended by adding the following: It shall be unlawful for a registered public accounting firm (and any associated person of that firm) that performs for any issuer any audit required by the rules of the Commission to provide to that issuer, contemporaneously with the audit, any non-audit service, including:*

    (1) bookkeeping or other services related to the accounting records or financial statements of the audit client;
    (2) financial information systems design and implementation;
    (3) appraisal or valuation services, fairness opinions, or contribution-in-kind reports;
    (4) actuarial services;
    (5) internal audit outsourcing services;
    (6) management functions or human resources;
    (7) broker or dealer, investment adviser, or investment banking services;
    (8) legal services and expert services unrelated to the audit; and
    (9) any other services that the Board determines, by regulation, is impermissible.

    PREAPPROVAL REQUIRED FOR NON-AUDIT SERVICES - *A registered public accounting firm may engage in any non-audit service, including tax services, that is not described above, for an audit client only if the activity is approved in advance by the audit committee of the client.*

    (b) EXEMPTION AUTHORITY - *The Board may, on a case-by-case basis, exempt any issuer, public accounting firm, or transaction from the prohibition provision to the extent that such exemption is necessary or appropriate in the public interest and is consistent with the protection of investors, and subject to review by the Commission.*

11. **Sarbanes-Oxley Section 203. AUDIT PARTNER ROTATION**

    a. CPA firms must rotate audit partners so that the same individual is not supervising a client's audit for an extended period of time.

    (j) *It shall be unlawful for a registered public accounting firm to provide audit services to an issuer if the lead (or coordinating) audit partner (having primary responsibility for the audit), or the audit partner responsible for reviewing the audit, has performed audit services for that issuer in each of the five previous fiscal years of that issuer.*

12. **Sarbanes-Oxley Section 302. CORPORATE RESPONSIBILITY FOR FINANCIAL REPORTS**
    (a) REGULATIONS REQUIRED - The SEC shall require, for each company filing periodic reports under the Securities Exchange Act of 1934, that the principal executive officer or officers and the principal financial officer or officers, or persons performing similar functions, certify in each annual or quarterly report filed or submitted under the act that--
    (1) the signing officer has reviewed the report;
    (2) based on the officer's knowledge, the report does not contain any untrue statement of a material fact or omit to state a material fact necessary in order to make the statements made, in light of the circumstances under which such statements were made, not misleading;
    (3) based on such officer's knowledge, the financial statements, and other financial information included in the report, fairly present in all material respects the financial condition and results of operations of the issuer as of, and for, the periods presented in the report;
    (4) the signing officers--
       (A) are responsible for establishing and maintaining internal controls;
       (B) have designed such internal controls to ensure that material information relating to the issuer and its consolidated subsidiaries is made known to such officers by others within those entities, particularly during the period in which the periodic reports are being prepared;
       (C) have evaluated the effectiveness of the issuer's internal controls as of a date within 90 days prior to the report; and
       (D) have presented in the report their conclusions about the effectiveness of their internal controls based on their evaluation as of that date;
    (5) the signing officers have disclosed to the issuer's auditors and the audit committee of the board of directors (or persons fulfilling the equivalent function)--
       (A) all significant deficiencies in the design or operation of internal controls which could adversely affect the issuer's ability to record, process, summarize, and report financial data and have identified for the issuer's auditors any material weaknesses in internal controls; and
       (B) any fraud, whether or not material, that involves management or other employees who have a significant role in the issuer's internal controls; and
    (6) the signing officers have indicated in the report whether or not there were significant changes in internal controls or in other factors that could significantly affect internal controls subsequent to the date of their evaluation, including any corrective actions with regard to significant deficiencies and material weaknesses.
    (b) FOREIGN REINCORPORATIONS HAVE NO EFFECT- Nothing in this section 302 shall be interpreted or applied in any way to allow any issuer to lessen the legal force of the statement required under this section 302, by an issuer having reincorporated or having engaged in any other transaction that resulted in the transfer of the corporate domicile or offices of the issuer from inside the United States to outside of the United States.

Stop and review! You have completed the outline for this subunit. Study multiple-choice questions 1 through 5 beginning on page 425.

12.2 RISK AND INTERNAL CONTROL

1. **The Assessment and Management of Risk**

    a. Every organization faces risks, that is, unforeseen obstacles to the pursuit of its objectives. Risks take many forms and can originate from inside or outside the organization. Examples include the following:

    1) A hacker may break into a university's information systems, changing grades and awarding unearned degrees.
    2) The CEO may bribe a member of Congress to introduce legislation favorable to the firm's business.
    3) A foreign government may be overthrown in a *coup d'etat*, followed by the expropriation of the firm's assets in that country.
    4) An accounts payable clerk may establish fictitious vendors in the company's information systems and receive checks in payment for nonexistent goods or services.
    5) A spike in interest rates may make the firm's long-term capital projects unprofitable.
    6) The introduction of a new technology may make one of the firm's premier products obsolete.

    b. **Risk assessment** is the process whereby management identifies the organization's vulnerabilities.

    1) All systems of internal control involve tradeoffs between cost and benefit. For this reason, no system of internal control can be said to be "100% effective." Organizations accept the fact that risk can only be mitigated, not eliminated.
    2) **Risk management** is the ongoing process of designing and operating internal controls that mitigate the risks identified in the organization's risk assessment.

    c. Risk can be quantified as a combination of two factors: the severity of consequences and the likelihood of occurrence. The expected value of a loss due to a risk exposure can thus be stated numerically as the product of the two factors.

    1) Risk can also be assessed in qualitative terms.
    2) EXAMPLE: A company is assessing the risks of its systems being penetrated by hackers.

Event	Consequences	Likelihood
Minor penetration	Annoyance	90%
Unauthorized viewing of internal databases	Public embarrassment, Loss of customer confidence	8%
Unauthorized alteration of internal databases	PR crisis, Customer defection	2%

    a) Although the occurrence of an annoyance-level incident is viewed as almost inevitable, the company will not find it worthwhile to institute the level of control necessary to prevent it.
    b) By contrast, the occurrence of a disastrous-level incident is seen as remote, but the consequences are so severe that the company is willing to institute costly internal controls to ensure its prevention.

    d. The AICPA audit risk model can be adapted to the system of internal control as follows:

    1) Inherent risk (IR) is the susceptibility of one of the company's objectives to obstacles arising from the nature of the objective. For example, a uranium mine is inherently riskier than a shopping mall.

2) Control risk (CR) is the risk that the controls put in place will fail to prevent an obstacle from interfering with the achievement of the objective. For example, a policy requiring two approvals for expenditures over a certain dollar amount could be bypassed by collusion.

3) Detection risk (DR) is the risk that an obstacle to an objective will not be detected before a loss has occurred. For example, an embezzlement that continues for a year before detection is much costlier than one that is discovered after 1 month.

4) Total risk (TR) may thus be stated as follows:

$$TR = IR \times CR \times DR$$

2. **The System of Internal Control**

   a. An organization establishes a system of internal control to help it manage many of the risks it faces. The IMA's *Management Accounting Glossary* defines internal control as follows:

   The whole system of controls (financial and otherwise) established by management to carry on the business of the enterprise in an orderly and efficient manner, to ensure adherence to management policies, safeguard the assets, and ensure as far as possible the completeness and accuracy of the records.

   b. The proper design and operation of an organization's system of internal controls is the responsibility of management.

      1) Section 404 of the Sarbanes-Oxley Act of 2002 requires publicly traded companies to issue a report stating that

         a) Management takes responsibility for establishing and maintaining the firm's system of internal controls and

         b) The system has been functioning effectively over the reporting period.

3. **Roles and Responsibilities Regarding Internal Control**

   a. **Responsible Parties**

      1) Board of Directors and Its Committees

         a) The entity's commitment to integrity and ethical values is reflected in the board's selections for the chief executive officer (CEO) and senior vice president positions.

         b) To be effective, board members should be objective, have knowledge of the organization's industry, and be willing to ask the relevant questions about management's decisions.

         c) Important subcommittees of the board, in organizations of sufficient size and complexity, include the following:

            i) Audit committee
            ii) Compensation committee
            iii) Nomination or governance committee
            iv) Finance committee
            v) Risk committee

      2) Senior Management

         a) Senior management is responsible for establishing and maintaining the organization's system of internal control.

         b) The CEO also establishes the tone at the top. Organizations inevitably reflect the ethical values and control consciousness of the CEO.

3) Internal Auditors

   a) Although management is ultimately responsible for the design and operation of the system of internal controls, an organization's internal audit function has a consulting and advisory role.

   b) Internal audit also evaluates the adequacy and effectiveness of internal control in response to risks in the entity's oversight, operations, and information systems. For example, internal audit evaluates controls over the following:

      i) Achievement of the organization's strategic objectives
      ii) Reliability and integrity of financial and operational information
      iii) Effectiveness and efficiency of operations and programs
      iv) Safeguarding of assets
      v) Compliance with laws, regulations, standards, policies, procedures, and contracts

   c) To remain independent in the conduct of these reviews, the internal audit function cannot be responsible for selecting and executing controls. This is solely the responsibility of management.

4) Other Entity Personnel

   a) Everyone in the organization must be aware that (s)he has a role to play in internal control, and every employee is expected to perform his or her appropriate control activities.

   b) In addition, all employees should understand that they are expected to inform those higher in the organization of instances of poor control.

b. **External Parties**

   1) External Auditors

      a) Traditionally, independent accountants have been required by their professional standards to consider the auditee's system of internal control as part of their audit of the entity's financial statements.

      b) This is no longer simply a good practice self-imposed by the accounting profession. The PCAOB has made it a legal requirement for auditors of public companies to examine and report on internal control.

   2) Legislators and Regulators

      a) Congress passed the Foreign Corrupt Practices Act and the Sarbanes-Oxley Act, both of which set legal requirements with regard to internal control.

   3) Parties Interacting with the Entity

      a) The following are examples of control-related information received from outside sources:

         i) A major customer informs management that a sales representative attempted to arrange a kickback scheme in return for the customer's business.
         ii) A supplier reveals inventory and shipping problems by complaining about incomplete orders.

      b) Parties without a supplier or customer relationship with the entity also may provide insight into the functioning of controls.

         i) As a condition for granting a loan, a bank may require that certain ratios be kept above or below specified levels. As a result, management may need to pay closer attention to controls over cash and inventory levels than it did previously.

SU 12: Internal Controls -- Corporate Governance

4) Financial Analysts, Bond Rating Agencies, and the News Media

a) The actions of these parties can inform an entity about how it is perceived by the world at large.

5) Outsourced Service Providers

a) Some of an entity's business functions, e.g., IT, human resources, or internal audit, may be performed by external service providers.

i) Accordingly, management must manage the risks of outsourcing. Thus, it must implement a means of evaluating the effectiveness of control over outsourced activities.

4. **Flowcharting**

a. Flowcharting is the representation of a process using pictorial symbols and can be useful in obtaining an understanding of internal control and in systems development.

1) Flowcharting symbols have been standardized by both the American National Standards Institute (ANSI) and the International Organization for Standardization (ISO).

2) Below are some standard flowcharting symbols representing process endpoints and connectors:

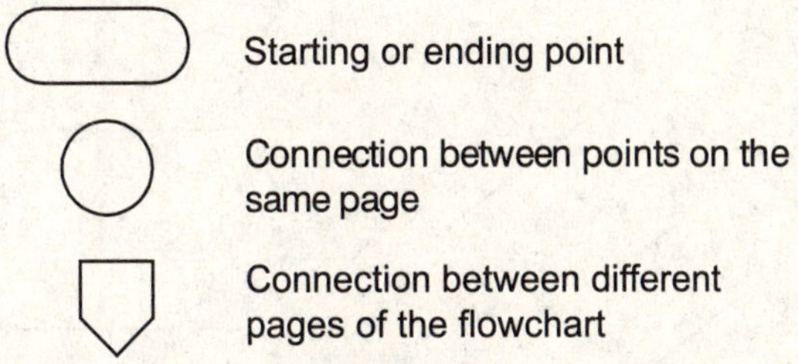

- Starting or ending point
- Connection between points on the same page
- Connection between different pages of the flowchart

Figure 12-2

3) Below are some standard flowcharting symbols representing processes:

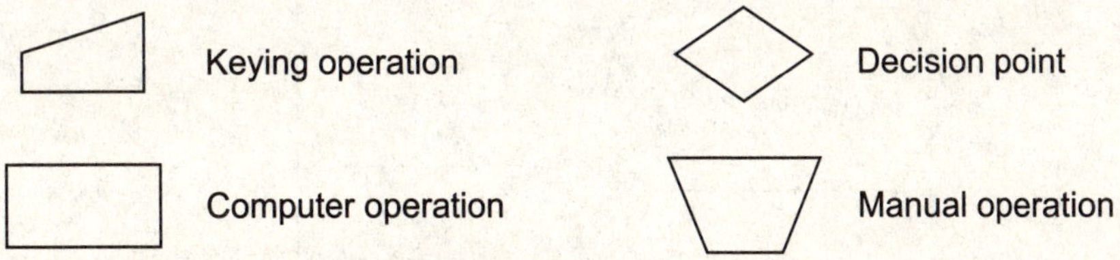

- Keying operation
- Decision point
- Computer operation
- Manual operation

Figure 12-3

4) Below are some standard flowcharting symbols representing input and output:

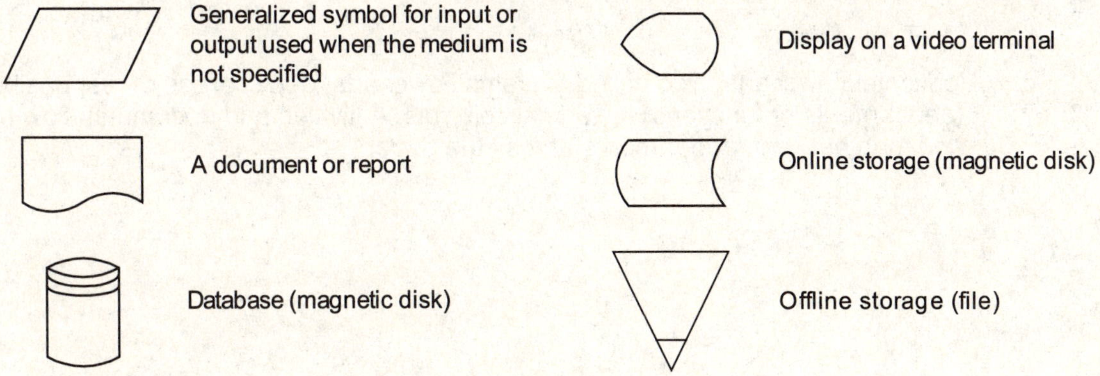

- Generalized symbol for input or output used when the medium is not specified
- Display on a video terminal
- A document or report
- Online storage (magnetic disk)
- Database (magnetic disk)
- Offline storage (file)

Figure 12-4

b. Vertical flowcharts present successive steps in a top-to-bottom format. Before the advent of object-oriented programming, flowcharts were a very common tool for computer programmers to design the flow of a new system. Below is an example of a simple vertical flowchart.

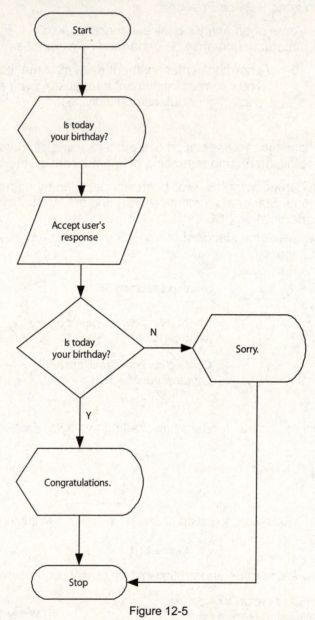

Figure 12-5

c. Horizontal flowcharts, also called systems flowcharts, depict areas of responsibility (departments or functions) in vertical columns. Activities and documents flow back and forth between departments across the page.

SU 12: Internal Controls -- Corporate Governance

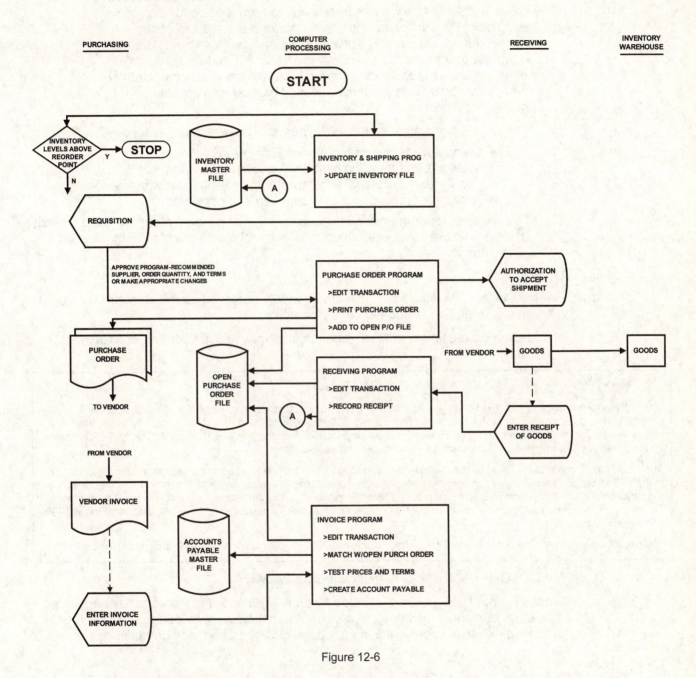

Figure 12-6

5. **PCAOB Approach**

   a. One of the requirements of the Sarbanes-Oxley Act is that the annual financial statement audit also address the firm's system of internal control.

      1) The PCAOB issued its Auditing Standard (AS) No. 5, "An Audit of Internal Control Over Financial Reporting That Is Integrated with An Audit of Financial Statements," to provide guidance when these two audits are integrated.

      2) AS 5 requires the external auditor to express an opinion on both the system of internal control and the fair presentation of financial statements.

b. AS 5 focuses on the existence of material weaknesses in internal control:

> *Because a company's internal control cannot be considered effective if one or more material weaknesses exist, to form a basis for expressing an opinion, the auditor must plan and perform the audit to obtain competent evidence that is sufficient to obtain reasonable assurance about whether material weaknesses exist as of the date specified in management's assessment. A material weakness in internal control over financial reporting may exist even when financial statements are not materially misstated.*

1) The AICPA's auditing standards define material weakness as follows:

    > *A material weakness is a deficiency, or combination of deficiencies, in internal control that results in a reasonable possibility that a material misstatement of the financial statements will not be prevented or timely detected and corrected.*

2) This financial reporting-oriented focus for internal controls stands in contrast with the broader view that internal controls are processes to aid the organization in achieving its goals.

6. **COSO Framework**

    a. *Internal Control – Integrated Framework* is widely accepted as the standard for the design and operation of internal control systems.

    1) However, regulatory or legal requirements may specify another control model or design.

Background

The Watergate investigations of 1973-74 revealed that U.S. companies were bribing government officials, politicians, and political parties in foreign countries. The result was the Foreign Corrupt Practices Act of 1977. The private sector also responded by forming the National Commission on Fraudulent Financial Reporting (NCFFR) in 1985. The NCFFR is known as the Treadway Commission because James C. Treadway was its first chair.

The Treadway Commission was originally sponsored and funded by five professional accounting organizations based in the United States. This group of five became known as the Committee of Sponsoring Organizations of the Treadway Commission (COSO). The Commission recommended that this group of five organizations cooperate in creating guidance for internal control. The result was *Internal Control – Integrated Framework*, published in 1992, which was modified in 1994 and again in 2013.

The executive summary is available at www.coso.org/documents/990025P_Executive_Summary_final_may20_e.pdf.

---

b. The COSO model defines internal control as follows:

> *Internal control is a process, effected by an entity's board of directors, management, and other personnel, designed to provide reasonable assurance regarding the achievement of objectives relating to operations, reporting, and compliance.*

c. Thus, internal control is

1) Intended to achieve three classes of objectives
2) An ongoing process
3) Effected by people at all organizational levels, e.g., the board, management, and all other employees
4) Able to provide reasonable, but not absolute, assurance
5) Adaptable to an entity's structure

7. **Objectives**
    a. The three classes of objectives direct organizations to the different (but overlapping) elements of control.
        1) **Operations**
            a) Operations objectives relate to achieving the entity's mission.
                i) Appropriate objectives include improving (a) financial performance, (b) productivity, (c) quality, (d) innovation, and (e) customer satisfaction.
            b) Operations objectives also include **safeguarding of assets**.
                i) Objectives related to protecting and preserving assets assist in risk assessment and development of mitigating controls.
                ii) Avoidance of waste, inefficiency, and bad business decisions relates to broader objectives than safeguarding of assets.
        2) **Reporting**
            a) To make sound decisions, stakeholders must have reliable, timely, and transparent financial information.
            b) Reports may be prepared for use by the organization and stakeholders.
            c) Objectives may relate to
                i) Financial and nonfinancial reporting
                ii) Internal or external reporting
        3) **Compliance**
            a) Entities are subject to laws, rules, and regulations that set minimum standards of conduct.
                i) Examples include taxation, environmental protection, and employee relations.
                ii) Compliance with internal policies and procedures is an operational matter.
        4) The following is a useful memory aid for the COSO classes of objectives:

            O = **O**perations
            R = **R**eporting
            C = **C**ompliance

    b. Linkage
        1) The entity's overall objectives must connect its particular capabilities and prospects with the objectives of its business units.
        2) As conditions change, the objectives (and related internal controls) of subunits must be altered to adapt to changes in the objectives of the entity as a whole.
    c. Achievement of Objectives
        1) An internal control system is more likely to provide reasonable assurance of achieving the reporting and compliance objectives than the operational objectives.
        2) Reporting and compliance objectives are responses to standards established by external parties, such as regulators.
            a) Thus, achieving these objectives depends on actions almost entirely within the entity's control.
        3) However, operational effectiveness may not be within the entity's control because it is affected by human judgment and many external factors.

8. **Components of Internal Control**

    a. Supporting the organization in its efforts to achieve objectives are the following five components of internal control:

        1) Control environment
        2) Risk assessment
        3) Control activities
        4) Information and communication
        5) Monitoring

    b. A useful memory aid for the COSO components of internal control is, "Controls stop **CRIME**."

        C = **C**ontrol activities
        R = **R**isk assessment
        I = **I**nformation and communication
        M = **M**onitoring
        E = Control **e**nvironment

9. **Control Environment**

    a. The control environment is a set of standards, processes, and structures that pervasively affects the system of internal control. Five principles relate to the control environment:

        1) The organization demonstrates a commitment to **integrity and ethical values** by

            a) Setting the tone at the top. Through words and actions, the board of directors and management communicate their attitude toward integrity and ethical values.
            b) Establishing standards of conduct. The board and management create expectations that should be understood at all organizational levels and by outside service providers and business partners.
            c) Evaluating the performance of individuals and teams based on the established standards of conduct.
            d) Correcting deviations in a timely and consistent manner.

        2) The board demonstrates independence from management and exercises **oversight** for internal control. The board

            a) Establishes oversight responsibility. The board identifies and accepts its oversight responsibilities.
            b) Applies relevant experience by defining, maintaining, and periodically evaluating the skills and expertise needed among its members to ask difficult questions of management and take appropriate actions.
            c) Operates independently. The board includes enough members who are independent and objective in evaluations and decision making.

                i) For example, in some jurisdictions, all members of the audit committee must be outside directors.

            d) Provides oversight. The board is responsible for oversight of management's design, implementation, and conduct of internal control.

3) Management establishes, with board oversight, **structures, reporting lines, and appropriate authorities and responsibilities**. Management

   a) Considers all structures of the entity. Variables considered in establishing organizational structures include the following:

      i) Nature of the business
      ii) Size and geographic scope of the entity
      iii) Risks, some of them outsourced, and connections with outside service providers and partners
      iv) Assignment of authority to different management levels
      v) Definition of reporting lines
      vi) Reporting requirements

   b) Establishes and evaluates reporting lines. The trend in corporate governance has been to allow employees closer to day-to-day operations to make decisions.

   c) Designs, assigns, and limits authorities and responsibilities.

4) The organization demonstrates a **commitment to attract, develop, and retain competent individuals** in alignment with objectives.

   a) Policies and practices reflect expectations of competence. Internal control is strengthened when management specifies what competencies are needed for particular jobs.

   b) The board and management evaluate competence and address shortcomings. Employees and outside service providers have the appropriate skills and knowledge to perform their jobs.

   c) The organization attracts, develops, and retains individuals. The organization is committed to hiring individuals who are competent and have integrity. Ongoing training and mentoring are necessary to adapt employees to the control requirements of a changing environment.

   d) Senior management and the board plan and prepare for succession.

5) The **organization holds individuals accountable** for their internal control responsibilities in pursuit of objectives. Management and the board

   a) Enforce accountability through structures, authorities, and responsibilities
   b) Establish performance measures, incentives, and rewards
   c) Evaluate performance measures, incentives, and rewards for ongoing relevance
   d) Consider excessive pressures
   e) Evaluate performance and reward or discipline individuals

10. **Risk Assessment**

    a. The risk assessment process encompasses an assessment of the risks themselves and the need to manage organizational change. This process is a basis for determining how the risks should be managed. Four principles relate to risk assessment:

       1) The organization **specifies objectives** with sufficient clarity to enable the identification and assessment of risks relating to five types of objectives.

          a) Operations
          b) External financial reporting
          c) External nonfinancial reporting
          d) Internal reporting
          e) Compliance

2) The organization **identifies** risks to the achievement of its objectives across the entity and **analyzes** risks to determine how the risks should be managed. Management must focus carefully on risks at all levels of the entity and take the necessary actions to manage them.

3) The organization considers the potential for fraud in **assessing fraud risks** to the achievement of objectives. The organization must

   a) Consider various types of fraud,
   b) Assess incentives and pressures,
   c) Assess opportunities, and
   d) Assess attitudes and rationalizations.

4) The organization **identifies and assesses changes** that could significantly affect the system of internal control.

   a) Significant changes could occur in an organization's external environment, business model, and leadership. Thus, internal controls must be adapted to the entity's changing circumstances.

11. **Control Activities**

    a. These policies and procedures help ensure that management directives are carried out. Whether automated or manual, they are applied at various levels of the entity and stages of processes. They may be preventive or detective, and segregation of duties is usually present. Three principles relate to control activities:

       1) The organization **selects and develops control activities** that contribute to the mitigation of risks to the achievement of objectives to acceptable levels.

       2) The organization selects and develops **general control activities** over technology to support the achievement of objectives.

       3) The organization **deploys control activities** through **policies** that establish what is expected and **procedures** that put policies into action.

12. **Information and Communication**

    a. Information systems enable the organization to obtain, generate, use, and communicate information to (1) maintain accountability and (2) measure and review performance. Three principles relate to information and communication:

       1) The organization obtains or generates and uses **relevant, quality information** to support the functioning of internal control.

       2) The organization **internally communicates** information, including objectives and responsibilities for internal control, necessary to support the function of internal control.

       3) The organization **communicates with external parties** regarding matters affecting the functioning of internal control.

13. **Monitoring Activities**

    a. Control systems and the way controls are applied change over time. Monitoring is a process that assesses the quality of internal control performance over time to ensure that controls continue to meet the needs of the organization. The following are two principles related to monitoring activities:

       1) The organization selects, develops, and performs **ongoing or separate evaluations (or both)** to determine whether the components of internal control are present and functioning.

       2) The organization **evaluates and communicates control deficiencies** in a timely manner.

SU 12: Internal Controls -- Corporate Governance

14. **Relationship of Objectives, Components, and Organizational Structure**

    a. The COSO model may be displayed as a cube with rows, slices, and columns. The rows are the five components, the slices are the three objectives, and the columns represent an entity's organizational structure.

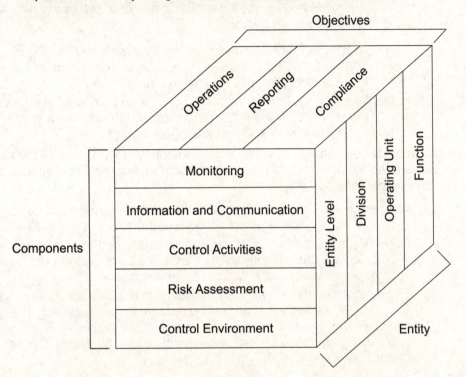

Figure 12-7

Stop and review! You have completed the outline for this subunit. Study multiple-choice questions 6 through 20 beginning on page 427.

12.3 INTERNAL AUDITING

1. **The Internal Audit Function**

    a. The growth and complexity of modern organizations has led to an accompanying growth in the field of internal auditing.

        1) An adequate internal audit activity is now considered to be so basic to the governance of a modern corporation that some stock exchanges require all companies registering to trade their stock to have one.

        2) Under the Foreign Corrupt Practices Act, organizations are expected to maintain reasonably detailed and accurate accounting records and a reasonably effective system of internal control. Maintaining an effective internal audit activity is an integral part of achieving this goal.

        3) Under the Sarbanes-Oxley Act of 2002, the CEO and CFO of a publicly traded company must certify to the effectiveness of the system of internal control.

b. The IIA defines internal auditing as follows:

Internal auditing is an independent, objective assurance and consulting activity designed to add value and improve an organization's operations. It helps an organization accomplish its objectives by bringing a systematic, disciplined approach to evaluate and improve the effectiveness of risk management, control, and governance processes.

1) The IIA's *International Standards for the Professional Practice of Internal Auditing* (the *Standards*) "provide guidance for the conduct of internal auditing at both the organizational and individual auditor levels."
2) In addition, The IIA has issued numerous Practice Advisories, which it refers to as "concise and timely guidance to assist internal auditors in applying Code of Ethics and *Standards* and promoting good practices."

c. The internal audit activity must be organizationally independent of the activities under audit. In addition, individual internal auditors must maintain an attitude of objectivity in carrying out their duties.

1) Independence, therefore, is an attribute of the internal audit department as a whole, while objectivity is an attribute of the auditors themselves.
2) Generally, the internal audit function is headed by the chief audit executive (CAE) who reports directly to the CEO. The CAE also should have direct, unhindered access to the board of directors.
3) The purpose, authority, and responsibility of the internal audit activity should be defined in a written charter. The charter should establish the internal audit activity's position within the organization; authorize access to records, personnel, and physical properties; and define the scope of internal audit activities.

2. **The Scope of Internal Auditing**

a. The three principal functions of internal auditing within a modern organization are to aid

1) Upper management in the maintenance of the firm's system of internal control
2) Upper management in improving the efficiency of the firm's operations
3) The external auditors in the conduct of the audit of financial statements

b. The scope of work performed by an internal audit department is much broader than that performed by the independent external auditor. In carrying out its basic functions, the internal audit activity can perform a wide variety of specific tasks, such as

1) Identifying and evaluating significant exposures to risk and contributing to the improvement of risk management and control systems
2) Evaluating the adequacy and effectiveness of controls encompassing the organization's governance, operations, and information systems and the promotion of their continuous improvement
3) Evaluating the reliability and integrity of financial and operational information
4) Evaluating the effectiveness and efficiency of operations
5) Evaluating the safeguarding of assets
6) Evaluating compliance with laws, regulations, and contracts
7) Ascertaining whether management has established adequate control criteria to evaluate the accomplishment of objectives and goals
8) Preventing and detecting fraud
9) Coordinating activities and sharing information with the external auditor

SU 12: Internal Controls -- Corporate Governance 421

3. **Incidents that Should Be Reported**

   a. The internal audit activity must report certain types of incidents that come to its attention to upper management and the board of directors. These include

   1) Fraud
   2) Illegal acts
   3) Material weaknesses and significant deficiencies in internal control
   4) Significant penetrations of information security systems

4. **Reporting on Internal Control**

   a. The board and internal audit function have interlocking goals. The core role of the CAE is to ensure that the board receives the support and assurance services it requests.

   b. One of the primary objectives of the board is oversight of financial reporting processes to ensure their reliability and fairness. The board and senior management typically request that the internal audit activity perform sufficient audit work and gather other available information during the year to form an opinion on the adequacy and effectiveness of the internal control processes.

   1) The CAE normally communicates that overall evaluation, on a timely basis, to the board. The board will evaluate the coverage and adequacy of the CAE's report.

5. **Financial Auditing**

   a. Internal auditors provide assurance regarding financial reporting to management and the board. For example, in many countries, laws require that management certify that the general-purpose financial statements are fairly stated in all material respects.

   1) Many countries also require management to provide an assessment of the organization's internal control over financial reporting. Internal auditors assist management in meeting these responsibilities.

   b. Reports of governance failures underscore the need for change to achieve greater accountability and transparency by all organizations. Senior management, boards, internal auditors, and external auditors are the basis of effective governance.

   1) Senior management has become more accountable (for example, as a result of legislation) for the information contained in financial reports. Thus, senior management and the board now tend to request more services from the internal audit activity.

      a) These requests include evaluating and improving the effectiveness of internal controls over financial reporting and the reliability and integrity of financial reports.

6. **Compliance Auditing**

   a. Internal auditors should assess whether the organization is in compliance with any applicable laws, regulations, or rules.

   1) They also should conduct follow-up and report on management's response to regulatory body reviews.
   2) An example would be an audit to determine whether a company is in compliance with pollution and environmental laws.

7. **Operational Auditing**

   a. *Sawyer's Internal Auditing: The Practice of Modern Internal Auditing* (Sawyer, Dittenhofer, and Graham, 5th ed., The IIA, 2003, p. 30) defines operational auditing as

   > *The comprehensive review of the varied functions within an enterprise to appraise the efficiency and economy of operations and the effectiveness with which those functions achieve their objectives.*

Current pronouncements of The IIA no longer use the term "operational auditing." However, the term is included in the IMA's Learning Outcome Statements for Part 1 of the CMA exam. Basically, an operational audit is an audit of the efficiency and effectiveness of operations.

    b. An operational audit is a thorough examination of a department, division, function, etc. Its purpose is to appraise managerial organization, performance, and techniques.

        1) An operational audit attempts to determine the extent to which organizational objectives have been achieved. It is a control technique that provides management with a method for evaluating the effectiveness of operating procedures and internal controls.

            a) The focus is on efficiency, effectiveness, and economy (these terms are sometimes called the "three Es of operational auditing").

        2) The report resulting from an operational audit consists primarily of specifying where problems exist or emphasizing the absence of problems.

        3) The internal auditor compares a department's operations with company policies and procedures, industry averages, and departmental trends.

            a) The basic tools of the internal auditor for operational auditing include

                i) Financial analysis
                ii) Observation of departmental activities
                iii) Questionnaire interviews of departmental employees

        4) The operational audit evolved as an extension of the typical financial audit in that it goes beyond what is ordinarily considered to be the accounting function, e.g.,

            a) Reviewing purchasing policies
            b) Appraising compliance with company policies and procedures
            c) Appraising safety standards and maintenance of equipment
            d) Reviewing production controls and scrap reporting
            e) Reviewing adequacy of facilities

    c. An operational audit is essentially a benchmarking activity. The auditor determines the benchmarking standards using industry averages, information from competitors, and common business sense, and assesses whether the department is operating efficiently, effectively, and economically.

    d. Internal auditors should not assume operating responsibilities. If senior management directs internal auditors to perform nonaudit work, they are not functioning as internal auditors.

8. **Internal Control According to The IIA**

    a. The purpose of control is to support risk management and achievement of objectives. Control ensures

        1) The reliability and integrity of information;
        2) Efficient and effective performance;
        3) Safeguarding of assets; and
        4) Compliance with laws, regulations, contracts.

    b. Senior management oversees the establishment, administration, and assessment of risk management and control processes.

    c. Line managers assess control in their areas.

    d. The CAE's goal is to obtain sufficient audit evidence to form an overall opinion on the **adequacy and effectiveness** of control.

        1) This opinion is communicated to senior management and the board.

e. To achieve this goal, the CAE develops the proposed internal audit plan to provide sufficient evidence to evaluate control. The plan should be flexible enough to permit adjustments during the year.

1) It covers all major operations and functions. It also gives special consideration to operations most affected by recent or expected changes.
2) Furthermore, the plan considers relevant work performed by others, including (a) management's assessments of risk management, control, and quality processes and (b) the work completed by external auditors.

f. The CAE evaluates the plan's coverage. If the scope of the plan is insufficient to permit expression of an opinion about risk management and control, the CAE informs senior management and the board about gaps in audit coverage.

g. The overall evaluation of control considers whether

1) Significant weaknesses or discrepancies exist,
2) Corrections or improvements were made, and
3) A pervasive condition leading to unacceptable risk exists.

h. Whether unacceptable risk exists depends on the nature and extent of risk exposure and level of consequences.

9. **Report on Control Processes**

a. Control criteria. The first element of the control process is to establish standards for the program or operation to be controlled. Acceptable industry standards, standards developed by professional associations, standards in law and government regulations, and other sound business practices are usually deemed to be appropriate criteria. The IIA has addressed this subject as follows:

1) Internal auditors should ascertain the extent to which operating and program goals and objectives have been established and conform to those of the organization.
2) Internal auditors should review operations and programs to ascertain the extent to which results are consistent with established goals and objectives to determine whether operations and programs are being implemented or performed as intended.
3) Adequate criteria are needed to evaluate controls. Internal auditors must ascertain the extent to which management has established adequate criteria to determine whether objectives and goals have been accomplished. If adequate, internal auditors must use such criteria in their evaluation. If inadequate, internal auditors must work with management to develop appropriate evaluation criteria.
4) During consulting engagements, internal auditors must address controls consistent with the engagement's objectives and be alert to significant control issues.

    a) Internal auditors must incorporate knowledge of controls gained from consulting engagements into evaluation of the organization's control processes.

b. Once the relevant internal controls have been identified, the internal auditor applies four types of procedures:

1) Make inquiries of appropriate personnel

    a) While simple answers to verbal questions are not considered a strong form of evidence, they can nonetheless be very informative, especially when employees describe their ordinary duties or when they admit that a given control procedure is often not followed.

2) Examine documentation

a) Even in a computerized environment, some control procedures leave a paper trail. For example, purchases of capital equipment may require the signature of a regional vice president.

b) In some computerized environments, signatures and other approvals can be tracked electronically. The internal auditor may require specialized knowledge to determine whether these controls are functioning properly.

3) Observe control-related activities

a) Because some control procedures may leave no audit trail of any kind, the internal auditor may need to watch them being performed to gain assurance about them functioning properly.

4) Reperform client procedures

a) Some types of control procedures can be effectively tested simply by the internal auditor reperforming the activity. For example, the extended price of a line item on an invoice should equal the quantity shipped times the unit price. The auditor can reperform this multiplication on a sample of invoices to check for a computer error or unauthorized overrides.

c. Any unexpected results from what was expected should be investigated and adequately explained.

d. The CAE's report on control processes is presented, usually once a year, to senior management and the board. It describes

1) The role of control processes,
2) The work performed, and
3) Any reliance on other assurance providers.

10. **Due Care in Internal Auditing**

a. Attribute Standard 1220, *Due Professional Care*, states "Internal auditors must apply the care and skill expected of a reasonably prudent and competent internal auditor. Due professional care does not imply infallibility."

1) Due professional care can be demonstrated if the auditor acted as any other auditor would have, given the same facts and circumstances.

b. The IIA provides specifics about the application of due care in Practice Advisory 1220-1, *Due Professional Care*:

1) "Exercising due professional care involves internal auditors being alert to the possibility of fraud, intentional wrongdoing, errors and omissions, inefficiency, waste, ineffectiveness, and conflicts of interest, as well as being alert to those conditions and activities where irregularities are most likely to occur" (para. 1).

2) "Due professional care implies reasonable care and competence, not infallibility or extraordinary performance. As such, due professional care requires the internal auditor to conduct examinations and verifications to a reasonable extent. Accordingly, internal auditors cannot give absolute assurance that noncompliance or irregularities do not exist. Nevertheless, the possibility of material irregularities or noncompliance needs to be considered whenever an internal auditor undertakes an internal audit assignment" (para. 2).

SU 12: Internal Controls -- Corporate Governance

c. The IIA provides the following Implementation Standards for the application of due care during assurance engagements.

1) Implementation Standard 1220.A1

Internal auditors must exercise due professional care by considering the

- Extent of work needed to achieve the engagement's objectives;
- Relative complexity, materiality, or significance of matters to which assurance procedures are applied;
- Adequacy and effectiveness of governance, risk management, and control processes;
- Probability of significant errors, fraud, or noncompliance; and
- Cost of assurance in relation to potential benefits.

2) Implementation Standard 1220.A2

In exercising due professional care, internal auditors must consider the use of technology-based audit and other data analysis techniques.

3) Implementation Standard 1220.A3

Internal auditors must be alert to the significant risks that might affect objectives, operations, or resources. However, assurance procedures alone, even when performed with due professional care, do not guarantee that all significant risks will be identified.

Stop and review! You have completed the outline for this subunit. Study multiple-choice questions 21 through 30 beginning on page 431.

QUESTIONS

12.1 Corporate Governance and Legal Aspects of Internal Control

1. The requirement of the Foreign Corrupt Practices Act of 1977 to devise and maintain adequate internal control is assigned in the act to the

A. Chief financial officer.
B. Board of directors.
C. Director of internal auditing.
D. Company as a whole with no designation of specific persons or positions.

Answer (D) is correct.
REQUIRED: The person in a company responsible for compliance with the FCPA.
DISCUSSION: The accounting requirements apply to all public companies that must register under the Securities Exchange Act of 1934. The responsibility is thus placed on companies, not individuals.
Answer (A) is incorrect. Compliance with the FCPA is not the specific responsibility of the chief financial officer. Answer (B) is incorrect. Compliance with the FCPA is not the specific responsibility of the board of directors. Answer (C) is incorrect. Compliance with the FCPA is not the specific responsibility of the director of internal auditing.

2. The Sarbanes-Oxley Act has strengthened auditor independence by requiring that management

A. Engage auditors to report in accordance with the Foreign Corrupt Practices Act.
B. Report the nature of disagreements with former auditors.
C. Select auditors through audit committees.
D. Hire a different CPA firm from the one that performs the audit to perform the company's tax work.

Answer (C) is correct.
REQUIRED: The Sarbanes-Oxley requirement that strengthened auditor independence.
DISCUSSION: The Sarbanes-Oxley Act requires that the audit committee of a public company hire and pay the external auditors. Such affiliation inhibits management from changing auditors to gain acceptance of a questionable accounting method. Also, a potential successor auditor must inquire of the predecessor auditor before accepting an engagement.
Answer (A) is incorrect. The SEC does not require an audit report in accordance with the FCPA. Answer (B) is incorrect. Reporting the nature of disagreements with auditors has been a long-time SEC requirement. Answer (D) is incorrect. The Sarbanes-Oxley Act does not restrict who may perform a company's tax work. Other types of engagements, such as the outsourcing of the internal audit function and certain consulting services, are limited.

3. A major impact of the Foreign Corrupt Practices Act of 1977 is that registrants subject to the Securities Exchange Act of 1934 are now required to

A. Keep records that reflect the transactions and dispositions of assets and to maintain a system of internal accounting controls.
B. Provide access to records by authorized agencies of the federal government.
C. Prepare financial statements in accord with international accounting standards.
D. Produce full, fair, and accurate periodic reports on foreign commerce and/or foreign political party affiliations.

Answer (A) is correct.
REQUIRED: The major impact of the Foreign Corrupt Practices Act of 1977.
DISCUSSION: The main purpose of the Foreign Corrupt Practices Act of 1977 is to prevent bribery by firms that do business in foreign countries. A major ramification is that it requires all companies that must register with the SEC under the Securities Exchange Act of 1934 to maintain adequate accounting records and a system of internal accounting control.
Answer (B) is incorrect. Authorized agents of the federal government already have access to records of SEC registrants. Answer (C) is incorrect. Although some international accounting standards have been promulgated, they are incomplete and have not gained widespread acceptance. Answer (D) is incorrect. There are no requirements for providing periodic reports on foreign commerce or foreign political party affiliations.

4. Section 201 of the Sarbanes-Oxley Act of 2002 prohibits audit firms from performing certain engagements for audit clients. Which of the following services is permitted under Section 201?

A. Preparation of tax returns.
B. Bookkeeping services.
C. Internal auditing outsourcing.
D. Actuarial services.

Answer (A) is correct.
REQUIRED: The service that is permitted under Section 201 of the Sarbanes-Oxley Act of 2002.
DISCUSSION: Tax services are not prohibited by Section 201.
Answer (B) is incorrect. Bookkeeping services are specifically prohibited by Section 201 of the Sarbanes-Oxley Act of 2002. Answer (C) is incorrect. Internal auditing outsourcing is specifically prohibited by Section 201 of the Sarbanes-Oxley Act of 2002. Answer (D) is incorrect. Actuarial services are specifically prohibited by Section 201 of the Sarbanes-Oxley Act of 2002.

5. Section 404 of the Sarbanes-Oxley Act of 2002 requires management of publicly traded corporations to do all of the following **except**

A. Establish and document internal control procedures and to include in their annual reports a report on the company's internal control over financial reporting.
B. Provide a report to include a statement of management's responsibility for internal control and of management's assessment of the effectiveness of internal control as of the end of the company's most recent fiscal year.
C. Provide an identification of the framework used to evaluate the effectiveness of internal control and a statement that the external auditor has issued an attestation report on management's assessment.
D. Provide a statement that the audit committee approves the choice of accounting policies and practices.

Answer (D) is correct.
REQUIRED: The false statement with regard to Section 404 of the Sarbanes-Oxley Act of 2002.
DISCUSSION: The Sarbanes-Oxley Act of 2002 imposes many requirements on management, boards of directors, and auditors. Section 404 deals with internal controls and reports thereon. It requires management to establish and document internal control procedures and to include in their annual reports a report on the company's internal control over financial reporting. The report is to include a statement of management's responsibility for internal control, management's assessment of the effectiveness of internal control as of the end of the most recent fiscal year, identification of the framework used to evaluate the effectiveness of internal control (such as the COSO report), and a statement that the external auditor has issued an attestation report on management's assessment. Because of this requirement, there are two audit opinions: one on internal control and one on the financial statements. Section 301 does address activities of the audit committee, but it contains no requirement that the audit committee approve the choice of accounting policies and practices. Section 204 states that the auditor must report to the audit committee all critical accounting policies and practices, alternative treatments of information discussed with management, implications of the alternatives, and the treatment preferred by the auditor.
Answer (A) is incorrect. These are true statements about Section 404 requirements. Answer (B) is incorrect. These are true statements about Section 404 requirements. Answer (C) is incorrect. These are true statements about Section 404 requirements.

12.2 Risk and Internal Control

6. Risk assessment is a process

A. Designed to identify potential events that may affect the entity.
B. That establishes policies and procedures to accomplish internal control objectives.
C. Of identifying and capturing information in a timely fashion.
D. That assesses the quality of internal control throughout the year.

Answer (A) is correct.
REQUIRED: The essence of the risk assessment process.
DISCUSSION: Every organization faces risks, that is, unforeseen obstacles to the pursuit of its objectives. Risks take many forms and can originate from within or from outside the organization. Risk assessment is the process whereby management identifies the organization's vulnerabilities.
Answer (B) is incorrect. Internal control objectives cannot be formulated until the organization knows what its vulnerabilities are. Answer (C) is incorrect. Identifying and capturing information in a timely fashion is a function of an information system, not of risk assessment. Answer (D) is incorrect. Assessing the quality of internal controls is a portion of the internal control department's ongoing duties; it is not a definition of risk assessment.

7. The primary responsibility for establishing and maintaining internal control rests with

A. The external auditor.
B. Management.
C. The controller.
D. The treasurer.

Answer (B) is correct.
REQUIRED: The person primarily responsible for establishing and maintaining internal control.
DISCUSSION: Establishing and maintaining internal control is the responsibility of management. Internal control is intended to provide reasonable assurance that the entity's objectives are achieved. Achievement of these objectives is the basic function of management.
Answer (A) is incorrect. Auditors must consider internal control, but they do not establish and maintain it. Answer (C) is incorrect. The controller is responsible only to the extent that (s)he is a part of the management team. Answer (D) is incorrect. The treasurer is responsible only to the extent that (s)he is a part of the management team.

8. There are three components of audit risk: inherent risk, control risk, and detection risk. Inherent risk is

A. The susceptibility of an assertion to a material misstatement, assuming that there are no related internal control structure policies or procedures.
B. The risk that the auditor may unknowingly fail to appropriately modify his or her opinion on financial statements that are materially misstated.
C. The risk that a material misstatement that could occur in an assertion will not be prevented or detected on a timely basis by the entity's internal control structure policies or procedures.
D. The risk that the auditor will not detect a material misstatement that exists in an assertion.

Answer (A) is correct.
REQUIRED: The definition of inherent risk.
DISCUSSION: According to AU 312, "Inherent risk is the susceptibility of an assertion to a material misstatement, assuming that there are no related internal control structure policies or procedures. The risk of such misstatement is greater for some assertions and related balances or classes than for others." Unlike detection risk, inherent risk and control risk "are independent of the audit." Furthermore, inherent risk and control risk are inversely related to detection risk. Thus, the lower the inherent risk, the higher the acceptable detection risk.
Answer (B) is incorrect. The risk that the auditor may unknowingly fail to appropriately modify his or her opinion on financial statements that are materially misstated is audit risk. Answer (C) is incorrect. The risk that a material misstatement that could occur in an assertion will not be prevented or detected on a timely basis by the entity's internal control structure policies or procedures is control risk. Answer (D) is incorrect. The risk that the auditor will not detect a material misstatement that exists in an assertion is detection risk.

9. Which of the following features of a large manufacturer's organizational structure is a control weakness?

A. The information systems department is headed by a vice president who reports directly to the president.
B. The chief financial officer is a vice president who reports to the chief executive officer.
C. The audit committee of the board consists of the chief executive officer, the chief financial officer, and a major shareholder.
D. The controller and treasurer report to the chief financial officer.

Answer (C) is correct.
REQUIRED: The control weakness in a large manufacturer's organizational structure.
DISCUSSION: The audit committee has a control function because of its oversight of internal as well as external auditing. It should be made up of directors who are independent of management. The authority and independence of the audit committee strengthen the position of the internal audit activity. The board should concur in the appointment or removal of the chief audit executive, who should have direct, regular communication with the board.
Answer (A) is incorrect. This reporting relationship is a strength. It prevents the information systems operation from being dominated by a user. Answer (B) is incorrect. It is a normal and appropriate reporting relationship. Answer (D) is incorrect. It is a normal and appropriate reporting relationship.

Questions 10 through 14 are based on the following information. This flowchart depicts the processing of daily cash receipts for Rockmart Manufacturing. Please note that some procedures are not shown in this flowchart.

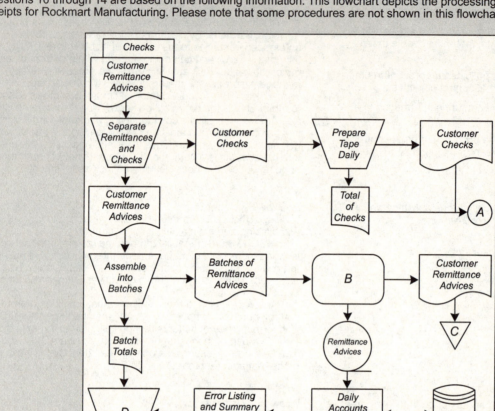

10. The customer checks accompanied by the control tape (refer to symbol A) are

A. Forwarded daily to the billing department for deposit.
B. Taken by the mail clerk to the bank for deposit daily.
C. Forwarded to the treasurer for deposit daily.
D. Accumulated for a week and then forwarded to the treasurer for deposit weekly.

Answer (C) is correct.
REQUIRED: The proper procedure for handling customer checks and the related control tape.
DISCUSSION: Symbol A is a connector between a point on this flowchart and another part of the flowchart not shown. The checks and the adding machine control tape should flow through symbol A to the treasurer's office. The treasurer is the custodian of funds and is responsible for deposit of daily receipts.
Answer (A) is incorrect. Recordkeepers perform functions that should be separate from custody of assets. Answer (B) is incorrect. The mail clerk should prepare a list of checks received before they are forwarded to the treasurer for deposit. Answer (D) is incorrect. Daily receipts should be deposited intact daily and then reconciled with the bank deposit records. Prompt deposit also safeguards assets and avoids loss of interest income.

11. What is the appropriate description that should be placed in symbol B?

A. Keying and verifying.
B. Error correction.
C. Collation of remittance advices.
D. Batch processing.

Answer (A) is correct.
REQUIRED: The appropriate description for symbol B.
DISCUSSION: Because the figure below symbol B signifies magnetic tape, the operation represented by symbol B must be keying the information onto the tape. Verifying the keyed data would also occur at this step.
Answer (B) is incorrect. Error correction occurs subsequently except for keying errors. Answer (C) is incorrect. Collation has already occurred. Answer (D) is incorrect. Batch processing describes the entire system.

12. The next action regarding the customer remittance advices (refer to symbol C) is to

A. Discard them immediately.
B. File them daily by batch number.
C. Forward them to the internal audit department for internal review.
D. Forward them to the treasurer to compare with the monthly bank statement.

Answer (B) is correct.
REQUIRED: The action taken regarding the customer remittance advices at symbol C.
DISCUSSION: All activity with respect to the paper documents most likely ceases at symbol C. Accordingly, the batched documents must be filed.
Answer (A) is incorrect. The documents should be kept for reference and audit. Answer (C) is incorrect. Internal auditors cannot feasibly review all documents regarding transactions even in an audit. Answer (D) is incorrect. Comparison by the treasurer would be inappropriate. (S)he has custody of cash.

13. What is the appropriate description that should be placed in symbol D?

A. Attach batch total to report and file.
B. Reconcile cash balances.
C. Compare batch total and correct as necessary.
D. Proof report.

Answer (C) is correct.
REQUIRED: The appropriate description for symbol D.
DISCUSSION: This flowcharting symbol indicates a manual operation or offline process. Because the input to this operation consists of an adding machine tape containing batch totals and a document containing summary information about the accounts receivable update and an error listing, the operation apparently involves comparing these items.
Answer (A) is incorrect. No filing symbol is given. Answer (B) is incorrect. The flowchart concerns daily receipts, not the reconciliation of cash balances. Answer (D) is incorrect. Symbol D indicates a comparison, not output in the form of a report.

14. What is the appropriate description that should be placed in symbol E?

A. Accounts receivable master file.
B. Bad debts master file.
C. Remittance advice master file.
D. Cash projection file.

Answer (A) is correct.
REQUIRED: The appropriate description of symbol E.
DISCUSSION: The flowcharting figure at symbol E indicates magnetic disk storage. Because it is an input and output for the daily computer processing of accounts receivable, it must be the accounts receivable master file.
Answer (B) is incorrect. Bad debts are not a part of processing daily receipts. Answer (C) is incorrect. The remittance advice master file was not used for the daily accounts receivable run. Answer (D) is incorrect. The cash projection file was not used for the daily accounts receivable run.

15. The graphic portrayal of the flow of data and the information processing of a system, including computer hardware, is **best** displayed in a

A. Data-flow diagram.
B. System flowchart.
C. Gantt chart.
D. Program flowchart.

Answer (B) is correct.
REQUIRED: The best method of displaying the flow of data and the information processing of a system.
DISCUSSION: A system flowchart is a graphic analysis of a data processing application, usually prepared by a systems analyst. The system flowchart is general and stresses flows of data, not computer program logic. A program flowchart is a graphic representation of the detailed steps and logic of an individual computer program.
Answer (A) is incorrect. A data-flow diagram would show only the flow of data, not the total system. Answer (C) is incorrect. A Gantt chart is a bar chart used to monitor the progress of large projects. Answer (D) is incorrect. A program flowchart shows only the details of a single program, not the entire computer system.

16. A director of a corporation is **best** characterized as a(n)

A. Agent.
B. Trustee.
C. Fiduciary.
D. Principal.

Answer (C) is correct.
REQUIRED: The best characterization of a corporate director.
DISCUSSION: Officers and employees as well as directors are fiduciaries with regard to the corporation. They owe a duty of loyalty, good faith, and fair dealing when transacting business with or on behalf of the company. This duty requires full disclosure of any personal interest in transactions with the corporation, avoidance of conflicts of interest and the making of secret profits, and placing the corporate interest ahead of personal gain.
Answer (A) is incorrect. A director is not an agent. (S)he cannot act alone to bind the corporation. As a group, directors control the corporation in a manner that agents could not. Answer (B) is incorrect. A trustee holds legal title to property used for the benefit of others. Answer (D) is incorrect. The corporation itself is the principal.

17. When management of the sales department has the opportunity to override the system of internal controls of the accounting department, a weakness exists in

A. Risk management.
B. Information and communication.
C. Monitoring.
D. The control environment.

Answer (D) is correct.
REQUIRED: The conceptual location of a weakness when one department can override another's internal controls.
DISCUSSION: An organization's control environment encompasses the attitudes and actions of the board of directors and upper management regarding the significance of control, i.e., the "tone at the top." One of the components of the control environment is the assignment of authority and responsibility. For example, management defines key areas of authority and responsibility by placing the information technology, financial accounting, and treasury functions under separate officers. When the management of one department can override the internal controls of another, authority and responsibility have not been properly assigned.
Answer (A) is incorrect. Risk management is the ongoing process of designing and operating internal controls that mitigate the risks identified in the organization's risk assessment. Answer (B) is incorrect. Information and communication are ongoing processes in every organization; they are not the basis for internal control. Answer (C) is incorrect. Monitoring cannot prevent damage done due to a system design flaw, such as one department being able to override another's internal controls.

18. One of the financial statement auditor's major concerns is to ascertain whether internal control is designed to provide reasonable assurance that

A. Profit margins are maximized, and operational efficiency is optimized.
B. The chief accounting officer reviews all accounting transactions.
C. Corporate morale problems are addressed immediately and effectively.
D. Financial reporting is reliable.

Answer (D) is correct.
REQUIRED: The objective of internal control.
DISCUSSION: Internal control is designed to provide reasonable assurance of the achievement of objectives in the categories of (1) reliability of financial reporting, (2) effectiveness and efficiency of operations, and (3) compliance with laws and regulations. Controls relevant to a financial statement audit ordinarily pertain to the objective of preparing external financial statements that are fairly presented in conformity with GAAP or another comprehensive basis of accounting.
Answer (A) is incorrect. Many factors beyond the purview of the auditor affect profits, and the controls related to operational efficiency are usually not directly relevant to an audit. Answer (B) is incorrect. The chief accounting officer need not review all accounting transactions. Answer (C) is incorrect. Controls relevant to a financial statement audit do not concern the treatment of corporate morale problems.

19. Basic to a proper control environment are the quality and integrity of personnel who must perform the prescribed procedures. Which is **not** a factor in providing for competent personnel?

A. Segregation of duties.
B. Hiring practices.
C. Training programs.
D. Performance evaluations.

Answer (A) is correct.
REQUIRED: The factor not related to competence of personnel.
DISCUSSION: Human resource policies and practices are a factor in the control environment component of internal control. They affect the entity's ability to employ sufficient competent personnel to accomplish its objectives. Policies and practices include those for hiring, orientation, training, evaluating, promoting, compensating, and remedial actions. Although control activities based on the segregation of duties are important to internal control, they do not in themselves promote employee competence.
Answer (B) is incorrect. Effective hiring practices result in selection of competent employees. Answer (C) is incorrect. Effective training programs increase the competence of employees. Answer (D) is incorrect. Performance evaluations improve competence by identifying substandard work and by serving as a basis for rewarding exceptional efforts.

20. Some account balances, such as those for pensions or leases, are the results of complex calculations. The susceptibility to material misstatements in these types of accounts is defined as

A. Audit risk.
B. Detection risk.
C. Sampling risk.
D. Inherent risk.

Answer (D) is correct.
REQUIRED: The susceptibility to material misstatements in account balances resulting from complex calculations.
DISCUSSION: Inherent risk is the susceptibility of an assertion to a material misstatement in the absence of related controls. This risk is greater for some assertions and related balances or classes than others. For example, complex calculations are more likely to be misstated than simple ones, and cash is more likely to be stolen than an inventory of coal. Inherent risk exists independently of the audit.
Answer (A) is incorrect. Audit risk is the risk that the auditor may unknowingly fail to appropriately modify an opinion on financial statements that are materially misstated. Answer (B) is incorrect. Detection risk is the risk that the auditor will not detect a material misstatement that exists in an assertion. Answer (C) is incorrect. Sampling risk is the risk that a particular sample may contain proportionately more or fewer monetary misstatements or deviations from controls than exist in the population as a whole.

12.3 Internal Auditing

21. From a modern internal auditing perspective, which one of the following statements represents the **most** important benefit of an internal auditing activity to management?

A. Assurance that published financial statements are correct.
B. Assurance that fraudulent activities will be detected.
C. Assurance that the organization is complying with legal requirements.
D. Assurance that there is reasonable control over day-to-day operations.

Answer (D) is correct.
REQUIRED: The most important benefit of an internal audit activity.
DISCUSSION: According to the definition of internal auditing, "Internal auditing is an independent, objective assurance and consulting activity designed to add value and improve an organization's operations. It helps an organization accomplish its objectives by bringing a systematic, disciplined approach to evaluate and improve the effectiveness of risk management, control, and governance processes." Thus, it helps the organization to maintain effective controls by evaluating their effectiveness and efficiency and by promoting continuous improvement (Standard 2120).
Answer (A) is incorrect. Published financial statements are only required to be fairly presented. Internal audit activities cannot ensure correctness. Answer (B) is incorrect. Internal auditing's responsibility with respect to fraud detection is to examine and evaluate the adequacy and effectiveness of internal control. Answer (C) is incorrect. Internal auditing evaluates and contributes to the improvement of risk management, control, and governance processes, but it cannot ensure compliance with legal requirements.

22. Which of the following activities is outside the scope of internal auditing?

A. Assessing an operating department's effectiveness in achieving stated organizational goals.
B. Safeguarding of assets.
C. Evaluating controls over compliance with laws and regulations.
D. Ascertaining the extent to which objectives and goals have been established.

Answer (B) is correct.
REQUIRED: The activity outside the scope of internal auditing.
DISCUSSION: Safeguarding assets is an operational activity and is therefore beyond the scope of the internal audit activity, which evaluates and contributes to the improvement of risk management, control, and governance processes. However, internal auditors should evaluate risk exposures relating to governance, operations, and information systems regarding the safeguarding of assets. Based on the risk assessment, they should evaluate the adequacy and effectiveness of controls encompassing governance, operations, and information systems. This evaluation extends to safeguarding of assets (Standards 2110.A2 and 2120.A1).
Answer (A) is incorrect. Internal auditors should ascertain the extent to which results are consistent with established goals and objectives (Standard 2120.A3). Answer (C) is incorrect. Evaluating controls over compliance with laws, regulations, and contracts is within the scope of internal auditing (Standard 2120.A1). Answer (D) is incorrect. Ascertaining the extent to which operating and program objectives and goals have been established is within the scope of internal auditing (Standard 2120.A2).

23. Internal auditing is a dynamic profession. Which of the following **best** describes the scope of internal auditing as it has developed to date?

A. Internal auditing involves evaluating the effectiveness and efficiency with which resources are employed.
B. Internal auditing involves evaluating compliance with laws, regulations, and contracts.
C. Internal auditing has evolved to verifying the existence of assets and reviewing the means of safeguarding assets.
D. Internal auditing has evolved to evaluating all risk management, control, and governance systems.

Answer (D) is correct.
REQUIRED: The scope of internal auditing.
DISCUSSION: The internal audit activity evaluates and contributes to the improvement of risk management, control, and governance processes using a systematic and disciplined approach (Standard 2100). According to PA 2100-1, internal auditors evaluate the whole management process of planning, organizing, and directing to determine whether reasonable assurance exists that objectives and goals will be achieved. These evaluations, in the aggregate, provide information to appraise the overall management process. All business systems, processes, operations, functions, and activities within the organization are subject to the internal auditors' evaluations. The comprehensive scope of work of internal auditing should provide reasonable assurance that management's

- Risk management system is effective.
- System of internal control is effective and efficient.
- Governance process is effective by establishing and preserving values, setting goals, monitoring activities and performance, and defining the measures of accountability.

Answer (A) is incorrect. Evaluating effectiveness and efficiency is an incomplete description of the scope of work of internal auditing. Answer (B) is incorrect. Evaluating compliance is an incomplete description of the scope of work of internal auditing. Answer (C) is incorrect. Verifying the existence of assets and reviewing the means of safeguarding assets are not the only functions of internal auditors.

24. Directors, management, external auditors, and internal auditors all play important roles in creating proper control processes. Senior management is primarily responsible for

A. Overseeing the establishment, administration, and assessment of control processes.
B. Reviewing the reliability and integrity of financial and operational information.
C. Ensuring that external and internal auditors oversee the administration of the system of risk management and control processes.
D. Implementing and monitoring controls designed by the board of directors.

Answer (A) is correct.
REQUIRED: The best description of senior management's responsibility.
DISCUSSION: Senior management's role is to oversee the establishment, administration, and assessment of the system of risk management and control processes. Among the responsibilities of the organization's line managers is the assessment of the control processes in their respective areas. Internal auditors provide varying degrees of assurance about the effectiveness of the risk management and control processes in select activities and functions of the organization (PA 2130-1).
Answer (B) is incorrect. Internal auditors are responsible for evaluating the adequacy and effectiveness of controls, including those relating to the reliability and integrity of financial and operational information (Standard 2130.A1). Answer (C) is incorrect. Senior management's role is to oversee the establishment, administration, and assessment of the system of risk management and control processes (PA 2130-1). Answer (D) is incorrect. The board has oversight responsibilities but ordinarily does not become involved in the details of operations.

25. The authority of the internal audit activity is limited to that granted by

A. The board and the controller.
B. Senior management and the *Standards*.
C. Management and the board.
D. The audit committee and the chief financial officer.

Answer (C) is correct.
REQUIRED: The source of authority of the internal audit activity.
DISCUSSION: The purpose, authority, and responsibility of the internal audit activity should be formally defined in a charter, consistent with the *Standards*, and approved by the board (Standard 1000). Furthermore, PA 1000-1 states that the CAE should seek approval of the charter by senior management. The charter should establish the internal audit activity's position within the organization; authorize access to records, personnel, and physical properties relevant to the performance of engagements; and define the scope of internal audit activities.
Answer (A) is incorrect. The controller is not the only member of management. Answer (B) is incorrect. The *Standards* provide no actual authority to the internal audit activity. Answer (D) is incorrect. Management and the board, not a committee of the board and a particular manager, endow the internal audit activity with its authority.

26. Internal auditing is an assurance and consulting activity. An example of an assurance service is a(n)

A. Advisory engagement.
B. Facilitation engagement.
C. Training engagement.
D. Compliance engagement.

Answer (D) is correct.
REQUIRED: The example of an assurance service.
DISCUSSION: According to the Glossary published by The IIA as part of the *Standards*, an assurance service is "an objective examination of evidence for the purpose of providing an independent assessment on risk management, control, or governance processes for the organization. Examples may include financial, performance, compliance, system security, and due diligence engagements."
Answer (A) is incorrect. Consulting services include "advisory and related client service activities, the nature and scope of which are agreed with the client and which are intended to add value and improve an organization's governance, risk management, and control processes without the internal auditor assuming management responsibility. Examples include counsel, advice, facilitation, and training." Answer (B) is incorrect. Consulting services include "advisory and related client service activities, the nature and scope of which are agreed with the client and which are intended to add value and improve an organization's governance, risk management, and control processes without the internal auditor assuming management responsibility. Examples include counsel, advice, facilitation, and training." Answer (C) is incorrect. Consulting services include "advisory and related client service activities, the nature and scope of which are agreed with the client and which are intended to add value and improve an organization's governance, risk management, and control processes without the internal auditor assuming management responsibility. Examples include counsel, advice, facilitation, and training."

27. Of the following, the primary objective of compliance testing is to determine whether

A. Procedures are regularly updated.
B. Financial statement line items are properly stated.
C. Controls are functioning as planned.
D. Collusion is taking place.

Answer (C) is correct.
REQUIRED: The primary objective of compliance testing.
DISCUSSION: Internal auditors should assess compliance in specific areas as part of their role in organizational governance. Compliance testing can be used to determine whether laws and regulations are being adhered to, as well as whether internal controls are functioning as designed.
Answer (A) is incorrect. Compliance testing involves assessing the everyday functioning of internal controls. Answer (B) is incorrect. The proper statement of financial statement line items is the purview of a financial audit, not a compliance audit. Answer (D) is incorrect. No type of testing can be sure of detecting instances of collusion.

28. Which of the following is **most** likely to be regarded as a strength in internal control in a traditional external audit?

A. The performance of financial audits by the internal audit activity.
B. The performance of operational engagements by internal auditors.
C. The routine supervisory review of production planning.
D. The existence of a preventive maintenance program.

Answer (A) is correct.
REQUIRED: The activity most likely regarded as a strong internal control in a traditional external audit.
DISCUSSION: The external auditor's traditional role is to perform an audit to determine whether the externally reported financial statements are fairly presented. Thus, a financial audit by the internal audit activity is relevant to the traditional external audit because it is an engagement in which the reliability and integrity of financial information is evaluated. Such an engagement is consistent with internal auditing standards. According to Standard 2130.A1, the internal audit activity must evaluate the adequacy and effectiveness of controls in responding to risks within the organization's governance, operations, and information systems. This evaluation extends to the (1) reliability and integrity of financial and operational information; (2) effectiveness and efficiency of operations; (3) safeguarding of assets; and (4) compliance with laws, regulations, and contracts.
Answer (B) is incorrect. Operational engagements are concerned with operational efficiency and effectiveness, matters that are not the primary focus of an external audit of financial statements. Answer (C) is incorrect. Routine supervisory review of production planning is a concern of management but does not directly affect the fair presentation of the financial statements. Answer (D) is incorrect. The existence of a preventive maintenance program is not directly relevant to a financial statement audit.

29. Which one of the following forms of audit is **most** likely to involve a review of an entity's performance of specific activities in comparison to organizational-specific objectives?

A. Information system audit.
B. Financial audit.
C. Operational audit.
D. Compliance audit.

Answer (C) is correct.
REQUIRED: The type of audit most likely to involve a review of an entity's performance of specific activities.
DISCUSSION: An operational audit is a thorough examination of a department, division, function, etc. Its purpose is to appraise managerial organization, performance, and techniques. An operational audit attempts to determine the extent to which organizational objectives have been achieved.
Answer (A) is incorrect. An information system audit involves examining the specific controls over information systems. Answer (B) is incorrect. A financial audit involves assessing the fair presentation of financial statements in accordance with U.S. GAAP. Answer (D) is incorrect. A compliance audit involves assessing the everyday functioning of internal controls.

30. The top-down approach to the audit of internal control over financial reporting can **best** be described as beginning

A. At the financial statement level, focusing on entity-level controls, and working down to significant accounts and disclosures and their relevant assertions.
B. With interviewing top management and observing the actions of top management with respect to the entity's control environment.
C. With considerations of the controls over assets and their related transactions, progressing to controls over liabilities and to controls over equities.
D. By identifying significant accounts and disclosures for each assertion that has a reasonable possibility of containing a material misstatement.

Answer (A) is correct.
REQUIRED: The definition of the top-down approach to auditing.
DISCUSSION: The top-down approach to the audit of internal controls over financial reporting is best described as beginning at the financial statement level, focusing on entity-level controls (the "top"), and working down to significant accounts and disclosures and their relevant assertions (the "bottom"). The top-down approach is also known as the risk-based approach.
Answer (B) is incorrect. This does not describe a specific approach to auditing. Interviewing top management and observing their actions is done in most audits in order to gain an understanding of the entity's control environment. Answer (C) is incorrect. This describes the balance sheet approach to auditing. Under the balance sheet approach, substantive procedures are focused on balance sheet accounts, with only limited procedures being carried out on income statement/profit and loss accounts. Answer (D) is incorrect. This describes the substantive procedures approach to auditing. Under this approach, audit resources are targeted on testing large or significant accounts, transactions, and disclosures without any particular focus on specified areas of the financial statements.

Access the CMA Review System from your Gleim Personal Classroom to continue your studies with exam-emulating multiple-choice questions!

12.4 ESSAY QUESTIONS

Scenario for Essay Questions 1, 2, 3

Micro Dynamics, a developer of database software packages, is a publicly held company whose stock is traded over the counter. The company recently received an enforcement release proceeding through an SEC Administrative Law Judge that cited the company for inadequate internal controls. In response, Micro Dynamics has agreed to establish an internal audit function and strengthen its audit committee.

A manager of the Internal Audit Department was recently hired as a result of the SEC enforcement action to establish an internal audit function. In addition, the composition of the audit committee has been changed to include all outside directors. Micro Dynamics has held its initial planning meeting to discuss the roles of the various participants in the internal control and financial reporting process. Participants at the meeting included the company president, the chief financial officer, a member of the audit committee, a partner from Micro Dynamics' external audit firm, and the newly appointed manager of the Internal Audit Department. Comments by the various meeting participants are presented below.

President: "We want to ensure that Micro Dynamics complies with the SEC's enforcement release and that we don't find ourselves in this position again. The Internal Audit Department should help to strengthen our internal control system by correcting the problems. I would like your thoughts on the proper reporting relationship for the manager of the Internal Audit Department."

Chief financial officer: "I think the manager of the Internal Audit Department should report to me since much of the department's work relates to financial issues. The audit committee should have oversight responsibilities."

Audit committee member: "I believe we should think through our roles more carefully. The Treadway Commission has recommended that the audit committee play a more important role in the financial reporting process; the duties of today's audit committee have expanded beyond the rubber-stamp approval. We need to have greater assurance that controls are in place and being followed."

External audit partner: "We need a close working relationship among all of our roles. The Internal Audit Department can play a significant role monitoring the control systems on a continuing basis and should have strong ties to your external audit firm."

Internal Audit Department manager: "The Internal Audit Department should be more involved in operational auditing, but also should play a significant monitoring role in the financial reporting area."

Questions

1. Describe the role of each of the following in the establishment, maintenance, and evaluation of Micro Dynamics' system of internal control:
    a. Management
    b. Audit committee
    c. External auditor
    d. Internal Audit Department

2. Describe the responsibilities that Micro Dynamics' audit committee has in the financial reporting process.

3. Discuss the characteristics of an audit committee in terms of the following:
    a. Composition, size, and term of membership
    b. Relationship with management, the external auditor, and the internal auditor

Essay Questions 1, 2, 3 — Unofficial Answers

1.
   a. Management has the overall responsibility for protecting company assets and, therefore, for establishing, maintaining, and evaluating the internal control system.
   b. The audit committee's primary responsibility involves assisting the board of directors in carrying out their responsibilities as they relate to the organization's accounting policies, internal control, and financial reporting practices. The audit committee assists management and the board in fulfilling their fiduciary and accountability responsibilities, and helps maintain a direct line of communication between the board and the external and internal auditors.
   c. The external auditor reviews the organization's control structure, including the control environment, accounting systems, and control procedures, in order to assess the control risks for financial statement assertions. In addition, the external auditor would inform the company of any material weaknesses found during the review.
   d. The Internal Audit Department performs both operational and financial audits to determine compliance with established policies and procedures, and reports its findings and recommendations to management or the audit committee for evaluation and corrective action. The Internal Audit Department may also assist the external auditors with their review of the internal control system.

2. The responsibilities of the Micro Dynamics' audit committee in the financial reporting process include
   a. Obtaining assurance that the organization's control system is adequate and effective, identifying risk and exposure, and ensuring that the financial disclosures made by management reasonably reflect the financial position, results of operations, and changes in cash flow
   b. Reviewing the progress of the audit and the final audit findings
   c. Acting as a liaison between the auditors and the board of directors

3.
   a. The audit committee should consist of at least three independent, outside directors. The maximum size may vary, but normally three to five members would be sufficient to allow each member to play an active role. The term is set by the board of directors and may vary but should include an arrangement to allow continuity to be maintained while rotating the membership.
   b. The audit committee is selected by the board of directors and assists the board of directors in carrying out their responsibilities concerning the organization's accounting policies, internal control, and financial reporting practices. The audit committee's oversight responsibilities that relate to the activities of management, the external auditor, and the internal auditor provide assurance to management and the public regarding the reliability and integrity of financial information. The audit committee also has the responsibility of selecting the external auditors, helping to resolve problems arising during the audit, and discussing the audit results with management and the external auditor.

Access the **CMA Review System** from your Gleim Personal Classroom to continue your studies with exam-emulating essay questions!

STUDY UNIT THIRTEEN
INTERNAL CONTROLS --
CONTROLS AND SECURITY MEASURES

(16 pages of outline)

13.1	Control Procedures	437
13.2	Systems Controls and Information Security	443
13.3	Security Measures and Business Continuity Planning	449
13.4	Essay Questions	461

This study unit is the **second of two** on **internal controls**. The relative weight assigned to this major topic in Part 1 of the exam is **15%**. The two study units are

Study Unit 12: Internal Controls -- Corporate Governance
Study Unit 13: Internal Controls -- Controls and Security Measures

If you are interested in reviewing more introductory or background material, go to www.gleim.com/CMAIntroVideos for a list of suggested third-party overviews of this topic. The following Gleim outline material is more than sufficient to help you pass the CMA exam; any additional introductory or background material is for your own personal enrichment.

13.1 CONTROL PROCEDURES

1. **The Control Process**

    a. Control requires feedback on the results of organizational activities for the purposes of measurement and correction.

    b. The control process includes

    1) Establishing standards for the operation to be controlled,
    2) Measuring performance against the standards,
    3) Examining and analyzing deviations,
    4) Taking corrective action, and
    5) Reappraising the standards based on experience.

    c. An evaluation-reward system should be implemented to encourage compliance with the control system.

    d. The costs of internal control must not be greater than its benefits.

2. **Types of Controls**

    a. Primary Controls

    1) **Preventive controls** deter the occurrence of unwanted events.

        a) Storing petty cash in a locked safe and segregation of duties are examples of this type of control.
        b) IT examples include (1) designing a database so that users cannot enter a letter in the field that stores a Social Security number and (2) requiring the number of invoices in a batch to be entered before processing begins.

    2) **Detective controls** alert the proper people after an unwanted event. They are effective when detection occurs before material harm occurs.

        a) For example, a batch of invoices submitted for processing may be rejected by the computer system. A detective control provides for automatic reporting of all rejected batches to the accounts payable department.
        b) Hash totals are commonly used to detect data entry errors but may also be used to test for completeness.
        c) A burglar alarm is another example.

3) **Corrective controls** correct the negative effects of unwanted events.

   a) An example is a requirement that all cost variances over a certain amount be justified.

4) **Directive controls** cause or encourage the occurrence of a desirable event.

   a) Policy and procedure manuals are common examples.

b. Secondary Controls

1) **Compensatory (mitigative) controls** may reduce risk when the primary controls are ineffective. However, they do not, by themselves, reduce risk to an acceptable level.

   a) An example is supervisory review when segregation of duties is not feasible.

2) **Complementary controls** work with other controls to reduce risk to an acceptable level.

   a) For example, separating the functions of accounting for and custody of cash receipts is complemented by obtaining deposit slips validated by the bank.

c. Time-Based Classification

1) **Feedback controls** report information about completed activities. They permit improvement in future performance by learning from past mistakes. Thus, corrective action occurs after the fact. Inspection of completed goods is an example.

2) **Concurrent controls** adjust ongoing processes. These real-time controls monitor activities in the present to prevent them from deviating too far from standards. An example is close supervision of production-line workers.

3) **Feedforward controls** anticipate and prevent problems. These controls require a long-term perspective. Organizational policies and procedures are examples.

d. Financial vs. Operating Controls

1) **Financial controls** should be based on relevant established accounting principles.

   a) Objectives of financial controls may include proper authorization; appropriate recordkeeping; safeguarding of assets; and compliance with laws, regulations, and contracts. These are sometimes called "accounting controls."

2) **Operating controls** apply to production and support activities. They are sometimes called "administrative controls."

   a) Because they may lack established criteria or standards, they should be based on management principles and methods. They also should be designed with regard to the management functions of planning, organizing, directing, and controlling.

e. People-Based vs. System-Based Controls

1) **People-based controls** are dependent on the intervention of humans for their proper operation, for example, regular performance of bank reconciliations.

   a) Checklists, such as lists of required procedures for month-end closing, can be valuable to ensure that people-based controls are executed when needed.

2) **System-based controls** are executed whenever needed with no human intervention.

   a) An example is code in a computerized purchasing system that prevents any purchase order over a certain monetary threshold from being submitted to the vendor without managerial approval.

   b) Other examples include control totals, reasonableness checks, and sequence tests.

3. **Control Activities**

   a. Control activities are designed and placed in operation to ensure that management's directives are executed. Thus, they should include the requisite steps to respond to the risks that threaten the attainment of organizational objectives.

      1) For this purpose, controls should be suitably designed to prevent or detect unfavorable conditions arising from particular risk exposures. They also should be placed in operation and operate effectively. If controls are not always in force, they cannot operate effectively, no matter how effective their design.

      2) Control procedures are implemented to manage or limit risk in accordance with the entity's risk assessments whenever risk exposures exist that threaten loss of assets or misstatements of accounting or management information.

      3) Controls can be identified in the following areas:

         a) Segregation of duties, including four basic functional responsibilities
         b) Independent checks and verification
         c) Safeguarding controls
         d) Prenumbered forms
         e) Specific document flow

4. **Segregation of Duties**

> This subunit describes the types and provides examples of segregation of duties. As a CMA candidate, you must be able to identify and explain proper segregation of duties procedures. However, you should also be able to apply this concept to many different functions within the internal control process.

   a. The **segregation of accounting duties** can enhance systems security. Segregation of duties involves the separation of the functions of authorization, recordkeeping, and asset custody so as to minimize the opportunities for a person to be able to perpetrate and conceal errors or fraud in the normal course of his or her duties.

      1) Four types of functional responsibilities should be segregated:

         a) The authority to execute transactions
         b) Recordkeeping of the transaction
         c) Custody of the assets affected by the transactions
         d) Periodic reconciliation of the existing assets to recorded amounts

      2) EXAMPLE: In the purchases-payables cycle,

         a) The authority to execute transactions is vested in the purchasing department, not the treasurer.
         b) Recordkeeping is done by accounts payable, not purchasing.
         c) Custody of the assets involved is vested in the warehouse, not inventory control.
         d) Periodic reconciliation of the existing assets to recorded amounts is performed by inventory control, not the warehouse.

3) EXAMPLE: In the sales-receivables cycle,
    a) The authority to execute transactions is vested in the sales department, not the treasurer.
    b) Recordkeeping is done by accounts receivable, not sales.
    c) Custody of the assets involved is vested in the warehouse (in the case of the merchandise) and the treasurer (in the case of the cash).
    d) Periodic reconciliation of the existing assets to recorded amounts is performed by the general ledger accounting group, not the treasurer.
4) EXAMPLE: In the payroll cycle,
    a) The authority to execute transactions is vested in the human resources department, which authorizes the hiring and termination of employees and their rates of pay and deductions.
    b) Recordkeeping is done by the payroll department.
    c) Custody of the assets involved is vested in the treasurer.
    d) Periodic reconciliation of the existing assets to recorded amounts is performed by the general ledger accounting group.
5) The following memory aid is for the functions that should be kept separate for proper segregation of duties:

A	Authorization
R	Recordkeeping
C	Custody
R	Reconciliation

5. **Independent Checks and Verification**
   a. The reconciliation of recorded accountability with the assets must be performed by a part of the organization either (1) unconnected with the original transaction or (2) without custody of the assets involved.
      1) A comparison revealing that the assets do not agree with the recorded accountability provides evidence of unrecorded or improperly recorded transactions.
         a) The converse, however, does not necessarily follow. For example, agreement of a cash count with the recorded balance does not provide evidence that all cash received has been properly recorded.
      2) The frequency of such comparisons for the purpose of safeguarding assets depends on the nature and amount of the assets involved and the cost of making the comparison.
         a) For example, cash may be counted daily but raw materials inventory only annually.
   b. EXAMPLE: The general ledger group performs monthly reconciliations of bank statements to the company's records. This is an independent check on the work of the treasury function.

6. **Safeguarding Controls**

    a. Safeguarding controls limit access to an organization's assets to authorized personnel. Access includes both direct physical access and indirect access through the preparation or processing of documents that authorize the use or disposition of assets.

    1) EXAMPLES:

        a) A lockbox system for collecting cash receipts from customers
        b) Daily, intact deposit of cash receipts after preparation and verification by two treasury employees
        c) Approval of credit memos by the credit department, not sales
        d) Writeoffs of uncollectible accounts by the supervisor of the credit department manager
        e) Unescorted access to computer operations center prohibited to (1) all non-information systems personnel and (2) all non-operations information system personnel, such as developers
        f) Online access to production application libraries prohibited to developers; online access to production databases prohibited to all users except the organizational "owners" of the data elements
        g) Direct deposit of pay in lieu of distribution of physical paychecks; unclaimed paychecks held by the treasurer, not payroll
        h) Holding of securities in safe deposit box; two employees always present when box is accessed
        i) Physical measures taken to protect assets from natural disasters, e.g., floods, wind damage, earthquakes

7. **Prenumbered Forms**

    a. Sequentially prenumbered forms are the basis for a strong set of internal controls. Receiving reports in the warehouse and purchase orders in the sales department are common examples.

    1) When every hardcopy form is prenumbered, all can be accounted for; e.g., the date of their use and the person who filled them out can be ascertained. Any document in the sequence that is missing can be flagged for special scrutiny when it is processed.

        a) During the periodic reconciliation, the verifying party can detect unrecorded and unauthorized transactions.

    2) This functionality can be achieved even in a paperless environment. Applications can be coded to sequentially number initiated transactions, and proper review and approval can be verified online.

    3) In addition to prenumbered forms, procedures ensuring that personnel do not receive documents inappropriate to their duties enhance internal control.

        a) For example, documents authorizing the writeoff of uncollectible receivables should not be routed to cashiers. These cashiers could later pocket the money if a written-off account was subsequently paid.

8. **Specific Document Flow**
   a. As an organization conducts business, documents and other evidence of business transactions should be created.
      1) Sequentially prenumbered forms increase the usability of this evidence.
   b. **Tracing and Vouching**
      1) **Tracing** follows a transaction forward from the triggering event to a resulting event, ensuring that the transaction was accounted for properly.
         a) Tracing is used to gain assurance that a liability was properly accrued for all goods received.
      2) **Vouching** tracks a result backward to the originating event, ensuring that a recorded amount is properly supported.
         a) Vouching is used to gain assurance that a receivable claimed is supported by a sale to a customer.

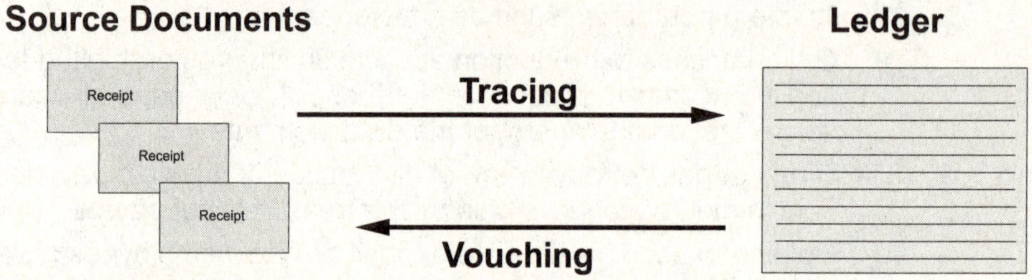

   Source Documents → Tracing → **Ledger**
   Ledger → Vouching → **Source Documents**

   Figure 13-1

   c. By searching for missing records in the document flow, auditors can detect errors or fraud.
   d. The chart below describes some of the possible procedures and the information they provide.

Procedures	Information Provided
Trace shipping documents with sales invoices and journal entries. Account for the numerical sequence of sales orders, shipping documents, invoices, etc.	Sales and Receivables were all accounted for.
Vouch sample of recorded sales to customer orders and shipping documents.	Sales occurred.
Trace cash receipts to specific accounts.	Accounts receivable are measured appropriately.
Vouch a sample of recorded cash receipts to accounts receivable and customer orders. Vouch a sample of recorded cash disbursements to approved vouchers.	Cash transactions occurred.
Vouch a sample of recorded purchases to documentation. Vouch a sample of recorded cost of sales to documentation.	Inventory transactions occurred.
Vouch a sample of recorded payables to documentation, e.g., requisitions, purchase orders, receiving reports, and approved invoices	Purchases occurred.
Trace subsequent payments to recorded payables. Collect supporting documentation and search for unmatched documents to determine whether relevant documents have been lost, misplaced, or misfiled.	Accounts Payable are all accounted for.

9. **Compensating Controls**

    a. Compensating controls replace the normal controls, such as segregation of duties, when the latter cannot feasibly be implemented.

    1) For example, in the finance and investment cycle, top management may authorize and execute investments and have access to the records, stock certificates, etc. The compensating control in this case is for at least two people to perform each function.

        a) Providing oversight is an alternative to the performance of each function by at least two people. Thus, the board may authorize an investment with other functions (custody of stock certificates, management of the portfolio, and oversight of recordkeeping) performed by a top manager.

    2) Other compensating controls in the finance and investment cycle include periodic communications with the board, oversight by a committee of the board, and internal auditing's reconciliation of the securities portfolio with the recorded information.

Stop and review! You have completed the outline for this subunit. Study multiple-choice questions 1 through 11 beginning on page 453.

13.2 SYSTEMS CONTROLS AND INFORMATION SECURITY

1. **Three Goals of Information Security**

    a. Availability is the ability of the intended and authorized users to access computer resources to meet organizational goals.

    b. Confidentiality is assurance of the secrecy of information that could adversely affect the organization if revealed to the public or competitors.

    c. Integrity is maintained by preventing the unauthorized or accidental modification of programs or data.

2. **Threats to Information Systems**

    a. **Input manipulation** is an intrusion into a system by exploiting a vulnerability in a legitimate electronic portal, such as the input boxes on a web page. An input box may call, for instance, for the user's address, but a knowledgeable hacker can implant HTML code in the input box that runs a system command giving him or her access to the organization's data.

    b. **Program alteration** is the deliberate changing of the processing routines of an application program. A famous, if apocryphal, example of long standing is a piece of code that directs all amounts less than one cent to be directed to the malicious programmer's bank account.

    c. **Direct file alteration** is the deliberate changing of data in a database to the intruder's advantage. A common example is a hacker who uses unauthorized access to change his or her course grades while bypassing the normal audit trail.

    d. **Data theft** is the surreptitious copying of critical data elements from an organization's databases. Social Security and credit card numbers are common targets of this type of attack.

    e. **Sabotage** is the disruption of an organization's systems, not for personal gain, but simply for revenge or in the spirit of vandalism. Changing a company's website to include unflattering information that is not immediately noticeable is an example. Another example is a disgruntled programmer who injects a logic bomb into an application that will disrupt processing long after the programmer's departure from the company.

f. **Viruses** are computer programs that propagate themselves from one computer to another without the user's knowledge. Some are written only for the programmer's amusement and are relatively harmless. This type of virus may cause a clever or annoying message to appear on the user's screen. Others are malicious and can cause great inconvenience and even loss of data to the user. A common way of spreading a virus is by email attachments and downloads.

g. **Logic bombs** also destroy data but, unlike viruses, they remain on a single computer and do not replicate. Often they lie dormant until triggered by some occurrence, such as the arrival of a certain date.

h. **Worms** are pieces of code that do not threaten the data on a computer (unlike viruses and logic bombs) but are destructive because of the rapidity with which they replicate themselves. A worm released onto the Internet will propagate from network to network, eventually overwhelming one or more servers with traffic.

i. **Trojan horses** are voluntarily installed on a computer by the user because they are masquerading as programs the user wants. While the program may present the user with, for instance, an entertaining video game, behind the scenes, it contains codes that a hacker can activate later to take over the computer, retrieving sensitive data from it or using it to launch proxy attacks on other computers.

   1) Viruses, worms, Trojan horses, etc., are often collectively referred to as malicious software, or malware.

j. **Back doors** are a means of obtaining access to a system while bypassing the usual password controls. IT personnel often deliberately design back doors into systems to allow system management during unusual circumstances. Hackers search for vulnerabilities in systems to exploit back doors for their own purposes.

k. **Spyware** spies on a user without his or her knowledge and collects data, such as a history of keystrokes. Programs that capture keystrokes are called **keylogger** software.

l. **Ransomware** holds a computer or files hostage and demands a ransom payment. Ransomware distributors do not really want to cause major trouble. They just want to take something hostage and get a quick payment from the computer user.

m. **Theft** becomes increasingly problematic with the higher portability of laptop and palmtop computers. All organizations must establish policies for the proper physical protection of computing infrastructure assets.

n. **Malware** is short for malicious software. Basically, the term "malware" encompasses all harmful software, including all of those listed above and on the previous page.

o. **Phishing** is the attempt to acquire sensitive information by pretending to be a trustworthy entity.

3. **Systems Development Controls**

   a. All information systems, automated or manual, perform four basic functions on information: input, processing, output, and storage.

      1) Proper management of the systems development process can enhance the accuracy, validity, safety, security, and adaptability of the controls over these functions.

   b. Effective systems development requires the setting of priorities. This can be achieved through a steering committee composed of managers from both the IT function and the end-user functions. The committee approves development projects, assigns resources, and reviews their progress.

      1) The steering committee also ensures that requests for new systems are aligned with the overall strategic plan of the organization.

      2) All newly developed systems should conform to established organizational standards for coding and documentation.

c. Changes to existing systems should be subject to the same strict controls. Requests for changes should be initiated by an end user and authorized by management or the steering committee.

1) All changes should be made to a working copy of the program. Production code should never be directly alterable by a programmer.
2) All changes should be adequately tested before being placed in production. The test results should be demonstrated for and accepted by the user who requested the change.
   a) Adequate testing must involve the use of incorrect data. The program must be able to appropriately handle data that do not conform to the ideal.
3) The changed program code should be stored in a secure library during testing and while awaiting migration into production.

d. Unauthorized changes to programs can be detected by code comparison. The version in use compared electronically to an archived version known to be "clean."

4. **Physical Controls**

   a. Physical controls limit physical access and environmental damage to computer equipment and important documents.

   1) Physical access. Only operators should be allowed unmonitored access to the computer center. This can be accomplished through the use of a guard desk, a keypad, or a magnetic card reader.
   2) Environmental controls. The computer center should be equipped with a cooling and heating system to maintain a year-round constant level of temperature and humidity, and a fire-suppression system.

5. **Logical Controls**

   a. Logical controls are established to limit system access in accordance with the principle that all persons should have access only to those elements of the organization's information systems that are necessary to perform their job duties. Logical controls have a double focus, authentication and authorization.

   1) **Authentication** is the act of ensuring that the person attempting to access the system is in fact who (s)he says (s)he is. The most widespread means of achieving this is through the use of IDs and passwords.
      a) Anyone attempting access to one of the organization's systems must supply a unique identifier (e.g., the person's name or other series of characters) and a password that is known only to that person and is not stored anywhere in the system in unencrypted format.
         i) Not even information security personnel should be able to view unencrypted passwords. Security personnel can change passwords, but the policy should require that the user immediately changes it to something secret.
      b) Password optimization
         i) Passwords should be difficult to guess.
            - A dialog can be designed to query the user for common names in his or her life (children, pets, sports teams) so that these words can be stored and never permitted by the system to be used as that person's password.
            - Ideally, passwords are at least eight characters long and contain both uppercase and lowercase letters and numerals.
         ii) The system should force passwords to be changed periodically, e.g., every 90 days.

c) Password fatigue results when users must log on to several systems in the course of a day. Users are likely to write down their IDs and passwords in such cases, defeating the purpose of automated authentication.

   i) Single sign-on can be the solution in well-managed systems environments. A single ID and password combination is required to allow a user access to all IT resources (s)he needs. A high level of maintenance and security consciousness is required to make single sign-on successful.

2) **Authorization** is the practice of ensuring that, once in the system, the user can only access those programs and data elements necessary to his or her job duties.

   a) In many cases, users should be able to view the contents of some data fields but not be able to change them.

   b) An example is an accounts receivable clerk who can view customers' credit limits but cannot change them. This same clerk can, however, change a customer's outstanding balance by entering or adjusting an invoice.

   c) To extend the example, only the head of the accounts receivable department should be able to execute the program that updates the accounts receivable master balance file. An individual clerk should have no such power.

6. **Input, Processing, and Output Controls**

    a. **Input controls** provide reasonable assurance that data submitted for processing are (1) authorized, (2) complete, and (3) accurate. These controls vary depending on whether input is entered in online or batch mode.

       1) Online input controls can be used when data are keyed into an input screen.

          a) Preformatting. The data entry screen mimics the old hardcopy document, forcing data entry in all necessary fields.

          b) Edit checks. The data entry screen prevents certain types of incorrect data from entering the system. For example, the system rejects any attempt to enter numerals in the Name box or letters in the Amount box. Dropdown menus can restrict the user's choices to only valid selections.

          c) Limit (reasonableness) checks. Certain amounts can be restricted to appropriate ranges, such as hours worked < 20 per day, or invoices over $100,000 requiring supervisor approval.

          d) Check digits. An algorithm is applied to any kind of serial identifier to derive a check digit. During data entry, the check digit is recomputed by the system to ensure proper entry. Requiring the full number including check digit to be keyed in all future data entry operations eliminates the possibility of dropped or transposed digits, etc.

       2) Batch input controls can be used when data are grouped for processing in "batches."

          a) Management release. A batch is not released for processing until a manager reviews and approves it.

          b) Record count. A batch is not released for processing unless the number of records in the batch, as reported by the system, matches the number calculated by the user.

          c) Financial total. A batch is not released for processing unless the sum of the dollar amounts of the individual items as reported by the system matches the amount calculated by the user.

d) Hash total. The arithmetic sum of a numeric field, which has no meaning by itself, can serve as a check that the same records that should have been processed were processed. An example is the sum of all Social Security numbers.

   i) This number is much too unwieldy to be calculated by the user, but once it is calculated by the system, it can follow the batch through subsequent stages of processing.

b. **Processing controls** provide reasonable assurance that (1) all data submitted for processing are processed and (2) only approved data are processed. These controls are built into the application code by programmers during the systems development process.

   1) Some processing controls repeat the steps performed by the input controls, such as limit checks and control totals.
   2) Validation. Identifiers are matched against master files to determine existence. For example, any accounts payable transaction in which the vendor number does not match a number on the vendor master file is rejected.
   3) Completeness. Any record with missing data is rejected.
   4) Arithmetic controls. Cross-footing compares an amount to the sum of its components. Zero-balance checking adds the debits and credits in a transaction or batch to ensure they sum to zero.
   5) Sequence check. Computer effort is expended most efficiently when data are processed in a logical order, such as by customer number. This check ensures the batch is sorted in this order before processing begins.
   6) Run-to-run control totals. The controls associated with a given batch are checked after each stage of processing to ensure all transactions have been processed.
   7) Key integrity. A record's "key" is the group of values in designated fields that uniquely identify the record. No application process should be able to alter the data in these key fields.

c. **Output controls** provide assurance that processing was complete and accurate.

   1) A complete audit trail should be generated by each process: batch number, time of submission, time of completion, number of records in batch, total dollars in batch, number of records rejected, total dollars rejected, etc.

      a) The audit trail is immediately submitted to a reasonableness check by the user, who is most qualified to judge the adequacy of processing and the proper treatment of erroneous transactions.

   2) Error listings report all transactions rejected by the system. These should be corrected and resubmitted by the user.

7. **Computer-Assisted Audit Techniques (CAATs)**

   a. Certain controls relating to the input, processing, and output of data are internal to the computer system.

      1) They should be tested by procedures that are not traditionally performed in a manual environment.
      2) Such techniques have been characterized as auditing around the computer or auditing through the computer.

b. **Auditing around the computer** is not appropriate when systems are sophisticated or the major controls are included in the computer programs. It may be appropriate for very simple systems that produce appropriate printed outputs.

   1) The auditor manually processes transactions and compares the results with the client's computer-processed results.
   2) Because only a small number of transactions can ordinarily be tested, the effectiveness of the tests of controls must be questioned.
   3) The computer is treated as a black box, and only inputs and outputs are evaluated.

c. **Auditing through the computer** uses the computer to test the processing logic and controls within the system and the records produced. This approach may be accomplished in several ways, including

   1) Processing test data
   2) Parallel simulation
   3) Generalized audit software
   4) Data extraction techniques
   5) Creation of an integrated test facility
   6) Programming embedded audit modules

d. Computer-assisted audit techniques may be systems- or transaction-based or may provide automated methods for extracting and analyzing data.

e. Test data consist of a set of dummy inputs containing both good and bad data elements. This approach subjects auditor-created data to the client's programs.

   1) The auditor can assess the controls embedded in the application by observing (a) whether the good data are correctly processed and (b) how well the system handles the bad input.
   2) Test data must never be mingled with real data, and test data must not be allowed to interfere with production processing. Monitoring by IT personnel is crucial when the auditor employs a test deck.

f. Parallel simulation subjects client data to auditor-created programs.

   1) The goal is to determine whether the data are subjected to the processes that the client claims the application performs.
   2) Parallel simulation requires the auditor to have considerable technical knowledge. The auditor also must have extensive communications with client personnel to learn the designed functions of the application being imitated.

g. Generalized audit software (GAS) packages allow the auditor to load a copy of the client's production data onto the auditor's own computer and perform various analytical procedures.

   1) The auditor can search for duplicate records, gaps in numerically sequenced records, high-monetary-amount transactions, suspect vendor numbers, etc. Control totals can be calculated, and balances can be stratified for receivables testing.
   2) The leading GAS packages are ACL (Audit Command Language) and IDEA (Interactive Data Extraction and Analysis).
   3) The hazards lie in ensuring that the data obtained are those required for the audit procedure being performed. Control totals and other methods are used for this purpose.

h. Spreadsheet analysis. Electronic spreadsheets, such as Microsoft Excel, permit easy analysis of huge amounts of client data and the performance of what-if scenarios.

i. Integrated test facility (ITF). In this approach, the auditor creates a fictitious entity (a department, vendor, employee, or product) on the client's live production system.

  1) All transactions associated with the dummy entity are processed by the live system, and the auditor can observe the results.
  2) Use of an ITF requires great care to ensure that no transactions associated with the dummy entity are included in production reports and output files.

j. An embedded audit module is an integral part of an application system. It is designed to identify and report actual transactions and other information that meet criteria having audit significance.

  1) An advantage is that it permits continuous monitoring of online, real-time systems.
  2) A disadvantage is that audit hooks must be programmed into the operating system and applications programs to permit insertion of audit modules.

k. Application tracing uses a feature of the programming language in which the application was written.

  1) Tracing aids computer programmers in following the step-by-step operation of a computer program's source code. It can be used by auditors for the same purpose.

l. System mapping is similar to application tracing. But mapping is performed by another computer program instead of by the auditor.

8. **Storage Controls**

  a. Dual write routines. The data can be stored on two separate physical devices (usually magnetic hard drives) so that a mishap to one does not destroy the organization's data set.

   1) Especially important in this regard is the technology known as RAID (redundant array of independent discs), a data storage virtualization technology that combines multiple physical disk drive components into a single logical unit for the purposes of data redundancy, performance, or both.

  b. Validity checks. Hardware that transmits or receives data compares the bits in each byte to the permissible combinations in order to determine whether they constitute a valid structure.

  c. Physical controls. Mounting hard drives in physically secure rooms and storing portable media in locked storage areas are vital to preventing the compromise of confidential data.

Stop and review! You have completed the outline for this subunit. Study multiple-choice questions 12 through 22 beginning on page 456.

13.3 SECURITY MEASURES AND BUSINESS CONTINUITY PLANNING

1. **Inherent Risks of the Internet**

  a. Password Attacks

   1) A brute-force attack uses password cracking software to try large numbers of letter and number combinations to access a network. A simple variation is the use of password cracking software that tries all the words in a dictionary.
   2) Passwords also may be compromised by Trojan horses, IP spoofing, and packet sniffers. Spoofing is identity misrepresentation in cyberspace, (e.g., using a false website to obtain visitor information). Sniffing is the use of software to eavesdrop on information sent by a user to the host computer of a website.

b. A man-in-the-middle attack takes advantage of networking packet sniffing and routing and transport protocols.

1) These attacks may be used to steal data, obtain access to the network during a rightful user's active session, analyze the traffic on the network to learn about its operations and users, insert new data or modify the data being transmitted, and deny service.
2) Encryption is the effective response to man-in-the-middle attacks. The encrypted data will be useless to the attacker unless it can be decrypted.

c. A denial-of-service (DoS) attack is an attempt to overload an organization's network with so many messages that it cannot function (i.e., induce a system crash).

1) A distributed denial-of-service (DDoS) attack comes from multiple sources, for example, the machines of several innocent parties infected by Trojan horses. When activated, these programs send messages to the target and leave the connection open.
2) A DoS attack may establish as many network connections as possible to exclude other users, thus overloading primary memory or corrupting file systems.

2. **Use of Data Encryption**

a. Encryption technology converts data into a code. Unauthorized users may still be able to access the data, but without the encryption key, they cannot decode it.

1) Encryption technology may be either hardware- or software-based. Two major types of encryption software exist.

b. **Public-key**, or asymmetric, encryption is the more secure of the two because it requires two keys: The public key for coding messages is widely known, but the private key for decoding messages is kept secret by the recipient.

1) The parties who wish to transmit coded messages must use algorithmically-related pairs of public and private keys.
2) The sender uses the recipient's public key, obtained from a directory, to encode the message, and transmits the message to the recipient. The recipient then uses the public key and the related private (secret) key to decode the message.
3) Neither party knows the other's private key. The related public key and private key pair is issued by a certificate authority (a third-party fiduciary, e.g., VeriSign or Thawte). However, the private key is issued only to one party.

   a) RSA, named for its developers (Rivest, Shamir, and Adelman), is the most commonly used public-key method.

c. **Private-key**, or symmetric, encryption is less secure because it requires only a single key for each pair of parties that want to send each other coded messages.

1) Data Encryption Standard (DES), a shared private-key method developed by the U.S. government, is the most prevalent secret-key method. It is based on numbers with 56 binary digits.
2) The Advanced Encryption Standard (AES) is a recently adopted cryptographic algorithm for use by U.S. government organizations to protect sensitive information. The AES will be widely used on a voluntary basis by organizations, institutions, and individuals as well as by the U.S. government.

3. **Firewalls**
    a. A firewall is a combination of hardware and software that separates an internal network from an external network, such as the Internet, and prevents passage of specific types of traffic.
        1) Firewall systems ordinarily produce reports on organization-wide Internet use, exception reports for unusual usage patterns, and system penetration-attempt reports. These reports are very helpful as a method of continuous monitoring, or logging, of the system.
        2) A firewall alone is not an adequate defense against computer viruses. Specialized anti-virus software is a must.

4. **Routine Backup and Offsite Rotation**
    a. It is a truth seldom grasped by those who are not computer professionals that an organization's data is more valuable than its hardware.
        1) Hardware can be replaced for a price, but each organization's data bundle is unique and is indispensable to carrying on business. If it is ever destroyed, it cannot be replaced. For this reason, periodic backup and rotation are essential.
    b. The offsite location must be temperature- and humidity-controlled and guarded against physical intrusion.
        1) Just as important, it must be geographically remote enough from the site of the organization's main operations that it would not be affected by the same natural disaster. It does the organization no good to have sound backup procedures if the files are not accessible or have been destroyed.
    c. A typical backup routine involves duplicating all data files and application programs once a month. (Application files must be backed up as well as data since programs change too.)
        1) Incremental changes, that is, only those data elements and programs that have changed since the last full monthly backup, are backed up every week and kept at the main processing center. (Transporting the weekly backups to the offsite location is generally not cost-effective.)
    d. In case of an interruption of normal processing, the organization's systems can be restored such that, at most, 3 weeks of business information is lost. This is not an ideal situation, but it is a far cry from a complete loss of a company's files, which could essentially put it out of business.

5. **Business Continuity Planning**
    a. Disaster planning is the name commonly given to this activity.
        1) Disaster recovery is the process of resuming normal information processing operations after the occurrence of a major interruption.
        2) Business continuity planning is the continuation of business by other means during the period in which computer processing is unavailable or less than normal.

b. Two major types of disasters must be planned for: those in which the data center is physically available and those in which it is not.
1) Examples of the first type of disaster are power failure, random intrusions such as viruses, and deliberate intrusions, such as hacking incidents.
a) The organization's physical facilities are sound, but immediate action is required to keep normal processing going.
2) The second type of disaster is much more serious. This type is caused by disasters, such as floods, fires, hurricanes, earthquakes, etc.
a) An occurrence of this type necessitates the existence of an alternate processing facility.
c. Dealing with Specific Types of Disasters
1) Power failures can be guarded against by the purchase of backup electrical generators. These can be programmed to automatically begin running as soon as a dip in the level of electric current is detected. This is a widespread practice in settings such as hospitals where 24-hour system availability is crucial.
2) Attacks such as viruses and denials-of-service call for a completely different response. The system must be brought down "gracefully" to halt the spread of the infection. The IT staff must be well trained in the nature of the latest virus threats to know how to isolate the damage and bring the system back to full operation.
3) The most extreme disaster is when the organization's main facility is rendered uninhabitable by flood, fire, earthquake, etc. It is to prepare for these cases that organizations contract for alternate processing facilities.
a) An alternate processing facility is a physical location maintained by an outside contractor for the express purpose of providing processing facilities for customers in case of disaster.
b) The recovery center, like the offsite storage location for backup files, must be far enough away that it will likely be unaffected by the same natural disaster that forced the abandonment of the main facility. Usually, companies contract for backup facilities in another city.
c) Once the determination is made that processing is no longer possible at the principal site, the backup files are retrieved from the secure storage location and taken to the recovery center.
d) Recovery centers can take many forms. Organizations determine which facility is best by calculating the tradeoff between the cost of the contract and the cost of downtime.
i) A **hot site** is a fully operational processing facility that is immediately available. A flying-start site is a hot site with the latest data and software that permit startup within a few minutes or even a few seconds.
ii) A **warm site** is a facility with limited hardware, such as communications and networking equipment, already installed but lacking the necessary servers and client terminals.
iii) A **cold site** is a shell facility lacking most infrastructure but readily available for the quick installation of hardware.

Stop and review! You have completed the outline for this subunit. Study multiple-choice questions 23 through 30 beginning on page 459.

QUESTIONS

13.1 Control Procedures

1. Internal controls may be preventive, detective, corrective, or directive. Which of the following is preventive?

A. Requiring two persons to open mail.
B. Reconciling the accounts receivable subsidiary file with the control account.
C. Using batch totals.
D. Preparing bank reconciliations.

Answer (A) is correct.
REQUIRED: The internal control that is preventive.
DISCUSSION: Preventive controls are designed to prevent an error or an irregularity. Detective and corrective controls attempt to identify and correct errors or irregularities that have already occurred. Preventive controls are usually more cost beneficial than detective or corrective controls. Assigning two individuals to open mail is an attempt to prevent misstatement of cash receipts.
Answer (B) is incorrect. Reconciling the subsidiary file with the master file may detect and lead to the correction of errors, but the control does not prevent errors. Answer (C) is incorrect. The use of batch totals may detect a missing or lost document but will not necessarily prevent a document from becoming lost. Answer (D) is incorrect. Bank reconciliations disclose errors in the accounts but have no preventive effect.

2. The procedure requiring preparation of a prelisting of incoming cash receipts, with copies of the prelist going to the cashier and to accounting, is an example of which type of control?

A. Preventive.
B. Corrective.
C. Detective.
D. Directive.

Answer (A) is correct.
REQUIRED: The kind of control exemplified by a prelist of cash receipts.
DISCUSSION: A prelisting of cash receipts in the form of checks is a preventive control. It is intended to deter undesirable events from occurring. Because fraud involving cash is most likely to occur before receipts are recorded, either remittance advices or a prelisting of checks should be prepared in the mail room so as to establish recorded accountability for cash as soon as possible. A cash register tape is a form of prelisting for cash received over the counter. One copy of a prelisting will go to accounting for posting to the cash receipts journal, and another is sent to the cashier for reconciliation with checks and currency received.
Answer (B) is incorrect. A corrective control rectifies an error or fraud. Answer (C) is incorrect. A detective control uncovers an error or fraud that has already occurred. Answer (D) is incorrect. A directive control causes or encourages a desirable event.

3. When an organization has strong internal control, management can expect various benefits. The benefit **least** likely to occur is

A. Reduced cost of an external audit.
B. Elimination of employee fraud.
C. Availability of reliable data for decision-making purposes.
D. Some assurance of compliance with the Foreign Corrupt Practices Act of 1977.

Answer (B) is correct.
REQUIRED: The least likely benefit from a strong internal control.
DISCUSSION: Even the best internal control cannot guarantee the complete elimination of employee fraud. Effective internal control will reduce the amount of employee fraud and probably detect losses on a timely basis.
Answer (A) is incorrect. It is a benefit of strong internal control. The cost of the external audit will be lower because of the reduction of the audit effort related to substantive testing. Answer (C) is incorrect. It is a benefit of strong internal control. Management will have better data for decision-making purposes. Answer (D) is incorrect. It is a benefit of strong internal control. Management will have some assurance of compliance with the FCPA.

4. In a well-designed internal control structure in which the cashier receives remittances from the mail room, the cashier should **not**

A. Endorse the checks.
B. Prepare the bank deposit slip.
C. Deposit remittances daily at a local bank.
D. Post the receipts to the accounts receivable subsidiary ledger cards.

Answer (D) is correct.
REQUIRED: The activity that the cashier should not perform.
DISCUSSION: The cashier is an assistant to the treasurer and thus performs an asset custody function. Individuals with custodial functions should not have access to the accounting records. If the cashier were allowed to post the receipts to the accounts receivable subsidiary ledger, an opportunity for embezzlement would arise that could be concealed by falsifying the books.

5. Accounting controls are concerned with the safeguarding of assets and the reliability of financial records. Consequently, these controls are designed to provide reasonable assurance that all of the following take place **except**

- A. Permitting access to assets in accordance with management's authorization.
- B. Executing transactions in accordance with management's general or specific authorization.
- C. Compliance with methods and procedures ensuring operational efficiency and adherence to managerial policies.
- D. Comparing recorded assets with existing assets at periodic intervals and taking appropriate action with respect to differences.

Answer (C) is correct.
REQUIRED: The item for which an accounting control does not provide reasonable assurance.
DISCUSSION: An accounting control is concerned with the safeguarding of assets and the reliability of financial records, whereas an operational or administrative control is concerned with operational efficiency and effectiveness. Thus, compliance with methods and procedures ensuring operational efficiency and adherence to managerial policies is an objective of an operational control.
Answer (A) is incorrect. Control objectives concerning the entity's ability to record, process, summarize, and report financial data include management authorization of access to assets. Answer (B) is incorrect. Control objectives concerning the entity's ability to record, process, summarize, and report financial data include proper authorization of transactions. Answer (D) is incorrect. Control objectives concerning the entity's ability to record, process, summarize, and report financial data include comparison of recorded accountability with assets at reasonable intervals.

6. One characteristic of an effective internal control structure is the proper segregation of duties. The combination of responsibilities that would **not** be considered a violation of segregation of functional responsibilities is

- A. Signing of paychecks and custody of blank payroll checks.
- B. Preparation of paychecks and check distribution.
- C. Approval of time cards and preparation of paychecks.
- D. Timekeeping and preparation of payroll journal entries.

Answer (D) is correct.
REQUIRED: The combination of responsibilities not considered a violation of the separation of duties requirement.
DISCUSSION: Combining the timekeeping function and the preparation of the payroll journal entries would not be improper because the employee has no access to assets or to employee records in the personnel department. Only through collusion could an embezzlement be perpetrated. Accordingly, the functions of authorization, recordkeeping, and custodianship remain separate.
Answer (A) is incorrect. Persons with recordkeeping but not custody of assets responsibilities should have access to blank checks, while the duty of signing checks (custodianship) should be assigned to persons (e.g., the treasurer) with no recordkeeping function. Answer (B) is incorrect. Payroll preparation and payment to employees should be segregated since they are incompatible recordkeeping and custodianship functions. Answer (C) is incorrect. Approval of time cards is an authorization function that is incompatible with the recordkeeping function of preparation of paychecks.

7. Auditors document their understanding of internal control with questionnaires, flowcharts, and narrative descriptions. A questionnaire consists of a series of questions concerning controls that auditors consider necessary to prevent or detect errors and fraud. The **most** appropriate question designed to contribute to the auditors' understanding of the completeness of the expenditure (purchases-payables) cycle concerns the

- A. Internal verification of quantities, prices, and mathematical accuracy of sales invoices.
- B. Use and accountability of prenumbered checks.
- C. Disposition of cash receipts.
- D. Qualifications of accounting personnel.

Answer (B) is correct.
REQUIRED: The most appropriate question designed to contribute to the auditors' understanding of the completeness of the expenditure cycle.
DISCUSSION: A completeness assertion concerns whether all transactions and accounts that should be presented in the financial statements are so presented. The exclusive use of sequentially numbered documents facilitates control over expenditures. An unexplained gap in the sequence alerts the auditor to the possibility that not all transactions have been recorded. A failure to use prenumbered checks would therefore suggest a higher assessment of control risk. If a company uses prenumbered checks, it should be easy to determine exactly which checks were used during a period.
Answer (A) is incorrect. Determination of proper amounts of sales invoices concerns the valuation assertion. Also, sales invoices are part of the sales-receivables (revenue) cycle. Answer (C) is incorrect. Cash receipts are part of the revenue cycle. Answer (D) is incorrect. Consideration of the qualifications of accounting personnel is not a test of controls over the completeness of any cycle. This procedure is appropriate during the consideration of the control environment.

8. Organizational independence is required in the processing of customers' orders in order to maintain an internal control structure. Which one of the following situations is **not** a proper separation of duties in the processing of orders from customers?

A. Approval by Credit Department of a sales order prepared by the Sales Department.

B. Shipping of goods by the Shipping Department that have been retrieved from stock by the Finished Goods Storeroom Department.

C. Invoice preparation by the Billing Department and posting to customers' accounts by the Accounts Receivable Department.

D. Approval of a sales credit memo because of a product return by the Sales Department with subsequent posting to the customer's account by the Accounts Receivable Department.

Answer (D) is correct.
REQUIRED: The situation not a proper separation of duties in the processing of customer orders.
DISCUSSION: Allowing a sales department to approve a credit memo without a receiving report would be dangerous. Sales personnel could overstate sales in one period and then reverse them in subsequent periods. Thus, a copy of the receiving report for returned goods should be sent to the billing department for preparation of a credit memo after approval by a responsible supervisor who is independent of the Sales Department.

9. Which one of the following situations represents an internal control weakness in the payroll department?

A. Payroll department personnel are rotated in their duties.

B. Paychecks are distributed by the employees' immediate supervisor.

C. Payroll records are reconciled with quarterly tax reports.

D. The timekeeping function is independent of the payroll department.

Answer (B) is correct.
REQUIRED: The internal control weakness in the payroll department.
DISCUSSION: Paychecks should not be distributed by supervisors because an unscrupulous person could terminate an employee and fail to report the termination. The supervisor could then clock in and out for the employee and keep the paycheck. A person unrelated to either payroll recordkeeping or the operating department should distribute checks.
Answer (A) is incorrect. Periodic rotation of payroll personnel inhibits the perpetration and concealment of fraud. Answer (C) is incorrect. This analytical procedure may detect a discrepancy. Answer (D) is incorrect. Timekeeping should be independent of asset custody and employee records.

10. Proper segregation of duties reduces the opportunities for persons to be in positions to both

A. Journalize entries and prepare financial statements.

B. Record cash receipts and cash disbursements.

C. Establish internal control and authorize transactions.

D. Perpetrate and conceal errors or fraud.

Answer (D) is correct.
REQUIRED: The effects of the segregation of duties and responsibilities.
DISCUSSION: Proper segregation of duties and responsibilities reduces the opportunity for an individual to both perpetrate and conceal an error or fraud in the normal course of his or her duties. Hence, different people should be assigned the responsibilities for authorizing transactions, recordkeeping, and asset custody.
Answer (A) is incorrect. Accountants typically journalize entries and prepare financial statements. Answer (B) is incorrect. Accountants may record both cash receipts and cash disbursements as long as they do not have custody of the cash. Answer (C) is incorrect. Management establishes internal control and ultimately has the responsibility to authorize transactions.

11. Which one of the following situations represents a strength of internal control for purchasing and accounts payable?

A. Prenumbered receiving reports are issued randomly.

B. Invoices are approved for payment by the purchasing department.

C. Unmatched receiving reports are reviewed on an annual basis.

D. Vendors' invoices are matched against purchase orders and receiving reports before a liability is recorded.

Answer (D) is correct.
REQUIRED: The strength in internal control relevant to purchasing and accounts payable.
DISCUSSION: A voucher should not be prepared for payment until the vendor's invoice has been matched against the corresponding purchase order and receiving report. This procedure provides assurance that a valid transaction has occurred and that the parties have agreed on the terms, such as price and quantity.
Answer (A) is incorrect. Prenumbered receiving reports should be issued sequentially. A gap in the sequence may indicate an erroneous or fraudulent transaction. Answer (B) is incorrect. The approval of an invoice for payment is a basic duty of the accounts payable department and would therefore not represent a strength of internal control for purchasing and accounts payable. Answer (C) is incorrect. Annual review of unmatched receiving reports is too infrequent. More frequent attention is necessary to remedy deficiencies in internal control.

13.2 Systems Controls and Information Security

12. Data processed by a computer system are usually transferred to some form of output medium for storage. However, the presence of computerized output does not, in and of itself, ensure the output's accuracy, completeness, or authenticity. For this assurance, various controls are needed. The major types of controls for this area include

A. Transaction controls, general controls, and printout controls.
B. Activity listings, echo checks, and pre-numbered forms.
C. Tape and disk output controls and printed output controls.
D. Input controls, tape and disk output controls, and printed output controls.

Answer (D) is correct.
REQUIRED: The major types of controls to ensure that computerized output is accurate, complete, and authentic.
DISCUSSION: Input controls provide reasonable assurance that data received for processing have been properly authorized, converted into machine-sensible form, and identified, and that data have not been lost, suppressed, added, duplicated, or otherwise improperly changed. Input controls also relate to rejections, correction, and resubmission of data that were initially incorrect. Output controls provide assurance that the processing result is accurate and that only authorized personnel receive the output.
Answer (A) is incorrect. General, transaction, and print-out controls do not ensure accuracy of inputs. Answer (B) is incorrect. An echo check, which is an input control over transmission along communications lines, does not ensure proper authorization of data. Neither do the other techniques ensure completeness of data. Answer (C) is incorrect. Output controls are insufficient to ensure completeness and accuracy of output. Input controls are also needed.

13. The use of a generalized audit software package

A. Relieves an auditor of the typical tasks of investigating exceptions, verifying sources of information, and evaluating reports.
B. Is a major aid in retrieving information from computerized files.
C. Overcomes the need for an auditor to learn much about computers.
D. Is a form of auditing around the computer.

Answer (B) is correct.
REQUIRED: The true statement about the use of a generalized audit software package.
DISCUSSION: The primary use of generalized computer programs is to select and summarize a client's records for additional testing. Generalized audit software packages permit the auditor to audit through the computer, to extract, compare, analyze, and summarize data and generate output as part of the audit program. They allow the auditor to exploit the computer to examine many more records than otherwise possible with far greater speed and accuracy.
Answer (A) is incorrect. The auditor must still use audit judgment. Answer (C) is incorrect. An auditor must have a knowledge of computer auditing to use a generalized software package. Answer (D) is incorrect. Using a generalized software package is a means of auditing through the computer.

14. An employee in the receiving department keyed in a shipment from a remote terminal and inadvertently omitted the purchase order number. The **best** systems control to detect this error would be

A. Batch total.
B. Completeness test.
C. Sequence check.
D. Reasonableness test.

Answer (B) is correct.
REQUIRED: The best systems control to detect the omission of a purchase order number on a receiving report keyed in from a remote terminal.
DISCUSSION: A completeness test checks that all data elements are entered before processing. An interactive system can be programmed to notify the user to enter the number before accepting the receiving report.
Answer (A) is incorrect. A batch total is a total of one information field (such as sales on invoices) for all records in a batch. Answer (C) is incorrect. A sequence check tests for the ordering, not omission, of records. Answer (D) is incorrect. A limit or reasonableness test checks the values of data items against established limits.

15. Control procedures over accounting information systems are referred to as general controls or application controls. The primary objective of application controls in a computer environment is to

A. Maintain the accuracy of the inputs, files, and outputs for specific applications.
B. Ensure the separation of incompatible functions in the data processing departments.
C. Provide controls over the electronic functioning of the hardware.
D. Plan for the protection of the facilities and backup for the systems.

Answer (A) is correct.
REQUIRED: The primary objective of application controls in a computer environment.
DISCUSSION: Application controls relate to specific tasks performed by the IT department. Their function is to provide reasonable assurance that recording, processing, and reporting of data are performed properly. Application controls are often categorized as input controls, processing controls, and output controls.
Answer (B) is incorrect. Separation of incompatible functions is a general, not an application, control. Answer (C) is incorrect. Hardware controls are general controls. Answer (D) is incorrect. Operating controls are general controls.

16. Which one of the following input validation routines is **not** likely to be appropriate in a real-time operation?

A. Sign check.
B. Reasonableness check.
C. Sequence check.
D. Redundant data check.

Answer (C) is correct.
REQUIRED: The input validation routine not appropriate in a real-time operation.
DISCUSSION: All of the terms listed refer to program controls to prescreen or edit data prior to processing, but the sequence check is most likely to be used only in batch processing. A sequence check tests to determine that records are in proper order. For example, a payroll input file would be sorted into Social Security number order. A sequence check could then be performed to verify record order. This control would not apply in a real-time operation because records would not be processed sequentially.
Answer (A) is incorrect. Sign checks test data for the appropriate arithmetic sign. For instance, hours worked in a payroll should always be a positive number. Answer (B) is incorrect. Reasonableness tests verify that the amounts of input or output fall within predetermined limits. Answer (D) is incorrect. A redundancy check requires transmission of additional data items to check a previously received data item; for example, a few letters of a customer's name could be matched against the name associated with the customer number.

17. The online data entry control called preformatting is

A. A program initiated prior to regular input to discover errors in data before entry so that the errors can be corrected.
B. A check to determine if all data items for a transaction have been entered by the terminal operator.
C. A series of requests for required input data that requires an acceptable response to each request before a subsequent request is made.
D. The display of a document with blanks for data items to be entered by the terminal operator.

Answer (D) is correct.
REQUIRED: The definition of preformatting.
DISCUSSION: To avoid data entry errors in online systems, a screen prompting approach may be used. The dialogue approach, for example, presents a series of questions to the operator. The preformatted screen approach involves the display on the CRT of a set of boxes for entry of specified data items. The format may even be in the form of a copy of a transaction document.
Answer (A) is incorrect. It describes an edit routine. Answer (B) is incorrect. It describes a completeness check. Answer (C) is incorrect. It describes prompting.

18. Routines that use the computer to check the validity and accuracy of transaction data during input are called

A. Operating systems.
B. Edit programs.
C. Compiler programs.
D. Integrated test facilities.

Answer (B) is correct.
REQUIRED: The routines that check the validity and accuracy of transaction data during input.
DISCUSSION: Special programs validate (edit) input data for completeness, validity, and accuracy. The edited data are then used in processing. The errors, omissions, or exceptions are printed on a report.
Answer (A) is incorrect. The operating system controls the overall functioning of the CPU and its online peripheral equipment. Answer (C) is incorrect. A compiler translates source programs written in a higher level language into machine language. Answer (D) is incorrect. An ITF uses simulated transactions to audit the processing system.

19. An example of an internal check is

A. Making sure that output is distributed to the proper people.
B. Monitoring the work of programmers.
C. Collecting accurate statistics of historical transactions while gathering data.
D. Recalculating an amount to ensure its accuracy.

Answer (D) is correct.
REQUIRED: The example of an internal check.
DISCUSSION: Arithmetic proof checks (recalculations) are performed by edit routines before data are processed. A simple example is comparing total debits and total credits.

20. A company employing an online computer system has terminals located in all operating departments for inquiry and updating purposes. Many of the company's employees have access to and are required to use the terminals. A control the company would incorporate to prevent an employee from making an unauthorized change to computer records unrelated to that employee's job would be to

A. Restrict the physical access to terminals.
B. Establish user codes and passwords.
C. Use validity checks.
D. Apply a compatibility test to transactions or inquiries entered by the user.

Answer (D) is correct.
REQUIRED: The control to prevent an unauthorized change in a computer record by an employee with online access.
DISCUSSION: A compatibility test is an access control used to ascertain whether a code number is compatible with the use to be made of the information requested. For example, a user may be authorized to enter only certain kinds of transaction data, to gain access only to certain information, to have access to but not update files, or to use the system only during certain hours.
Answer (A) is incorrect. The employees must have access to the system. Thus, the restriction of access would not solve the problem. Answer (B) is incorrect. The employees must have access to the system. Thus, user codes and passwords would not solve the problem. Answer (C) is incorrect. A validity check is used to compare input identification numbers with acceptable numbers.

21. In entering the billing address for a new client in a company's computerized database, a clerk erroneously entered a nonexistent zip code. As a result, the first month's bill mailed to the new client was returned to the company. Which one of the following would **most** likely have led to discovery of the error at the time of entry into the company's computerized database?

A. Limit test.
B. Validity test.
C. Parity test.
D. Record count test.

Answer (B) is correct.
REQUIRED: The best computerized control for preventing an erroneous zip code from being entered.
DISCUSSION: In validity tests, values entered into the system are compared against master files of valid data. In this case, a master file of all zip codes recognized in the U.S. is held in memory and each time a clerk enters data in the zip code field, the clerk's entry is compared to the list of valid values. If the zip code entered does not match any entry in the master file, data entry is halted and the clerk is advised to reenter the data.
Answer (A) is incorrect. A limit test deals with quantified data, such as preventing hours worked in a single week from exceeding 100 without special authorization. Answer (C) is incorrect. A parity test is a means of ensuring whether the correct number of binary bits has been transmitted. Answer (D) is incorrect. A record count test is a batch-level control for ensuring that the correct number of records has been processed in a batch.

22. In the organization of the information systems function, the **most** important segregation of duties is

A. Not allowing the data librarian to assist in data processing operations.
B. Assuring that those responsible for programming the system do not have access to data processing operations.
C. Having a separate information officer at the top level of the organization outside of the accounting function.
D. Using different programming personnel to maintain utility programs from those who maintain the application programs.

Answer (B) is correct.
REQUIRED: The most important segregation of duties in the information systems function.
DISCUSSION: Segregation of duties is a general control that is vital in a computerized environment. Some segregation of duties common in noncomputerized environments may not be feasible in a computer environment. However, certain tasks should not be combined. Systems analysts, for example, should be separate from programmers and computer operators. Programmers design, write, test, and document specific programs required by the system developed by the analysts. Both programmers and analysts may be able to modify programs, data files, and controls and should therefore have no access to computer equipment and files or to copies of programs used in production. Operators should not be assigned programming duties or responsibility for systems design and should have no opportunity to make changes in programs and systems.
Answer (A) is incorrect. Librarians maintain control over documentation, programs, and data files; they should have no access to equipment, but they can assist in data processing operations. Answer (C) is incorrect. A separate information officer outside of the accounting function would not be as critical a separation of duties as that between programmers and processors. Answer (D) is incorrect. Programmers usually handle all types of programs.

13.3 Security Measures and Business Continuity Planning

23. Which of the following is a computer program that appears to be legitimate but performs some illicit activity when it is run?

A. Hoax virus.
B. Web crawler.
C. Trojan horse.
D. Killer application.

Answer (C) is correct.
REQUIRED: The apparently legitimate computer program that performs an illicit activity.
DISCUSSION: A Trojan horse is a computer program that appears friendly, for example, a game, but that actually contains an application destructive to the computer system.
Answer (A) is incorrect. A hoax virus is a false notice about the existence of a computer virus. It is usually disseminated through use of distribution lists and is sent by email or via an internal network. Answer (B) is incorrect. A web crawler (a spider or bot) is a computer program created to access and read information on websites. The results are included as entries in the index of a search engine. Answer (D) is incorrect. A killer application is one that is so useful that it may justify widespread adoption of a new technology.

24. Which of the following is used for Internet security as opposed to data transmissions over secured transmission lines?

A. Firewalls.
B. Mapping.
C. Parallel simulation.
D. Concurrency controls.

Answer (A) is correct.
REQUIRED: The control that is used for Internet security.
DISCUSSION: Firewalls separate an internal network from an external network (such as the Internet) and prevent passage of specific types of traffic.
Answer (B) is incorrect. Mapping involves monitoring the execution of an application program to determine certain statistical information about a computer run. Answer (C) is incorrect. Parallel simulation involves the use of specially prepared application-type programs to process transactions that have also been run in routine processing. Answer (D) is incorrect. Concurrency controls manage situations in which two or more programs attempt to use a file or database at the same time.

25. A company's management is concerned about computer data eavesdropping and wants to maintain the confidentiality of its information as it is transmitted. The company should utilize

A. Data encryption.
B. Dial back systems.
C. Message acknowledgment procedures.
D. Password codes.

Answer (A) is correct.
REQUIRED: The most effective countermeasure against data eavesdropping.
DISCUSSION: The most effective preventive measure against unauthorized interception of data is encryption. Encryption technology converts data into a code. Unauthorized users may still be able to access the data, but without the encryption key, they will be unable to decode the information. Encryption technology may be either hardware- or software-based.
Answer (B) is incorrect. Dial back systems are a primitive countermeasure that are only appropriate to old-style dialup modem connections. Answer (C) is incorrect. Message acknowledgment procedures are a means only for affirming that a message has been received by the intended party; they do not provide any means of alert in case of interception by an unintended party. Answer (D) is incorrect. Password codes must be assigned and saved on specific systems; they are not applicable to ongoing electronic transmission.

26. Which one of the following would **most** compromise the use of the grandfather-father-son principle of file retention as protection against loss or damage of master files?

A. Use of magnetic tape.
B. Inadequate ventilation.
C. Storing of all files in one location.
D. Failure to encrypt data.

Answer (C) is correct.
REQUIRED: The practice most likely to compromise computer file backup-and-rotation procedures.
DISCUSSION: The offsite location where an organization's computer backup files are kept must be temperature- and humidity-controlled and guarded against intrusion just as the main processing center is. Just as important, it must be geographically remote enough from the site of the organization's main operations that it would not be affected by the same natural disaster. It does an organization no good to have sound backup procedures if the files are not accessible or have been destroyed.
Answer (A) is incorrect. Magnetic tape is a sound, though slow, medium for the storage of backup files. Answer (B) is incorrect. Inadequate ventilation, while undesirable, is not the most compromising of the choices. Answer (D) is incorrect. If data will only be used on equipment owned by the organization and will not be transmitted over network lines, leaving it unencrypted will not compromise the soundness of backup-and-rotation procedures.

27. A critical aspect of a disaster recovery plan is to be able to regain operational capability as soon as possible. In order to accomplish this, an organization can have an arrangement with its computer hardware vendor to have a fully operational facility available that is configured to the user's specific needs. This is **best** known as a(n)

A. Uninterruptible power system.
B. Parallel system.
C. Cold site.
D. Hot site.

Answer (D) is correct.
REQUIRED: The fully operational facility that is configured to the user's specific needs.
DISCUSSION: A disaster recovery plan may include a contract with an external contingency facility vendor. Depending on the organization's needs, the contingency facility may be a hot site or a cold site. A hot site is an arrangement with a vendor for a fully operational facility that is configured to the user's specific needs and that will be available within 24 hours. A hot site may also be fixed or portable and is recommended for an organization that cannot afford for its computer system to be down for even one day.
Answer (A) is incorrect. An uninterruptible power system is a system that is fully protected by a generator or battery backup to prevent data destruction and downtime from electrical power outages. Answer (B) is incorrect. A parallel system exists if a company maintains an identical system to the main system. Answer (C) is incorrect. A cold site is a cheaper alternative to a hot site. It is a shell facility suitable for the quick installation of computer equipment. It provides a prebuilt, environmentally controlled area with raised flooring, electrical power, and appropriate plumbing.

28. Confidential data can be securely transmitted over the Internet by using

A. Single-use passwords.
B. Firewalls.
C. Encryption.
D. Digital signatures.

Answer (C) is correct.
REQUIRED: The method of securely transmitting data over the Internet.
DISCUSSION: Encryption technology converts data into code. Unauthorized users may still be able to access the data but, without the encryption key, they will be unable to decode the information.
Answer (A) is incorrect. Single-use passwords are a tool for permitting one-time access to a system. Answer (B) is incorrect. A firewall is a combination of hardware and software that separates an internal network from an external network and prevents passage of certain types of traffic. Answer (D) is incorrect. A digital signature is a means of verifying electronically that a certain party was the one who sent a given message.

29. Managers at a consumer products company purchased personal computer software from only recognized vendors, and prohibited employees from installing nonauthorized software on their personal computers. To minimize the likelihood of computer viruses infecting any of its systems, the company should also

A. Restore infected systems with authorized versions.
B. Recompile infected programs from source code backups.
C. Institute program change control procedures.
D. Test all new software on a stand-alone personal computer.

Answer (D) is correct.
REQUIRED: The best protection against viruses.
DISCUSSION: Software from recognized sources should be tested in quarantine (for example, in a test/development machine or a stand-alone personal computer) because even vendor-supplied software may be infected with viruses. The software should be run with a vaccine program and tested for the existence of logic bombs, etc.
Answer (A) is incorrect. If viruses infect a system, the company should restore the system with authorized software, but this procedure does not minimize the likelihood of initial infection. Answer (B) is incorrect. If viruses infect programs that the company created, it should recompile the programs from source code backups, but this procedure does not minimize the likelihood of initial infection. Answer (C) is incorrect. Instituting program change control procedures is good practice but does not minimize the likelihood of the system's being infected initially.

30. Which of the following is an indication that a computer virus is present?

A. Frequent power surges that harm computer equipment.
B. Unexplainable losses of or changes to data.
C. Inadequate backup, recovery, and contingency plans.
D. Numerous copyright violations due to unauthorized use of purchased software.

Answer (B) is correct.
REQUIRED: The indicator of a computer virus.
DISCUSSION: The effects of computer viruses range from harmless messages to complete destruction of all data within the system. A symptom of a virus would be the unexplained loss of or change to data.
Answer (A) is incorrect. Power surges are caused by hardware or power supply problems. Answer (C) is incorrect. Inadequate back-up, recovery, and contingency plans are operating policy weaknesses. Answer (D) is incorrect. Copyright violations represent policy or compliance problems.

13.4 ESSAY QUESTIONS

Scenario for Essay Questions 1, 2

The internal audit department of Sachem Manufacturing Company is considering the purchase of computer software that will aid in the auditing process. Sachem's financial and manufacturing control systems are completely automated on a powerful networked server. Melinda Robinson, the director of internal audit, believes that Sachem should acquire computer audit software to assist in the financial and procedure audits that her department conducts. The types of software packages that Robinson is considering are described below.

- A generalized audit software (GAS) package that assists in basic audit work such as the retrieval of live data from large computer files. The department would review this information using conventional audit investigation techniques. More specifically, the department could perform criteria selection, sampling, basic computations for quantitative analysis, record handling, graphical analysis, and the printing of output (i.e., confirmations).
- An integrated test facility (ITF) package that uses, monitors, and controls "dummy" test data through existing programs and checks the existence and adequacy of program data entry controls and processing controls.
- A control flowcharting package that provides a graphical presentation of the data flow of information through a system, pinpointing control strengths and weaknesses.
- A program (parallel) simulation and modeling package that uses actual data to conduct the same systemized process by using a different computer-logic program developed by the auditor. The package can also be used to seek answers to difficult audit problems (involving many comparisons and computations) within statistically acceptable confidence limits.

Questions

1. Without regard to any specific computer audit software, identify the general advantages to the internal auditor of using computer audit software to assist with audits.
2. Describe the audit purpose facilitated and the procedural steps to be followed by the internal auditor to use a(n)
    a. Generalized audit software package
    b. Integrated test facility package
    c. Control flowcharting package
    d. Program (parallel) simulation and modeling package

Essay Questions 1, 2 — Unofficial Answers

1. General advantages to the internal auditor of using computer audit software to assist with audits include the following:

    a. Audits can be more efficient, saving labor time spent on routine calculations. The routine operations of footing extensions, transcription between reports, and report generation are computer generated as a result of the software.
    b. The auditor's time spent on the audit is more analytical than clerical.
    c. The auditor is able to examine more records and extract desired data more readily through ad hoc reporting.
    d. Computer-generated reports and schedules are more objective and professional, improving data communication.
    e. Audit sampling is improved. Any bias in sample selection is eliminated because of assured randomness. This has a direct effect on sampling precision, reliability, and audit accuracy.

2. Many tools have been created to help auditors achieve different objectives.

    a. The purpose of generalized audit software (GAS) programs is to perform a variety of auditing operations on the computer files used to store the information. The steps to be followed by the internal auditor to use generalized computer audit software would include

        - Planning and designing the audit application.
        - Ensuring that the output and final reports are generated from the files being tested.

    b. The purpose of integrated test facility (ITF) packages is to test both source data controls and processing controls. The steps to be followed by the internal auditor to use an ITF include

        - Selection and preparation of the test transactions to be passed through the ITF. These transactions must be representative of all of the transactions the dummy unit emulates. All types of valid and invalid transactions must be used and blended with regular transactions over time to adequately test the system's responses under normal conditions.
        - Review of all output and processing routines including a comparison of actual results to predetermined results.

    c. The purpose of a control flowcharting package is to interpret the program source code and generate a program flowchart corresponding to it in order to facilitate the review of internal controls. The steps to be followed by the internal auditor to use a control flowcharting package would include the following:

        - Establish the audit objective by identifying the systems and programs to be tested.
        - Review manuals and documentation of the system and interview relevant personnel to get an overview of the operations to be tested.

    d. The purpose of a parallel simulation package is to ensure that organizational objectives are being met, ensure compliance to technical standards, and detect unauthorized program changes. The steps to be followed by the internal auditor to use a parallel simulation package include the following:

        - Run the same data used in the company's current application program using the "simulated" application program.
        - Compare the results from the "simulated" application with the results from the company's current application program to verify that objectives are being met.

APPENDIX A
PV/FV TABLES

PRESENT VALUE OF AN ANNUITY

	1%	2%	3%	4%	5%	6%	7%	8%	9%	10%	12%	14%	16%	18%	20%	
1	0.990	0.980	0.971	0.962	0.952	0.943	0.935	0.926	0.917	0.909	0.893	0.877	0.862	0.847	0.833	1
2	1.970	1.942	1.913	1.886	1.859	1.833	1.808	1.783	1.759	1.736	1.690	1.647	1.605	1.566	1.528	2
3	2.941	2.884	2.829	2.775	2.723	2.673	2.624	2.577	2.531	2.487	2.402	2.322	2.246	2.174	2.106	3
4	3.902	3.808	3.717	3.630	3.546	3.465	3.387	3.312	3.240	3.170	3.037	2.914	2.798	2.690	2.589	4
5	4.853	4.713	4.580	4.452	4.329	4.212	4.100	3.993	3.890	3.791	3.605	3.433	3.274	3.127	2.991	5
6	5.795	5.601	5.417	5.242	5.076	4.917	4.767	4.623	4.486	4.355	4.111	3.889	3.685	3.498	3.326	6
7	6.728	6.472	6.230	6.002	5.786	5.582	5.389	5.206	5.033	4.868	4.564	4.288	4.039	3.812	3.605	7
8	7.652	7.325	7.020	6.733	6.463	6.210	5.971	5.747	5.535	5.335	4.968	4.639	4.344	4.078	3.837	8
9	8.566	8.162	7.786	7.435	7.108	6.802	6.515	6.247	5.995	5.759	5.328	4.946	4.607	4.303	4.031	9
10	9.471	8.983	8.530	8.111	7.722	7.360	7.024	6.710	6.418	6.145	5.650	5.216	4.833	4.494	4.192	10
11	10.368	9.787	9.253	8.760	8.306	7.887	7.499	7.139	6.805	6.495	5.938	5.453	5.029	4.656	4.327	11
12	11.255	10.575	9.954	9.385	8.863	8.384	7.943	7.536	7.161	6.814	6.194	5.660	5.197	4.793	4.439	12
13	12.134	11.348	10.635	9.986	9.394	8.853	8.358	7.904	7.487	7.103	6.424	5.842	5.342	4.910	4.533	13
14	13.004	12.106	11.296	10.563	9.899	9.295	8.745	8.244	7.786	7.367	6.628	6.002	5.468	5.008	4.611	14
15	13.865	12.849	11.938	11.118	10.380	9.712	9.108	8.559	8.061	7.606	6.811	6.142	5.575	5.092	4.675	15
16	14.718	13.578	12.561	11.652	10.838	10.106	9.447	8.851	8.313	7.824	6.974	6.265	5.668	5.162	4.730	16
18	16.398	14.992	13.754	12.659	11.690	10.828	10.059	9.372	8.756	8.201	7.250	6.467	5.818	5.273	4.812	18
20	18.046	16.351	14.877	13.590	12.462	11.470	10.594	9.818	9.129	8.514	7.469	6.623	5.929	5.353	4.870	20
22	19.660	17.658	15.937	14.451	13.163	12.042	11.061	10.201	9.442	8.772	7.645	6.743	6.011	5.410	4.909	22
24	21.243	18.914	16.936	15.247	13.799	12.550	11.469	10.529	9.707	8.985	7.784	6.835	6.073	5.451	4.937	24
26	22.795	20.121	17.877	15.983	14.375	13.003	11.826	10.810	9.929	9.161	7.896	6.906	6.118	5.480	4.956	26
28	24.316	21.281	18.764	16.663	14.898	13.406	12.137	11.051	10.116	9.307	7.984	6.961	6.152	5.502	4.970	28
30	25.808	22.396	19.600	17.292	15.372	13.765	12.409	11.258	10.274	9.427	8.055	7.003	6.177	5.517	4.979	30
32	27.270	23.468	20.389	17.874	15.803	14.084	12.647	11.435	10.406	9.526	8.112	7.035	6.196	5.528	4.985	32
34	28.703	24.499	21.132	18.411	16.193	14.368	12.854	11.587	10.518	9.609	8.157	7.060	6.210	5.536	4.990	34
36	30.108	25.489	21.832	18.908	16.547	14.621	13.035	11.717	10.612	9.677	8.192	7.079	6.220	5.541	4.993	36
38	31.485	26.441	22.492	19.368	16.868	14.846	13.193	11.829	10.691	9.733	8.221	7.094	6.228	5.545	4.995	38
40	32.835	27.355	23.115	19.793	17.159	15.046	13.332	11.925	10.757	9.779	8.244	7.105	6.233	5.548	4.997	40

PRESENT VALUE OF $1

	1%	2%	3%	4%	5%	6%	7%	8%	9%	10%	12%	14%	16%	18%	20%	
1	0.990	0.980	0.971	0.962	0.952	0.943	0.935	0.926	0.917	0.909	0.893	0.877	0.862	0.847	0.833	1
2	0.980	0.961	0.943	0.925	0.907	0.890	0.873	0.857	0.842	0.826	0.797	0.769	0.743	0.718	0.694	2
3	0.971	0.942	0.915	0.889	0.864	0.840	0.816	0.794	0.772	0.751	0.712	0.675	0.641	0.609	0.579	3
4	0.961	0.924	0.888	0.855	0.823	0.792	0.763	0.735	0.708	0.683	0.636	0.592	0.552	0.516	0.482	4
5	0.951	0.906	0.863	0.822	0.784	0.747	0.713	0.681	0.650	0.621	0.567	0.519	0.476	0.437	0.402	5
6	0.942	0.888	0.837	0.790	0.746	0.705	0.666	0.630	0.596	0.564	0.507	0.456	0.410	0.370	0.335	6
7	0.933	0.871	0.813	0.760	0.711	0.665	0.623	0.583	0.547	0.513	0.452	0.400	0.354	0.314	0.279	7
8	0.923	0.853	0.789	0.731	0.677	0.627	0.582	0.540	0.502	0.467	0.404	0.351	0.305	0.266	0.233	8
9	0.914	0.837	0.766	0.703	0.645	0.592	0.544	0.500	0.460	0.424	0.361	0.308	0.263	0.225	0.194	9
10	0.905	0.820	0.744	0.676	0.614	0.558	0.508	0.463	0.422	0.386	0.322	0.270	0.227	0.191	0.162	10
11	0.896	0.804	0.722	0.650	0.585	0.527	0.475	0.429	0.388	0.350	0.287	0.237	0.195	0.162	0.135	11
12	0.887	0.788	0.701	0.625	0.557	0.497	0.444	0.397	0.356	0.319	0.257	0.208	0.168	0.137	0.112	12
13	0.879	0.773	0.681	0.601	0.530	0.469	0.415	0.368	0.326	0.290	0.229	0.182	0.145	0.116	0.093	13
14	0.870	0.758	0.661	0.577	0.505	0.442	0.388	0.340	0.299	0.263	0.205	0.160	0.125	0.099	0.078	14
15	0.861	0.743	0.642	0.555	0.481	0.417	0.362	0.315	0.275	0.239	0.183	0.140	0.108	0.084	0.065	15
16	0.853	0.728	0.623	0.534	0.458	0.394	0.339	0.292	0.252	0.218	0.163	0.123	0.093	0.071	0.054	16
18	0.836	0.700	0.587	0.494	0.416	0.350	0.296	0.250	0.212	0.180	0.130	0.095	0.069	0.051	0.038	18
20	0.820	0.673	0.554	0.456	0.377	0.312	0.258	0.215	0.178	0.149	0.104	0.073	0.051	0.037	0.026	20
22	0.803	0.647	0.522	0.422	0.342	0.278	0.226	0.184	0.150	0.123	0.083	0.056	0.038	0.026	0.018	22
24	0.788	0.622	0.492	0.390	0.310	0.247	0.197	0.158	0.126	0.102	0.066	0.043	0.028	0.019	0.013	24
26	0.772	0.598	0.464	0.361	0.281	0.220	0.172	0.135	0.106	0.084	0.053	0.033	0.021	0.014	0.009	26
28	0.757	0.574	0.437	0.333	0.255	0.196	0.150	0.116	0.090	0.069	0.042	0.026	0.016	0.010	0.006	28
30	0.742	0.552	0.412	0.308	0.231	0.174	0.131	0.099	0.075	0.057	0.033	0.020	0.012	0.007	0.004	30
32	0.727	0.531	0.388	0.285	0.210	0.155	0.115	0.085	0.063	0.047	0.027	0.015	0.009	0.005	0.003	32
34	0.713	0.510	0.366	0.264	0.190	0.138	0.100	0.073	0.053	0.039	0.021	0.012	0.006	0.004	0.002	34
36	0.699	0.490	0.345	0.244	0.173	0.123	0.088	0.063	0.045	0.032	0.017	0.009	0.005	0.003	0.001	36
38	0.685	0.471	0.325	0.225	0.157	0.109	0.076	0.054	0.038	0.027	0.013	0.007	0.004	0.002	0.001	38
40	0.672	0.453	0.307	0.208	0.142	0.097	0.067	0.046	0.032	0.022	0.011	0.005	0.003	0.001	0.001	40

FUTURE VALUE OF AN ANNUITY

	1%	2%	3%	4%	5%	6%	7%	8%	9%	10%	12%	14%	16%	18%	20%	
1	1.000	1.000	1.000	1.000	1.000	1.000	1.000	1.000	1.000	1.000	1.000	1.000	1.000	1.000	1.000	1
2	2.010	2.020	2.030	2.040	2.050	2.060	2.070	2.080	2.090	2.100	2.120	2.140	2.160	2.180	2.200	2
3	3.030	3.060	3.091	3.122	3.153	3.184	3.215	3.246	3.278	3.310	3.374	3.440	3.506	3.572	3.640	3
4	4.060	4.122	4.184	4.246	4.310	4.375	4.440	4.506	4.573	4.641	4.779	4.921	5.066	5.215	5.368	4
5	5.101	5.204	5.309	5.416	5.526	5.637	5.751	5.867	5.985	6.105	6.353	6.610	6.877	7.154	7.442	5
6	6.152	6.308	6.468	6.633	6.802	6.975	7.153	7.336	7.523	7.716	8.115	8.536	8.977	9.442	9.930	6
7	7.214	7.434	7.662	7.898	8.142	8.394	8.654	8.923	9.200	9.487	10.089	10.730	11.414	12.142	12.916	7
8	8.286	8.583	8.892	9.214	9.549	9.897	10.260	10.637	11.028	11.436	12.300	13.233	14.240	15.327	16.499	8
9	9.369	9.755	10.159	10.583	11.027	11.491	11.978	12.488	13.021	13.579	14.776	16.085	17.519	19.086	20.799	9
10	10.462	10.950	11.464	12.006	12.578	13.181	13.816	14.487	15.193	15.937	17.549	19.337	21.321	23.521	25.959	10
11	11.567	12.169	12.808	13.486	14.207	14.972	15.784	16.645	17.560	18.531	20.655	23.045	25.733	28.755	32.150	11
12	12.683	13.412	14.192	15.026	15.917	16.870	17.888	18.977	20.141	21.384	24.133	27.271	30.850	34.931	39.581	12
13	13.809	14.680	15.618	16.627	17.713	18.882	20.141	21.495	22.953	24.523	28.029	32.089	36.786	42.219	48.497	13
14	14.947	15.974	17.086	18.292	19.599	21.015	22.550	24.215	26.019	27.975	32.393	37.581	43.672	50.818	59.196	14
15	16.097	17.293	18.599	20.024	21.579	23.276	25.129	27.152	29.361	31.772	37.280	43.842	51.660	60.965	72.035	15
16	17.258	18.639	20.157	21.825	23.657	25.673	27.888	30.324	33.003	35.950	42.753	50.980	60.925	72.939	87.442	16
18	19.615	21.412	23.414	25.645	28.132	30.906	33.999	37.450	41.301	45.599	55.750	68.394	84.141	103.740	128.117	18
20	22.019	24.297	26.870	29.778	33.066	36.786	40.995	45.762	51.160	57.275	72.052	91.025	115.380	146.628	186.688	20
22	24.472	27.299	30.537	34.248	38.505	43.392	49.006	55.457	62.873	71.403	92.503	120.436	157.415	206.345	271.031	22
24	26.973	30.422	34.426	39.083	44.502	50.816	58.177	66.765	76.790	88.497	118.155	158.659	213.978	289.494	392.484	24
26	29.526	33.671	38.553	44.312	51.113	59.156	68.676	79.954	93.324	109.182	150.334	208.333	290.088	405.272	567.377	26
28	32.129	37.051	42.931	49.968	58.403	68.528	80.698	95.339	112.968	134.210	190.699	272.889	392.503	566.481	819.223	28
30	34.785	40.568	47.575	56.085	66.439	79.058	94.461	113.283	136.308	164.494	241.333	356.787	530.312	790.948	1181.882	30
32	37.494	44.227	52.503	62.701	75.299	90.890	110.218	134.214	164.037	201.138	304.848	465.820	715.747	1103.496	1704.109	32
34	40.258	48.034	57.730	69.858	85.067	104.184	128.259	158.627	196.982	245.477	384.521	607.520	965.270	1538.688	2456.118	34
36	43.077	51.994	63.276	77.598	95.836	119.121	148.913	187.102	236.125	299.127	484.463	791.673	1301.027	2144.649	3539.009	36
38	45.953	56.115	69.159	85.970	107.710	135.904	172.561	220.316	282.630	364.043	609.831	1030.998	1752.822	2988.389	5098.373	38
40	48.886	60.402	75.401	95.026	120.800	154.762	199.635	259.057	337.882	442.593	767.091	1342.025	2360.757	4163.213	7343.858	40

FUTURE VALUE OF $1

	1%	2%	3%	4%	5%	6%	7%	8%	9%	10%	12%	14%	16%	18%	20%	
1	1.010	1.020	1.030	1.040	1.050	1.060	1.070	1.080	1.090	1.100	1.120	1.140	1.160	1.180	1.200	1
2	1.020	1.040	1.061	1.082	1.103	1.124	1.145	1.166	1.188	1.210	1.254	1.300	1.346	1.392	1.440	2
3	1.030	1.061	1.093	1.125	1.158	1.191	1.225	1.260	1.295	1.331	1.405	1.482	1.561	1.643	1.728	3
4	1.041	1.082	1.126	1.170	1.216	1.262	1.311	1.360	1.412	1.464	1.574	1.689	1.811	1.939	2.074	4
5	1.051	1.104	1.159	1.217	1.276	1.338	1.403	1.469	1.539	1.611	1.762	1.925	2.100	2.288	2.488	5
6	1.062	1.126	1.194	1.265	1.340	1.419	1.501	1.587	1.677	1.772	1.974	2.195	2.436	2.700	2.986	6
7	1.072	1.149	1.230	1.316	1.407	1.504	1.606	1.714	1.828	1.949	2.211	2.502	2.826	3.185	3.583	7
8	1.083	1.172	1.267	1.369	1.477	1.594	1.718	1.851	1.993	2.144	2.476	2.853	3.278	3.759	4.300	8
9	1.094	1.195	1.305	1.423	1.551	1.689	1.838	1.999	2.172	2.358	2.773	3.252	3.803	4.435	5.160	9
10	1.105	1.219	1.344	1.480	1.629	1.791	1.967	2.159	2.367	2.594	3.106	3.707	4.411	5.234	6.192	10
11	1.116	1.243	1.384	1.539	1.710	1.898	2.105	2.332	2.580	2.853	3.479	4.226	5.117	6.176	7.430	11
12	1.127	1.268	1.426	1.601	1.796	2.012	2.252	2.518	2.813	3.138	3.896	4.818	5.936	7.288	8.916	12
13	1.138	1.294	1.469	1.665	1.886	2.133	2.410	2.720	3.066	3.452	4.363	5.492	6.886	8.599	10.699	13
14	1.149	1.319	1.513	1.732	1.980	2.261	2.579	2.937	3.342	3.797	4.887	6.261	7.988	10.147	12.839	14
15	1.161	1.346	1.558	1.801	2.079	2.397	2.759	3.172	3.642	4.177	5.474	7.138	9.266	11.974	15.407	15
16	1.173	1.373	1.605	1.873	2.183	2.540	2.952	3.426	3.970	4.595	6.130	8.137	10.748	14.129	18.488	16
18	1.196	1.428	1.702	2.026	2.407	2.854	3.380	3.996	4.717	5.560	7.690	10.575	14.463	19.673	26.623	18
20	1.220	1.486	1.806	2.191	2.653	3.207	3.870	4.661	5.604	6.727	9.646	13.743	19.461	27.393	38.338	20
22	1.245	1.546	1.916	2.370	2.925	3.604	4.430	5.437	6.659	8.140	12.100	17.861	26.186	38.142	55.206	22
24	1.270	1.608	2.033	2.563	3.225	4.049	5.072	6.341	7.911	9.850	15.179	23.212	35.236	53.109	79.497	24
26	1.295	1.673	2.157	2.772	3.556	4.549	5.807	7.396	9.399	11.918	19.040	30.167	47.414	73.949	114.475	26
28	1.321	1.741	2.288	2.999	3.920	5.112	6.649	8.627	11.167	14.421	23.884	39.204	63.800	102.967	164.845	28
30	1.348	1.811	2.427	3.243	4.322	5.743	7.612	10.063	13.268	17.449	29.960	50.950	85.850	143.371	237.376	30
32	1.375	1.885	2.575	3.508	4.765	6.453	8.715	11.737	15.763	21.114	37.582	66.215	115.520	199.629	341.822	32
34	1.403	1.961	2.732	3.794	5.253	7.251	9.978	13.690	18.728	25.548	47.143	86.053	155.443	277.964	492.224	34
36	1.431	2.040	2.898	4.104	5.792	8.147	11.424	15.968	22.251	30.913	59.136	111.834	209.164	387.037	708.802	36
38	1.460	2.122	3.075	4.439	6.385	9.154	13.079	18.625	26.437	37.404	74.180	145.340	281.452	538.910	1020.675	38
40	1.489	2.208	3.262	4.801	7.040	10.286	14.974	21.725	31.409	45.259	93.051	188.884	378.721	750.378	1469.772	40

APPENDIX B
SAMPLE FINANCIAL STATEMENTS

We have annotated these audited financial statements to show how the various elements interrelate. For instance, (a) is the year-end balance of cash and equivalents; this annotation is found on both the balance sheet and the statement of cash flows.

FORD MOTOR COMPANY AND SUBSIDIARIES
CONSOLIDATED INCOME STATEMENT
(in millions, except per share amounts)

	For the years ended December 31,		
	2012	2011	2010
Revenues			
Automotive	$126,567	$128,168	$119,280
Financial Services	7,685	8,096	9,674
Total revenues	134,252	136,264	128,954
Costs and expenses			
Automotive cost of sales	112,578	113,345	104,451
Selling, administrative and other expenses	12,182	11,578	11,909
Financial Services interest expense	3,115	3,614	4,345
Financial Services provision for credit and insurance losses	86	(33)	(216)
Total costs and expenses	127,961	128,504	120,489
Automotive interest expense	713	817	1,807
Automotive interest income and other non-operating income/(expense), net	1,185	825	(362)
Financial Services other income/(loss), net	369	413	315
Equity in net income/(loss) of affiliated companies	588	500	538
Income before income taxes	7,720	8,681	7,149
Provision for/(Benefit from) income taxes	2,056	(11,541)	592
Net income	5,664 (a)	20,222 (b)	6,557 (c)
Less: Income/(Loss) attributable to noncontrolling interests	(1)	9	(4)
Net income/(loss) attributable to Ford Motor Company	$ 5,665 (v)	$ 20,213	$ 6,561

AMOUNTS PER SHARE ATTRIBUTABLE TO FORD MOTOR COMPANY COMMON AND CLASS B STOCK

Basic income	$ 1.48	$ 5.33	$ 1.90
Diluted income	$ 1.42	$ 4.94	$ 1.66
Cash dividends declared	$ 0.15	$ 0.05	$ —

CONSOLIDATED STATEMENT OF COMPREHENSIVE INCOME
(in millions)

	For the years ended December 31,		
	2012	2011	2010
Net income	$ 5,664	$ 20,222	$ 6,557
Other comprehensive income/(loss), net of tax			
Foreign currency translation	142	(720)	(2,234)
Derivative instruments	6	(152)	(24)
Pension and other postretirement benefits	(4,268)	(3,553)	(1,190)
Net holding gain/(loss)	–	2	(2)
Total other comprehensive income/(loss), net of tax	(4,120) (d)	(4,423) (e)	(3,450) (f)
Comprehensive income	1,544	15,799	3,107
Less: Comprehensive income/(loss) attributable to noncontrolling interests	(1)	7	(5)
Comprehensive income attributable to Ford Motor Company	$ 1,545	$ 15,792	$ 3,112

FORD MOTOR COMPANY AND SUBSIDIARIES
CONSOLIDATED BALANCE SHEET
(in millions)

	December 31, 2012		December 31, 2011	
ASSETS				
Cash and cash equivalents	$ 15,659	(g)	$ 17,148	(h)
Marketable securities	20,284		18,618	
Finance receivables, net	71,510		69,976	
Other receivables, net	10,828		8,565	
Net investment in operating leases	16,451		12,838	
Inventories	7,362		5,901	
Equity in net assets of affiliated companies	3,246		2,936	
Net property	24,942		22,371	
Deferred income taxes	15,185		15,125	
Net intangible assets	87		100	
Other assets	5,000		4,770	
Total assets	$190,554		$178,348	
LIABILITIES				
Payables	$ 19,308		$ 17,724	
Accrued liabilities and deferred revenue	49,407		45,369	
Debt	105,058		99,488	
Deferred income taxes	470		696	
Total liabilities	$174,243		$163,277	
Redeemable noncontrolling interest	322		—	
EQUITY				
Capital stock				
Common Stock, par value $0.01 per share (3,745 million shares issued)	$ 39	(i)	$ 37	(j)
Class B Stock, par value $0.01 per share (71 million shares issued)	1	(i)	1	(j)
Capital in excess of par value of stock	20,976	(k)	20,905	(l)
Retained earnings	18,077	(m)	12,985	(n)
Accumulated other comprehensive income/(loss)	(22,854)	(o)	(18,734)	(p)
Treasury stock	(292)	(q)	(166)	(r)
Total equity attributable to Ford Motor Company	$ 15,947	(s)	$ 15,028	(t)
Equity attributable to noncontrolling interests	42		43	
Total equity	$ 15,989		$ 15,071	
Total liabilities and equity	$190,554		$178,348	

FORD MOTOR COMPANY AND SUBSIDIARIES
CONDENSED SECTOR STATEMENT OF CASH FLOWS
(in millions)

	For the year ended December 31, 2012		
	Automotive	Financial Services	Total
Cash flows from operating activities of continuing operations			
Net cash provided by/(used in) operating activities (Notes)	$ 6,266	$ 3,957	$ 10,223 (u)
Cash flows from investing activities of continuing operations			
Capital expenditures	(5,459)	(29)	(5,488)
Acquisitions of retail and other finance receivables and operating leases	–	(39,151)	(39,151)
Collections of retail and other finance receivables and operating leases	–	32,333	32,333
Net collections/(acquisitions) of wholesale receivables	–	(1,235)	(1,235)
Purchases of securities	(73,100)	(22,035)	(95,135)
Sales and maturities of securities	70,202	23,748	93,950
Cash change due to initial consolidation of businesses	191	–	191
Proceeds from sale of business	54	12	66
Settlements of derivatives	(788)	51	(737)
Investing activity (to)/from Financial Services	925	–	925
Elimination of cash balances upon disposition of discontinued/held-for-sale operations	–	–	–
Other	(49)	(12)	(61)
Net cash provided by/(used in) investing activities	(8,024)	(6,318)	(14,342)
Cash flows from financing activities of continuing operations			
Cash dividends	(763)	–	(763)
Purchases of Common Stock	(125)	–	(125)
Changes in short-term debt	154	1,054	1,208
Proceeds from issuance of other debt	1,553	30,883	32,436
Principal payments on other debt	(810)	(28,601)	(29,411)
Financing activity to/(from) Automotive	–	(925)	(925)
Other	31	128	159
Net cash provided by/(used in) financing activities	40	2,539	2,579
Effect of exchange rate changes on cash and cash equivalents	–	51	51
Net increase/(decrease) in cash and cash equivalents	$ (1,718)	$ 229	$ (1,489)
Cash and cash equivalents at January 1	$ 7,965	$ 9,183	$ 17,148 (h)
Net increase/(decrease) in cash and cash equivalents	(1,718)	229	(1,489)
Cash and cash equivalents at December 31	$ 6,247	$ 9,412	$ 15,659 (g)

FORD MOTOR COMPANY AND SUBSIDIARIES
NOTES TO THE FINANCIAL STATEMENTS

The reconciliation of *Net income attributable to Ford Motor Company* to *Net cash provided by/(used in) operating activities* for the year ended December 31 was as follows (in millions):

	2012		
	Automotive	Financial Services	Total
Net income attributable to Ford Motor Company	$ 4,466	$ 1,199	$ 5,665 (v)
Depreciation and special tools amortization	3,655	2,524	6,179
Other amortization	43	(1,018)	(975)
Provision for credit and insurance losses	6	86	92
Net (gain)/loss on extinguishment of debt	–	14	14
Net (gain)/loss on investment securities	(89)	(16)	(105)
Dividends in excess of equity investment earnings	20	–	20
Foreign currency adjustments	(121)	5	(116)
Net (gain)/loss on sale of businesses	183	4	187
Gain on changes in investments in affiliates	(780)	–	(780)
Stock compensation	134	6	140
Cash changes in operating assets and liabilities were as follows:			
Provision for deferred income taxes	1,444	545	1,989
Decrease/(increase) in intersector receivables/payables	899	(899)	–
Decrease/(increase) in accounts receivable and other assets	(2,335)	713	(1,622)
Decrease/(increase) in inventory	(1,401)	–	(1,401)
Increase/(decrease) in accounts payable and accrued and other liabilities	(520)	1,005	485
Other	662	(211)	451
Net cash provided by/(used in) operating activities	$ 6,266	$ 3,957	$ 10,223 (u)

FORD MOTOR COMPANY AND SUBSIDIARIES
CONSOLIDATED STATEMENT OF EQUITY
(in millions)

	Equity/(Deficit) Attributable to Ford Motor Company						Equity/ (Deficit) Attributable to Non-controlling Interests	Total Equity/ (Deficit)
	Capital Stock	Cap. in Excess of Par Value of Stock	Retained Earnings/ (Accumulated Deficit)	Accumulated Other Comprehensive Income/(Loss)	Treasury Stock	Total		
Balance at December 31, 2009	$34	$16,786	$(13,599)	$(10,864)	$(177)	$ (7,820)	$38	$ (7,782)
Net income	–	–	6,561	–	–	6,561	(4)	6,557 (c)
Other comprehensive income/(loss), net of tax	–	–	–	(3,449)	–	(3,449)	(1)	(3,450) (f)
Common stock issued (including share-based compensation impacts)	4	4,017	–	–	–	4,021	–	4,021
Treasury stock/other	–	–	–	–	14	14	–	14
Cash dividends declared	–	–	–	–	–	–	(2)	(2)
Balance at December 31, 2010	$38	$20,803	$ (7,038)	$(14,313)	$(163)	$ (673)	$31	$ (642)
Balance at December 31, 2010	$38	$20,803	$ (7,038)	$(14,313)	$(163)	$ (673)	$31	$ (642)
Net income	–	–	20,213	–	–	20,213	4	20,222 (b)
Other comprehensive income/(loss), net of tax	–	–	–	(4,421)	–	(4,421)	(2)	(4,423) (e)
Common stock issued (including share-based compensation impacts)	–	102	–	–	–	102	–	102
Treasury stock/other	–	–	–	–	(3)	(3)	5	2
Cash dividends declared	–	–	(190)	–	–	(190)	–	(190)
Balance at December 31, 2011	$38 (j)	$20,905 (l)	$ 12,985 (n)	$(18,734) (p)	$(166) (r)	$15,028 (t)	$43	$15,071
Balance at December 31, 2011	$38	$20,905	$ 12,985	$(18,734)	$(166)	$15,028	$ 43	$15,071
Net income	–	–	5,665	–	–	5,665	(1)	5,664 (a)
Other compensation income/(loss), net of tax	–	–	–	(4,120)	–	(4,120)	–	(4,120) (d)
Common stock issued (including share-based compensation impacts)	2	71	–	–	–	73	–	73
Treasury stock/other	–	–	–	–	(126)	(126)	–	(126)
Cash dividends declared	–	–	(573)	–	–	(573)	–	(573)
Balance at December 31, 2012	$40 (i)	$20,976 (k)	$ 18,077 (m)	$(22,854) (o)	$(292) (q)	$15,947 (s)	$42	$15,989

APPENDIX C
GLOSSARY OF ACCOUNTING TERMS
U.S. TO BRITISH VS. BRITISH TO U.S.

U.S. TO BRITISH

U.S.	British
Accounts payable	Trade creditors
Accounts receivable	Trade debtors
Accrual	Provision (for liability or charge)
Accumulated depreciation	Aggregate depreciation
Additional paid-in capital	Share premium account
Allowance	Provision (for diminution in value)
Allowance for doubtful accounts	Provision for bad debt
Annual Stockholders' Meeting	Annual General Meeting
Authorized capital stock	Authorized share capital
Bellweather stock	Barometer stock
Bylaws	Articles of Association
Bond	Loan finance
Capital lease	Finance lease
Certificate of Incorporation	Memorandum of Association
Checking account	Current account
Common stock	Ordinary shares
Consumer price index	Retail price index
Corporation	Company
Cost of goods sold	Cost of sales
Credit Memorandum	Credit note
Equity	Reserves
Equity interest	Ownership interest
Financial statements	Accounts
Income statement	Profit and loss account
Income taxes	Taxation
Inventories	Stocks
Investment bank	Merchant bank
Labor union	Trade union
Land	Freehold
Lease with bargain purchase option	Hire purchase contract
Liabilities	Creditors
Listed company	Quoted company
Long-term investments	Fixed asset investments
Long-term lease	Long leasehold
Merchandise trade	Visible trade
Mutual funds	Unit trusts
Net income	Net profit
Note payable	Bill payable
Note receivable	Bill receivable
Paid-in surplus	Share premium
Par value	Nominal value
Pooling of interests method	Merger accounting
Preferred stock	Preference share
Prime rate	Base rate
Property, plant, and equipment	Tangible fixed assets
Provision for bad debts	Charge
Purchase method	Acquisition accounting
Purchase on account	Purchase on credit
Retained earnings	Profit and loss account
Real estate	Property
Revenue	Income
Reversal of accrual	Release of provision
Sales on account	Sales on credit
Sales/revenue	Turnover
Savings and loan association	Building society
Shareholders' equity	Shareholders' funds
Stock	Inventory
Stockholder	Shareholder
Stock dividend	Bonus share
Stockholders' equity	Share capital and reserves or Shareholders' funds
Taxable income	Taxable profit
Treasury bonds	Gilt-edged stock (gilts)

BRITISH TO U.S.

British	U.S.
Accounts	Financial statements
Acquisition accounting	Purchase method
Aggregate depreciation	Accumulated depreciation
Annual General Meeting	Annual Stockholders' Meeting
Articles of Association	Bylaws
Authorized share capital	Authorized capital stock
Barometer stock	Bellweather stock
Base rate	Prime rate
Bill payable	Note payable
Bill receivable	Note receivable
Bonus share	Stock dividend
Building society	Savings and loan association
Charge	Provision for bad debts
Company	Corporation
Cost of sales	Cost of goods sold
Credit note	Credit Memorandum
Creditors	Liabilities
Current account	Checking account
Finance lease	Capital lease
Fixed asset investments	Long-term investments
Freehold	Land
Gilt-edged stock (gilts)	Treasury bonds
Hire purchase contract	Lease with bargain purchase option
Income	Revenue
Inventory	Stock
Loan finance	Bond
Long leasehold	Long-term lease
Memorandum of Association	Certificate of Incorporation
Merchant bank	Investment bank
Merger accounting	Pooling of interests method
Net profit	Net income
Nominal value	Par value
Ordinary shares	Common stock
Ownership interest	Equity interest
Preference share	Preferred stock
Profit and loss account	Income statement
Profit and loss account	Retained earnings
Property	Real estate
Provision for bad debt	Allowance for doubtful accounts
Provision (for diminution in value)	Allowance
Provision (for liability or charge)	Accrual
Purchase on credit	Purchase on account
Quoted company	Listed company
Release of provision	Reversal of accrual
Reserves	Equity
Retail price index	Consumer price index
Sales on credit	Sales on account
Share capital and reserves or Shareholders' funds	Stockholders' equity
Shareholder	Stockholder
Shareholders' funds	Shareholders' equity
Share premium	Paid-in surplus
Share premium account	Additional paid-in capital
Stocks	Inventories
Tangible fixed assets	Property, plant, and equipment
Taxable profit	Taxable income
Taxation	Income taxes
Trade creditors	Accounts payable
Trade debtors	Accounts receivable
Trade union	Labor union
Turnover	Sales/revenue
Unit trusts	Mutual funds
Visible trade	Merchandise trade

APPENDIX D
ICMA CONTENT SPECIFICATION
OUTLINES AND CROSS-REFERENCES

The following pages consist of a reprint of the ICMA's Content Specification Outlines (CSOs) and related information for Part 1, effective January 1, 2015. In addition, we have provided cross-references to the Gleim CMA study units. Please use these CSOs as reference material only. The ICMA's CSOs have been carefully analyzed and have been incorporated into Study Units 1 through 13 to provide systematic and rational coverage of exam topics.

We believe we provide comprehensive coverage of the subject matter tested on the CMA exam. If, after taking the exam, you feel that certain topics, concepts, etc., tested were not covered or were inadequately covered, please go to www.gleim.com/feedbackCMA1. We do not want information about CMA questions, only information/feedback about our CMA Review System's coverage.

Effective January 1, 2015

Content Specification Outlines
Certified Management Accountant (CMA) Examinations

The content specification outlines presented on pages 475 through 476 represent the body of knowledge that will be covered on the CMA examinations. The outlines may be changed in the future when new subject matter becomes part of the common body of knowledge.

Candidates for the CMA designation are required to take and pass Parts 1 and 2.

Candidates are responsible for being informed on the most recent developments in the areas covered in the outlines. This includes understanding of public pronouncements issued by accounting organizations as well as being up-to-date on recent developments reported in current accounting, financial and business periodicals.

The content specification outlines serve several purposes. The outlines are intended to:

- Establish the foundation from which each examination will be developed.
- Provide a basis for consistent coverage on each examination.
- Communicate to interested parties more detail as to the content of each examination part.
- Assist candidates in their preparation for each examination.
- Provide information to those who offer courses designed to aid candidates in preparing for the examinations.

Important additional information about the content specification outlines and the examinations is listed below and on the following page.

1. The coverage percentage given for each major topic within each examination part represents the relative weight given to that topic in an examination part. The number of questions presented in each major topic area approximates this percentage.

2. Each examination will sample from the subject areas contained within each major topic area to meet the relative weight specifications. No relative weights have been assigned to the subject areas within each major topic. No inference should be made from the order in which the subject areas are listed or from the number of subject areas as to the relative weight or importance of any of the subjects.

3. Each major topic within each examination part has been assigned a coverage level designating the depth and breadth of topic coverage, ranging from an introductory knowledge of a subject area (Level A) to a thorough understanding of and ability to apply the essentials of a subject area (Level C). Detailed explanations of the coverage levels and the skills expected of candidates are presented on the following page.

4. The topics for Parts 1 and 2 have been selected to minimize the overlapping of subject areas among the examination parts. The topics within an examination part and the subject areas within topics may be combined in individual questions.

5. With regard to U.S. Federal income taxation issues, candidates will be expected to understand the impact of income taxes when reporting and analyzing financial results. In addition, the tax code provisions that impact decisions (e.g., depreciation, interest, etc.) will be tested.

6. Candidates for the CMA designation are assumed to have knowledge of the following: preparation of financial statements, business economics, time-value of money concepts, statistics and probability.

7. Parts 1 and 2 are four-hour exams, and each contains 100 multiple-choice questions and 2 essay questions. Candidates will have three hours to complete the multiple-choice questions and one hour to complete the essay section. A small number of the multiple-choice questions on each exam are being validated for future use and will not count in the final score.

8. For the essay questions, both written and quantitative responses will be required. Candidates will be expected to present written answers that are responsive to the question asked, presented in a logical manner, and demonstrate an appropriate understanding of the subject matter. It should be noted that candidates are expected to have working knowledge in the use of word processing and electronic spreadsheets.

In order to more clearly define the topical knowledge required by a candidate, varying levels of coverage for the treatment of major topics of the content specification outlines have been identified and defined. The cognitive skills that a successful candidate should possess and that should be tested on the examinations can be defined as follows:

Knowledge: Ability to remember previously learned material such as specific facts, criteria, techniques, principles, and procedures (i.e., identify, define, list).

Comprehension: Ability to grasp and interpret the meaning of material (i.e., classify, explain, distinguish between).

Application: Ability to use learned material in new and concrete situations (i.e., demonstrate, predict, solve, modify, relate).

Analysis: Ability to break down material into its component parts so that its organizational structure can be understood; ability to recognize causal relationships, discriminate between behaviors, and identify elements that are relevant to the validation of a judgment (i.e., differentiate, estimate, order).

Synthesis: Ability to put parts together to form a new whole or proposed set of operations; ability to relate ideas and formulate hypotheses (i.e., combine, formulate, revise).

Evaluation: Ability to judge the value of material for a given purpose on the basis of consistency, logical accuracy, and comparison to standards; ability to appraise judgments involved in the selection of a course of action (i.e., criticize, justify, conclude).

The three levels of coverage can be defined as follows:

Level A: Requiring the skill levels of knowledge and comprehension.

Level B: Requiring the skill levels of knowledge, comprehension, application, and analysis.

Level C: Requiring all six skill levels, knowledge, comprehension, application, analysis, synthesis, and evaluation.

The levels of coverage as they apply to each of the major topics of the Content Specification Outlines are shown on the following pages with each topic listing. The levels represent the manner in which topic areas are to be treated and represent ceilings, i.e., a topic area designated as Level C may contain requirements at the "A," "B," or "C" level, but a topic designated as Level B will not contain requirements at the "C" level.

CMA Content Specification Overview

Part 1 *Financial Reporting, Planning, Performance, and Control*
(4 hours – 100 questions and 2 essay questions)

Topic	Percentage	Level
External Financial Reporting Decisions	15%	Level C
Planning, Budgeting and Forecasting	30%	Level C
Performance Management	20%	Level C
Cost Management	20%	Level C
Internal Controls	15%	Level C

Candidates for the CMA designation are assumed to have knowledge of the following: preparation of financial statements, business economics, time-value of money concepts, statistics and probability. Questions in both parts of the CMA exam will assume that the successful candidate can effectively integrate and synthesize this knowledge with the specific topics covered in the content specification outline.

On the following pages, we have reproduced verbatim the ICMA's Content Specification Outlines (CSOs) for Part 1. We also have provided cross-references to the study units and subunits in this book that correspond to the CSOs' coverage. If one entry appears above a list, it applies to all items in that list.

Appendix D: ICMA Content Specification Outlines and Cross-References

Part 1 – Financial Reporting, Planning, Performance, and Control

A. **External Financial Reporting Decisions (15% - Levels A, B, and C)**

1. *Financial statements*
    a. Balance sheet (1.2)
    b. Income statement (1.3)
    c. Statement of changes in equity (1.4)
    d. Statement of cash flows (1.5)

2. *Recognition, measurement, valuation, and disclosure*
    a. Asset valuation (2.1-2.5, 3.1-3.4)
    b. Valuation of liabilities (2.8, 3.5-3.6)
    c. Equity transactions (2.7)
    d. Revenue recognition (1.6-1.7)
    e. Income measurement (1.6-1.7)
    f. Major differences between U.S. GAAP and IFRS (SUs 1-3)

B. **Planning, Budgeting and Forecasting (30% - Levels A, B, and C)**

1. *Strategic Planning*
    a. Analysis of external and internal factors affecting strategy (SU 8)
    b. Long-term mission and goals (SU 8)
    c. Alignment of tactics with long-term strategic goals (SU 8)
    d. Strategic planning models and analytical techniques (8.1-8.4)
    e. Characteristics of successful strategic planning process (8.5-8.7)

2. *Budgeting concepts*
    a. Operations and performance goals (9.1)
    b. Characteristics of a successful budget process (9.1)
    c. Resource allocation (9.1)
    d. Other budgeting concepts (9.2)

3. *Forecasting techniques*
    a. Regression analysis (8.1)
    b. Learning curve analysis (8.2)
    c. Expected value (8.3)

4. *Budgeting methodologies*
    a. Annual business plans (master budgets) (9.3)
    b. Project budgeting (9.4)
    c. Activity-based budgeting (9.4)
    d. Zero-based budgeting (9.4)
    e. Continuous (rolling) budgets (9.4)
    f. Flexible budgeting (10.2)

5. *Annual profit plan and supporting schedules*
    a. Operational budgets (9.5-9.6)
    b. Financial budgets (9.7-9.8)
    c. Capital budgets (9.3)

6. *Top-level planning and analysis*
    a. Pro forma income (9.9)
    b. Financial statement projections (9.9)
    c. Cash flow projections (9.9)

C. **Performance Management (20% - Levels A, B, and C)**

1. *Cost and variance measures*
    a. Comparison of actual to planned results (10.1)
    b. Use of flexible budgets to analyze performance (10.2)
    c. Management by exception (10.1)
    d. Use of standard cost systems (10.2)
    e. Analysis of variation from standard cost expectations (10.3-10.8)

2. *Responsibility centers and reporting segments*
    a. Types of responsibility centers (11.1)
    b. Transfer pricing models (11.6)
    c. Reporting of organizational segments (11.2-11.3)

3. *Performance measures*
    a. Product profitability analysis (11.2)
    b. Business unit profitability analysis (11.2)
    c. Customer profitability analysis (11.2)
    d. Return on investment (11.3-11.4)
    e. Residual income (11.3-11.4)
    f. Investment base issues (11.3-11.4)
    g. Key performance indicators (KPIs) (8.6)
    h. Balanced scorecard (8.6)

D. Cost Management (20% - Levels A, B, and C)

   1. *Measurement concepts*
       a. Cost behavior and cost objects (4.1-4.3)
       b. Actual and normal costs (4.4, 6.4-6.5)
       c. Standard costs (4.4, 6.4-6.5)
       d. Absorption (full) costing (6.1-6.2)
       e. Variable (direct) costing (6.1-6.2)
       f. Joint and by-product costing (6.3)

   2. *Costing systems*
       a. Job order costing (5.1)
       b. Process costing (5.3)
       c. Activity-based costing (5.2)
       d. Life-cycle costing (5.4)

   3. *Overhead costs*
       a. Fixed and variable overhead expenses (6.4-6.5)
       b. Plant-wide versus departmental overhead (6.4)
       c. Determination of allocation base (6.4-6.5)
       d. Allocation of service department costs (6.6-6.7)

   4. *Supply Chain Management*
       a. Lean manufacturing (7.1)
       b. Enterprise resource planning (ERP) (7.2)
       c. Theory of constraints and throughput costing (7.3)
       d. Capacity management and analysis (7.4)

   5. *Business process improvement*
       a. Value chain analysis (7.5)
       b. Value-added concepts (7.5)
       c. Process analysis (7.6)
       d. Activity-based management (5.3, 7.6)
       e. Continuous improvement concepts (5.3, 7.6)
       f. Best practice analysis (7.6)
       g. Cost of quality analysis (7.6)
       h. Efficient accounting processes (7.6)

E. Internal Controls (15% - Levels A, B, and C)

   1. *Governance, risk, and compliance*
       a. Internal control structure and management philosophy (12.2)
       b. Internal control policies for safeguarding and assurance (13.1)
       c. Internal control risk (12.2, 13.1)
       d. Corporate governance (12.1)
       e. External audit requirements (12.1)

   2. *Internal auditing*
       a. Responsibility and authority of the internal audit function (12.3)
       b. Types of audits conducted by internal auditors (12.3)

   3. *System controls and security measures*
       a. General accounting system controls (13.2)
       b. Application and transaction controls (13.2)
       c. Network controls (13.3)
       d. Backup controls (13.3)
       e. Business continuity planning (13.3)

APPENDIX E
ICMA SUGGESTED READING LIST
(As printed in the ICMA's 2016 CMA Handbook)

The following ICMA suggested reading list is reproduced to give you an overview of the scope of Part 1. You will not have time to study these texts. Our CMA Review System is complete and thorough and is designed to maximize your study time. Candidates are expected to stay up-to-date by reading articles from journals, newspapers, and professional publications.

Part 1 – Financial Reporting, Planning, Performance, and Control

External Financial Reporting Decisions

Kieso, Donald E., Weygandt, Jerry J., and Warfield, Terry D., *Intermediate Accounting*, 15th edition, Wiley & Sons, Hoboken, NJ, 2011.

Nikolai, Loren A., Bazley, John D., and Jones, Jefferson P., *Intermediate Accounting*, 11th edition, South-Western Cengage Learning, Mason, OH, 2010.

Hoyle, Joe B., Schaefer, Thomas F., and Doupnik, Timothy S., *Advanced Accounting*, 11th edition, McGraw Hill, New York, NY, 2013.

Planning, Budgeting and Forecasting

Wheelen, Thomas L., et. al., *Strategic Management and Business Policy: Globalization, Innovation and Sustainability*, 14th edition, Prentice Hall, Upper Saddle River, NJ, 2014.

Blocher, Edward J., Stout, David E., Juras, Paul E., and Cokins, Gary, *Cost Management: A Strategic Emphasis*, 6th edition, McGraw Hill, New York, NY, 2013.

Horngren, Charles T., Datar, Srikant, and Rajan, Madhav, *Cost Accounting: A Managerial Emphasis*, 14th edition, Prentice-Hall, Upper Saddle River, NJ, 2012.

Anderson, David R., Sweeney, Dennis J., Williams, Thomas A., Camm, Jeff, and Martin, R. Kipp, *Quantitative Methods for Business, 11th Edition*, Mason, Ohio: South Western, 2010.

Performance Management

Blocher, Edward J., Stout, David E., Juras, Paul E., and Cokins, Gary, *Cost Management: A Strategic Emphasis*, 6th edition, McGraw Hill, New York, NY, 2013.

Horngren, Charles T., Datar, Srikant, and Rajan, Madhav, *Cost Accounting: A Managerial Emphasis*, 14th edition, Prentice-Hall, Upper Saddle River, NJ, 2012.

Cost Management

Blocher, Edward J., Stout, David E., Juras, Paul E., and Cokins, Gary, *Cost Management: A Strategic Emphasis*, 6th edition, McGraw Hill, New York, NY, 2013.

Horngren, Charles T., Datar, Srikant, and Rajan, Madhav, *Cost Accounting: A Managerial Emphasis*, 14th edition, Prentice-Hall, Upper Saddle River, NJ, 2012.

Internal Controls

Simkin, Mark G., Rose, Jacob M., Norman, Carolyn S., *Core Concepts of Accounting Information Systems*, 12th edition, John Wiley & Sons, Hoboken, NJ, 2012.

Bodnar, George H., and Hopwood, William S., *Accounting Information Systems*, 10th edition, Prentice-Hall, Upper Saddle River, NJ, 2010.

Sawyer's Guide for Internal Auditors, 6th edition, The Institute of Internal Auditors Research Foundation (IIARF), Altamonte Springs, FL, 2012.

Candidates Love Gleim CMA Review

See what our candidates are saying about what makes Gleim CMA the #1 CMA Prep Course.

" I liked the way Gleim's Personal Counselors guided and motivated me all the time. I also liked the variety of questions with detailed answers to help you understand the topic. Gleim Review system helped me to understand the topics, read big questions quickly, and answer them in a short time. I would definitely recommend Gleim.

—Murtaza Pitolwala, Sultanate of Oman

" The Gleim Review System offers bite size materials that allowed me to take advantage of my limited time and helped me to focus. The questions are very similar to the exam. It helped me to familiarize myself with the content and the style of the exam. A must have product that you will never regret!

—Alan Li, CMA

" Not only did the Gleim Review System prepare me with the material to pass on the first attempt, it also made me feel comfortable going into the exam, as I knew exactly what to expect. Gleim worked well for me because of the variety of mediums through which one can choose to study. For me, I really grasped the concepts through the professor-led instructional videos. My personal counselor assisted and cheered me on along the whole way as well, which is a neat feature that I was thankful to have.

—Brandi Dominique, CMA

INDEX

Abnormal spoilage
   Definition of. 125
   Job-order costing. 144
   Process costing. 160
Absorption (full) costing. 126, 179
Accounting equation. 12
Accounts receivable. 45
Accrual basis. 11
Activity
   Analysis. 146, 232
   -Based
      Budgeting. 297
      Costing (ABC). 128, 144
      Management (ABM). 149, 231
      Systems. 146
   Drivers. 148
Actual costing. 127
After-purchase costs. 161
AICPA audit risk model. 408
Allocation base. 190
Allowance for uncollectible accounts. 46
Amortization of
   Discount. 101
   Premium. 101
Analysis
   Best practice. 235
   PEST. 266
   SWOT. 259, 265
Annual
   Interest expense. 101
   Profit plan. 293
Area office profitability analysis. 378
Assumptions of planning. 271
Asymmetric encryption. 450
Audit
   Compliance. 421
   Operational. 421
   Trail. 447
Auditing Standard
   2. 405
   5. . . . . 405, 413
Authentication. 445
Authorization. 446
Avoidable costs. 123

Back doors. 444
Backlash effect. 230
Backup. 451
Backward (upstream) integration. 261
Bad debt expense. 46
Balance sheet. 12
Balanced scorecard. 235, 265
Bargaining power. 261
Barriers, entry. 261
Batch-level activities. 146
Benchmarking. 234
Benefit received. 382
Best practice analysis. 235
Bill of materials (BOM). 218
Board of directors. 288, 409

Bond
   Discount. 101
   Effective-interest. 101
   Premium. 101
Bonds. 100
   Carrying amount. 101
   Issuance. 100
   Sold at
      Discount. 100
      Premium. 100
Boston Consulting Group (BCG). 263
Bottleneck. 221, 231
Brand identity. 261
Brute-force attack. 449
Budget. 285, 293
   Breakeven point. 304
   Capital. 306
   Cash
      Example of. 308
      Order of preparation. 295
      Purpose of. 306
   Committee. 288
   Continuous (rolling). 299
   Contribution margin. 304
   Controllability. 291
   Cost of goods sold, example of. 303
   Cycle. 317
   Direct
      Labor, example of. 301
      Materials, example of. 301
   Ending finished goods inventory. 303
   Expense, order of preparation. 295
   Financial. 294, 306
   Fixed overhead, example of. 303
   Gross margin. 304
   Manual. 290
   Master (comprehensive). 293
   Nonmanufacturing, example of. 305
   Operating. 293, 300
   Participation. 288
   Planning calendar. 290
   Production
      Example of. 300
      Order of preparation. 294
   Project. 296
   Purchases, order of preparation. 295
   Revisions. 291
   Sales
      Example of. 300
      Order of preparation. 294
   Variable overhead, example of. 302
Budgetary slack. 288
Budgeting. 285
   Activity-based. 297
   Incremental. 298
   Process. 291
   Zero-based (ZBB). 298
Build strategy. 264
Bullwhip effect. 230
Business
   Continuity. 451
   Process reengineering (BPR). 233

Buyer bargaining power............... 261
By-products....................... 125, 188

Capacity
   Expansion...................... 226
   Factors, transfer pricing........... 385
   Normal..................... 126, 191
   Planning....................... 225
   Practical................... 126, 191
   Theoretical (ideal)............ 126, 191
Capital expenditures................ 295
Carrying costs..................... 126
Cash
   Budget..................... 306, 307
      Order of preparation.......... 295
   Collection schedule............... 306
   Cows.......................... 264
   Disbursements schedule........... 307
   Flow............................ 23
Cellular organization................ 217
Certificate authority................ 450
CMA exam.......................... 1
Coefficient of
   Correlation.................... 247
   Determination.................. 248
Cold site......................... 452
Committed costs................... 123
Common costs
   Allocation of................... 382
   Definition of................... 120
Compensating controls.............. 443
Compensatory (mitigative) controls.... 438
Competitive
   Forces........................ 260
   Strategies..................... 262
Complementary controls............. 438
Completed-contract method........... 30
Compliance objectives.............. 415
Computer-assisted audit techniques (CAATs).... 447
Concurrent controls................ 438
Conformance costs................. 236
Consolidated financial statements..... 65
Constant gross-margin percentage NRV method.. 187
Constraint........................ 221
Continuous improvement process (CIP)....... 231
Contribution margin................ 126
Control.......................... 286
   Activities.................. 418, 439
   Compensatory (mitigative)....... 438
   Complementary................ 438
   Corrective.................... 438
   Criteria....................... 423
   Detective..................... 437
   Environment.................. 416
   Feedback..................... 438
   Financial..................... 438
   Internal................... 405, 419
   Operating.................... 438
   People-based................. 438
   Preventive................... 437
   Risk (CR).................... 409
   System-based................. 439
Controllability..................... 376
Controllable costs.................. 123

Controls
   Compensating................. 443
   Safeguarding.................. 441
Conversion costs................... 118
Corporate governance............... 399
Corporations formation.............. 400
Corrective controls................. 438
Correlation analysis................ 247
Corrupt payments.................. 403
COSO
   Components of internal control.... 416
   Framework, Internal control...... 414
   Objectives.................... 415
Cosourcing....................... 220
Cost............................ 118
   Accounting.................... 117
   Accumulation systems........... 141
   Behavior..................... 120
   Center....................... 375
   Driver
      Activity-based costing........ 150
      Definition of................ 118
      Overhead allocation.......... 190
   Focus........................ 262
   Historical..................... 124
   Incurrence.................... 230
   Leadership.................... 262
   Management terminology......... 117
   Objects................... 118, 148
   Of goods sold budget............ 303
   Pools.................. 120, 146, 148
   Recovery method................ 29
   Standards.................... 292
   Strategy...................... 263
   Structure, transfer pricing....... 385
   Switching.................. 260, 261
   Target........................ 161
Costing
   Absorption (full)............ 126, 179
   Activity-based (ABC).......... 128, 144
   Actual........................ 127
   Extended normal............... 127
   Job-order................. 127, 141
   Life-cycle.............. 128, 160, 230
   Normal....................... 127
      Example.................. 193
   Peanut-butter................. 145
   Process................... 128, 152
   Standard..................... 128
   Target........................ 129
   Throughput (supervariable)....... 221
   Variable (direct)............ 126, 180

Costs
    After-purchase. 161
    Avoidable. 123
    Carrying. 126
    Central
        Administration. 383
        Support. 382
    Committed. 123
    Common
        Allocation of. 382
        Definition of. 120
    Conformance. 236
    Controllable. 123, 291
    Conversion. 118
    Currently attainable (practical) standards. 293
    Differential. 124
    Direct. 120
    Discretionary. 124
    Economic. 124
    Engineered. 124
    Environmental. 236
    Fixed. 121
    Fringe benefits. 302
    Full absorption. 384
    Ideal (theoretical) standards. 293
    Imputed. 124
    Incremental. 124
    Indirect. 120, 382
    Joint (common). 185
        Definition of. 125
    Locked-in (designed-in). 230
    Manufacturing. 118
    Marginal. 123
    Mixed (semivariable). 122
    Nonconformance. 236
    Noncontrollable. 123, 291
    Nonmanufacturing. 119
    Nonvalue-added. 232
    Opportunity. 124, 225
    Outlay (out-of-pocket). 124
    Overhead. 189
    Period. 119
    Prime. 118
    Product (inventoriable). 119
    Quality. 235
    Relevant. 124
    Resource. 147
    Selling (marketing). 119
    Separable. 125, 186
    Service (support). 195
    Sunk. 124
    Transferred-in. 126
    Value-adding. 126, 232
    Variable. 120, 384
Critical success factors. 230
Currently attainable (practical) standards. 293
Customer profitability analysis. 378

Data theft. 443
Delivery strategy. 263
Denial-of-service (DoS) attack. 450
Deposit method. 30
Depreciation. 82
Detection risk (DR). 409
Detective controls. 437

Differential costs. 124
Differentiation. 262
    Product. 260
Direct
    Costs. 120
    File alteration. 443
    Labor. 118
        Variances. 346
    Materials. 118
        Variances. 344
    Method of calculation. 196
Directive controls. 438
Directors. 400
Disaster
    Planning. 451
    Recovery. 451
Discretionary costs. 124
Divest strategy. 264
Dogs. 264
Drum-buffer-rope (DBR). 223
Dual
    Pricing. 387
    -Rate allocation. 198

Economic costs. 124
Effectiveness. 271
Efficiency. 271
Electronic data interchange (EDI) in JIT. 217
Encryption. 450
Engineered costs. 124
Enterprise resource planning. 220
Entry barriers. 261
Environmental controls. 445
Equipment purchases. 295
Equivalent units of production. 154
Error listings. 447
Estimated net realizable value (NRV) method. . . . 187
Expected value. 253
    Of perfect information (EVPI). 256
Expenses, administrative. 119
Extended normal costing. 127
External
    Auditors. 410
    Parties. 410

Facility-sustaining activities. 147
Factoring. 48
Factory operating costs. 118
Feedback controls. 437, 438
Feedforward controls. 438
FIFO. 55
Financial
    Accounting. 117
    Auditing. 421
    Controls. 438
    Reporting, general-purpose. 9
    Statement relationships. 11
Financing
    Activities. 24
    Reporting. 10
Firewall. 451
Five competitive forces. 260

Fixed
    Costs. 121
        Overhead variance. 351
Flesher, Dale L. iii
Flexibility strategy. 263
Flexible budget variance
    Definition of. 339
    Formula. 343
Flowcharting. 411
Focused differentiation. 262
Forecasting. 247, 270
Foreign Corrupt Practices Act of 1977. 403
Four-way overhead variance analysis. 352
Fringe benefits, cost. 302

Gains. 15
Gleim, Irvin N. iii
Goal
    Budget. 289
    Congruence. 235, 376, 385
Goodwill. 64
Governance. 399
    Practices. 399
Gross
    Margin. 126
    Profit
        Margin. 52
        Percentage. 28
Growth-share matrix. 263, 264

Harvest strategy. 264
High-low method. 122
Historical cost. 124
Hold strategy. 264
Homoscedasticity. 250
Hot site. 452

Ideal (theoretical) standards. 293
IFRS
    Impairment of PPE. 82
    Intangible assets, impairment. 88
    LIFO. 57
    Long-term construction contracts. 32
    Lower of cost or market. 59
    Measurement of PPE. 85
    Revenue recognition. 28
Impairment. 85
Imputed costs. 124
Income
    Residual. 379
    Statement. 15
    Taxes. 94
Incremental
    Costs. 124
    Method. 383
Indirect
    Costs. 120
    Labor. 118
    Materials. 118
Industry
    Life cycle. 260
    Situation, budget. 291

Information
    And communication. 418
    Security. 443
Inherent risk (IR). 408
Input
    Controls. 446
    Manipulation. 443
Insourcing. 220
Installment method. 28
Intangible assets. 87
    Impairment. 89
Internal
    Auditing. 419
    Auditors. 410
    Control. 405, 419
        Responsible parties. 409
International Financial Reporting Standards (IFRS)
    Impairment of PPE. 82
    Intangible assets impairment. 88
    LIFO. 57
    Long-term construction contracts. 32
    Lower of cost or market. 59
    Measurement of PPE. 85
    Revenue recognition. 28
Intraentity transactions. 66
Inventory. 49
    Average method. 54
    First-in, first-out (FIFO). 55
    Last-in, First-out (LIFO). 56
    Lower of cost or market (LCM). 58
    Periodic. 50
    Perpetual. 50
    Specific identification. 54
Invested capital. 380
Investing activities. 23
Investment
    Bases. 380
    Center. 376
    Intensity. 260

Job
    Cost sheets. 141
    -Order costing. 127, 141
Joint
    (Common) costs. 185
        Definition of. 125
    Products
        Allocation of. 186
        Definition of. 185
Just-in-time (JIT). 215

Kaizen. 231
Kanban. 216
Key performance indicators (KPIs). 265

Lagging indicators. 266
Leading indicators. 266
Lean operation. 215

Learning
   Curve analysis. 251
   Model
      Cumulative average-time. 252
      Incremental unit-time. 252
Leases. 90
Least-squares analysis. 249
Legislators and regulators. 410
Life cycle
   Costing. 128, 160
   Industry. 260
Linear-cost functions. 123
Locked-in (designed-in) costs. 230
Logic bombs. 444
Logical controls. 445
Long-term construction contracts. 30

Malicious software (malware). 444
Man-in-the-middle attack. 450
Management
   Accounting. 117
   By
      Exception. 129
      Objectives (MBO). 270, 272
   Plan. 287
Manufacturing
   Cells. 217
   Costs. 118
   Overhead. 118, 142
   Resource planning (MRP II). 220
Marginal costs. 123
Market
   Growth rate (MGR). 263
   Price. 384
Master production schedule (MPS). 218
Material weaknesses. 405, 414
Materials requirements planning (MRP). 218
Maturity date. 101
Measurement, PPE. 81
Method
   Acquisition. 64
   Equity. 63
Mission statement. 258, 270
Mix variance. 349
Mixed (semivariable) costs. 122
Monitoring activities. 418
Motivation. 376
   Budget. 286

Negotiation. 385
Nonconformance costs. 236
Noncontrollable costs. 123
Noncontrolling interest. 64
Nonlinear-cost function. 123
Nonmanufacturing costs. 119
Nonvalue-added
   Activity. 149, 232
   Costs. 232

Normal
   Costing. 127
      Example. 193
   Spoilage
      Definition of. 125
      Job-order costing. 144
      Process costing. 160

Officers. 400
Offsite location. 451
Operating
   Activities. 23
   Controls. 438
Operations
   Objectives. 415
   Strategy. 263
Opportunity costs. 124
Organizational culture. 272
Outlay (out-of-pocket) costs. 124
Output controls. 447
Outsourcing. 220
Overhead. 189
   Application rate
      Calculation of. 190
      Departmental vs. plantwide. 191
      Job-order costing. 142
      Single-rate vs. dual-rate. 198
   Variances. 349

Password. 445
   Attacks. 449
   Fatigue. 446
   Optimization. 445
Payoff table. 253
PCAOB. 405
Peanut-butter costing. 145
People-based controls. 438
Percentage-of-completion method. 30
Perfect information. 256
Performance measures. 377, 379
Period costs. 119
Physical
   Access. 445
   Controls. 445
Planning. 287
   Capacity. 225
Policies. 272
Porter, Michael E. 226, 260
   Five competitive forces. 260
Portfolio analysis, Boston Consulting Group (BCG). 263
Power bargaining. 261
Premises of planning. 271
Preventive controls. 437
Prime costs. 118
Private-key encryption. 450
Pro forma
   Balance sheet. 312
   Income statement. 310
   Operating income. 305
   Statement of cash flows. 312
Procedures. 272

Process. 233
   Analysis. 230
   Costing. 128, 152
   Value analysis. 149, 231
Processing controls. 447
Product
   -Cost cross-subsidization. 145
   Differentiation. 260
   (Inventoriable) costs. 119, 179
   Profitability analysis. 377
   -Sustaining activities. 147
Profit
   Center. 376
   Plan. 285
      Annual. 293
Program alteration. 443
Progress billings. 32
Property, plant, and equipment (PPE). 81
Public-key encryption. 450
Pull system. 216
Push system. 218

Quality strategy. 263
Question marks. 264

RAID. 449
Reasonable assurance. 403
Reciprocal method of calculation. 197
Regression analysis. 248
Relative market share (RMS). 263
Relevant
   Costs. 124
   Range. 120, 123
Reporting objectives. 415
Residual income. 379
Resource
   Costs. 147
   Drivers. 147
Responsibility centers. 375
Return on investment (ROI). 379
Revenue
   Center. 376
   Recognition after delivery. 27
Rework. 125
Risk. 408
   Assessment. 408, 417
   Management. 408
      Activities. 400
      Owners. 401
Rivalry among existing firms. 260
Rules. 272

Sabotage. 443
Safeguarding controls. 441
Sales
   Forecast. 300
   Value at split-off method. 186
   Variances. 356
   -Volume variance
      Definition of. 339
      Formula. 343
Sarbanes-Oxley Act. 404, 406, 409

Scrap. 125
Securities
   Available-for-sale. 61
   Held-to-maturity. 60
   Trading. 60
Security. 449
Segment reporting. 377
Segmental performance. 385
Segregation of duties. 439
Senior management. 409
Sensitivity analysis. 256
Separable costs. 125
Service
   Department costs. 195
   Providers. 411
   Strategy. 263
Shareholder. 400
Single sign-on. 446
Situational analysis. 259
Sniffing. 449
Split-off point. 125, 186
Spoilage
   Definition of. 125
   Job-order costing. 144
   Process costing. 160
Spoofing. 449
Stakeholders. 399, 401
Stand-alone method. 383
Standard costs. 292
Stars. 264
Statement
   Of
      Cash flows. 22
      Changes in equity. 18
      Comprehensive income. 17
      Financial position. 12
      Retained earnings. 19
   On Management Accounting
      (SMA). 225, 228, 234, 235
Static budget. 341
   Variance
      Definition of. 339
      Formula. 342
Step-
   Cost function. 123
   Down method of calculation. 197
Storage controls. 449
Strategic
   Business units (SBUs). 263, 375
      Life cycle. 264
      Management. 258
      Planning. 270
Substitutes. 261
Sunk costs. 124
Supervariable costing. 221
Suppliers' bargaining power. 262
Supply chain. 229
Switching costs. 260, 261
SWOT analysis. 259
Symmetric encryption. 450
System
   -Based controls. 439
   Of internal control. 409
Systems development controls. 444

Target
  Cost. 161
  Costing. 129
  Price. 161
Tax
  Factors, transfer pricing. 385
  Income. 94
Theft. 444
Theory of constraints (TOC)
  Definition of. 221
  Example of. 224
  Steps in an analysis. 221
Threat of
  Entry. 261
  Substitutes. 261
Three-way overhead variance analysis. 352
Throughput
  Costing. 221
  Margin. 221
Total
  Industry capacity. 227
  Risk (TR). 409
Tracing. 442
Traditional
  -Based systems. 146
  (Volume-based) costing system. 145, 146
Transfer pricing. 384, 385
Transferred-in costs. 126
Treadway Commission. 414
Trojan horses. 444
Two-way overhead variance analysis. 353

Unit-level activities. 146
Upstream (backward) integration. 261
Users of financial statements. 10

Value
  -Adding
    Activity. 149, 232
    Costs. 126, 232
  Chain. 160, 228
    Analysis. 227
  Engineering. 161, 230
  Expected. 253
Variable
  Costs. 120
  (Direct) costing. 126, 180
  Overhead variance. 349
Variance
  Analysis. 337
  Direct
    Labor. 346
    Materials. 344
  Efficiency. 340
  Mix and yield. 348
  Overhead. 349
  Sales. 356
  Spending. 350
Vertical integration. 261
Viruses. 444
Volume-based systems. 145

Vouching. 442

Warm site. 452
Waste. 125
Whole-life costs. 161
Worms. 444

Yield variance. 349

Notes

Notes